High
Anxiety

◆

Arts and Politics of the Everyday

*Patricia Mellencamp, Meaghan Morris, and Andrew Ross,
series editors*

High Anxiety

---◆---

CASTASTROPHE, SCANDAL, AGE, & COMEDY

---◆---

Patricia Mellencamp

Indiana University Press

---◆---

Bloomington and Indianapolis

The photographs from *Eternal Frame* are reprinted here by
permission of Chip Lord. Photo credit: Diane Andrews Hall.

Final photograph by Dae Mellencamp, Brown University, 1990.

Covers of the *National Examiner* and *Weekly World News* are reproduced by permission.

A shorter version of "Disastrous Events" appeared in *Logics of Television: Essays in Cultural
Criticism,* edited by Patricia Mellencamp (Indiana University Press, 1990), and a shorter
version of "Lucy" appeared in *Studies in Entertainment: Critical Approaches to Mass Culture,*
edited by Tania Modleski (Indiana University Press, 1986).

Excerpts from *The Search for Signs of Intelligent Life in the Universe,* by Jane Wagner
(Harper and Row, 1987), are reprinted by permission.

The paper used in this publication meets the minimum requirements of American
National Standard for Information Sciences—Permanence of Paper for Printed
Library Materials, ANSI Z39.48-1984.

Manufactured in the United States of America

Library of Congress Cataloging-in-Publication Data

Mellencamp, Patricia.
    High anxiety : catastrophe, scandal, age, and comedy / by Patricia
Mellencamp.
      p. cm. — (Arts and politics of the everyday)
    Includes bibliographical references and index.
    ISBN 0-253-33744-5 (alk. paper). — ISBN 0-253-20735-5 (pbk.)
    1. Television broadcasting—Social aspects—United States.
    2. United States—Popular culture.   3. Women in television.
    I. Title. II. Series.
    PN1992.6.M44   1992
    302.23′45′0973—dc20   91-46255

1 2 3 4 5   96 95 94 93 92

To Dae and Rob Mellencamp

———————————◆———————————

one

day

at

a

time

"Lucy and Superman," Episode #166 (January 14, 1957, CBS)

Contents

Preface

Time/Travel

In David Lodge's parody of upper-class academia and high theory, appropriately titled *Small World*, Morris Zapp, the hip semiotician or postmodern critic, assesses the scholarly world as composed of cities strung together by identical airports, a topography of conference topics. Zapp: "Zurich is Joyce. Amsterdam is Semiotics. Vienna is Narrative. Or is it Narrative in Amsterdam and Semiotics in Vienna . . .? Anyway, Jerusalem I *do* know is about the Future of Criticism. . . ." Persse McGarrigle, the young assistant professor, chases his dream girl and scholarship through international airports and universities alike. However, rather than the male hero's passion, time and surveillance rather than romance and mystery dominate and narrate airports—oases of anxiety and boredom more than desire.

The pedestrian acts of waiting and meeting are punctuated by checking out the "times" electronically posted on banks of black-and-white TV monitors, which resemble video art installations. The iconography is simple math, strings of disparate cities divided into arrivals and departures, beginnings and endings. As in high-tech airport architecture, the lines of destination are rhomboid, going off in all directions like the airline maps in on-flight magazines. Corporate terrain is not clear, no longer determined by name and linked to place. American used to be just that; Pan American flew to South America; Trans World did just what its name implied—there were corporate and international territories, a spatial plan. Now there are cat's-cradle graphs which overlap, deregulated.

Airports, like shopping malls, are modern spaces of duty-free purchase and passage. On the planes and flat escalators, we move forward but appear to remain in place; we are moving and being moved, somewhere between active and passive. We are unable to tell arrivees from departees, beginnings from endings. There is no narrative other than coming or going, either here or there, no public identity, no nationality, only the mission and desire of being "on time" while feeling timeless, contextless, unmoored, noplace, in an anonymity of suspended time. Regularity is broken by forced delay—the disruption of scheduled time by mechanical error (for which the passengers are compensated) or the vagaries of nature (whose foibles and cost we bear). Time's extension *and* collapse into international, standardized zones traverse seasons. Night and day are marked only by food—if it's breakfast, it must be morning and time to chat.

Thus, the commandeering of tourists by terrorists, the taking of travelers from their unseen anonymity into context and history—turning the national into the international, which airports already are—*randomly* transforms passengers into bystanders, partisans in a political drama, witnesses of confrontation and negotiation. Hostages embody the nightmare of waiting or being trapped in airports and airplanes, our fears of death in flight, as well as the risk of live theater. These are epics of time more than space, of waiting more than acting, hence suitable to TV special-event coverage. The random move from bored obscurity to dangerous celebrity is a surrealist one: there is no reason for the selection of hostages, determined only by destination and chance. The terror is the missing cause-effect logic. Hostage dramas thus represent not the complexity of the political issues which triggered their coverage, but images and reports of waiting, the suspension of time, and anxiety—the very experience of flight and temporality, boring *and* deathly.

Like passengers and their families, TV waits, counting time against death threats. Waiting by/with TV for the resolution of the Iranian "hostage crisis" metamorphosed into a late-night television show, *Nightline*, and the making of a TV news star, Ted Koppel, whose topics are often the management of crises. In August 1990, that crisis (and Carter's failure) was remembered as the primal scene of the crisis in Iraq, another hostage drama. (Like ABC and Iran, CBS considered creating its own Iraq "hostage watch" program.) However fraught with anxiety and potential shock, this is not dialectic time—this is what Walter Benjamin might call homogeneous time, empty time.

Yet commercial TV—so in chronotopic sync with airports—flowing forth from little airport sets mounted on individual chairs, with slots for quarters of time, has been anomalous in those spaces. Perhaps watching TV (unlike watching censored movies on the plane's monitor) is too repetitive of enforced waiting (one of the best places, along with libraries, to watch people read is at the airport). Or airport time misregisters with TV time, one obsession canceling out or magnifying the other. However, while watching TV seems out of place (at least for now, pre–Ted Turner's Airport Channel)—either too fragmented, too nationally determined, or too embarrassing to do in public, unlike legit reading, no matter how pulpy—TV is everywhere, monitoring time, surveying our bodies, X-raying our lingerie and birth-control devices, uncovering fruit, drugs, and weapons, and recording our automobile license plates outside the parking structure. We watch time on banks of television monitors while discreetly mounted surveillance cameras monitor our view and every move, "security" measures which will protect us from terrorist acts.

We might feel safely anxious and anonymous in the crowd of imagined obscurity, but we have appeared and been recorded on television, like all the other hostages, yet not broadcast on the nightly news. (If we have been to the bank, visited the museum, and gone shopping, we have made several guest appearances on TV.) Like the airplane, television is a time machine. Unlike the airlines, U.S. TV is rarely late and never early.

Acknowledgments

This book is fat and funny—not as daunting as its hefty size implies. It is a serious and comic (perhaps wacky) look at the state of culture, premised, I believe, on women's everyday life and logic. Just as the 1990s are replaying earlier decades, including the 1890s, numbered sections echo and replay each other. They can be read sporadically and out of order, although there is an argument and a movement—from catastrophe to comedy, from fear to laughter, from men's thought to women's. The line of thought is marked by roman numerals (I-XVIII) which move *through* chapters and the book. My intellectual focus has changed—from desire to anxiety, from sex to money, from youth to age, from film to television, from theory to the everyday, and, to a degree, from academia to journalism. I have always loved comedy and admired funny women.

The sections document an epistemology, a subjectivity of contradiction, remodeling Freud (a makeover) by reading obsession through fear and anxiety rather than desire and pleasure, through the money, more than the sexual, economy. Ironically, feminists have relentlessly talked sex for almost twenty years. For me, the boom is long gone—or has soured to an obsession. It's time to talk self-love, knowledge, and power (and money) rather than romance, sex, and power (and desire).

For me, identity and satisfaction come from work, wisdom, and the small pleasures—coffee in the morning, a book at night, a movie with good friends. Aging has taught me that daily life is not a rehearsal but the big event. From gossip, I learned that a "quidnunc" is a busybody (a great term) who loves gossip. From personal experience, I know that Freud's model of loss and shock is dead right. I am no stranger to profound fear and high anxiety.

This is a book that tried to live in the present. Unfortunately, but amusingly, my attempt to keep it current led, with each production phase, to updates and additions. The words and pages grew, like Topsy or an obsession, into a fat text, as I breathlessly tried to stay apace with popular culture and the market.

It all began with "*I Love Lucy*" in 1982. I wanted to write a feminist critique which could explain my response to the series and begin an analysis of women and comedy. Few feminist scholars then (or now) took either comedy or television seriously. They were wrong—about *Lucy's* triviality and situation comedy's irrelevance. Lucille Ball was a brilliant performer;

the model of contradiction I arduously uncovered in the series (apparent like the purloined letter *and* hence very difficult to initially see), although inflected by history, holds true for many cultural artifacts.

This series has been on the air every day for forty years, *roughly* paralleling my conscious life (as an early "boomer"). This time-span coincided with the Cold War, an era of clammy fear and wild anxiety, and the glory years of U.S. network television. I dedicate this book to Lucy and the many funny and clever women who grew up with her—amidst all the contradictions applied to working women everywhere.

All my love and respect . . .

To Mary Yelanjian for her research; to Dae Mellencamp, Tara McPherson, Rob Mellencamp, and Jim Castonguay for their analyses of TV; to Mimi White, Andrew Ross, and Meaghan Morris for their revisions; to Lily Tomlin for her corrections, and to Jane Wagner for her generosity.

To the women of *The Milwaukee Journal*—Jacquelyn Mitchard, Jacquelyn Gray, and especially Lois Blinkhorn—for their critiques of popular culture and women's lives; to the many reporters of *The Wall Street Journal* (Robert Johnson, Teri Agins, John Keller, Lee Berton, Richard Gibson, Dana Milbank, Kathleen Deveny, Ellen Graham, and others) who write with such acumen and wit about corporate-commodity culture; and to my mother, Peg Jewson, for sharing her knowledge of "the market."

To my friends in academia Maggie Morse, Eileen Meehan, Judine Mayerle, Kathleen Rowe, and Sonja Rein for their writing on TV; to Kathleen Woodward for her book on aging and her encouragement; and to academics, authors of books, I have never met—Patricia Spacks, Dolores Hayden, Susan Strasser, and Susan Porter Benson—for their erudition.

To Marge Rock, Sharon Coffman, and Betsy Van Horne, who helped me understand fear and quell anxiety. To Peg and Bob Jewson, my parents, and Nancy Mooney, my sister, who enabled me to live through shocking events.

My deepest gratitude belongs to Rob and Dae, who grew up so brilliantly and lovingly while I was writing this book and helped me to do the same.

Patricia Mellencamp, October 28, 1991
Sadgurunath Maharaj ki Jay!

PART I

PACKAGING THE
DIFFERENCE

Franchise Culture

I know what you're thinkin'; you're thinkin' I'm
crazy. You think I give a hoot? You people look
at my shopping bags, call me crazy 'cause I save
this junk. What should we call the ones who
buy it?

— Trudy, the Bag Lady, in Jane Wagner's

The Search for Signs of Intelligent Life in the Universe[1]

I begin with the personal—trivial and catastrophic. First, the mundane.
In 1987, I moved from my home of twenty years and decided to buy
new kitchen appliances, a simple task, or so I foolishly imagined. After
freeway trekking to outpost warehouses containing *hundreds* of models, I
felt like my brain had been involved in a collision. Like VCRs, all the
stoves and refrigerators looked identical, yet the salesmen talked as if they
were radically different. Brand name no longer guaranteed style and
features. More perplexing was the discovery that only a few companies
manufactured components, packaged and sold under different names.
Was money the *only* measure of (almost imperceptible) difference? The
"choice" was up to me! Salesmen warily eyed me as an antediluvian
consumer. (Repair folk greet my original 1981 IBM PC, a brief moment of
either Apple *or* IBM, as if it were a relic of a pre-electronic era.)

Seeing the difference amidst infinitesimal differentiation stymied me.
Porcelain, a commonplace for old refrigerators, had become a pricey item.
The formerly ordinary (or the real) had become a luxury, turning me into
an elitist, but a cheap one who wanted to find the best buy. Given the rash
of products and my savvy disbelief in salesmen, a bargain was no small
task. When everything is constantly and unpredictably on sale or dis-
counted, with no retail norm, bargains become relative rather than season-
ally fixed. Eventually paranoiac, trusting no one, I still think I could have
gotten a better deal.

While roaming the city on my anxious mission, I began to ponder the
imponderable: "Why did McDonald's, Burger King, and Wendy's build
franchises on the same corner or strip? After all, they sell the same product,
don't they? The burger story, is, of course, the same as the refrigerator
tale—a story of diversity, differentiation, and free choice. Many fretful
miles later, my car broke. Not only was I subjected to the deceptive wiles
and astronomical cost estimates of mechanics talking car parts, but I now
had the additional freedom of going to national franchises which special-

ized in parts and services (like Midas Muffler) rather than my locally owned all-service dealer.

Let's make a deal and discerning difference became all-consuming, my life's work. Gradually it dawned on me that these mundane events also applied to popular media, especially television, where decentralization and differentiation *seemed* to rule, appearing to grant me freedom of diversity.

My shopping (by now I was driving with the single-mindedness of Al Unser) was derailed by a medical disaster. After a series of tests and biopsies on my son, the surgeon said, "It looks like lymphoma." I remember visually receding. Sound become barely audible. My body was separated from reality as if encased in thick glass. Only my eyes allowed the real in, and if I closed them, I was shielded from bombardment. It was like floating in an air-proof bubble. Fear and anxiety, which were almost unbearable, had, for a moment, been physically mediated. Freud's analysis of shock in *Inhibitions, Symptoms and Anxiety* perfectly described my reaction. These experiences triggered anxiety and paralyzed action. So I watched TV.

While daytime talk was filled with confession and revelation, not to reveal either the personal or the political appeared to be the rule of late-night talk. Also, political difference, like many binarisms, no longer was discernible. One night in his opening monologue, Carson made jokes about Bush, who gave a speech in a flag factory, then "had a fitting." The next night, the target was Dukakis, "Zorba the Clerk." I compared Gary Shandling on Carson to Woody Allen's guest stints on Jack Paar in the '60s and '70s, and Carson to Paar.

Amidst Allen's intellectual neurosis and sexual angst, he expressed a political position and parodied high culture from Strindberg to philosophy. Shandling reacts to the foibles of everyday life, with neither a pro nor a con. We knew where Bob Hope's political allegiances lay, unlike Jay Leno's. David Letterman, another comedian of everyday life, with tics, quirks, and obsessions including his bad haircuts and lopsided sport coats, has no stands on issues—particularly when compared to Paar. And if Dave does let an opinion slip, like his digs at NBC, he will retract his aside or deny it, which might have been simulated anyway.

That Bob Hope is old-fashioned (less so after the War in the Gulf TV tributes, including one at his home!) while Jay Leno is with it is more than a difference of age. Leno's comedy is derived from the *overt* contradictions of popular culture, particularly advertising and television *as* our daily life. The everyday is defined *as* popular culture, which includes politics and economics. We get his jokes because the contradictions are very familiar. That Leno is also the private star of corporate conventions, as is Bill Cosby (like Bob Hope), testifies that his comedy is not threatening but economically lucrative. The joke as critique functions as a sell. Leno turns consumer culture (more aptly, its publicity and purchase) into parody which the informed and with-it audience can play and applaud—and knowingly buy. We might watch six hours of daily television, but we also understand the absurdity of Leno's "readings" of *TV Guide* and his acute "deconstruction" of commercials. Those TV programmers and advertising rapscallions, or show biz structuralists, aren't fooling us!

Critically, however, what is funny, what is being critiqued, is not the commodity but its packaging, not commerce or capitalism but its ploys and techniques—advertising and politics as absurd but never successfully manipulative. Thus, simultaneously inside and outside parodic consumption (or guilty purchase), we fancy ourselves as neither naive nor resistant but smart and complicit.

Although the standups now sit down, some things never change: late night is still a masculine preserve (with, significantly, Arsenio Hall breaking the race barrier). The divide between telling and not telling is gendered, although Hall reveals more. Equally, like Bob Hope, the binarism of political position seems very old fashioned. The best jokes are about contradictions, particularly of popular culture.

High Anxiety

Television embodies contradictions—rather than an "either/or" logic, one of "both/and," an *inclusive* logic of creation/cancellation in which mimicry and simulation are stolid cornerstones rather than lofty embellishments. *(Marxists might say, "So what? Capitalism always embodies contradiction!" For television, however, contradictions are not concealed but overtly declared, often directly, like Jay Leno's act.)* The logic of television is akin to that proposed by Robert Venturi in the 1960s for an architecture of "complexity and contradiction": "I am for richness of meaning rather than clarity of meaning; for the implicit function as well as the explicit function. I prefer 'both-and' to 'either-or' "[2] For Venturi, both-and "emphasizes double meanings," the non sequitur and the duality—or what Joseph Albers calls "the discrepancy between physical fact and psychic effect" (27).

This style *can* be political: it "must embody the difficult unity of inclusion rather than the easy unity of exclusion. More is not less" (23). A model of difficult inclusion, unlike the exclusionary tactics of binarisms and irrevocable differences, is promising. Like Venturi, "I like . . . hybrid rather than 'pure' . . . boring as well as 'interesting,' conventional rather than 'designed,' accommodating rather than excluding, redundant rather than simple . . . inconsistent and equivocal rather than direct and clear. I am for messy vitality over obvious unity" (22). (Also, as Engels and Hegel pointed out, quantity can take a leap into quality, or molecules of water can become a waterfall.)

(Hipper critics will say, "So what! This is by now old hat postmodernism." However, most PM critiques dropped contradiction in favor of bricolage, and history in

a rush to label the present as new, and paid scant attention to subjectivity. Only the rare schizophrenic [1.5%, according to the government study] appeared as the post-modern subject [or the "PMS"], appropriately "feminized" given Fredric Jameson's gendering of the schizophrenic.)[3]

The cultural logic of television—a "messy vitality"—can also be mind-boggling, imitating the "diphasic" quality of obsessional neuroses, what Freud calls in *Inhibitions, Symptoms and Anxiety* (1926) "the power of ambiv-alence": "one action is cancelled out by a second, so that it is as though neither action had taken place, whereas, in reality, both have."[4] In other words, more can appear to be less.

Every week for seven years, Lucy, the chorus girl/clown, complained that Ricky was preventing her from becoming a star. For twenty-four min-utes, she valiantly tried to escape domesticity by getting a job in show busi-ness. After a tour de force performance of physical comedy, in the inevita-ble reversal and failure of the end, she resigned to stay happily at home serving big and little Ricky. The ultimate "creation/cancellation"—the se-ries' premise, which was portrayed in brilliant performances and then de-nied weekly—was that Lucy was not star material. For keeping her home and out of show business, Lucy throws a pie in Ricky's face during his solo performance at the Tropicana (in "The Ballet").

However, Ricky gets the last laugh by dumping a bucket of water (rigged over the apartment's front door) on her head when she arrives home; in the twenty-second end of this episode, Lucy recants her actions by saying, "You were right all along, Ricky. Forgive me?" Laughter. Applause. Seven days later, Lucy repeats her break for freedom, her anarchism against wifery. To rephrase Freud: "An action which carries out a certain injunc-tion is immediately succeeded by another action which stops or undoes the first one." The affect (drawn for Freud from war neuroses and for me from popular culture) is one of anxiety.

A front-page headline in *The Milwaukee Journal* (November 1, 1988)— STUDY FINDS MUCH MENTAL ILLNESS—supported my personal Amana thesis of anxiety. (For some reason—a *headline* that we are all basically nuts, or the officialese of data, or 18,000 phobics gathered in one place taking a multiple-choice test or singing the Coke anthem—this study amused me.) "Almost one-third of all Americans suffer from acute mental illness during their lifetimes and, at any one moment, major mental disorders afflict almost 15% of the nation's population, according to new findings from the largest study of its kind ever conducted" (1A). The U.S. as a manic laboratory for high-tech stress, as Meaghan Morris so archly and acerbically asserted one afternoon[5]—its scientific "research and development" prior to the international exportation of anxiety—was statistically verified in this National Institute of Mental Health document.

My tongue-in-cheekiness aside, the figures were startling, particularly the prevalence of obsessive-compulsive disorder (repetitive behavior of, for example, washing and checking rituals), "26 to 60 [some spread!] times

Figure 2

greater than previously thought. Instead of being rare, the disease is commonplace." Shortly thereafter, OCD became a topic on *Oprah Winfrey*, with testimonial sufferers arrayed across the stage.

This $20 million *official government* study of 18,599 people discovered that "huge proportions of people with debilitating phobias and major depression . . . simply find ways to cope with their symptoms and live their lives as best they can, never coming in contact with mental health workers." That these wacked-out citizens might be in self-help therapy groups for alcoholics, overeaters, or sexual addicts is, strangely, not considered. Tops on the list were drug abuse (16.4%), followed by anxiety disorders (phobias, panic disorder, and OCD, 14.6%), with schizophrenia as rare (1.5%) (6A). No wonder Freud devoted more papers to obsessional neurosis than any other topic. The study bleakly concluded with economics—most people cannot afford care: "Mental health care is increasingly becoming an opportunity only for the affluent," a finding poignantly and daily visible in the rising number of homeless people. Or, alternatives to "mental health" professionals are being sought.

Even the most staid profession, accounting—"people who once acted like members of a quiet gentleman's club"—"has been transformed into a Darwinian jungle" as a result of client mergers, litigation, layoffs, and competition.[6] "Internecine battles among accounting-firm leaders have brought chaos to once-serene professional organizations," engaged in the "survival of the fittest." (The return of Darwinian thought is widespread.) The language of warfare (or the cave man) is typical of financial reporting. Although macho might be adorned in horn-rimmed glasses and a Brooks Brothers suit, business is still a men's club.

Alas, the profession seems to be plagued by an outbreak of neurasthenia. "Accountants are leaving the business in droves. Those who remain . . . have become so anxiety-ridden that . . . their health is in peril." Over one hundred firms regularly consult with psychologists for stress management. "As the pressure mounts, some go berserk. . . . We give them quick psychiatric help." Lawrence Nelson became "so stressed out" that he overate, lost sleep, and was divorced. "Many of us are in a panic." There have been sightings of formerly mild-mannered accountants screaming and throwing water goblets at each other. A survey of fifty firms revealed that "the incidence of coronaries, ulcers and back problems among partners has risen 30% in the past three years." These years have seen the great junk-bond trader scandals—accountants' clients. Liability insurance has tripled.

Accountants use variable systems, presumed to be true and absolute rather than creative and arbitrary. Although a new accounting system can change the picture and forecast, numerical calculations are taken as a measure of the real—which can be worth millions of dollars on the stock market. Quarterly reports, particularly profits/losses and "earnings," are the clues to a stock's worth and a company's value, assayed every three months. Immediate and continual gain is the goal—resembling an obsession, a spreading logic of infinitely more. Because accounting is predicated on a binary logic of debits or credits, gains or losses, the emergence of an econo-logic of both/and, where debit and credit are interchangeable, where investment and consumption can be the same (for example, buying art, going back to school, physical fitness), has caused high anxiety.

The recent plunge of Orion Pictures stock, from $15 to less than $2, is a financial scandal attributed to "creative" accounting and explained by obsession. Orion, under the leadership of Arthur Krim, "cooked the books," taking the company, the producer of prestigious films, from negative to positive quarterly reports. "Instead of writing off failed films, it was carrying many of them on its books as assets." Thus, "Orion recorded profits every year but 1986 [and] showed 'rising assets,' " actually failed films not written down. Krim, the CEO, was "driven to keep looking successful," a drive that "bordered on the disastrous."[7]

And, like most things, including the turn-of-the-century corporate practice of "differentiation," the outbreak of OCD is not necessarily new. In 1908, Freud quoted writers on neurasthenia, a modern disorder which "Beard [a New York neurologist] believed he had discovered . . . in America" (like Morris). After noting that the doctor, not the disease, was American, the author (Binswanger) then tied the symptoms to modern life: "the unbridled lust and haste for gold and possessions" and "immense advances in technical spheres which have reduced . . . limitations of time and space where communication is concerned."[8] Another writer worries that "all is hurry and agitation: night is used for travel, day for business; even 'holiday trips' keep the nervous system on the rack. . . . The exhausted nerves seek recuperation in increased stimulation, in highly seasoned pleasures" (22). (Unfortunately, at this early date, Freud reduced these symptoms to the cause of sexual repression, an ad nauseam position which he would later revise.)

In *No Place of Grace*, T. J. Jackson Lears traces neurasthenia, or what Freud calls "modern nervousness," back to "the cultural turmoil of the late nineteenth century," which he labels "a neurasthenia epidemic."[9] In this icebox era, "nervous prostration" was the "disease of the age" (49); neurasthenia was characterized by "a paralysis of the will," the sufferer "tortured by indecision and doubt" (50). For George Miller Beard, who viewed the neurasthenic body as a small machine low on energy supply, the cause was civilization—new technologies such as electricity and the telegraph; mass transit, particularly trolleys and the railroad; cities; the periodical press; Fordist-Taylorist methods of factory production—and the cold and dry weather.

Like Freud, Lears quotes Miller Beard's *American Nervousness* (1880), a compendium of fear—of contamination, of being alone, of society. Practitioners advocated many cures. Scarcity therapy was one method. "Letting go" was another (53). Linking therapy (which, for Lears, is bad) with consumerism (also bad), a position with which I disagree, Lears evaluates this ongoing "therapeutic world view" as the "evasive banality [of] modern culture" (55) (a phrase he might apply to this book). What he fails to note is that "neurasthenia"—obsessions and addictions—can be fatal as well as fashionable. Having a middle-class history does not mean that something is banal or over.

For Miller Beard, neurasthenics were frequently middle-class white women, imagined as constitutionally weaker than men and hence more affected by civilization than men.[10] More unsettling is a 1990 international study (covering Europe, Africa, and North America) by the American Psychological Association which discovered that "women are twice as likely as men to experience depression."[11] Among the causes, which also include the biological, are sexual abuse, unhappy marriages, poverty (75% of the poor are woman), race, age, addiction, and, significantly, being a "professional woman." It's not easy being a woman, in 1890 or 1990, and living a logic of contradiction which asks us to work against our best interests, to "freely choose" the dubious pleasures of wifery and economic subservience. Yet, no matter how acute the reasons for our depression, I question the conclusion. As Miller Beard discovered in 1870, sexual impotence was a widespread problem—but men didn't talk about it.

However, there is help for the postmodern neurasthenic—if she can afford it.[12] The production of anxiety and its cures are costly. Charles of the Ritz has begun to market "Disaster Cream," while Estee Lauder sells "Skin Defender Lotion," and the Golden Door, "Crisis Cream." Almay has "Stress Cream" and "Stress Eye Gel"; Aveda offers "Calming Nutrients"; and Origins sells "Stress Buffer" and "Peace of Mind" in jars. The latest in makeup ingredients include caviar, gold, cashmere, and pearl to upscale the appeal and the price. If measured by the pound or gallon, makeup, sold by fractions of an ounce, costs more than precious stones or metals.

Some anxiety potions are turn-of-the century reprises of neurasthenia. Ellon Bach's "Rescue Remedy" should be used "when life's demands overwhelm you"—in effect, constantly. This sixty-year-old wonder cure-all, marketed in 1991 via a direct-mail campaign, can "help you handle emergencies and everyday upsets calmly." Rescue Remedy is "the perfect aid in relieving nervousness accompanying business meetings or public speaking, fear of flying, job interviews. . . . It can be used when fearful, after an injury, accident, upon receiving bad news, or even in the dentist's chair." The next scene is my favorite: "Sprayed from an atomizer, it can bring a sense of calm to stressful surroundings . . . alleviating fear and terror; compulsions or obsessions; grief and trauma; irritability and restlessness." *Some cure!*

Rescue Remedy will not create positive emotions such as happiness, but it will "help you alleviate feelings." Or, Rescue Remedy Cream can be externally applied "if you're experiencing any discomfort at all." The 1960s drug culture promised untold experiences of ecstasy. However disastrous, its logic was additive (and addictive). The 1990s health culture mediates the negative effects of a stressed, polluted, addicted environment—a logic of creation/cancellation.

The 1991 Remedy differs from the original. The reissue is touted as "all natural," is meted out in small vials, and is expensive—the critical distinction. Packaging makes the difference, and price creates the value. If it's costly (and old-fashioned), it must be good—as Thorstein Veblen essayed years ago. The homemade and the natural, including patent medicines, jam, bread, and ice cream, which used to be domestic, inexpensive, and ordinary (tied to women's work), are now upscale products, costly, and unusual (linked to entrepreneurs like Ben and Jerry of liberal ice cream fame, or even *Mrs.* Field of chocolate-chip cookie renown). The price for moving from domesticity to the marketplace is high, providing some measure of the real value of women's home labor.

Contradictory logic and compulsive repetition triggering anxiety are the main lines of this book's argument, under the rubrics catastrophe, scandal, age, and comedy. It is not so much the two terms of the contradiction but their juxtaposition that counts. This is a tentacled logic that crosscuts and blends forms of cultural commerce—leveling differences among media. The logic of contradiction, which refigures cause-effect outcomes, disguised by repetition (a purloined letter ploy) is familiar (if not immediately, then unconsciously) to women, who have gotten the short and confusing shrift of the "double standard" for years.

Economics, itself a genre of popular culture—the stock market—provides a frame, some amusing examples, and the perfect contradiction, that of spend/save, urged in the same breath as the cure for the monetary health of the nation. Spend/save is a logic of cancellation comparable to eat/diet—the effects of fast-food franchisers are offset by weight-loss franchisers.

One econotext is the decline of the U.S. dollar and the emergence of several economic superpowers, displacing the post–World War II dominance of Wall Street—a realignment of monetary power and subjectivity. Another is the creation of transmedia oligopolies, such as Time-Warner or Sony-Columbia-CBS Records—companies dealing in representations which are, unlike steel ingots, relatively intangible—immaterial like money, and unpredictable like the stock market. As Douglas Gomery, Eileen Meehan, and others have argued, the monopolistic structure of the major Hollywood studios (in spite of the Paramount antitrust decree of 1948) has powerfully reemerged—diversified and deregulated.[13] Amidst wild product and system proliferation, only a few corporate players produce the technology and the programming for television. Thus, the replay of the same, differentiated on hundreds of channels and across media, is not surprising.

While I see the present as thoroughly inflected by history's inevitable return, I suspect that old-fashioned policies of "deregulation," "privatization," "the marketplace," "diversity," or the "free flow of information" (processes of differentiation) have pummeled, battered, and perhaps reshaped subjectivity, caught amidst the shift from a product economy to a service and information economy, from work to leisure *as* work, what I call franchise culture and what critics, influenced by neoclassical economists, have labeled "neo-" or "post-Fordism."

As with Scylla and Charybdis, or a rock and a hard place, it is not easy to tell the difference between work and leisure, between anxiety and pleasure. Are we having fun yet? is a good question for the late 1980s and 1990s. I don't think this is a new subjectivity, but rather a "new and improved" version of an aging model which has been working out. Charting the course of change is difficult when the progression is one step forward, two steps back, along with a ninety-degree turn to the political right. In contrast to Rosalind Coward's premise in *Female Desires* that "our desire [is] constantly courted,"[14] I submit that anxiety is courted as much as, or more than, women's desire. Guilty pleasure is anxious more than desirous, conscious as well as unconscious. Money more than sex is the (un)repressed focus.

A Method to the Madness

Along with corporate economics and subjectivity, I will simultaneously focus on representation (until recently considered an intangible yet one of the most profitable, and tangible, U.S. commodities—the TV syndication market and movies), including sexual and chronological differences. At the moment of seeming dispersion and pluralism, whether corporate, technological, or social, apparati of representation enact a resolute containment. This is not surprising given media conglomerates—more products, big audiences, but fewer producers. Thus, not only do television and other forms of cultural commerce embody a both/and logic, but so does my critique. I raid several disciplines and my own life, thereby committing two scholarly crimes: the lack of expertise and the presence of personal experience. Scholars in many fields, for example Henri Lefebvre, Michel Foucault, Michel de Certeau, and Iurii Lotman, have taken everyday life as the object of their theories. However, for Lotman, the everyday can become a legitimate scholarly object only when it is removed in time, place, or culture, with most documents written by an external observer. To be in the everyday is presumed "natural" rather than cultural. It is only when the everyday is historical or "foreign," argues Lotman, that it can be experienced aesthetically and taken scholastically or seriously.[15]

This "defamiliarization," paradoxically a lack of personal experience and immediate knowledge so familiar to anthropologists and tourists, grants validity to research. However, as feminism has so brilliantly disputed the equation of gender, sex, and nature, wherein biology is destiny, it has also demonstrated that it is possible to be both inside and outside systems, including the contradictions of gender, popular culture, and daily life, *at the same time*.[16] The subject can simultaneously be the external observer. Cultural time, like style, aided and abetted by technology, has speeded up, enabling the critic to see its passage and its return. History, a "tiger's leap into the past,"[17] rewinds and then fast-forwards. For example, leopard, cheetah, and ocelot spots turned up on clothes shown for fall 1989 in Milan, Paris, and New York, along with tiger and zebra stripes. "Animal patterns [were] big fashion news." But animal stripes and spots were big news for fall 1987 and fall 1984. "How can they be new now? Is fall 1987 so long ago?"[18]

In this opening foray, I will look briefly at more traditional communications studies which paint a scholarly and statistical picture of (1) economic deregulation and (2) the TV world of representation. Without any arrogance, I can say that these studies, which came at the end, verify my assertions, gleaned from critical rather than statistical observation of everyday life. Throughout the book, I use data, including theories, as backup, not premise.

(After sending my son's tissue to experts around the country, including a slide appearance at a national medical conference, and after three months of torture including bone-marrow extraction, the by-now slew of doctors reversed their diagnosis. There was no scientific explanation for the weird cell structure other than my son might be an alien. So much for the twilight zone of science and rationality. I eventually bought a white Kitchenaid, with black decorator doors. As I waited, anxiety lessened, absorbed by the body slowly, over time. Expectation of a crisis can, however, partially recall the moment.)

I

◆

Differentiation

Mr. Nabisco, sir! You could be the first to sell
the concept of munching to the Third World.
We got an untapped market here! Those
countries got millions and millions of people
don't even know where their next meal is
comin' from. So the idea of eatin' between meals
is somthin' just never occurred to 'em!"

—Trudy, the Bag Lady

Passionate Consumption

John Berger's 1972 assessment of the replacement of political choice by a
polynomial begetting of new and improved products (his second major argument in *Ways of Seeing*)—a dizzying reiteration, an endogamy of the
same as difference—is right on the money.[19] The only difference is packaging. Tylenol sells "pain relief" as an aside: in the beginning, there were
tablets, then capsules, then caplets; today there are "new extra strength *gel
caps*, not capsules. It's not a capsule, it's better." (This is not easy to swal-
low. Jay Leno scales his verbal register of incredulity: A *gel cap*?) The 1989
Infiniti ads carried this edict too far, absenting the car altogether in favor of
a TV haiku. Why?

An elegant brochure/mailing explained: "Simple. Owning an Infiniti is not for everyone. First, each Infiniti is built in strict, limited quantities. . . . Second, from a philosophical point of view, Infiniti is . . . an iconoclast's car. It is for those who are very comfortable with themselves . . . those who would rather lead than follow . . . those who believe luxury is more a personal reward than a public statement. As you can see, that eliminates a lot of the car-buying public. [Sales dropped.] And leaves those like you. [Nissan stock plummeted from 24 to 12.] That is why you will want to send for a special video we have created. It will let you see more, experience more. . . . Send for your copy of the Infiniti video, 'Infiniti Unlocked,' today." Infiniti, after all, is not a car but a tasteful experience which many chose not to have.

In *Consuming Passionately in California*, Judith Williamson stars as an intrepid but distraught shopper at Target, the lead in a Hollywood musical, and a Marxist critic. In this "Esther Williams goes radical" B-videotape, the romance and familialism of the Hollywood musical are linked to consumerism. This Paper Tiger TV tape, a parodic version of Berger, invents the swimming sock, which, to my amazement, I later learned is a real product. (Nike introduced Aqua Sox in 1987 for water sports. "Although they retain a level of dorkiness comparable to golf shoes, waders, and inflatable vests," by 1989 Nike couldn't stock the shelves fast enough.)[20] In the videotape's big number, Busby Berkeley on a shoestring (bad pun), the male chorus role-reverses and stages an aquatic spectacle—a commercial for swimming socks. Williamson plays Esther.

Entering Target is accompanied by "Heaven, I'm in heaven." Punctuating the movie clips and re-creation is Williamson's analysis of a sock advert in voiceover. To expand, capitalism seeks markets. One target is the body, which is redefined, locating more functions, which in turn need new products. Ironically, the focus is the foot, an old-fashioned sexual fetish here analyzed as a commodity fetish. "We can't change the world, but we can change our socks." Or, "It's not a shoe, it's a revolution," as the actual ad for Nike Air Jordans goes. Who would have imagined socks for walking, power-walking, running, tennis (singles and doubles, winter and summer, indoor and outdoor, humid and dry, foot, ankle, and mid-calf, tasseled or not, and resolutely, as wanton socks are wont to do, sexed, men's and women's), basketball, ad infinitum, in all colors and many textures. There are even bisexual Sox Shop franchises in the corners of shopping arcades.

Amidst all this *differentiation*, the political concept of *differences*, along with meaningful choices, is arduous to maintain. The high cost of Nikes, a status symbol within black communities, has been targeted as the cause of gang violence and at least one death. Shoes are a big target of theft at homeless shelters. Along with designer children (and babies), African-Americans and other minorities are new and profitable demographic targets— paradoxically enabling African-Americans to enter representation at the movies and on television, initially in commercials but increasingly on regular programming. Procter and Gamble has a special and successful division for "minority" publicity, a model which is being rapidly copied by other corporations. Spiraling consumerism has debits and credits other than money.

Spiegel has hooked up with *Ebony* magazine "to develop a fashion line and catalog aimed at black women. The venture underscores a movement by mainstream marketers [mainstream rather than white] to target minority groups." This is the big ploy for "new audiences," and a sign that what economists call discretionary income, and credit, are now available to more people. "The marketers are discovering that minority consumers often spend a higher percentage of their income on fashion and beauty products than do consumers overall." (The avoidance of the adjective *white* is astonishing because it is unnecessary. The "consumer" is presumed to be white.) Another reason for the new "minority" marketing is that "the black population, with an estimated $250 billion in annual purchasing power, is growing twice as quickly as the general U.S. population [white customers are "overall," "general," and "mainstream"]."[21] Given that two-thirds of the GNP in the 1991 second-quarter report (this is two-thirds of a $5.6 trillion annual economy, but who's counting?) came from consumer spending, shopping is indeed power.[22]

The line will be called E style, "especially designed for black women" who want "bold colors" and styles, for urban professionals who have been "abandoned by the department stores who pay little attention" to their skin-care, sizing, color, and fabric "needs." True enough, but desire is more accurate than need. For Spiegel, "this venture marks another attempt to broaden its appeal by targeting new types of customers. The company went after large women in the early 1980s . . . and recently introduced" a children's line. What is disturbing about this report is the silencing of black women's voices, the avoidance of the joint partner in this venture, the "publisher" of *Ebony*, quoted as "Mrs. Rice of Johnson Publications," "dressed in a bold red suit and gold blouse," only at the end, and then as a potential buyer of the E-line and a wife.[23] Michele Wallace might call this "the invisibility blues."

Kentucky Fried Chicken Australia Ltd "will launch a large expansion programme . . . extending its presence into the South Pacific with a potential target of 500 outlets. . . . In French Polynesia, the indigenous people are earning pretty good money and they are looking for somewhere to spend it." In its battle with McDonald's and Pizza Hut, KFC "had to differentiate its product," changing its image "away from being a meal replacement" toward the concept of munching, as Jane Wagner so accurately parodied. KFC introduced a new snack line, called "non-whole-meal products," a singularly thudding term. Spending $20 million on advertising, KFC targeted "towns with populations of between 10,000 and 15,000."[24]

Claiming that Kentucky Fried Chicken was "enriching China's great culinary traditions," the company opened China's first fast-food restaurant in November 1987. "From a red-and-white chicken bucket two stories high, the likeness of Col. Harlan Sanders beamed benevolently." The 500-seat restaurant "offers a view of the mausoleum where Mao Tse-tung's embalmed body is on public view, of Qianmen Gate at the south end of the square, and of the Great Hall of the People, the seat of government," "the best location in the world." In this joint $1 million venture, KFC owns 60 percent; the copartners include the Beijing Travel and Tourism Corporation.[25]

Along with the formerly untapped markets of African and Hispanic Americans, indigenous peoples, and socialist countries, children, including babies, are a big target. The Juvenile Products Manufacturers Association "has grown from 29 member companies in 1962 to 210 last year. Sales jumped from $700 million in 1978 to $1.8 billion in 1987," with a record $2 billion in 1988. As in the film *Baby Boom*, "babies can sample organic baby food at a baby bar in Bellini, a San Francisco boutique for the underaged."[26]

"Infant fragrances are becoming increasingly popular. . . . With more women becoming parents at an older age, parents have more sophisticated attitudes about products for children," including "exposing their children to sensory experiences." Along with the dubious "sophistication," older women must have more money or be more gullible. A dozen "scents" for babies are now in the stores, for high prices. Of course, all of this was preceded by market research, a fringe entrepreneur—90 percent of female infants "preferred to interact with scented objects." Thus, research, with its gender bias extending to babies and perfume, uncovers new targets for old products, creating little renifleurs (Freud's notion in "The Rat Man" which I discuss later) very early.

Other infant (no longer "baby") products include womb sounds/music (which Stuart, the lawyer and new father on *L.A. Law*, used, along with other baby gadgets, child-raising issues, and psychologies), designer kid clothes, and car seats approved by the Federal Aviation Administration for use on airplanes. Soon, under the guise of safety, babies will have to buy airline tickets. All this is very profitable. "Children have a $130 billion influence on household purchases . . . particularly food, toys, clothing, and cars."[27]

The new baby boom (which has struck actresses and TV newswomen, who, unlike Murphy Brown, are leaving the airwaves in droves) can be perversely seen as a campaign to create little consumers and shore up the crumbling family—the prime marketing target. Or, it can be paranoiacally imagined as a ploy to take women out of the paid labor market and into domesticity, a traffic which historically emerges during times of high unemployment. Connie Chung (and her desire to beat the clock and become pregnant) has been the most visible in the tabloids and on late-night monologues, including a *Saturday Night Live* remote "pregnancy watch" outside her home, but the ranks of the maternal include Deborah Norville, her replacement, Katie Couric, and Meredith Vieira on *60 Minutes*. While motherhood and women's desire became news, a good thing, the economics of maternity leave are being contested. Perhaps the joke was on women after all: Norville and Vieira will be replaced, and Chung will take a cut in her million-dollar salary. The choices for newsmaking women are not as clear-cut as for men.

In spite of this, TV characters, who are often actresses pregnant in "real" life, are choosing their professions and motherhood but not marriage. Mary Jo on *Designing Women* underwent artificial insemination; Rosie O'Neill talked about it with her psychiatrist. Murphy Brown and Teddy on *Sisters* are pregnant and unmarried. On *Cheers*, Rebecca thought she might be pregnant, as did Hannah on *Anything but Love* and Ava (who is married) on *Evening Shade*. Although unhinging motherhood from marriage, "TV's baby boom carries the uncomfortable hint that a woman needs a child to be complete."[28]

The wild and predictable proliferation of products such as diapers (for old and young, male and female, day and night, white or in color), socks, and zany cereal, manufactured by the same few companies and boxed in ever-increasing sizes, demands cavernous warehouse super-markets like Pick 'n' Save for display. These architectural designs resemble the air port hangar or the 1920s/30s industrial plant. Those Fordist assembly-line tactics of incremental divisions of labor and Taylorist time are practiced on our bodies by Nautilus machines during workouts and on hamburgers by minimum-wage retirees, teenagers, and mothers. Leisure and fast food are very disciplined. Like burgers, the packaging of television has been redesigned and recalibrated. There is infinitely more television, available on seventy-plus channels, for twenty-four hours per day. However, unlike the quantum leap of theoretical physics, which overthrew geometry along with Newton's laws of motion, and despite Time-Warner's 200-channel experiment, this is often more of the same, including a multiple appeal to the new paradox of local, mass, subcultural (Taco Bell) audiences.

On the designer surface, diversification (including technologies) appears to complicate specialization and standardization, the twin principles of turn-of-the-century monopoly capitalism. Nothing prepared me for one hundred Elvis impersonators gyrating patriotically beneath the Statue of Liberty or the Elvis Presley charge card, "part of the rapidly growing affinity group market. . . . Just say, charge it to the King!" who is dead although resuscitated by necrophilia.

While burgers and fries are still the old-fashioned claim to fame and product, what McDonald's has always sold cheaply is our valuable time— a system of speed, a temporal model of labor efficiency, a meticulously clean, antiseptic service, now addressed to (grand)parents, which cheerfully saves us time. Only a happier, faster, more fastidious apparatus (who among you, when traveling, uses the restrooms at local filling stations any longer?), not a better hamburger, will upset its dominance—the value of diversified (or, theoretically speaking, heterogeneous), antiseptic, packaged-to-go haste.

The hugely profitable Domino's pizza will be free if home delivery (contracted as piecemeal pizza incentives to local, off-time, spiritually inspired entrepreneurs who *believe* in Domino's profits) takes longer than thirty minutes from the time of the call. Toll House "ready-bake" cookies concluded a recent commercial with "Fast at Last" as their new slogan; American Airlines is now sold as an "on-time machine," while we drive through Tyme machines to punch out money.

While the U.S. television networks block and barter chunks of time, in other service industries, time as velocity has become virtue and sales pitch. Accelerated time is time saved. The rapidly expanding and profitable service industries are dividing and multiplying labor into discrete, timed units—a move from (local) centralization (e.g., all-service garages or department stores) to (national) dispersity—local franchises of international monopolies for fast services, like Midas Muffler or McDonald's or cable TV. Franchise (ironically meaning liberty or freedom from restriction or servitude) culture is trademark culture—a minutely disciplined culture of service. The guarantee is that the Big Mac will be *exactly* the same in Moscow as in Washington.

What will shock and please Soviet temporality will be not uniformity but rather speed and system of incremental labor—Taylor's 1911 (and earlier) schema of timed "scientific management," *without* Taylor's monetary incentives (which Domino's instated. For Taylor, increased profits would result from paying the most efficient workers the highest wages).[29] Whereas the Soviet system of purchase necessitates standing in three lines—one for selection, one for payment, one for pickup—McDonald's has only one line, in Moscow a very long one.

As the luxurious, turn-of-the-century department store goes into receivership or bankruptcy, after the mergers and takovers during the 1980s by international corporate moguls, warehouse discount stores have eliminated decor and services, often instantiating an older method of purchase, which demands waiting. At American, a Milwaukee furniture and appliance discounter, after the dilemma of selecting among hundreds of television monitors, purchase is time-consuming, necessitating two separate transactions. In the $30 billion home-furnishings industry, a Swedish company, Ikea, "is packing its stores [200,000 square feet, visible from major highways] with shoppers" with its "philosophy which calls for each of us to do a little in order to save a lot." "Working against Ikea . . . is the anxiety many people seem to feel about shopping for furniture . . . even worse than buying a car." That consuming is anxious more than pleasurable is a refrain of its coverage. The company's intensive advertising is smart-aleck, hip: "It's a big country. Someone's got to furnish it." Like Frito-Lay executives, Ikea executives understand "what their customers need" and give it to them—mainly furniture, which this Swedish company designs—using

1,500 suppliers in more than forty-five countries to supply components.[30] Even bookcases are multicultural in this era of international trade.

Retailers are being undersold by warehouse discounters—Wal-Mart, K-Mart, and Target, who in turn capitalize on manufacturers of name brands (see below). The challenging competitor to both the retailer and the discounter is the new discount-designer mall with "manufacturer owned outlet stores selling big-name goods at 25% to 70% off. . . . With an upscale look and names like Donna Karan New York, Liz Claiborne . . . the factory outlets let shoppers feed their brand-name cravings without paying department store markets." Perhaps due to consumers' "obsession with trendy brands," these malls have doubled in the past four years, to about 275, with annual sales of "$6.3 billion, making it the fastest growing segment of the retail industry."[31]

Like so many other products signaling an increase in "discretionary income," triggering the insatiable desire for what are called "positional goods" (scarce and hence pricey items such as famous paintings and admission to Ivy League colleges), the proliferation of these gigantic malls is "aimed at upscale shoppers." They "capitalize on the shift to the self-disciplined '90s from the self-indulgent '80s," ironically suggesting that the '90s will be the same as the '80s but at bargain prices. "I'm 40 years old and my free-spending mentality has changed, but I don't want to give up all the niceties. . . . I just want to pay less." Or, more can be gained for less. Our obsessions will be cheaper.

These upscale outlets are small, pleasant shops which provide sales services. They no longer sell seconds or flawed merchandise—in other words, products are manufactured for the outlets, cutting out the retailing "middlemen," and "reaching customers who wouldn't normally buy their luxury items." However, if everyone can afford luxury, dependent on scarcity, is it still luxury? or just everyday life? Luxury and elitism are, after all, historical. The outlets placate retailers by locating outside cities (where the real estate is substantially cheaper—some favor!) and selling last year's line. These are small concessions to their double dealing; the manufacturers are getting it both ways and are not talking. "It's too sensitive an issue with retailers," says the Donna Karan rep (B6). As retaliation, retailers are either dropping lines or building their own outlets, where they sell leftovers to shoppers, imagined as obsessives.

(However, monetary profits aside, few financial analysts understand the psychic payoff of buying more for less. The thrill of a bargain depends on knowledge—of fashion, style, quality, detail, and original price. Unless one knows that a DKNY blazer sells for $450, the $90 price tag is no big deal. The pleasure is the thrill of getting away with something and of having the shopper's savvy of recognizing a good deal (and knowing upscale brands). (My sister's metaphor for bargaining is quite different. Her thrill is that of the hunt—tracking one's prey.)

Not all is harmonious in the discount stores. "A decade ago, lured by the temptation to increase sales, RCA began selling to national retail chains like Kmart," in effect competing with its own dealers and distributors (with 25,000 small retailers who returned a healthy profit to RCA), who went out of business. Thomson S.A. of France, which bought the company in 1987 from General Electric, has reversed this tactic, ordering a "new line of high-end products" and new services for small dealers. Thomson S.A. concluded that discount retailers "force down prices and use manufacturers' brand names to lure consumers into the store only to switch them to cheaper, no-name brands," known as "bait-and-switch."[32] The return to small dealers secures the strength of brand names. By seeking greater control over distribution, manufacturers protect the power of their brand name—one key to franchise culture.

Differentiation has become the hue and cry of advertising under the rubric "individualized" (*presumably* different from "mass") marketing. This new coinage is even older than Bach's Remedies yet depends, paradoxically, on electronic technology. "Direct" or "personalized" marketing is made possible by computers and will really catch hold when ads can be "electronically delivered" to homes.[33] Thus, new houses are being wired with remote-controlled hookup systems which enable an entire house, not just a TV, to be electronically plugged in. One analogy for "direct" marketing is that advertising will become "personalized just the way the listening experience has been miniaturized by the Sony Walkman" (B4).

Along with the skyrocketing expenditure on advertising in the 1980s— the U.S. spends 50 percent more than other countries, averaging almost "$6 a week on every man, woman, and child in the U.S."; the Anheuser-Busch Company "now spends $9 marketing a barrel of beer, compared with $3 in 1980"—the proliferation of products and the capabilities of the computer to gather and collate personal data triggered this emphasis on the individual. As I said, this tactic is new, technologically speaking (although telephones and the mail have been available for years!), and old at the same time—encouraging brand and company loyalty, seeking likely targets rather than just a mass audience or "blaring the message to everyone," establishing a "lasting dialogue or closer relationship with their customers," and "paying attention to what the customer wants."[34] However, while this old-fashioned or postmodern customer is no longer the mass audience modernism, the individual is a statistic, a lifestyle, or a profile, not a person.

"Betcha Can't Eat Just One"

Comparable to the overt logic of contradiction, this is a "reversal of the ad strategy that prompted Vance Packard's 1950 classic, 'The Hidden Persuaders.' Rather than trying to manipulate consumers to letting the consumers manipulate them . . . markets are exploring every facet of consumer behavior—from obvious things such as taste preferences, to more subtle psychological desires. . . . At Frito-Lay, this approach has become something of an obsession." For "snack" foods, obsession is the right word; Robert Johnson's piece in *The Wall Street Journal* is brilliant. "Snack food research and development costs . . . have about doubled in the past decade—to between $20 million and $30 million a year. At the same time, the company says it is spending proportionately less on advertising." Thus, the costs, and the jobs, remain in-house. Frito-Lay's healthy profits are attributed to research, not addictive eating behavior, science and psychology accounting for their share of the market climbing to 33.5 percent from 25 percent within a decade.[35]

According to *Snack Food* magazine, yet another fringe entrepreneur (*Nails* is another magazine, addressed to the nail-care industry, splitting off from hairstylists, and, like the atom, dividing or specializing into hands or feet), "pretax profit margins approach a whopping 20 cents on every retail-sales dollar" (B1). As with the history of another "inferior" (cheap) food product, popcorn (and movies), the profits from starch are substantial. Like the ever-growing paper containers (yet another booming industry) for popcorn and soda, the bags are getting bigger. "No one walks around with a 6½ ounce Pepsi anymore. That's a child's size, an embarrassment. We want that to be true of small bags of potato chips too. We want to load the consumer up with bigger bags." (Soon we will need porters in movie theaters to carry our snack food for us.)

A typical adult eats seventy-two potato chips at a sitting (but who's counting?). Because over 65 percent of chips are "eaten in private," they are a perfect TV snack (although Pepsico is eyeing movie theater concession stands, with their profitable markup). One psychologist, perhaps a nutty professor, suggests that potato chips "confer some of the merriment and excitement of snacks eaten previously at a party." Potato chips as Happy Days! Amazing! Like the expansion of TV channels and the spread of addiction therapies, the potato chip economy is booming—a $4 billion market, with consumption topping six pounds per person in the U.S., or a hundred one-ounce vending-machine bags per person per year. One executive poetically assesses that "young people are learning to graze on potato chips, the way cows eat grass." These browsers and grazers "expect the potato chip to be there as on-demand feeding," yet another eloquent figuration of the chip consumer.

Mr. Lay, who founded the company in 1929, learned about consumer preferences from conversations with grocery-store owners and gas-station managers as he hawked his wares from his Ford pickup. Now Pepsico, the conglomerate owner, the perfect double whammy of salt/soda, has a Frito-Lay sales force of 10,000, "each equipped with a hand-held computer that can advise headquarters." I can see Steve Martin in this role. At their "Potato Chip Pentagon," a closely guarded building in Dallas, five hundred chemists, engineers, and psychologists work, "leaving no consumer preference to guesswork." Their primary tool is a "$40,000 simulated human mouth made of aluminum to measure the jaw power it takes to crunch single chips." (Leno does not have to look too far for his parodies of popular culture. Capitalism can be very funny.) "We have to have a fanaticism about this to deliver just the right feeling to the mouth. . . . We have to be perfect; after all, no one really *needs* a potato chip." "But many people *want* them."

The distinction between need and want is a good analysis of psychoanalytic desire, which is as insatiable as eating potato chips. In their Lacanian search for the perfect taste (endless, like desire or eating enough chips), the company conducts six thousand consumer taste tests to develop six new varieties per year. "Knowing more about the consumers than the consumers themselves know is an important goal at Frito-Lay," which, like psychoanalysts or drug counselors, has savvy ways to measure chip intake in spite of denials by crunchers who claim to eat sprouts, not chips.

While the company realizes that "the basic snack-chip market remains anyone with a mouth,' " a stupefying remark, Frito-Lay also acknowledges difference (in video portraits of chip consumers), and hence markets eighty-five regional brands. "There's really no national snack-food market anymore." Sour cream is popular in the Midwest, vinegar in the Northeast, and mesquite in the Southwest and California. Northerners "like their chips fried a bit longer than the typical 2½ minutes." Yet, I wonder whether this new regionalism, or even (mass) localism, is another ploy of diversity as a marketing tactic. After the market has exploded, nationally or mass-culturally, it implodes, dividing itself in order to multiply, like *Aliens* or Procter and Gamble. (I can imagine some research VP inventing a *soft* chip for the baby, excuse me, infant, market. This idea is not far-fetched. I remember an episode of *Burns and Allen*. It wasn't Gracie putting a pen in the electric pencil sharpener that was funny for the laugh track; it was the superfluity of the electric sharpener itself—now an office essential rather than a joke.)

"Little wonder that some consumers can barely keep up with all their options. When Frito-Lay set up a display of its new Cheetos, 'Paws'—a corn snack in the shape of a cheetah's foot—near the petfood aisle, confusion set in. 'Are Paws for my cat or me?' " No stand-up comic could have made up this product, its name—or this story.

The snack-food industry has recently undertaken its most contradictory endeavor—making its products fit the new ecological and healthy lifestyle of low fat, salt, and sugar, the McLean culture. McDonald's has led the way, introducing a low-fat burger and recyclable paper wrappings. Frito-Lay has been quieter, lowering the salt count without letting anyone know, and substituting "cooking" for "fried," a word which was corporately banned. As Dwight Riskey, a research VP, says, "Consumers won't sacrifice taste for health in snacks" (B2). However, Riskey's either-or logic is out of date; consumers want both/and. Given chips' high fat content, about 70 percent, a healthy chip is quite an order.

An updated Darwinian food chain might be something like this: Frito-Lay spends $30 million to create the perfect compulsive taste, setting off the crazy desire to eat between meals, called "snacking"; Jenny Craig counters by opening weight-watch centers which forbid fat, salt, and eating between meals. (Oprah Winfrey, the host of a daytime talk show, confesses to a food addiction, particularly salt and chips; after losing sixty pounds by not eating, she gains the weight, and more, back. To paraphrase Jane Wagner, "I have lost the same twenty pounds so many times that my cellulite is experiencing deja-vu.") Frito-Lay responds by creating the low-fat diet chip; Jenny Craig sells her own brand of no-cal chips. In this no-cal Nirvana of "on-demand feeding," we could munch constantly, at exorbitant cost, without gaining weight (as in *Defending Your Life*). We *can* have our cake and eat it! If the snack industry succeeds, the centuries-old differences between breakfast, lunch, and dinner will be elided, differentiated.

Just as truth is stranger than fiction, the market outruns imagination. "Fast food's flight from fat is accelerating." Low-cal, low-fat burgers hawked by McDonald's and Hardee's are nothing compared to the new alliance: Burger King is teaming with Weight Watchers (owned by H. J. Heinz) in a Florida marketing test. The new Burger King menu includes Weight Watchers low-cal pancakes, lasagna, and fettucine, along with Weight Watchers popcorn, brownies, and salad dressing. "Offering customers Weight Watchers lasagna as an alternative to a Whopper" provides something for everyone, a perfect double logic.[36] Procter and Gamble, "hungry for a bite of the rich chocolate market," might have discovered the key to the low-cal candy bar. "Anything that reduces the guilt could be a big hit." Given that our average U.S. consumption of chocolate is eleven pounds per person, P & G stands to profit.[37]

PepsiCo, the "parent company" of Frito-Lay, also owns Pizza Hut, Kentucky Fried Chicken (relabeled, in this era of no fat, KFC), and Taco Bell. PepsiCo considers its new big rival to be McDonald's—quoting its stock price along with Coca Cola's. "Pepsi is conceding the international coke war to Coca Cola." Although PepsiCo is not on "a global beverage quest," it is on an international fast-food quest. KFC has higher profit margins abroad than domestically. PepsiCo has been opening "fast-food places at the rate of three a day," becoming the biggest restaurant business, second in profit only to McDonald's.[38]

As of June 1991, Frito-Lay was PepsiCo's "flagship business," the biggest source of profit. By September 1991, the Frito-Lay picture was not so rosy. "The snack-food giant is slicing 800 administrative and managerial jobs from its headquarters in Plano, Texas. . . . Frito-Lay, with 42% of PepsiCo's profits, had a 9% drop in earnings. . . . It doesn't expect profit margins to improve this year."[39] Ah, the vagaries of the market.

The move from mass-media advertising to direct marketing via mail and telephone shifts profits away from television, newspapers, and magazines. These tactics cost more per targeted consumer and hence make economic sense only when advertisers "know enough about a household." I smell a new (old) business here. While Frito-Lay has its own research staff, data entrepreneurs compile and resell lists, a lucrative trade of information enabled by computers. The industry bootlegs and recycles data scavenged from the public domain, including registrations (which state governments sell) and birth records; financial transactions such as mortgages, loans, and credit purchases; and subscription lists of journals and newspapers.

Their electronic data bases "include nearly every household in America, with address, phone number, estimated income and information on purchasing habits."[40] What is intriguing is the tautological logic—data come from a previous purchase, either a product or a credit card, a birth or a death. Or, as the industry bluntly puts it, "what they have, what they buy and what they can afford." And then we die. This closed circuit of consumption unto death leads to the conclusive claim that "using data on their customers' habits and preferences, advertisers can now pitch individuals with laser-beam precision." Three companies presently dominate this unregulated business—R. L. Polk, Connelley Marketing, and Metromail—which is becoming intensely competitive. Some companies specialize. "Senior Citizens Unlimited combs driver licenses and voter registrations for its data base of 40 million Americans over 50."

Telephone companies are also moving into the business rather than serving merely as the carrier. For example, in a great gambit, a recent advert "promoted an 800 number one could call to learn the latest pollen count. The phone computers kept a record of the thousands who called, matched them to names and addresses, and all were sent a mailing by Warner-Lambert for Benadryl antihistamine."

Death and the Market

"Meanwhile, the industry keeps thinking of new twists." Lifestyle Change Communications, Inc., of Atlanta includes in its compilations a question about a recent death in the family. According to Robert Perlstein, the company's president, "Death has always been a negative life-style change nobody thought could be sold, but I differ. . . . I think it's a very good market" (A12). And, indeed, he is right. Business is booming, as the 77 million baby boomers will "soon begin reaching middle age and dying in increasing numbers."[41] In order to dispel their negative image, funeral homes, a $3 billion-a-year industry regulated in 1984 under the funeral rule, now provide aftercare services. These include anniversary mailings, group counseling, and memorial tributes—video tapes or tree plantings. One package includes free limousine services for a wedding in the family of the deceased.[42] Some homes have hired a "bereavement-services director" to handle aftercare. Again, Leno would love not only the idea of death as "a negative life-style change," but also a "bereavement services director" trying to give death an upbeat image.

It would appear that differentiation is only as limited as our imaginations, that generating products and services appears to be an infinite process. And where there is a service, there will be byproducts, particularly books and magazines. *Caregivers Quarterly* provides information on death and dying to eight hundred ministers in Minnesota. The main journals, however, are *Cemetery Management, Catholic Cemetery,* and *American Cemetery,* the "least grave" magazine of cemetery management, with a sense of humor for cemeterians. "Make money the Modern Way. Urn it," is their slogan. The magazine reprints "Far Side" cartoons and features "Funerals of the Famous."[43] Even dead celebrities other than Elvis are fascinating in this gossip culture.

However, differentiation has one limit that even death cannot outwit— memory. Given the average daily exposure to 300 ad messages, 9,900 per month, or 109,500 per year, "some 80% of Americans can't remember the typical commercial one day after they have seen it," resulting in a case of "national amnesia." New research suggests that ads which either are too fast or tax "both the left and right hemisphere" leave viewers "baffled." (One advertising research center recently closed, "otherwise we'd all be in rubber rooms.")[44] To counter forgetting, Inner Response, a research firm in Charlotte, North Carolina, uses EEGs, tracing electrical activity within the brain, performing brain-wave analysis. "The magic formula may lie in the growing body of research on emotions," the link between memory and feelings.

Since the War in the Gulf, and the many TV advertising cancellations, marketing professors have claimed that "a sad ad placed within a sad program . . . was 40% more effective than a happy ad in the same program, and 15% more forceful than a sad ad placed within a happy program." The sad-ad, sad-program combo beat out a "feel good ad within an upbeat program." Ad execs questioned the feasibility of putting this theory into practice, wondering how to classify *L.A. Law* or *Knot's Landing* ("Television Commercial Evaluation in the Context of Program Induced Mood: Congruency vs. Consistency Effects" by Michael A. Kamins).[45]

This new magic formula of affect is apparent even on the NBC *Nightly News,* which now closes with a feeling spot. In the future, if feelings continue their positive trend, anchors may even be allowed expressions of affect. Although fear has been the leading emotion for decades, producing anxiety which necessitates therapy, who knows what affects will become stylish in the 1990s once therapy has enabled us to identify our real feelings which can then be diversified. Then, as now, affect, along with time, will mean money.

Another aftereffect of the war was an "about-face" in network policy regarding commercials during catastrophe coverage. After Kennedy's assassination, the networks had suspended commercials for close to four days. However, in 1992 "viewers are very sophisticated." They know that commercials are "necessary to produce and cover the story." A more feasible argument than audience sophistication (from the networks!) is the decline in network ratings, the ascension of CNN, and the drop in advertisers during the War in the Gulf coverage. "Even after the war ended, many sponsors pulled their TV spots every time controversy reared its head." The Soviet coup and the Hill-Thomas hearings "prompted an advertiser exodus."

To counter this trend, and noble TV history, the Network Television Association, a trade group for the three networks, blanketed "3,000 ad executives with a new, 16 minute videotape"—"Advertising during Times of Crisis." An executive VP for NBC News states that crises "captivate" people, "gluing them to their TV screens." The tape argues that "people don't mind ads interrupting crises coverage," wielding viewer statistics as evidence. For example, "seven out of ten people surveyed thought advertisers were doing a public service." After statistics, network executives promise sensitivity. "Ads won't be placed next to footage of blood and body bags." The gore will be mediated by "a pad section or explainer section." Mainly, the tape emphasizes high ratings. The Hill-Thomas hearings "drew about a 22 share. The audience is full of news junkies." (*Wall Street Journal*, January 27, 1992, B5.)

As Freud knew so well, "the untrustworthiness of our memory" (SE X, 243) has always been "the weak spot in our mental life." Long before brainwave marketeers, Freud asserted that we believe in memory "without having the slightest guarantee of its trustworthiness." This uncertainty spreads over "the entire past." Obsession, or compulsion, is an "attempt at a compensation for this doubt" (SE X, 234).

II

◆

Obsession
(Not *Just* a Perfume)

The artsy, angst-laden ads for Calvin Klein's *Obsession* have a long and romantic history—that of melancholia, the agon of tortured men, sometimes
geniuses, although Lady Macbeth is a perfect case study (as is Captain Ahab).
One predominant fear used to be plague, then syphilis, replaced by cancer
and more recently AIDS.[46] Death, war, spaces, and fear of traveling have been
constant. As Calvin Klein knows, (and now Estee Lauder, with its perfume
Knowing competing with Klein's *Obsession*), obsession depends upon repetition and differentiation—the Frito-Lay method of research and marketing.[47]
Comparable to differentiation, with its turn-of-the-century corporate origins,[48]
therapy for obsession can be traced to the same time period: the 1903 theories
of Pierre Janet, a French medical psychologist whose methods are being clin-
ically revived in the U.S., and the 1909 publication of Freud's "Notes upon a
Case of Obsessional Neurosis" (the year he visited the U.S.), ignominiously
labeled the Rat Man.

While Janet described successful treatment of rituals with behavioral
techniques, often confronting imaginary fears,[49] "prolonged exposure to
an obsessional stimulus"[50] (like watching the War in the Gulf), by 1920
treatment had turned away from symptoms and rituals and toward the unconscious conflicts assumed to underlie them, away from the present and
into the patient's past. According to behaviorists, Oedipus did little to im-

prove treatment.[51] "Behavior" or "Reality" therapy exists in the present, treating immediate rituals. Psychoanalysis traces these displaced symptoms back to their presumed cause—a search for an origin (like authorship), an answer which will resolve the dilemma.[52]

This shift from the wildly popular neurasthenia (from 1869 to 1920) to obsession around 1920 can also be explained by the establishment of certification boards which regulated the therapy business—medicine was professionalized: standardized, specialized, and centralized; like corporations, it also monopolized. Prior to medical "specialization," an early instance of bodily differentiation, a plethora of practitioners had diagnosed and treated neurasthenia; after this, alienists, rechristened "psychiatrists," would be its analysts. In the U.S. in the 1950s, amidst an outbreak of Cold War fear and anxiety, behavior therapies competed with psychoanalysis, gaining ascendancy; learning theories applied to phobic disorders were applied to OCD symptoms, reducing compulsive rituals by confronting imaginary fears.

Recent therapies for OCD are a bricolage of Janet, Beard, and behaviorism, with spiritual beliefs, often Eastern, mixed with Jungian-Freudianisms. The 12 Steps of Alcoholics Anonymous (which is free) are at the base of other therapies, differentiated to deal with various problems—which, like cars, cleansers, and lipstick, have multiplied. Like other forms of cultural commerce, therapies, and therapists, have been deregulated, turning therapy into a booming entrepreneurial or do-it-yourself industry. Therapy is a profitable enterprise, a service with tangible by-products—books, journals, and real estate: meeting places and treatment centers. Once one enters the circuit of self-help and therapy, one service and product leads to another. Because there is no cure, only the continual process of recovery, this endless chain can be costly.

Formerly, like the Platonic mind/body split of Western philosophy, mental disorders were also divided—into cognitive and affective. Of the latter, three are termed "anxiety disorders"—phobias, neuroses, and obsessive-compulsive disorders (OCD).[53] Along with anxiety, they are also defined by fear, as is neurasthenia. The division between thought and feelings, or head and heart, is paradoxical because obsessive/compulsive neurosis consists of involuntary *thoughts* triggering *affect*—doubt, fear, and anxiety. Or, "intrusive disturbing thoughts and repetitious, stereotyped actions." Edna Foa and Gail Steketee separate "thoughts and images and actions that elicit anxiety as obsessions" from "overt behaviors that reduce anxiety into compulsions."[54] Freud proposed three forms of obsessions: ideas, affects, and actions.

The cause, the source of the fear, is usually missing. Like Freud's model of shock in *Inhibitions, Symptoms and Anxiety* (in the next chapter), the anxiety lacks an object. "An external, precipitating event, radiation or an auto accident, is generally not present"; a passing thought becomes "a source of unremitting anguish and disabilities." The obsession "becomes autonomous, evolving into a threat of its own."[55] The relation between anxiety and the lack of an object, the perceived separation from the real, is more than interesting as an analysis of contemporary, electronic culture.

A significant debate still rages around cause-effect—whether the compulsive situations *cause* or *reduce* anxiety. Behaviorists such as Foa and Steketee argue that the ritual reduces discomfort and yet is experienced as pressure. For psychoanalysis, rituals are the outcome of anxiety. For cognitive or structuralist therapy, rituals are anxiety-producing. For example, Graham Reed claims that obsessions and compulsive rituals are internal, are resisted, and lead to interference. Resistance is the struggle against an intrusive thought— often an exhausting battle which results in extreme fatigue.[56] Another dispute is whether to define OCD as its form or its content. These either/or arguments resemble the pattern and effects of OCD, which derails cause-effect logic.

Most psychiatrists (behavioral and phenomenological) describe OCD as the *contents* of the behavior. Rituals of cleaning and washing, counting, checking, or ruminating on an idea, enacted in an exact chain, consume more and more time, often preventing the victims from leaving their homes. (Think of continual catastrophe coverage, necessitating more TV, or the FCC lifting of *all* restrictions on commercial time per hour.) Some patients spend up to six hours or more dressing (or "watching" TV). Others wash their hands one hundred times, then soak them in caustic disinfectants, a ritual based on a fear of contamination which can spread to other parts of the house or body, virtually taking up one's entire life.[57] One twenty-two-year-old woman "had an intense fear of contamination from dogs. . . . The problem generalized to include many areas of England; even reading or hearing about these places triggers prolonged washing rituals. Her fears led to repeated changes of residence."

Rituals have a strict sequence. If interrupted, the compulsion will begin over again until it is completed. Rituals are repetitive and stereotyped (like sitcoms), becoming progressively complex and time-consuming (like catastrophe coverage). While this behavior ranges from the normal to the nuts, compulsive thought exists in our everyday life. The domino theory of foreign policy (so vehemently argued for Korea and Vietnam) which accompanied cold wars of containment resembles this logic on a global scale. The spread of the 1991 War in the Gulf was constantly imagined. Television heightens rumor and fear while simultaneously assuaging our fears—a logic of creation/cancellation comparable to Eat!/Diet! The coverage of catastrophe involves what communication scholars call a disaster array, comparable to the feeding frenzy of fish, or obsession. Thus, the "War in the Gulf" revived the cold war fear of Stalinism regarding the Soviet actions in the Baltic states. In the 1987 coverage of "Black Monday," anchors raised the specter of the stock market crash of 1929. The historical devastation of San Francisco (along with the prediction of "the Big One" for Los Angeles) was invoked during the 1989 continual coverage of "The Great Quake." History becomes fear, triggering obsession. TV created fear, which necessitated more TV, coverage spreading throughout the day, to all channels. Constant viewing and channel switching are audience rituals which uncannily resemble classic OCD behavior.

Less seriously, corporate logic, under the guise of "diversification," appears to be dominated by obsession. Take Liz Claiborne, "the cherished choice of the working woman . . . arguably the most powerful label in retailing. It isn't enough. No matter that . . . Claiborne dominates as much as half of the women's apparel floor space." Or the company's "double-digit" growth. "It still isn't enough." Just like desire, obsession has no end, spreading rhizomatically, like crab grass. Success (or money) breeds the desire for more. Hence Liz (as aficionados refer to the label, although she sold out and retired in 1989) needs to "recruit new customers and expand into new merchandise areas"—diversification. They've already moved into several apparel "niches," large sizes and menswear. The next big step is into athletic shoes (they've got to be kidding!)—make that "fashion athletic shoes that coordinate with a collection of Claiborne clothes."[58]

(By 2000, buying "tennis shoes" will take several weeks. Alas, after choosing a shoe, with the consultation of a foot-fitness expert, will come the anguish of selecting socks, with a retail psychologist on hand. Only then will shoe fetishism, with its Victorian history, take its place as a major postmodern addiction. Twelve Step Groups will take on literal meaning as barefoot sufferers speak about the inability to stop looking for the perfect "athletic shoe." I remember an era of two choices, inevitably picking U.S. Keds, Canvas Flyers, which returned in 1990, forty years later, as a new style—the ALL SPORT SHOE! When memory does work, commercial culture is *very* funny.)

Obsession—a thought process, a logic which drives the behavior—is tautological, administering *and* defusing fear and anxiety, with both temporal and spatial manifestations. Another woman "restrained her child in one room which was kept entirely germ free. She opened and closed all doors with her feet in order to avoid contaminating her hands." "A 42 year old woman practiced hand-washing and house-cleaning rituals over a 26 year period. . . . She found it impossible to truncate her rituals in order to prepare dinner . . . or get to bed."[59] As if to trigger or appeal to obsessions, advertisers have differentiated bodily and household zones of odor and dirt, necessitating additional cleaning products, proliferating like TV channels and commercial time slots.

In "Three Kinds of Dirt," Judith Williamson consulted the *Hoover Book of Home Management*, discovering not three but five kinds of carpet dirt. "The product" sells itself as "the 'answer' to a 'problem,'" while in fact the product itself defines the problem it claims to solve," a circular logic which resembles obsessive-compulsive thought. Products redefine the world by "creating new categories out of previously undifferentiated areas of experience."[60] (Personal products also re-create our bodies, locating malfeasances in hygiene or aesthetics which necessitate specialized products—another tautological logic.)

Like saving time (and fast franchises), alleviating fear has become a profitable enterprise. "Franchisers are cashing in on Americans' phobias. Fearful of using public toilets? Swishers International sprays restroom fixtures weekly with a germicide. . . . Guilt-ridden about letting your kids go to fat in front of the television? Discovery Zone offers fitness centers for pre-teens. . . . Worried that the used car you want to buy is a lemon in disguise? Car Checkers of America will inspect everything." The owners of these firms say that they have "caught on with franchisees because they ease current anxieties: fears about diseases, baby boomers' anguish over their tot's fitness, and . . . [the] consumer's growing price consciousness."[61]

Regarding checking rituals, a male nurse "had to ensure that no one had been inadvertently locked in a room or been trapped in a manhole, that no babies had been dumped into dustbins or bushes."[62] A woman teacher "spent up to three hours each night checking doors, gas taps, windows, plugs, and switches before going to bed." "A 19 year old clerk carried out four hours of checking rituals after other members of his family went to bed" (116). The *Today Show* used to announce what we would see next week or the next day. Then it announced what we could expect in the next hour or half-hour. Now it repetitively and compulsively checks on its own content, counting down to the next segment, the next minute's topic. Soon, the program will consist only of the ritual of repeated promos and expectations. The American Express ad for travelers' checks, like those for burglar alarm systems, trigger other fears and checking rituals. Overt guilt is a recent appeal as Sandy Duncan switches to a new brand of Wheat Thins, feeling "no guilt," and anxious businessmen fret over their inadequate telephone system, shot with hand-held cameras.

The last episodes of the 1990 season of *thirtysomething* concerned male anxiety, structured around Elliot's ability to direct a TV promotion/commercial, and the subsequent corporate-raider takeover of the ad agency, with Michael playing an inside mole. In the name of childhood friendship—his commitment to the fired Elliot—he conspired to overthrow Miles, the owner, and failed. High (corporate) Anxiety was not the outcome but the very substance and basis of these episodes, filled with fretful musical scoring. Advertising became high, deadly serious drama. The corporate domain of anxiety, linked to men, money, and success in advertising, is reversed for women on this series, tied to affairs of the body, domesticity, and ecology. At home, although illustrating children's books, Elliot's wife developed ovarian cancer and survived chemo- and radiation therapy, while the very pregnant Hope worked on ecology issues and considered having an affair with an environmental activist.

As Sasha Torres sees it, this now-canceled series, like *The Wonder Years* and *L.A. Law*, appealed to baby boomers who, she imagines, resembled the series' characters—"white, educated, urban, upper-middle class, and well-endowed with cultural capital."[63] In this post-feminist world, sexual difference doesn't matter anymore.

Reed argues that form, not content, is determinant: "*What* is thought is not so significant as *how* the thought is reached and maintained."[64] Reed's three criteria are that "the worry has a compulsive quality, that the individual regards it as irrational, and that he [she] struggles unsuccessfully to rid himself [herself] of it. The content of the experience is beside the point" (41). Yet Reed endorses Janet, whose study of content had five categories—sacrilege, crime, self-shame, shame of one's body, and hypochondria, contents which referred to the individual rather than to objects in the outside world (26). The accuracy of Janet's taxonomy regarding TV commercials suggests that women's anxiety and shame, not our pleasure or desire, are being simultaneously courted and fostered.

That TV appeals to bodily and self-shame and hypochondria goes without saying. That shame is gendered and at the base of addiction is rarely noted. Some psychiatrists hesitantly acknowledge that OCD shares symptoms with addiction, anorexia nervosa, and posttraumatic stress syndrome. All involve "intrusive, reprehensible thoughts or images that are resisted. . . . The intrusive content frequently shifts to new preoccupations."[65] Addictive logic is destructive and inverse—addicts repeat the same behavior, expecting different results, rather than changing initial actions. Cause-effect logic is perversely out of whack with reality: "I drink (drug, eat, shop, gamble) because I have problems," rather than "drinking (etcetera) is my problem." For Janet, the patient "is not only relatively incapable of appropriate response to reality but is unaware of his incapacity." Denial is a powerful stranglehold, difficult to break and infinitely more complex than lying. "Emotional disturbance is the result, not the cause, of this subjective inadequacy" with reality (77).

Janet points to the futility of "intellectual activity which does not culminate in interaction with reality. If intellectual elaborations are not related to real outcomes or experience, they do not facilitate the individual's healthy development." Thoughts can become "substitutes for reality behaviors so that the sufferer increasingly postpones activity in favour of internal debate" (79). Reality and thought are equal dilemmas. After the Rat Man analysis, "omnipotence of thought" becomes a favorite Freudian term.[66]

"Rat Man"

Because Freud understood contradictory logic and wrote a history of patriarchy, his work can provide insights into the workings of familialism as well as capitalism. Because television is filled with talking heads (more than faces), as is psychoanalysis, a further affinity exists. As Mahony suggests, Freud's context was the " 'Era of Second Orality' [a good slogan for dentists] ushered in by . . . telephone and radio, which introduce a senso-rial shift from . . . scriptorial and typographic traditions" (134). Redun-dancy "characterizes oral thought and speech," television, and Freud's style of writing, which Mahony describes as a "temporal flow" which en-gages with an unseen audience—an apt analysis of TV as well as *The Stan-dard Edition*. *Beyond the Pleasure Principle*'s child's game of fort/da, linked to the death drive, the compulsion to repeat, and the mastery of mother and unpleasure, is not surprisingly an appropriate model for TV conventions, programming, *and* addictive behavior.

Freud wrote more about obsessive-compulsive neurosis than any other topic, devoting fourteen major papers to it. His first was in 1894, his most famous in 1909—"Notes upon a Case of Obsessional Neurosis," the Rat Man (aka Dr. Ernst Lanzer, "revealed for the first time" in 1986 by Ma-hony); *Beyond the Pleasure Principle* and "The 'Uncanny' " in 1919; and in 1926, the substantial revision, *Inhibitions, Symptoms and Anxiety*. For Freud, "obsessional neurosis is unquestionably the most interesting and repaying subject of analytic research" (Mahony, 20). The oversight of this work in contemporary cultural theory is surprising, particularly since Walter Ben-jamin *predicated* his analysis of the experience of modernity/shock/information in "On Some Motifs in Baudelaire" on Freud—"Freud's fun-damental thought, on which these remarks are based."[67]

Given Freud's inscription of a female subject in *Inhibitions, Symptoms and Anxiety*, obsession is more pertinent for women than the Lacanian model of male desire and female lack. The fifteen-year focus of feminist theory on sexuality and desire, modeled on metaphors of vision, has created a real blind spot. The dominant model of psychoanalysis developed for cinema is based on the unconscious, desire, and the male subject. It relies on voy-eurism and scopophilia, desirous seeing from a distance. Obsessional neu-rosis shifts to include the conscious, love/loss, and the female subject. Obsession depends on knowing, on epistemophilia—on thought (and per-haps smell) rather than sight. This is a model of anxiety rather than plea-sure, an economics of money more than libido.

Freud's theory of anxiety—which can lack an object (as do the majority of fears)—resembles franchise (or service) and electronic culture, particularly television and computers, media wherein tangibility is a secondary stage, an aftereffect. (Tangible objects, often women, are central for scopophilia and voyeurism.) The relation between anxiety and the lack of an object is also a fear of contemporary theorists. Think of Baudrillard's acute anxiety about the state of simulated culture and missing referents. Or, as Felix Guattari writes of Lacan's "concept of the unconscious that tends essen-tially to divide desire from reality": "To believe that desire can only be based (symbolically) on its own impotence, its own castration, implies a complete set of political and micro-political assumptions."[68] In many ways, the insatiable nature of Lacanian desire resembles obsession or addiction.

What is rarely noted is that obsessional neurosis is tied to thought and is aural more than visual. U.S. television (broadcast, cable, and satellite)—embodying contradictions and erasing boundaries between media and spaces—is obsessed with speaking bodies which filter and mediate the "world" by words. And while obsession is everywhere, it is not the only subjectivity.

Freud's comparison between hysteria and obsessionality is helpful in charting differences between subjectivities. Hysteria is linked to *visual* memory, while obsessionality is tied to *thoughts,* to *words. Studies in Hysteria* states that "whereas the memories of hysterical patients usually return in pictorial form, the memories of obsessionals return as thoughts" (Freud, 280). By *Totem and Taboo* (1913), hysteria is a "gesture-language" and obsessionality a "thought-language" (Mahony, 169), with hysteria "similar to the picture language of dreams" (170). Perhaps most critical, obsession "functions between the conscious and the unconscious rather than between the unconscious and the preconscious" (147). Obsessionality is more "readily comprehensible than hysteria in that its language is closer to the expressive form of our conscious thought" (169).

For Freud, obsessional thoughts are hybrids which accept certain premises of the obsession that "they are combating, and thus, while using the weapons of reason, are established upon a basis of pathological thought" which he labels *deliria* (SE X, 222). The obsessional idea thus retains traces of the original struggle—which is why the cancellation is not readily apparent.

The techniques of obsessionality—techniques which Benjamin cited in his critique of "information" and newspapers—are applicable to commercial culture. Pushing the "date of the first occurrence" "further back as the analysis proceeds," constantly finding fresh "first occasions for the appearance of the obsession" (SE X, 229), is another ploy. For many critics, the most troubling aspect of television is the missing first occasion, caught up in reruns and TV references, labeled simulation. TV anchors try, during catastrophe coverage, to locate a first cause, an origin, providing us with a cause-effect logic which covers up omission and ellipsis.

Another tactic is avoidance of facts which would help in solving the conflict, along with a "predilection" for "uncertainty and doubt." "The chief subjects . . . are paternity, length of life, life after death, and memory" (SE X, 233)—a virtual compendium of soap-opera topics, particularly the "doubt of love" which results in paralyzing indecision, enabled by the "weak spot in the security of our mental life—the untrustworthiness of our memory." With Bobby's infamous return to *Dallas,* after a season-long dream, TV took this "weak spot" too far, straining all credulity.

Days of Our Lives gave more narrative credit to its long-term viewers—adept in serial conventions, including the replacement of actors playing a recurring role. The return of Marlena and Roman Brady, both narratively dead, was also a resurrection of two performers who had left the show five and seven years earlier. In contrast to the shock tactic of *Dallas, Days* tied memory to story, creating a new memory for and with us. The return was foreshadowed and gradual—beginning in August 1991, and realized only in October. The story is that Victor Kuriakis, for some vague, conspiratorial gain which is either high finance or criminal (or both), held them prisoner on some Latin American island—Marlena in a coma and Roman in chains. The Lazarus tale was no small task, given that a new actor had replaced Roman (the plastic-surgery ploy), slept with Marlena, and, after her death, raised her/his children. The two Romans, the real and the impersonation, were with Marlena in the jungle, then back in Salem. Fortunately, the fake Roman (aka John Black) is in love with Isabella, who is conveniently pregnant.

The differences (simplified, to be sure) between logics of hysteria and obsessional neurosis are instructive. Hysteria satisfies opposing impulses simultaneously, and obsessionality satisfies opposing impulses through sequential acts (Mahony, 168). In hysteria, "two birds are killed with one stone. In contrast, a contiguity marks the diphasic obsession, acts where a first activity is undone by the second" (57). At the base of obsessionality are what Freud called reproaches; at the base of hysteria is conflict (153). Both are the result of holding opposing or contradictory thoughts. Both logics apply in different measures to television and other cultural objects. The patient had "two separate and contradictory convictions. . . . His oscillation between these two views obviously depended upon his momentary attitude towards his obsessional disorder" (SE X, 229–30).

More pertinent for my argument is Freud's assessment that the subject— a female subject—has two "different outlooks upon life." "She puts forward the first of them (easy-going and lively) as her official ego, while in fact she is dominated by the second (gloomy and ascetic)." Although he is, as usual, negative when speaking of women, "she" becomes a subject. Behind her gloom and asceticism are "long-repressed wishful impulses" (SE X, 248). "Long-repressed" resembles Freud's anatomy of "humour," predicated on rage. Rather than directing anger outward, the subject takes anger inward. Rather than railing against social conditions, TV urges us to change our bodies, our clothes, our lifestyles.

However, women's "long-repressed wishful impulses" are being expressed—a frightening scenario for men as *A Question of Silence*, the film by Marlene Gorris, revealed. A spate of 1991 films with aggressive female protagonists raises the issue of women and violence. *Thelma and Louise* is a violent response to rape and sexism of all varieties. *The Silence of the Lambs* investigates male sexual perversion, dramatizing the aggression of the now-famous "male gaze" along with serial killers and cannibalism. As in *La Femme Nikita*, the women shoot to kill. *V. I. Warshawski* and *Terminator 2* portray tough, strong women skilled in the martial arts. In all these films, male institutions, including psychoanalysis in *Silence* and *Terminator*, are under investigation by women who take action. *Impromptu*, *Truth or Dare*, and *Switch* trespass and invert the decorum of gender prescriptions.

While I would argue that a logic of obsession (ideas, affects, and actions) producing High Anxiety is currently rampant and fashionable, particularly in the corporate world, U.S. TV switches address and enunciation, positioning the viewer across a spectrum of subjectivities which are, however double-voiced, consistent within form or genre, for example, soap opera, commercials, late-night talk, news and catastrophe, and situation comedy, and contained by heterosexuality and familialism, the basis of the cultural economy. TV's proclivity for parody involves the displacement of the conventions and enunciation of one form into another.

TV manufactures fear, uncertainty, and doubt. Perhaps over time, it fosters OCD and addiction; at least Adrienne Rich and Betty Ford believe it does. TV can be watched at the Betty Ford Center only on Saturday nights after 7:00 P.M. Hitting bottom in her made-for-TV movie, Gena Rowlands as Betty Ford sits in front of TV's flickering lights, drunk, inarticulate. She has chosen TV (and drinking) over a dinner made by her son.

The traits of compulsion—repetition, stereotypy, rituals, indecision, ruminations—along with sexual difference (more washers are female, more checkers are male), uncannily apply to TV and the stock market, as do the contradictory, sequential logic and techniques of obsessionality. No wonder studies in 1989 revealed an astonishing increase of OCD in the United States, with headlines shouting the high anxiety level of a nation. And, these figures were compiled after the end of the Cold War, fully one year before Iraq invaded Kuwait. The anxiety level two weeks, 15,000 "sorties," and many TV hours after the initial U.S. bomb attack could be measured only on the Richter scale. But that is another story. Suffice it to say for now that psychoanalysis and economics may not be so far apart as they seem. The theoretical object of one is sex, the other money. Both relentlessly focus on the white, middle-class family of capitalism.

Money and Culture

In "Rat Man," a telling title, Freud *equates rats with money*, "the whole complex of money interests which centred around his father's legacy to him" (SE X, 213; see chapter XII for further elaboration of this case). While this central linkage between obsession and money is crucial to me, Freud, alas, after hearing his patient cite numerous incidents and thoughts about money (in fact, the triggering event involves spectacles and money), its payment and exchange, runs the analysis back to infantile sexuality— where it has unfortunately remained, unexplored in relation to modernity or postmodernity. For many academics and moralists, money, it appears, is filthy, as it was for Freud, connected with the Rat Man's painful dreams of anal torture and excrement. (This disdain becomes apparent in the discussion of marketed gossip, called "dirt.")

While Freud is not at all interested in the money economy and its circulation, immediately shifting his interpretation of the rats from money to children(!) and the sexual/familial economy, an early essay by Georg Simmel, "Money and Modern Culture" (1896), makes money central to obsessive logic.[69] He argues a both/and logic comparable to Freud, closer to simultaneity than to sequentiality. The key to, and the dilemma of, modernity for Simmel is that money, which is a means, becomes an end, a goal, what he calls the "colonization of ends by means" (25).

A central issue of postmodernity is the inversion of cause-effect, means-ends, form-content logics, comparable to debit/credit, no longer clearly discernible binarisms. While postmodern critics predictably argue that binarisms no longer apply, it's trickier than this. Often, the former binarism is upside down, or politically reversed like a mirror image. Fred Block touches on this when he suggests that double-entry bookkeeping is similar to the schemes of premodern people for organizing reality; accounting is comparable "to the complex kinship systems analyzed by structural anthropologists."[70] These systems, which are arbitrary, create the appearance of certitude, ward off uncertainty and close down options (33), particularly for women and people of color, I would add.

"A feeling of tension, expectation . . . runs through modernity . . . as if the main event, the central point of life . . . were yet to come. [This] is the emotional outcome . . . of the *compulsion* [my emphasis] to build one means on top of another." Simmel's astute analysis of desire, yearning not for that which is distant but for "that which is not owned but seems to be becoming nearer," is perfect (27). (In many ways, Lacanian desire resembles obsession.) Endlessness causes anxiety—the state of waiting, of expectation, of anticipating a future which is always delayed. For Simmel, this endless desire, where money (not sex, as the Lacanian model would have it) becomes the goal, is "the reason for the restlessness . . . the unrelenting character of modern life."

Updating desire by a hundred years, Block argues that postindustrial upward mobility belongs to the U.S. majority rather than the few: by the 1950s, food had moved upward; by 1973, the majority of laborers owned homes; for the past twenty years, the shift is "toward quality in consumption" (181). The majority of consumers have more "discretionary income" and can buy "positional goods"—desirable because scarce—like fancy houses, classy cars, and country-club memberships. However, the pleasure of purchase is dubious. These pricey items have "insidious characteristics": "whatever one attains, there will be positional goods that are even more exclusive and valuable. It is difficult to find . . . satisfaction. . . . The pursuit tends to produce disappointment" (182).

For Simmel, however, although "the desire for money is the permanent disposition that the mind displays in an established money economy," this can be taken both positively *and* negatively, as a stimulus to cultural development and to the demise of values. For Simmel, the money economy is paradoxical, separating people *and* creating strong economic bonds.

"Money makes the division of production possible and money inevitably ties people together." Like F. W. Taylor, Simmel linked money with time, punctuality with the monetary system. However, this did not apply to domestic labor, which didn't count. While wives didn't exchange time for money, they understood, as white women and African-Americans have for centuries, Simmel's central proposition: the exchange of money involves a relation "between freedom and dependence" (21). What Simmel fails to note is that these double meanings split according to gender and race. When people have no money and cannot own property, when people can be bought and sold for money, Simmel's system becomes infinitely complex, involving no freedom, only constraints. Lucy and Ethel struggled comically with this paradox for seven prime-time years.

Two of Simmel's concepts are particularly pertinent to my argument, and to television—"restless flow" posits the circulation of money as an equalization, a wearing-down process, which has indeed occurred in relation to class and money; "flow" anticipates Raymond Williams's analysis of U.S. TV; the "transformation of stability to instability that characterizes . . . philosophy . . . and the economic cosmos" relates history to catastrophe, linked to economics. Suggesting the catastrophe theory of Rene Thom, this is the potential of crisis that best defines the (1) high drama of capitalist economics on the stock market and on television, (2) world history as a series of catastrophes, and (3) addiction, or obsession—the state of constant, tautological crisis, pending disaster and last-minute reprieves. Unlike neoclassical economists, and in accord with Block, Simmel sees a mutuality between the trends of history and economics. He concludes with a metaphor of the tautological, contradictory logic of modernity: "The money economy might resemble the mythical spear that is itself capable of healing the wounds it inflicts" (30).

III

Deregulation

Business art is the step that comes after Art. . . .
I wanted to be an Art Businessman or a
Business Artist. Being good in business is the
most fascinating kind of art. . . . Making money
is art and working is art and good business is
the best art.

—Andy Warhol,
The Philosophy of Andy Warhol

Econologic: "The Luster of Capital"

For Berger, "The choice of what one eats (or wears or drives) takes the place of significant political choice. Publicity helps to mask and compensate for all that is undemocratic with society. And it also masks what is happening in the rest of the world. Publicity [which is *eventless*] . . . explains everything in its own terms" (149). I wonder whether in the 1990s, *unmasking* and the frenetic *production of events* produce comparable effects.

The 1980s return of neoclassical economics—turn-of-the-century theory which became reality during the Reagan years—suggests that Berger might need to be revised. With the revival of neoclassicalism, the public debate no longer concerned what kind of society we wanted and aspired to be, but what the needs of the economy were—so neatly demonstrated by the War in the Gulf coverage, which intercut the war budget and stock market reports with military news. As a primer for anyone not familiar with this terrain, I will skip through Fred Block's *Postindustrial Possibilities*.

First, neoclassicalism treats the economy as a separate realm. Its second premise is that individuals act rationally—an old notion of Taylorism and advertising, overthrown by 1910, according to Susan Strasser: "The argument over scientific marketing reflected a larger question about human nature. The economists who had followed Adam Smith had come to believe in 'the market' as an impersonal realm . . . where individuals operated rationally, according to self-interest . . . 'economic man' . . . but others were coming to conceive of buyers as irrational, a view that predominated by 1910" (158). Block's third feature is that neoclassicalism "naturalizes" the market—a notion which Marx critiqued via the "commodity fetish" (30–31). Economic institutions are social creations, cultural and historical rather than natural entities. Block points out that all work, especially women's, was not counted, and that accounting systems were built from arbitrary conventions yet "create the appearance of certitude" (33).

The neoclassical model, furthermore, is based on the spot market, one-time transactions with multiple buyers and sellers, quite unlike most transactions, for example, the retail trade where prices are relatively fixed. Block does not opt for a Marxist position; rather, he critiques an either/or debate, advocating the work of Karl Polanyi, a Hungarian refugee intellectual who taught at Columbia during the 1950s. As Polanyi saw it, nineteenth-century capitalism was formed by two opposing movements—the first was laissez-faire capitalism, with no government regulation; the second sought "to protect society from the market through the formation of labor unions and government regulations" (39). For Polanyi, the capitalist economy was "constituted by these two movements together"; he argued the interrelationship between markets, state actions, and forms of social regulation (41).

Block details this model, wherein there are checks and limits on marketedness—the public and nonprofit sectors, the growth of corporations, and the rise of professionalism. Vertical integration, advertising, and the development of brand names are limits to competition instated by corporations. "Cannibalization" is another old tactic becoming very popular—one company selling two competing products or services—like Pizza Hut and Taco Bell (owned by PepsiCo). Professionalism creates a monopoly in certain labor markets, like psychoanalysis, and regulates through codes of ethics (62). Comparable to Simmel, Block argues that "the most serious danger in all of this is that financial activity . . . becomes the central economic activity of the society" (72). In many ways, this is what occurred during the 1980s when the financial markets, brokerage firms, became inordinately powerful. In the financial markets, one can make huge amounts of money in a short time, which cannot be done by manufacturing a product or managing a firm. The astronomical amounts of money were held to no calculation, to no standard.

Eric Alliez and Michel Feher, drawing on neoclassical economics, detail changes in the market around three dates: the 1949 postwar surplus economy, the 1960s series of economic crises and inflation, and the 1980s, for them an era of neoconservative consumerism and waste.[71] Post–World War II consumption has reached a saturation point, and capitalism has entered a neo-Fordist (or post-Fordist) regime. Without increasing productivity, capitalism has made other adjustments—through *incorporation* and differentiation. What this cogent synthesis of neoclassicalism fails to note is that for women and racial minorities, the dawn of neo-Fordism is not news. To their formulation, I would add gender and revise their straight line of history by suggesting two steps forward and one back, wherein the new frequently looks like, or is, the old, repackaged. As with burgers, we are told that it is different or new.

For example: One new look in 1991 is old, or middle-aged, uncannily familiar as Brigitte Bardot of 1959, or Barbie. Farah Fawcett has embodied this look for years, although she updated it by working out. Professionalizing the look, Deborah Norville (*Today Show*, NBC) was a Donna Rice (of the Gary Hart scandal) lookalike who resembled Fawn Hall (Oliver North's secretary). Then came Ivana Trump, Faith Ford (Corky Sherwood on *Murphy Brown*), and even Candice Bergen playing the irascible Murphy—a grouchy anti-Barbie. Like Ivana, dumped for a younger Barbie, Marla Maples, Jane Fonda had breast implants and plastic surgery after Tom Hayden left her for a younger woman. Yet Barbie is too flip for an analysis. This "look" is a memory—of the constancy of self-image as a young woman. The return of Bardot reminds us that fashion rewinds history, our own and others', played out on our bodies.

Under the old-fashioned but high-tech auspices of Reaganomics and econoBush, corporate time might have jumped back to a pre-Fordist configuration, just before the Andrew Carnegie monopolists, a time of *unregulated* (rather than de- or reregulated) competition and corporate practices. The undoing of labor unions, the unwriting of guarantees and contracts, echoes this premodernist period. Early Taylorism (1903–1915) saw the shift from domestic to factory production, from the local, small-time entrepreneur (or mom-and-pop store) to the national corporate hierarchy, capped off by standardization, specialization (and professionalism, certified by specialty boards), and vertical monopoly.

In many ways (grossly simplified, granted), television continues to refigure early film history (particularly production and distribution but including exhibition): at the marketed inception (for film, the early 1900s; for TV, the late 1940s), the concern with technological invention, innovation, and novelty more than product or content; the shift of production centers from the East to the West Coast; the financial centers' location on the East Coast;

and the changes (1) from sale by the foot to rental (the video cassette market does both), (2) from local to national and international exchanges, (3) from the unpredictability and cost-inefficiency of documentary to the cost-accounting of narrative and continuity style (here I think about the news division cutbacks, particularly at CBS), (4) from products of short duration to feature-length (on TV in the late 1940s, the news was five minutes, then fifteen; programs were often fifteen minutes as well), (5) to competing technologies (the Kinetoscope versus the Vitagraph, the varying color systems of CBS and NBC), (6) from unregulation to standardization and monopolies (the Motion Picture Patents Company, the Big Five; the network monopoly, cable TV) and back again, and (7) from anonymous authors and actors to auteurs and stars.

For Alliez and Feher, Fordism has changed from a "regime of production" to a "regime of accumulation" which revolves around time rather than space. The change was dependent upon turning the Fordist producer into a consumer, a turn-of-the-century practice which comes as no surprise to women working in department and clothing stores. (Susan Porter Benson's cleverly titled *Counter Culture* is a wonderful history of the department store and women's places within it. Via empirical research, she models contradiction and inscribes women's presence and culture, which the male ownership and management never could dominate or manage. See my last chapter for elaboration.)

What Alliez and Feher don't emphasize is that within the "regime of accumulation," there are few distinctions between saving and spending. My bank grants the same gold card privileges for either $15,000 of credit or debt. Huge junk-bond debts are the new sign of conspicuous wealth, with late million-dollar interest payments reported with bated breath by gossip columnists, along with cutbacks in million-dollar lifestyles. Venture capitalists come to the rescue of other high-rolling players, bailing them out with multi-million-dollar loans and "restructuring." Credit, and debt, leads to more rather than less credit, deferring payment. Many people cannot afford debt and do not qualify for credit—they cannot be saved or bailed out. They never enter the "regime of accumulation." They are subjects only for welfare, if they are lucky. The poor can do little for the "health" of the economy, dependent on credit and consumer spending as it is.

The system of production referred to as Fordist involved centralized employment (for example, the development of Hollywood film studios), a hierarchical division of labor (producer, director, screenwriter, cinematographer) which enabled "more skilled" workers to be paid higher wages, and the separation of conception from execution, or management from labor. For Fordism, labor and production were the same, with the worker cut off from the product and profits. In "neo-Fordism," there is an inverse relation between labor time and production; productivity now depends on transferring labor income to capital—to a reduction of the payroll rather than increasing the buying power of wage earners (which Taylor strongly advocated). This change in the "factory regime" involves decentralization —the rediscovery of the entrepreneurial spirit of subcontracting, franchises, and part-time employees, dispersed rather than centralized places of employment.

Franchise operations of local (and national) ownership, such as Baskin Robbins, Subway, Dunkin' Donut, and their forebear, McDonald's, are echoes of mom-and-pop stores, possible because of specialization—cones or burgers—and standardization of equipment, labor, and food, prepackaged and shipped in bulk from the chain. After location surveys (they must be kidding!), local entrepreneurs endure a rigorous qualification scrutiny (including lengthy interviews and a detailed financial investigation), buy a franchise, go to training school (they must graduate), and then pay a percentage of their profits to the chain. The rates vary; Subway takes 8 percent, McDonald's 12 percent. All the workers at Subway *must* wear the standard uniform, down to the silly hat, or risk franchise loss.[72] In turn, franchisers pay minimum wage to part-timers, doing away with benefits.

Franchising has a long history—for example, U.S. oil companies, Coca Cola, and Fred Harvey/Howard Johnson's Restaurants, the latter built alongside the railroad as it moved West. After World War II there was a big increase in local, independent fast-food enterprises—with, however, a high failure rate. During the 1970s, fast and casual food joints—Laugh-in, Black Angus, Herky's, Barnacle Bill's, and Here's Johnny—were hawked by franchise companies along with mufflers, pies, childcare, and brakes. Taxonomy of products didn't matter—franchise "knowhow" did. While the franchisees received a brand name or trademark, promotional materials, special decor, and secret recipes, what they really bought was neither visible nor tangible: expertise—the managerial techniques of franchising. What franchisers sold was not a product but a system, applicable to virtually any service, of standardization and specialization—a reprise of F. W. Taylor echoed by Foucault's *Discipline and Punish,* uniform down to granules of salt.

One recent trend is for franchisees to take "the ultimate step and acquire the franchising firm." However, this is risky business. "When they have to make the global decisions that affect all franchisees, they find it very difficult."[73] One famous franchise agent who succeeded big-time was Ray Kroc, just a milkshake machine salesman when Dick McDonald and his brother Maurice, aka Mac, "dreamed up the concept of 'fast food' and opened the nation's first fast-food restaurant [in San Bernadino] in 1948." (So much for history as we know it.) They eliminated the carhops of drive-ins, "pared down the menu," cut prices, and standardized production ("10 burgers to the pound, all with mustard, ketchup, pickle and onion). The aim was to fill orders in 20 seconds rather than 20 minutes." "Five years later . . . they introduced the Golden Arches, based on Dick McDonald's own sketches." They sold franchises for a flat fee of $1,000. "They had sold

21 McDonald's franchises and had opened nine restaurants before Mr. Kroc entered the picture in 1955, when the brothers hired him as a franchise agent."[74] (Is nothing sacred?)

Kroc formed Franchise Realty Corp., opening outlets nationally and aggressively, changing the name to McDonald's Corp. in 1960. Unlike the McDonalds, Kroc didn't let the cold weather of the north intimidate him. Shortly thereafter, the McDonald brothers sold out to Kroc for $2.7 million. Kroc founded the business, not the burger; the corporation, not the concept. Ray Kroc died in 1984, but Dick McDonald recently said, while eating a burrito at McDonald's: "Too many items slow the system down. They should be very careful, or fast food will be history" (A10). PepsiCo's test of "casual dining" suggests McDonald might be right.

While the brothers gave up more than $15 million/year in franchise fees, the fate of Becky McGammon and her company, Mom's Best Cookies, is worse. Between its founding in 1981 and its recent Chapter 11, sales zoomed from nothing to $1.9 million. After her marriage broke up, McGammon turned to a neighbor, Mr. Jones, a "marketing executive with Coca Cola." He invested in the company, with controlling interest, and became president, putting Becky's picture on the cookie label. However, after one year, they no longer spoke to each other; Jones asked McGammon to fill in for the receptionist and to travel with delivery people for promotion. The final ignominy occurred in 1990—Mom was fired, and in turn sued the company.[75] So much for love, the main ingredient of Mom's Best Cookies.

Among the 9 million "home professionals," "entrepreneurs who have started their own businesses," "are many former managers who were laid off by corporations."[76] "Many of the new telecommuters [salaried workers at home] and home entrepreneurs are women who want to spend more time with their children."[77] Popular cultural productions generate spinoff enterprises—like the videotape and transcript services for the daytime talk shows and *60 Minutes.* Spike Lee sells spinoff film products, including T-shirts, in his own store, a Bed-Stuy mom-and-pop enterprise. *Twin Peaks,* on again and off again through 1991, had plans to market cherry pie from the Double R Diner, Dr. Jacoby ties, Audrey Horne sweaters and saddle shoes, Sheriff Truman hats, woodsmen jackets, and Dale Cooper–approved coffee, along with Laura Palmer's diary.[78] Yet this is not new in the 1990s but a reprise of Disney's clever marketing in the 1930s and '40s, when Shirley Temple products, along with Mickey Mouse, were enormously profitable. In the 1950s, Desi Arnaz negotiated product tie-ins, along with the creation of Ricardo merchandise, from Desi smoking jackets and Lucy lingerie to bedroom furniture.

Consumer durables are essential to this process, a boon to office equipment dealers, as is the "freedom" to cross boundaries of the factory, the school, the home, and the supermarket, actualizing freedom while guaranteeing subjection. One McDonald's ad is testimony by a young uniformed mother; her "flexible" schedule enables her to be a full-time mom. *"I Love*

Lucy" is a virtual history of 1950s upward mobility as the freedom to purchase washers, driers, fashion, and finally a car; to travel, first to California then to Europe; and at last, to buy a suburban home in Connecticut. From being the manager of a club, Ricky becomes an owner. Like Porter's model, this process involved a contradiction: Lucy was the consummate consumer, as was Ethel, with no economic independence. Her buying scams became story and problem, her lack of power necessitating lies and subservience to Ricky. Her full-time job as a housewife was consuming, yet she was imagined as not working. Thus, Ricky worked while Lucy schemed and shopped. Fred Mertz, Fordist that he was, divided the world into earners and spenders, men and women, husbands and wives. Women were the targets, the critical consumers of Fordism, with little access to the realm of production. Fordism's courting/disdain for the consumer is equivalent to the double whammy applied to women—everything and nothing at the same time. While few women are CEOs, the status of shopping has changed—in 1991 consumption is in the national interest, our patriotic duty.

In the neo-Fordist regime, class interests are converted into demands for consumption. Yet this conversion is paradoxical—the former purview of the rich, for example international travel, is now more accessible, not a bad thing. Paradoxically, "provisionals" are historical, not forever. In 1990, the art market boom slumped, with auction houses "rolling back price estimates" to 1987/88 levels, rollbacks "from 25% for corporate-lobby mainstay Frank Stella to about 65% for . . . Roy Lichtenstein." In 1991, buyers (unlike art historians) "weren't sure what art is worth." This uncertainty is the "result of the deflation . . . of the wealth arena." (The wealth arena?) Jean Dubuffet is a good example. "Dubuffet was well-suited to fast turn-over, because the artist was known to art-hungry Japanese collectors." Then the Japanese market nose-dived. "At the major auctions in May, four Dubuffets went on the block. . . . None of them sold." However, "art prices are always tricky to track; unlike stocks and bonds, many works of art are unique."[79]

Or, mechanically reproducible, a challenge to the high cost of aura. Although the prices for famous photographs now run to six figures, "collectors are combing the photography market for bargains." However, reproducibility perplexes collector/investors. "It's a hornet's nest," says one appraiser.[80] Authenticity is up for grabs—just how far away from the original negative can a work of art be before it becomes popular culture? Or how many copies before it transforms into mass culture?

"Right now, antique jewelry—dating from the early 1800s to the 1940s—is perhaps the single strongest sector of the art market," with collectors paying incredible prices. Antique jewelry, like art history, is divided into periods and styles, with Victorian, Art Deco, and "Retro" the current faves. Signed pieces, along with items made by famous jewelers, are hot. The reason for this new status is that the federal government's new 10 percent luxury tax—on furs, boats, and jewelry over $10,000—exempts antique jewelry. Another reason is the Persian Gulf war; jewelry is easily transportable, "an investment that's attractive during periods of political instability."[81]

Other luxury items are slow sellers: "Dom Perignon sales are flat. Steuben crystal is collecting dust. . . . Cartier is having trouble moving $10,000 watches." The price of Beluga caviar was slashed to $395 an ounce from $695. The price of Farraris has been halved, from $300,000 to $150,000. Sad, sad. But does anyone care? And if so, why? Because "conventional wisdom holds that the upper end of the market is recession-proof." This has not been true of the late 1980s/'90s recession—less of a "blue-collar downturn" and extending "higher into the quasi-elite." (Quasi-elite?) "A larger issue seems to be the broad backlash against the conspicuous consumption of the 1980s, a decade when the luxury market grew at an annual rate of 10% in many sectors." "These days, ostentation is almost looked down upon." "People want to live well for less."[82] (This slump has affected magazines that rely on luxury advertising—which has shifted its appeal from status.)

As the service sector expands, the boundaries between production (going to work at the factory), consumption (shopping at the mall), and reproduction (coming home) are also blurred. The workday overflows; work, life, and leisure become inseparable, just as the distinctions between domestic space and the workplace disappear. For women, they were always the same. "The logic of capital once confined to market investments has permeated the domestic space of the household, inscribing itself on the bodies of individuals."[83]

Thus, *Time* magazine proclaims the glory of new domestic entrepreneurs, mainly women, working at home, never noting that now women have two full-time jobs. Under the rubric "the freedom to stay at home," women must stay home, all the time. This can be either a benefit or a disciplinary tactic of containment. Thus, the acclaimed blessing can be, at the same time, an exploitation, a tactic of divide and conquer, a divestment of space and equipment expense, now borne by the home worker rather than the company. The function of consumer durables, recently electronics, to enable or keep women within domesticity never ceases to amaze me.

A more conservative double whammy is blatantly proclaimed by *Good Housekeeping*'s "New Traditionalist" campaign: "She was searching for something to believe in—and look what she found. Her husband, her children, her home, herself. She's the contemporary woman who has made a new commitment to the traditional values. . . . She wasn't following a trend. She made her own choices. . . . Market researchers are calling it the biggest social movement since the sixties."[84] All the steps here are backward. The new is old. Even Freud cautioned that "marriage . . . has long ceased to be a panacea for the nervous sufferings of women. . . . A girl must be very healthy to 'stand' marriage."[85] That the new spatial politics are not being hotly contested might have something to do with neo-Ford-ism: space is subsumed under time, permeated by capital. Individuals are not so much *subjected to* but rather *incorporated by* capital—a costly illusion of free choice.

Alliez and Feher assess that workers no longer identify with abstract labor, or with organizations, or with production, but with capital. Subjects become investors in their own lives, which in turn, as gossip demonstrates, are human capital. Goods and services are equal to time saved and stored. Thus, in a dizzying tautology, we work to make money to pay for goods and services which will save time, which will enable us to work for money to pay . . . ad infinitum. The goal is to produce the maximum amount of time (commodity enjoyment) within a minimum amount of time (com-modity production). The result is that everyone works very hard for this time. We buy, save, spend, waste time—a precious commodity linked to obsession.

Paradoxically, to save time by acquiring goods and services, people must defer enjoyment. Pleasure is replaced by anxiety, or work becomes leisure. Perhaps there is a certain rebellious logic to women's staying home. I re-peat: the most time is devoted to earning money to buy more machines to save time to earn more money. "The colonization of time and not the com-modification of labor . . . was always the . . . destination of econologic" (Rajan). Fordism (capitalism) had free time. Neo-Fordism (neocapitalism) is a totality of time.

"As more companies go global, executives have less time to call their own," reachable by fax and telephone, talking with London early in the morning and Tokyo late at night, and traveling the rest of the time. Within international business, "it's almost impossible to separate your work from your personal life."[86] "The emphasis . . . on career . . . and making . . . money hasn't made them very happy." The status symbol of the 1990s will be leisure time, not money. However, as Block points out, there is a big difference between voluntary and involuntary leisure. A fly in this neat ointment are recent studies which clearly indicate that professionals enjoy work more than leisure.[87]

Among the poor or lower-class or, in Milwaukee, unemployed African-Americans, more time is spent on fewer commodities. People with time on their hands, like the African-American men sitting on the street in Lee's *Do the Right Thing*, the poor or the unemployed, are waste products. To have time, particularly too much time, is a sign of laziness, failure, poverty, or old age. How to spend time is indeed a political issue—George Bush golfed, fished, and steadfastly vacationed on the coast of Maine during the first weeks of the Iraq oil crisis (August 1991), his golf cart a high-tech com-munication module and his advisors decked out in leisure clothes.[88]

For Berger, writing in the early 1970s, we live not in the present but in a delayed, imaginary future; "for publicity the present is by definition insuf-ficient" (144); "the working self envies the consuming self" (149). Publicity uses the past to sell a future, making us discontent with ourselves in the present. "All publicity works upon anxiety. The sum of everything is money, to get money is to overcome anxiety" (143). Money has replaced sex, while lifestyle has replaced liberation: "To be able to buy is the same thing as being sexually desirable."

As a follower of F. W. Taylor said a long time ago, "the *dollar* is the final term" (6). Minute time studies were prerequisites for scientific management; time became money, except for women, whose (labor) time was free (often incorrectly confused with free time). Standards of higher pay for speed and skill were mainly applied to work performed in the factory; housework was low-paying or free, even when domestic engineers like Mary Pattison scientifically measured tasks.[89] Monetary models derived for production did not apply to the realms of reproduction or consumption—the spaces in which women worked.

Rajan argues that Fordism brought labor power, not individual time, under its sway. In post-Fordism, capital has permeated individual time, with each individual's lifetime a resource to be exploited. For male theorists, this is a bad thing. I think it has to do with women. Perhaps what is occurring is that women and their work are entering the sphere of production, altering its very conception. The inclusion of women's work in the Gross National Product appears to erase distinctions between work, home, and leisure—distinctions for men, as is the notion of "free time." Feminists might find women's daily lives, including the contradictory logic of which women are subjects *and* to which they are subjected, as the structuring principle of post-Fordism.

Because "nobody makes two-layer cakes or deep fries chicken anymore," Procter and Gamble is replacing Duncan Hines and Crisco with cosmetics, getting into the "beauty-care business" by buying cosmetics companies for two years (Noxell, Cover Girl, Clarion, and recently Revlon). As P and G so presciently said, "This is a business where packaging counts more than product quality." However, despite their astuteness or cynicism (and because of ecological pollution), the emphasis is increasingly on skin protection, not just appearance—the new-style health of the 1980s. In many ways, the 1990 profile of P and G products documents the trend of the 1980s and 1990s—47 percent in "personal care," 32 percent in laundry and cleaning, 13 percent in food, and 6 percent in pulp and chemicals. The move of this Cincinnati company from housework to masquerade, from soap to cosmetics, from the kitchen to the office and the party, traces the path of women from 1890 to 1990, from domesticity to the marketplace. P and G also represents the new internationalism. They market what they call "world brands," the same products with different names: Pert is the world's best-selling shampoo; in Britain it is called Vidal Sassoon and in Japan, Rejoy.[90]

Unlike the old and respected domestic conglomerate P and G, yet profiting from comparable trends, the nail-care business is an entrepreneurial upstart. As documented by *NAILS* magazine, "this little piggy went to market" is a $2 billion business. *NAILS* has 42,000 subscribers, with *The Nail Report* and *Nail Pro* entering the market—a service resulting in byproducts. The primary readers belong to the National Nail Technicians Group (NNTG), an industry dominated by "Vietnamese refugees in the West Coast, Cubans in the South, and Koreans in the Northeast," a multi-culturalism quite in contrast to the makeup of U.S. corporations. The "great American nail boom began in the 1970s with the large female migration from home to workplace."[91] (The dominance of refugees suggests that U.S. foreign policy, particularly the Cold War and policies of containment such as Korea and Vietnam, were also contributing factors. That these services are primarily women's work, hence of low status, which can then be linked to race, makes this slippery terrain. Beauty care is, after all, highly political—perhaps the best instance of "the personal is political.")

Just as the improved technique of Spandex enabled girdle innovation (and differentiation), dentists' glues and acrylics for teeth were "modified to work on nails. Lowly manicurists broke out of the beauty-parlor substrate and opened nails-only specialty salons." Today, there are over 40,000 salons and 200,000 "nail technicians," no longer just manicurists. Recently, toenails have surfaced, although "lots of nail techs don't do toes." So much for the mystique of foot fetishism. However, a new machine, the "European Touch Whirlpool Pedicure Spa," is changing this. The new entrepreneur is located in "the mysterious Lake Michigan port of Milwaukee" (which sounds like the sister city of *Twin Peaks*). Walt Disney was right all along—it *is* a small world, after all.

Unfortunately, in the lofty, immaterial ether of high finance, women are still largely invisible at the top. In a two-page spread of *The Wall Street Journal* in April 1991—"Executive Pay"—listing the salaries and bonuses of the heads of major U.S. corporations, there were no women. Only three women are CEOs in the Fortune 500 companies. Fortunately, there is a bit of good news: Time Warner Inc named Lisa Valk, formerly publisher of the profitable *People*, as the publisher of *Time*—"the first woman to hold the power position." This "bold move" will put executives (read, the former publisher) in place to "take the magazine franchises deeper into TV and cable" and "to expand . . . international business, especially in Asia."[92]

What is critical, along with gender as it blurs manmade distinctions of public/private, production/reproduction, product/service, labor/capital, debit/credit, product/waste, is that art and thought are also subjected to the criteria of the market—the rapidity of conception and comprehension, the profusion of references. This assessment of "information" is uncannily accurate for television, a medium of time and information which it can escalate to a crisis. Via research and development, (1) information has become *production*; (2) electronic applications rely on the ability to quantify information; and (3) information is merchandise. Thus the market, and television, promotes information that is easily negotiable. This analysis recapitulates the development of the classical continuity style in cinema, a set of "easily negotiable" conventions in play by 1915, according to Bordwell, Staiger, and Thompson,[93] and Benjamin's analysis of newspaper techniques of "information."[94]

The key argument, endlessly used to bash TV, is that information is governed by market criteria, which the networks, the raters (from Hooper and radio to A. C. Nielson), and the advertisers have known for years.[95] The cost of information, measured in time necessary for formulation and comprehension, must be minimized while its exchange value is increased by the multiplication of references, clearly apparent in the repetition of catastrophe coverage and the circulation of gossip (and the redundancy of Hollywood narrative). Thus, only information which sells well, or circulates rapidly, is promoted. In many ways, film economic history and television predate or parallel Alliez and Feher. And no wonder, given that reconfigured Hollywood producers, like the heyday of the studio system, oversee the majority of U.S. popular cultural products.

Given corporate in-bred ownership, one medium feeds another until, for example, *Batman* was everywhere, and might be again when the sequel is released. One crucial econotext is thus the creation and "restless flow" of transmedia oligopolies like Time-Warner or Sony-Columbia-CBS (which often appear to compete with themselves, cannibalizing their own creations). Studios such as Paramount consider joint ventures with Philips Electronics of the Netherlands, along with merging with NBC, owned by General Electric. Meanwhile, Time-Warner, which refused Paramount Communications Inc.'s offer of purchase two years ago, meets with Canal Plus A.A. of France and Toshiba Corp. of Japan to "strike a complex series of deals," like a country, or a general, making alliances with "strategic partners," while selling two million shares of "toymaker Hasbro on the open market," and offering additional stock in a public sale to offset its debit level. United Artists Entertainment Co. refuses takeover bids by Tele-Communications Inc., which already owns 46 percent of UA stock. Let's Make a Deal meets a corporate incestuousness right out of a 1991 *Dynasty* reunion.

The monopolistic structure of the major Hollywood studios has powerfully reemerged—diversified, deregulated, operating and owned transnationally.

I repeat. Only a few corporate players produce the technology and the programming for television and other cultural products. Hence, the same artifact is marketed cross-culturally as a book, a film, a food product, a song, a toy, and a costume—Batman, the Terminator. Targeted or cross-promotions go even further and treat movies as individual brands, not singular products. The publicity machine of trademark or franchise culture, the world of "product placement," doesn't involve the exchange of cash. Critically, promotion costs the producers nothing except a reference: "In return for getting a product featured in a film, a marketer . . . will develop a promotion around the movie."[96]

While none of this is new, dating back to at least the 1860s, business is booming. The summer of 1991 saw "Thirst Terminator" collectors' cups and "Prince of Thieves" cereal. Paramount linked up with K-mart and Chrysler for a sweepstakes program promoting four films simultaneously. Carolco's licensing president figures that by letting Subway use ten to fifteen seconds of *Terminator* footage, they gained $5 to $6 million in advertising. (Licensing involves sales of "brands," often difficult to distinguish from advertising, which is tax-deductible as a business expense, unlike licensing, which is a profit, unless no money is exchanged. No wonder accountants are flipped out! Many things come from nothing.) However, the most amazing lure was that considered by CBS—offering viewer points comparable to airlines' frequent flyer miles; more points would be granted for lower-rated programs.

Not only a Mouseketeer, Mickey Mouse has been an exemplary franchise marketeer. Disney has recently expanded into magazines, buying *Discover*, the science magazine, and hiring a vice-president of publishing. Michael Eisner, the chairman, assured the public that this new venture would be family-oriented (unlike many Touchstone films)—tied to "children's books, a children's magazine, TV specials for the Disney pay cable channel, and theme park attractions. . . . This is an extension of the Disney franchise."[97] Rather than licensing its characters to other publishers as it has done in the past, Disney's new mandate is vertical integration—baldly stated.

For a detailed analysis of the new constellation of TV corporate technologies and players, see Meehan's "Towards a Third Vision of an Information Society." Meehan's reading of duality complicates the simplicity of Alliez and Feher's information assessment: "For just as producers are always and simultaneously making a commodity containing the most accessible content—that is, the dominant ideology—so too are producers constructing a cultural artifact whose ability to resonate with different collectivities depends on a combination of elements from the cultural fund. And these collectivities . . . 'read' the televisual text in a multiplicity of ways" (454). For her, the problem is one of "captur[ing] dualities and lay[ing] bare their interconnections," a Marxist model of contradiction, not, however, as is Benson, concerned with gender or derived from feminism.[98]

Like time and information, cultural products are increasingly immaterial —the "experience" of an Infiniti in ads which didn't show the car. The land of Infiniti is where the libidinal investment is measured by intangible qualities which make up lifestyle, the contours of identity as taste. While money matters, it is not the only thing. Electronic products, like "filmless photographs," are also objectless, posing the dilemma for Eastman Kodak of competing with itself or losing out. Kodak has chosen a hybrid, a camera which combines "real" film with discs, a both-and logic which enables Kodak to have it both ways.

Neoclassical economists ceaselessly repeat that since time and information have become key commodities (an idea which is, at the least, ninety years old yet reappears as new), "econologic" concerns "the immaterial," a realm which was previously cordoned off to economics. However, money, and its value, have been symbolic, immaterial for decades; only the effects of money are tangible, visible as power. Retroactively, in this era of electronic transactions and credit, money becomes material and unessential, at the same time. The linkage of money and time is also reversing. Time used to result in money; now money can buy time. Through the stock market, economics have become representation, no longer just a calculating analysis. The market has become entertainment, popular culture, with its own programs, networks, and celebrities, its regular slot on the network nightly news, its own journals and magazines, and its own brand of obsession. The market can be watched all day on TV as information; it is also high drama, a powerful "Let's Make a Deal." FNN might not be that different from the Home Shopping Channel. The libidinal investment might resemble the art of shopping, albeit masculine and hence legit, and the market, a giant electronic designer discount mall.

Thus, the market is work, leisure, and life, both an object and its interpretation. Its logic is one of prophecy, reversal, and high risk, presented as statistic, flow chart, and annual report. Amidst a sea of numbers and a torrent of data, ups and downs, highs and lows, opening and closing, the bottom line is luck, and money—earnings, profits, dividends, losses. Currently, the health of the economy is dependent on IBM—which has such a large share of the market that its loss is a national loss. With the exception of the military, for whom cost is not an object, the market has overrun the state—which is tied to broadcasting. General Norman Schwarzkopf's expression of gratitude to the press for its coverage of U.S. invasion maneuvers, a military deceit which fooled Iraq (and the press), is the downside of this trade-off.

The market has, at most, a three-month attention span—with a rigid rule: each quarter must be better, a logic of more. The same is not enough. Annual corporate reports compare quarters to the previous year in order to chart growth. While the market appears to have a memory, albeit a short one, it can just as quickly forget. Headlines in the *Wall Street Journal* chart amnesia: November 19, 1991: "Stocks Climb, but Signs of Weakness Linger"; November 20, 1991: "Industrials Tumble 41.15 Points; Gloom Spreads to Bonds, Dollars"; December 27, 1991: "Industrial Average Soars to Record"; and December 31, 1991: "Stocks Soar 62.39 Points to New Record." From the depths to new heights in one month—a euphoria very different from *Time*'s year-end depression.

TV and the FCC

At its marketed inception in the 1940s, owing to the public nature of the airwaves (which "belong to the people"), TV was legally declared a service (rather than a product). Thereby the networks were prevented, in those antitrust days, from owning the majority of their programs or products; they were barred from a vertically integrated monopoly. From the late 1940s on, many programs and series were produced, and owned, by Hollywood studios. Like other service industries, the television industry appears to be shifting away from centralization, from network television (an amalgam of the local and the national, with regional differences, including accents, now vanishing) to national cable channels or superstations specializing in money, weather, prayer, shopping, movies, sports, news, medicine, and, recently, genres or styles, for example, the new documentary channel, and address (Lifetime is pitched to women). These services (products?) are picked up by local, competing cable franchises such as Viacom or Warners, which are national monopolies (which may soon be reregulated). (Paradoxically, amidst all this seeming dispersion and plethora of programs, the battle is over TV's object [or product] status and is being waged between two big players—the Hollywood studios and the TV networks, excluding Fox, Rupert Murdoch's fourth network.)

Along with the acclaimed diversity, pluralism, and freedom of choice (public arguments determined by product rather than service and defended as the "free flow of information" guaranteed under the First Amendment) signaled by this new electronic/satellite constellation, this liberated or deregulated economics of broadcasting (denotatively meaning disbandment, decentralization, and hence accurate but now termed "narrowcasting") and "point-to-point" can also be read as standardization and specialization aided and abetted by differentiation—the principles of Fordism. Centrism is cleverly disguised as intangible dispersion. Under the uniformity of local franchises (national monopolies) and transmedia conglomerates (oligopolies), we are being rapidly disenfranchised of differences. History repeats itself, deregulated, differentiated.

However, if corporate technologies of electronic invention, distribution, and exhibition determine the argument (what Raymond Williams critiqued as "technological determinism"), along with marketing tactics and transnational enterprises, television appears to be very different, at least on first anarchic glance at zapping, VCRs, cable, and satellite transmission/ reception (technology's decentrist, pluralist promise for the video guerrillas of the counterculture in the 1960s).[99]

In "The Impact of Television Deregulation on Private and Public Interests," Victor Ferrall, Jr., traces the path of FCC deregulation in the 1980s under the tutelage of its chair, Mark Fowler, for whom "marketplace" meant no regulation.[100] The belief in the recession-proof profitability of television stations was a critical motivator for early 1980s takeovers by "leverage buyers and corporate raiders," new groups of investors who upped station selling prices (8). The markets with five stations jumped by 85 percent during the 1980s, increasing the demand for programs: "The economic consequences of this development of five-station markets cannot be overstated" (9).

Regarding cable, "a monopoly toll-gate," only 22 percent of households were wired in 1980. Arbitron upped this figure in 1988 to 52.5 percent (47 million). Unlike the networks, this chartered monopoly "derives revenues from both advertisers and subscribers." Advertising sales were $58 million in 1980, climbing to $1.45 billion in 1988 (12–13). It is not surprising that "station and network audience shares began a slow but steady decline that is continuing" (13), a decline translated into dollars, since advertising costs are based on viewers (or time spent, human capital now differentiated by demographics, with women between 18 and 49 as a favored target given their shopping labor, and blacks gaining popularity). The "reregulation" bill for cable TV pending in Congress is also not surprising.

Paradoxically with the support of broadcasters, Fowler "obliterated" "fifty years of regulatory accretion" (15), enabling poorly financed, inexperienced nonbroadcasters to enter the business. Ferrall succinctly summarizes the massive and rapid rescinding, paralleling the policies of Reagan's presidency and called "deregulation." In 1984, the former seven-station rule was increased; now twelve stations could be owned (16). The three-year rule of ownership (three years before sale and license renewal) was repealed, increasing station prices which, like other real estate, could be traded faster. Rather than detailed financial statements and solid economic support, buyers now declared monetary capability "by checking a 'yes' box" (17). "Lottery procedures," including a "Kenolike gambling device," are used to award "low-power television grants" (18).

As Ferrall points out, "The concept of localism was at the heart of regulation" (18). The effect of lifting program requirements has been a decrease in local programming and an increase in "commercial time available for sale" (19). (The significant exception was "obscene and indecent programming"; in fact, "strict new limits" of "FCC decency scrutiny" were imposed [19–20].) Previously commercial time had been limited to sixteen minutes per hour. In 1984, all limits were taken off. "Two immediate results" were the Home Shopping Network and syndicated home shopping programs (20–21). The marketplace would "do the right thing," an argument which also led to the elimination of requirements for news and public-service programming.

The turn of the screw came when these rescindments backfired to a degree. For station operators, the result of deregulation "would be profit-reducing competition." The catch-22 was that unlike other commodities in an open marketplace, TV programming was free, so to speak. The *output* of programs is fixed by the number of channels and the number of waking hours in the day. And the price of programs is also fixed, at zero" (25). "Unlike the inventory of most oligopoly sellers, however, commercial time is ephemeral and totally perishable. . . . With every tick of the clock, a part of their inventory is lost forever" (27–28). Or, to take this further, TV's ultimate commodity is time, just as the audience spends time. Critics disparage TV as a waste of time. For these and other reasons, "broadcasters . . . made an economic miscalculation in supporting . . . deregulation initiatives" (29).

Along with not being profitable, as Ferrall argues, deregulation has so far not led to innovation: "Marketplace competition in television has bred program sameness." Imitation and repetition might be more accurate. (His absolutism is not mine.) While "voice diversity" has increased, competition and lower profitability have "reduced diversity," seeking a "still lower common denominator for programming." This argument coincides remarkably with Alliez and Feher on "information." For Ferrall, "a thousand different speakers asserting the same point of view are . . . less diverse . . . than two speakers asserting contrasting viewpoints" (30), a recapitulation of the shift from binarisms to pluralism.

One rule, however, has not been completely rescinded—the Final Interest and Syndication Rules. "Fin-syn" has "blocked TV networks from the rerun business [the lucrative syndication market] and allowed the [Hollywood] studios to dominate this $5.7 billion-a-year global market." These rules, imposed at the behest of Hollywood studios, were enacted in 1970 when "the networks held 90% of the television audience and were virtually the only buyers of programming. Today, they hold only 60% of viewers, and programming is purchased by hundreds of independent stations, dozens of cable channels, and Fox Broadcasting." Rather than promoting diversity, the rules "cemented the dominance of Hollywood's big studios. Last year the eight largest studios controlled 63% of the $3.4 billion syndication market in the U.S. and 80% of the $2.3 billion market overseas . . . supplying over 70% of the prime-time shows." "This [syndicated] market is expected to almost double by 1995, to $10.6 billion." Hollywood, led by Jack Valenti, blocked the latest attempts at deregulation, to the confused amazement of the FCC chair, Alfred Sikes, congressional leaders, and the networks.[101] Imagining Ronald Reagan's influential blessing of Hollywood would not be paranoiac.

The network system is definitely under siege—after a fifty-year reign. After the success of CNN and news, Ted Turner began to capitalize on time—linking television to waiting (and to buying): "placing thousands of TV sets just about anywhere people have to stand in line—shopping malls, banks, fast-food restaurants, supermarkets, and public transportation." In other words, literally commercial television, selling when people are already buying—double-whammy TV. In 1991, standees, or waiters, can watch a channel cleverly named Checkout Channel. For the supermarket experiment, Turner "will pay for everything: the monitors, a satellite dish, installation, maintenance, programming." Checkout will cost $50 million, reaching 5,000 stores and 75 million viewers. The future for waiting television is promising: "Any retail environment with queuing will be a target," says the vice-president of Turner Private Networks, Inc. Turner and his competition, CNBC and Whittle Communications, are negotiating with health clubs, malls, hospitals, and airports. Whittle already "runs hourlong video programs in 20,000 medical offices."

Contradicting my opening assertion that TV is not watched in airports, Turner's Airport Channel will be installed in July 1991 in Atlanta, Chicago, and Dallas. "It will provide travel spots, weather and business news. . . . Having a captive audience also means advertisers won't have to battle what has become a major nemesis: the remote control." Initial tests document a recall for the Checkout Channel of 31.5 percent versus 17.5 percent for the same ads on network TV.[102] McDonald's is "exploring" installation of "television sets with exclusive programming" in 8,600 stores—another example of "out-of-home" TV developed by Turner Private Networks. The McDonald's network could reach an audience of 18 million (*Wall Street Journal*, November 19, 1991, B8).

Because the network audience is shrinking and aging, a station in Miami is revamping its news format—a thirty-year staple, the "Eyewitness News" format created in 1965 by Al Primo on KYW in Philadelphia. One trademark was happy talk between anchors, reporters, and weathermen (or persons). In a grab for younger audiences, anchors, the "ubiquitous over-the-shoulder graphics," and sports will be missing. The new format will have a "casually dressed host who strolls through the newsroom and chats with reporters, sometimes interrupting someone typing a story." The "host" will break in to ask reporters questions. Reports can run as long as seven minutes, "an eternity in local news, where the average piece lasts 90 seconds." The format is called an "environmental newscast," where viewers can see spilled coffee, cameras and wires.

As an afternote: just when the network decline seemed inevitable, the fall 1991 season premiered to high ratings—in the 70 percent primetime range. "There seems to be no sign of erosion this year."[103] I guess it's not over until it's over.

The Global Village or the New World Information Order?

As I have briefly suggested, deregulation, a neoconservative gambit, overlaps with the technological dreams of the countercultural video guerrillas.[104] These video visionaries lauded electronic technologies, which then were *alternative*, marginal not mainstream, especially the computer, cable and satellite TV, and home video equipment, particularly the cassette recorder. With this technology, radical politics could bypass institutions and nations and go directly to the people, producing alternatives to corporate America, elided with science, the military, and commercial television. The new technologies would create, along with drugs, antimaterial "lifestyles" of ecology and equality. Video visionaries imagined the world as a global village, radically hooked up, connected by satellites and other technologies. However, the counterculture dreams, particularly its visions for liberating electronic technology, have been realized by commerce in 1991: AT&T has "spanned the globe," creating a global village quite different from the visionaries of the late 1960s.

"National barriers are breaking down, allowing competition in markets that were protected before. Deregulation and privatization of national communications companies are speeding the breakdown." All the countercultural goals are inverted—cooperation has become "competition," communities are "markets." Rather than goals of ecology, equality, and love, "today's major players"—AT&T, Britain's Cable & Wireless, and Japan's Nippon Telegraph and Telephone—"want to capture revenue from both ends of a call." International "telecommunications" is a booming industry. With deregulation and privatization, "national phone monopolies are slowly disappearing." The U.S., Britain, France, and Japan have "opened their markets to outside competitors." Systems are so complex that only the wealthy can get into the bidding. This is leading to consolidations— Southwestern Bell has hooked up with Telefonos de Mexico, and Telefonica de Espana S.A. of Spain has purchased phone properties in Argentina and Chile (R4). International systems, "global voice, data, and video networks," often are owned by corporations like Ford.

One of the "largest corporate communications networks" is VISA— linked to MCI and AT&T—handling "three billion transactions/year, averaging 1.9 seconds each." They have two "smart-switch" centers in the U.S., two in Britain, and one in Tokyo, "all processing traffic from banking centers in more than 100 countries." Visa doesn't worry about a "network catastrophe": "if San Mateo goes out, Basingstoke [England] could take over without any noticeable degradation in service." However cavalier about catastrophe, they nicely summed up postmodernism, including the difficulty of locating origins: "We want a payment system that's superior to cash."[105] Tangible objects, like money or even burgers, are no longer our main cultural objects—suggesting that time is no longer linked to money or to space. Time has become relative, curved, linked to speed, as physics has known for years. And for many of us, outside the spaces and calculations of time and money, this might be a very good thing.

One paradox of contemporary culture is the gradual swing of notions such as technology from formerly left advocacy to practices of commerce and conservatism—capitalism's ability to "incorporate." Unlike the Reaganomics of national deregulation, some communication scholars have argued that international deregulation, a conservative politics, can also be taken liberally to anarchistically via video "piracy." (This might be a leftover, pun intended, from the protest, countercultural heydays. Many stalwarts of the U.S. left, particularly Marxists, clung to premises which had long been appropriated.) For international communication studies, deregulation has resulted in "piracy." The video cassette recorder and satellite reception have challenged the economics and one-way flow of Western media, overthrowing Marxists' "media imperialism" thesis along the way. Momentarily, the take on the national scene is not the same as on the international.

As Raymond Williams pointed out years ago, national transmission (and real estate—stations in major cities) and clear, private reception (and the sale of TV sets or "consumer durables") rather than content or product have long been network, corporate concerns—resembling what "video guerrillas," in their critique of network or "beast television" as product culture, hailed in the mid-1960s as "process" culture.[106] These arguments and issues have now taken on an international scope, including Ted Turner's banishment of the word "foreign" from his network.

Colleen Roach assesses U.S. arguments within the New World Information and Communication Order, after the U.S. had withdrawn its membership in UNESCO. "The imperative for U.S. transnational telecommunications business interests is concretely reflected in the 'deregulatory fever' and the move toward the privatization of the public sector."[107] Across a wide variety of issues, the U.S. advocates a "market economy" for the solution of problems, including world population and Africa's economic crisis. The U.S. stance is against "government control" of media, a freedom-of-speech issue which is also a claim for expanded markets (39). As Roach points out, while U.S. programs dominate international markets, the U.S. imports almost nothing—in 1983, only 2 percent for total imports of commercial and public broadcast stations (44). The "free flow of information" is one-way rather than reciprocal; with cinema, this has been the historical case for decades.

Douglas Boyd analyzes "Third World Pirating of U.S. Films and Television Programs from Satellites." Satellites orbit in the " 'Clark Belt,' 22,300 miles high. Because a satellite's 'footprint' is usually quite broad, anyone possessing the proper equipment can receive a down-link signal if within its footprint, thus making piracy easy. In most countries piracy is not illegal."[108] The impact of the new technology and piracy question "the original media/cultural imperialism assumptions" (150), different in the 1980s from what they were in the 1960s. Because there is a lack of international agreements, with the legality of satellite usage under the auspices of the International Telecommunications Convention and Union (founded in 1865), along with a lack of enthusiasm, the U.S. "has taken direct action to stop satellite piracy" (154–55).

In 1983, antipiracy provisions were placed in the government's economic recovery acts. According to Boyd, nations taking satellite programming without agreement may have economic benefits withheld, at least in the Caribbean Basin. However, the stricture and penalty apply only to "government-owned" entities. To counter piracy, HBO has "invested heavily in scrambling technology." Descramblers are available, though, "despite the U.S. State Department ban on their export without a license" (156).

In a case study of Turkey and the VCR, Christine Ogan argues that "decentralization" requires a rethinking of "the media imperialism thesis."[109] "Although a hypodermic theory of media effects had been abandoned for Americans and other Western viewers, Third World audiences were assumed to soak up the . . . values of the foreign media products they viewed." In some Third World countries, distributors don't bother to market or sell their products, given the impossibility of competing with the black market. The Motion Picture Association of America claims million-dollar losses from cassette piracy, with tapes circulating before the film is released (96). She suggests that VCRs will enable owners to "avoid" foreign material in favor of domestically produced content (97). A law against piracy was passed only in 1987 (98), after cassette stores went into business around the country, with Turkish films "far more popular than foreign films" (101).

Ogan goes so far as to suggest that video "can restore local cultural fare to the people," citing a video linkage between Indian villages in Brazil as an example. The chief of the tribe plans to use video technology to preserve the local culture. "Given that the white man has little interest in us, we have to act on our own" (104). Perhaps the dreams of the video guerrillas of the late '60s, and Paper Tiger TV today, will be realized. If so, they will be inflected by fast food, along with technology.

Or tribal dreams will be realized by Imax—a film technology using a wide film strip and huge, unwieldy film cameras, with a projection that is fifty feet high and seventy feet wide. World Odyssey of California came up with this profitable attraction: "Tourists would travel to remote towns on the edge of national parks, view a film about the park on a giant Imax screen, stay overnight in an adjoining motel, and then leave without having to set foot in or damage the park itself." Through Imax, the "experience" of the park would be "heightened, with the advantage of taking us back in history." The tourists "won't have to sweat. . . . There's a market for this."

Indeed there is. These attractions, so perplexing to environmentalists, already exist near the Alamo, Niagara Falls, and the Grand Canyon (which attracts 600,000 visitors annually at $6 each).[110] Equally paradoxical is that the real is a scarce (natural) resource that must be preserved, *and* the real is insufficient, improved by film technique and story. In order to save the real from tourism, an on-site tourist attraction, better than the real and almost as big, is just the profitable answer. Whoa! What a thought process! Through Imax, the Mormons, who control the technique and fund the films, are preserving the ecology, making money, and revising national history. At the Polynesian Village in Hawaii, a Mormon enterprise, one can view the neocolonial effects—real and Imaxed—of this revisionist "history" applied to indigenous peoples as a tourist attraction. It is not a pretty political picture.

Wisconsin is exploring "tribal tourism opportunities," particularly for the Lac de Flambeau Chippewa Indian reservation. The first sign that tourism might aid a poverty economy came from substantial bingo profits. The first step has been to change the reservation sign, adding "Welcome" and "Please Hurry Back."[111] The important realization was that sightseeing and history were linked, tied together as tourism by the authentic, the real. To exploit their history or be exploited as history seems to be the question for the tribal leaders. So far, the tribes have control, and the fare is plain and simple. Tours visit a museum, the tribal campgrounds, an old Indian village, with seasonal events like wild rice harvesting and powwow dancing during the summer, and end with an Indian meal of venison, wild rice, and cranberries, prepared by local residents. Forty percent of the visitors are from Europe, particularly Germany.

The Oneida tribe, with a 65,000-acre reservation in Wisconsin, is showcasing its matriarchal lineage—women select the male chief, make war, and pass on their family names to their husbands and children. I wonder what Imax would do to tribal history determined by women. Rather than becoming authentic and profitable objects for Mormon attractions, Native Americans can retain, and profit from, their own history by controlling the means of production. The incredible success of *Dances with Wolves*, albeit from a white man's view, suggests that the terrain has become highly popular.

IV

♦

Representing Difference(s)

To return to U.S. network TV, shifting away from technology, industry, and audience to representation. It is usually argued that television in the 1990s is not the same theoretical object as television of the late 1940s and 1950s, that television has aged. Distribution and reception (the quality and quantity) have substantially changed. Television is going new places—to the supermarket and dentist's office—and doing new things—giving us medical advice, providing therapy, and analyzing the stock market. Increasingly, our experience of the real comes from television. However, it might be more accurate to argue that television is simultaneously different *and* the same, like plastic surgery, both old and new, depending on where one is looking or politically sitting. What hasn't changed is the trade-off of drama for commerce and the number of male over female performers.

Given U.S. TV's (1) reliance on parody, an internal referentiality to itself and other media's forms, styles, and characters, incorporating historical audiences in on the joke (or process), (2) enunciation along a spectrum of live/recorded, direct/indirect address, the presence of audiences and laugh tracks, (3) recycling of old and familiar formats, genres, and stars as programming techniques (*Roseanne* is a return of *Lucy*, with a feminist, working-class, standup comedy, late 1980s twist), (4) representation of motherhood, marriage, and the family home, (5) dominance of white male characters on particularly news but also entertainment, and (6) representation of women and race, TV history, or what I would call "a tiger's leap into fashion," is remarkably consistent—or, better, fashionable.

"Egad, It's Plaid"

For example, when women and their issues are "in style" as they were in the early 1970s, we will, as with padded shoulders in 1988, see them on television. Women's "lib" was both joke and story on the old *Bob Newhart*. In 1986, feminism, even lesbianism, is introduced into *L.A. Law* as issue or shocking event, then turned into gossip or scandal—transformed into crazy idiosyncrasy and hence contained like all the "strong," single professional women who were coupled to perfect mates in amazing speed. (The high style of this show, in addition to the designer suits of the women, is one of cultural shock from current public issues usually concerning sex [impotency, lesbianism, mental disability and sterilization, age]. The tactics surprise us because they are barely foreshadowed—like women kissing, or Roz falling down an elevator shaft, or Arnie and Roxanne, en flagrante, crashing through a partner's ceiling; and they break serial conventions—letting a major character die and then showing her lying in her coffin.)

Fashion, particularly the return of the 1940s in the mid- to late 1980s, might just result in the undoing of the television's hierarchy. Although secondary in status, women are now physically bigger than men on TV: Jane Pauley was larger than Bryant Gumbel on the *Today Show*, while Connie Chung was larger than Tom Brokaw on the NBC *Nightly News*; Michael Dukakis looked tiny by comparison. However, as women are returning to domesticity in the early 1990s, their shoulders are shrinking back to early 1960s size. The latest scoop is that the 1940s will return to Paris in 1992—save your shoulder pads and long skirts.

More amazing, "High-fashion designers are parading their rap-inspired clothes and accessories down the runways of 7th Ave. and Paris. No kidding. . . . Socialites and rich chicks can dress like home girls, too." Isaac Mizrahi was inspired by the elevator operator in his building: "The most stylish people are the home girls and the home boys." Huge gold chains, knuckle rings, glitzy pendants, feathers, lycra, quilted satin, and gold vinyl are the signs of rap style. However influenced by young African-American men, Mizrahi's internationalism is "multicultural." Native American, Sephardic Jewish, and Scottish tartan mix it up with black-rap; a "silver trench coat" is dedicated to the Guardian Angels, and a long hooded coat to the Bedouins.

Sandra Bernhard wore "a gold dollar sign pendant hanging from the rope chain around her neck, a Star of David belt buckle, a knuckle ring and a black cap" and "displayed plenty of attitude" on David Letterman. More demurely, Donna Karan and Anne Klein styles have street savvy—big zippers, lycra, and tight lines.[112] Culture moves up—from teenagers, the streets, low prices, and makeshift to high style, showrooms, and astronomical prices—then filters down to the middle class and outlet stores. Style often begins with African-Americans; here it begins with the rap subculture.

However, by fall 1991, a conservative to right-wing reaction occurred, containing all this new multicultural radicalism with the oldest, boldest Anglo-Saxonism.[113] "Family colors are turning up on boxer shorts, baseball caps, sequined cocktail dresses," oven mitts, and furniture, chosen from among the registered "2,200 tartans," supposedly protected. "But Americans don't stand on ceremony." "In pushing plaids, anxious retailers are probably assuming that slaves to fashion currently have closets full of taupe and black but nowhere near enough tartan. . . . But egad! Why plaid? It isn't news—and it has a checkered past. Junior Leaguers . . . doomed it to dowdiness after years and years of wearing floor-length tartan hostess skirts and velvet headbands at Christmas time. Golfers with a penchant for goofy prints made a plaid situation worse. Boxy and busy, plaids have always been hard to wear without coming across like an overstuffed chair or a rec-room couch that doesn't show dirt."

Ralph Lauren, the upper-class ethnicity-designer, is "at the cutting edge of plaid this year." However, "since Seventh Avenue has always believed in imitation, it isn't certain just who was first to go plaid. But Isaac Mizrahi . . . known for his witty creations, is getting most of the credit. . . . Twyla Tharp . . . hired [him] to design tartan tutus for her ballet, 'Brief Fling.' " In a great tag line to a witty piece, Agins writes: "So it's a case of 'the good, the plaid and the ugly'—a line borrowed from President Bush's favorite Off Broadway musical, 'Forever Plaid' " (A2). The big question is, why plaid? "Fashion marketers can concoct a rationale for anything. Plaids, they say, are wholesome and honest, durable and economical, the perfect back-to-basics couture for people who are fed up with frivolity and artifice." A return to political conservatism (a racial reactionism) might be more accurate.

Dressing professional women for success throughout the 1980s catapulted many retail/designers into high profits and onto the Dow Jones. In the 1990s, "women have scaled down clothing purchases . . . as the frenzied consumerism of the 1980s has faded." (For the market, history takes hours or days, at the most, weeks. Thus, the 1980s can fade so quickly.) Designers have developed secondary lines—one reason for the jump of 23 percent last year in Liz Claiborne profits. Ann Taylor, owned by the Jones Apparel Group, went public this year—unusual for an apparel company, viewed by Wall Street as "too volatile." (Just like a woman?) Conversely, the prices of Donna Karan (Murphy Brown's favorite) and Giorgio Armani have skyrocketed to $1,500 for a jacket, and $2,500 for a suit. Imitations used to appear two years later; now the time lag is only two months.[114]

In obvious ways, Marx's "commodity fetish"—wherein the fashion, or product, conceals labor, separating the laborer from the product and its profits—perfectly suits the garment industry. The price of apparel can be lowered, and costly detail can be added, because labor has shifted to third world countries. The industry is booming in Bangladesh—a real quandary for a feminist, political analysis. In ten years, the industry has jumped from $3.7 to $750 million, making "garments the country's largest export."[115] The labor-intensive work (so far only assembly) has displaced jute and tea. The change from agriculture to industrialization, along with the move of women from the home to the factory, is a tremendous social upheaval. Because Bangladesh is so poor, so out of sync with technology, corporations can aid *and* profiteer, exploit *and* assist.

The mainly female work force is doubly complex given that the country is Islamic. In order to employ women, an Islamic country had to be desperately poor and uneducated (or extremely wealthy and educated). The history of the garment industry repeats itself. "Women . . . are earning between $40 and $55 per month," an exploitative wage which for Marcus W. Brauchli, the reporter, is a big gain over the "projected 1991 national per-capita income of $202 a year," and their husbands' $1 per day as rickshaw drivers. No matter what the measure, poor is still poor. I wonder whether having a job "is giving women an independent role." Fourteen hours per day at the factory might lead to exhaustion more than independence.

Islamic law allows a man four wives—who cannot own property. Here, the kinship system coincides with money: women are properties that make money—like capitalism. Given their new income-earning potential, females are becoming more valuable, maybe more independent.

Not a Pretty Picture

In regard to the history of representation of women, the claimed impetus behind TV content analyses is "the concern for social equity, or what might otherwise be described as an assault on the supremacy of the White middle class male."[116] If this is the case, then the disdain or distaste which analyses of the TV text (a concept which for me can include program, flow, context, historical audiences, and technology) have encountered, and the haste with which content studies have been dismissed by cultural studies advocates as old hat and naive, might suggest more than a debate with the serious flaws and limits of quantitative analysis. Like feminist criticism, these studies of "characters" pointed to "television's underrepresentation of women and minority groups and its promulgation of sexual, racial, socioeconomic, and occupational stereotypes" (534).

To chart a profile of the TV gender and race balance, a pell-mell riff of statistical quotations, first by the team of Seggar, Hafen, and Hannonen-Gladden: "In 1971, the distribution was 79.2 percent male and 20.8 percent female; in 1973, it was 74.4 percent male and 25.6 percent female; in 1975 68.5 percent male and 31.5 percent female; and finally in 1980, males represented 60.9 percent and 39.1 percent were female. The trend over the decade shows an increase . . . for females. A change of 18.3 percent over the ten years is a change of considerable substance. Stated another way, the ratio of males to females portrayed had changed from 4:1 in 1971 to 3:2 in 1980. [However, males are still in the lead, contrary to many critics' assumptions of the "feminization" of mass culture and TV.] From data presented elsewhere: from the early 1950s a significant drop in the . . . representation of women occurred steadily to a low in 1971."[117] The upswing began in 1973.

Nancy Signorielli paints a portrait with which viewers are familiar: "When women do appear, however, they usually are younger than the men, are more attractive and nurturing, are quite often portrayed in the context of home and family, and are likely to be married. Women who are employed (not usually those who are also married) are cast in traditionally female occupations—nurses, secretaries, waitresses and sometimes teachers. Men . . . are generally portrayed as older, more powerful and potent and proportionately fewer are married. More men are employed and they usually work in high prestige and traditionally masculine occupations. . . . Marriage, home, family and romance" are presented as the domain of the female.[118]

Regarding work, "over one-quarter of the women and 10 percent of the men" do not hold jobs; however, they are not unemployed. "Rather, an occupation is not part of their characterization." Three-fourths of men and half of the women have specific occupations; "the rest are housewives, criminals, retired, or not otherwise employed. . . ." Married women are the least likely group to be portrayed as employed—only 28.3 percent on TV and over 50 percent in real life. "For male characters, marital status is not related to employment status." Formerly married women are presented less traditionally—they are older, have jobs, are not involved in a romantic relationship; they are less attractive, somewhat unhappy, a little selfish, and less feminine. Formerly married men do not differ as much (594).

Kalisch and Kalisch summarize previous research, as social science is wont to do. For example, Thorow's conclusions that on soap operas, "female characters issue directives in 46% of the male-female interactions; on prime-time series, men do the ordering and advising in 70% of the male-female exchanges."[119] In a study of sitcoms and crime dramas, "Lemon found that in all programs men tend to dominate women," at home as well as on the streets (535). A 1981 study of competence revealed that in family and violent shows, "males made almost twice as many statements as females; there were no sex differences for daytime serials."[120] The family shows tended to depict people as being in control and responsible for their lives; in daytime serials, people were . . . characterized as controlled by forces external to the self" (542). "Males talked significantly more than females on violent and family shows" (545). To no one's surprise, Downs and Gowan state that "the sex and age differences found for reinforcement and punishment suggest that television continues to be heavily dominated by adult male performers. . . . Little progress has been made toward an equalization of the sexes on television. Adult males are far more likely than adult females or children to give or receive responses in general."[121] A study by Weibel argues that "television portrays a higher number of exceptional men than it does exceptional women."[122] More literally, the representation of television nurses has not changed in thirty years—female, Caucasian, under thirty-five, single, childless, and subordinate to the superior, heroic physician (539).

Yet, these statistical studies of wildly divergent, questionable sampling (from 16,688 characters for a nine-year period to four programs taken from a single week, restating, but never directly except as "scientific method," the dilemma of defining, or locating, the TV text),[123] witnessed by "trained observers," sometimes a lonely graduate student counting and annotating characters and roles, drastically flatten the landscape of television, annulling differences while they point to problems.[124] Equally absent are any intimations of aesthetics or "complexity and contradictions."

Content analysis can be the flip side of audience research. As Susan Strasser points out, academia and business have been in alignment since the early 1900s; along with F. W. Taylor and other "scientific engineers," the earliest corporate psychologists (including Hugo Munsterberg) held professorships at Harvard, Columbia, Yale, NYU, and Wisconsin. When John B. Watson "lost his Johns Hopkins job for sexual misbehavior in 1920 . . . he went to work for J. Walter Thompson."[125] The field of audience research—tied to "scientific principles" derived for industrialism as were many aspects of life in the early 1900s, including housework—has been "burgeoning" since 1900. Media scholars in the 1980s, initially connected with Birmingham in England, would rediscover the audience.

Sometimes empiricism is downright ridiculous. "One does wonder about these scientists. One bloke wanted to establish the parts of the body which attracted each sex. To this end he constructed a huge Mad Max visor, equipped it with a video camera and placed it on the head of a conscript. This poor, overloaded person was then sent into a singles bar, where the camera recorded the point where his gaze wandered. The scientist proudly announced that humans stared at each other's crotches." (So much for Laura Mulvey's famous argument.) As the satirist Richard Glover writes, the more likely explanation was that "the bloke" was too embarrassed to look anyone in the face. "In Australia we have a name for people like that. In America they're apparently called research psychologists."[126]

More disturbing than the status of white women, however, are the figures charting a severe decline in the representation of blacks and other minorities (which is changing in the 1990s). From 1970 to 1980, (1) whites enhanced their overall domination, (2) blacks had a representation of only 6 to 8 percent, and (3) other minorities were virtually excluded from portrayal. The study concludes that the black female has become almost invisible, and appearances by other minorities have dropped, while the representation of white women has increased. The percentage of whites, both male and female, has increased in major roles, while the percentage of blacks of both sexes has decreased in major roles.[127] Granted that the figures are pre-Cosby and pre-Hall (Eddie Murphy, Michael Jackson, the Jesse Jackson campaign, and Oprah Winfrey), these remarkably stable findings replicate a report from 1969 to 1974: white males were overrepresented, females underrepresented, and minority females almost invisible.[128] This trade-off, of delimited, equivocal gains for white women and losses for women of color, is a disconcerting turn of events.

Critical Differences

Television's patronizing "coverage" of Jesse Jackson's presidential campaign triggered Michele Wallace's essay "Invisibility Blues."[129] In a wide-ranging review of television news, she goes on to wonder whether "Black Monday"—with its (in)advertent racism—referred to 1887 or 1987 (93). She asks, "What is a black viewer supposed to wish for Oprah Winfrey, Bill Cosby, Eddie Murphy, Action Jackson, Spike Lee and Prince? What's changed? Has Tonto walked away from the Lone Ranger yet? Has Rochester handed Benny his notice?" Blacks "neither own nor manage . . . publishing companies, magazines, televisions, film studios, museums, theaters."

Wallace links economics, conditions of production, to representation, tying "victimization" to "flawed, inadequate representation" (242). (Winfrey, who owns a substantial production facility in Chicago, along with her own syndicated program, is a significant exception—which Wallace doesn't emphasize.) Black women have largely been erased from representation and politics, excluded from "the issues." "As blacks who are not men, and women who are not white, it simply wasn't safe to accept any representation of the [presidential] candidates . . . in television news . . . in the newspapers . . . or on the 'left' or 'right' " (245). This is powerful thought.

Wallace is critical of *The Women of Brewster Place*, a mini-series from Gloria Naylor's novel, produced by and starring Winfrey and other black women, which was briefly a series: "the series simply confirmed television's currently deplorable record on black female characterization . . . tragic chippies and weeping mothers" (246). The biggest discrepancy for Wallace is the difference between the "daytime" and the "nighttime Oprah." "Fat, old, and poor" versus "her elegant couture wardrobe . . . her meteoric success." "Don't worry, be rich," says the "daytime Oprah." Although Winfrey *has* control over her conditions of production, along with being visible for over five hours per week on television—quite a heroic accomplishment for anyone—one image did play against the other, troubling the receptive waters of the series, which was canceled.

Jacqueline Bobo and Ellen Seiter begin their analysis of this series with Aida Hurtado's assertion that the public-private distinction "is relevant only for the white middle and upper classes since historically the American state has intervened constantly in the private lives and domestic arrangements of the working class."[130] Hurtado's argument is that white feminism, ironically like *Oprah Winfrey*, seeks to make private issues public. On the contrary, "feminists of color" deal with public issues such as affirmative action and prison reform. However true this has been and still is, Hurtado ignores the unconscious, the place of contradiction, and the fact that sexual abuse, rape, and sexual harassment are neither public nor private —but issues which demonstrate that these demarcations were drawn only to keep women in their place and quiet. Sexual issues were seen as private, not public, matters—a distinction disputed by the Senate testimony of Anita Hill.

Bobo's and Seiter's subsequent reading of *The Women of Brewster Place* is divergent from Wallace, including the emphasis on its director, Donna Deitch, a woman whose film *Desert Hearts* dealt with lesbian relationships. The "themes" of the novel and series are a "sense of community, female bonding, and overcoming adversity"—significant because they are "not normally found in television plots" (294). (Daytime soaps might challenge this rarity, as do trauma-of-the-week TV movies.) The series is exceptional because "the black community is used for survival rather than individual advancement and upward mobility . . . contain[ing] . . . values that are starkly opposed to the values of the mainstream white culture and economy."

In the tradition of black women writers, the series "is a scrutiny of sexism and of violence against black women by black men" (296). Unlike Wallace, who sees the women playing stereotypical or prototypical roles, these co-writers argue that "the television version of *The Women of Brewster Place* . . . violates expectations about representations of black women . . . from movies and television series"—a "natural" connection to sexuality, a relationship "to whites as domestic servant, and a role in the nuclear family as a domineering or restraining force." These opposed interpretations are a good sign of the times.

"Race" will not yield a singular "truth" or "answers" for black or white women—who can learn from black women and find their own answers.

Anita Hill

During the October 1991 Senate hearings, two black lawyers—a male judge and a female professor—became enigmatic and fascinating "others" for the white male senators on the Judicial Committee. While the white senators looked to Anita Hill and Clarence Thomas for answers, labeled truth, they failed to realize that this was impossible: the white senators represented the double-edged problem—sexism and racism. Although the investigation involved what Thomas had said to Hill ten years earlier, what was on trial, in many ways, was senatorial ignorance. Whether staged or not, we watched incredulous senators, like crocodiles, attempt to overcome disavowal, their disbelief, inadvertently airing their collective unconscious in public, like dirty laundry or skeletons in closets. Sometimes embarrassing, often infuriating, their stupidity was staggering. At the end, they were exhausted, as were the newsmen/anchors. After this four-day big battle with the unconscious, the whole nation, we were told, could get some well-deserved sleep. Although women were everywhere as expert witnesses— pro/con, feminist or not, all the judges were men.

The hearing of the Senate Judiciary Committee on the confirmation of a black judge, Clarence Thomas, to the U.S. Supreme Court, regarding Hill's charge of sexual harassment, will enter the pantheon of noble hearings of TV history—Army-McCarthy (Communist conspiracy), Kefauver (organized crime), along with Watergate and Iran-Contra. All involved scandal, the repetition of illegal activities (the crimes here were sexual), and the law of the land. In these televised hearings, major institutions run by men are momentarily on trial. Once hooked, the audience responds obsessively; TV takes over daily life; TV demands more TV—OK because this is important TV, "patriarchy under brief siege" TV. Whew, say the male lawmakers, nothing changed. Because Hill-Thomas constant coverage continued on Saturday and Sunday, the networks had a serious dilemma—sporadically intercutting their regularly scheduled sports programming. There was little difference. The U.S. Senate is an old boys' club—which still believes in double standards and men's jokes, just like the locker room after the game.

Constant coverage was an intensive seminar in racism and sexism for men and group therapy for women—involving resistance and identification. What feminist theory, albeit white with all its blind spots, has been arguing for over fifteen years is the importance of the unconscious, held to the private sphere by psychoanalysts, priests, and lawyers alike. Women, including Winfrey and now Anita Hill, are breaking these barriers, are refusing to keep secrets which work to their disadvantage or illness. Racism and sexism, aided and abetted by the unconscious, work by a double-whammy logic of blaming the victim, the logic of sexual harassment. This is the quintessential logic of cancellation—often with deadly consequences.

Significantly, Anita Hill's long and impressive day of testimony on October 11, 1991, when "regular narrative programming" was canceled by all three networks in favor of constant coverage, could prove to be a decisive event of change—for women of color, particularly African-American women. She revealed little affect, which impressed the senators. Thomas, on the other hand, appeared to be near implosion, a body of contained rage, which also impressed the senators. Listening to Hill teach the panel of judges—the white senators—about sexism was in many ways an extraordinary event. The balance of power, for a moment, flowed upstream, against the physical arrangement of white masculine power, itself on trial.

Like the Olympic coverage in the late 1980s, Hill's appearance, as well as the testimony of many black men and women for both sides, could alter the bleak statistics of television representation. Hill, referred to as Professor Hill, demonstrated that the entire nation was fascinated by an intelligent black woman talking, listening, and detailing for men what has been a feminist issue for years. And while the issue is a public one, it is also private—involving shame, guilt, confusion, embarrassment. For many women, keeping these things private is part of the public problem. Hill faced women's painful dilemma, turned to comedy by Gracie Allen: women are not to be believed, or trusted. Women, enigmatic others, cannot be taken at their word.

There are other signs that things (on daytime soaps and primetime sitcoms) are changing: African-American women have roles on *The Young and the Restless* (two gorgeous sisters—one a doctor, the other a dropout who learned to read and now is working at Jabot cosmetics—and their aunt, Mamie, the familiar housekeeper for John Abbott, the president of Jabot); *Days of Our Lives* (a quirky fortuneteller–con artist who unabashedly and comically turns men into sexual objects); *General Hospital* (the long-time character of Simone, married to the chief of staff's son. (*In Living Color* is a great parody of an old NBC slogan, one of the many daily clichéd racisms, like "Black Monday.")

The makeup of the TV audience suggests that things might improve for women. For primetime in 1991, the figures are 42 percent men to 46 percent women. Many programs were pitched to women—*Roseanne, Designing Women, Rosie O'Neill, Sisters,* and the *Cosby Show.* (Fox counterscheduled the *Simpsons* and *In Living Color,* addressed more to men, comparable to other Fox programs pitched to a younger audience. ABC Entertainment VP Ted Harbert says, "We have always been and will always be basically a female-oriented medium."

There are additional limits to content analyses. For me, Charlie's Angels are not Cagney and Lacey, and the historical, aesthetic, and political differences are telling. *One Life to Live* (ABC, New York) is not *Days of Our Lives,* an NBC (California) soap opera which has changed drastically within the past three years. Formerly the purview of mid-age but beautiful women, often with professional careers or dedicated to domesticity, the women on *Days* grew younger in the late 1980s, more glamorized, more dependent on men each week. Their jobs were vague, volunteer positions. They rarely stayed home, except to ponder criminal or personal mysteries. Whether working with gang violence or homeless children who could not speak, or both at the same time, they had no discernible source of income (although the plucky, feisty, and beautiful Jennifer Horton is a journalist and an intelligent woman), neither husbands nor wealthy parents. At the same time, their men, usually official or unofficial detectives, failed miserably to protect them; they never solved crimes which, like the many multiple murder/rape cases, dragged on for months. Middle-class clothing and makeup fashions start here, while middle-age women move to the periphery or off the show, not even good for being mothers, advice givers, dragon ladies, or meddlers.

For long-term viewers, the message was loud and clear: after a certain age, women are marginal-to-unnecessary beings, leading dull, asexual lives. The 1990 return of Julie, presumably from a long stint in Europe, as a high-powered, glamorous, wealthy entrepreneur savvy in the ways and wiles of high finance and corporate maneuvering, is a countermove. However, Victor has questioned her sex appeal and sex life, preferring a much younger woman, Carly, to her. The return of Marlena in the summer of 1991 has shifted the balance of power, and story interest, back to mature women. *Days*'s narrative switches feel like interactive TV—plugged into popular culture trends, with the audience calling the shots.

While the *genre* soap opera has been analyzed, there are also critical differences within and among serials, rapidly changing rather than remaining the same, particularly the lack of repetition of crucial narrative scenes. Like the rest of culture, soaps are faster, diversified, the same *and* different. "The family," imagined as monolithic, is also varied; parenthood and marriage have diversified, along with cultural artifacts. Single-parent sitcoms from *Lucy* after Desi on represent different family configurations, including the recent plethora of single-father shows, the latest trend, which, of course, has a historical lineage; John Forsythe was a wealthy single parent, as was Bill Bixby. Amidst TV's generic sameness, specificity and history can also be claimed—maintaining differences rather than collapsing them via content analyses, global theory, or audience demographics. I have argued, for example, that although they fit into the sitcom generic slot, the strategies of Lucy and Gracie were almost diametrically opposed. Every week Lucy lost, while Gracie won; each feisty female, however, was contained by the end. For me, the difference, whether funny or not, counts.

In an era of mass diversity of sameness, the identification of differences and the delicate maintenance of contradiction and "the difficult unity of inclusion," rather than the manufacture of indifference and exclusion, is a critical project. As one content analyst asserts: "Television's chief significance as a medium has resided in its sheer impact; in its rapid infiltration into everyday American life; in the fact that its images—for all their transience, smallness, sameness, and mediocrity—have wafted, year after year, into the consciousness of hundreds of millions of viewers."[131]

Yet there is still one more story to be told, one which presupposes, as Foucault argues, an original identity, "the belief that there must be, in an author's thought, a point where contradictions are resolved, where the incompatible elements can be *shown* to cohere around a fundamental and

originating contradiction."[132] The author, "a principle of unity," neutralized the "contradictions that are found in a series of texts." The trouble
with television might be its downplay of authorship and its preference for
"personalities." For many critics, the era still hailed as most significant was
TV's Golden Age, a time of famous authors (and live broadcasts). However, as Foucault asked: "Is it not necessary to draw a line between those
who believe that we can situate our present discontinuities within the historical and transcendental tradition of the nineteenth century and those
who are making a great effort to liberate themselves . . . from this conceptual framework?" We should "examine the empty space left by the author's
disappearance, we should attentively observe, along its gaps and fault
lines, its new demarcations and the reapportionment of this void" (17).
This "new demarcation" would perhaps reveal a "messy vitality."

However, just as the corporate realm might be recapitulating the nineteenth century, authorship also isn't dead, it is figured differently, sometimes collectively; perhaps it has been dispersed, pluralized, incorporated.
What is becoming apparent is that women like Jane Wagner write and
produce, along with relate and portray, more of the stories. The awards
and million-dollar deals of Susan Harris (*Soap*), Linda Bloodworth-
Thomason (*Designing Women*) and Diane English (*Murphy Brown*) declare
their real authority. Harris has four sitcoms in the 1991 season—*Golden
Girls, Empty Nest, Nurses,* and *Good and Evil.* In 1990 Bloodworth-Thomason
added *Evening Shade* to her kudos. Her deal requires CBS to "buy five
shows over the next eight years from the Thomasons' company, Mozark
Productions, for $45 million," "paying full production costs instead of the
usual portion." This could mean $100,000/week in fees.[133] What is more
important is the control over, and ownership of, the series by these famous, and glamorous, "writer-producers." (Diane English appears in fashion commercials.)

While in 1991 five sitcoms made the top-ten primetime programs, with
sitcom a staple supporting television for almost fifty years, the real authorizes "serious" (and scandalous) television (as it used to authorize
cinema—hence all the theoretical debates about film's relation to reality).
But exactly what is real is up for grabs—particularly in the news division
debate regarding staged re-creation of events. As a funnier example, ABC
rejected an ad for Yoplait frozen yogurt because it "contained simulated
news techniques. Such representations are reserved specifically for actual
news broadcasts." In the ad, a woman, identified as a "Frozen Yogurt Reporter," "interviews a police detective intent on dusting empty yogurt cartons for tongue prints." "The crime: theft. The loot: frozen yogurt." CBS
requested a disclaimer because "commercials are not actual news." It
would appear that the real or the "actual" has, like the rest of life, become
a style which is taken very seriously indeed.[134]

At the same time, as a local promo goes, the real is there, waiting for us.
"If you have this piece of equipment [a portable video camcorder], you can

be a TV 6 news reporter." A shot of a dopey guy with his camcorder on ready alert cuts away to a shot of a house burning. "Just send your footage to us." This real can be catastrophic—a shot of a local helicopter crashing— or comic—a baseball player losing his pants while catching a high fly ball and falling over a fence. The latter won the $100,000 prize on *America's Funniest Home Videos.* "I Witness Video" is a new series of shocking eyewitness clips submitted by viewers, who make appearances reliving their recorded experience. The real, it would appear, is worth something—money or fifteen seconds of celebrity.

PART II

BEYOND THE PLEASURE PRINCIPLE OF
TELEVISION

TV Time, History, and Catastrophe

U.S. network television is a disciplinary time machine, a metronome rigorously apportioning the present, rerunning TV history, and anxiously awaiting the future. The hours, days, and television seasons are seriated, scheduled, and traded in ten-second increments modeled on the modern workweek—daytime, primetime, late night, or weekend. Time itself is a gendered, hierarchized commodity capitalizing on leisure. Along with selling public time and service for private homes (paradoxically over an electromagnetic spectrum which "belongs to the people"), TV quantifies the body, collectively imagined by the networks as "the audience"—measured by statistics, demographics, and people meters, correlated with supermarket purchases, and bartered according to calculations of time spent/money made. (Subcultural, in-person studies of specific local audiences depict other, idiosyncratic versions of the TV homebody, rephrasing the network obsession with "shares.") The expenditure of time, unlike cinema's tallies of box-office attendance/receipts (and spatial aesthetics), is what counts. Our time is money. Television is a machine capitalizing on the fear of the passage of time—as aging and death; like sponsors, for whom time is money, we can also buy or stop time.

TV's "flow" of entertainment is an economics, including libidinal, which resembles Newtonian time—an old-fashioned view of history as relatively static, slowly changing, a notion emblematized by Darwin. Along with its origin in tourism—reportedly Raymond Williams came up with "flow" in a San Francisco hotel room—the structural model has another U.S. lineage, a pragmatist dimension, from William James and others who argued around 1890 that time was a flux rather than a sum of discrete units, that human consciousness was a stream rather than a configuration of separate faculties; James wrote in 1894: "Consciousness does not appear to itself chopped up into bits. . . . It is nothing jointed; it flows. . . . A river or a stream are the metaphors. . . . Let us call it the stream of thought, of consciousness."[1]

As Susan Strasser points out, "flow" and "continuous process" production were assembly-line principles employed by nineteenth-century companies (prior to 1913 and Henry Ford's Model T) which "packed meat, brewed beer, and canned vegetables using conveyer systems, rollers, and gravity slides that sent materials through the production process automatically, in a continuous stream. The idea had been used in flour milling for over a century."[2] (In their early years, the Hollywood studios adopted the continuity script method of production, which also incorporated "assembly-line" business practices.)[3]

(A recent two-part commercial for Excedrin demonstrates the confident hold of flow, of continuity rather than rupture: in part one, a man with a headache takes an aspirin, seemingly a conclusion; but after two ads and station promos, the commercial returns like a program, incorporating the time lapse into the sell and brief narrative: two minutes later, the man's headache is gone. The interruption itself has been fragmented, mimicking conventions of program and flow. This tactic was used in a different way by the Ragu spaghetti sauce commercials which were miniature sitcoms, replete with laugh tracks and applause, planned as a long-running series. Television or publicity is one step ahead of its theorists; theory is humbled, taken from the realm of academia into popular culture, made accessible and parodic; our cultural objects are, like physics' unpredictable atoms or terrorists, moving, unstable targets.)

Turn-of-the-century Joycean figurations of time split public time, the time of crowds—the newly instituted world standard time which crossed national boundaries like the wireless, regulating war, railroads, and masses alike—from private time, which, like memory, was capricious; both added simultaneity to successive time. Freud's theory of childhood and memory elucidates this temporal model, perfectly applicable to television programming: TV reruns and remakes Freud's "repetition compulsion": "Theoretically, every earlier state of content could thus be restored to memory again even if its elements have long ago exchanged all their original connections for more recent ones."[4] For Freud, as for Newton, Darwin, and reruns of "I Love Lucy," time is "embedded in our embryonic beings . . . in which every experience leaves a trace."

However, the memories TV recalls via constant reruns, remakes, and parody, the past it re-creates, rarely summon or echo personal experience—what Benjamin in "On Some Motifs in Baudelaire," referring to Bergson's "theory of experience" and Proust, called involuntary memory. Rather, TV schedules memories of television, perhaps, as Benjamin argues, resulting in an "atrophy" of experience. TV's peculiarly democratic past is infrequently idiosyncratic. As exemplified by *Leave it to Beaver* and the return of June Cleaver in name to *Roseanne*'s promo and in body to *Baby Boom* (canceled), TV's history personally, parodically belongs to everyone, whether alive or dead when it happened. "Therefore Proust, summing up, says that the past is 'somewhere beyond the reach of the intellect, and unmistakably present in some material object (or in the sensation which such an object arouses in us). . . . As for that object, it depends entirely on chance whether we come upon it before we die or whether we never encounter it."[5] Roland Barthes, in *Camera Lucida*, came upon the material object, the old photograph of his mother as a child, before he died.

TV is rarely the material object setting off involuntary (personal) memory, causing us to assimilate "the information it supplies as part of [our] own experience." "Where there is experience in the strict sense of the word, certain contents of the individual past combine with material of the collective past."[6] Rather than this amalgam of involuntary/voluntary memory, shifting from conscious to unconscious, from collective to individual past, in the realm of experience—as Marguerite Duras did in *The Lover* or as occurred during the twenty-fifth-year commemoration of Kennedy's assassination—television's intention "is just the opposite, and it is achieved: to isolate what happens from the realm in which it could affect the experience of the reader."[7]

TV triggers memories of TV in an endless chain of TV referentiality. The newspaper techniques Benjamin cites are applicable to TV: "brevity, comprehensibility, and above all, lack of connection between the individual news items."[8] Instead of experience and memory, television's past, whether funny or not, evokes laughter and distance. It is a disassociated, dated history, out of sync with the present, with nothing, now, to do with us—it is over and thus, paradoxically, ahistorical or nostalgic, at least for most critics. With its raw appeals to, and erasures of, affect (see Parts II and III), television is a medium of remembrance more than memory: "The function of remembrance," Reik writes, "is the protection of impressions; memory aims at their disintegration. Remembrance is essentially conservative, memory is destructive."[9] TV enacts the contradiction of destructive conservation.

However, Benjamin's model of history as revolutionary or catastrophic exists as an inside premise of television's rhetoric. Like Proust, who "immediately confronts this involuntary memory with a voluntary memory, one that is in the service of the intellect," or Benjamin in his encounters with the everyday or artifacts of popular culture which set off memories of, for example, the Berlin of his childhood, and in his formulations of time in "Theses on the Philosophy of History," we can analyze the present of television through our personal, generational, and intellectual histories. This "dialectical" or materialistic analysis might "blast a specific era out of the homogeneous course of history—blasting a specific life out of the era or a specific work out of the lifework [which] is preserved—and at the same time cancelled,"[10] what I call, following Freud's cue as does Benjamin, television's process of creation/cancellation. Like Benjamin's famous formulation, TV partially gives us "a conception of the present as the 'time of the now' which is shot through with chips of Messianic time."[11]

This conception of the eruption of the past into the present as a simultaneity is based on Freud's model of shock, which, along with the Soviet revolution, influenced Benjamin: "To articulate the past historically . . . means to seize hold of a memory as it flashes up at a moment of danger. . . . fashion is a tiger's leap into the past. . . . The same leap in the open air of history is the dialectical one. . . . Where thinking suddenly stops in a configuration pregnant with tensions, it gives that configuration a shock . . . a revolutionary chance in the fight for the oppressed past."[12] While TV is usually a tiger's leap into fashion, a medium of remembrance rather than memory, it operates, particularly during catastrophe coverage—"the configuration of shock"—"as if" there might be a revolutionary chance. Catastrophe coverage, "the time of the now," is represented as a moment when thinking stops, a moment of danger that might portend change, which paradoxically is both thrill and preclusion. To suggest mechanisms of this containment is the goal of this analysis, which, perhaps parroting Freud's tedious, humorless style of rephrasing, or like the depleted TV coverage of parades and elections, unstylishly resorts to a determined repetition. (Could anything be more tedious than watching parades on television?)

Paralleling TV's temporal effects, anxiety is television's affect. If this is so, then we might consider shifting our analysis from theories of pleasure to include theories of unpleasure (and paradoxically, from constructs of work to models of leisure *as* work), moving *Beyond the Pleasure Principle* to *Inhibitions, Symptoms and Anxiety*, away from desire, lack, castration, Oedipus, the unconscious and toward anxiety (and Colonus), loss, separation, the conscious, and, particularly for me (but also for Freud), women.

Successive, simultaneous time, measured by regular, on-the-half-hour programming (a historical expansion and contraction of the 15-minute radio and early TV base program unit), indefinitely multiplied by (point-to-point) cable and satellite transmission, hypostatized by familiar formats and aging stars in reruns and remakes, trivialized by scandal and gossip, is disrupted by the discontinuity of catastrophe coverage. So-called heterogeneity or diversity ceases, as do commercials and TV continuity time, as we focus on a single event. My temporal model of television incorporates the aging body (including plastic surgery, masquerade, and sexual difference) and speaks about gossip/scandal (including talk show "pluralism" and differentiation as difference), which are figured later.[13]

Newton's project of charting an unchanging universe—the equivalent of plastic surgery—was doomed, as are our sagging, wrinkled bodies, by his own laws of gravity: the natural state of matter (at least for now) is chaos, disorder. Einstein and relativity sketched an artistic universe where space is curved, the path of light is bent, and time is slowed. TV time of regularity and repetition, continuity and "normalcy," contains the potential of interruption, the thrill of live coverage of death events. It is here, in the potential and promise of disruption—a shift between the safe assurance of successive time and story and the break-in of the discontinuity of the real in which the future hangs in the balance, the intrusion of shock, trauma, disaster, crisis—that TV's spectatorial mechanism of disavowal, which is retroactive, operates most palpably.

If a program begins off the half-hour, or we hear the alarm "We interrupt this regularly scheduled program," a catastrophe or political event has occurred;[14] that it is still not on the air reassures us that it was not a nuclear catastrophe, at least in the U.S. Our disasters require "continual coverage," nation over narrative; those of other countries are not worth a missed soap opera. Most critical, the U.S. network trade of time for money was, until 1991, suspended during catastrophe coverage, formatted events too portentous for commercials. The news division's takeover of entertainment is also the daytime replacement of women by men. The break-in or disruption of continuity flow or narrative normalcy has rigid rules: in addition to the rare, unscheduled presidential address or news conference, it must be economic (commercials, station IDs, promos, market crises) or deathly. Imagine a mid-program break to the zoo, the classroom, or an art event. (Constant coverage of hearings is a planned event which hooks audiences in other obsessive ways.)

V

◆

Shocking Thoughts

Theories of catastrophe—mathematical (René Thom); psychoanalytic (Sigmund Freud); socio/geo/logical (the journal *Disasters*); historical materialist or dialectical (Benjamin); artistic (Andy Warhol in painting, Bruce Conner in film and sculpture, and Ant Farm and Steve Fagin in video); biblical (the catastrophists and TV evangelists); figural/aesthetic (Baudrillard and Derrida's "nuclear criticism"—a critique of other apocalyptics); and literal (U.S. nuclear actions, testing, and policy)—are predicated on models of time and fear of death (functioning as denial/disavowal and loss, of power/mastery). In fact, catastrophe discourses echo each other across history, context, and discipline in quite remarkable ways, with a political distinction which breaks down into two opposing categories: those that embrace and detail the paradox of contradiction (and discontinuity); and those premised on apocalyptic, evolutionary, but invisible answers or originary causes—Baudrillard, the biblical catastrophists, and the U.S. government.[15] (Sociology tries to treadle both ways via empiricism.)

"Jump Behavior": René Thom

René Thom's mathematical system of topology (presented in academic papers in the late '50s, with his book appearing in 1972) is a qualitative rather than quantitative way of analyzing change that is not smooth but rather discontinuous. Rather than a scientific theory, Thom's is an "art of models."[16] While this resonates of simulation, suggesting Baudrillard, who, like Thom, has the will to totalizing answers, Thom is undone by observation, along with the magnitude of his "text" which includes the everyday. "Catastrophe theory" is concerned with "sudden and discrete changes, the stability of forms, and the creation of forms."[17] "Form" and "model" are crucial terms for his analysis of catastrophe—"jump behavior"[18] resulting from a state of conflict. Catastrophe is a problem of "the succession of form," and relies on "local models" applicable to common, everyday experience. "Our everyday may be a tissue of ordinary catastrophes, but our death is a generalized catastrophe."[19] "Many phenomena of common experience [are] in themselves trivial . . . but is it not possible that a 'theory' launched for such homely phenomena might, in the end, be more profitable for science?"[20] His homely examples are cracks in a wall and the shape of a cloud, which suggest a "structural stability" of recurrent, identifiable elements. I would add television to the list of the homely.

As this theory is dependent on form, so is my model of TV catastrophe—form historically turned into learned convention. Catastrophe occurs for "formal reasons,"[21] is a process involving the creation or destruction of forms, their disappearance and replacement. As Woodcock and Davis point out, the models must depict both continuous and discontinuous change, summarizing the appearance and disappearance of stability: "To change discontinuously is to pass through non-equilibrium states." "The abrupt bursting of a bubble, the transition from ice at its melting point to water at its freezing point, the shift in the unconscious in the process of getting a joke or pun"[22] are examples of shifting moments of discontinuity and transformation.

The similarity between comedy and catastrophe is a fascinating one, suggesting a relationship between laughter and shock. Thom argues that these transitions are discontinuous because the intervening states of passage from one state to another are not stable. However, they are brief eruptions, as they are rare on television, in comparison to the time spent in stable states. (CNN inverts this formula, seeking nonequilibrium as its norm.) "Jump behavior" is a state of unstable passage, signaled by the network news announcer's vocal break-in with a visual logo and the abrupt cutaway, *off the half-hour*, to the news studio and the anchorman, a discontinuous shift from the taped and rehearsed into the live, irregular, and unpredictable which disrupts TV's "structural stability"—a catastrophe of TV "normalcy," continuity, and narrative. (For CNN, nothing is disrupted but rather *incorporated*. Catastrophe fits snugly into their continuity: the normal state of the news, a genre determined by crisis, is bad.) The pleasure of familiar repetition of the same as difference turns into the unpleasure of repetition, moving "beyond the pleasure principle." Many viewers of afternoon soap operas expressed their displeasure via the mail, angry that Chernobyl replaced thirty minutes of *One Life to Live*.

"From Libido to Anxiety": Sigmund Freud

As Thom's allusions to the double dealing of the joke work suggest, and as Benjamin argued, Freud rather snugly adheres to a catastrophe model. Two texts, *Inhibitions, Symptoms and Anxiety* (1925–26) and *Beyond the Pleasure Principle*, are central to my argument. Revising his position in 1926, Freud writes: "I can no longer maintain this view . . . of the transformation of libido into anxiety."[23] This is almost an inversion for Freud: now rather than anxiety as the result of repression, repression is a consequence of anxiety. "Anxiety is a reaction to a situation of danger" predicated on a fear of "being abandoned by the protecting super ego" (128). Anxiety both is an "affect" ("every affect . . . is only a reminiscence of an event" [133]) and is "freshly created out of the economic conditions of the situation" (130)— conventions of catastrophe coverage, the event being covered, and audience response. We respond to TV interruptions of announcements of airline crashes and nuclear accidents with an affect of anxiety, which TV can decide to exacerbate by "staying on the air," eradicating the regularly scheduled entertainment, a narrative catastrophe.

Anxiety is "something that is felt," "a very marked character of unpleasure" (132) unlike tension, pain, or mourning—although these are later stages of catastrophe coverage. (Grief is a reaction to actual loss, anxiety to the possibility of loss.) Anxiety is a "physiological, motor manifestation" based upon "an increase of excitation which produces unpleasure which finds relief through acts of discharge" (133).

The historical and *crucial* difference between Benjamin, Freud, and television is that television is shock *and* therapy; it both produces *and* discharges anxiety. Whereas for Benjamin, shock came from the public "crowd" of modernity (and historical events), and for Freud the experience or affect was, with the critical exception of war neuroses, individuated, TV administers shock and ameliorates the collective affects, imagined as shared, perhaps uniform. Via repetition, information, and constant coverage, TV is both a source and solution.

The origin of anxiety is traced back to birth and then fear of castration, both of which are dismissed as explanations (to be honest, castration, Freud's favorite answer on *Jeopardy*, is abandoned rather sadly, or at least nostalgically); Freud finally settles on "missing someone who is loved and longed for" (136) as his favored analysis—not an answer/cause he savors like the former. "Longing turns into anxiety" for the child (the subject of psychoanalysis). This text circles around the mother. "The situation, then, which it regards as a 'danger' and against which it wants to be safeguarded is that of non-satisfication, of a *growing tension due to need*, against which it is helpless." In relation to the imperfect body addressed by commercials and explanations of the causes and even "facts" of catastrophe, TV preys on/creates nonsatisfaction, all the while staying on the air, waiting, repeating. In this "situation of non-satisfaction the amounts of stimulation rise to an unpleasurable height without its being possible for them to be mastered . . . or discharged" (137). Zapruder's film footage of Kennedy's assassination was endlessly repeated; the thirty-second *Challenger* explosion was re-run hundreds of times—attempts at mastery and discharge. (These are open-ended times in which narrative and closure are absent.)

As in the rest of Freud, sexual difference circulates; however, in this text, there is a fascinating, albeit awkwardly reluctant, if not begrudging, reversal—an almost whispered inscription of female subjectivity: "It is precisely in women that the danger-situation of loss of object seems to have retained the most effect." And, sounding like an ad copy man on Madison Avenue, aware of feminism: "All we need to do is to make a slight modification in *our* description of *their* [my emphasis] determinant of anxiety," which, he asserts, is the loss not merely of an object but of "the object's love" (143). Given the "determinant" of "their" or female anxiety (unstated though it is, from the daughter's or mother's subjective position), Freud cautions us to "put ourselves on guard against over-estimating that factor [castration] since it could not be a decisive one for the female sex, who are undoubtedly more subject to neuroses than men." While I doubt the neurotic claim, castration is not decisive.

(On the same page, Freud reverses himself. After aligning women with neuroses, farther down he links hysteria with women and "obsessional neurosis . . . with masculinity." By mentioning castration so often as an explanation for almost everything, he inscribes his arduous difficulty relinquishing it. Also, when he does refer to mother, he does so almost as an afterthought, for example, "such as mother" when referring to children's fear of the dark [136].)

Along with a backhanded privileging of women, albeit neurotic females, there is another crucial distinction from pleasure, his theory of desire and the unconscious. In unpleasure and anxiety, "the ego is the actual seat of anxiety" (140). In current grey-tone ads for telephone and computer systems, middle-management/aged men and a few discriminately placed women, with furtive brows and worried glances, haltingly, quizzically fret anxiously in piercing, abrupt closeups about their wrongly chosen business system while vérité-style hand-held camera shots literally signify "high anxiety." (TV coopts yet another tactic of the counterculture, cinéma vérité, direct cinema, or hand-held video, for commodity culture as "art"—a double-whammy recuperation.)

Thus, while one dominant model of psychoanalysis developed for cinema is based on the unconscious, the male subject, desire/castration/lack, and Oedipus, this construct shifts to include the ego, the female subject, love/loss, with a subjective, hesitant place reserved for mother (no small gain)—critical distinctions which, for me, go a long way toward theorizing the mechanisms of both the TV text and its audience, with, however, historical differences, including the permutation and rearrangement of every-day U.S. life, politics, and culture by television.[24]

If the "danger-situation changes . . . the impulse [anxiety] will run its course under an automatic influence . . . the influence of the compulsion to repeat . . . as though the danger-situation that had been overcome still existed" (153). That everyday and catastrophic television rely on repetition (an economic "compulsion to repeat") like no other activity (or medium) except assembly-line production is not without consequence. The sheer repetition of coverage serves a hypothetical purpose of "as if"—operating on the pretense that "the danger situation still existed." Even Freud's description of anxiety resembles television. For example, as Freud often does, he tacks on an intriguing addendum which relates "angst" to expectation —"anxiety *about* something. It has a quality of *indefiniteness* and *lack of object.*" As with television itself, a central trait of catastrophe coverage is indefiniteness; coverage involves a search for the answer, the explanation—in short, the object. On a metaphorical level, indefiniteness and lack of object define television (and neoclassical economics)—electronic, erasable circuitry with no visible, material base until transmitted. Freud differentiates "realist anxiety"—"about a known danger"—from "neurotic anxiety" —"a danger that has still to be discovered" (165). TV vacillates between realistic and neurotic coverage. The live, videotaped murder of Lee Harvey Oswald by Jack Ruby, rerun like the Zapruder film, triggered neurotic anxiety; Black Monday anchors awaited, like network vultures, a crash after the fall, prophesying back to 1929, the realist harbinger of the neurotic future.

To doggedly restate my earlier argument: Freud argues that "there are two reactions to real danger. One is an affective reaction, an outbreak of anxiety. The other is a protective action" (165). With its strategy of creation/contradiction/cancellation, TV is both the outbreak and the protective action, the latter accomplished by repetition, finding answers, and the rare result of assigning guilt. Like a doctor detailing medical procedures to a patient before and after surgery, information here provides a therapeutic service, a ritual akin to prayer or chanting. Cloaked as an episteme, a desire to know, it soothes our anxiety, protecting us from fear. Thus, information, the raison d'être of coverage, becomes story, therapy, and collective ritual. Later it will become myth.

I can find no better description of catastrophe coverage than "Anxiety is . . . an expectation of a trauma, and . . . a repetition of it in a mitigated form. . . . Expectation belongs to the danger-situation, whereas its *indefiniteness* and *lack of object* belong to the traumatic situation of helplessness—the situation which is anticipated in the danger situation" (166). Although TV situations are mainly comedy, the TV spectator anticipates, fears, then relishes the danger situation: "a recognized, remembered, expected situation of helplessness. Anxiety is the original reaction to helplessness. . . . The ego . . . repeats it actively in a weakened version. . . . What is of decisive importance is the first displacement of the anxiety reaction from its origin in the situation of helplessness" (166–67). Expectation is displaced anxiety. We await catastrophe as the ultimate promise and noble dream of television—when time is open-ended, commercial-free, and we are helpless. However, the audience is not passive but expectant; agitated by TV, it partakes of masochism, is soothed by mundane ritual, and is contained by contradiction.

The place of mother (and the determinance for Freud's prior writing of sexual difference) suggests that the response to catastrophe will necessarily be different for men and women. Madelon Sprengnether's interpretation of these texts is rather different from mine. Our disagreement would hinge, I believe, on whether or not "castration" is a sexually neutral term. *Webster's Unabridged* supports my masculine reading of the act of castration: "1. To geld; to remove the testicles of; to emasculate. 2. to cut out or revise, thereby depriving of essential vigor or significance [hardly a satisfactory definition of birth]. 3. in botany, to take away the stamens [which destroys reproduction]." For me, castration is singularly masculine, and has little to do with women, let alone birth. I see separation and castration as distinct: separation is actual and beneficial; castration is symbolic and detrimental; separation functions consciously, and castration, unconsciously. Sprengnether, on the other hand, interprets "castration as separation—not of the phallus from the male body, but of the infant from the maternal body."[25]

However, by equating castration with (as) separation, and hence birth, Sprengnether can make Mother (and birth), not Father, the originary term —no small move. This pre-Oedipal mother is, however, ambivalent— desirable and repugnant: a "point of origin" and "death." This originary, or "spectral," woman may not be so different from the old double-whammy of plenitude and fear, the virgin/whore evoked by fear of castration.

Whereas anxiety is my focus, central to Sprengnether's reading is Freud's debate, stated and read between the lines, with Otto Rank's theory of birth trauma, which challenges Oedipus and hence Freud's theory. Because refuting Rank is, for Sprengnether, the key subtext, or pretense, Freud's argument is viewed not as contradictory but as ambivalent or unstable—back and forth, progress and retreat, an "undoing action" (142) she attributes to Freud's avoidance of the pre-Oedipal mother. Our differences might depend on what we were looking for in the first place. Her assessment that "Freud's obsession with Rank . . . acts simultaneously as a denial and as an acknowledgement of his interest [in the mother-infant relationship]" is one of many acute remarks. Yet, I wonder if Rank was the obsession or its displacement.

Gilles Deleuze's work on masochism is helpful in this regard because the scenario, the contract, revolves around "mother." As Sonja Rein has so lucidly argued: "What is important in masochism is the desire to return to the mother. . . . Thus, the masochist demands that he be beaten in order that the image of his father in him . . . is diminished." However, as Rein points out, "What is important for Deleuze is the nature of the agreement made between the masochist and his torturer. . . . The contract functions . . . to invest the mother image with the symbolic power of the law."[26] The image of the mother in catastrophe events does not function as law—rather as loss; the image circulates within an economy of anxiety, not one of desire. Yet, like masochism, mother is at least subjectively there, albeit leftover. However, the audience does make a contract with TV during catastrophe coverage, a painful ritual which mirrors masochistic (un)pleasure.

VI

♦

Disastrous Events

Before the Fall, After the Fall: Baby Jessica and Black Monday

U. S. TV was on disorder alert, in a frenzy of disequilibrium, anticipating a danger situation, in October 1987. Daytime entertainment was interrupted, punctuated by crises which failed to escalate to catastrophe. Issues were conflated and strangely gendered. Milwaukee was in a virtual frenzy of local news as a result of fires in the racially segregated core district—black children were dying by the dozens. The image of conflagration was lifted off by satellite and picked up in Sydney. Eventually, this local spectacle was analyzed in the newspapers as an issue of poverty, migration from the South, families living together in crowded, flimsy homes, without heat and using space heaters to keep warm, families headed by young women without jobs or husbands. The families were black, the landlords were white.

After the hideous deaths of so many local black children, and the single solution of installing fire alarms(!), the local, revved-up audience saw the blonde Baby Jessica emerge as a national star on Friday, October 16, in a TV nightmare of entrapment (Fig. 3). TV kept breaking in; Connie Chung was not at the scene but more prestigiously at the catastrophe helm in New York, the throne of power, prestige, and stability usually occupied by an-

Figure 3

chormen, in this NBC case Tom Brokaw, who was off for the weekend. While diagrams graphed Baby Jessica's (and our) Freudian nightmare, the camera focused on the rigging, a cable surrounded by men and media—in a Texas town, Midland, depleted by the U.S. oil crisis, an image right out of *Radio Days* and the Depression, this time with a happy ending. There was little to see except the same cable and the passage of time; little to tell except the local story of the uncanny accident, teenage parentage, and community heroicism. (The barely repressed issue was oil and energy, a U.S. economic crisis which erupted in Iraq in August 1990.) Drilling miscalculations were delays prolonging the suspense and time of coverage. Once the classic story of dead or alive had begun, the networks couldn't quit; it was only a matter of time, which would tell. She was rescued, alive, looking like a little mummy, on NBC just before *Miami Vice*.

The next day, the story of Baby Jessica shifted to surgical details—her damaged foot and face. The drama of the separation of mother and child continued, but Nancy Reagan's breast, cancer, and gender were added to the surgical agenda. Enter the symbolic mother. The two dramas were positioned together in the newspapers; the female body became headlines, a front-page event. Baby Jessica and Nancy were stories of loss and separa-

Figure 4

tion for women. Although the coverage was mediated by men, particularly the medical news briefings, Connie Chung was one initial narrator; the female reporter covering Nancy wore a remarkably similar red dress. On Saturday, Jessica was "serious but stable" (Fig. 4). By Sunday's headlines, Nancy was fine, and Jessica's foot would be saved (Fig. 5). (The Jessica story continued: the *Oprah Winfrey* show visited Midland with a program dedicated to Jessica, capitalizing on the bizarre vis-à-vis personal compassion. Later, participants in the rescue wrangled over monies for selling the rights to the story—organizing into unions for profits. Made into a TV movie in 1989/90, the scenario reappeared in August 1990 on *Days of Our Lives*, as Sean Douglas fell down a well, "just like Baby Jessica.")

The coverage and the events were the made-for-TV reenactment of *Inhibitions, Symptoms and Anxiety*, including birth, loss, and several mothers—Jessica's teenage mother, Nancy Reagan, and Connie Chung. Along with helplessness, there was no visible object, only waiting, indefiniteness, and the expectation of either alive or dead. The weekend bodily drama of anxiety seemed suspiciously anachronistic (like the emergence of high-style Bakhtin), a symptom of something else. Black Monday and the stock-market plunge interrupted *Days of Our Lives*, the soap in the 12 noon slot, with

Figure 5

another version of the fall and loss—this time of money, not mother/child (Fig. 6). Tom Brokaw was back as the NBC anchor, trying to explain this crisis of capitalism via talking heads, shots of the New York Stock Exchange, Wall Street, and, later, international exchanges.

While it was argued that the problem was electronic, set off by computer trading via satellite transmission across standardized international time zones, it was difficult for the U.S. audience to believe that the world and business carried on while it slept. The stammering reports, interspersed irregularly throughout the day, revealed a dual dilemma—significant for cultural studies scholars as well as the sad yuppies who were interviewed en masse on PBS financial programs, stricken with grief at the loss of million-dollar condos, BMW's and Porsches (Porsche suspended manufacture after the crash): (1) the inability to analyze electronic, computerized conditions of production and transmission, and (2) the difficulty of imagining international, rather than nationally determined, boundaries, economic structures, times, and points of view. The ultimate catastrophe for television would be a crisis of capitalism, resulting in change, which could unravel or alter TV's economic/commercial base, above which catastrophe coverage is a superstructural raison d'être. (For example, one reason for TV's rigid tem-

Figure 6

porality is to notify advertisers of the seconds their ads will air; different times have different costs.)

It is not surprising that these four days revealed a very old-fashioned sexual hierarchy of power: with women on the side of babies and the body—the visible referent, and men aligned with money and technology—the invisible symbolic. Yet, perhaps this move of the surgical body from scandal magazines to the nightly news might portend a challenge to the propriety or decorum called power. Granted that Reagan's (Ronald's) colon and nose had been spotlighted previously, Nancy's breast took over the headlines. And hers was not the only newsworthy surgical breast in 1987 (as Jessica Hahn revealed).

While it has been theorized in philosophy and art since the early 1900s that simultaneity replaced succession, that electronics annihilated space and time and extended the present, we are still caught in our thinking about television around the turn of the century (which, given neoclassical economics and the snug fit of a Freudian model, might be apt if we keep in mind that Freud is only one among several models, for example Jean Baudrillard and Gilles Deleuze and Felix Guattari).

The stock-market coverage frantically tried to locate a place or context, and an object—like the sinking of the *Titanic*. If, as for Stephen Kern, the *Titanic* is a historical border between the present as a series of local events (local news coverage and horizon-to-horizon transmitting towers) and a simultaneity of multiple, distant events (network, nightly news, and satellite transmission), then we have entered another historical phase. If in the *Titanic* "we recognize with a sense near to awe that we have been almost witness of a great ship in her death agonies," our history might be determined by what we cannot see.[27] In the 1987 crisis, electronic technology was no longer only the means of transmission and salvation but was also, like the *Titanic*, part of the problem—and an invisible, international, simultaneous crisis at that. As with time and money, the stock and trade of television, there was no stable, tangible object, only effects and victims (who made personal appearances on TV or committed suicide—an exaggerated recreation of 1929) (Fig. 7). Our history might be determined by aftereffects.

Coverage of the Iraq oil crisis in August 1990, a military action ostensibly initiated in the name of Kuwait rather than money and energy, regularly intercut the military buildup and stock-market reports (in a cause-effect logic), awaiting a war and a recession, with no pretense that economics were not the determinant issue and fear, the real source of national anxiety. The irrationality of predicting either war or the stock market was covered up by cause-effect logic. CNN's coverage, titled "The Crisis in the Gulf," was particularly direct in this regard, interviewing stock-market experts more than government officials. And even with military spokesmen, the economic cost of the action was at issue. Editorials in newspapers urged the populace not to put off purchase of consumer items, thereby undermining the economy; to continue to regularly shop was an act of national support.

Coverage was also a network battle, with Koppel beating out Rather by getting into Iraq first. CNN beat ABC and CBS, along with NBC. That CBS was spending $1.5 million to keep Rather's CBS crew on location may have led to the resignation of the head of the news division and the paring down of all the network news divisions after the war ended. The staff of network news was one casualty in the ratings war of cost effectiveness. (I will return to the War in the Gulf.)

(Having taken on national news, CNN and other cable channels are beginning to compete with local news. They plan to beat local stations with news items on leisure and shopping, what could be called "good news," reported by anchors who stand up rather than sit behind desks. For example, Turner Broadcasting System, Inc., "is encouraging operators to insert five minute of local news every half hour into its Headline News network," which reaches six million homes. James P. Mooney, president of the National Cable Television Association, said that "the next big breakthrough in cable programming" will be local news, appealing because of its high ratings [*The Wall Street Journal*, June 18, 1991, B1].)

Figure 7

Death, Shock, Art:
Kennedy, Walter Benjamin, and *Eternal Frame*

The assassination of John F. Kennedy set the pattern for catastrophe coverage. Zapruder's amateur/tourist movie footage was endlessly rerun on television and scrutinized for clues. Because it had been recorded, the image, aligned with reality and tragic drama, would yield an answer, a truth, if, like the riddle of the Sphinx, we could only get closer, deconstruct it. A shift from cinema to television was dramatized by the murder of Lee Harvey Oswald by Jack Ruby, live on television and rerun.

It could be argued that the assassination, not initially covered by the networks, was the first and last time for a united television audience: everyone compulsively remembered and minutely described, again and again, like reruns, where *they were*, in real life, and where they were in relation to television, representation, a cultural moment when television and our daily lives were still separate but merging. While our emotional experience of the event came from television, our bodies remained distinct from television; "meaning" occurred to us in specific places. This is comparable to Benjamin's use of Freud and "shock": "Perhaps the special achievement of shock defense may be seen in its function of assigning to an incident a precise point in time in consciousness at the cost of the integrity of its contents."[28]

Along with a precise time as a shock defense, viewers remembered where they were when they heard the news—a place contiguous to a television set. We took our grief into public places and watched TV together. The assigning of a time at the cost of content for Benjamin "would be a peak achievement of the intellect; it would turn the incident into a moment that has been lived" (163). The assassination—"a moment that has been lived" between individual memory and collective ritual, a moment that tended toward destruction rather than remembrance—and its coverage marked the passage from experience to information (the physical to simulation), from the *public crowd* as the source of shock ("collisions . . . nervous impulses . . . in rapid succession, like . . . electric energy" [175] . . . "an experience" of the "passerby" which corresponds to "what the worker experiences at his machine" [176]) to the *private audience* of television; in the '60s, we were still on the threshold.

The difference between the private *audience* of television and the public *crowd* of mass culture is a historically crucial distinction. Drawing on Freud's theory of stimulus-response in *Beyond the Pleasure Principle*, which was modeled on the mass experience of shell shock during World War I, Benjamin's theory of modernity speaks of shocks from the external world—of traumatic shocks which "break through the protective shield." For Benjamin, strolling through the streets and arcades of Berlin and Paris with Baudelaire as his imaginary companion, shocks came from the crowd, the wares, and the passersby (as well as Fordist systems of labor). As he wrote of Baudelaire, "The crowd—no subject was more entitled to the attention of 19th century writers" (166).

Film, a collective public exhibition unlike the private reception of television (which is a historical rather than ontological case), was an analogue for, an experience of, modernity as a series of shocks: "like the energy from a battery . . . a reservoir of electric energy . . . the experience of the shock." Hence, film as "perception in the form of shocks was established as a formal principle" (175). For Benjamin, Sergei Eisenstein's theory of conflict and dialectical editing—a series of shocks, of conflict within and between shots, sequences, and spectators—overlaps with Freud. (Benjamin had been in Moscow.) Benjamin's argument (from Eisenstein and Pavlov's reflex psychology along with William James) applies military (Freud) and revolutionary (Einstein/Marx) aetiologies to the experience of the city and popular culture—which includes electrical technologies. Although compared to the assembly line, this is a shift from work to leisure, from Great Events to everyday life.

"Nervous impulses" and "electric energy" portend electronic culture and its reception—the creation/mediation of the shocking experience of modernity. For Benjamin, the "crisis of reproduction" manifests itself as a "crisis in perception": "To perceive the aura of an object we look at means to invest it with the ability to look at us in return."[29] On television, invested with direct looks and address, we are never in danger of being seen, for as yet there is no return, only its aura, an aftereffect. (However, interactive and reciprocal TV will soon be available, along with cyberspace actuality — like the vacation in the ironically titled *Total Recall*.) As Wolfgang Schivelbusch points out, the relation "between subject and outside world [was] a synthesis. . . . The stimulus shield . . . *is* [the] outer world . . . absorbed and interiorized" by the subject.[30] Benjamin more fancifully writes that "the man who loses his capacity for experiencing feels as though he is dropped from the calendar. The big-city dweller knows this feeling on Sundays . . . the poor souls that wander restlessly, but outside of history"[31] (a good definition of football fans).

The Kennedy assassination marked a cultural shift from public to private reception, from film to television. We told stories about our personal experience of the event, set off by a film of the real; after this, we would speak of television and representation. (*Eternal Frame*, a performance/videotape by Ant Farm, restages the *film* of the assassination as simulation.)

The constant coverage of the assassination was cited by TV journalists as realizing television's potential for collective identification—television's democratic dream that by informing us and setting a good, calm, and rational example via the autocratic anchors, the populace will be united, soothed, and finally ennobled by repetition of and patient waiting for information. As I argued earlier, TV administers and cushions shocks, is both the traumatic shock and Freud's protective "shield" which protects against excess excitation . . . and also transmits excitation from the outside to the inside of the organism."[32] This double function of "transmission and protection" is temporal, and is accomplished by narration—"temporizing the traumatic effects of an excess of energy . . . the death drive as another name for a story," according to Samuel Weber (145). Like the joke technique (described by Freud as an envelope or a container), TV envelops the shock, delivering *and* cushioning us from stimuli which it regulates in acceptable levels—like the dosage of microwave ovens—turning news or shock into story and tragic drama. Rather than an excess of stimuli which set off for Benjamin private recollection and memory, such as the assassination coverage initially provided, TV administers then defuses stimuli in containing doses.

Television promises shock and trauma containment over time, via narration of the real. As Weber states, Freud's analysis of abstract time was connected to the psychic real as an *aftereffect* of events. This aftereffect is separate yet necessarily dependent on the event; examples are the "dream, in the narration that disfigures it, the joke, in the laughter that displaces it," citations which recall Thom. Like "The Return to Space," as the October 1988 *Discovery* flight was titled by CBS, "aftereffects repeat the event they follow, but they also alter it and it is precisely this process of repetitive alteration that renders the event psychically 'real' "(147). The stories do not merely repeat an event but each other, in a sequence that is both successive and simultaneous. (The Great Quake coverage best illustrates this process, with its endless repetition of the three primal scenes.) Catastrophe coverage, rendering events psychically real, is "repetitive alteration" or disfigural representation resulting in aftereffects which read back, creating further disfiguration. In Weber's view, this process is stoppable for Freud, in the end, by myth and eros—a conclusion to which I will return.

Freud's analysis of consciousness as precisely "not consciousness *of* anything, and even less . . . self-consciousness," might describe the role of the anchor—along with repetition and narration, another means of cushioning excess. Covering catastrophes is the ultimate test of the top anchor's (usually a man) mettle, his stamina measured by words, information, and calm demeanor. (The Los Angeles news announcer who panicked during the 1987 earthquake and ducked under his desk miserably failed anchor protocol, becoming a joke for late-night comics.) Television fancies that if we have enough news, if it stays on the air with us, a vigil like sitting up with a sick or dying friend, we will behave like adults. Or, the stock-market coverage of "Black Monday" demonstrates that television can also, like computer trading, panic us, creating a need *for* television. What was innovative then has become protocol which we have come to expect and which plays into and creates those expectations.

Eternal Frame

Eternal Frame, a 1975 performance and videotape made by Ant Farm and T. R. Uthco, is a simulation of a catastrophe—of the *film* of John Kennedy's assassination in Dallas. The re-creation dissects representation, moving from the grainy film *image* imprinted in our memory as Greek tragedy, through the *copy* of the actor's preparations, rehearsal, and performance, to a *model*—the videotape. Thus, it shifts from film to television, without a real except the Zapruder film. The copy matches the original, which is only an image—an indelible one. That historical, silent image—along with the spectatorial mechanisms of disavowal or suspension of disbelief (reception) —is the mystery rather than who killed Kennedy and how, the usual concerns brought to bear on the Zapruder footage, painfully re-enacted in Oliver Stone's *JFK* in 1991.

Unlike Baudrillard's theory of the simulacrum (which in large part was predicated on one of his trips to the U.S., on his real experience of exported representations of the U.S. in films and television, an example of tourism producing theory), the videotape works through a series of contradictions, not the least of which is a definition of "art." It argues television as historography, as a set of social relations *and* as a challenge to history and mastery which can provide a truth, a real.

Figure 8

At the same time, the performance and tape grant answers and closure and reveal mastery through professionalism—the satisfactory perfection of their re-creation and its effects. The British television trial, broadcast on HBO, of Lee Harvey Oswald (which adjudged him guilty, to no one's amazement), the first in a series of planned restagings of history as court-room drama, a revival of "You Were/Are There," conducted by real lawyers interrogating experts, witnesses, and culprits and based on real evidence and documents, is a simpler investigatory simulation—looking for an imaginary real rather than interrogating its displaced representation.

As the poster announcing the showing of the videotape to a San Francisco art audience states, the piece is "An Authentic Remake of the Original J.F.K. Assassination." Early in the tape, the artist/president, Doug Hall, reprising his uncanny impersonation of Kennedy in *Media Burn*, declares: "I am in reality nothing more than another image on your television set. . . . I am in reality nothing more than another face on your screen. . . . I am in reality only another link in that chain of pictures which makes up the sum total of information accessible to us all as Americans. . . . Like my predecessors, the content of the image is no different from the image itself." While Kennedy's death was, as the tape asserts, both a real and an image death, far from liquidating representation, it enthroned the film image. *Eternal Frame* critiques that powerful hold of the image as history on our memory and emotions. (*JFK* undermines the image by rapid-fire words and rapid editing.)

For Baudrillard, simulation is infinitely more dangerous than an actual crime, "since it always suggests . . . that law and order themselves might really be nothing more than simulations."[33] (This was the premise of the conspiracy theorists after Jack Ruby's shooting of Oswald on TV. It is an apt analysis of the Iran/Contra hearings, particularly Oliver North's testimony. If we take this in an opposite direction, nuclear war had better be a simulation.) Like law and order, simulation versus realism is also an issue for art critics as well as TV news. Near the end of the tape, a middle-aged man, whose reactions were recorded outside the San Francisco theater after he saw the videotape, speaks for Baudrillard's insistence on denotative distinctions, on his desire for referents. "They didn't use anything original at all." They should have "either told what happened or made up their own story. . . . They took a theme of a real man getting killed and they played little games with it."

As *Eternal Frame* suggests, not only the assassination of Kennedy but particularly the circulation and repeated viewing of the amateur/tourist movie footage (which has been endlessly rerun on television and scrutinized by real and amateur detectives) signaled the end of (imagined) mastery via brave individuality written in narrative accounts of cause-effect logic and closure. Because it had been recorded, the image, elided to reality and tragic drama, would yield an answer, a truth, if, like the riddle of the Sphinx, we could only get closer, could deconstruct it. But when deconstruction failed, re-creation, or simulation, was the next logical step—a cultural shift analogous to the move from cinema to television as the dominant theoretical object or culture metaphor (Fig. 9).

After a rerun of the brief "original" (the Zapruder film is shorter than I remembered, a clip lengthened by history, slow motion, and stop-frame analysis), the reenactment of the assassination becomes, as the spectators of the rehearsals and real thing acknowledge, "more real" (there are progressively fewer errors or deviations from convention and expectations) until it is encapsulated as "art" and replayed for us as image, which it always was. The first rehearsal of the assassination occurs in a car in front of rear-screen projection, flattening depth like a '40s Hitchcock automobile ride. The studio is replaced by location shooting in Dallas, the scene of the real and artistic crime. Rehearsals of the event are intercut with backstage costuming and interviews with Jack (Hall) and Jackie (played by Doug Michaels), who comment on dress rehearsals, acting, and masquerade. Sexual difference is inscribed as a simulation: Jackie is played perfectly by a man in a pink suit and pillbox hat.

The hesitant actors, leery of, indeed fearing, reprisal, believing their act to be scandalous or sacrilegious (overstating the radical effects of art), emerge for the final performance and restage the event for passersby, who appear to deeply enjoy it (as tourism, as "live" TV). The final color reenactment is then rerun as a rhapsody six times from various angles, becoming "authentic" and emotive in the process as patriotic music crescendoes on the soundtrack.

Figure 9

The level of the real intensifies when the tourist audiences react—at one moment with tears. This audience of casual passersby re-creates that historical audience which lined the street (and Zapruder's film) for Kennedy's motorcade, later to become witnesses, critics, and stand-ins or extras for the nation-audience. Thus, the real players simulated an image, turning a film into a live performance which is measured by historical audiences against the famous footage as reality, or later in the tape against standards of "art." That both memory and aesthetics, or history and art, are slippery calls emerges in the irony that the standard of the real is a bad "original" film, famous because of its singularity and hence "aura." Its existence is both the ultimate amateur filmmaker's fantasy and nightmare. "This is really bad taste," remarks Hall when watching their rear-screen footage on a television monitor in a hotel room.

The distance between *Eternal Frame* and Baudrillard can be measured by their conceptions of the audience. Baudrillard's mass audience is passive, fascinated, silent, outside; Ant Farm's series of inscribed audiences are vocal, actively involved in critique or, surprisingly, disavowal, yet producing, not merely consuming or escaping, meaning. One position is conservative, humorless, and without irony, predicated as it is on a model drawn from commerce; the other is refreshing. The spectators of the piece in Dallas compare the live performance to the real thing which is being re-created, they imagine, as a tourist attraction(!) rather than "art": "I saw it on television after it happened. . . . It looks so real now. . . . The characters look so real." Shots of these tourists photographing the re-creation remind us of the anonymous maker of the original: Zapruder was just a person in the crowd filming Kennedy, and his film was introduced as evidence in the investigation, an unnerving way to become an artist. "He's re-enacting it. . . . I'm glad we were here. . . . It was so beautiful. . . . " After the performance, an incredulous Doug Hall comments: "I thought the most interesting thing was watching the people enjoy it so much. . . . How could they enjoy it so much?" This is the critical question of catastrophe coverage.

However unexpected this response of spectator *enjoyment* by the performers who drastically misjudged reception and pleasure on many accounts, *Eternal Frame* incorporates response. Its various audiences exist in a dialogue with the re-creation, acting as a corrective and participant/observer. (When the audacious performers, secure in the acceptance of their masquerade as tourism, enter the Kennedy Museum, a place of souvenirs, they disrupt the sanctity of Kennedy as commerce and are kicked out.) The "live" event was edited into a videotape for a San Francisco art audience, which responded with the following remarks, later incorporated into the final piece: "bad taste but impressive," causing "bad dreams, disturbing but entertaining." Reception ("reciprocity," "feedback") alters interpretation.

This sophisticated construction of and respect for audiences is a canny treatise on reception and context which resembles Gilles Deleuze's model of simulation. For Deleuze, the simulacrum circumvents mastery because it already includes the spectator, the angle of the observer. Thus the spectator/auditor is in tandem with the maker and can transform and deform the images. (I note the keen resemblance here to Freud's model of the joke, detailed later.) Deleuze argues that the simulacrum "subverts the world of representation" and is not a degraded copy but rather a positive one which denies privileged points of view and hierarchies.[34] Clearly another modeling of power is at stake—one which might unsettle "classical" scholars as well as patriarchy's parameters. Particularly intriguing in both the tape and Deleuze is the inclusion of the spectator's point of view in the very *definition* of the simulacrum—a position which is consonant with *Eternal Frame* and the practice of Ant Farm, with their predilection for art as events which critique and incorporate "the media" and audiences.[35]

Sublime Visions:
The *Challenger* Explosion

The *Challenger* explosion (January 28, 1986) exploded the modernist myth of technology (and also the Western frontier myth of the necessity of humans for space exploration) as unifying a dispersed audience. In this case the national audience was symbolically fragmented—comparable to the unseeable and horrific imaginary nightmare of the human astronaut bodies, knowing and alive for seconds, plunging at unfathomable speed into oblivion. The technological catastrophe, our telescopic, distanced view of an abstract speck, collided with the chance personal drama of a mother and father at the liftoff watching—and then, in an instant and a glance, *knowing*, turning away—their teacher/daughter/mother blown up in space, unnecessarily. At that poignant moment, we were truly in the position of voyeurs, catching a glimpse of something private we shouldn't have seen and, in contrast to the Kennedy assassination, unable to really see what happened. We saw only the beautiful "aftereffect," the clouds of white, billowing smoke against a deep blue sky, reminiscent of the spectacular clouds after a nuclear explosion. This image of Christa MacAuliffe's mother and father staged Freud's trauma of separation, as the images of Jacqueline Kennedy in the motorcade car and beside the coffin restaged mother-child and loss. Mourning, with affects different from anxiety, was a later stage of coverage/response.

In keeping with the myth of the frontier which has dominated the U.S. space program, MacAuliffe was the adventurous schoolmarm from the Western genre, an Easterner who had won a contest to bring civilization to space via the one-room satellite schoolhouse, conquering space and winning audiences with knowledge. Represented as mother/daughter/teacher/ amateur, she dominated coverage before and after the explosion, an unusual situation of a woman being the focus of news and then catastrophe. That she was more like us increased (1) our identification and (2) our shock: because a mother of young children was aboard, we believed that the shuttle missions were surefire, foolproof occurrences. However determined by being "the first," the press became fascinated with a woman's work and home life, which was news before her death became an event. (Notice how few obituaries are of women—like their lives, women's deaths are not as newsworthy as men's.)

While verbal facts and accounts detailing the horror of error and technological failure were piled onto that distant fragmentation to explain it, scientifically, we imagined, from the audio tapes, the personal nightmare and terror inside the shuttle. Did they know? For how long? Afterward, as in a search for conspiracists, the ocean floor was combed in mourning, the fragments of bodies and machine brought back to create a funeral pyre—to retrieve, and later reconstruct, the real.

Standing by in Concord to record MacAuliffe's students celebrate her liftoff and subsequent space lecture, TV reran her death back in time, showing the initial register of the students' shock, disbelief, grief; twenty-five TV news crews descended on the town afterward and recorded weeping schoolchildren and trauma management—a pedagogical model for audiences of TV catastrophe, taking us from anxiety to grief and vicarious mourning, with psychological advice. The shift into mourning and pedagogy, for example, the historical details of a presidential funeral in Kennedy's case, is a significant part of the reassurance stage of catastrophe coverage, fear turning to grief, acceptance of loss, and a return to normalcy.

NASA, or the "once-proud NASA, trying to regain its pride," was investigated as a trial of errors rather than murder, with videotaped evidence endlessly repeated. Seeing was not believing in this instance. While disavowal could not function in either tragedy as reassurance for onlookers or spectators, the difference between these two events is profound, and historical: The horror of Kennedy was in what we saw; the terror of *Challenger* was what we could not see—the bodies, the premises of the entire space program, the loss of technological superiority. The concern after the assassination was who shot Kennedy; the worry after *Challenger* was over communication satellites and space insurance—corporate purviews—and U.S. space potency. The irony was that we saw so little of a communication mission for corporate profits which included product tie-ins. Spiegel's 1986 catalogue advertised an indoor/outdoor *Challenger* tent in which children could watch MacAuliffe's lecture.

CBS's "Return to Space" in October 1988 reenacted the scenario of *Challenger*, remembering that primal scene of which this was the successful and professional remake. Countdown was scheduled for a weekday morning (rather than a cynical primetime slot), with a huge live audience of Florida tourists. Sitting behind a sleek desk in the modern studio mise-en-scène with Dan Rather was a former astronaut; rather than the usual tech talk, he described his *feelings* of anxiety when walking to the launch pad and sitting in the cockpit during liftoff. A teacher and a finalist in the contest which MacAuliffe had won was interviewed along with his students, remembering and rewriting the horror of that earlier scene; these students were older, fewer. The explosion footage was rerun as the danger situation—this horrific image had served as a trailer, rerun for two years to prepare us for the anxiety of this event. While the digital clock in the lower corner of the screen counted down, calm Dan reminded us of his and our anxious states. I was completely nervous—exactly as I was supposed to be. As with the second 1988 presidential debate, anxiety was a precondition or lure rather than a result of viewing. Without a catastrophe, the affects of coverage had been simulated by reruns, reminiscences. The return, both sequel and remake, resulted in mastery by NASA and the networks, who truly dazzled us with technique.

A telescopic, wide-angle zoom of the launch pad, clearly shot from a heavenly angle, opened the enclosed, framed broadcast, which included commercials—blatant clues that they expected no problems. A concluding zoom of the launch from this same godly view was poetically repeated at the end. The critical seventy-three seconds were clearly and multiply visible this time; the editing, camera placement, and clarity were technically remarkable, efficiently scripted. The visual and verbal style was rehearsed, not catastrophic—we should have relaxed. Blue-screened or keyed in as backdrop, the rumbling, fiery rocket, shuttle, and launchpad appeared to be right behind Dan's desk, with coverage dominating or equated with its subject, visible through a "picture window." There were no glitches by NASA or CBS; the smooth professionalism, resembling an error-free simulation rather than live coverage, and a performed, public emotionalism akin to the nightly news, as much as the successful mission, reassured us that the U.S. had not lost its standing in technocracy or in space. The two-year run of the explosion ended its long engagement (only to return, like Baby Jessica, as a made-for-TV movie).

One protagonist of the initial drama was resolutely absent but determinantly figured as memory—Christa MacAuliffe (the aftereffect that was contained, erased, as women are in TV—and newspaper—news). There were no women on board this flight. While one critic has argued that the sick jokes, mainly focused on MacAuliffe, which circulated after the *Challenger* tragedy testified to regard and identification with her, I suggest the opposite, more in line with Freud. ("Where did MacAuliffe spend her summer vacation? All over Florida.")[36] Like the objects of Freud's jokes which are women, she is strangely at fault, guilty. While NASA took the rap, a nonprofessional, a space amateur, is also to blame. When women assume subjectivity in masculine enclaves, claiming an equal if not superior status (as Joan Rivers did on Carson), disloyalty (not a better job) or disaster is the result. Thus, it is logical to banish women from that endeavor, at least momentarily. Women, as leftovers or aftereffects, become the objects of jokes or malicious gossip, their asserted subjectivity the real target, analyzed, like Lucy, as lack of ability.

Baudrillard's prognoses of cultural elided with nuclear catastrophe are, like postmodernism, linked to or derived from television, particularly its instantaneous capacity to present "live" coverage of death events, both shocking and mollifying the audience, mediating and exacerbating the effects of the real—rerun and transformed into representation. We can await "live" catastrophe on TV, signaled by ruptures in the flow of programs, a disruption of time, TV's constancy. Catastrophe argues for the importance, the urgent value, the truth of television and its watching which will be good for us—providing catharsis or, better, mastery, via repetition of the same which is fascinating, mesmerizing.

Catastrophe coverage thus functions *Beyond the Pleasure Principle* as an essentially verbal rendering of "fort da!" hinged on a "compulsively repeated" visual detail (Baby Jessica's cable, the thirty-second explosion, rifle shots, a buckled bridge or collapsed freeway) to acknowledge then alleviate fear and pain—the audience and the anchor, like the child, achieving mastery over loss, the departure and return and, perhaps in the end, control of the mother, depending on who is throwing the ball. Perhaps masochistically, pleasure, aligned with death rather than life, a ritual determined by the mother rather than the father, comes from that game of repetition, with catastrophe as potent TV, coded as exception, yet one that doesn't come from TV techniques, which are usually of extremely poor quality—shaky, minimal, indecipherable images, awkward editing glitches, missed cues and connections, filler speech and delimited language, endless repetition of the same facts and simple arguments—like Muzak, yet overwhelming narrative, regular programming as we wait with the anchor for either further events and analysis or a conclusion before TV normalcy can return.

In the attempt to theorize, I have ignored specificity in two areas: textual analysis of crisis coverage, and the variations among the three major networks, differences multiplied when CNN is considered. Different disfigurements create different aftereffects. In *Nightly Horrors: Crisis Coverage by Television Network News*, Dan Nimno and James E. Combs operate on the now-axiomatic premise that U.S. TV news is story or narrative in which the hero motif is central, as is melodrama. Their detailed content analysis of recent crises covered by NBC, CBS, and ABC, ranging from Jonestown to Three Mile Island, revealed variant patterns—what might be termed symptoms of ideology. NBC was more educational and contextual, acceptant of "the human condition"; CBS emphasized technology, which was sometimes represented as a monster, and searched for the high-tech causes of failures; ABC had the greatest appeal to anxiety, running interviews with survivors and heroes and citations of victim tolls rather than emphasizing the facts of the stories, whereas CBS appealed to experts and factual detail. While NBC had more and variant sources and location shots, ABC tended to remain in the studio. NBC's pluralist approach was more assuring than alarming, with more "straight" news placed in context. ABC, in contrast, depicted helplessness, chaos; Ted Koppel's ABC reports often contributed to a narrative of chaos and frustration in which no one was in control. (That Koppel is now the very powerful and famous host of *Nightline*, in rigorous control of looks and content, is not insignificant; the program grew, like Topsy, from temporary coverage of the Iranian hostage crisis, the institutionalization of catastrophe *as* news format and content rather than the reportage of catastrophe *on* the news or as a special event; it is still a crisis program.) CBS had narratives of diplomacy, with technology their recurring star and issue; NBC used colloquialisms, in a low-key, conversational style. No matter what the content, the form of the three networks tended to similarity.[37]

Our crises are frequently technological—a historical argument. That the technological serves as a symptom, cover-up, or declaration of economics is also historical. The increasing emphasis on economics, for example during the crisis in Iraq, suggests that money has become interesting and entertaining to the majority of viewers, now fascinated by capital as is *Entertainment Tonight*. (Lists of films' box-office revenues used to appear in *Variety*, a show-business newspaper. Now, even ten-year-olds discuss ticket receipts, listed in local newspapers. And, of course, the obvious: increasingly, small investors play the market. Watching the market throughout the day on investment channels is entertainment for the domestic investor, at work, at home.)

Disaster Studies

The field of disaster studies is a collaboration between academic sociology and behavioral psychology, sponsored by federal and local agencies, with titles like *Organized Behavior in Disaster, The Disaster Handbook,* and *System Responses to Disaster* and professional journals such as *Disasters.* The field also provides a model for TV catastrophe, addressing a problem of contemporary theory as well—the conflation of natural with technological. "The problem of taxonomy is the most pressing issue confronting the field at this time."[38] *Behavior and Attitudes under Crisis Conditions* defines disasters as "forces of nature" and catastrophe as "man-made hazard actualizations"— the latter a good definition of TV coverage. This text divides disasters accordingly: Natural (eighteen), Technology (nuclear, building collapses, energy shortfall), Discrete Accidents (with beginnings and endings, like toxic fumes, industrial/transportation accidents), Socio-political (war, assassinations, hostaging, terrorism), Epidemics and Disease.[39]

The conflation of natural/technological by the Federal Emergency Management Agency in Washington is predicated on response—a "response to a crisis is phenomenological evidence of a crisis, which is dependent on perception which abruptly changes normalcy to crisis."[40] Also, as with the stock-market coverage, "there are cumulative implications of trends of threat." No matter what the event, the response—termed "crisis expectant" and "crisis surge"—is uncannily similar and predictable. The public will (1) seek information, (2) confirm warnings, (3) tend to evacuate, and (4) unite in groups, particularly families, to ease tension. However, rather than evacuate, TV urges us to stay home, to continue watching. Meaghan Morris argues that the ultimate catastrophe for the audience is silence on TV (which might occur if Los Angeles earthquakes into the Pacific Ocean during entertainment programming;[41] we feared this had happened in San Francisco when transmission of the 1989 World Series was interrupted by an earthquake). However, the ultimate catastrophe for TV would be coverage without an audience—either a ratings dilemma or a sign that disaster had eradicated viewers.

Like Thom and Freud, disaster studies position "normalcy" against crisis, arguing that "daily life is dependent on continuities, on repetition. . . . A disruption of normalcy produces stress," "either by the event or the perception of a threat."[42] Along with Thom's emphasis on form and structural stability, disaster studies add perception, as does Freud, a response not dependent on the type of event. For me, the conventions of catastrophe coverage, mapped over the event, trigger and sustain audience response, and hence are determining. These conventions can transform a personal accident such as Baby Jessica's into a national catastrophe, watched by millions. Disaster studies emphasize temporality: the timing of crisis events "cannot be encompassed."[43] Catastrophe coverage is open-ended; it ceases only when it has an answer or becomes exhausted from repetition. Once on the air, Connie had to keep going, although there was little new to tell.

A contradiction emerges in these manuals: disaster analyses, like the stock-market coverage, are predicated on the belief that people will panic. (TV participated in the stock-market panic, coverage creating a "crisis surge.")[44] Yet, studies repeatedly demonstrate that this is resolutely not usually the case; instead of panicking, people confirm, reconfirm, and often deny the message. TV, believing that it is in control and we are not, is a source of reconfirmation; rarely does it deny—if it did, we would not need to watch. Disaster subcultures are people with experience in "repetitive situations,"[45] like the TV audience familiar with conventions. That a subculture of catastrophe operates via TV is demonstrated by televangelism (which appeals to personal crises and apocalypse, with a serious decline in viewers attributed to the recent scandals) and the creation of midday "newsbreaks" which combine the style of catastrophe break-ins (by a news announcer at a studio desk in New York or Washington) with the temporality of commercials and announcements. When a "newsbreak" comes on, Cher or Liz might have been married or England destroyed. Via metonymy and remembrance, catastrophe style, like avant-garde techniques on MTV, has become regular yet unsettling flow. The popularity of CNN, which transmits international crises all day and into the night, is another sign of a disaster subculture, as is the stock market.

In the famous 1920 Halifax case study which poetically and rigorously analyzed the harbor explosion and fire that decimated the city, Prince points to the difference between catastrophe and crisis—"an instant when change one way or another is impending. Crises are those critical moments which . . . are big with destiny. . . . The term [precedes] change."[46] Prince criticizes the failure to distinguish between that which occasions the crisis and the crisis itself—a dilemma for television, my argument, and contemporary culture, which conflate the two. For him, "crises precede catastrophes . . . and catastrophes generate the crisis-situation . . . the disintegration of the normal by shock and calamity" (21). After noting that change is only a premium in science, a nice notion, his crucial argument is that "catastrophe always means social change. There is not always progress" (32). TV mitigates against change by equating crisis and catastrophe and defusing both via repetition. Unlike the Halifax disaster, which "smashed through social divisions, traditions,"[47] TV upholds institutions via containment. Catastrophe threatens "conventionality, custom, and law"— which TV, as exemplar, defends. In an argument remarkably similar to Freud's, Prince argues that victims repeat the initial shock, "reproducing the tragic or terrible scenes," deny them, or commit suicide.[48]

Prince accords import to communication agencies which set a good example that can be imitated. Heroes, what he calls a "disaster protocracy," emerge—"often men were surprised at their own power for prolonged effort under the excitement of catastrophe."[49] These heroes are the anchors or the chance reporters on the scene—established stars or emerging stars. Prince cites the "stimulus" of the lookers-on: "Citizens of Halifax knew they were not 'unobserved.' Halifax simply had to make good. She was bonded to the world" (78–79). However, one notion is anathema to television: "A disaster event happens in a particular social context. . . . Our primary focus is on the community as the locus of the event and as the social system that copes with the physical impact." While this was initially and later partially true for San Francisco in 1989, what media events can also do to "disaster events" is erase "the particular social context." What DeBord called "the society of the spectacle" has become the culture of catastrophe, with a historical shift from nuclear to eco-catastrophe (ecology and economics).

Seeing Is Believing: "The Great Quake"

The San Francisco earthquake shorted out the broadcast of the third game of the 1989 World Series on ABC (Tuesday, October 17). For the TV spectator, the moment of static was perfect Freud: "the first determinant of anxiety . . . is loss of perception of the object (which is equated with loss of the object itself)."[50] Whether the lost object was the game or part of the country was up for grabs. The initial events of this fifteen-second disaster, a TV catastrophe, were replayed on the networks and CNN from Tuesday through Thursday evening and beyond. Coverage focused on three scenes which became primal evidence: the buckling of the Bay Bridge, the fire in the Marina District, and the collapse of the Nimitz Freeway. The original footage on Tuesday night came from aerial shots. By Wednesday, star anchors were on the ground and at the now-famous scenes. (This happened in Iraq only *after* the war—with the agonizing scenes of the Kurdish refugees.) Many initial local reporters were women; the national network takeover of the story was by men. The repetition and permutation by commentary of these brief scenes during hundreds of TV hours was staggering. Three silent, distanced images sustained billions of words.

The natural was indistinguishable from the technological—architecture, transportation, and communication systems. "A natural disaster is usually also an information disaster."[51] All the signs of the event, including the seismograph, were indexical. The moment was irretrievably historical. For three days, television tried to recapture, to re-create, fifteen seconds of historical time. Through an "interplay between liveness and historicity,"[52] TV was "rewriting history in the present" (291). As Mimi White so intelligently writes, "The institution of television . . . becomes the guarantee of history, even as it invokes history to validate its own presence at an event" (285). The networks toured us through a shaken San Francisco as it recovered from a tremor of 6.9. It took us from shock to aftershock, from loss to grief, from reality to therapy, posttraumatic stress, and depression—from crisis to normalcy. TV also escalated a crisis mentality by citing a rising death toll (far beyond actuality) and geological, scientific predictions of "the Big One" for Los Angeles. Paradoxically, while reporting affect, television tried to show very little of it, preferring information to emotion. The coverage jibed with Freud and with communication studies of risk and disaster which I will intersperse in this chronological account.

On ABC, Tuesday evening, the content of the broadcast was haphazard and repetitious, a time of fear and anxious waiting, of pauses and attempts to locate experts and eyewitnesses. Other than Koppel's stardom, there was little hierarchy. While the facts remained the same, airtime was filled up with maps, graphics, and voiceovers, particularly telephone calls from local citizens who talked with Koppel on the air. Alone at the catastrophe helm, Koppel looked off camera, to the right, when talking on the telephone; when he addressed us, updating latecomers and explaining the absence of the ballgame, he looked straight out, shifting in his chair. (As they had done with Hurricane Hugo, AT&T capitalized on their system's heroic stature in subsequent commercials.)

During this disaster watch, ABC searched for filler, cutting to the inside of the Goodyear Blimp to interview the pilot, who didn't respond, yet another lapse in communication. The president of the international association of firemen appeared in a Washington TV studio, looking out of place. There were cuts to the White House regarding disaster relief; footage from KGO, the ABC affiliate, was interspersed with scenes from Candlestick Park, replaying the cancellation of the game by the commissioner of baseball, Fay Vincent, assuring us that there was no danger, and leaving the park for lack of electricity. After we saw that Candlestick Park was still standing, there was a respite, a moment of denial and security, along with an inability to hook up with the West Coast. Many viewers were irritated that the Series had been canceled, its future scheduling the central question rather than the quake. Cutaways to Vincent, in retrospect, were a strange but logical displacement, indicative of the sheer economics of professional sports and suggestive of denial in spite of the evidence.

Network coverage was a calm stammer, a professional search for information from virtually any source, including anonymous telephone callers. "Information is hard to come by . . . even more difficult is the communication system" (Koppel). While repeating the same clips, the coverage changed: from sparse to full, with a plethora of experts and bland officials, edited montages, and victim interviews. Within two days, coverage became a mammoth orchestration, a weeklong event in a famous tourist city, San Francisco (rather than Oakland, or San Jose and Santa Cruz, cities nearer the "epicenter"). Like the quake-proof architecture, this TV event was a technological tour de force, a reassurance of the restoration of order and communication.

Shots of the fire, the buckled bridge, and the freeway repeated all evening. Koppel missed the significance of the collapsed double-decker freeway—that cars and their drivers were trapped underneath, sandwiched in the wreckage. Only at 10:30, on *Nightline*, was the freeway read properly by ABC. The fear in the beginning was of broken gas mains and fire—invoking the quake's famous forebear. Fear then focused on the rising death toll. The "severity" of disasters is judged by "the number of deaths and injuries, extent of property damage, and geographic scope,"[53] with a nationalistic bent to which I will return. The decision was finally made to stay on the air through *Nightline*, the severity (and the location) demanding constant and live coverage.

Local Midwest news cut in at 10, scavenging network footage and mimicking the national big-time by sending local reporters to San Francisco. (The descent of technology and personnel must have been "seen as intrusive, a nuisance, and a drain on resources like time."[54] Rarely, however, was the presence of the media and their management visible.) In remote broadcasts, Milwaukee news focused on local calls to relatives, sports fans in local bars, a local fire with firemen on the scene, and a radon alert with a report of cancer deaths—a disaster array parasitically feeding off the affects of the San Francisco calamity. The local weatherman gave yet another history of earthquakes on the same map as the day's temperatures. He was upbeat, concluding with "Geology and earthquake stuff is very complicated." The sports announcer replayed the Vincent footage at the stadium. The earthquake was neatly divided into local genres—news, weather, and sports.

The *Nightline* logo and commercials, particularly the Infiniti ads for Nissan serenity and tranquility, reassured us that things had calmed down, along with providing commercial irony. "The California Earthquake" had reordered its initial three hours of material and represented the event in a more orderly fashion, subdivided into local reporters, bystanders, and victims on the scene: the reporters on the top of the bridge, at the fire, and at the collapse of the Nimitz Freeway in Oakland were all women. Reminiscence began, only four hours after the event, in interviews with Al Michaels re-creating the moment at Candlestick, and Fay Vincent. ABC was not yet sure whether the quake or the Series was the bigger story.

The earlier coverage relied on local reporters (many of whom were women) and affiliates, even cutting to their newsrooms. Just as the network replaced the local, and men took over from women, officials replaced the average citizenry: "What is covered is the 'official view' [measured at 78 percent of sources] of the disaster, and the activity of formal, traditional emergency organizations."[55] (The preference is for "law enforcement and fire departments," 31 percent of sources, city and county agencies, 24 percent.) Normalcy is thus the reemergence of official hierarchy—the dominance of white men, of patriarchy. Interviews with doctors of emergency medicine with disaster experience, along with seismologists—experts on quakes and prevention—added scientificity, the calm and the terror of data. A seismologist complained about spending most of her time answering journalists' questions. Bureaucrats from the Federal Emergency Management Agency informed us about disaster protocol amidst commercials for Allstate's prompt payment of claims for Hurricane Hugo. Benefits were discussed along with hazards and risks, with insurance agents assuming official status. As with cars and commuter traffic, private property was a key issue. The shattered houses in the background would be demolished on Jennings's ABC special program the following night. The TV death toll mounted to fifty.

The freeway collapse, which was "going to be very bad news," was repeated, followed by another Infiniti commercial of trees swaying in a gentle breeze—a harsh contrast. The freeway image was analyzed as the death trap it was. The upper ramp had collapsed on the lower, entombing invisible, unknown, as yet uncounted commuters. After three hours of replay, the nightmare of entrapment, the terror of being buried alive, finally became visible, the scene of an ongoing drama, a rescue which was only beginning. An image became a story of heroism, with a future. The Nimitz would become the primal scene of the fifteen-second, 6.9 quake. Koppel's misinterpretation was a challenge to the truth of vision, to the veracity of TV images.

The initial coverage from the Goodyear Blimp, amateur video, and helicopter shots taken by KCO couldn't get close enough. Electronic technology had been derailed; the desire to see, more accurately, the desire to know, was also thwarted. (Throughout the War in the Gulf, with the exception of Peter Arnett's radio reports, we stayed above, or away from, Iraq. Our point of view was aligned with airborne technology—military or communications—and machines rather than the earthbound eyes and bodies of humans.) The startling images yielded little information. In fact, the long shots from the blimp, with the exception of the buckled bridge and a contained fire, revealed a rather tranquil city, not at all like movie scenes of earthquakes or earthquakes in Third World locales. Repetition triggered the desire for more, creating a desire for TV. It was only from the ground and from words added to the images that the scale of the quake became apparent. Presence, being there or living there, granted expertise. The star anchors flocked to the primal scenes, endorsing the truth of vision and the restoration of communication and normalcy: Jennings (ABC) to Market Street and Rather (CBS) to the Nimitz freeway (a dig at Koppel?).

At the end of *Nightline* on Tuesday, Koppel was not reassuring, fanning the flames by reporting the smell of gasoline and urging people to stay in their homes. After "the story of the night, possibly the story of the month," latecomers were updated. "It's been, of course, a very long evening, and events are still unfolding, as we've tried to keep you up to date all evening long. In the event that some of you have tuned in late, all this began at 5:04, and we first became aware of it as the opening of the World Series was interrupted when the electricity went out, that was caused by an earthquake. . . . ABC will keep you up to date throughout the night. We will be with you. There will be reports on shows tomorrow. . . . Goodnight." Alone in our homes, yet watched over by ABC, our public guardian, we, the audience, were in touch, connected.

The *Today Show*, "The Morning After," was broadcast from Chicago, with explanations of their inability to get to San Francisco. In a portent of personnel change, Deborah Norville reported the more prestigious facts, and Jane Pauley took personal-interest stories, the realm of affect. The fatality count continued to climb in this extended broadcast, which ran until 10:30 rather than 9:00. Willard Scott, the weatherman, made everyone laugh and celebrated the heroicism of television in times of crises. As in previous reports, "the Big One" was predicted for Los Angeles, upping the ante of fear and anxiety. Norville quoted a 60 percent chance for Los Angeles.

The three primal scenes were replayed throughout Wednesday's coverage, each time with different audio tracks. The visual and the aural, like time itself, were out of sync, taken out of context. Stan Lai, a resident of the Marina District, was interviewed in the first of a series of reminiscences from victims, the stories of "Where were you when the quake hit?" While he spoke, shots of the fire burning yesterday were intercut today. The chief engineer from a TV station, Don Sharp, described why he was on the Bay Bridge, his voice over old footage; their telephone hookup disconnected, a sign of the live. The famous footage was cut into a presidential press session as if to illustrate Bush's words, "It's being reported very thoroughly on the television." Gumbel discussed "the limits of science" with structural engineers 2,700 miles away, repeating shots of the freeway collapse. A presumably live helicopter shot of the freeway was accompanied by questions: "How can the concrete be moved? Who is inside? Is it deathly silent up there? Can you hear anything? Nothing." As in the previous evening's overage, silence was unacceptable and a sign of death; words were a lifeline.

The ebullient Scott and Pauley extolled "ordinary people, plain folk," wondering about the rescue workers' families, their personal lives. Red Cross personnel discussed anxiety—the therapeutic stage had begun. At the conclusion, *Today* recapitulated the trauma—now a rerun of TV coverage—and added an upbeat ending: electricity and transportation were being restored, the spirit of the people was rising from chaos, a new day was dawning. Suddenly, Gumbel, in a fit of nostalgia and pride, congratulated himself and/as TV: "We've been sitting here for three hours now. . . . This is kind of television in its purest sense. . . . I mean, we don't have any computerized routines, we don't have any scripts, we're having trouble with the picture and the sound, it's kind of the old 'what can you see and what can you tell us.' " Everyone agreed that "it's really kind of refreshing." The good old pre-high-tech days became a time of inventive individualism; verbal glitches and visual minimalism were signs of the live and the real—history in the making.

CNN interviewed participants who had lost their homes in the Marina District. Comparable to other disasters, a "dominant visual image. . . was the portrayal of people as victims rather than as capable of mitigating their circumstances."[56] This might have been the audience's real nightmare, the destruction of private property as much as the loss of life, with economics (and home insurance) as a catastrophe. One victim, hoping to get back into his collapsed apartment building before demolition, was asked about his "feelings": "just shock, you didn't believe it." Syndicated TV has feelings, emotions; network TV wards them off and covers them with women. (After CNN's ratings victory in the War in the Gulf, network news began to experiment with affect in "feeling" spots, concluding with good news of exceptional individuals.)

Another realization slowly dawned—that the epicenter was in Santa Cruz, down the coast, not here. And while the destruction of the shopping mall in the heart of that quaint town was noted, the coverage remained based in San Francisco. There was continual reference to San Francisco as a tourist haven of familiar landmarks. The Marina District became a site for tourist buses. The bridge became a problem for rush-hour traffic and, by Thursday, a source of lawsuits.

As I stated, two of the three famous scenes became backdrops for the anchor stars, now on the historical scenes: NBC *Nightly News* broadcast from the Marina District, CBS "Special Report" from the freeway, and ABC's "The Great Quake" from the Marina District. The restoration of formatted, encapsulated information, including credits, logos, and commercials, signaled the return of the normal. Brokaw cited statistics and the still-climbing death toll, announcing that full power was being restored. The Bay Bridge, 880, was the biggest problem; George Lewis interviewed Dan Ruby, whose son was missing, trapped in the freeway. The eyewitnesses were black, Hispanic, Chinese, another class of victims, another part of the area, and another issue.

In a special edition of *48 Hours*, Dan Rather was in Oakland in front of the 880 freeway, bringing experts and witnesses from offscreen into on-camera interviews. "We'll be looking at death, damage, destruction, from the area south of here" was a montage of disaster capped by the CBS logo "CBS News, Special Report." The disaster footage had become a snappy disaster sequel. Calling attention to other cities, he noted the San Francisco bias, shifting to San Jose and Santa Cruz. CBS's catchy logo of seismographic markings framed a history of earthquakes by Washington experts, replete with scientific data. With constant looks back at the freeway and descriptions of the bodies and the operations, Rather interviewed a survivor who repeated that this was real, not a movie. As he crawled out of his car, he saw a live brain on the pavement; "body parts were all around." Along with economics, the difference between reality and representation became a central issue—one of the spectatorial mechanism of disavowal.

In "The Great Quake" (ABC, Wednesday, 9 P.M.), Peter Jennings was standing on a street in the Marina District; the noisy demolition of a collapsed apartment building was visible and audible. The broadcast was an *analysis* of catastrophe coverage which began by reporting "something good that man did today"—the successful launch of the *Galileo* space probe. The intercut color footage of the separation in space demonstrated technical wizardry. The elision of the memory of the *Challenger* explosion and the San Francisco earthquake, of the technological and the natural, became a tribute to "the people," the future, and technology. *Galileo* would produce "a wealth of knowledge for man" (the gender bias of newsspeak). "When the space shuttle lifted off today, we were reminded, for a moment, of the *Challenger* disaster. . . . We always are."

The memory of *Challenger*, like Kennedy's assassination, haunts catastrophe coverage—a genre hawked as TV's finer moments. The fond remembrance reminds us how valuable television is. This linkage of disasters is what communication scholars call a "disaster array," comparable to the feeding frenzy of fish. News shifted throughout "the day after" between the launch and the quake. What united these disparate events was television's obsession with technology and hence with itself—its autocratic role in times of national travail. Jennings reminisced: "We were all united by television, the disaster almost unfolded in front of us. . . . We hung in front of our television sets, waiting for information to eke out from the cape. [Disaster news travels fasts: Within a half-hour, '69 percent of adults . . . had learned about' the *Challenger* explosion, '58 percent' from either television or radio.[57]] Well, in many respects, this was the same thing last night," as Beth Nissan recalls."

The "united" TV audience is the measure of catastrophe coverage, an audience of high ratings that television appears to throw to the wind in its pursuit of the real and emotive in tour de force technological endeavors. One could cynically imagine ABC, bereft of its sports broadcast, capitalizing on the disaster, forcing NBC and CBS to begin competitive break-in coverage, which they did around 7:40. ABC had the advantage, there live to cover baseball.

The ABC insert by Beth Nissan, a montage of the famous quake scenes, was an elegy of the disaster, beginning with TV static—the interruption of the World Series, and the words from someone in the ABC booth, "We are having an earth . . . " The loss of entertainment, the eradication of information, the interruption of communication, are indexical signs of catastrophe. "It is only the complete absence of representation, video black and silent audio, which is unacceptable."[58] The substitution of reruns (*Roseanne*, with break-ins by Koppel on ABC) suggested that the disruption might be a glitch in ABC's hook-up to the coast. Eventually television confirmed our fears, necessitating constant television to inform us that the world was not OK, and then reassure us that the world or we would be and are OK.

Nissan's montage replayed the familiar images, obsessively rerun in attempts to retrieve a real. The natural and the technological—the quake and the loss of the television image—were equated; television was fascinated with itself: "All last night, there were audible aftershocks and visible fault lines in the normal [shots of the bridge]; the television picture, the picture that is always, always there [a shot of a scene from a sitcom, *Perfect Strangers*, with the two leads bound in ropes, held hostage by a character with dynamite strapped to his body, then static], fell from the screen, broke into static [shots of static]. When it came back, it could only bring us the news in fractions, in numbers. Without telephones, without fax machines, news came through the way it used to [shot of Koppel in his big anchor moment]. Person to person, millions of Americans watched that one fire last night, until they finally went to bed [shot of the fire], remembering everyone they ever knew who lived on the jagged Western edge. Then, a new day is born, to recovery, passing from night to daytime, reminding us of how little control we have." Rather than history being made by others, "we" become witness/participants making history with TV.

Jennings complimented Michaels, as earlier he had complimented Koppel: "Reminded me of the great Jim McKay during the Munich Olympics." A protocracy of anchors is one fallout of catastrophe, a potential fame-making moment. "It's a tremendous tragedy, but it's also a great moment in the history of California; they'll be back, they'll be all the way back." The euphoria which follows shock set in, particularly for the exuberant anchors, who provided hope and optimism.

The Great Quake had already become a Great TV Moment and a reminder that this was a catastrophe of technology—of transportation systems, of electricity, the indices the absence of television and the lack of telephone lines, with the telephone emerging as the truly amazing device of simultaneity and reciprocity it has always been. Rather than gathering together, people watched television and talked on the phone—private pursuits. "The more civilized the schedule and the more efficient the technology, the more catastrophic is destruction when it collapses. There is an exact ratio between the level of technology with which nature is controlled [quake-proof structures] and the degree of severity of its accidents."[59] To a degree, Schivelbusch's analysis is only partially accurate; most of the buildings and transportation systems survived. However, the disaster had an economic aftershock—the big business of tourism, which fell off drastically.

Montage segments, short clips, and bits (bytes) of data were framed and connected by commercials for Miracle Whip, Allstate Insurance, and Actifed. The concluding credits of "The Great Quake"—run over a seismograph superimposed on the famous scenes, framed by portentous music and computer graphics—clinched the return of normalcy, signaled by (1) scripted, edited news, (2) the inclusion of commercials, and (3) the one-hour format where time is neatly segmented and can close. The time was no longer the present but was safely historical, over. History had become three TV images.

In "Earthquake Aftershock" (*Today* on Thursday), a Red Cross volunteer, Marty, again raised the issue of representation and the real, the spectatorial mechanism of disavowal. "It's one thing to see it on the camera; it's another to come down here and look at it." Pauley: "What's the difference between what you see on TV and what you see with your own eyes?" Marty: "When you see it on TV, it's like watching a movie; you get the idea that it's staged, although you know it's really happened. . . . You have to come down here to see it's actually happened . . . to see these houses tilted over and crumbling, huge gaps in the street." Another "guest" (Patricia Lee) extolled the therapeutic effect of television for grieving. A psychiatrist analyzed posttraumatic stress syndrome, providing therapy. After interviews with those left homeless, Sal Bordlee, a State Farm Insurance agent, estimated that only 30 percent of them had quake insurance. Allstate had moved agents into the area from North Carolina. Increasingly, coverage focused on the cost of the quake, which was mounting like the death toll.

In a long and moving interview on CNN, live at 1:24, Thursday, Donna Luporini, a student living on loans, imagined what she would retrieve from her apartment before demolition: her birds, her books, her telephone book, and her purse for ID. "I would like to get a few things. I have nothing. I don't even have shoes." She kept looking at the building, a lost object, realizing that her home was gone and that she would have to begin her life "from scratch." "I grew up here; you know it's coming, yet we still stay here. . . . I never thought it would happen to me. I never thought my building would collapse." Disaster denial.

By the Thursday night news, the scene shifted to the freeway, the waiting relatives, and the emotional aftereffects—death, anger, grief, and mourning. Rather was in Oakland. The show opened with a snappy montage of numbers counting down in the corner, caught in a 3-D floating television camera. "The crushing, ripping force of the earthquake which hit here almost forty-eight hours ago is giving way to the tough aftershock of reality. Many of the things you normally count on still don't work—roads, bridges, phones, water." Bodies being lifted out of the collapsed freeway by rescue crews were shown, with Rather overshadowing the freeway image. "Grim work, a grim wait." "The Wait" included a brief glimpse of the rescue crew managing the spectacle of the press, letting the hordes of cameramen in sporadically. "You have to not get emotionally involved to do your job," said a rescue worker. "It's like hell up there." Daniel, the father, wanted to go up and search and was prevented from doing so. We watched him receive the bad news about the death of his son.

However, this coverage was different; it focused on the "Tenderloin District," on poor people—blacks, the homeless—people with nothing to lose "who are close to the breaking point." These were people with no families, no homes, no place to go, an ongoing rather than catastrophic nightmare of having nothing. A baseball owner (Oakland A's) came to the rescue, giving food to the homeless. Another hero was black, the Reverend Cecil Williams, tending to his flock of the homeless. The coverage also emphasized stress, emotional aftershock, and psychiatry; for example, Milton Miller, trauma psychiatrist: "The moment will intrude into dreams, things will look different, flashbacks, the passage of time allows memory to fade. . . . The pain recedes and is diluted." Rather than receding, television provided flashbacks, reliving the shock of the initial moment, replaying the primal scene. As if on unconscious cue, the program cut back to the ballpark and the big fire, forty-three hours later.

Wearing a jean jacket over his shirt rather than a blazer (as if to identify with his subjects and locale), Rather interviewed a black family. They went back to their apartment, pointing out the cracks in the building. "I have nothing to go home to." This linkage of poverty and race with continual loss rather than crisis homelessness is another disaster, one which is neither natural nor technological but social and political. (The emergence of this issue was replaced by the rescue of a trapped driver, who died a few days later.) There is a politics to catastrophe, one which has to do with change and the potential of progress.

Catastrophe politics also concern nation and trade. In "Whose Lives Count?", a 1986 study of 1976 earthquakes, William Adams wonders how news media "prioritize the rest of the world."[60] The study tested the hypothesis that "the amount of attention" reflects "the magnitude of the disaster." After discovering that "coverage priorities on all three networks were highly similar" (115), the study uncovered huge disparities. "Western Europe (Italy) is indisputably on top. Eastern Europe (Romania) is a distant second and Latin America . . . a distant third. The least relative news time is given to the Middle East . . . and to Asia" (117). The War in Iraq redrew the U.S. map of the world—on television.

The factors influencing time and coverage were first and foremost the "number of U.S. tourists," followed by the "severity of the news event" and the "distance from New York City" (119). Other correlates are intriguing: tourism had a "correlation of .84 with U.S. exports; .91 with the ethnic ancestry of elite journalists; and .66 with the ancestry of the U.S. public." "This further suggests that the tourism variable is a reasonable and convenient surrogate for the sociocultural affinity of the U.S. for other countries" (12). The study concludes that "earthquakes, typhoons, and floods in the Third World, given their severity, have received proportionately little attention," with violence and conflict receiving comparable minimal treatment.

"Where earthquakes occur makes a great deal of difference" (121). "Overall, the globe is prioritized so that the death of one Western European equaled three Eastern Europeans equaled 9 Latin Americans equaled 11 Middle Easterners equaled 12 Asians." (The application of this bias to the Iraq War overlaps with the constant citation that Saddam Hussein has little concern for life. The perverse odds of the body count, however, increased; the death of one American equaled thousands of Iraqis. In fact, their bodies didn't count.) Strangely, in San Francisco, a city of intermixed races, including large Asian and Hispanic populations, this international racial bias was repeated as a national prejudice. Disaster events, it would appear, are unnatural constructs of sexual, racial, and ethnic differences, linked to an economics of tourism and trade. Coverage remained in "this city beside the bay," with its spectacular tourist backdrops, memorable to many in the audience.

As I worked on these videotapes (simultaneously with the ongoing live courage), the repetition caused me to lose a sense of time, including the present tense I was in. The barrage of fragmented repetition set off a strange amnesia, to a degree akin to Fredric Jameson's description of the modern schizophrenic.[61] The VCR's capacity for time shifting, fast-forward and reverse, along with zapping from channel to channel, confuses TV's metronomic system. I could make temporal distinctions based only on what the reporters were wearing, and whether or not they were in California. Night and day were demarcations, although the days began to blend into each other as did the three networks, repeating the same footage, all looking and sounding alike. Even night and day were not clear, given the time delay from the coast. Ironically, this timelessness resembled the experience of traumatic shock when time vanishes, when time itself is painful, when the past casts a pall over the present, making it unbearable. We were receiving information, yet we learned little we didn't know immediately. The coverage was a search for rationality (through technology and individualism)—an impossibility, demonstrating (as Nissan declared) how little control we have.

The CNN coverage had a different effect on me than the networks. Its continual focus on the story upped the anxiety ante. Yet affect seemed real, personal; I could remember moments in detail, like Donna's story. The long interviews with residents and insurance adjusters (including payments to clients by Allstate agents), sharing intimate recall of their experiences, stopped time, which was linked to a place rather than funneled through the egos of star anchormen who transform local catastrophe into national celebrity, the context only themselves *as* television. For CNN, San Francisco was a rehearsal for "the Big One"—the War with Iraq.

Aerial Views: Operation Desert Storm

Catastrophes, whether natural or technological, are significantly different from the temporality, intentionality, and logistics for war, a planned rather than unexpected event. Yet while the cause is different, the effects (and even logistics) are comparable. For the loser, war resembles catastrophe;

for the victor, war can result in economic gain. In this brief analysis, I am referring *only* to the televised war, not to political policy, the Middle East, or even the war itself.

"Operation Desert Storm" was cast not as an economic struggle but as an apocalyptic religious battle between good and evil, Bush versus Saddam (his first name). The War was a robust revival of rugged individualism, a high-tech frontierism, with events attributed to people, not economic, political, or religious causes. The War was a chest-thumping staging of masculinity, with muscular, tough heroes—Schwarzkopf (already parodied by Jonathan Winters in commercials for America West airlines), Colin Powell, and the U.S. military machine—routing wimps, Hussein, and the entire inept Iraqi army. (The forces of other nations, which had their own briefings, were loyal, but not nearly as potent or virile as the U.S. forces; it proved a good time to bash Japan, which didn't fight.)

Paradoxically, the censorship of coverage, a system of reporter pools, turned a lusty war into pedagogy (and budgetary cost accounting). The majority of airtime was devoted to lectures by retired real and armchair generals about the strategy, the weapons, and the results (with virtually no evidence of the latter, neither the infamous Bomb Assessment Damage evidence nor reports of the Iraqi casualties and devastation). This was a war of words (and experts), not bodies (and grunts); it concerned theory more than experience, intellect more than affect—which came later. Although the reporters had to pass a physical exam to qualify for a field pool, as we heard and saw it, it was a war fought by aging men in their late fifties or sixties, many of them verging on hefty to fat, armed and wrestling with statistics, logistics, graphs, and war phraseology. The best soldiers were the best lecturers, the most articulate and precise briefers. One emotively illustrated lecture on TV catapaulted "Stormin' Norman" into history, the pantheon of military greats, and million-dollar book contracts. (His next speech cost $50,000.) We saw very little but learned about the "new" upscaled and postmodern military. During the war, the military dropped its commercials. It no longer needed to pay for TV publicity, which it now received for free.

In spite of its video classroom appearance of "Quiz the Professor" in camouflage fatigues, the networks adopted interruptive catastrophe rather than educational TV style, including initial expectations of a rapid, contained conclusion, and predictions of a disaster array, particularly the intervention of Israel. While everything was revealed to us as planned, except the outcome (which presumably came as somewhat of a surprise to the U.S. military), the coverage behaved as if everything were chaos, unpredictable. Thus, censorship, and the delimited coverage, quickly became an issue of patriotism. From being a hero, Peter Arnett of CNN became suspect for his coverage from Baghdad—where he chose, and was allowed, to stay. Bombing Iraqi television stations became a military act.

The initial shock was administered first to a U.S. and then to an international audience on January 16, 1991, during the nightly news at 6:00 EST; network and CNN journalists, on the scene, reported bombs falling on Baghdad. On ABC, Peter Jennings was talking to his man in Baghdad, who called back when the war began. CNN stayed on the air that night and the next day, for sixteen hours, with satellite-transmitted verbal reports— telephone linkups that re-created the good old days of radio, paradoxically by a pricey ($16,000 per month), high-tech "four-wire" that needs no technicians and can function when local wires are down. Like cable television, CNN, which broadcasts to 103 countries, was given a monopoly clearance by Iraq. The three reporters on the scene were catapulted into the Edward R. Murrow galaxy of heroic reporters—one side effect of fame-making catastrophe journalism. NBC's Arthur Kent, whom Johnny Carson called "the stud among the Scuds," is becoming a leather-bomber-jacketed icon reminiscent of World War II. The truly revolutionary technology is, of course, very old-fashioned—the telephone, a two-way, simultaneous device, unlike the one-way of our TV reception. In many ways, the coverage—along with the public illustrated lecture of maps, charts, graphs, and granular-to-bad aerial views—was radio. The irony of watching reporters talk on the telephone on television is significant. The real winner was CNN—stealing the network show and hastening the decline of the network news divisions.

CNN and the U.S. networks began constant coverage, which lasted until Friday the 18th at noon, when soap operas returned and interruptive, called "expanded," coverage began. With the exception of the Fox network and Arsenio Hall, who kept reiterating his gung-ho–to-macho support of "my boys" amidst jokes and interviews, late night returned to normal only on January 26, when an NBC *Saturday Night Live* repeat also returned. Carson and Letterman were replaced by network war news, with programs at the ready to replace them after their return if "the situation warrants it." When they returned two weeks later, their monologues parodied television's war coverage: "After two weeks, Tom Brokaw had his anchor chair surgically removed." "Is CNN's Wolf Blitzer a weapon or a reporter?" "Iraqi TV also wanted to hire retired generals, only there weren't any. Hussein had killed them." *People* magazine criticized NBC-TV for the festive apparel worn by female anchors: "The network's female correspondents and commentators often seemed wildly overdressed." What they failed to note was that many CNN anchors/reporters were women. During the reign of continual coverage, TV stations in Sydney, Australia, hooked up with one of the networks or CNN, shocking Australia with the first instance of constant coverage, which transfixed and obsessed audiences for a comparable time span—perhaps with heightened anxiety given its stature as a first-time event.

Within four days, the war shifted from news and catastrophe to regular series and catastrophe, replete with network theme music, graphics, logos, and titles—"Showdown in the Gulf," "War in the Gulf." Interruptive coverage, the earmark of catastrophe, became the hallmark of local stations, which were selling themselves as twenty-four-hour stations," the local trying to imitate the latest catastrophe winner, CNN, with local reporters now telephoning back randomly intercut reports from Israel about local citizens abroad. A Milwaukee woman throwing pots in Israel became our expert.

For CNN, the all-news network, constant coverage is its raison d'être, its norm rather than an exception. Hence, it's not surprising that a war would catapult it into international fame—guaranteed by the military endorsement on both sides of the struggle. CNN has everything to gain from war and catastrophe and constant coverage; the networks have advertising revenue tied to narrative sponsorship to lose. Hence their 1992 campaign for ad revenue during crises. The formerly little channel that could has, like *Nightline* and the hostage crises, the making of Ted Koppel, and the regular nightly catastrophe slot, been catapulted into fame. A twenty-four-hour crisis channel was there when the war needed it (although it pretended to be a reluctant subject, keeping the press at bay but using it for great publicity).

The global village, the dream of the visionary counterculture and video guerrillas, a satellite network that would bypass national boundaries and differences, going directly to the people, had been realized and inverted—in the name of war, not the sought-for peace of the 1960s. Another 1960s memory and protest, Vietnam, had also been revised, its history vanquished, replaced by the virility of victory. (Another counterculture dream, of the alternative family as a producing rather than consuming unit, has also been derealized. I return to this in the last chapter.) The U.S. at least had moved from the 1960s left to the right. Self-reliance, individualism, and fundamentalism ruled the day; Billy Graham crusaded with God for Bush in the White House, and Saddam Hussein invoked God's name against the forces of Satan, Islam versus the Infidels. Israel and the Jews watched the Muslims and Christians fight it out. The swing to the far right, the war between good and evil, was enthusiastically sanctioned on the religious program *The 700 Club*, and among Zionists everywhere, including Phyllis Chesler.

The U.S. audience, caught in fear and anxiety, failed to notice the many anomalous incongruities—the "relaxed" Saddam (trivialized by Bush's referring to him by his first name) was deceitful; the "composed" vacationing Bush was a good leader. U.S. tactics were brave and civilized; Saddam's were barbaric and broke all the rules of the Geneva accords—as if war techniques could ever be good. Fifteen thousand bombing sorties in Iraq were sanitized by their aerial views and "smart bomb" claims, while fifteen missiles in Israel were barbaric and stupid, their effects viewed from the ground. Our technology was better, more intelligent, than theirs—Scuds became a joke, while Patriots made Raytheon stock climb. Despite all the women in the U.S. military—still banned from fighting (what a threat that would be to masculinity; what fear and male anxiety a battalion of fighting females would arouse)—this was indeed a war of virility, which was also corporate, economic.

The most troublesome contradiction, along with the public acceptance of censorship, was the linkage between the military and TV coverage. Each network had resident ex-generals as expert commentators serving a function comparable to scientists during space launches, or older and wiser journalists during the now-infrequent TV news editorials. Each morning, like good soldiers, we watched the 9 A.M. military briefing conducted by the army, presumably for reporters. Our war instructors wore combat fatigues and were pedagogically armed with maps, pointers, and TV. Like film instructors, they stood beside TV monitors closely analyzing the sortie footage of bombings, pointing out details yet refusing specificity; we watched granular images we would see later that day, taken out of context and accompanied by different words and voices. The images were from the pilot's viewpoint when he was firing at the impersonal "target." The clips lacked so much specificity, and were of such poor quality, they could have been shot anywhere. Because they were bad and barely decipherable, they must be real.

In Freud's model of obsession, one means of distortion is removing the idea from the "situation in which it originated" and in which it could be comprehensible. An interval of time is inserted, like the interruptive flow of TV commercials and promos, leading causal connections astray, and "taking the obsession out of its particular setting by being *generalized*" (SE X, 246). The images were removed from context; war was seen from the air, where its effects could not be seen. The cause-effect logic of dropping bombs on cities was defused. The claim that no civilian targets were being hit, and that the bombs hit only their computerized targets, altered the context, again derailing cause-effect logic.

Another means by which "obsession is protected against conscious attempts at solution" is the choice of an indefinite or ambiguous wording, a wording resembling the style of TV anchors, which "works its way into the deliria, furthering the misunderstanding" rather than the original notion. Within hours, we were bombarded by military terminology—euphemisms, such as the poetic "Operation Desert Storm," for killing people. Reporters and viewers studied and learned new terms and phraseology—that of an ambiguous wording, terms of deliria. None was perhaps more ignominious than the BDA, the "Bomb Damage Assessment"; this close analysis of pilots' footage was not forthcoming, was constantly promised but delayed. And there were outright lies: "precision bombing" was striking only military targets, not civilians.

Catastrophe coverage and reception are remarkably akin to the revisions and process of obsession/compulsion. Simply put, TV causes anxiety (obsessive thought), which necessitates more TV viewing (compulsion), which raises the ante of fear, ad infinitum, in an endless tautology of viewing triggering anxiety/anxiety triggering viewing—an interchangeability of cause and effect. In contrast to the postmodern schizophrenic and the loss of history, the key point is that "repression is effected not by means of amnesia but by a severance of causal connections brought about by a withdrawal of affect." By banishing bodies, by eliminating shots of the people on the ground, TV withdrew affect, thereby severing causal connections. Rather than being a medium of either amnesia, as TV is for Fredric Jameson and other theorists of postmodernism, or emotion and affect, as argued by cultural studies and feminism, *TV severs causal connections by withdrawing affect*. To express emotions is to be memorable and moving yet ineffective, out of control, like the anchorman who ducked beneath his desk during an earthquake, or the mourning black mothers in Milwaukee whose children died in inner-city fires, or female political candidates such as Pat Schroeder, who cried when withdrawing her candidacy for national office. While there are famous moments of TV history including Walter Cronkite's emotion when hearing of Kennedy's assassination, these are exceptions, not the rule. (Cronkite looked down, wiped his eyes, paused, gulped. It took only a few seconds—minimal emotion.)

For Freud, these "repressed connections appear to persist in some kind of shadowy form (. . . an endopsychic perception), and they are thus transferred, by a process of projection, into the external world, where they bear witness to what has been effaced from consciousness" (SE X, 231–32). The dead and maimed bodies and the wreckage of war which had been "effaced from consciousness" returned as an "endopsychic perception" after Iraq withdrew from Kuwait. However, they were taken out of context— displaced to the plight of the Kurds. For weeks, the networks showed shots of the refugee camps and interviewed the cold, hungry, sick, and dying inhabitants. These repeated scenes of wandering, grieving families and children bore witness "to what has been effaced from consciousness," the effects of U.S. war technology on the civilians of Iraq. The imbalance of the war dead—less than 100 U.S. soldiers, more than 100,000 Iraqis—is a figure which has been neutralized, a number which may come back to haunt us. The ghostly scenes of the Kurds, in endless, homeless circles of Dante's hell, were the spectral negatives of the U.S. soldiers, coming home. The inability of helicopters to distribute food was a pathetic commentary on the previous glorification of air technology. The scene on the ground was a hellish nightmare of disease and cold, wet starvation—the effect of the war blamed on Hussein.

Isolation is a strategy which "remov[es] the possibility of contact," which describes what eradicating images of the body did. Isolation is identical to Benjamin's brevity and disconnectedness of news items. TV is an endopsychic displacement, a "shadowy form" which "bears witness" to the external world rather than reiterating or effacing or simulating reality. During the War, reporters gathered at a briefing tent in Saudi Arabia, listening to generals and lieutenants and watching monitors. We watched them as they bore witness to a war, just as the reporters standing outside the White

House, or in front of Big Ben or at the Marina District, do. We were, in one sense, all reporters for this war, taking our cues from the generals.

Aerial (pilots') views and military cartography took over, replicating the battle plan, *Top Gun* now live TV, as television redrew the map of the world, much like the surrealists or fifteenth-century explorers and map-makers. The Middle East, whose disasters, with the exception of Israel, had rarely been covered, grew more prominent on our map of the world. In a fall 1990 special program, after the invasion of Kuwait, Peter Jennings walked on an extraordinary ABC map of the Middle East. On this map, the theater of war, the perspectives were multiple, his points illustrated by his movements over the cartography which filled the TV monitor. TV remakes the world by what it represents. There were only "targets" on the military's uninhabited map, a world like an empty Rod Serling town which contained only buildings without people. As Homi Bhabbha wrote, "The modern colonizing imagination conceives of its dependencies as a territory, never as a people."

In many ways, the disaster in the Middle East is still not being covered. Like the rhetorical premises of good versus evil, the devastation was seen from a godly point of view which abstracted details. "They" were a map, without bodies or identities other than Saddam Hussein. "We" were individuals, real people. Thus, the war happened to U.S. soldiers and, particularly, to U.S. families. Local stations broadcast from living rooms as mothers, wives, and children saw their soldiers on TV inserts, or talked in remote hookups on the telephone. In fact, what mattered, along with individualism, what was at stake, was the family, which was happy and ideal. This has always been the great romance of war—the separation and reuniting of couples and families. Video eulogies, tributes, and ceremonies for dead U.S. soldiers re-created the pain of separation (literalizing *Inhibitions, Symptoms and Anxiety*). These tragic moments of loss were few compared to the plethora of airport family reunions—which became almost its own genre. The *Nightly News* closed each evening with touching airport scenes of tears, hugs, kisses. The cause, the War in Iraq, and its effect, U.S. families together, over time provided a strange logic. All of the contained affect of the previous weeks spilled out of the TV screens as "family." High Anxiety turned to High Romance, family togetherness.

While depicted as a crisis of familialism, healed by a resurgence of old-fashioned values like patriotism, the war concerned nation and trade, revising the statistics of "Whose Lives Count?" While the economics of oil and its major players were not overtly stated as cause, the linkage of disaster to economics was directly acknowledged during coverage. During constant coverage, the stock market, which plummeted after Iraq's invasion of Kuwait in August 1990 and soared when Iraq withdrew in 1991, was given substantial time, particularly on CNN. Economics later included the daily costs of the war, the debits and credits of the U.S. and other nations. The war budget was tabulated on a daily basis. As I said, oil politics, predictably enough, were rarely mentioned, other than gasoline prices and the Dow Jones increase in value of oil stocks on the U.S. market. While Schwarzkopf was everywhere during and after the war, the real power may have been invisible.

Operative on all coverage were (1) the stylistic and rhetorical conventions of catastrophe coverage, a disruption of normalcy derived from events which are open-ended (presumably unplanned, unpredictable), and (2) the imposition of a logic of creation/cancellation which separates technology from the body. Aerial footage—the now-famous scenes of the explosions over Baghdad, a granular aesthetic of pyrotechnics endlessly replayed, and the grainy aerial views from the bombers—was the creation stage; cancellation involved verbal denial that civilians were being hit. The logic was akin to nuclear disavowal: elaborately staged spectacles of nuclear bomb explosions were the creation. Denials of radiation's harmful bodily effects were the cancellation. Comparable to nuclear capacity argued as defense rather than offense, the massive bombing of Iraq was depicted as defensive—to save the lives of U.S. soldiers on the ground. Although I discuss nuclear disavowal in more detail later, suffice it to say that the overall logic separated cause from effect, technology from the body—if precautions were taken, radiation would not hurt the body. This ranges from a logic of denial (it's bad but necessary) to a logic of repudiation (of reality)— the effects of thousands of bombing raids, the euphemistic "sorties." Or, as Freud wrote: "there are two kinds of knowledge, and it is just as reasonable to hold that the patient 'knows' his traumas as that he does *not* 'know' them. For he knows them in that he has not forgotten them, and he does not know them in that he is unaware of their significance" (SE X, 196).

As I have repeated, a convention of catastrophe coverage is minimal, shaky images. Glitches in the coverage, usually due to a breakdown in technology, are equated with the real, the unstable, and the urgent. The restoration of "professional quality" is the return of order or normalcy, which is fallaciously presumed to be peace. History might demonstrate that peace is the disruption of the normal. (Culture produces fear, crises, anxiety more than serenity.) A strange paradox dominated the coverage of Iraq: minimal coverage, the sign of the real, was due to censorship, to the military's showing and allowing indecipherable images taken from distant hotel rooms or fighter planes. At the same time that communication technologies were minimal, the military technology was flaunted and fetishized. Along with military censorship of images and words, the fear that Iraq would use chemical weapons kept reporters inside, wearing gas masks, often inaudible.

What is even more paradoxical is that television, even in uncensored times, has "a limited inventory" of images for communicating disaster: computer graphics; historical footage; Department of Defense footage; and scenes of everyday life with an ironic voiceover. Thus, even without censorship, an outpour of images might not have been forthcoming, reliant as the medium is on words and talking heads—the predilection for the presence of the star anchor or reporter standing in for the visual; we see reporters, not events. As Vietnam demonstrated, the networks followed the lead of the government and the military rather than critiquing the war. Thus, the coverage, or its censorship, concealed TV's lack of reliance on visuals in the news, its opposition another pretense like the normalcy of peace.

The patriotic tech talk, constant coverage, and paucity of images concealed the larger fact that the premises of the military invasion had not been debated for long, in spite of the praise heaped on Congress and the last-minute debate and pro-Bush decision. Amid catastrophe style, war, the quintessential illogic, was represented as a rational, controlled, contained endeavor.

The Machine That Killed Bad People

The Machine That Killed Bad People, a 1990 videotape by Steve Fagin, is a rendering of catastrophe (the collapse of the Marcos regime) and scandal (Imelda's spending sprees and governmental graft). Avant-garde formalism meets the techniques of CNN and syndicated TV, unraveling network news coverage of the Philippines.

After the snap election of 1986 in the Philippines, Marcos's opponents Juan Enrile and General Benigno Ramos, in alliance with Cardinal Sin and Corazon Aquino, were jousting for power—with General Fabian Ver on Marcos's side. In one of the many extraordinary clips interwoven in *The Machine That Killed Bad People*, Marcos went on live TV, hoping to be picked up by the U.S. networks. In a family melodrama right out of *Dynasty*, Marcos played Lear in a season-ending cliffhanger climax. Imelda and other family members framed him while children clambered onto Imelda's lap and wandered in front of the president/grandfather. The scene was informal, almost casual. This tone was undercut by General Ver, from stage right, wearing his combat fatigues, issuing growling, guttural reports of outside chaos and awaiting Marcos's commands to action. While the scene was staged, Ver's interruption of Marcos was very transgressive, akin to Schwarzkopf interrupting Bush.

The long and rambling TV appearance (like Nixon's tortured farewell press conference), orchestrated for U.S. television and politicians, was a simulation of mastery now in chaotic decline. Technology failed Marcos just as neocolonialism had served him. Fagin describes these fifty minutes as a "drama of duration: the untelling of a dictatorship. . . . TV had been reversed and now power flowed upstream. A dictator under surveillance, television stripping the emperor bare. A whole nation watched a machine hand out its own justice, as spectacle toppled before the wrath of the real."[62]

The differences between U.S. and Filipino TV conventions and the chasm between the industrialized U.S. and the agricultural Philippines are startling. A high-tech electronics clashes with a low-tech colonized culture, revealing a time warp. Marcos had become an impersonation, a mimicry kowtowing to U.S. power rather than outwitting it. Video, imitating syndicated studio style and replaying live TV clips and home movies, *reveals* rather than represses cultural, political, and economic differences.

The struggle for power was electronic, mediated by colonialism—U.S. politicians and the CIA in lockstep with corporations and journalism. This intervention has been economically and psychically internalized within Filipino culture, where, in spite of everything, America still means superior. All sides courted the seal of U.S. media approval and legitimacy—a pipeline to U.S. support. (Stanley Karnow reports that in 1985, Cory Aquino had met Abe Rosenthal of the *New York Times;* reputedly, Rosenthal found her "vacant."[63] Afterward, she played poorly in the *Times*, which cast a pall of personal ineptness over her leadership which still persists.) To cover the events of the 1986 election, the TV networks had fielded crews and celebrity anchors. The elections were perfect TV fare—gossip and catastrophe as primetime political soaps. Marcos would be interviewed on CBS only by Dan Rather. General Ramos and Marcos appeared on *Meet the Press*, with Marcos declaring: "I don't believe President Reagan would ask me to step down."

The equally strenuous job in the U.S. was to convince Reagan to depose his old friend, which, after assurances of U.S. asylum, finally occurred indirectly. Imelda and Ferdinand, "show biz to the end . . . with a retinue of sixty . . . left the Malacanang palace, after singing a farewell duet, 'Because of You.' " They flew to Guam and then Hawaii. "Once aloft, Imelda began to sing 'New York, New York' " (422). The show tunes, like the Marcoses' group performances of them, are transformed in *The Machine* from a U.S. media joke into signs of cultural difference, the Filipino tradition of minus-one singing, imported from Japan, for which Imelda had a real talent. Her singing transfixed Lyndon Johnson, who was also fascinated with her young beauty, as were the U.S. media in the late 1960s. After Cory Aquino was inaugurated, it was all Reagan's advisors could do to convince him not to visit the Marcoses in Hawaii—no small task given his commitment to the couple.

Before his decline, Marcos had alienated the ruling families in the oligarchic culture, including the business community and the Catholic church, his early supporters. These powerful families shifted their allegiance to Cory Aquino, who represented the old oligarchy that Marcos had dispossessed (423). Karnow argues that his economic failure, virtually bankrupting the country, more than revolutionary or reform fervor, resulted in his deposition. In many ways, nothing has changed; given the role of kinship as the cornerstone of the political system, change could occur only if the powerful families relinquished, or were dispossessed of, their land, the source of their power.[64]

Armed with an introduction to a family clan tied to the intelligentsia, Fagin traveled to the Philippines on a three-month journey. This experience of culture shock infuses *The Machine*, which unravels a complex history of colonialism, whether governmental, corporate, or psychic. For Homi Bhabha, colonialism functions within the contradiction of recognition and disavowal of "racial/historical/cultural differences" which places the "colonized [as] a fixed reality which is . . . entirely knowable and visible."[65] He calls this "a complex articulation of the troops of fetishism" (29). That Fagin takes fetishism literally in the shopping channel inserts and the rape machine at the end is not insignificant. In addition, he doesn't minimize, as does Bhabha, that in Freud's construction, it is the woman's body which is the source of the fetishistic disavowal for the man. For Freud, "woman" embodies contradiction.

There is a snug fit between Bhabha's model of fetishistic disavowal and colonialism—wherein race is visible and clearly not a secret (like Foucault's repudiation of Freud's repression hypothesis, arguing instead that the secret that is sex/identity is loudly proclaimed)—and the defining logic of U.S. television which also operates via overt, declared contradictions, a logic of both/and rather than either/or. Like colonialist discourse, TV overtly speaks with a forked tongue, declaring its contradictions, unlike cinema, which is more seamless. Unlike Freud's fetish, for TV and colonialism there is no reassuring object. *The Machine* reveals the mechanism of all three fetishes—the woman, the colonial subject, and television—as logics of contradictions.

The unbelievable scene of hands-on surgery in the fourth section, "Tourism," stages this psychic mechanism. This is shocker, drop-dead footage of "Alex Orbito, Faith Healer and Travel Agent" from Manila, who doesn't want to promote his mystical talents, only heal. With Fagin's voice outside the frame lending veracity, there is an uninterrupted shot of hands-on stomach surgery on a middle-age, middle-class American woman. She lies on Orbito's desk; the camera zooms in on her body as his hands create a gaping wound with red fluid, then its resuturing and cleaning. She sits up, perkily smiles, and testifies: "This man has saved my life twice. . . . It doesn't hurt; it feels good." This scene is an assault on Western surgery and a challenge to both fetishistic disavowal and the truth of vision. The woman's testimony is linked to tourism and the tape's shopping channel re-creations, which also include comments from happy customers.

Imelda, a central figuration, no longer serves as an easy target, a cultural joke of bad taste, a cover-up for real corruption. Rather, she is a leftover, a symptom, the result of colonialism—neither Filipino nor American, without identity yet so well known as a celebrity caricature. Fagin gives her a fictive identity, that of a tragic heroine of the late nineteenth century. Neither is the blame placed singly on Marcos. The strands of power—visible and invisible, audible and inaudible—are full of anomalies and cultural difference, yet replete with greed and covert acts turned corrupt and personal.

The Machine embodies two models of time and history: successive, moving chronologically from Marcos to Aquino, and simultaneous, doubling back like memory or shock. The collision of the everyday with shocking or catastrophic scenes culminates in an extraordinary, macabre performance at the end: the bloody coupling/rape of the Filipino emblem, an eagle, by a Cyclopean U.S. phallic rocket/dollar—a perverse, violent, fire-breathing machine. The metaphor of rape is staged earlier, over a Filipino woman's body tended by surgeons, lying on top of a map of the world, a body which has replaced the corporate station logo, KSKY, which has a bleeding eye in its last letter. Rape is literal in the child prostitution trade near the U.S. military bases. The Cyclopean eye/phallus/money machine reminded me of Bhabha's description of the colonizer: "Their governance is overwhelmed by . . . an exciting pleasure . . . which might turn into a Cyclopean policy."[66]

The tape stages what Graham Pechey calls "the theatre of history," a strategy of decolonization, with a critical relation between performance and writing.[67] Fagin's technique is rigorously thought out. He rips off abstract formalism, commercial TV tactics, cinéma vérité, guerrilla video, performance art, and acting methods. This bricolage, of familiar, mundane techniques combined with high art formalism, unsettles the relation between person and actor, the real and the simulated, the documented and the re-created, the historical and the experiential or personal.

Super VHS, shot in hand-held vérité style with the color removed, is used in two recurring conversational tableaux: the first, an activist land reformer and priest meeting with constituents in Ilocas Norte, Marcos country; and the second, a dinner-table interview with an activist lawyer, his articulate wife, and a former political prisoner. These clearly privileged sections retain the liberal to Marxist politics-style of cinéma vérité (including "real" locales) and raise deeply serious, straightforward issues: the presence of U.S. business and military bases.

A variant of this hand-held, black-and-white format is the granular Fisher-Price video or toy footage (reminiscent of avant-garde films) of Ron Vawter as Alden Pyle. This toughly sensitive reporter/agent is closeted in his hotel room, reading or writing about events; his experience is mediated, fantasmatic. Pyle is a condensation of Vawter, the ex-Marine and off-Broadway actor, Fagin, and Edward Lansdale, a CIA operative in the Philippines and Vietnam. The simulated and the real elide and collide; history is impersonated.

Lansdale was Oliver North's hero and the model for the characters of both *The Ugly* and *The Quiet American*. In the first novel, he is Colonel Hillendale, anticommunist crusader. In the second, by Graham Greene, he is Pyle, teaching democracy to the peasants to "resist the communist menace." Lansdale, who died in 1987, wrote, "I took my American values into these Asian struggles." Karnow argues that "the clue to Lansdale was his youth in the advertising trade" (348). Vawter/Pyle also suggests a Jack Smith performance in a Ken Jacobs film or Martin Sheen going nuts in his hotel room in *Apocalypse Now*. This Fisher-Price footage is shot (by Leslie Thornton) and edited in tight, fragmented images, bound in further by a black matte frame.

As Pyle writes and reads, the text, which is shown in lettered, broken closeups, is also heard. "Under the Marcoses, this place was a kleptocracy. Imelda would go into Tiffany's on Fifth Avenue, a Unesco check made out to the Philippines neatly folded in one of her native bags. . . . Now, like a character from 'Dawn of the Dead,' she haunts the malls of Hawaii."

The "I" of Pyle's text is the "I" of Fagin's experience, an alter ego acting out fictive history. Critique and autobiography are presented as performance more than documentary experience. Regarding his introduction and the taping of the coffin of Marcos's mother:

> When I first arrived I thought it to be my good luck. Drop the right name, doors, now even coffins opened, everyone seemed to know one another, and they were so closely knit. . . . That's what an oligarchy feels like. The wake . . . longer than a mini-series, but not quite long enough for syndication. The paid mourners, the mother in state, well lit, just enough flowers to fill the frame. The right had become so accessible. Once arrogant and removed, they saw their last hope as American television. The left, on the other hand, was cautious. Maybe their image would be seen by the vigilant death squads, perhaps you're in the CIA, oh yes, a concerned writer. Know an issue in a weekend and show it in a thirty second balanced featurette. . . . I insisted the camera should shoot directly into the casket. . . . The sequence was shot a second time. A retake. What did I expect? The corpse to blow its lines, to blink, to sneeze? Only the camera made death feel near. . . .

We see Marcos's dead mother, who bears an uncanny resemblance to her son, preserved and waiting, later.

A hand-held camera brushes over the items on Pyle's desk. This incidental detail is reminiscent of the throwaway newspaper item which first attracted Fagin to this project. It described "the objects left on Ferdinand Marcos' desk the day he departed from the Philippines. . . . An exploration of the objects left behind, on a day that would prove to be historic, could function as insight into the configurations of power, the random and the everyday."

This personal image reminds me of the CNN reporter covering the 1989 earthquake in San Francisco (coincident with Fagin's editing; like this tape's conclusion, catastrophe was linked to baseball), asking the now-homeless standing outside their collapsed apartments to describe what they had taken when they fled, or what they would retrieve during their fifteen-minute visitation before demolition. To Fagin's not surprising good luck, Marcos "took the gold bullion rather than the home movies" which Fagin "accessed." While copying TV technique, we are not held in by conventions of flow or narrative containment. Rather, we are displaced within a chain of associations where one catastrophe slides into another or, just as unexpectedly, jumps back, like the flash of personal memory. Time, like history and disaster, is a series of unexpected simultaneities.

Connie Lansdale is the anchorwoman played by Constance DeJong. This condensation of herself, Connie Chung, and Edward Lansdale embodies TV grammar, linking segments and contents. She reports the weather and the price of Filipino commodities. Her intonation is undifferentiated, an affectless monotone. Her "professionalism," a lack of emotion, is in high contrast to the dramatic performance of Vawter. Behind her are bizarre, Giotto-inspired murals of Christian allegories. She exists in a satellite studio suspended above the earth, completely removed from any social context. Her intonation, English, and TV nonsequiturs are superimposed on the world, flattening it into sense, eradicating differences. Like TV, Connie smooths over any disruption by failing to notice any difference.

Given that network TV news studios are increasingly run by remote-control cameras, with computers picking up satellite feeds from around the world which are then stored in memory banks for instant access, they can be anywhere and don't need anyone to be present; anchors can be keyed in (like being beamed aboard the *Enterprise*). The network valuation of being on the scene is an old-fashioned realist (Baudrillard) claim, one which denies the very electronic technology enabling the broadcast or point-to-point transmission—an interesting contradiction. Although we couldn't see either Koppel or Rather in Iraq in August 1990, they were *there*, as their voice broadcasts informed us.

The postproduction mix of hard-core TV graphics and flashy but commonplace editing linkages subverts the visual and aural grammar of TV flow. These linking and packaging techniques of logos, promos, phrases, ID's, and graphics (which grab our attention, promise a future, and erase memory) are crucial for TV continuity and normalcy; they are devices which we ignore or endure. In nonplussed manner, these visual and spoken connectives can link the weather to an assassination, an artificial cause-effect illogic. Fagin fills these empty markers with conflicting content, forcing them to "mean" differently. These repetitions lack redundancy, unlike TV. While many references are immediately recognizable, over time they assume an intellectual complexity they didn't initially warrant. TV's intricate grammar has been deformed through what Eisenstein called vertical and intellectual montage and revised by language.

The TV precursors are neither the networks nor PBS but programs made for syndication: the Home Shopping Channel, *America's Ten Most Wanted*, (and other re-creations of sensational events), magazine format shows *Entertainment Tonight* and *Inside Edition*, and particularly CNN, the cable news channel. The alternation of techniques resembles channel zapping; the return to the same scene with different commentary suggests instant replay, multiple viewings, or time shifting. The shopping channel re-creations, miniature compositions hawking compact discs, necklaces, or cellular telephones, are commodity tableaux with spiders, snakes, and frogs in the mise-en-scène—scenes which illustrate Bhabha's analogy between the fetish and colonialism. A long-fingernailed hand caresses the glitzy merchandise, while on-the-air telephone chats with TV viewers meld into accounts of the graft of Marcos cronies. The consumerism of shopping, like Imelda's shoes, is peanuts compared to official graft.

"Hello shoppers. Welcome to some are smarter than others. Our featured shopper is Marcos' crony, Herminio Disini, who masterminded the fattest single contract ever landed in the Philippines, the Westinghouse nuclear power plant in Bataan, build on a site subject to tidal waves, 5 miles from a volcano and 25 miles from a geological fault. Disini was paid a commission by Westinghouse of 59 million dollars and Disini companies [were] in charge of civil works, engineering, communication and insurance. . . . The eventual cost was 2.2 billion dollars. Remember to stay home and shop. If you ever want to get a taste of what it would be like if World War Three broke out, go to a shopping mall between now and Christmas."

The lowly shopping channel turns to critique, to style which can be filled with alternative content. TV's lack of connection between random events, its brevity of items, begin to hookup and make sense. Voices are dispersed, wrenched from a single, authorial viewpoint. Power is no longer a one-way street, on the side only of the colonizer. The tape "reconstructs a process of cultural resistance and . . . disruption, by writing a text that can answer colonialism back."[68]

Along with catastrophe, the tape circles around gossip and scandal, particularly in the second section, "The Marcoses." The focus is on Imelda. A patron of the arts with an affinity for other wealthy patrons, she hung out with the Whitneys, Rockefellers, and Fords, courting celebrities and politicians with her dazzling entertainment. Her famous friends, including the pages of *Women's Wear Daily*, abandoned her in the end; her taste, formerly stylish, soured to tacky, excessive. "I have surpassed Cinderella," she declared as she invented a fairytale of a life which included singing for Irving Berlin and meeting Douglas MacArthur. She was, as the tape so poignantly remarks, a "twentieth-century Emma Bovary, an ambitious girl from the provinces who had dreams which were the symptoms of her century. The difference between them is that Imelda's dreams came true. First as daydream and finally as nightmare."

As official culture revised it, Imelda's life resembles a soap opera, perhaps starring Joan Collins. After facing Marcos's myriad and public sexual affairs, for which Benigno Aquino was also famous, she "buckled under the pressure and flew to New York to consult a psychiatrist—who prescribed tranquilizers and advised: Either quit Marcos or adapt to his lifestyle. She adapted . . . but she was never fully stable. Her subsequent shopping binges and insomniac soliloquies plainly reflected manic [or addictive] tendencies" (Karnow, 375). Thus, like so many women, she was tranquilized and adapted, explaining her shoe closet—a compulsive obsession so typical of addiction (as is Valium).

However, like Emma Bovary, the fairytale princess was not always a joke, not always "stout and a bit blowsy" and "tacky." In 1966, *Life* compared her to Jackie Kennedy with Eleanor Roosevelt's energy, while *Time* praised "Marcos' dynamic, selfless leadership." It is as if Imelda froze in that earlier and happier image—wearing one of her many '60s/'70s formal gowns to her 1989 hearing in New York, held in a Jackie time warp, surrounded by mocking media, alone, pathetic, sad rather than funny. Women must scrutinize the objects of men's jokes, often, like Freud, at (rather than about) women's expense.

Karnow's take on Imelda is typical; she is ridiculous, out of control, grotesque, just like an aging woman. He dishes out the gossip. "Arriving in Tokyo, Rome or Paris, she would buy racks of clothes and trays of diamonds. . . . She squandered $12 million on jewelry in a single day in Geneva. . . . Bloomingdale's opened especially for her on Sunday" (373). The abandoned loot, like the conclusion of *Citizen Kane* and her shopping sprees, is displaced in the tape onto parodies of the shopping channel and governmental greed.

The Machine opens with an image of the televised assassination attempt on Imelda in 1972—a clip which was played as a continuous loop for hours on Filipino television. Section two features home movie footage of Imelda's birthday party. In a setting resonant of a U.S. country club, the partygoers sing show tunes; Imelda takes the microphone and the singing lead. She is sweetly gracious, very beautiful, the center of attention and adoration. The scene will return, with a different text—like the obsessive return to key moments in catastrophe coverage, or key plays in sports, trying to understand events by repeating them, piling on diverse interpretations or facts.

At this point, the performance of DeJong as the anchorwoman takes on texture and resonance. She becomes more than an impassive connective fixture shuffling papers and tells parables about Imelda. The first is of Maria Malibran, the opera singer, who had been forced to sing the role of Desdemona in Rossini's *Othello*. Like Emma Bovary and Lady Macbeth (and their obsessions or addictions), Imelda takes on fictive and tragic/pathetic stature. The words cue us to the novelistic dimensions of the text and to the paucity of language on TV, blanded into a delimited uniformity. History, story, and allegory blend, retaining a nineteenth-century flavor.

Then the words referring back to her assassination footage: "Imelda arose, the morning after the assassination attempt, in the manner of the hysteric who, after a hectic day of being beaten, tortured and defeated by her symptoms, awakes refreshed. . . . Later in the day, watching the events in an endless loop on television, she puzzled. Why had Ver's security standing by not rushed to her rescue? Ver politely explained, his men had wished to give her center stage, to remain out of camera range." The third tale is Imelda's own fairytale: "Imelda sang to Berlin 'You Are My Sunshine.' She had been told this was the anthem of the American liberation. Despite Berlin's praises, Imelda decided not to pursue a singing career." Imelda's life as fantasy, as Hollywood movie, suggests another reason for the close affinity with the Reagans.

After shots of the very famous shoe and dress closets, and another shopping channel insert, the tape returns to Marcos on formerly live, but now dead, TV, followed by a visit to his mother's funeral and a look inside the coffin, staging Vawter's earlier words. Dona Josepha looks exactly like the aging, ill Marcos, then holed up in seclusion in Hawaii. The visit reminds me of the *National Enquirer* paying relatives for photographs of Elvis in his coffin. Even the tabloid was astonished at how many family mourners complied. The winning photograph became headlines. In this mise-en-scène of sensational kitsch, more than death or grief, the camera goes into the coffin for a closeup. The mother's death scene, reminiscent of the son's TV appearance, is framed by ironic logos and pop music.

The relations between TV and tourism are clear. This is not, however, a tracing of the West superimposed over another culture, resulting in the TV mirror image of the U.S. Filipino voices are everywhere; cultural artifacts are taken seriously. The collision is that of electronic culture with folk culture. The local, in which colonized subjects speak, undermines the global.

While 1980s theorists of postmodernism mourned our entrapment in the present, Deleuze and Guattari advocate the present-tense quality of history. The parallel of this tape with Deleuze and Guattari is close. *The Machine That Killed Bad People* is an *agencement*, with "lines of . . . segmentation, strata, territorialities; but also lines of flight, movements of deterritorialization."[69] One line of flight is the New People's Army—a movement of deterritorialization, a claim for land reform, a class struggle. Set against this is an arborescent logic of hierarchy, of filiation, the clan system which owns the land and U.S. interests. *The Machine* is a rhizome which connects "organizations of power, and events in the arts, sciences, and social struggles" (12).

This is a revision of 1960s countercultural protest movements and liberation struggles, the context of the first-generation video artists, a time of mobile and shifting alliances such as the women's movement, civil rights, arts activism, and the antiwar movement. This first wave of video understood the power and techniques of television, arguing that video should provide alternatives. Video was process, diversity, and heterogeneity; commercial or "beast" TV meant product, centrality, and homogeneity, with spokesmen speaking above and for us. As Michael Shamberg wrote in *Guerrilla TV*: "Because radio men have been unable to model a visual language, only abnormal modes of behavior are considered news. . . . A lack of a true video grammar . . . also means that the actual experience of being at an event can't be communicated and therefore isn't considered news."[70]

The "video freaks' " assessment of commercial TV, linked to official, governmental culture, was uncannily accurate and predictive. Akin to TV, "government is geared towards crisis management, to anticipatory response" (14). Along with crisis and catastrophe, media celebrity was another earmark of product culture: "Abbie Hoffman thinks he's getting his message across by going on the Dick Cavett show, but as somebody . . . once said: 'The revolution ended when Abbie Hoffman shut up for the first commercial.' " "No alternate cultural vision is going to succeed in Media America unless it has its own alternate information structures, not just alternate content pumped across the existing ones. And that's what videotape . . . is ultimately all about" (27).

The spirit of the tape reminds me of TVTV's brilliant and powerful *Four More Years*, which was alternative coverage of the 1972 GOP convention, the year Marcos imposed martial law on the Philippines. The roving hippie reporters took their hand-held video camera onto the convention floor, charting a binary divide between the middle-class, suited conventioneers and the protesters outside the convention walls, with Vietnam Vets against the War, including the now-famous Ron Kovic, author of *Born on the Fourth of July*, chanting "Tricky Dicky's Got to Go," trying to shout down the GOP's Nixon slogan, "Four More Years." Along with charting an era which protested war and imperialism, the reporters interviewed the network stars as much as the politicians, while the networks statically recorded official history, remaining above events in their booths.

Four More Years became history of the '80s, of political events (the move to the right, fundamentalism, and Reagan, a star of the tape), and of TV style (and even TV theory, with a long debate on the real or simulated enthusiasm of youth for Nixon predictive of Baudrillard, a mid-1980s hand-wringing era that might, thank God, be over). Video guerrillas disavowed retaining any distinction between the real and simulation. What is striking about *Four More Years*, nineteen years later, is the tape's radical aesthetics, its vision of video's capacity to inscribe a history of the present which is valid and moving today rather than distanced and over.

Four More Years takes to positive ends Fredric Jameson's condemnation of network television: "The disappearance of a sense of history, the way in which our entire contemporary social system has . . . begun to lose its capacity to retain its own past, has begun to live in a perpetual present," with media figured as "agents" for our "historical amnesia."[71] Rather than amnesia, *Four More Years* inscribes memory akin to Benjamin's "conception of the present as the 'time of the now' which is shot through with chips of Messianic time,"[72] causing us to assimilate "the information it supplies as part of [our] own experience."[73] "Where there is experience in the strict sense of the word, certain contents of the individual past combine with material of the collective past" (159).

Fagin takes Benjamin's negative examples of information—"brevity, comprehensibility, and above all, lack of connection between the individual news items" (158) (so prescient a description of commercial TV)—to

positive ends. The very defining features of postmodernism for Jameson—
"the transformation of reality into images, the fragmentation of time into a
series of perpetual presents"—are Fagin's primary tactics for this history of
the present.[74] History is not over but ongoing. Neither is history linear,
chronological, or univocal.

Bakhtin's dialogical culture describes the tape's double-directed hybrid
tactics. Benita Parry suggests that the position of "hybridity" can "circum-
vent, challenge, and refuse colonial authority."[75] Against the centripetal
notion of TVspeak, Bakhtin prefers dispersity, plurality, and decentering,
without closure or identification.[76] "The productivity of the event does not
lie in the fusion of all into one, but in . . . my nonfusion, in the reliance
upon the privilege afforded me by my unique position, outside" (108).

Popular culture which is "free, full of ambivalent laughter . . . disparagement and unseemly behavior, familiar contact with everybody and everything," with respect for the "repertory of small, everyday genres," is
preferred to official culture, which is monologic: "monolithically serious
and somber, beholden to strict hierarchical order, filled with fear, dogma-
tism, devotion, and pretense" (178). Guerrilla video versus TV news.

"Intonation" for Bakhtin is "at the boundary between the verbal and the
nonverbal, the said and the unsaid" (46). Intonation is directed toward life
and the listener as ally or witness. Thus, we engage in a dialogue. Significantly for Bakhtin, the "other" is not located in the unconscious, as it is for
Freud and Lacan, but in the social, in language. Thus, expression organizes
experience rather than the other way around—a concept highly pertinent
to television. Also applicable to television is Bakhtin's idea of "character
zones"—"from . . . alien expressive elements into authorial discourses—
ellipsis, questions, exclamations—characters' voices intermingle with authors' voices."[77]

The Machine is not a monologic condemnation of U.S. imperialism, what
Parry calls "the eurovision of the metropolitan left" (51). The final two
scenes explode. The first is an interview with Father Gerry Cabillo, the jovial land-reform activist: "We were always dictated upon. . . . We should
run on our own . . . self-determination . . . masters of our own destiny."
Immediately, Connie says: "Welcome back to the USA." She reads a letter,
discovered by accident, written by Lansdale to his father in 1951. After
writing about the World Series, he criticizes the Europeans, who don't realize the importance of "oppression, communism, atheism. . . . It's really
true, the fate of the world is in our hands and we just have to round the
Filipinos into shape. My advertising experience comes in handy. . . .
Sometimes this war makes me feel like a kid again back in Detroit. Often
it's games and pranks that work. . . . But at least it's a Christian country."
It is Christmas: "It sure is festive, a bit too festive, almost pagan. Now I
understand what McKinley meant when he said we had to Christianize
them. Wait till next year, Your loving son."

For Bhabha, "the modern colonizing imagination conceives of its dependencies as a territory, never as a people." Bhabha might call this "muscular Christianity and the civilizing mission, a vigorous despotism."[78] This is a boyhood dream, that of an adolescent male, the good son: "Sometimes this war makes me feel like a kid again back in Detroit." "P.S. Tell Mom to send some of her cookies." As this letter, imagined by Fagin, is being read by DeJong/Lansdale, it assumes a nefarious actuality. Off to the side, the fierce and malevolent machine, clanking violently, shuddering and bloody, is relentlessly, blindly smashing into the Filipino emblem.

When I saw the tape, the letter sounded like another era. However, Dan Rather's August 1990 interviews with young U.S. soldiers on ships sent to the Persian Gulf and Iraq reminded me of these youthful American words. While *The Machine* is specific to the Philippines, it also demonstrates that U.S. values continue to repeat themselves over time and continents. History continues to jump into the present, hanging over our heads like the sword of Damocles. Nowhere were "muscular Christianity and the civilizing mission" more operative than in the Bikini Atoll nuclear experiments— my last tale of catastrophe.

Nuclear Disavowal

While Freud's is an apt theory for television, there are historical flaws: television addresses an older audience (and generational audiences), not easily recapitulated by childhood and Oedipus, Freud's focus. The Cold War was television's context, a history predicated on a defensive nuclear imaginary —an image of death that turned many of us into neurotics. The Cold War qualifies the interpretation of Freud as analyzed by Weber: "the very impulse to move beyond the pleasure principle to repetition, and beyond repetition to the death drive, also impels him to move beyond the death drive . . . toward a very different 'place' . . . in which the repetition of the same becomes the repetition of difference" (130). Although Weber's fatal conclusion of sexual difference, or death in the form of "the passive female,"[79] is not new or unimportant, as the dead MacAuliffe and pink-suited Jackie illustrate, Weber finds at the end of Freud's thought "a myth which counterbalances the death drive"[80]—love stories, eros.

Although George Bush declared the end of the Cold War in his 1992 State of the Union address, I want to partially disagree with Weber, and update Freud's historical assertion that "the unconscious seems to contain nothing that could give any content to our concept of the annihilation of life."[81] The second half of the twentieth century had an image of doomsday and annihilation which Freud could not have imagined. This image haunted the unconscious, politics, art, and criticism; it was not a love story and, like "The Return to Space," excluded the female. With the abrupt end to the Cold War in 1988, a virtual suspension of disbelief, its image has shifted from testing in 1946 and Operation Crossroads to simulation and Troop Test

Smokey, from avid discussion to silence, from civil defense to its futility, and from visual representation in government experiments and art to theory. The logic of governmental, nuclear argument was one of contradiction: a process of creation—showing us the visual spectacle of the bomb's capacity in elaborately staged films—and cancellation—the verbal denial that nuclear power would be offensively used. If precautions were taken, radiation's harmful bodily effects were also denied, disingenuously.

The nuclear image, with its logic of conscious disavowal, including our reception, is historical. Like a few of us, this imaginary real has aged, its terror contained by forty years of disavowal. We grew up with it, terrified; my very Catholic grandmother convinced me that every airplane sound signaled imminent death from Russian planes. Duck and cover in school encouraged fear of Soviet attack—the contradictory premise of U.S. *defensive*(!) policy—the ultimate exemplar of a logic of creation/cancellation. This is the repressed of catastrophe coverage, haunting its form; this could be its content, and we are almost relieved when it is not. (That the imaginary hold of this apocalyptic fear of the Soviet Union, and "Red" China, is over is demonstrated by the recent governmental acknowledgment that nuclear plants do have real and destructive effects on the human body.)

Along with television comedy, which distracted us by the "liberation" of laughter, these two institutions of Cold War foreign and domestic containment determined the '50s and audience memories. The U.S. imaginary was arrested at that adolescent moment which refused passage into the symbolic and resisted aging (with the necrophiliac resuscitation and sightings of the real Elvis and the photographed nude Marilyn as rituals of this arrested process); the Cold War generations of parents and children addressed by television are now well into middle and verging on old age. The historical point marked a move away from the real which could destroy us, into the imaginary, into simulation as positive, with offense figured by the government as defense, the rhetorical disavowal (and lie) of safe nuclear policy. Television rather than cinema became culture's dominant "theoretical object"—only recently recognized, albeit usually unstated, in the boom in postmodernism. Early stages of postmodernism can be glimpsed in the '50s selling of television, coincident with and party to the rapid expansion of consumer markets, nuclear experiments, and the development of nuclear rhetoric. Shopping in the new centers was sold to the populace as one patriotic way of easing fear of "the bomb."

To set the historical scene: The location is the Bikini Atoll in 1946. Amidst swaying palm trees, "natives" sit in circles, smiling and quietly listening to U.S. military personnel while a movie is being shot. The "natives" are extras, not the stars of this military event staged for the media. The soldiers stand above them and the scene, superior, their uniforms an ominous, foreign intrusion. Commodore Wyatt is an early theorist of contemporary catastrophe. His filmed prologue, with a reflexive nod to the "film apparatus," is a justification of imperialism. This live event, more suited to De

Mille or Griffith, is a spectacle staged as an act of kindly fathers for polite children, the natives: "They're willing to go and leave everything in God's hands." The live audience was huge: 42,000 soldiers were watching; 200 warships were anchored; 140 planes circled overhead; 200 goats, 200 pigs, and 4,000 rats were tested in this fourth atomic bomb test—Operation Crossroads, July 1, 1946. As with earlier experiments, the demarcation between spectators and victims was a slim one.

This is the famous footage, an aesthetic nightmare subsequently watched by millions, an aftereffect imprinted in our memories rather than its conditions of production—the eradication of the islanders' home and culture.[82] Shot from a godly point of view, up in the heavens, from many angles, the sublime spectacle of atomic catastrophe, aided and abetted by cinema, has erased history rather than recorded it. We remember only the fetish—not the ruins which the beautiful, powerful image disavows, like the effects of radiation on bodies.

The linkage of God with U.S. military power and racist conventions of representation on sound and image tracks which subsume the voice of the "natives" are inflammatory issues. So is the metaphor of rape, coded by the juxtaposition of shots of soldiers, young women smiling, and the demolition of the island, an act concluded by the satiating, peaceful tumescence of the mushroom cloud. However, here I am concerned with technological catastrophe as imperialism, reduced to an image and traded across media, nations, cultures, and time. The image eradicates history and contains differences—of gender, race, culture. We are left with a timeless, aesthetic aftereffect with can be replayed in politics, science, philosophy, and art.

Catastrophe, produced in the name of the real (or science/technology), became an international phantasm, an assertion of nation and masculinity. The Bikini detonation was a powerful commodity fetish exchanged for history, its sublime magnitude blocking analysis. For contemporary theory, the image founds totalizing systems which invoke and make the specter safe. While the participants in a colloquium held in April 1984 at Cornell University, "Nuclear Criticism,"[83] reiterate that we have never had an atomic war, I wonder if the subjects of the destruction of Hiroshima, Nagasaki, and the Bikini Atoll (and U.S. victims of nuclear tests) would agree. Turned into objects, history, like "Scene 2, Take 26," has sublated their voice.

This image stalks our cultural history, is refigured, like God, in the Baudrillard boom. Once a visible or metonymic referent, coincident with the marketing of television as Joyce Nelson argues,[84] it is now an ineffable image of containment. While repetition (and the end of the Cold War) might have exhausted its effectiveness, it has neither aged nor changed, an assertion documented in a study of TV nuclear coverage by David Rubin and Constance Cummings. Their network analysis focused on three 1983 events—nuclear winter, *The Day After* (a TV film), and Reagan's nuclear plans—and began by posing a perplexing conundrum: given that nuclear war, at least until 1988 or 1989, served as a "*cantus firmus* to modern life . . . the media should be filled on a daily basis with images and information."[85]

As any TV viewer knows, this was resolutely not the case; in fact, exactly the opposite is true. For example, from 1982 to 1986, when Reagan "began to talk publicly of the need to dominate a nuclear war at every force level, to provide nuclear options for the president," the networks presented only "24 stories," totaling "48 minutes and 40 seconds on evening news programs" (45). Supported by statistical data, the authors conclude that TV is unwilling "to question the [any] administration's nuclear policy" (52). TV's predilection for "events," along with the " 'taboo' against reporting repetitive stories" (40), is the reason for this avoidance of public debate.

Particularly fascinating is their discovery that "television has acquired only a limited inventory of metonymical images for communicating the horror of nuclear war" (53). These images cluster into four groups, comparable to the visuals of the San Francisco quake: computer graphics, historical footage (of Hiroshima and Nagasaki), Department of Defense footage (of test explosions and missile liftoffs), and scenes of everyday life with an ironic voiceover (53–54). "Nor has television advanced from the familiar images of the 1950s and 1960s in its portrayal of nuclear threat. Little imagination has been employed in communicating how thoroughly the nuclear culture has invaded American life" (56). Like the high secrecy of the Manhattan Project, the nuclear regime has remained largely invisible and unexamined, dependent on the initial images derived from the 1940s and 1950s, replayed fetishes, like Marilyn and Elvis.

To theorize this avoidance, I will briefly detour and elaborate Liz Gross' schema of disavowal, denial or negation, and repudiation.[86] Denial is a "lifting of repression," although not "an acceptance of what is repressed." Nuclear war is hideous but not possible. Or, yes, I am frequently drunk and disorderly, but I do not have a problem with alcohol. Repudiation "involves the rejection of an idea" from external reality rather than the id. We could survive or win a nuclear war. Or, as the Northwest pilot argues, "I am an alcoholic, therefore I can drink more." Or, more commonly, "If I wanted to, I could stop drinking tomorrow." Here, the "real has never been signified." Disavowal exists somewhere between denial and repudiation. "The fetishist maintains two attitudes," a contradictory logic. Like Freud's sexual fetish, an ideal or sublimity which wards off fear of castration and death, disavowal (and denial and repudiation) has functioned for the nuclear regime all too effectively.

The consensual denial was summed up by Reagan in his response to the film *The Day After*: "Nuclear war would be horrible, and that's why we're doing what we're doing [building a bigger arsenal], so there won't be one." Journalistic logic is equally convoluted: because nuclear devastation is a given, it's not newsworthy. Thus, journalists "disengage from the subject rather than [seizing] it with missionary zeal" (56). For "disengage," one could substitute deny or repudiate.

Under the warning "This is a test," the *Milwaukee Journal* reported the following event "as though it were really happening. But it is not. There has been no accident. This is a test."[87] Then followed a lengthy piece, with photos of a "make-believe victim," on a "make-believe" accident at the Zion Nuclear Power Station in Illinois. "Officials from Commonwealth Edison Co. and federal officials are acting as though a nuclear accident is under way." The simulation, or "make-believe," continued for four days, with such reports as "134,000 evacuees in Illinois were told that they could not return to their homes. . . . Wisconsin's 5,500 evacuees remained out of the area Wednesday, but dairy farmers were given the status of emergency workers . . . allowing them to return temporarily to their farms to tend their cattle." Then, the amazing tidbit, resonant of 1950s assurances about radiation's lack of danger: "The herds were brought inside and fed stored feed to prevent them from accumulating radiation in their milk." The last story was "Mock Disaster Wasn't Totally Believable." Three Mile Island was the remembered primal scene in all the coverage.

That a mock accident was staged when there are so many that have been real and repressed by the government is more than ironic. Under the Freedom of Information Act, evidence of 1950s disasters is being unearthed. Nuclear history is being taken out of the public-secret realm and revised; or, better, nuclear history of the 1950s is being written for the first time in the 1990s.

As unbelievable as the newspaper coverage was, it didn't match a news release by the IRS in March 1989.[88] The new IRS manual has a section, "National Emergency Operations," added at the urging of the Federal Emergency Management Agency. "In the event of a national emergency [especially resulting from nuclear attack] the primary function of the service is to support the secretary of the Treasury." "The IRS expects to be out assessing and collecting taxes within 30 days of the nuclear holocaust, clad in appropriate nuclear winter clothing, like lead galoshes. . . . Collecting taxes will be the thrust of the post-nuclear Internal Revenue Service." Unless a neighborhood gets a direct hit of a megaton or two, "enforced collection of delinquent accounts will be continued." Who needs theory when everyday life contains such items?

Cummings and Rubin conclude that "it is difficult to imagine a major government initiative that has moved so inexorably through planning, funding, and execution with less public participation. . . . The government has structured today's nuclear regime with little public participation." Television has been a "silent, willing partner . . . in keeping nuclear issues below the threshold of national consciousness" (56). Of course, this place below consciousness might be the unconscious, the realm of disavowal. Like the Manhattan Project, the nuclear regime is a place of secrecy and invisibility, the realm of Oedipus. "The bomb . . . accelerated . . . reliance on the publicity value of military technology," a reliance "on a weapon's image rather than its use."[89] On the surface, this is substantially different from the iconography of the "manned" Space Program—its modern publicity advocating the myth of the West and the frontier: "If this apparently unrestricted media coverage tended to obscure more than it revealed . . . it nevertheless increased the display value of each flight" (200).

For Joyce Nelson, TV's statistical complicity in the "nuclear regime" would come as no surprise: "Virtually the same corporations developed TV and . . . nuclear power systems. . . . Television and the bomb [two mass media] cannot help but be intertwined in an ideological embrace" (12). Her argument sets the body, "with all its humbling imperfections," as "standing in the way of efficiency" (15)—against microelectronic technology of information, which is "being constituted not as a liberating technology, but as one that will facilitate the rule of capital across ever wider spheres of social existence" (14). More radically, or paranoiacally, depending on whether disavowal or repudiation (an unconscious repression or an overt lie) was the government tactic, she asserts that television "united the populace around all technological advance" (26), including nuclear weapons. Hers is a brilliantly sceptical and fascinating book.

Troop Test Smokey is the 1950 simulation in the Nevada desert of an atomic war. The atomic test is real; the fighting is not. The Soviet Union "has the bomb"—for the U.S., a real catastrophe. Bomb bipolarity or dichotomy was a nightmare and the linchpin of military/economic policy; proliferation was even more frightening. Only the U.S., we knew in our hearts intolerant of cultural difference, would behave responsibly. For the film, the mythical enemy has landed on the coast of California. This experimental war/training film neatly coincides with Foucault's *Discipline and Punish*, and is a literalism, twenty or more years before the fact, of Baudrillard's *Simulations*.

The soldier/teacher, like Commodore Wyatt soon to be a theorist of nuclear criticism, informs his students/spectators/soldiers about simulating nuclear fighting: "You are here to participate in an atomic maneuver. This explosion is one of the most beautiful sights ever seen by man. You're probably saying, 'So it's beautiful. What makes it so dangerous?' " The sergeant's Kantian response to the limits of mere beauty is the sublime—anticipating the return of Longinus to literary criticism by almost forty years. Or, is his stance more in line with Baudrillard? The sublime of danger is aligned with the invisible, the ineffable, if you will the hyperreal (radiation, "the least important as far as the soldier on the ground"): "You can't feel radiation, see it, smell it, or taste it." Like TV and videotape, only the mediation of a machine, the Geiger counter (or bodily aftereffects), can prove, or measure, radiation. Seeing is not necessarily believing. The mastery inherent in sight, where "I see" means "I understand," is upset.

In this atomic theater of the '50s absurd, now a thing of the past like drive-in movies, or more ominously hidden underground or buried in classified government reports, Troop Test Smokey resembles the grandiosity of the Hollywood spectacle rather than a humble army training film. Initially, the unsuspecting soldiers in the Nevada desert are historical spectators, wearing special spectacles and watching the explosion from their dugouts. Then they become performers, walking toward the cloud for an encounter with the imaginary or "mythical" enemy. Finally, they are victims of the test's fallout and of Cold War history: the collective suit by the soldiers for damages due to radiation poisoning was finally denied in the summer of 1987 by the U.S. courts. Thus, they join the Bikini Islanders in experiencing the real or physical, bodily (and denied) rather than simulated or ineffable effects of catastrophe.

From the designs of late '40s and '50s atomic testing, nuclear maneuvers increasingly moved to simulation, as did nuclear policy predicated on deterrence—almost literalizing Baudrillard's edict to *Forget Foucault!* Nuclear thought and catastrophe migrated to art and theory. Comparable to a Bruce Conner film, in "Nuclear Criticism" Francis Ferguson depicts the "nuclear as the unthinkable," "the most recent version of the notion of the sublime . . . that alternative to the beautiful."[90] In the same journal, Jacques Derrida argues "that subject cannot be a nameable subject, nor that referent a nameable referent. . . . Then the perspective of nuclear war allows us to re-elaborate the question of the referent. What is a referent? . . . To elaborate the question of the . . . transcendental ego, the transcendental subject, Husserl's phenomenology needed, at some point, the fiction of total chaos."[91] For Derrida, literature, like television, then "speaks to other things," puts off the "encounter with the wholly other." "This is the only invention possible" (28). Nuclear criticism is Kantian criticism—"thought about the limits of experience as a thought of finitude" (30).

V. I. Arnold, a Soviet mathematician, criticizes Thom's stylistic incomprehensibility and his mystical bent: "Catastrophe theory . . . favorizes a Heraclitian view of the universe, of a world which is the continual theatre of the battle between archetypes." He quotes Thom: "It is a fundamentally polytheistic outlook. . . . In all things one must learn to recognize the hand of the Gods."[92] It appears that fundamentalism is not only the purview of television evangelists.

Arnold begins his *Catastrophe Theory* with a scathing critique of the mass-media circulation of catastrophe theory (Thom's work appeared as a "pocket book," something which had not happened in math since cybernetics, from which "catastrophe theory derived many of its advertising techniques" [2]), specifically mentioning *Newsweek*, and the hundreds of applications ranging from alcohol studies to prison uprisings to heartbeat, particle theory, hydrology, and the censorship of erotic literature, a virtual Borges taxonomy. Arnold concludes with the following dig: "In the early seventies catastrophe theory rapidly became a fashionable and widely publicized theory which by its all-embracing pretensions called to mind the pseudo-scientific theories of the past century." That lofty science descended to lowly mass culture, to a wild dispersity akin to Nutrasweet, irks this scientist.

Like theory, media events erase "the particular social context," including victims. Which brings me back to the "natives" of the Bikini Atoll—without point-of-view shots or language in the clip. As Michel de Certeau writes: "The concept-city is decaying. . . . The ministers of knowledge have always assumed that the whole universe was threatened by the very changes that affected their . . . positions. They transmute the misfortune of their theories into theories of misfortune. . . . They transform their bewilderment into 'catastrophes'. . . . They seek to enclose the people in the 'panic' of their discourses."[93]

Catastrophists

During the decade-long boom in the U.S. of televangelism, each nepotistic ministry built its own TV studio, leisure/vacation center, college, or TV network, along with the massive lease of airtime purchased with untaxed revenues. Now derailed by gossip and trials, they preached a late seventeenth- and eighteenth-century fundamentalist version of measuring history and time—paradoxically by employing TV's conventions of the live via direct address, dispersed production, and distribution—cable, satellite, and global transmission. In many ways, televangelism adopted the practices of the counterculture, who urged video guerrillas to bypass the networks and commerce with the new, available technologies, going directly to the people.

Their forebears, the early catastrophists, were a less scandalous lot, scholars rather than preachers (or politicians). Divided into various specialties, for example, the Neptunists and the Plutonists, *Genesis* and geology were combined in a system to explain the history of the earth—no small task. They compressed the geologic record into the literal time zones of the Bible. Earthquakes, volcanic eruptions, and tidal waves were cataclysmic events which coincided with God's invention. Fossils being excavated were ascribed to a universal deluge. Doomsday was figured as a great flood or a comet colliding with the sun. While the present was smooth, the past was not. They looked back at the historical record, at the artifacts of the earth, in order to make sense to the present.[94]

A fast and simple summary: "Catastrophism" was the theory which unified the archeological knowledge being unearthed by miners, engineers, and farmers. The disciples of Abraham Gottlob Werner at Freiburg were known as Neptunists. His students applied Werner's observations in Saxony to the entire world. For Werner (1787), the earth was a "child of time and has been built up gradually" (88). One of my favorite catastrophists, a precursor of contemporary French theory, was Georges Louis Leclerc, Comte de Buffon. Among his many pursuits, which included law, medicine, and natural science, he translated Newton's new mathematics of calculus into French. This dazzling, resplendent figure in the Paris of Louis

XV, "who could write only when caparisoned in all the elegance of silk, lace, and braided wig" (89), escaped the censure of both the church and secular critics to become the Isaac Asimov of his time, publishing fifty volumes called *Natural History*. Like so many modern theorists, he wanted one concept that would unify the age of the earth, the existence of fossils, and biblical catastrophe, finding his answer in a series of great floods.

Cuvier picked up where Buffon left off—developing the theory of correlation: that parts of an organism are interrelated and the shape of missing parts can be deduced from the available parts. He inspired even Balzac, who called him a great poet who populated the world with gigantic lizards. Like Newton, who created a clockwork universe, Cuvier created a static order of species, each relegated to a time and place, each wiped out in turn by a great catastrophe, a "frightful occurrence." "The evidences of those great and terrible events are everywhere to be seen by anyone who knows how to read the record of the rocks." Today, rather than the rocks, we might go to the Vanderbilt television archives for evidence of "frightful occurrences."

James Hutton examined the evidence of the present in order to understand the past in his classic *Theory of the Earth*, read in 1785. Hutton ruled out the catastrophic concept, allowing time into the model, unlike the limited time of the catastrophists. For Hutton, the earth had always existed; he thereby ran afoul of the church, which accused him of atheism. Hutton viewed the earth as a self-renewing world machine. Charles Lyell picked up the notion that the present was the key to the past, switching his position from Neptunist to Plutonist. His book *Principles of Geology* was a bestseller which used the catastrophists' time frame (which dated the birth of the earth to 4004) as a straw-man argument.

Lyell assumed that natural laws were constant, uniform in time and space; that the present could explain the past; that geologic change was slow, gradual, and steady (a uniformity of rate ruled out catastrophic event explanations); and that the earth has been essentially the same since its formation. His theory was called "uniformitarianism." Modern geology is a blend of both schools, of Lyell's uniformitarianism and the scientific catastrophism of Cuvier. (Lyell freed the mode from a church-decreed time frame.) Yet, as Loren Eiseley points out (100), it is the "Christian world which finally gave birth . . . to the experimental method of science itself." As Eiseley suggests in *Darwin's Century*, faith was translated into scientific method. That Darwin is making a comeback is a sign of the times.

As the story goes, Darwin, initially a catastrophist, set out on a voyage to substantiate the Book of Genesis. Onboard the *Beagle* in 1831, he read Lyell's book. Voila! Darwin, a tourist in South America, then challenged Cuvier, inadvertently creating laws applicable to television ratings and programming: offspring (new programs) are produced in excess of the number that can survive; populations (primetime) remain constant, hence there is a high death rate (series cancellation); survival (ratings) is a struggle; competitors (formats or genres) vary in small ways which will effect their chances; the organism best able to survive (the #1 rated series) will transmit its traits (TV's repetitive return of the same). Darwin (like Brandon Tartikoff, the legendary programming wizard at NBC, now the president of Paramount) had the theory of evolution but no idea how it occurred until he read Thomas Malthus on population (110)—the key to overpopulation was disease and sickness. Like communication scholars, Darwin observed and described, amassing data.

Far from being undone by observation, catastrophic thought is alive and well in the 1990s: the greenhouse effect, pollution of water and air, the dumping of waste and chemicals, the trade deficit/S&L debacle, illness from radiation and electromagnetic fields, overpopulation, and the threat of war (in Iraq, a trade war, with fundamentalist, religious overtones). Yet, as the disaster manuals predict, people fail to heed the warnings, preferring denial. The effects of natural catastrophe multiply within the technological environment—nuclear plants are built on earthquake fault lines in California. The scientific community warns us about South American deforestation, the extinction of species, the depletion of natural resources, energy, and nuclear winter, but, it would appear, few are listening.

Everyone is at the mall, shopping, one defense urged on us as a salve for our fear. In a 1954 film and TV ad campaign by a chain of department stores in the newly emerging shopping centers, we were urged to assuage our Cold War fears of the Soviet Union and nuclear annihilation by shopping, a patriotic act which would rescue the U.S. economy. As Susan Strasser warns, "The ecological consequences of unlimited market creation demand a public discourse about matters generally considered private."[95] Like John Berger in *Ways of Seeing*, she argues that consumer products "have embodied progress and promised convenient solutions to problems throughout the twentieth century. They have provided satisfactions and pastimes that have diverted people from the political area." She also goes further than Berger: "There are no convenient solutions to the environmental challenge. . . . New strategies must come . . . from a political process that addresses inherent conflicts and competing interests." Thus, planning must not be "left to private industrial firms," the vagaries of either "the marketplace" or "deregulation." Equally, this new public discourse must "challenge the fundamental 'privacy' of our buying habits, recognizing that production and consumption" (economics and daily life) are intertwined (291).

Rather than shopping or politicizing ecology issues, De Certeau suggests another way out of catastrophe. His Diogenes is Foucault: "one can analyze the microbe-like, singular and plural practices which an urbanistic system was supposed to administer or suppress . . . following the swarming activity of everyday regulations and surreptitious creativities that are concealed by the discourses of organizations." This is, in a manner of speaking, history, one which includes the present, with personal experience engaging the past; this is not immutable history or a catalogue of seismic events, but history of the everyday, where women are clearly visible and audible.

De Certeau verges on eliminating the border between public and private, its maintenance, like borders in the Middle East and Israel, a political issue. As Judith Allen argues: "Historians' commitment to an unexamined public/ private split, typical of Western notions of male rationality, produces a number of patriarchal effects in historical work. Symptomatically enough, published history was dominated by works of political, diplomatic and military history, and studies of great men and great ideas."[96] I would add that TV news, including catastrophe, is dominated in the same way. It must deem events important—death or money—before breaking in, suggesting that, at least on the surface, Baby Jessica was a rare event. Bush and Hussein at the OK Corral or the Baghdad Café illustrate the pleasure of flexing military might and masculinism. Two weeks into the fray, there was virtually no public dissent on U.S. television or in the newspapers. Like Doug Hall, I wonder: How can television and audiences so enjoy a military buildup?

For Mimi White, "Television's production of history and subjectivity [is] constituted simultaneously as past and present, old and new, here and there, live and preserved, ended and open-ended" (296). This is a both/and logic, one which aligns history with the subject and theory. This history crosses the border between the past and the present and other traditional lines of demarcation—particularly news and entertainment. I would add reconfiguring the border between private and public—particularly since privacy, as Strasser argues, is a recent historical construct. For Strasser, "the historical process of market creation" is at the "intersection of public and private life" (290). Gossip is located at the same intersection, a demarcation which is no longer legal—a topic to which I will soon turn.

Unlike the claims of disaster studies (Prince), Thom, and Benjamin for catastrophe, U.S. television is a model not of change but of incremental stasis, continuity, repetition; rather than wild heterogeneity, the return of the same, often *as* the same, albeit on 100 channels; along with desire and pleasure, unpleasure, anxiety, and boredom. Repeats and remakes, like the instant playback of sports, are games of mastery via a compulsive yet voracious repetition. This is not without consequence and is not a condemnation. However, critical models predicated on radical dispersity or pluralist reception (along with theories which rely on referents/realism, cause-effect/either-or dualisms, along with detectable authors and tangible objects) are limited in relation to television.

Television contains (and pleasures) us by contradictions, positing us in a halfway house, a netherworld between subject/object—half-subject, half-object: rather than an "either/or" logic, one of "both/and." TV pinpoints our loneliness by providing companionship, advice, consolation, prayer, and therapy, assuring us we are not alone by assembling audiences who have fun together. It materializes reality by simulation; obsesses with time while eradicating it; and repeats catastrophes which tell us that we are safe. TV catastrophes construct us as victims and onlookers or audience, a division replicated in interviews with emotional eyewitnesses or actual victims, intercut with the anchor's direct address to us; thus, we are held between shifting identifications with the emotive participants and the unemotive or "rational" anchor—linked to the safety of usually him, not them, in an investigative search for truth or an outpouring of human compassion. In relation to victims, our response is usually an anti-identification, the relief of "not me" resulting in gratitude. It might be argued that catastrophe coverage can function to ensure our feelings of well-being and good fortune. This would hold true for our response to anonymous victims and bystanders. Celebrities or public figures elicit *very* different responses, however. Depending on our personal experiences, we have several choices. The assurance for the viewer of catastrophe is that it is happening, but elsewhere; or, it already happened and is now historical, over. The tantalizing threat, the true danger, of catastrophe is the here and now; if it were happening to us, we wouldn't be watching television.

We exist as vicarious participants whose presence is critical, acknowledged, and flattered, yet we are never in danger of being touched, seen, or heard; neither do we need to act (the only action TV requests—along with buying—is dialing the telephone). Television's participatory nonparticipation of direct looks and address, structures of the joke and parody which incorporate us, the presence of onscreen audiences, laugh tracks, viewer mail, telephone polls, pleas for money, measuring us and charging accordingly, is the ultimate reassurance of our status as safe outsider, yet holding an opinion as involved, concerned citizens. We are safe, at home, perhaps in bed, away from the crowd.

However, television is a medium of containment with a significant difference from nuclear discourse (and the War in Iraq)—TV invokes the palpable body, often female, which nuclear policy and criticism have disavowed, eradicated. Although the network "news" division is still a strong masculine preserve, TV's address incorporates women as half-subjects, half-objects in need of physical improvement and domestication, but also critically *as* subjects. This enunciation, and its specific textual practices amidst the changing conditions of production which increasingly but sparingly include women as producers, writers, and directors as well as performers and reporters, bears careful scrutiny. Instead of merely being satisfied that television acknowledges that women do indeed exist, we must analyze the terms of the enunciation. After all, contradiction and simulation are not new(s) to women.

This book's progression from catastrophe to comedy, from Walter Benjamin to Lily Tomlin, is away from men and toward women.[97] The models of subjectivity are inflected by Freud, revealing similarities between crises and jokes. The argument somewhat perversely inverts traditional value distinctions: news-entertainment, mainstream-tabloid press, official culture-popular culture. Although I promised not to repeat this to *anyone*, and if you promise to keep this a secret . . .

PART III

Gossip and Scandal

The old flatterer took for granted that the King
was an ordinary man, and set to work to make
him out extraordinary. The newer and cleverer
flatterer takes for granted that he is extraordinary, and that therefore even ordinary things
about him will be of interest.

—G. K. Chesterton,
All Things Considered (1908)

Everybody loves gossip. Inquiring minds want
to know, and I'm not shy about asking.
Gossip is important. Gossip is history that
hasn't aged.

—Joan Rivers, TV Promos (September 1989)

Mediated gossip about sensational strangers and short- or long-term celebrities is a fallout of franchise culture—of information, services, leisure
work, and therapy. Not surprisingly, the gossip trade has legal and corporate underpinnings. A series of Supreme Court rulings since 1964 on libel
and slander, along with the federal policy of deregulation which enabled
the expansion, from the 1960s to the 1990s, of cable and satellite broadcasting, paved the profitable way. Deregulated talk was free content for the
new venues. In its redundant, repetitive circulation, mediated gossip is a
paradigm of neo-Fordism—the titillation of the "luster of capital." Gossip
is not so much information that is produced (linked to labor or production)
but second-hand talk that is consumed, recycled, and refashioned (akin to
leisure or reproduction).

Gossip is a genre, with its own conventions. It (1) traverses media and
formats (which are rigidly hierarchized and stylized according to education
and profession)—whether tabloid, mainstream, or upscale press, or TV,
whether syndicated series or nightly news; (2) dissolves the distinctions between therapy, confession, and information; and (3) is a symptom of the
shifting border between private and public domains and issues.

Public gossip is legalized as a contest between individual rights to privacy and the First Amendment—the public's right to know. An ironic tautology is at stake: while individual rights are vanishing everywhere, particularly in defamation law, gossip is obsessed, in a very old-fashioned way,
with individuals—their scandals, idiosyncrasies, and daily lives; gossip
verifies and proclaims a star system, one linked to television culture, a medium of institutional/anonymous/collective authorship.

Mediated gossip's obsessive repetitions and star system stage an episte-mophilia as much as a scopophilia, the desire to know along with the de-sire to see. In epistemophilia, "the thought process itself becomes sexual-ized, for the sexual pleasure which is normally attached to the content of thought becomes shifted on to the act of thinking itself, and the satisfaction derived from reaching the conclusion of a line of thought is experienced as a *sexual* satisfaction" (SE X, 245). Like *Citizen Kane's* investigation of a life's meaning, a futile search for a secret that would explain things, gossip both grants *and* thwarts epistemophilic satisfaction—providing tantalizing tid-bits but rarely the "truth," the real. Gossip searches for the authentic be-hind the representation, and paradoxically enacts the impossibility of knowing: we are intimate with the public persona, the familiar tics, habits, and performed behavior, yet can never know the "real" person. A third person, neither private nor public, is what we get. Subjects become third-person objects which are spoken for and about. Often this hybrid in the form of Johnny Carson or Oprah Winfrey will directly address us as an "I," speaking to a "you," a familiar, conversational encounter. However, the "you" is always an object, the audience, never singular, always collective, while the speaking "I" is he or she.

In the telling, the promise is that the image, the person, will be revealed or explained by the words. This is not the simple search for a real, or ref-erents, or authenticity à la Baudrillard. Rather, as Dean MacCannell so in-ventively suggests, it is exactly the *inverse* of Walter Benjamin's analysis of "the structure of attraction": "The work [or persona] becomes 'authentic' only after the first copy of it is produced. The reproductions [or gossip] *are* the aura, and the ritual, far from being a point of origin, *derives* from the relationship between the original object [person] and its socially con-structed importance" [gossip's circulation and reception].[1]

Gossip is almost archaic, a symptom of another era—like Bakhtin's Ra-belaisian, grotesque body, and the uncivilized body beneath Freud's expe-rience of the uncanny, both currently fashionable. The old, rude, and noisy erupts into the sleek design and quiet hum of the electronic new. That the body—its contours and its excesses exploited and contained within a deco-rum of class and gender—is often gossip's focus is almost a defining fea-ture. Paradoxically, while the focus on the body is old-fashioned, the law has deregulated bodies. Gossip transforms personalities into raw capital.

Thus, gossip is also emblematic of the modern world, "composed of movements and life-styles that exhibit neither 'leadership' nor 'organiza-tion.' . . . World views and life-styles emerge from and dissolve into cul-tural productions" (31). I will return to MacCannell's theses regarding work and leisure, the shift from industrial production to cultural production, from the commodity to experience and affect, at the end of this chapter. For now, suffice it to say that gossip is a cultural production which keenly re-sembles tourism (and catastrophe), a mediated form of sightseeing.

I will first meander through the licentious terrain of academic gossip theory, from journalists, anthropologists, sociologists, and literary critics, including Patricia Spacks's classy book *Gossip*, while detailing a model derived from the electronic and tabloid press, psychoanalysis, and addiction therapy, with small doses of Mikhail Bakhtin, Michel Foucault, and Gilles Deleuze/Felix Guattari tossed in, along with brief mention of 1980s films which star gossip: *Cry in the Dark* and *Dangerous Liaisons* (with two versions, a brilliant one directed by Stephen Frears, and a banal one by Milos Forman). Then I sketch a rank amateur's simple version of libel and slander law, historically predicated on direct or in-person speech and written texts and now, like academia, grappling with defining broadcast, electronic technologies.

There are critical and telling differences between gossip law and gossip theory, between legal and academic definitions and evaluations. Gossip Law is related to money, corporate practices, print, and electronic mass culture. Gossip Theory is predicated on oral folk culture and local community, and is antimoney. For academics, mass culture's linkage to the market and money, so determining of the new economics of desire, as Warhol so well knew, is offensive to repugnant.

Along this rambling way I will consider the relation between gossip, biography, the everyday (and news), which now include confession and/as therapy. The third section involves media artifacts, with analyses of (1) the U.S. tabloid press (particularly the *National Enquirer*), (2) syndicated TV series, specifically *Entertainment Tonight* and daytime talk shows, and (3) the tribulations and media trial of Tammy Faye and Jim Bakker. The fourth and last section, dealing with gossip and affect, argues that over time gossip is narrativized, transformed into biography, story, romance, and history. Thus, this authorless and illegitimate genre is authorized and sanctified over time by narrative and made respectable. Whether narrative and authorship function as conservative restraints is open to question. In fact, television's relation to narrative and authorship emerges as a critical issue.

My zigzag careening between esteemed and disparaged artifacts, ranging from the scholastic to the scandalous, is akin to gossip style and circulation: a layout and movement which can be rigidly and chaotically arborescent, segmented, and predictable, but also unexpected, rhizomatic—without hierarchy or defined beginnings and endings, a series of middles, of crazy connections, with their own rules and logic. Gossip enacts both sides of Deleuze and Guattari's fanciful models of logic. Gossip is both thuddingly predictable, like Vanna White, and wildly paranoiac—capable of derailing careers, as it did with Gary Hart (the U.S. presidency) and John Tower (secretary of defense).

Secret Pleasures

As a technique, gossip combines indirect with direct address, a dialogue resembling Freud's triadic structure of the joke: a first-person jokester addresses a third-person auditor about a missing second person, an aural circuit completed by laughter. Like the joke, the gossiper and the gossipee share private information about an absent third party, the gossiped-about (terms Ogden Nash coined in a limerick, "I'm a Stranger Here Myself"). Gossip's *form* of secrecy is comparable to what Freud calls the joke's envelope or container. Missing in the analogy is the joke's conclusion (laughter, a mutual slippage into the unconscious). Rather than satiation, gossip's thrill is in the retelling despite promises and safeguards against repetition. Gossip elicits denial: "Please don't repeat this" or "I promised not to tell anyone." Like jokes, gossip is taken out of context and circulates as authorless, continuing until it is exhausted. Or, like the child's game of "telephone," gossip embellishes what was said and who said it. And like tendentious jokes, gossip frequently revolves around sex as the secret.

Obviously, the print and electronic tabloids are monologues or imaginary dialogues, without reciprocity (other than ratings and TV conventions of participation), without the physical presence of Freud's third-person listener. However, TV gossip has techniques: the gossipee's absent-presence is coded by direct looks and address to an audience, just as laughter encoding a "live" audience marks the auditor's place in situation comedy. Both tactics, including the presence of a studio audience, occur on late-night talk shows. The centrality of listening, of sound as much as sight, figures us as *écouteurs* more than voyeurs.

While the gossipee, the audience, is only imagined (unless there is a co-anchor), media gossip, unlike personal confabs, often materializes the gossiped-about (Freud's second-person object) in photographs, clips, or interviews. For the tabloids, capturing the person visually in a compromising photograph or an interview is half the game; elusiveness and unavailability of the gossip quarry up the ante, fueling the paranoiac form. Privacy and silence are construed as signs of secrecy suggestive of hidden content. Madonna/Warren Beatty watchers staked out the couple's every move during the filming and release of *Dick Tracy*, reportedly a two-week stand cleverly extended into a long-term relationship with hints of marriage as a publicity ruse. Gossip capitalized on Beatty's Don Juan reputation, this time sponsored by Disney, the film's producer. The elusive Beatty was also interviewed by Barbara Walters, his previous unavailability serving as a ratings lure.

Jackie Onassis has legally enjoined photographers to stay away; only after her facelift did we see legit photos. There was Onassis, on the cover of *Vanity Fair*, looking beautiful, not a day over thirty-five. Sightings of Elvis take unavailability, along with necrophilia, to extremes. Greta Garbo's fame rested on her glamorous face of perpetual youth and her legendary unavailability. The grainy photograph of her as an old woman reprinted after her death appeared almost as a sacrilege. Or, gossip is courted as publicity by Pia Zadora and Grace Jones. The classy will dodge and avoid, the crass will seek and reveal, and a third option, the Warhol maneuver, combines both.

Along with being profitable, talk about gossip is also fashionable. Investigative and parodic gossip, written with an educated, witty-to-arch tongue-in-cheek about the powerful and the intelligent, as well as the popular and crass, as in *Spy*, is sophisticatedly "in." This is gossip for the new intelligentsia, gossip that proclaims rather than undermines class allegiance. Ironically, *Spy*'s parody relies on knowledge of trashier gossip, popular culture, *and* official or serious culture. For *Spy*, the divide between high and low culture is not just incorrect, it is passé. This parodic upscaling of gossip into clever reportage is a posture of pure ambivalence. (This is different from "It's bad but I like it" or outright repudiation, as in intellectuals' denials in the 1960s and 1970s that they watched TV or owned sets.) More frequently, gossip is predictably divided into good and bad camps.

The ethical taxonomy depends on (1) the gossiper's motivation, social or class strata, and gender and (2) the medium. Regarding the latter, it is not so much the medium, although writing style does count, as the implied or actual audience or readership. For example, *Spy*, *Harper's* and perhaps *Fame* are read by more respectable people than the *Star* and hence are imagined as classier purveyors. (The number of black women who buy the *National Enquirer* suggests that the audience bias is racial as well as stylistic, economic, and educational.) That the *Enquirer* is pitched to women, in contrast to the crossover readership of *Spy* and *Fame*, adds a sexual bias. (What we admit we read determines who we publicly are—heaven forbid that we be seriously rather than parodically positioned with the working-class poor!) Tabloid gossip is deplorable, TV bad but interesting, while literary gossip ranges from better to legit. Private gossip by decorous participants is infinitely more valued than public gossip, with "private gossip" almost an oxymoron in the 1990s.

When gossip was packaged as "entertainment news" on TV, recapitulating the history of male gossip columnists such as Walter Winchell and Ed Sullivan, men co-anchored the programs, as reporters. If, like PBS, *Masterpiece Theater*, and Robin Leach, they had British accents, so much the better and more respectable. The reports of Princess Di's brother on *Today* during the royal wedding were one of gossip's most legitimate and democratic moments; the viscount became just a regular guy, interested in a career in journalism, while the events he covered merited this royal treatment and presumably transcended the merely personal and anecdotal—that rare ether where personal gossip can become national headlines or the highest level of politics: *Scandal*. Then, the personal lives of blacks such as Marion Barry, Martin Luther King, or Allan Boesak in South America can enter mainstream headlines. Thus, gossip is evaluated according to (1) an ethics of authorial intentions (the status and style of the gossiper), (2) a hierarchy of media, and (3) the implied class/education of the reader or viewer, the gossipee. In addition to the status and gender of the gossiper, the class, gender, race, and profession of the gossiped-about also make a crucial difference, just as differences between spoken, written, and televised gossip count.

In many literary accounts, gossip has been the realm of the cynical sophisticate, with implied tributes to an Oscar Wilde pithiness. The two film versions of *Dangerous Liaisons* (1987 and 1989, one directed by Stephen Frears, the other, *Valmont*, by Milos Forman), based on a novel by a woman, were not merely coincidental releases and are not without a cautionary moral in a witty text which takes the effects of gossip on people's lives very seriously. Comparable to the analyses of literary gossip scholars, here gossip, elided with sex, is power, a force manipulated by a woman, which turns to tragedy in the end, wreaking vengeance on all the players, including the perpetrator, who above all else must not reveal her feelings or her desire. Unlike this narrativized gossip, scandals which have descended to the masses, and which, as with Jim and Tammy Faye Bakker and other supermarket commodities, have become available to everyone, are scorned and the sad state of culture is bemoaned. Among the markers of class difference in the U.S. (including money, job, gender, and race), gossip is a symptomatic sign: there is upper-, middle-, and working-class gossip, with stories increasingly crossing over, just as gossip traverses media boundaries. Gossip is imagined as belonging to the private realm, like secrets (and duplicity). This is also the space of women.

It is telling, like gossip itself, that the scorned or trivial pursuits are usually linked to women, while the big issues, including national and foreign (a word forbidden by Ted Turner on CNN, replaced with "international") policy and corporate takeovers, are left to men. When the corporate trial is tied to a woman, such as Leona Helmsley, she is accused of being a tough broad who was rough on her employees, and found guilty not only of being excessive and greedy but of not being nice, of being an improper woman. Thus, her aging downfall is just; she is a gold digger without the polish of class, voice, and quiet manners. While she lived lavishly in Manhattan, she was still from Queens. Perhaps her real crime was operating powerfully in a man's domain—real-estate deals and tax loopholes almost incidental to media coverage.[2] Charles Keating of the savings-and-loan scandal, in spite of the mind-boggling monetary magnitude of his crimes, is figured with a high-powered dignity; the junk bond wizard, Michael Milken, is reported to be a family man, of humble to homely domestic taste.

Gossip's grotesque body of excessive bad taste is a lower-class body, frequently a female body, while the upper-class body of the news (and its scandals) is sleek, refined, tasteful, discreet, often a male. Women as excess, one version of which is affect (or its absence, which can also signal guilt—a real double whammy), belong in the tabloids—the place of the body and the emotions. Men belong in the legitimate newspapers and magazines—the domain of the intellect and rational thought—an artificial, Platonic divide reiterated by the difference between daytime and prime-time TV, a barrier which *Oprah*, like gossip, is rampantly crossing. The accepted difference between news and gossip, one proclaimed by the network news divisions, is also the difference between men and women.

Face-ism: "Women through *Time*"

Hundreds of statistical communication studies document this division in representation—the landscape of everyday life which is so commonplace, its blatant sexism often remains unnoticed. In "Women through *Time*: Who Gets Covered?" the authors report that women are "pictured on only 14% of covers of *Time* since 1923."[3] "By featuring personalities on [its] covers, as opposed to events, ideas, or themes," *Time* has always practiced "personality journalism," with cover stories built around an individual (890). Thus, history is the biography of great men. Women's lives apparently have not been deemed newsworthy or historical. An earlier study of photographs on the inside pages revealed that "women were infrequently pictured, with men predominant in all occupational roles except those of spouse. When a woman was depicted, she was most often seen as an artist/entertainer, spouse or socialite" (891).

Along with a Caucasian U.S. and Western European bias, the authors anticipated and discovered similar findings for the covers. In some years, only one woman made the cover—Jaclyn Smith (a TV actress, formerly one of *Charlie's Angels*) in 1982 and Beth Heiden (an athlete) in 1980 (and Eleanora Duse in 1923, Amy Lowell in 1925, and Katherine Cornell, Judith Anderson, and Ruth Gordon together in 1942) (896). Making the number of women represented even smaller is the fact that cover girls repeat: Queen Elizabeth has six covers, Pat Nixon five, and Betty Ford four. Wife and national mother appear to be the jobs valued most by *Time*.

(However, things might be changing for women [for worse, with the new anti-abortion rulings, and for better, on *Time*'s covers]. The October 14, 1991, Jodie Foster head-and-shoulders cover, "A Director Is Born," was exceptional, including an inside story on women directors in Hollywood. The next week, October 21, 1991, Clarence Hill and Anita Thomas faced off, in closeup. The featuring of African-American faces on *Time* suggests that history might be changing. Inside, the stories attacked the Senate, with Barbara Ehrenreich writing the prestigious editorial at the end, as she often does. In the same concluding spot in the October 28, 1991, issue, Lance Morrow wrote: "The hearings were a bad moment for middle-aged white men. The Senate Judiciary Committee sat arrayed in its Caucasian glory, like Muppets of Bomfog and Claghorn, each Senator more confused and senescent and miserable and lost to pomposity than the last." However, his conclusion was with Thomas—"He will surprise them all."

Ehrenreich concluded with "the need to start populating positions of power with people of more than one sex. On some subjects, for reasons both historic and tragic, women know best.")

In the late-night opening monologues of the *Tonight Show* hosts Johnny Carson and Jay Leno, which are based on daily news events, women are not faring well. The rare women guests, particularly on Leno, adorned in the 1991 return of the little dress of the 1960s, seem self-conscious, uncomfortable as they tug and pull at skimpy garb. The gender of the late-night jokes' objects is telling: out of 3,025 jokes on late night, seventeen of the top twenty topics were men—political leaders or businessmen. The three women were Tammy Faye Bakker, with sixteen; Barbara Bush, with fifteen; and Imelda Marcos, with twelve—all wives of famous men. The leaders were Dan Quayle, George Bush, and Saddam Hussein. The only Democrat in the top twenty, Michael Dukakis, was last.[4]

"Faces in the News" measured the "face-ism" index and summarized findings that photos of males represented more of the face and head than photos of females.[5] Based on over 1,700 photos, an earlier study of mainstream news magazines found a face-ism index of .65 for males and .45 for females: "The essence of a woman is thought to reside more generally in her body," while "the essence of man is in his face" (72). Face-ism has been studied over a six-century span, with the differential increasing. "Faces in the News" discovered that women in politics "received the same facial prominence as men, while actresses, a frequently depicted female occupation, received substantially less" (70). Instead of faces, actresses were represented by their bodies.

This study recapitulated data that 81 percent of the photographs in the *Washington Post* and the *Los Angeles Times* were of men, while one-fourth of all females depicted in the *Washington Post* were brides. Goffman's studies revealed that females were "frequently shown in prostrate positions, while males were often shown in elevated positions above a female. Commercials directed primarily to boys . . . have higher levels of inanimate action, more scene changes, higher rates of cuts, and more noise than those directed to girls" (71). Like life, it appears that continuity style is also gendered—an intriguing assertion.

One common thread of content analyses is that when women are represented, they are rarely public officials or involved in public work. When infrequently represented, women are private citizens (likely to be mothers, daughters, wives), while men run the government and society.[6] When women are referred to in print, reporters often use their first names ("Nixon Assures Golda Mideast Will Balance"), avoid professional titles, and emphasize women's marital status.[7] More startling is the statistic that over 83 percent of newspaper obituaries are of men. Like their lives, women's deaths are not as newsworthy as men's. As the author writes, "Perhaps women never die, they just fade away."[8]

Another analyst argues that the news is event- rather than issue-oriented; women's *issues* are rarely taken as or transformed into *events*. However, these results are derived from mainstream newspapers and magazines, primarily *Time* and *Newsweek*. Perhaps the tabloids and gossip, rather than journalism and news (in tandem with biography and history), are more disposed to women.

Trivial Pursuits: Harping at *Harper's*

To answer the great intellectual question about the meaning of the popularity of gossip, *Harper's* assembled Lewis Lapham, the editor; Liz Smith, syndicated gossip columnist (lampooned in *Spy*); Barbara Howar, formerly a Washington party giver and later a correspondent for *Entertainment Tonight*; William Buckley; John Gross, book reviewer for the *New York Times*; Mark Crispin Miller, who "taught writing at Johns Hopkins along with writing on mass culture"; and Robert Darnton, a history professor at Princeton, to converse at Maxim's in New York.[9]

After our need was traced back to an analysis by Sally Quinn (a reporter for the *Washington Post*) that gossip was the methadone after the heroin of Watergate, the distinction between private and public was quickly brought up: public gossip needed checking and verification. (The veracity accorded to *Spy* is derived from in-depth gossip research; Woodward and Bernstein transformed Watergate gossip into history through research and verification [and the ultimate secrecy, the identity of Deep Throat].) William Buckley seemed to have no scruples about gossip as he Cheshire-catted the two gossip columnists into proclaiming a deep gossip ethics—refusing to report the date of the marriage when stating the birth of a child.

Miller raised the literary scholar's distinction between gossip as communitarian and television, a central difference for Patricia Spacks and an ontology which reveals the old saws high/low, art/mass culture, or the written text versus the electronic or imagistic text—the aural versus the visual, the difference between listening and seeing (with sound ranked below sight by most scholars). Gossip tied to TV celebrities (who don't have other jobs, like president) is the worst kind.

Smith emphasized that gossip ethics are historical—the press wouldn't touch Kennedy and Monroe because reporters and country alike used to respect presidents. (The *New York Times* rule had not yet passed.) As Gary Hart's demise demonstrated, via reportage of his dangerous liaison with Donna Rice, accompanied later by photographs on the *Monkey Business* (a scoop by the *National Enquirer*, a proud tabloid moment), this is no longer historically the case. Lapham, the editor, and Miller, the college professor, argue the inverse of Spacks: gossip attacks the weak and protects the powerful—as the Kennedy example illustrates—throwing in the private life of Jean Seberg as a counterexample but neglecting gender difference.

However, the second distinction, an argument which is central to

Spacks, which makes today's gossip worse than the court of Louis XV, is that "gossip today has a market value" (40). That this deregulated economics, with money and lifestyle replacing sex and liberation, is the new ritual or figuration of desire is not considered. The market value ups the ante, increases the desire, transforming leisure into work and profit—one earmark of a service rather than product culture, an economy predicated on intangibles and the qualities derived from commodities rather than the mere possession of commodities.

Buckley points out that gossip used to function via a class system (presumably a good thing, connoting discretion and good taste)—until television (42). The intriguing paradox is then posed: There is more gossip about fewer and fewer people who must be identifiable. Like neo-Fordism, this is one leveling function of the national and international scope of television. The process of differentiation collides with the repetition compulsion—the twin mechanisms of TV, gossip, and cultural production, repeating in leisure and recreation the methods of assembly-line production, of Taylorism and Fordism (the turn-of-the-century version still operative in the Soviet Union).

The luminaries agree that life has assumed more importance than work, that a leisure of the self has overwhelmed work (a privilege which used to belong only to the rich but is now available to everyone). For them, this shift is not necessarily a good thing. The "life" has value as a gimmick for the sale of the book, the movie, or the TV series. After arguing the spillover benefits of gossip, for example, Betty Ford's alcoholism leading to public awareness/acceptance and the formation of the clinic, the symposium at Maxim's concludes by attributing to Cher, "that wonderful philosopher," a line from Lily Tomlin/Jane Wagner: "If we're all going to be famous for fifteen minutes, will there be room for all of us at Betty Ford?" However chic and journalistic, many of the major issues of gossip sociology are touched upon.

A more cynical version of gossip's concerns is represented in a new magazine, *Fame*.[10] The sagacity of Warhol's critique and enactment of commodity culture politics is apparent in the shift from pop to postmodernism, with his shopping sprees now legendary and his daily life logged as gossip of the rich and famous in the rather shocking publication of his diaries. Before this, there was *Interview* magazine, the starmaking of his own stable of performers on film, including the 16mm portraits of visitors to the Factory, and *Andy Warhol's 15 Minutes*, a half-hour magazine-format show featuring interviews and comedy skits with the interviewees. Produced by Warhol (of course), the show ran from 1979 to 1987, first on Manhattan Cable and then on Madison Square Garden TV, with a few episodes on MTV and *Saturday Night Live*.[11] More important was the manufacture and packaging of his daily life as a celebrity, which has resulted in enormous profits from his art and the event status of retrospectives of his work. Warhol lived an economics of desire which had less to do with sex and more to do with shopping, money, and gossip. *Fame* is a degraded Warholian text, a new magazine hawked for the 1990s.

The glossy ad reveals a woman in shocking pink lingerie, her posterior provocatively stuck in our faces, with a pouty, handsome man wearing business garb: feminism gone awry. The eclectic array of concerns and experts includes psychology, with analyses by Dr. Herbert Freudenberger, the man who coined the term "burnout." The wonderfully named Freudenberger (which synthesizes Freud and McDonald's; self-help meets fast food) will provide advice on success, survival, and satisfaction. "Each time out" there will be updates on the new, "anything and everything that's forward and exciting, from the ultimate in ultra-tech . . . to the latest developments in medical progress," with stories about "the famous getting together." Readers of *Fame* will be "united in the common bond," a "quotient of success." And *Fame* will, of course, explore "Aging and Its Antidotes" (as if we could be cured of age, represented as a disease or weakness) in a column on health, which is advice on how to remain young. There will also be regular columns by a divorce lawyer, and another on great automobiles, written by a woman, entitled "Carnal Knowledge." The rural, or the local, is also included, with a column on small-town fame. Paul Newman, in his sixties but not looking a day over thirty-five, is on the advert. "In the 1990s, it will be FAME!"—which Warhol turned into a theoretical object.

Cars, therapy, youth/health, celebrity gossip, and tech-toys fashion a profile of the late 1980s hip reader. Yet it's not the commodity per se that counts; rather, as Dean MacCannell argues, it's the experience, the affect: "the common bond," the "quotient of success," "everything that's forward and exciting." As I wrote earlier, Nissan's costly 1989 ad campaign for its new car, the Infiniti, did not show the car, only the experience, the "feeling" of the car, a Zen-like, transcendentalist ecstasy of tranquility derived from nature scenes, a haiku affect of high-tech luxury. As Jay Leno quipped, car sales were slow, but nature was selling fast.

With the exception of cars, ultra-tech, and high fashion (and the money to buy pricey items), the concerns reiterate those of the tabloid rags, here upscaled, trendy, pitched to a collective "in group" rather than a lonely, bored housewife. Money (and taste) is the difference. *Fame* also addresses issues discussed by cultural studies critics, just as the *Harper's* confab restates scholarly assessments of gossip.

VII

♦

Gossip Theory

Scholars, Tourists, Ecouteurs

I will pedantically and doggedly flip through the history of sociologists' explorations of gossip, noting that gossip scholars are often anthropologists, comparable to being tourists or foreigners. The researcher steps out of his or her cultural milieu, travels to another country, class, race, age, or time period, and assumes the position of an onlooker, an overhearer, outside the action as the safe, distanced observer rather than participant— somewhat akin to the TV audience of catastrophe or gossip. Thus, the scholar's presence/absence adds a fourth dimension to the gossip triad— the silent witness, the voice of authority, neutrality, behavioral science. Omniscience granted by uninvolvement and lack of knowledge becomes the basis for scholarship rather than informed experience, presumably beyond our capability to analyze. This stance of observer or witness is comparable to that of the TV anchor, the smooth, professional performance of uninvolvement, a relay and point of identification for the audience. Paradoxically, in a culture defined by "experience" and affect, as both MacCannell and Larry Grossberg argue, scholarship and news devalue both.

As I have stated, among gossip critics of all persuasions, gossip (1) contains a moral dimension (a religious leftover like defamation law), (2) is locked into the values of personal, communal speech, and (3) is predicated on a folk rather than a mass culture view of the world. Folk culture is good, mass culture is bad, like the bipolarity of gossip, simultaneously evaluated as benign or malignant. Good gossip serves a socially useful purpose, fostering solidarity and communal identity, and encouraging normative behavior; bad gossip is malicious, scandalous, and disruptive of community. Rather than contradiction, a both/and logic, sociology posits an either/or bipolarity which necessitates a moral evaluation. To grasp the workings of culture in the '90s we must not, as Roland Barthes claimed, change just the object itself, but precisely the way we think about the artifact.

The classic study is "Gossip and Scandal" by Max Gluckman, a British professor of social anthropology who studied the Zulu. He ranges from Jane Austen's *Emma* to the Makah Indians in Puget Sound, illustrating the maintenance of groups and community via gossip—which can exclude and include at the same time. Gossip creates a past history, a badge of membership; the "more exclusive a group," the greater its gossiping—working to exclude minority groups, increasing group unity.[12] Gossip is, as Foucault might argue, about power/knowledge, a productive network of daily exclusions and inclusions, a machinery no one sees, a productive network of pleasure, of evasion and containment.

In "Gossip, Networks and Culture in a Black America Ghetto," Ulf Hannerz, a Swedish scholar, journeys to a "lower-class Negro neighborhood," a tourist bringing anthropology and linguistics to unfamiliar terrain.[13] Not surprisingly, he links gossip to community life, presuming that gossip is informal, private, with two people talking about a missing third person. He discovers that gossip operates because of the discrepancies between "impression" and "reality"—as the downfall of Gary Hart so admirably illustrates. "The less such a discrepancy exists, the less likely is it that the person involved is a favored object of gossip" (38). Keeping up appearances is not only costly; the manufactured and/or fascinating image becomes a target for investigation.

The elevation of secrets to a structuring form is an incentive for their uncovering, as Deleuze and Guattari argue. Here, of course, Baudrillard also comes into play, negatively, with his mourning of the divide between the imaginary (the hyperreal) and the referent (the real), as does addictive therapy, which involves the telling of secrets and a dismantling of "the face"— dissolving discrepancies between impression and reality. For Hannerz, "bad gossip" is the deflation of the claimed identity of a third person (38). Women's age, or rather finding out their true age—Zsa Zsa Gabor; Paulette Goddard's obituary, which uncovered a seven-year discrepancy; or the news item "Jane Fonda, 50, fell off her bicycle in Toronto"—is one of gossip's favorite pursuits, comparable to discovering whether or not a woman has had plastic surgery, with before and after charts in *Spy* detailing operations. If the patient 'fessed up, like Angela Lansbury in April 1989 about her chin tucks and facelifts, there would be nothing hidden and therefore little to tell. Public testimonials, or first-person speech, defuse the bystander/third-person search for the truth behind the face. Secrecy involves a blurring of the real with questions of honesty. (Unless first-person accounts conflict—as in the Hill and Thomas hearings.) (I will return to secrecy later, particularly to Deleuze and Guattari's critique of psychoanalysis as a structuring secret.)

Hannerz posits three qualifications for in-personal gossip which distinguish it from mediated gossip: (1) information is regarded as gossip only when gossiper and gossipee have previous awareness, usually personal knowledge, of the gossiped-about (39); (2) gossip implies scarce information; and (3) the function of gossip is linked to local context. I will elaborate these three differences for celebrity gossip. Personal knowledge is no longer a prerequisite for either gossiper or audience—resulting in an imaginary, shared intimacy, a familiarity with a persona neither public nor private. The process is one of collective identification with behavioral *aspects* or traits of people rather than primary identification, with being or having the person.

Acting out primary identification with the *person* is not normal. Paradoxically, this error, a failed reality check which involves the psychic mechanism of repudiation rather than the usual mechanisms of disavowal or denial (negation)—a model I have taken from Liz Gross—is logical, the effect of taking TV conventions *literally*. While Johnny Carson (the boyish "Johnny") behaves as if he were my close friend, speaking directly and informally to me as does "Dave" Letterman, he is not. Thus, if seminormal, viewers hold contradictory beliefs, a structure of disavowal, or we deny, which involves affirmation and negation at the same time. Repudiation, "a rejection of or detachment from a piece of reality," is a psychosis, the paranoiac effect of late-night TV hosts and their fanatical fans so cogently played out in Martin Scorsese's *King of Comedy*, in which Sandra Bernhard and Robert De Niro kidnap Jerry Lewis as the late-night talk-show host, and so perversely acted out in real life in the attacks on young female actresses such as Jody Foster by violently adoring male fans who stalk and would kill their victims, or the woman who claims to be married to David Letterman and keeps breaking into his house.

Second, mediated gossip is not scarce but plentiful, albeit massively redundant—the paradox of scarcity in a land of plenty, repetition amidst incremental differentiation. We have obsessed over Liz, Marilyn, and Elvis (silk-screened so presciently by Warhol) for almost forty years on a daily basis. Not a day has gone by for the past five years that I have not encountered at least one reference to Presley. Our lack of personal knowledge paradoxically triggers an epistemophilia and a scopophilia (the desires to know and see), a desire for intimacy which points to our lack of knowledge. Television's predication on loss, inadequacy, and anxiety triggers more feelings of loss and anxiety, exemplified by repetition akin to obsessional neurosis: repeating the same actions, each time expecting a different result but never getting one.

Reading the same stories about the same resuscitated celebrities demonstrates addictive logic (this time, I will not drink too much); we expect answers and explanations but get only the same data. For Elvis, Marilyn, and Liz, while journalists keep searching for futile explanations, the answer is simple. Addiction leads to illness, catastrophe, and eventually death; no other interpretation except knowledge of addiction is necessary. The mechanism for this repetitive coverage and its reception is negation or denial, which is a "lifting of repression, though not of course an acceptance of what is repressed . . . a kind of intellectual acceptance of the repressed."

In relation to local history and context, Hannerz's third attribute of personal gossip, media gossip is unmoored and transformed, like the image of the catastrophe, taken out of everyday life and into public life. For example, a local gossip item regarding two blonde thirty-six-year-old twins who had appeared years ago in a joint *Playboy* spread and then in B-films but gave all that up for a love relationship with an eighty-six-year-old local and very wealthy financier, was reported in Milwaukee after the IRS accused the gravity-defying, curvaceous twins of not paying taxes on what reportedly was payment for their sexual labor. Rather than work, the twins claimed love and gift status for over $1 million and hence didn't report the money as income. The IRS sided with the financier's socially connected family. While love versus work was the sexual and legal ground for the action, as well as the titillation, their crime was not sexual but monetary— neither sex nor its sale, prostitution, but income-tax evasion.

A Current Affair descended on Milwaukee, fueling and inflating the local story, with the main twin presented in daily life as sweet, innocent, and making a direct national appeal for her decency, her honesty, her pursuit and entrapment by the nefarious IRS—the sweet young thing versus the bullying bureaucracy which was about to take away her lake home and her dog. Around the same time as that national story, the twins were arrested for drunken and disorderly behavior and resisting arrest at a local south side tavern. While the law does badger women, even Zsa Zsa Gabor (who had a bottle of booze in her car when she was stopped by the traffic cop), turning them into lewd or excessive jokes, addiction might be the problem which remains peripheral, a symptom rather than the cause, signaled only by emotional excess which, as with Zsa Zsa and Tammy Faye, becomes a long-playing, late-night joke. The twins, like Zsa Zsa, were found guilty (of tax default along with greed, the crime of the late 1980s) and were sentenced to jail and drug-rehabilitation halfway houses.

If context and process are so critical, the same information can or cannot be gossip. Confidentiality is a key issue for the government and gossip (along with 12 Step programs, which depend on group anonymity), a privilege legally granted to priests, lawyers, and doctors. In these sacrosanct professions, gossip becomes fact, information, the key to the unconscious, the solution to the crime, or the sin that needs forgiveness. In many ways, these closed domains maintain private shame. For private gossip, informality and privacy are two criteria which separate it from mediated gossip, which is formatted, formal and public (37). That Roseanne Barr had a seventeen-year-old daughter whom she had given up for adoption would not be gossip when told to a priest, a social worker, or a psychoanalyst. For the priest, the information becomes a confession; for the social worker, a problem; for the analyst, a piece of the puzzle or an explanation. (Psychotherapy transforms gossip into autobiography and analysis.)

Losing It: Roseanne and Oprah

In the tabloids, it was painful gossip, accompanied by a photograph of the young woman, looking a bit startled. On *Oprah Winfrey*, where Barr was hawking her new book and her new fiancé, the same scandal became personal confession and an attack on the cruelty of the tabloid press, claiming rights of privacy for one's family. I empathized while perversely waiting for the "real" story, the truth. What a thrill, and legit at that. Yes, she had an illegitimate (a word which Barr corrected) daughter and had been blackmailed with a birth certificate by the tabloid to tell the story. She refused. They printed the photograph. She was here to tell the truth, which also demonstrated that scandal, like sex, is indeed historical. Ingrid Bergman's post–World War II affair/child with Roberto Rossellini, and her "abandonment" of her U.S. husband/doctor and daughter, resulted in her condemnation and exile from the U.S. for years.

The irony was that the result of two programs to squelch gossip was the reported catfight over Barr's weight, presumably triggered by Oprah's backstage suggestions that Barr needed to lose, or was unhappy with, weight. This tidbit hit other venues within twenty-four hours, documenting the gossip/star status of both Barr and Winfrey. Neither is a version of the thin, classical body of cinema or fashion magazines; both are astronomically successful. Both are in direct and immediate control of their business empires, fashioned around their personalities, emotions, bodies, and experiences.

Experience, along with sheer "personality," lends authority and strength to these women. Experience forms the basis of Barr's feminist standup act, her sitcom (and squabbles over integrity and realism), and Winfrey's status as knowing interviewer. Both had it rough; both are survivors who emerged with good senses of humor. Their lives have become emblems of their power and the foundation for their respective acts. Both women address other women's lives on the basis of "having been there." Both are inspirational success stories right out of folklore or *Reader's Digest* of the '30s. Both are economically successful versions of women's everyday lives, warts, pounds, and all, which, in many ways, have been turned to profit. Both work behind the scenes and on the air with other women. Both illustrate that feminism, like experience, honesty, and revelation, can be profitable. At the same time, their respective rampant heterosexual need for a mate undermines their feminism; Barr changed her name to Arnold.

These women are also opposites: Barr is the bad girl, the naughty star fighting with a string of producers, unconcerned about weight and dieting, wearing sloppy jeans on her show, a working-class woman with a messy, undecorated house and noisy, fighting children. She is also scandalous off the show, mooning at football games, turning herself into a public spectacle. Winfrey is the good girl; her show is harmonious, the set impeccable, a slick, smooth mise-en-scène of women, friendship, and expensive fashion, with addictions, dieting, and other bodily problems a constant focus of this upscaled middle-class environ. *Roseanne* emblematizes the kind of problems for which *Oprah* provides therapy and group solace. Barr, however, refuses to define herself as a problem, an inadequacy in need of a cure.

After Oprah's major on-the-air weight loss, culminating in an episode in which she hauled eighty pounds of fat onto the stage in a wagon while wearing and gleefully modeling her size 8 Calvins, weight became the program's central obsession, along with spirituality/faith and addiction, with Oprah confessing on *Inside Edition* that she had regained twelve (make that seventy and climbing) pounds and was a food addict with a serious problem. (Barr has confessed to the same addiction.) In 1991, Barr (now Arnold) revealed her family's sexual abuse, as did Oprah. This came after her marriage and 12 Step program. Oprah's "spirituality"—attributable to black religious fundamentalism—is very familiar to anyone who has experienced a 12 Step program. A comparable faith is declared by performers during their acceptance speeches on award shows, adding God to the list of mother, father, agent, producer, and head of studio.

This unpredictable circulation of gossip which can break out from its containment (the Barr scandal) and take another direction (a catfight over weight) is analyzed in an eccentric but then serious 1908 study more relevant to academia (where gossip levels the distinction between the personal and the professional, with the occupational virtually becoming the personal. I often wonder if any profession is as gossip-prone as academia, where words are the biggest, if not only, commodity). In "The Psychology of Gossip," J. D. Logan proclaimed similarities between the gossip and the genius.[14] This likeness is due to comparable thought processes: gossips and geniuses alike think via unexpected connections between thoughts, with a logic of remote and unpredictable linkages which traverse the sane and the silly, the rational and the grotesque, the relevant and the irrelevant—like magazine shows, the format of the tabloid press. I could cheekily update and label this logic one of rhizomatic thinking, or describe the style as a postmodern one of pastiche, eclecticism, and bricolage. Logan was indeed ahead of his time.

Picking up on sexual difference, he decides that "those of our fellows whom we designate as garrulous old women, or slaves of literal fact, and those whom we designate as scandalmongers, are at fault in the mind . . . peculiar brain processes." As does Spacks, Doctor Logan cites amiable gossips, the nurse in Romeo and Juliet, Miss Bates in *Emma*, Mrs. Poyser in

Adam Bede, and various characters in Dickens. The difference "between the gossip mind and the original mind is that the latter ignores all trivial, grotesque and irrelevant suggestions and conserves only those which bear strictly on the topic. . . . The thoughts of the genius have connection, coherence, and unity"—invoking William James, the "process of . . . analyzing a whole into recognizable parts" (107).

Perhaps we could divide academia according to geniuses and gossips, men versus women, with masculinism arguing rational cause-effect and linear logic (what Deleuze and Guattari would call "arborescent" thinking) and feminism arguing discontinuity, rupture, and contradictions. That gossip, like TV, does not obey the rules of coherence, unity, and connections, along with originality and authorship, is not insignificant. To a degree, gossip trashes the long paternity of sacred narrative conventions and Cartesian logic. Like TV, gossip is closer to Bakhtin's grotesque, unofficial culture, a crude rather than artistic version of Barthes's hermeneutic code, with a preference for performance and the proairetic codes.

However, to J. D. Logan's credit, and awareness of academia, he includes the bore and the scandalmonger along with the gossip. Bores are usually men "who revere every fact equally—a slow, deadly treadmill of flat reminiscences" (110) comparable to television news, catastrophe coverage, or certain historical writings. His analysis of the gossip's and genius's thought process does resemble television's segmented, disconnected flow: "the power of each is to make novel or original connections between ideas; but this power which seems so original is, after all, wholly unoriginal, since it depends on the automatic reproduction of remote fragments of experience by total recall" (111). Television increasingly presents "remote fragments" which refer back to television's history, encasing us in a TV logic, or "total recall," without clear origin. TV commercials can be imagined as "remote fragments," illogical connections.

Another study, "Gossip and Marketplace Psychology" by Ralph L. Rosnow, posits an economics of gossip which is not merely "idle chatter" but "small talk with social purposes," argued as a valuable commodity.[15] He ties gossip to capitalist marketing practices, which, amidst graphs and charts, he terms "redistributive, exchange, and reciprocative." Exchange is the worst because it is sold to the highest bidder; redistributive is dispersed from a central source—normative gossip involving socialization which can also be exploitative, like entertainment gossip; the third involves reciprocity, as in Yerkovich and Spacks's models. For Rosnow, like most critics, gossip must be freely exchanged. When money is involved, as it is in mediated gossip, then it is tainted.

The denial or, better, repudiation that money matters is outmoded in the 1990s—particularly after the 1980s shopping spree which has turned the world into a mall or shopping binge, with countries, along with individuals, massively in debt. Tourism, so internationally commonplace for the postmodern scholar, has always been inseparable from shopping, sometimes called collecting. Florence might be seen as an open-air mall, with hundreds of shops and art sites, alternating art (which no one can afford) and fashion (which we can buy). Do we see the Ponte Vecchio and history or the glitter of gold in the many jewelry displays on that old covered bridge? Or are these inextricable, with tourism as historical, meaningful shopping? That the Kremlin is located just opposite the world's largest covered mall, the GUM department store, is ironic for the USSR, its political system failing in consumption. GUM has few items to buy, and those available are massively repetitious, sold in stalls as at a county fair. In addition, there are stores where only tourists can shop, revealing a double shopping standard. The relation between the conclusion of the Cold War and international shopping is perhaps not as trivial as it might seem. When the loftier "economics" or "conditions of production" are the terms, the focus is usually on the corporation or the plant, until recently a male preserve. Shopping shifts the issue to the intrepid consumer, who is often a female. Military purchases can also be thought of as shopping; if women were the buyers for the military, expenditures would be drastically reduced.

In an extended study, Rosnow and Gary Alan Fine extended gossip to politics, distinguishing between rumor and gossip by arguing that rumor is extended over time, and has results (Watergate, Irangate, Gary Hart, Jim Bakker), while gossips merely vanishes.[16] Perhaps like electronic artifacts, with no material base until transmitted, gossip is equally ephemeral, a commodity with no tangible base, a medium of aftereffects. At the same time, gossip is predicated on corporality (like the Watergate break-in), which is as real, perhaps, as anything gets. Like other scholars, Rosnow and Fine distinguish between good and bad gossip. While anthropologists endorse the normative power of gossip—its socialization function as a means of containment—Spacks challenges this stance, from women's points of view, arguing gossip as potential resistance to dominant or official culture.

Sally Yerkovich, who has the insight of someone familiar with the experience of gossiping, argues that congeniality, interaction, and familiarity of the participants are critical ingredients for the pleasures of gossip.[17] Participants must know enough about the people involved to experience the "thrill of revelation" (196). This explains the repetition of mediated gossip which, over time, familiarizes us with the gossiped-about. While television promises the "thrill of revelation," interaction and personal familiarity are re-created via direct address. For Yerkovich, gossip is a ritual and a contract, with its own rules of the game. For example, before gossiping, participants usually exchange biographies, suggesting that gossiping about enables us to identify people to gossip with—gossip as a warm-up for friendship and intimacy. Yerkovich emphasizes mutual recognition of a group of names, pointing out that rarely are relatives or close personal friends the object. The transaction identifies passive and active gossipers with a mutual interest in gossiping, assigning players "gossip reputations."

Most TV talk shows begin with chitchat, pleasantries, and capsule biographies, warming up before the meatier topics, which rarely emerge yet are promised. The *Today Show* used to announce its topics for the next week, then the next day, then the next hour; Katie Couric now gleefully enthuses about the next minute. Soon the program will consist of only promos and promises. Like airports and TV, gossip involves expectation, anticipation as much as the payoff. Joan Rivers proclaims her gossip reputation. Her presumption is that everyone else really wants to know about sex and that she is the consummate questioner. She promises the ultimate, the public telling of a private secret. Joan cajoles guests by pretending that millions are not watching, feigning the behavior of private gossip, a standing joke of repudiation. Rarely are the contents of secrets revealed—the play (anticipation/expection) is on the *form* more than the content of secrets.

As Yerkovich cannily points out, the presence of a Gossip will inhibit gossip—the participants fearing that they will in turn be gossiped about. This prohibition seems to work the other way for celebrity gossip and on daytime television—with guests, particularly those who are not celebrities, eager to reveal the most extraordinary and intimate things. Like virtually every critic, Yerkovich also polarizes gossip, ranking participants as congenial or benign gossipers and unwitting or knowing troublemakers who can inhibit the gossip. Although she doesn't gender the players, I would argue that men are viewed as benign, while women are frequently granted troublemaker status—like D. W. Griffith's portrayal of the malicious gossiper Martha Perkins in *Way Down East*, or the roving gangs of old spinster gossips in his Biograph films. Old, unattractive, and unmarried women attack sweet young things with gossip.[18] "Once the situation is defined as having appropriate personnel, the gossiping may begin" (195). Like daily syndicated programs, gossiping builds up over time, with later conversations "developing the initial characterization" (196). TV hosts, like guests, have reputations and develop the gossip terrain, over time.

In a number-crunching analysis of newspaper columns, Jack Levin and Allan J. Kimmel, like virtually every other scholar, assert that "informal gossip often has a moral or normative orientation."[19] That gossip mediates against change, that it exists in the present as a containment but one which promises the new, is a central contradiction, one in line with other entertainment machines of containment such as cinema and television. This study covered the period 1954–1975, spanning the time of the two critical Supreme Count decisions. In order to qualify as a gossip column, the material had to "focus on the personal lives of well-known individuals" (170). From the 1950s, the authors examined the columns of Earl Wilson, Dorothy Kilgallen, Ed Sullivan, Walter Winchell, Louella Parsons, and Hedda Hopper, for example. From the 1970s, they studied Marilyn Beck, Earl Wilson, and Suzy.

The results of the quantitative analysis revealed that 60 percent of the gossiped-about were men, 90 percent were white, and 68 percent were stars or celebrity show people. However, a reduction from the '50s to the

'70s did occur in the show people category, a slippage matched by an increase in politicians, which jumped from 2 to 8 percent to 14 percent in the '70s. Over one-half of the gossip was concerned with occupational roles rather than private lives—a critical distinction which forms the basis for *Entertainment Tonight*, a line which it constantly crosses, suggesting the elisions of the distinction work-leisure, as well as public-private. Romance accounted for 22 percent of all gossip in the 1950s, declining to 19 percent in the '70s—shifts accompanying social variations. The resurrection of romance, including weddings, engagements, and couples dating, as late 1980s/1990s gossip, is symptomatic of the revival of marriage and heterosexual familialism as a leisure pursuit.

During over a decade's resistance in the '60s and '70s to institutions of the family, Levin and Kimmel discovered that "almost one-half of all gossip was centrally concerned with the prescription or proscription of some behavior or attitude" (173), with normative gossip increasing from 42 percent to 60 percent. Gossip did function as a medium of containment, with columns shifting from description to evaluation and including mainly socially approved behavior. Disapproved activities were usually minor "infractions of everyday rules" rather than criminal activities. Columnists focused on "eccentricity rather than evil" (174), "small talk about small rules," heaping praise rather than criticism, and avoiding controversy. Although occupational gossip continues to increase, so it appears eccentricities have shifted to include criminal acts, with the number of gossiped-about in jail steadily on the rise. Leona awaits incarceration, while Imelda was acquitted after a lengthy U.S. trial; Jim is behind bars. Significantly, however, the gossiped-about were in the main white, male, and in show business. The rise in the number of women as gossip topics in the 1980s and 1990s might paradoxically document an increase in status, an ambivalent gain rather than a loss.

Given these statistics, and the number of male gossipers, the equation of gossip with women must indeed be an old wives' tale, or a "straw-woman" argument. In "How the 'Gossip' Became a Woman," Alexander Rysman traces the etymology of the term, as does Spacks.[20] The word moves from its origins in "godparent," "Good Sib," to "gossip," linked to small-town, rural settings. The next step is to Samuel Johnson quoting Shakespeare, and equating gossip with the female attendant at a birth. "The word acquires its unfortunate connotations only after it starts to be applied to women" (178). This study invokes Gluckman and James West's (a pseudonym for Withers) earlier report of Plainville, where Withers argued that gossip among professionals and other groups maintained solidarity and identity.

Rysman addresses sexual difference, which is at the core of gossip, illustrated by the resentment in Withers toward old women. Rysman describes a poignant scene of the two most feared old gossips in Withers's study—alone, talking only with each other, and spending most of the time staring out of their respective windows. "The meaning of 'gossip' lies in its inconsistent use. The noun is a negative stereotype used against women. . . . If two people engage in the same behavior, talking too much, the woman is likely to be called a gossip, while the man will not. Ironically, a man who talks too much is often called 'an old woman' " (179). Thus, gossip embodies chronological and sexual difference. Gossip has been historically tied to a negative image of the body—old, wrinkled, and female. Originally, it meant to be a companion—a function which television serves for many viewers in collective identification with on- and off-the-air participants, including Phil and Oprah, who really care about us.

This linkage of age and women with gossip, fueled by fear, has not vanished in our culture. Old age and gossip have both been given bad names—and gendered. (This view of gossip functions contradictorily: exemplifying *and* controlling "female solidarity" and the validity of women's speech.) When gossip entered television as regular, syndicated programming, it was transformed into "news" by the hiring of young male anchors or very young and perky female anchors; gone were the older women of the gossip columns. The male anchor (and the bright young blonde) grants a patina of legitimacy to gossip, as he does to nightly news.

Taking Things Literately: Patricia Spacks

In a 1977 essay covering a literary terrain comparable to Spacks, Homer Obed Brown points to the "uncertain status" of gossip by raising the critical issue of authorship. "If it is groundless and self-constituting, it is because communities are so. It establishes an authority without an author. This ambiguity of gossip is emblematic of its riddle of narrative voice (and perhaps of language itself): who (or what) speaks (writes)?" And what is a narrator "but a web of conventions, received ideas, inventions—personal, communal, traditional."[21] Brown's "web of convention" echoes Foucault's analysis of modes of authorship as various sites, and Bakhtin's social horizons and intonation wherein the speaking subject embodies a history of "received ideas." It is gossip's "parentless drift," an unresolvable ambiguity derived from speech, that is crucial. Gossip embodies dispersion, displacement, appropriation. Thus, the search for the origin of the word in "godparent" runs contrary to the very function of gossip, like the joke, without origin, lacking proper lineage.

Patricia Spacks's intelligent, classy study of gossip as narrative in literature revives what she argues has been considered a debased form linked to women.[22] For Spacks, on the contrary, gossip is a participatory form which can create intimacy, undermine power, serve eroticism, and propel stories. Gossip is a central method of the novel which she compares to the less esteemed forms of biography and letters. The key for her valuation of gossip is granting it the sanction of "narrative, interpretations, judgement." The gossip sequence creates "rhythm," story (13). "Gossip claims other people's experience by interpreting it into story" (11). Gossip enters the realm of the pleasure of the text.

Spacks's analysis *depends* on the lack of an audience: "No spectator watches . . . no auditor listens." Serious gossip involves a dyad or a small group; real gossip is private, not public, talk. "The presence of even a single observer would change the conversation's character: no longer true gossip, only a simulacrum." To be serious, gossip must be in person and oral. Spacks, like Adrienne Rich, prefers oral culture, presumed as community. She shares Baudrillard's disdain and notion of the simulacrum as false, thus partaking of a Platonic model of the real. Against valued gossip (or the real), whose function is creating intimacy, is set idle talk (the simulacrum), wherein gossip's consequences are uncontrollable and incalculable; this is gossip of "blunted awareness" (3–4).

Moral bipolarity structures her thought: the good practice "takes place in private, at leisure, in a context of trust, usually among no more than two or three people. Such gossip . . . may use the stuff of scandal but . . . it provides a resource for the subordinated . . . a crucial form of solidarity" (5). The (romanticized) relationship the talk sustains is what is at stake more than the information. The intimacy of gossip "bears about it a faint flavor of the erotic . . . an implicit voyeurism . . . an erotics of power." "These private forms of power supplement the more public ones" (11). Thus, gossip has "subversive implications" (12). However, "subversion" (of what exactly?) is only imaginary, akin to reading a good novel. It is the pleasure of the text rather than of politics; it is the woman-behind-the-man ploy, a version of domestic power which accepts, to a degree, the efficacy of subordination, making the best of a bad thing. This tactic of valorization, called resistance, might serve to prevent women from speaking out, in public and private, directly, in order to have an effect other than vague, erotic, voyeuristic "subversion" or "resistance."

Because her argument rescues gossip for women, turning it into a good critical object, *Gossip*'s morality is postmodern, to a degree. It is also conservatively old-fashioned, like the Supreme Court, locked within print and the novelistic. *Gossip* sternly admonishes electronic and tabloid media, sanctioning gossip only in the realm of good literature and genteel, decorous daily life, staunchly defending the tasteful borders between aesthetic culture and crass/mass culture, the dominion of the private over the public sphere. *People* "imitates and debases social functions of oral gossip. . . . It corresponds rather precisely to prostitution" (67–68), an interesting, feminine metaphor, replicating the good girl/bad girl split of '50s female culture. Via the exchange of money, popular culture becomes the bad object, set against an oral culture of personal contact. The media (which appear not to include books) only parody and reduce gossip. Spacks prefers to "ignore *People* and its shady relatives" (68).

What restores gossip for Spacks is (1) its fostering of community, the personal relations which TV is always accused of replacing and denying, and (2) its linkage with respectable narrative, authorship, and good intentions, the *Masterpiece Theatre* model of the proper world. Unmoored from a complex narrative system, an elaboration of the hermeneutic code, gossip becomes suspect, authorless, and for profit: "It makes money, and often it makes money its subject" (a good definition of 1990s culture and desire which also explains the current fascination with gossip). For her, *People* parodies gossip's system of exchange; rather than being a discourse about power, gossip in this instance becomes power, paradoxically as in *Dangerous Liaisons*. Spacks prefers free gossip from the point of the subordinated, like public television. For many intellectuals, the exchange of money, rather than embodying postmodern desire, is undesirable, a very bad thing.

While invoking Bakhtin, Spacks misses his historical spirit. Bakhtin's admonition of Lucien Le Febvre could be applied to *Gossip*: "Only the serious level of thought and culture exists in his mind. . . . Le Febvre actually remains within its official framework."[23] Mediated gossip resembles Bakhtin's description of carnival, unofficial culture, sanctioned but potentially transgressive. In this regard, Spacks's analysis applies perfectly to postmodern culture: "Much gossip delights by an aesthetic of surfaces. It dwells on specific personal particulars. . . . The assumed triviality of gossip has constituted one basis for attack. . . . It might equally well supply a ground for defense. To make something out of nothing is gossip's special creativity" (15). Like postmodernism, gossip is marked by a lack of struggle, an undifferentiated kind of intelligibility, "for which nothing is closed off any longer." "Gossip's assertions exist for their own sake, referring to nothing beneath the apparent. Anyone can gossip" (16–17). Rather than deep structures demanding deconstruction by experts, gossip is an aesthetic of surfaces, perhaps leading nowhere in particular. "Gossip insists on its own frivolity" (6). What you see and hear is what you get, triggering, like Frito-Lay, a desire for more.

Perhaps as with Spacks's analogy between serious personal gossip, literature, and narrative, an electronic, postmodern comparison could be drawn between television and media gossip's devaluation or revision of narrative, favoring a performative or proairetic code over the hermeneutic, a mode of distracted rather than contemplative viewing, a "structure of attractions" rather than decipherment, where the experience and affect count more than the narrative, the ultimate commodity of classical literature and cinema, with an erotics circulating around money rather than sex. (Accompanying the shift from cinema to television might be the move from "rational thought" and sex to affect and money.) Paradoxically, TV also provides massive doses of story and drama, twenty-four hours of miniature narratives, whether labeled news or soap opera. Television, eventually including gossip, has been thoroughly narrativized, is an onslaught of story, in its own fashion.

The split between the private and the public, the concern of so many commentators on gossip and cultural critics who bemoan the depleted state of culture, is a spatial model with delimited options for women. The breakdown of borders might have a great deal to do with women escaping their confinement to domesticity. Gossip blurs the "boundaries between the personal and the widely known, it implicitly challenges the separation of realms. . . . Gossip interprets public facts in private terms" (262). Or, TV and tabloid gossip work oppositely: private secrets such as child and sexual abuse and addiction have become public issues. Or, women's issues, including rape, have become public events. The Palm Beach Kennedy scandal is a tale of power, sex, and addiction. By naming the accuser, the rape victim, the *New York Times* crossed over the private/public line. Like television's present structure of domestic receivers in private homes, which bring international accounts of UN assemblies, presidential announcements, and news of Cher in the same one-minute newsbreak, breaking into the everyday with the national trauma of Baby Jessica and Nancy Reagan's breast surgery, the realms are no longer separate.

The big difference is that "instead of fostering closeness, this kind of gossip . . . creates loneliness," which I suspect is at least partially true. Oprah, Phil, and Geraldo address loneliness by assembling surrogate audiences, involving home viewers by telephone call-ins, and mailing transcripts to viewers, creating an electronic dialogue with millions. This audience is addressed as both individual and collective, a cross between a personal conversation, group therapy, and a town meeting.

At the same time that her model represents a disregard of popular culture, Spacks also takes on serious and official literary culture as she inverts the usual values of affect versus intellect: "The value of gossip . . . is to create and intensify human connection and to enlarge self-knowledge predicated more on emotion than on thought" (18–19). Here, *Gossip*'s theory of "emotional speculation" (3), with a chapter, "How It Feels," hooks up with the affective concerns of MacCannell and Grossberg, along with self-help therapies and feelings, which I will postpone. For now, suffice it to say that Oprah and Phil are representatives of current therapies designed to "enlarge self-knowledge predicated more on emotion than thought."

A Cry in the Dark

A Cry in the Dark, a 1988 film directed by Fred Shepisi, portrays Spacks's negative assessment of tabloid gossip. It was based on the "true story" of Lindy Chamberlain, an Australian housewife accused, found guilty, and then acquitted of murdering her baby daughter, Azaria. Lindy is played in a black wig and with Australian inflection by Meryl Streep. The incident, hearings, and trials surrounding this Seventh-Day Adventist family (which includes two boys) and the events that occurred during their vacation, a camping trip at Uluru (Ayers Rock), became a national spectacle and scandal, with motherhood and Christian fundamentalism on trial along with Lindy's lack of emotions. The powerful film meticulously re-creates events: the visit to the mysterious, spellbinding rock formation, a tourist site surrounded by amateur photographers; the campsite evening dinner when the Chamberlain baby was snatched from the tent and killed by a dingo, a wild Australian dog; the Chamberlains' relationship and everyday life in the suburbs of Queensland; the initial and subsequent investigation and trial of Lindy; the pursuit of the press and the public; her imprisonment, the birth of her new daughter, and, at last, her release and acquittal.

The film brilliantly figures the tabloid and mainstream press as anonymous, collective harpies committed to Chamberlain's guilt no matter what the evidence to the contrary. Reporters and photographers, armed with pencils, aggressive cameras, microphones, and condescending disbelief, assault Lindy and her family. In numerous intercut scenes of anonymous citizens, in conversational settings at work, during dinners or parties, or on the street discussing the case, gossip is figured as a mean-spirited leisure activity. Private gossip becomes rumor, a figural, *collective* character, circulating anonymously, like wildfire fueled by the popular press. Rumor has a life of its own—an assemblage of many mouths. Lindy is under scrutiny, unable to escape the ruthless gaze, malevolent words, and cavalierly malicious exploitation of the press. Equally, she is the object of talk by righteously vindictive strangers. Thus, gossip and its receivers, who, participate in vengeful and insidious circulation, a nasty and malign pleasure, are portrayed as treacherous and uncontrollable. The police, in tandem with the press, including women's magazines, relentlessly pursue the Chamberlains, intent on assigning guilt. Unlike publicity and "the people," including the jury, courtroom bystanders, and groups of casual gossipers, the law, in the form of sympathetic, older male judges, supports Lindy.

The triggering event, a wild dog snatching a baby from a tent and killing it, is perfect tabloid fare, unbelievable, grotesque, shocking, an aberration of the everyday happening to ordinary people. Thus, the "people's" response of disbelief is akin to the disavowal invoked by tabloid headlines of abnormalities and strange events: an average housewife undergoes an extraordinary event; beneath calm familialism and domesticity lies horror which turns to scandal. The film, like the trial, re-creates the primal scene, making the impossible—a dingo removing a baby's clothes without shredding them—possible. This evidence, of the dingo's eating habits and the eventual location of a missing piece of baby clothing, linked to Lindy and the truth of her story, was challenged by forensics experts and laboratory scientificity, the signs of her guilt which, along with manufactured evidence that she slit her baby's throat, were ultimately proven wrong. After over five years in prison, during which time she gave birth to another baby daughter, Lindy was released.

What was on trial as much as the incredulity of the event was the truth of women's speech and Lindy's *lack* of emotions—anonymous witnesses accused her of having no feelings, of being cold, heartless, unlike a woman, particularly a mother who has lost a child. Whether excessively emotive, like Tammy Faye, or controlled and determined, like Lindy, women lose to an overriding assessment of their guilt, usually in trials of their body and affect. In the film, Streep's eyes, along with private scenes with the children, let us know that she is not impassive. In contrast to the real media blitz, we have privileged glimpses and, unlike the gossipers in the film, can take the high road in the case.

Along with an indictment of the tabloid press, other issues pertinent to contemporary culture circulate. Foremost is the Chamberlains' fundamentalist faith: Michael Chamberlain, beautifully underplayed by Sam Neill, is a minister who campaigns against smoking and doesn't drink, even speaking against alcohol at the campsite. After the tragedy, and throughout the ordeal, he proclaims faith in God's plan; arguing acceptance, he refuses accusation and anger. Gossip and rumor label the death as a ritual, a religious sacrifice, a murder. Fundamentalist faith can be frightening, another aberration.

Another issue is the economics of tourism. The film includes slides of the family vacation, a time of togetherness turned into a nightmare. Uluru, the location of the trip, is a big tourist attraction/spectacle; it was argued that the fear of dingos, labeled dingoism, would hurt tourism, an increasingly profitable industry critically dependent on family travel—quality-time vacations. Areas of many nations are economically dependent on tourism; a big and powerful lobby in northern Wisconsin is battling tribes of Native Americans over treaty rights. That tourism has to do with land rights, and therefore the rights of indigenous people, is briefly inscribed—shots of Aborigines at Uluru, a later mention of the trackers, and shots of Aborigine women in prison with and supportive of Lindy, and mothers (the press pities her husband raising two children on his own).

TV, in the form of casual, vapid talk shows and news reporters hyping the case, is also critiqued. After trying to quell rumor by granting a TV interview where she doesn't play well, Lindy refuses to emote for either the media or the jury, vowing that she "will not show them anything."

At the same time, the film is a defense of family, motherhood, and the Church, firmly grounded on the details of everyday life. After an establishing shot, the opening scene occurs in a church, with a closeup of the baby at her christening ceremony. The image of mother and child will return throughout the film, becoming a publicity poster for Lindy's defense. In the beginning, the family is secure and intact, amidst a larger Christian family, until the violence at Uluru. After this, the family and motherhood, the bedrock of civilization, it would appear, are under siege. After the trials and tribulations—including Michael's momentary loss of faith, his gradual emotional crumbling, and his being a bad and ineffective witness for his wife at the trial, while Lindy becomes stronger, more resolved, and more pregnant, and the dissolution of their relationship from tender readings of the Bible in bed to quarrels about her weight—this Christian family is restored, with a new daughter.

In the last scene, the family is standing again in church, applauded by the congregation. The strong woman of faith has kept the family intact, with the baby as the quintessential object of desire. The words printed over the freeze frame regarding the "importance of innocence to innocent people" end with legality and justice. The image in the church instates the importance of family, and motherhood, to Australian culture. Narrative and the law have quelled gossip and scandal.

VIII

Gossip Law

Prior to 1964 in the U.S., defamation, which includes libel and slander, was a matter of state law. "Damage was . . . presumed . . . from the publication of the libel itself, without any evidence to show actual harm of any kind."[24] In a series of rulings since 1964, the U.S. Supreme Court has made it increasingly difficult for public figures and private citizens to win a libel suit against a publication. The decisions, predicated on print culture, are also attempts to categorize and define new media and (inadvertently?) come to terms with modern corporate practices. As I hinted above, recent free-speech rulings (often liberal issues) are strangely in line with policies of deregulation sought by conservatives and corporations alike. The struggle, cast between the rights of free speech and the rights of reputation, is one between the audience and the individual (with the lines redrawn in the audience's favor by network television "giving the audience what it wants," along with much contemporary scholarship, also fascinated in recent years with the audience and reception, as are direct-marketers and Frito-Lay.)

A striking if not uncanny parallel between legal and theoretical discourses emerges, revealing a legal base for theory which we imagined was radically new. Ironically, while the law coincides with scholarly debates, it simultaneously mandates postmodern corporate practices of franchise culture and deregulation. For example, the change in defamation from state to national law parallels and supports the solidification of the national television network horizon-to-horizon system, the installation of point-to-point cable and satellite, the growth of syndicated programming, and the super-market expansion of the tabloid press. It would appear that issues of free speech, so dear to the left, can also benefit the expansion of capitalism.

Before I elaborate two landmark cases—*New York Times v. Sullivan* (1964) and *Gertz v. Welch* (1974, with Welch a stand-in for the John Birch Society, a right-wing organization)—I will present a brief, legally unsophisticated history of what I call gossip law, a laywoman's brazen excursion which rudely sidetracks into television theory. Under the law of defamation, there are two forms of action for defamatory publications: libel, "which originally concerned written or printed words," and slander, "which was usually oral." "Libel was criminal in its origin and . . . is a common law crime, while slander was never criminal in itself" (Prosser and Keeton, 785). They are usually separate in common-law courts, with libel as the greater wrong. Thus, the hierarchy of the printed word over the spoken word is maintained in law as it is in criticism. Libel was eventually ex-tended to include "pictures, signs, statues, motion pictures," and inappro-priate behavior such as dishonoring a valid check or following someone for a long period of time. "Libel is that which is communicated by the sense of sight, or perhaps also by touch and smell, while slander involves the sense of hearing" (786). Like modern theory, predicated on metaphors and ap-parati of vision, an ideology of vision in which "I see" means "I under-stand," the court also ranks the senses. Vision is dominant, its crimes the most offensive. Sight or seeing is imagined as more physical, more real than sound (hearing)—not surprising in law or literary theory based on print culture.

However, as life and law would have it, this is not always the case: read-ing a defamatory writing aloud is a publication of libel. In many ways, the distinction is based on the existence of a tangible object, a concrete written or recorded rather than spoken and unrecorded text. "The sound in a 'talk-ing' picture is libel, since it accompanies and is identified with the film," a material object. This stance also accords with the subservient role most film theorists and historians have assigned to sound, viewed as subordinate to the image. "Defamation by radio and television is . . . still a subject of vi-olent debate" (apparent in the caution of TV programs regarding slander-ous content), logical given the historical lag of the law along with the lower status and relative intangibility of TV—without an object until transmitted, with videotape a material base less visible than the film strip.

However, the predominance of videotape over live (and then kine-scoped) broadcasting, along with the cheap availability of cassettes and the prevalence of VCRs, gives pause to the continuing veracity of this analysis. While the courts are wildly divided, words are considered to be libel if read from a script but slander if the speaker did not use a text— again, the printed word/tangible object bias, which is historical and hence will change. The use of cue cards on late-night talk shows would presumably be libel; the host's ad-lib banter, or what there is of it, would be slander. The huge cue cards could, à la Oliver North, of course be shredded. The ugly term "defamacast" was coined in *American Broadcasting–Paramount Theaters Inc v. Simpson* (1962). Critically, it is agreed by legal experts that "television will follow radio, wherever radio may be going, rather than an analogy to motion pictures" (787). Unlike the tabloids and print (libel), TV gossip might fall into the realm of slander, not as tangible and apparent as print and libel and hence requiring additional proof of damage by the victim.

However, the economic merger of print journalism, film, and TV corporately and within the cassette phenomenon and satellite broadcasting is cause for serious reflection on any distinctions between film and television, libel and slander—formerly imagined as distinct regimes, now merging within multi-media international corporations and post-1964 gossip law. Intriguingly, the older legal determinants coincide with TV theorists who emphasize the centrality of talk to television, its corporate lineage with radio, and the inapplicability of film theory to TV.

Prior to the seventeenth century, ecclesiastical courts handled defamation, which was ruled a sin, accounting for the moral evaluation of gossip by virtually all modern scholars of gossip. By the sixteenth century, common courts had added slander, setting up a division between spiritual and temporal damage (786)—another basis for gossip ethics. Gossip has a long moral, religious history which is piously invoked by postmodern advocates and detractors alike. Defamation law arose in the seventeenth century with the advent of printing (hence its bias toward written texts), in relation to political libel, protections which were later extended to nonpolitical libel. Modern defamation is handled under tort law—which refers to general breaches of public contract, to which all people are subject, rather than crimes or breaches of contract. From the beginning of the nineteenth century until 1964, any libel, as distinct from the same charges leveled by slander, was actionable without proving any impairment to reputation or other harm. This was not the case for slander, which had to demonstrate what was called "temporal" damage (788)—proving actual damage.

However, there were exceptions which required no proof of damage and which are still operative today: (1) charging a criminal offense or (2) a "loathsome disease," and (3) charges effecting business, trade, or profession (788–93). Modern statutes and rulings added a fourth category as an exception: the imputation of unchastity to a woman (33, 793). For men, an unchastity claim was not slander, more a fact of life or badge of honor. For fear of discrimination in this legal double standard, the latter claim has been modified to include sexual misconduct by members of either sex, a change perhaps accounting for the revelation of sexual misconduct followed by the quick demise of Gary Hart's presidential campaign. The loathsome disease protection came from a fear of social ostracism—with slander again becoming a prevalent fear in the era of AIDS, hence all the debates over testing and the confidentiality of results. Formerly the category applied to venereal diseases such as syphilis, or leprosy and insanity, which were regarded as permanent or incurable, unlike other contagious diseases like tuberculosis or smallpox (790). Today, insanity, like syphilis, is not included because it is no longer viewed as permanent and incurable. Thus, slander is historical. In 1990, women's rapid weight gain is more slanderous than unchastity or addiction and, for Liz Taylor and other female celebrities, worse than insanity. It would appear that, as with age, there is a double standard of weight.

Regarding the protection of a trade or profession, the charge must be directly related to business: to accuse a doctor of consorting with prostitutes would not apply; to accuse a surgeon of being a butcher or a chauffeur of being a drunk would apply (791). "The effect of a charge that the plaintiff is insolvent, illiterate, a coward, or has been seen drunk, may depend upon whether he is a merchant, a professor, a soldier, or a clergyman" (792). (Apparent as well is that drunkenness is seen as unseemly behavior rather than as an addictive disease.) Unchastity was originally regarded as a "spiritual" matter—a sin and not actionable without proof of damage—the loss of a marriage. This was changed in England in 1891 by the Slander of Women Act. With these four exceptions, "all other slanderous words . . . are actionable only upon proof of 'special' damage" (793)—proof which must be *economically* demonstrated.

What one legal scholar calls "the libel revolution" was initiated in 1964 by *New York Times v. Sullivan* (1). The Supreme Court overturned the defamation ruling of a lower court (along with a long history of legal precedence) by adding the stipulation of intent, what is called "actual malice": "a publisher must actually know that statements are false before publishing or act with such recklessness and indifference to the truth . . . that misconduct can be inferred" (1). This doctrine is known as the *"New York Times* rule" and applies to public figures and officials. For private citizens, "actual malice" was not required to prove libel. Because the stricture of actual malice applies mainly to public figures, a series of subsequent cases have, like Linnaeus, relabeled humanity and expanded the public categorization—not unpredictable due to the proliferation of media tabloids and the expansion of TV talk-show programming. Individuals who have "voluntarily injected themselves into a public controversy" are ignobly taxonomized as "limited-purpose public figures." This legal precedent which turns private citizens into public figures without grounds for libel damages is a strong explanation for the profitable increase in media gossip, particularly tabloid magazines and syndicated TV programs. In an uncanny way, these rulings have mandated Warhol's decree about fifteen-minute celebrity, turning it into law, along with erasing the divide between private and public spaces, personae, and actions.

The second landmark case which continued the drastic alteration of well over 150 years of legal precedent was *Gertz v. Welch* (1974). Here the Supreme Court confirmed that the plaintiff, Gertz, was a private citizen; however, the Court "rejected liability without proof of fault. . . . Mere defamatory publication and falsity were found insufficient" (5) grounds—even for private citizens. *Gertz* abrogated the presumed damage rule when a publication "is made through a public medium and honestly" (796). Following the precedent of the *New York Times* rule and its invocation of First Amendment/freedom of speech rights, the Supreme Court held that the First Amendment does not permit recovery of presumed or punitive damages unless the plaintiff establishes clearly that the defendant "had knowledge of the falsity or acted in reckless disregard of the truth of the defamatory matter published" (796).

An interesting sidelight of *Gertz* was the Court's distinction between fact and opinion: "only statements of fact as opposed to statements of opinion could be considered defamatory" (5), which further opened the legal doors for mediated innuendo (along with providing legal grounds for Baudrillard). (The Court importantly argued that there could be "no such thing as a false idea.") This distinction—between fact and opinion, news and editorial, truth and interpretation, or real and re-creation/simulation—is at the very base of TV news logic (which includes demarcated editorials authored by retired anchormen, wise sages presumably above the fray of facts with lofty analysis; the declaration of personal but informed "opinion" cleverly designates the rest of the news as fact, hence authorless, the anchor merely a channel through which facts pass). The truth of TV news is dependent on a Platonic belief in its factually based reality, like the writings of Baudrillard, who shares anchors' commitment to referents and realism (albeit dystopically for Baudrillard in the case of TV).

Like origin, truth, and realism, authorship circulates in these two benchmark cases as a key point: in *New York Times*, "actual malice" involves intent; in *Gertz*, fact versus opinion concerns enunciation and address. It would appear that for both the law and academia, the most troubling aspects of modern media are the lack of clearly defined object status (the tangible commodity as a product) and the dilemma of discerning authorship. Or, argued positively, the law charts the move from a culture of single, precious, ontological objects created by individual authors or artists to a culture of multiply mediated artifacts created by diverse and dispersed systems of authorship, moving from paper/print to electronics, from single to collective authorship.

To reiterate contemporary law, at least through 1990: The *New York Times* case established that a publisher must know that statements are false or act with indifference as to truth or falsity. The rule was then extended from public officials to a category called public figures or "limited-purpose public figures." Both required not only proof of a defamatory statement but proof of actual malice. The arguments for these decisions involved (1) free speech, (2) the presumed tendency toward media self-censorship without these legal guarantees, and (3) the ability of public officials or figures to answer the charges—a burden assumed when they enter the public arena (2–3). Contrary to these arguments is the right to protection of the private reputation or personality. However, even for private citizens such as Gertz, "the Court rejected liability without proof of fault. . . . Mere defamatory publication and falsity were found insufficient" (5). While the *New York Times* requirement of actual malice was not forced on Gertz, he was still required to prove negligence in some form. And even if negligence occurred, actual damages as opposed to presumed damages to reputation remain to be proven. Gertz argued that if libel law remained "wide open," there would be "bankrupting judgments against the media," and "consequently self-censorship to avoid economic disaster" (16). According to legal scholars, "a constitutional privilege to defame others has been extended to the media—it is not clear whether that same privilege extends to all persons" (796).

The legal logic—which has severed the Fordist border between public and private and challenged both form and content of secrecy—overtly a free (or deregulated) speech issue of the modern era, also harks back to older law and culture. To a degree, the logic enacts a tautology that serves business ("the press and broadcasting" [796]) rather than individuals: the increase of venues (syndicated programming, tabloids, magazines) enabled by the 1964 decision voraciously demands more people as topics, information sites, or problems, transforming private citizens into public performers, which the law then mandates has deprived them of their right to claim defamation. Arguing First Amendment rights of the free flow of information (also derived from a different historical period, and initially there to protect "free and unrestricted criticism of government" [1]), the law provides old or realistic legal grounds for current or postmodern defamation, suggesting that perhaps content, like form, does matter. (The law which protected individuals from government now protects businesses from individuals.) In effect, although with countervailing loopholes, the law, in tandem with the deregulation and expansion of corporate media, has sanctified the transformation of formerly private conversations into public social problems, turning the personal, the intimate, the confidential, and the shocking into mediated gossip and public scandal or political issue. Private, individual conversation and behavior have become public group therapy and event.

The second coming of the gossip trade—which hit big in the 1970s, with a TV surge in the mid-1980s coincident with the national hookup of cable wiring and satellite launchings, which created channels and markets for syndicated programming—can be explained by the legal superstructure guaranteeing the rights of the press, ensuring the free flow of public information at the cost of the protection of private reputation. After all, the airwaves belong to the people. In fact, reputations gradually became a major topic of television, with tabloid gossip functioning as a joke for late-night comics and situation comedy, along with making regular, serious appearances on the nightly news. It would seem that Generoso Pope, the founder of the *National Enquirer*, and Rupert Murdoch, the Australian media baron/ press lord—objects of journalists' derision and primetime attack on, for example, *60 Minutes*—have had the last and profitable laugh.

At the same time, increasing numbers of suits were filed against Pope and other publishers—paradoxical given the new and bad legal odds. And while the jury awards were huge, albeit rare, they were peanuts compared to tabloid profits. Several cases were won on the grounds of "actual malice," publishing with "serious doubt as to the truth of his publication" (19). In a suit by Johnny Carson against the *National Insider*, the court found sheer fabrication of the charge that he moved the *Tonight Show* to California in order to be near the "woman who broke up his marriage" (20).

The Carol Burnett case—hailed by entertainers, who viewed Burnett as a noble heroine—was similar. The story that Burnett was drunk and boisterous in a restaurant, offering fellow patrons bites of her dessert and haranguing Henry Kissinger, was proven to be fabrication and triggered eight other suits. "The paper ran a brief retraction but failed to get [Burnett's] suit dismissed when two restaurant employees swore affidavits saying they had told the paper before publication that the story was not true."[25] In this case, a reporter who had verified the report had insisted that it was inaccurate.[26] The California courts awarded Burnett $1.6 million in 1981. This was the first libel action against the *National Enquirer* to be tried since Pope bought the paper in 1952.[27] The *Enquirer* cleverly retorted that Carol Burnett was the "first person to be adjudicated 'not the life of the party.' "

Other cases involved Rory Calhoun, after an item reporting that he had cancer cost him TV roles; Paul Lynde, regarding his outrageous behavior on *Hollywood Squares*; and Shirley Jones regarding drunkenness. The *National Enquirer* countered with its procedure which (1) required reporters to tape-record interviews and (2) spent $2 million to verify articles (practices instantiated only in 1976, after a searing story on *60 Minutes*). It was revealed during the trials that the tabloid paid thousands for tips.[28]

As I have repeatedly stated, what is at stake is a contest between the rights of free speech and personal reputation, which, as the oldest court have decreed, can be temporal or spiritual. The few victories notwithstanding, recent decisions illustrate that personal reputation is declining as a valuable or necessary asset—or, that what constitutes reputation has radically changed. At the same time, the Court has mandated against the value of secrecy, enabling the transformation of private shame, like addiction, into public claim and testimony. I will return to secrecy later. For now, the struggle can be cast as the rights of the private individual, or the performer, versus the public audience—with the audience winning. This claim is in line with the TV networks' defense, argued since the quiz show scandals of the 1950s and mandated by the economics and "democracy" of the ratings, of "giving the people what they want."[29] However, as Eileen Meehan has demonstrated in her history and analysis of the ratings, just exactly who "the people" are is skewed and illusory—with the same class-biased ratings being sold through newer scientificity and technology to competing interests—the advertiser and network.[30]

The legal, formerly ecclesiastical and moral difference between slander and libel provides the basis for gossip scholars' distinctions between good (private and oral) and bad (public and written/televised) gossip. While general publication permits juries to "assume that there has been harm to reputation" which might deserve compensatory damages, "it is not so obvious that any impairment of reputation will . . . result from the publication of libel privately to one or more persons who may or may not believe the statement" (797). Thus, defamation must be communicated, what the courts call "publication"; if words, they must be overheard. Nor is it sufficient that they were mailed, or were contained in an unsealed letter, unless it can be proven that a third person read them. So much for the blackmailing *form* of secrecy—the proof is in telling, in the *content*. Furthermore, "it must be shown that the utterance was understood" as defamatory, including the comprehension of foreign words" (798). Thus, the courts have charted an interpretive theory of reception, one version of reader-response criticism (the opposite of Lacan's analysis of Poe's "The Purloined Letter").

In addition, the courts have debated exactly what constitutes a "publication," a haggling which overlaps with issues of authorship and media definitions predicated on ontology. Given the law's historical perch on the printed or personally spoken word (a bias reiterated and sanctioned by gossip scholars), and an older culture of in-person encounters and transactions, and what Raymond Williams calls discrete events opposed to television's indiscrete "flow," along with single-authored books, one can imagine the quandary the courts, like TV scholars, are in regarding television's very definition in an era of cable, satellite broadcasting, and international syndication, to say nothing of the dilemmas caused by TV's penchant for repetition, reruns, and anonymous, collective authors/producers—defining traits of television production which resemble the collective authorship and circulation of jokes.

For the courts, "every repetition of a defamation is a publication itself, even though the repeater states the source . . . or makes it clear that he does not . . . believe the imputation" (799). "Every sale" of "each single copy of a newspaper" constitutes a publication. However, "the majority of U.S. courts" treat an edition as one publication (800). "There may be several publishers of defamatory matter contained in a book or magazine, or broadcast over radio and television. The author of a book is a publisher; so is the book publisher" (803). The same holds true for a columnist and the newspaper, a reporter and the television station. The latter half of the dyad is considered a primary publisher and is subject to liability.

Secondary publishers are those who supply equipment, like the telephone company and, one would presume, cable and satellite transmitters, although this is up for legal grabs. Disseminators are distinguished from primary publishers. Whether held as primary or not, TV stations will most likely not be held responsible unless malice is proved. These niggling but pertinent distinctions raise other issues: whether television is a product (owning programs/series as commodities) or a service (a system of distribution and reception) or both; and questions of authorship and ownership. While the recent struggle between the Hollywood studios and the networks, a dispute involving the FCC and Congress, has resulted in a significant change, because TV has been historically defined as a service until very recently, few programs other than news and soap operas are network-owned (accounting for the increase in primetime magazine/news shows, owned by the networks and anchored by star reporters in a time of dwindling network shares). Furthermore, authors of programs were, until recently, rarely the owners, with several key exceptions, for example, Lucille Ball and Desi Arnaz, (stars, not writers) or Stephen Cannell and Steven Bochco. (Author-producers often own their TV series.) The legal trajectory parallels Jane Gaines's argument regarding the switch from copyright law to trademark law, with a change in the latter from protecting the customer or consumer—a guarantee of quality—to protecting corporate ownership of property.[31]

Other avenues of the law complicate this amateur's portrait. One is the right of privacy, turn-of-the-century laws which can overlap with defamation: defamation involves harm, while privacy hurts sensibilities (159). Privacy law involves appropriating an image without consent. One kind of privacy claim "arises in cases where facts of a highly personal nature are publicly revealed. As the alleged events actually occurred and there is no question as to the truth of the statements made, there can be no suit for defamation where truth is a complete defense" (175). The "embarrassing fact" doctrine poses the question of when privacy ends and history begins, addressing the distinction between biography and gossip (178). An aspect of privacy law or invasion is the claim that one has placed a party in a false light, an old-fashioned term labeled "false light privacy invasion": "Falsity is required and truth negates the charge" (181).

To make things even more complex, there also exists a right of publicity—the "right to protect what may be a valuable property right in one's name and likeness" (189). Thus, a Jackie Onassis lookalike lost in court (193). This right to the personal exploitation of one's identity can last after death, when self-image becomes an estate, as with Elvis. Tennessee passed a statute to protect the "holder of rights in post-mortem publicity" (195), thereby enabling Priscilla Presley as guardian to capitalize on her dead former husband's past, including turning Graceland into a tourist mecca and gift shop, producing a 1990 television series about the young Elvis which transformed gossip into story, and issuing an Elvis credit card. The rights of privacy and publicity both concern identity or likeness as property (189); as Liz Taylor argues, she is her own most valuable commodity. Previously, this applied to sight more than sound. Cases such as Bette Midler's recent claim for the identity of her voice are changing this bias.

Increasingly, gossiped-abouts, made famous by media coverage, are selling the rights of their lives, their likenesses and stories, to television. Celebrity becomes character, gossip events become narrative, made-for-TV movies, as TV devours its own production, or capitalizes on the publicity it generates. In a strange way, TV pays for what it created in the first place. I will return to these issues with the Bakker scandal.

IX

✦

Gossip and the Market

Women and the *National Enquirer*

Generoso (Gene) Pope, formerly editor of an Italian-language paper in New York, bought the *National Enquirer* in 1952 after noticing "how accidents drew crowds."[32] A few years later, Andy Warhol evinced a comparable fascination with death and disaster in his car crash series of the 1960s; another of Warhol's gruesome images of sensationalism was the electric chair (unveiling the modern and recent privacy of the execution hidden from view, unlike the formerly public spectacle of the quartering so dramatically reenacted in the opening of *Discipline and Punish*).[33] In fact, sensation and popular culture were topics for tabloids and artists alike (via pop art) in this period, with Warhol eventually founding a celebrity/gossip magazine, *Interview*. And like Pope, "Warhol was always more interested, I think, in the production and consumption of *individualism*—the ideological commodity of personalities, stars, celebrities, and fans."[34] In a clear reciprocity, using comparable techniques of mass production for his silkscreens of Elvis, Marilyn, Liz, and Jackie, Warhol set (or copied) the agenda for (of) the tabloids.

Famous 1962 *Enquirer* headlines are typical of the tabloid's content in the "gory" days of "cannibalism, sadism," and perversion (topics which recall film theorists' analyses of Hitchcock films or the film spectator): "Mom Boiled Her Baby and Ate Her," or "I Cut Out Her Heart and Stomped on

It."[35] These abnormalities and aberrations—shocking incredulities related as snappy headlines in the yellow journalism, matter-of-fact, carny-barker style which capitalizes on *and* defuses the gore and the reality—form our dominant images of the tabloids in the 1990s. However, while still featuring undecorous grotesqueries which were reported somewhere in Denmark—eliciting disavowal, disbelief, and amazed laughter (the slip into the unconscious of disavowal is compatible with Freud's model of a joke)[36]—a critical transformation has occurred, albeit usually unremarked. The tabloids have gone semilegit, with a profiteering twist that is addressed to women.

In 1968, four years after *New York Times v. Sullivan* (and coincident with the public emergence of the women's movement), Pope revamped the paper's content and instigated a new and economically brilliant strategy of distribution and sales.[37] The stories changed to a popular-culture/working-class respectability, a scatter-shot combination of the occult, the quasi and real scientific/medical, and gossip by and about media celebrities, primarily TV and film stars. The violent sex, horror, and bloody SF were dropped in favor of age, weight, alcoholism, and divorce—women's issues which have become topics of daytime talk shows and self-help books in the 1980s and 1990s. Along with the altered contents, the *Enquirer* moved from the male sites of newsstands and tobacco shops into supermarkets, women's domain of domestic shopping and familial consumption. The price rose from five to twenty (recently seventy-five climbing to ninety-five in July 1991) cents as the enunciation shifted gears and addressed women.[38] If readership counts, the *National Enquirer* could be labeled a woman's magazine.

For me the issue of reception, or readership, is both critical and paradoxical. While the audience of the tabloids is made up primarily of white women, including working-class or unemployed women, women's issues and the domestic sphere are depicted as grotesque, abnormal. Women, and their bodies, are the aberration, the scandal, a conservative echo of the liberal women's movement. (For Geraldo in the 1990s, *feminism* is an outrageous position.) And, while enunciation capitalizes on a female readership, the top dogs, along with the "conditions of production," are male, with reporters and editors often from England, Scotland, and Australia, countries with recent heady histories of sensational journalism. Media manipulative theory would assess that women are cultural dopes, with the rags as bad-faith, cynical objects. However, the cross-pollination between the tabloids and art, the influence of tabloid content on mainstream media, the revival of Bakhtin's writings in the academy, particularly the grotesque versus the classical body, along with the female readership, suggest that the tabloid phenomenon is more (and less) than initially meets the disparaging eye.

Along with rearranging the borders between scandal and the everyday, catastrophe and normalcy, reconfiguring private spaces and the public spheres, the tabloids' focus on the female body as a problem which needs a cure has crossed over into legit culture. Indeed, the contours of the body have changed, as Roseanne Barr's and Bette Midler's stardom suggest. Formerly domestic or women's issues such as daycare, drug addiction, and child abuse have become public issue and policy—for both Democrats and Republicans. The women's movement identified women's issues as liberal or radical; the tabloids addressed women and domesticity *as* a fundamentalist problem. Both attacked Western, Platonic logic and its institutions—medicine, law, and science. Both—one from the left, the other from the right—precipitated the crossover of women's issues into the public sphere.

Accompanying the tabloids' focus on the *middle-aged* female body has been a revision of domesticity (and romance). Rather than being a soothing, calm respite from the turmoil and travail of the public sphere, the domestic, or the private, has become a fount of trouble, conflict, anguish, and crime. This formerly imagined Taylorist space of respite from work and free time can be foul, traumatic. Like *Murder, She Wrote,* the tabloids often portray an archaic violence beneath the veneer of domesticity and publicity; the private unconscious has gone massively public. At the same time, the tabloids are quintessential cogs in the tired publicity machinery of what Guattari calls an "unrepentant familialism,"[39] which fragments issues and people into innuendo and rumor. In their focus on TV performers and programs, the tabloids brazenly proclaim what cultural studies scholars are so laboriously arguing: that television has permuted and rearranged daily, political, and economic life. Habermas's famous description of the noble "public sphere" as distinguished from state apparati, market economics, and private domains is an idealistic imaginary, dissolved by the publicity/celebrity machine. Rather than Habermas's formulation of the public sphere in which private citizens spoke about public issues, the inverse is true: public figures detailing private issues, transforming them into public events and policies.

Pope's journalistic makeover and chain-store, franchise distribution were wildly profitable, paralleling and taking advantage of the growth of regional and national supermarket chains which were rapidly replacing corner mom-and-pop grocery stores. Along with content and address pitched to women, Pope's inventive distribution system, involving infighting and payoffs for shelf or display space, is one key to the tabloid's analysis and to its profits. Percentages of sales are given to the retailer and the distributor, along with an allowance to salespersons for each "retail display."[40] "Among the thousands of items sold by a modern supermarket, *TV Guide* and the *Enquirer* are consistently among the ten most profitable" (78), with the *Enquirer* second only to *TV Guide.* These are fascinating figures.

Pope's marketing maneuver, a piggyback tactic of distribution, spawned imitators and competitors who copied his system along with his rude, noisy format and eye-grabbing headlines of the unbelievable—the horrific, personal catastrophe, scandal, and gossip pitched to women. At the height of the "grisly period," "circulation stalled at about 1,000,000." After the re-vamping, by 1972, it had climbed to 2,600,000, with approximately 1,000 new racks installed per week.[41] By 1978, circulation figures had climbed to 5.7 million copies, challenged by Rupert Murdoch's *Star* (begun in 1974 as a direct attack on Pope's territory), which had a 3.3 million circulation. The *Globe* has always been a distant third, with circulation of 1.7 million. In 1978, the *Enquirer* cleared $15 million, the same as the *New York Times* on four times more expenditure.[42]

On the increasingly crowded magazine racks near checkout counters, gossip is an everyday, packaged commodity like soap, cereal, toilet paper, or soda pop. The tabloids have become a welcome distraction from the ir-ritation of waiting in endless lines in giant warehouse supermarkets. Gro-cery shoppers peruse or comment on the headlines, with a kitsch chicness, embarrassment at reading such low-level news, or a serious interest. For the tabloids, the familial context of sales and standing-in-line reading and reception has everything to do with the change in content: miracle diets, celebrity gossip (particularly disease, divorce, addiction, *bad* fashion, and *lack* of taste), astrology predictions, cures for aging, UFO citings, foolish government expenditure, along with strange babies and psychics, crowd the flimsy, tacky, garish pages. "The supermarket managers don't want us to upset their patrons," said Tony Miles, executive publisher of *Globe* Com-munications.[43]

On original-cast episodes of *Designing Women,* Charlene, who takes the tabloids seriously to literally, frequently begins episodes by citing the latest tidbit making the tabloid rounds—a recent sighting of Elvis, for example. Gossip is both joke and sign of Charlene's relatively uneducated status, her history as small-town working- rather than middle-class. The other women, from middle- to upper-class backgrounds, respond with degrees of disavowal or condescension. This spectrum is directly related to class/ education, which correlates with feminist awareness. To complicate biolog-ical or social determinism, of the two sisters, Julia and Suzanne, one is a radical feminist, the other a beauty queen and southern belle. Their diver-gent popular culture takes were portrayed during their trip to Graceland. Charlene is a big fan of Elvis, as, it turns out, are the other women, with varying degrees of serious to flip fandom. On another episode, all the women fondly remember Lucy's exploits and the friendship between Lucy and Ethel, pulling a Lucy-like caper against a sexist photographer. Charlene's many references to "I Love Lucy" pay homage to the artistry of Lucille Ball and the series. This situation comedy about southern women and female friendship—more important than male desire or dates— addresses a range of women's issues, both tabloid topics and feminist pol-itics, complicating any notion of popular culture as a monolithic sameness. The women also represent various stages of middle age and weight, with a

1989 episode devoted to Suzanne's weight gain, which was simultaneously a hot topic of the tabloids. Julia is a fiery feminist activist, becoming involved in political disputes and current affairs, with episodes devoted to AIDS, racism, and sexism. Suzanne lives her past as a reigning beauty queen.

While men and dates are often topics on episodes, and sometimes men are guest stars, it's the women's friendship and comedy, centered on their workplace, that counts. The rivalry and power ploys are among women—not between women competing for men. These women care for each other and dress for themselves rather than for male approval. Suzanne is a funny throwback to the dinosaur era when male desire was the measure of women. Critical for sitcom, as Tara McPherson has pointed out, and in contrast to *The Golden Girls*, the characters are not frozen into a typology but can and do change, sharing the spotlight and hierarchy. Charlene lost weight, had a makeover, went to college, met an upper-class military man, was married, had a baby, and left the show in 1991.

Because episodes acknowledge tabloids, the dispute between Delta Burke and the producers, writer/producer Linda Bloodworth Thomason and her husband, was ironic, chronicled blow by blow in the tabloid press and on talk-tabloid TV. Gerald McRaney of *Major Dad* and Burke, married in "real" life, became a hot couple in 1991, as the War in the Gulf turned him into a fashionable Marine, and her weight garnered her tabloid headlines. (After the long-playing feud, Burke was fired, replaced by Julia Duffy.) Paradoxically, the publicity about the show and the stars in women's magazines runs counter to the self-sufficiency of the program's characters, as if to contain the show's feminism—featuring the actresses' heterosexual qualities and relationships by focusing on the importance of men and romance. Taken together, the series and the publicity form a contradiction between what Dean MacCannell might call onstage and backstage authenticity.

Like food products and TV channels, the tabloids have proliferated. By the 1980s, six tabloids in the U.S. reached 50 million readers per week (1). Along with Pope's and Murdoch's papers, the *Globe* also produces the *National Examiner* and the *Sun*. Another critical fact is the location of the tabloid press in the South (like *Designing Women*, which is set in Atlanta) rather than on the East Coast, addressing an older and less educated readership, along with right-wing or conservative constituencies, and located near cheaper real estate and labor. The *Enquirer*, which pays relatively high reporter salaries, is produced in Lantana, Florida. The *Globe* (with three tabloids, including the *National Examiner*) is in Boca Raton, near the *Enquirer*, with its smaller but spicier black-and-white *Weekly World News*, the market leader (9). The South is also the locale of the televangelists' TV studios, ministries, and broadcasts, with their version of scandal, doomsday catastrophe, miraculous cures, spirituality, and prophecy addressing a comparable audience with overlapping crises content. Murdoch's *Star* is located in Tarrytown, New York, rather than in Tabloid Valley.

In April 1990, the new owner of the *National Enquirer* (with circulation figures estimated at 4.1 million), the Manhattan-based G. P. Group, agreed to buy the *Star* from Murdoch for $400 million. "The *Star* will operate separately from its new sister publication. So on the surface at least the tussling tabs will still vie for the dirt on wayward celebrities and errrant aliens."[44] Thus, the tabloids' merger represents the new trend toward monopoly under the auspices of marketplace deregulation. (It's difficult to imagine the government bringing an antitrust suit against the tabloids.) As with McDonald's and Wendy's, the same will be bartered via differentiation, differences no longer derived from a locale, (the South), or a regional or working-class audience, or a peculiar entrepreneurial effort (Pope, who died in 1988), but from a respectable, anonymous East Coast publishing corporation. The use of "sister" accurately genders the "dirt" along with the audience. The G. P. Group, now based in Lantana, issued a public stock offering of 43 percent in 1991. This formerly "family owned, generous publisher" is now owned by Macfadden Holdings and Boston Ventures, who initially cut back the staff and costs because of flagging sales— 82 percent from newsstands. Macfadden also publishes the low-cost, high-profit *True Story* and *Modern Romance*. The new company will distribute the *Enquirer* in the U.K. and is planning spinoff products.[45]

The clever early entrepreneurs targeted their audience as consisting of "chiefly white women of middle age or older," with estimates of 90 percent female readership, with 85 percent of copies sold in supermarkets. "These women will not buy something that is too horrific or shocking. When the buyers were men, the emphasis was on sex, crime, and gore."[46] That the tabloids do not appeal primarily to romance, sexuality, or high fashion is significant. The *educated denial of these rags*, linked to unofficial or illegitimate rather than official, respectable culture—to TV rather than cinema, painting, or literature, to astrology rather than psychology or psychoanalysis, to weird alchemy rather than serious science, to miracle cures rather than medicine, to mysticism rather than rational thought (Fig. 10), to familial aberrations rather than weddings and romance, to alcoholism and divorce rather than fund-raising balls, and, perhaps, most critical, to the body rather than the mind—*serves* in many ways *as unwitting defense of Western, Platonic, masculine thought*. Along with sexual and chronological difference—with audiences consisting of older women—class difference might also have something to do with critics' denegation and readers' denial.

To counter Murdoch's blitz in 1974, Pope spent money on advertising, in the mid-1980s, with the sale to the G. P. Group, taking this campaign to television with the "inquiring minds want to know" blitz, which returned as Joan Rivers's slogan in 1989. The middle-classing of a degraded

Figure 10

object entered phase two, this time appealing to a female television audience. Under pressure from the *Star*, along with high-priced ads, the quality
of the tabloid was upgraded to include better paper and color. Unlike
Time and other official magazines, the tabloids don't depend on advertising (which consists largely of gimmicks like miracle weight-loss belts,
hair-loss potions, and blackhead removers), which presumably grants
them an independence which advertiser-dependent media, most magazines and television, do not have.[47] At the same time, the tabloids are
inextricable from TV culture. Initially, TV provided the content. The
exchange has become a two-way process, with tabloids stories providing
material for standup comics on late-night TV and, in the case of Gary Hart,
editorials on NBC's *Nightly News*. The tabloids broke the Hart-Rice boat
scoop photos, and reported on Roseanne Barr's illegitimate daughter—
a failed blackmail which became the content of two episodes of Oprah in
1989.

As I pointed out in Part I, TV is taking on the tabloids directly. Turner Broadcasting System, Inc., is competing for tabloid market space by installing TV monitors at checkout lines in supermarkets. Supermarket programming "will include two minutes of ads for every five minutes of news and entertainment." Rates will be expensive, comparable to network scales, and will bring in $100 million a year by 1993. The five-minute segments are timed to coincide with the four-minute waiting-in-line time, and will include "live broadcasts, upbeat music, and fast-paced news tidbits," varying content to coincide with the business time of day.

All of this location marketing is part of the new tactics of advertising. "Traditional media have lost some efficiency in terms of reaching people," says one corporate marketing exec. It enables cable broadcasters to profiteer, with this enterprise an unregulated spinoff of their cable programs.[48] It has taken over forty years, but TV reception, imagined as a public endeavor in the '30s, marketed as a domestic, private affair in the 1950s, now sees an open public space—that of tourism, shopping, and fast food. Surveillance TVs have been watching us in public for years. Now we will be able to watch TV in public—"out-of-home" or out-house TV.

Iain Calder, the editor-in-chief and president of the *Enquirer*, has worked there for twenty-four years. The structure is as follows: A group of article editors have their own staff of reporters, mainly British, who compete for story space; the more stories, the higher their salaries. The reporters agree that, except for the perennial favorite, Liz, "there is no big star today—like Jackie Kennedy, Elvis, Princess Grace; Rock Hudson and Liberace dying of AIDS provided us with exclusives. Joan Collins was big but is fading. [Or, as with Elvis or Rock Hudson, there will be more than one remake of the sensationalized life. Remakes of the real have been speeded up—with made-for-TV movies on Baby Jessica and *Challenger* coming close on the heels of the "real" TV event.] Vanna White turned out to be a flash in the pan."[49] All the tabloids pay for stories, with the *Enquirer* offering $50,000 early on for the first hard evidence of UFOs. Reporters blackmail celebrities with photos in exchange for interviews; agents are a good source of dirt about clients; celebrities identify themselves as their own "best friend" (9).

In accord with the profile of the audience, it is logical that *Reader's Digest* of the 1930s was Pope's model. It provided stories "about triumphs in adversity, breakthroughs in medicine, UFOs and nutrition." For Pope, "the most important element was that most of it was uplifting,"[50] the inspirational version of what the old yellow journalists called "gee-whiz" journalism, a term coined by Joseph Pulitzer, and "Hey Martha," which are the "sit up in bed kind" of stories (78) (Fig. 11). There is a very old-fashioned feeling about the tabloids, which recall an era when commodities were not plentiful. Another prevalent strategy is called "hit and run"— journalism which makes a story out of one fact. This fact is featured as the headline and is usually defused by the accompanying story; the uncanny

SURVIVORS OF 1936 PLANE CRASH FOUND!

Two men and a woman who survived a plane crash 52 years ago have been found alive and well on a remote South Seas island, stunned authorities report. "They are real-life Robinson Crusoes. It's an incredible story," one of their rescuers said. WORLD EXCLUSIVE REPORT, PHOTOS INSIDE!

WEEKLY WORLD

NEWS

January 31, 1989   30507   70¢

BRIDE IN CHAINS!
Hubby and landlady made her a slave, say police

Birth certificates prove their age, say doctors!

COUPLE, 70, HASN'T AGED IN 35 YEARS

HUSBAND: 'Nobody believes we were born in 1918'
WIFE: 'My friends are wrinkled — and jealous'

Seven space alien bodies found at site of UFO crash!

SURGERY NIGHTMARE!
Horrified patient is castrated by mistake!

The eeriest photo ever of a ghost!
CHILLING PIX inside

SEX CHANGE SHOCKER!
Can you guess which one's daddy?
The answer's inside

JUNK FOOD
makes you smarter, says new study

Woman killed over a $500 lottery ticket

Figure 11

is made commonplace, banal, or inspirational, as are most of the stories. When Elvis died, the *Enquirer* handed out cameras to relatives to snap the dead idol, amazed that so many loved ones complied. The winning photo was on page one. To the *Digest* formula, Pope added photographs and stories about TV and movie celebrities, consumer topics, and psychic phenomena. The relation to *TV Guide* is more than competitive; the tabloids are linked to TV culture, mass media rather than art or high culture. Dissension on the sets of top TV shows is a big item, along with new romances, boorish behavior, and the messy divorces of TV stars. Roseanne Barr fit all the categories perfectly and was a big tabloid star in 1989/1990. Oprah Winfrey's penchant for food, clothes, spirituality, and self-help qualified her for tabloid stardom as well. As I stated earlier, after the two-part Barr appearance attacking the tabloid tale of her daughter, and, as with many talk-show topics, coinciding with the publication of her autobiography and recently announced engagement, the tabloids reported a feud between Winfrey and Barr over weight. Reportedly, the newly slim Oprah had suggested that Barr needed to lose weight and could not possibly be happy and fat.[51]

"We know our average reader watches TV and she is interested in losing weight and what we try to do is fill a void in her life on a weekly basis," said Donald McLachan, a Scot who is a *Globe* associate editor. "When you get past our headlines, you find we are real down-home, like neighbors sharing gossip with neighbors in a small town, except we give more glamorous gossip than what they get at the parish door."[52] Other editors agree that the readers must never feel like they are missing something—parties, money, prestige, fashion, or cultural events—the case with much celebrity gossip that tells us about experiences from which we are excluded or commodities we cannot afford. Thus, the tabloids are very different from most newspaper gossip columns and *People*. The concern is the flawed rather than idealized body, a working-class, often older, grotesque body rather than the middle- or upper-class, classical body of glamor and high fashion. The body taken to task, or the body which is repellent and/or fascinating, is not necessarily thin, young, or beautiful. Perhaps this is a body of identity rather than envy, of sameness rather than otherness, of self rather than ideal; for many this body might be seen as acceptable and attractive.

Age and weight are recurring issues of the tabloids—often as headlines; for example, the *National Examiner*'s "How to Look 30 at 50" (Fig. 12), a theoretical capsule of chronology disavowal.[53] Today women proclaim rather than deny their real age, but they must not look it. Along with women's issues, the *Examiner* retains vestiges of the older style. The top or drop-dead headline of this edition is an experience of Freud's uncanny: "Jealous Dog Savages Young Bride at Altar." Other subsidiary stories include Liz Taylor and George Hamilton, plus a third on Diana Ross: "New Mom Will Be a Grandmom Soon," another version of not looking one's

Figure 12

age. A violent aberration, age, and TV stars involve incredulity and inspirational self-help. The inside story on looking thirty asserts "that the theory of growing old gracefully is outdated. You don't see your average 50-plus star with naturally gray hair, peering through granny glasses over a bundle of darning." Joan Collins, Jane Fonda, and Elizabeth Taylor are the role models for the self-help tips: diet, work out, dye your hair—gossip which resembles the older Hollywood fanzines. Diana Ross "refuses to consider her age an obstacle." That the tabloids focus on age might have, along with audience demographics, encouraged the growth of glossy magazines specifically addressed to older women is not an unreasonable argument.

The May 10, 1988, issue follows the same formula. The shocker story is "Mom, 54, Pregnant with Her 45th Child": the secondary item is "Amazing $3 Face Cream Takes 20 Years Off Your Age"; peripheral items include "Intimate Love Secrets Cher Shares with Her Tender Toy Boy" and "New

MOM, 54, PREGNANT WITH HER 45th CHILD

NATIONAL

Examiner 69¢

May 10, 1988   AMERICA'S FASTEST GROWING WEEKLY

Intimate love secrets Cher shares with her tender toy boy

AMAZING $3 FACE CREAM TAKES 20 YRS OFF YOUR AGE

The untold story

Is JoBeth Williams the latest victim of Poltergeist curse?

SWAGGART'S BIZARRE PLOT TO STAY IN POWER

New nude shock for Vanna

Figure 13

Nude Shock for Vanna" (Fig. 13). Women and their bodies are the aberration and the problem which can be cured. The fifty-four-year-old mom is a "washerwoman from Santiago, Chile"; the tale is an inspiration-survival piece of humble poverty and close family ties, reported amidst werewolf/vampire sightings, deformed children, psychic predictions, reports of aliens, and ads for youth formulas and diets.[54] Along with aliens, Elvis is regularly cited, recognized by his picture in the *National Examiner*. The Elvis story traveled into the mainstream press, eventually becoming a cover on *Newsweek*, accompanied by an Elvis watch. The ghost of Elvis makes regular appearances on David Letterman.

My favorite issue is an edition of the *Weekly World News*, another Pope tabloid. The stories include "Trucker in Hospital after UFO Horrors," a clash with aliens, a prehistoric lizard that ate sixteen people, the revival of a brain frozen in 1921, the prediction of a Doomsday meteor in 1990 (later, headlines on the NBC *Nightly News*), and a ninety-five-year-old "papa." However, the headlines are what make this a treasured edition: "Mom, 51,

Figure 14

Hasn't Aged since 18!" and "PHOTO INSIDE: See Tammy Faye without Makeup"—which we indeed do (figs. 14, 15, 16).[55] I will return to the ageless nightmare in the next chapter.

Idle Chatter: Syndication and Tabloid Talk

> We did some studies, Howard. We're still working on when superficiality began showing up in human nature. Nothin' in our studies gives us a clear picture as to the chain of events that must've taken place. We can only speculate. At one point, Howard, we were hunters and gatherers and then seems like, all of a sudden, we became partygoers.
>
> —Trudy, the Bag Lady

I'm confused about who the news belongs to.
... If your name's in the news, then the news
should be paying you. Because it's *your news*
and they're taking it and selling it as their
product. But then they always say that they're
helping you. ... If people didn't give the news
their news, and if everybody kept their news to
themselves, the news wouldn't have any news.

—Andy Warhol,
The Philosophy of Andy Warhol, p. 78

Entertainment Tonight is a gossip case in point—with plans in 1985 for a
magazine backed by Simon and Schuster, owned by Gulf and Western:[56]
an intriguing tautology given that its progenitor was a magazine. As *Reader's Digest* was the inspiration for the *Enquirer*, the role model was the astonishing success of *People* in the 1970s, a magazine which itself imitated a
television format and was predicated on the "now famous Stoller's Law of
Famous Covers": "young is better than old, pretty is better than ugly, TV is
better than music, music is better than movies, movies are better than
sports, anything is better than politics."[57] This assessment of what sells, a

Figure 15

virtual hierarchy of celebrity culture, by Stoller, the managing editor, re-calls the tabloids, with, however, critical differences: youth, rock and roll, and money culture.

In 1985, Patricia Ryan became the editor, adding "celebrity death" cov-ers. Best-selling issues have included the deaths of Princes Grace, Joan Riv-ers's husband, and Richard Burton (23). *People* and its imitators blur the line between television and print while also appealing to female audiences, transforming celebrity and women's "issues" into headlines. In all the magazines which followed—*Us*, edited by Jann Wenner, formerly editor of *Rolling Stone*; *ET Magazine*; and Stoller's *Picture Week*—people became gos-sip news because their images were on television; creating a television ver-sion of *People* was a logical step.

George Merlis, who created *Good Morning, America* for ABC, then created the CBS *Morning News*, was the initial executive producer of *ET*, produced by Paramount Television. The format is a series of short, interchangeable spots, "little movies, little plays," distributed by satellite to 135 markets in one hour. *ET* gained credibility by covering John Belushi's death, compet-ing with the newspapers. Paramount TV insists that they are doing "enter-tainment news"; another term is "infotainment," as ungainly as the legal coinage "defamacast." As proof of their newsworthiness, in December 1981 they hired Jim Bellows, a newspaper man from the *Los Angeles Herald Examiner*, making him managing editor. With at least a $20 million budget and "the largest staff of any show outside the network news and sports corporations (125 in LA and New York)," *ET* was, until 1983, the most ex-pensive syndicated TV program, reaching Australia and New Zealand, with a world audience of 20 million.[58] Fandom is not a sub- but rather a mass cult.

The key to *ET* is that it talks money and is part of the phenomenon it covers, a wheel in the publicity machine it seeks to explain, perpetuating rather than puncturing gossip. It treats its visits and reports as events in themselves. (While network teams of hundreds descending on a news story such as the San Francisco earthquake, Lindy Chamberlain, or Christa MacAuliffe's hometown is quite an event of logistics and technology, broadcast news rarely analyzes its presence as the star-studded spectacle it is, preferring instead to efface its transformative presence, there but as invisible wit-ness.) The thirty-minute show begins with brief reports, sometimes an ex-clusive, then a spotlight feature. Short takes such as celebrity birthdays, gossip disguised as remembrance or tribute, or still photos and brief clips link the segments. When *ET* covered the Democratic National Convention, it interviewed star anchors, exalting their super-celebrity status.

Partial *ET* imitators *A Current Affair* and *Inside Edition*, magazine-format (with "magazine concept" derived from Pat Weaver's career at NBC) half-hour syndicated series, capitalize on gossip, old and current regional crime, and consumer advocacy, and take advantage of the rights granted the media under defamation law and the recent developments in liability law. A legal paradox regarding liability is operative. In contrast to defamation law, it has been ruled that the cost of injury from defective products should be paid by industry, not the individual consumer. Scholars have argued that "the modern victim of a defamatory comment is not entirely unlike a victim of a commercial product."[59] In the main it would appear that the law protects tangible objects rather than the intangibles of our selves, our reputations, which now appear to be cheap and available.

Inside Edition, the left version of Maury Povich's *A Current Affair*, includes reports by political and consumer advocate Ralph Nader urging us to write to our reps in congress, harking back to his role in the late '60s and '70s, when consumerism was a populist movement which championed the power of ordinary citizens to strike back, transforming local issues into national events. In a convoluted sense, these syndicated programs critique the official news of their lofty counterparts, which in turn, as their ratings decline, imitate syndicated techniques by adding consumer advocacy, gossip, and leisure. CNN—Ted Turner's all-news channel—is more the progenitor of syndicated *style* than network news.

Kevin Glynn applies Pierre Bourdieu's model of popular taste to "tabloid television," gonzo journalism, "trash TV," as Povich hyped his program on promos.[60] Bakhtin's split between official or mainstream culture, the nightly news, and unofficial culture, the tabloids, along with Foucault's model of normalization in the disciplinary society (without, however, citing *Discipline and Punish*), are theories wielded to defend tabloid fare. The program "produces a nightly inventory of abnormality, an excessive display . . . of deviance" (30). "Normalization" is set against tabloid TV: "The tabloids' deviant images challenge . . . the normal in ways that straight news texts don't. . . . The normal is disfigured or defamiliarized," placing the spectator "uncomfortably, yet also pleasurably . . . between the normal and the abnormal" (31). The similarity to the *Enquirer*, along with a resemblance to catastrophe coverage and my earlier arguments, is striking.

However, Glynn's major premise is the audience—a populist celebraton of "the people" as "skeptical," "cynical," or "critical readers," terms which remain undefined and interchangeable while resonating of Peter Skloterdik's typology of cynicism. These clever "readers," "subordinates" who "take real pleasure" in stories of "breakdown" and the "abnormal," are *presumed* to be not only real but akin to the lives of viewers outside official culture. These "readers" move "skillfully and steathily through the tabloid text . . . discriminately activating some of the potential meanings . . . and ignoring or resisting others." (Ignoring might be sleeping, resisting might be cooking, while activating might be watching.) This *major* and unexamined premise of the people (their viewing habits predicated on attention, never mind analysis) as Derridean deconstructors enables Glynn's conclusion: "*A Current Affair* and other tabloid texts must be read as primary sites of rupture in the ideological fabric of bourgeois culture." Evaluation of tabloid TV as both good and political is the result. Significantly, the difference is more than meets most scholars' eyes: it is the difference between news produced by Hollywood studios and news produced by the TV networks.

"The audience" functions as a figure for the scholar's exuberance for the abnormal, *his* pleasures and deconstructions, *his* place as subordinated. However, for the academic—whose experiences are not acknowledged—pleasure might be even greater: in direct proportion to the power of seeing degraded texts through theoretical eyes, the thrill of making synaptic connections between Bakhtin and Povich, and a perverse delight I share.

Along with covering up the personal, the experiential, speaking for audiences is comparable to the networks giving the people what they want. Or, as Meaghan Morris argues, unexamined invocations of "the people" sweep aside the difference between the culture studied and the cultural student. John Caughie cautions intellectuals against the celebration of experiences we presumably are not having. Like other cultures, minorities, and now subversive television audiences, women have also been spoken for, a tactic which comes after they have been overlooked.

My third point of difference concerns repetition and style. While on the surface, "tabloid television texts . . . aren't univocal" (over time, there are significant differences among series), over the span of a series, content, like the thuddingly repetitive style, becomes uncannily predictable, hence normal. Excess, tabloid TV's defining trait, is rigorously contained by repetition. The structure or format of *A Current Affair literally* repeats the same material (1) as a promo for the next day's show, (2) as an opening trailer for the upcoming show, (3) then just prior to the spot, and (4) as the segment itself. There is little difference between promotion (trailers) and coverage (as there is little difference between the carny barker's pitch and the sideshow inside)—an extension of twenty- to thirty-second spots into a half-hour program which rarely provides the promised, additional information, explanation, or answer to the promos' enigma. The program's lack of closure, its paucity and incompleteness (not open-endedness) amidst claims of satiation and answers, is not without interest. Thus, programs return to previous stories (or repeat themselves as new), on guard, for us, piquing our interest, which is then argued as our own creation.

Thus, the series capitalize on (or cannibalize) themselves (and their limited resources) as much as on scandal and other events. They are economical (cheap) and tautological, tactics tied together by repetition, a cost-efficient style which *repetition as hype* covers up. Cynicism is more an attribute of the producers, the Povich ploy addressed to viewers, a fundamentalist preacher stance with which viewers might identify. Like carny barkers hawking the abnormal in the sideshow tent, the style advocates that if you show something enough times, and shout it loudly and abnormally enough (a repetition which might be predicated on a belief in the audience as unintelligent or distracted), "readers" will think the material is new and different. Style and structure (and a sameness repudiated by promos), along with Povich's noisy, savvy personality, are uncannily predictable and, for some, a repetition verging on boredom.

Paralleling the proliferation of media celebrities, fast-food chains, super-market products, and the tabloids, the number of TV stations and channels continued to grow in the 1980s, including a fourth network, Fox (another Murdoch enterprise), like its progenitor, Dumont, the fourth network until 1956. This expansion via cable hookups and satellite downlinks has resulted in a decline in network ratings and has created venues and demand for syndicated TV programs, some of which have become wildly profitable commodities, particularly quiz shows, *Jeopardy* and *Wheel of Fortune*, court programs, tabloid news, and daytime talk—Phil, Oprah, and Geraldo, with Oprah raking in the bucks. Like religious TV moguls, Winfrey equipped her own production facility in Chicago and branched into a short-lived (canceled) primetime series, *The Women of Brewster Place*, a weekly reprise of her earlier miniseries in which she (along with other black actresses and actors) played dumpy and middle-to-older-age rather than fashionably youthful as on her talk show. Like the owners of other syndicated programs, Winfrey's production company retains control of her work and profits. Unlike late-night talk shows, the daytime shows are not affiliated with the networks. And while syndicated programs have lower status and production costs, as daytime does in general, this may not be the case forever. Increasingly, like *Oprah*, *Jeopardy*, and the new *Monopoly*, syndicated programs have nighttime, bigger-bucks versions.

These series are distributed, sold and marketed, independently to local independent and network-affiliated stations and competitively time-shifted on local schedules, filling in the non-network blocks of daily programming, often, as in the case of *Geraldo* and *Oprah* in Milwaukee, competing with each other. There were ninety-six syndicated first-run shows at the start of the 1987-88 season, compared to eighty-eight in 1986 and twenty-five in 1980. (In 1991-92, there were only nine new programs from major producers.) Many series were produced by small companies, recently bought out or facing competition from Hollywood's biggest studios, which have been expanding rapidly into first-run syndication, companies with huge sales staffs for marketing and the bucks for development.[61] The battleground for syndication profits has been the FCC feud between the studios and the networks, with Hollywood holding its ground, signaled by Brandon Tartikoff's leaving NBC for Paramount Pictures. Rumor is that Paramount would like to buy a network, as General Electric purchased NBC in 1986. Gossip and news might then be inseparable.

The advantage to local stations includes programming for ratings and the sale of commercial time, garnering more profits than during network broadcasts. In addition to buying syndicated shows, local stations are increasingly linked to cable and satellite stations, connected by downlinks, particularly to CNN, which they selectively broadcast during early morning hours or catastrophes and upsetting events. The hold of the networks on their affiliates is gradually weakening. Previously, without a network affiliation, and without a high-frequency spectrum allocation, local independent stations made few profits. This is changing. The new deregulatory decrees by the FCC have also freed stations from local coverage and public service, enabling them to capitalize more profitably on their time sold.

International and cable deregulation have opened up markets previously regulated by the FCC in the U.S. and abroad, the lure and legal grounds of syndication, with *Oprah* playing in Japan—which amazes me. One can imagine a Samurai version of *Geraldo*. In fact, because the network decline in audience share—from 87 percent six years ago to 70 percent in 1988 and dropping in the 1990s to 60 percent (only to rise from these ashes to 70 percent again in fall '91), sometimes drastically, as in the case of Dan Rather on CBS and *Today* on NBC—has resulted in lowered profits for first-run and rerun network shows, first-run syndication has become more attractive to the big studios as the fastest-growing and potentially most profitable market.

For example, *Wheel* generates $400,000 per episode from fees paid by local stations and advertisers. *Wheel*, the electronic version of Hangman, makes "more than $100 million dollars through fees and advertising" (21), with costs of $8 million, for Merv Griffin Enterprises and King World Productions, the unit of the Coca-Cola Company/Columbia Pictures Industries that produces the show. (Assigning clear ownership amidst the rapid turnover/cross-media mergers of multinational corporations is no easy task.) "In the first quarter of 1990, King World had revenue of $168.4 million, up more than 20% from last year, chiefly because of *Wheel, Jeopardy!* and *The Oprah Winfrey Show.*"[62]

In the November (1989) ratings, *Wheel* was the number one show in syndication (14.1, each point representing 921,000 homes with televisions), followed by *Jeopardy* (12.4), with *Cosby* reruns a distant third (9.7), followed by *Winfrey* (9.6). Ratings translate into rates charged advertisers and thus mean money. And, the ratings are sold to TV stations and advertisers alike, presumably and economically speaking, competing interests. The profits from *Wheel* enabled Merv, crooner, friend of the Gabor sisters, and former talk-show host with a wicked gossip reputation, to go head to real-estate-mogul head with Donald Trump over a resort empire. His momentary victory may be souring to a Chapter 11. This may also be the fate of Trump, the victim of declining real-estate values and mind-boggling interest payments on credit, which is debt by another name. Three of Lorimar's syndicated shows, *The People's Court, Love Connection,* and *Superior Court,* "bring in annual revenues of $45 million and generate $16 million in operating income,"[63] mainly from *The People's Court*. The big players in 1990 are King World, Warner Brothers, Paramount, Columbia, Buena Vista (a subsidiary of Walt Disney Co.), MCA Inc. (the parent of Universal Studios), and Viacom. Many of these producers are heavily invested in cable

TV, film, and music production. Bigger players, including two Japanese companies, are now the corporate owners of the studios. (Amidst the corporate paucity of language, "reregulation" looms as a check to this free-market flow, increasingly monopolized by big companies, with "flow" the capitalist, international realization of Raymond Williams's analysis of the programming structure of U.S. TV.) The owners are bigger, fewer, and in flux.

(The price for sitcoms has increased drastically since 1976 when *Mary Tyler Moore* reruns sold for "$15,000 per episode. Less than a year later, the price per episode for *Happy Days* in New York was $35,000." Two years later, *Three's Company* went for $89,300, with *Cosby* topping off in New York in 1986 for $349,440 per episode.[64] These figures are declining, at least for the moment.)

Loose Talk: Oprah, Geraldo, and Phil

> I kept the TV on all the time, especially while people were telling their problems—when I got my first TV set, I stopped caring so much about having close relationships with other people.
>
> Right when I was being shot, and ever since, I knew that I was watching television. . . . I didn't know . . . that Bobby Kennedy had been shot the day after I was. . . . And then I heard the word "Kennedy" and that brought me back to the television world again.
>
> —Andy Warhol[65]

While Tabloid Valley is in the South, suggesting regional difference (with joint ownership of the *Enquirer* and the *Star* recently shifting to the East Coast, "the national" is replacing the regional, as it already has with local news and weather formats, increasingly national in scope), syndicated daytime talk is a Middle American, or Midwest, phenomenon. Phil Donahue emerged from Cincinnati, then moved to New York; Sally Jessy Raphael's show is produced in Cleveland, and Oprah Winfrey's in Chicago. Geraldo Rivera is a street-smart East Coaster, feisty more than sensitive, aggressive rather than affective, although he has his moments of intense feelings.

With the exception of the Irish-American, boyish, white Phil (although his commitment to women, emotion, liberal causes, and the expression of feelings, long before these attributes became fashionable, differentiates him from primetime anchors, known for their rationality, or late-night hosts, renowned for their wit), the three hosts diverge from the usual TV anchor: Sally is middle-aged; Oprah is African-American; Geraldo is Hispanic-American. Winfrey is, however, exceptional—personally and politically. She controls her own conditions of production *and* shares her experiences, with a canny eye on the TV audience *and* women's issues.

The format of all four one-hour programs is remarkably consistent, particularly the centrality of the audience, collectively embodying an issue, disease, or tragedy; the privileging of reception and listening; and the stardom of the host, a hybrid of MC, good conversationalist, informed citizen, emotional surrogate, therapist, and final authority, differentiated just enough to make a diference. The address and the enunciation are presumably to women, as are the audiences primarily female, with issues linked to women and the family, including deviances from and threats to this norm. The topics are a crossbreed of gossip (sensation and celebrity), group therapy (including public testimonial), and self-help. While expertise and knowledge are invoked, often in the physical form of professionals who are usually authors, the final arbiter is personal experience, including that of the host who drops in "private," confessional details. Although celebrities make regular appearances, ordinary people are valued, granted the expertise of experience.

And while rational thought—in the form of the outside expert or analyst speaking from the distanced third person of scholarship (usually hawking a new book around which the topic is arranged)—is included, first-person accounts, stagings of affect, count more than intellect or third-person analyses. The hierarchy between mind and body, between thought and feeling, is dissolved, with the latter, traditionally aligned with women, emerging as most valued. Walking or running around the mise-en-scène, mediating stage and studio audience, stopping to take questions from the live audience and listen to on-the-air telephone calls from the TV audience (with cutaways to people listening), the host can align him- or herself with any and every position—embodied as "persons" who are half-object, half-subject, both spoken about and speaking. Significantly, the hosts, unlike many of the interrupting guests, are superb listeners, letting others be heard and allowing new information to sway them.

The hosts take the new politics of pluralism and deregulation to shocking limits, sanctifying scandal and blanding the aberrant. "Female Impersonators. See Sexual Odysseys on Donahue at Four" is accompanied by a still photo of Phil. Nothing is too weird for these intelligent hosts, our role models, to take sensitively. On one of the many episodes on prostitution, the first witness claimed that she became a call girl after watching "*I Love Lucy*" and noticing that housewives were unpaid prostitutes. Another outfront "lady of the evening" provoked laughter by remembering that her first client, an insurance salesman, had the "smallest penis I have ever seen." The daytime "liberal" is full of empathy with everyone and everything. Thus, Oprah can "hear" bigots *and* understand audience rage at their remarks, all bipolarities eventually tamed and soothed by information funneled through the host's calm equanimity. Identification, particularly that of "being," is reserved for the famous, socially adept hosts who have star entrances, regular applause, and innumerable medium to close shots. These gregarious, opinionated hosts-in-the-audience make strong assertions, then modify or retract them after eliciting more information or experience from the onstage guests.

Geraldo, however, is not so cautious, often stating his own disgust (which might be feigned). On an episode devoted to doctors and sexual abuse, with a statistic of 13 percent as a scare tactic, plus an opening warning to send the children out of the room (presumably to the TVs in their bedrooms), Geraldo introduced the living topic: three guests who had been raped by an osteopath, a gynecologist, and an eye doctor. Newspaper headlines of these events preceded witnesses' testimony, accompanied by Geraldo's and the audience's *response* (the programs' main goal is to elicit strong response which, with the addition of information, must then be revised; a knee-jerk reaction is transformed into a liberal position). During the tale of the gynecologist, there are cutaways to the audience listening, watching. What are they thinking? Geraldo responds by calling the doctor "crud, slime." Then, on cue, the husband stands and is asked how he felt when the doctor touched the woman's vagina. (The audience placement is engineered; the closing segments of *Donahue* often are interviews with people who could have been onstage, suggesting a surplus of topic material.) He says something. Geraldo's moral outrage: "This is infuriating, sickening." A gasp is heard from the audience after the woman reports that her baby died. Geraldo seals our anger by reporting that the "guy" is still practicing, after thirty-one additional complaints.

Paradoxically, while involved and professing social and political preferences, often the hosts greet all positions with the same decorum or value, their performed level of personal affect and pluralism a conduit for audience response, a model of proper TV reception, which, as I stated, emphasizes listening. Pluralism, called "keeping an open mind" or "listening to both sides of the issue," is the valued virtue of the enlightened citizen, presented with a spectrum of testimonial about sex, rape, incest, handicaps, bodily disfigurations, political movements, new therapies, and addictions. After staging and provoking dissent and difference, in the end, the hosts come to a benign understanding of *all* opinions. The real scandal of Morton Downey, along with an abrasive crudity, is that he actually advocated a clearly discernible position rather than endorsing pluralism or ambivalence.

Because issues and medical abnormalities are exemplified *as* individual people, sitting up on the stage literally embodying the topic across a spectrum of difference, the involved hosts endorse humanity in all its foibles. Guests, even celebrities, represent an aspect of a problem, rarely a self with an identity beyond the topic. People are speaking evidence of a problem or a disease. Their problem defines their identity. The group topic is spread across the stage in a spectrum of bodies, for example, pro and con fat, stage left to right. If we have the ailment or dilemma, we can indulge in primary identification. Or we identify not with the person or expert but with the specific topic, usually a problem, another form of collective identification with experiences and emotions as symptoms which we might share. Or we can identify with the famous hosts. All versions involve identifying with the "real," the experiential. The fake sexual surrogate and her mate who garnered stints on *Geraldo* and *Sally* in the summer of 1987, and returned to *Sally* to be chastised after the revelation that they were actors, reveal the collapse of person-issue-truth, not Foucault's speaking eye but a speaking problem or talking symptom. Like socks and the body, daytime talk depends on generating more problems. Only on daytime talk could close friendship be a problem, not a pleasure.

With issues personalized, represented by first-person confessional bodies, pluralism takes tabloid scandal very empathetically indeed, granting it the truth of experience, the truth of ordinary personness, thereby transforming scandal into the urgency of the everyday. To disagree is to discount a person with a problem. Dissent is also the sign of enlightenment.

That the onstage problems are surrounded by an audience (or plants) composed of those familiar with or suffering from the problem suggests that the dilemma is more widespread, of greater import, than we initially imagined. Things, like best friendships, which we may not have imagined as problems can become dilemmas. Topics range from the aberrant made normal to the everyday made extraordinary. Thus, nymphomania, frigidity, and prostitution join weight loss and political candidates in the weekly fare. A list of 1989 episodes from *Geraldo* (more sensationally titled, more lurid than the other series) includes "Older Men, Younger Women," "Addicted to Love," "Homeless Children," "Vacation Horror Stories," "Diet Junkies," "Monstrous Crimes," "Cocaine Ladies," "Chastity," "The Serial Rapists," "Pregnant in Prison," "Women Who Date Married Men," "Campus Rape," "Kidnapped Kids," "Mothers of Slain Prostitutes," "Battered Lesbians—Battered Lovers," "Marrying a Prostitute," "When Men Become Women," "Hotel Horror Stories," "Men and Rape," and "Real Life Rain-Men." Whew! The real geniuses are the inventors of topics—masters of differentiation.

The programs depend on generating collective topics (often derived from recently published books, but including film releases and television series), linked to individuals, all transformed into middle-class problems of serious proportions. Although we may never have sexual allergies to our husbands' bodily fluids and need the serum injection discovered by a mild-mannered allergist/gynecologist from Cleveland, or die of asphyxiation from masturbating while hanging from a rope in a closet, or live in a nudist colony, or marry an old rich man, or have a penile implant, or see the live Elvis, it will be edifying and courageous for informed citizens and liberal grownups concerned about difference to sit in a TV studio and talk calmly to naked guests describing their experiences in nudist colonies in medium to close-up for the home viewer who cannot see what the studio audience is faced with. We have been exhorted that we must overcome our prejudice or disgust and finally not make a judgment about an issue that most likely will never directly involve but indirectly effects us all. However, we must feel, we must become involved, we must care about the experiences of others. The promo for *Sally Jessy Raphael* says, "Join me for interesting and sometimes surprising discussions. Join me and see how you *feel*" [my emphasis]. After all, this is the naked truth; issues are only human and must not be moralistically judged. However, we must all make personal choices. Right and wrong are personal choices, not institutional constraints.

Along with endorsing personal experiences and the veracity of affect, these programs are how-to manuals of television reception, paradoxically aligned with "good conversation." The success or failure of the shows depends on aural effect, visual, impassioned response, the reception of television. At home, alone, we are all connected; an audience has been assembled to address our loneliness and personal problems. Programs which return to former guests demonstrate the effectiveness of TV. An episode of *Oprah* concerned program success: a husband and wife reunited by on-TV therapy, a man who found a job through the program, the use of the Heimlich maneuver to save a life, the reunion of a mother and daughter.

Primetime talk is carefully scripted around an informality of distraction and the trivial. The style is a *rehearsed spontaneity* of guest and host (rarely with audience response other than applause for the hosts) reacting to the immediate or the mundane, a style of cutaways to banter and incidentals. Radically unlike primetime, daytime talk, scripted with an eye on audience response, relentlessly focuses on serious, albeit titillating, issues. Daytime talk involves a precise topic with no deviation, whereas nighttime plays out demure avoidance of any topic or revelation other than the routine of everyday life as a celebrity. Not to reveal one's personal life or political position—which revelation, paradoxically, functions as expectation and game for the late-night audience, which awaits a slip, a clue, failing to note that the rules have changed—is the late-night rule. In many ways, daytime shows are how-to manuals for serious conversation, unlike the determinedly adolescent banter of late-night; rigid rules are enforced by the host, who keeps everyone on the topic. To deviate to incidentals (or aspects of our lives other than the problem) and to go on too long are serious errors. After all, we are only problems, not fascinating celebrities. Finally, we care little about persons except for their particular experience or affliction.

Critically, guests speak for themselves, rather than indirectly. While therapists hawk their latest co-dependency treatise, they also bring along speaking subjects as living examples. This is in contrast to personal or mediated gossip, which is dependent on absent people as objects. This is a therapeutic gossip of enunciation, of direct adress, rather than gossip depending only on the enounced, the absent–gossiped-about. As I stated, the key is embodying people as positions, bravely coming forward with their problem in the hope of helping others. Airing the intimate, the secret, or the painful in public is valued, taking women's private issues into the public sphere and defusing shame, guilt, and fear along the way. For the participants, one can only imagine the effects of the program—confession, absolution, publicity, fifteen minutes of fame. It is not too far-fetched to imagine daytime talk as the electronic, syndicated version of conscious-ness-raising groups of the women's movement. Women's experiences, along with their emotions, are validated by the topic and the host. The transformation of gossip, or secrets, into electronic therapy devalues the formerly sanctioned places of secrets—medicine, the law, and psychiatry. The shift is away from experts and toward self-help, away from individu-ality and toward a group or collective ethos.

At the same time, particularly on *Geraldo*, women's issues, including feminism, are abnormalities or scandals, with women held to the body, to sheer affect, a postmodern symptom of Freud's hysteric. "Women and Madness" (*Geraldo*, December 11, 1989) included "Dr. Kate Millett (Former Mental Patient)" sitting onstage amidst other "Former Mental Pa-tients" not so famous. In the audience were "Dr. Phyllis Chesler, Psychologist/Author, *Women and Madness*," along with a spectrum of other experts: "Dr. Magda Denes, Mental Institution Advocate," and "Dr. Seth Farber, Therapist, Anti-Mental Institution." Geraldo opened the episode with his capsule rhetoric of quasi-yellow journalism: "Let's say a woman decides to get a full-time job or maybe have an abortion or to reject mar-riage, decide against children, or maybe even live with a man or a woman in a nontraditional relationship. Does that woman run the risk of being la-beled not just unhappy or abnormal, but maybe even crazy? That's what Phyllis Chesler alleged back in 1972 when she published her controversial book *Women and Madness*. Well, seventeen years later, the book has just been updated and reprinted, and these ladies [!] are here to tell us that, tragically, women, far more than men, are at risk of falling into the clutches of a mental health system that punishes independence as if it were a dis-ease." Then follows a capsule of the guest witnesses' experiences, with overtones of tabloid headlines: "Susan Thornton-Smith was turned into a drug zombie." "When Kate Millett, the noted feminist and author of *Sexual Politics*, was thirty-five years old, her family had her committed to a mental hospital. They apparently thought her radical ideas proved that Kate was crazy."

After Kate's opening tale, a debate between pro and con, Denes and Chesler, occurs. Denes is drastically outnumbered, the enemy on the at-tack and the defensive. Respites occur for commercials: "We'll talk about that. Got to take a break. This could be a miniseries. Women and madness, our focus. Be right back." Geraldo has, by far, the majority of comments. Although they are often brief remarks or directives such as "Hold it!" the comments control the editing, resulting in the majority of shots being of Geraldo. On this episode, from a total of 233 remarks, suggesting a fragmented hour not counting cutaways to commercials and promos, Gerald spoke 75 times, Denes 47, Chesler 16, Millet 14, with the remaining six guests and studio audience completing the total.[66]

Any Woman's Blues

"Any Woman's Blues: Jong . . . Steinem . . . Somers" (March 1, 1990) coincided with the publication of Erica Jong's new book. Geraldo's opening: "I'm going to give you the plot right now. Twisted passion dominates the life of a thirty-nine-year old self-proclaimed sexaholic female artist who becomes obsessively involved with an abusive twenty-five-year-old man. . . . That's the plot of an explicit new book that was the focus of a panel discussion last night at the 92nd Street Y, here in Manhattan," which featured Suzanne Somers (of *Three's Company* fame), a personal expert on addiction; Gloria Steinem, feminist; and Jong, talking about "love addiction and the implications of Erica's wild story of an older woman addicted to a younger man." Like her book, which also details the heroine's involvement in Alcoholics Anonymous, which is treated as a revelation, Jong's opening proclaims the value of great sex for women, in effect proclaiming her sexual appetite and prowess. Drug and alcohol addiction are dropped in favor of sex addiction and whether or not it is gendered.

Raoul Felder, divorce lawyer, is there as "resident male chauvinist" who asserts that there are both obsessive men and obsessive women: "I don't think a smart woman is going to do a stupid thing like getting involved with a guy who's going to ruin her career unless she's a self-destructive sort of crazy person." Steinem disagrees thoroughly, arguing the difference of women's lives and experiences. Dr. Helen Fisher, anthropologist, cites Barbados as another cultural example, a place where the women are rich and powerful. Amazing! Somers details her serious knowledge of co-dependency, drawn from being the child of an alcoholic and later involved in an addictive relationship.

Like Jong's book, feminism, along with addiction and obsession, is another scandal, a problem which is capitalized upon. The feud is between Steinem and Felder. All the women are there to help us by being open and honest. That the session is also a sales pitch is, of course, not acknowledged. However, the mutual exchange between publishing and television, between profiteering and therapeutic philanthropy, like the crossover ownership of print and TV venues, should be emphatically noted.

In *Any Woman's Blues*, a multiplicity of women's voices exists almost as a cover-up, concealing whether or not Jong or anyone is a alcoholic.[67] The novel is introduced by Caryl Fleishmann-Stanger, Ph.D. and Chair, Department of English, who has discovered a manuscript written by the now-dead Isadora Wing, who died in a "tragic flight with her fourth and last husband, the noted conductor and composer Sebastian Wanderlust." Dr. Fleishmann-Stanger posits the feminism of Wing, her lineage with and differences from Sylvia Plath and Anne Sexton, informing us that the author of the earlier book of poems *Vaginal Flowers* "nearly always wrote her 'novels' in response to disastrous events in her life." The stand-in for the now-fictive author is Leila Sand, a middle-aged, wealthy, famous, jet-setting painter/protagonist adored and desired by many men the world round, interrupted in the text by arguments or dialogues with the intrusive "author," Isadora Wing, breaking into the fiction, challenging the actions and motives of Sand. Wing is strong. Sand is the victim of her desires, which she exults and enjoys. Bessie Smith, the voice of the blues (and a strong victim? along with being an addict), is frequently quoted at the beginning of chapters—Leila Sand's alter identity as a black woman. Jong invoking Smith is, like the comparison to Plath and Sexton, romantic rather than political, the romantic claptrap of the self-destructive artist rather than addict. Isadora Wing writes an afterword, describing the plane crash and her discovery of work and self-identity, concluding an unfinished story, the novel proper.

Thus, Jong egomaniacally and fatuously splits herself into the intellectual and feminist (Fleishmann-Stanger); the artist/poet—Plath, Sexton, Smith; the liberated sensualist, recovering addict, and consummately successful and brilliant painter Leila Sand; and the biographical Wing—presumably self-reflexive tactics but, more to the point, denials and grandiose claims. Somehow the protagonist emerges as pathetic, unable to take herself seriously. She is figured, whether multiple or autobiographical or not, as a bricolage of contemporary therapeutic trends, ensnared in the accouterments of wealth, fame, and her brand of sexual gratification, wherein lust and romance (with all the gushy trappings of Harlequin) are thinly disguised as feminist desire and politics. Her concerns reiterate and upper-class the fascinations of the tabloid press.

However, someone has been in addictive therapy; unfortunately, the analysand is only a beginner, still living romance while labeling it a problem. Extrapolating ourselves from the unconscious takes great effort, literally changing the way we think. I doubt if the story of recovery—which moves inward, away from ego, pride, and romance, toward humility, wisdom, and serenity—would be a best-seller, or a topic on *Geraldo*. It is always the flailing, adolescent struggle of romance and sex, particularly addictive sex, that sells. Appropriately, Ann Barr Snitow has pointed to the relationship between romance and pornography.

Famous artists and writers, fashion designers, and international luxury hotels, scenes for endless trysts, are named in this lifestyle of the jet-setting rich and famous which Steinem calls "the truth." Along the way, almost in the middle, Leila joins AA, with the book citing the 12 Steps and describing both closed meetings and the program (breaking, to a degree, the tradition of AA's anonymity, which keeps it out of the terrain of fame and publicity; Jong turns AA to profit), presumably an item of strange fascination to the uninitiated, like the SM scene of flogging and titillation. And while alcoholism is one problem, placed in the middle and framed by intense sex and expensive fashion, it, like her twin daughters, is incidental or peripheral, displaced onto sexual addiction—the fuel and fascination of the novel, as is money. Thus, as with *Geraldo* (where Jong acknowledges that money, like sex, is a serious addiction) and the tabloids, the novel and the narrative capitalize on sexual addiction, an excuse which for Jong is always a pleasure, never an agony, like her drinking. The heroine works her way through various men and sexual scenes to recover from her addiction to a younger man, Dart, having many incidental relapses into sex and drink along the way. No matter; death is only a romantic, Amelia Earhart fiction here. Alcoholism has all the seriousness of flu, with fewer symptoms than a cold.

As in her previous novels, Jong is obsessed with sex, a '60s version of women's lib now transformed into a problem—our heroine still seeks what she calls "the land of fuck." Or, "That Dart loved my work was the icing on the cock." After affairs and relapses with rich men, with signs of money everywhere plentiful, and a sadomasochistic fling with a Sadian Madame Ada in New York, she travels to Venice, where she has a passionate affair with an Italian while sleeping at night with her composer-friend, whom she eventually marries, in the South Pacific. No one wears condoms; sex lasts for eternities and can happen anytime, all the time. Yet, it is updated to addiction status—the disease of the late 1980s and early 1990s.

At the same and paradoxical time, observations are right-on regarding early sobriety, where the world is a fog, where every old experience becomes brand new and unfamiliar—"Going to parties stone cold sober is new for me. . . . I see too much, feel too much, am too aware of all the lying" (16). "How sharp is the regret of early sobriety! All those wasted nights. . . . Who was the loser? No one but me. I missed my life" (197). Someone has undergone therapy, someone has experienced addiction. Unfortunately, addiction becomes profitable narrative and scintillation; recovery becomes fashion rather than collective survival. No one suffers, really; no one is suicidal, really. The book is stuck in early recovery, that rush of enthusiasm for the new fad, a brief respite from all the heady materialism. Sand is only a rash beginner; her relapse is inevitable.

Shady Relatives: Jim and Tammy Faye Bakker

Until recently, religious TV was a thriving, money-raising form of syndication, with relatively high ratings. For example, Pat Robertson turned a dilapidated Virginia television station into a religious empire, CBN. It buys airtime on 158 local stations to present *The 700 Club*, paying for it with donations from viewers. CBN also sells airtime to other television ministers who want to reach the CBN audience. CBN Cable provides "family entertainment" to 39 million fee-paying subscribers.[68] The 200-acre CBN complex in Virginia Beach prohibits smoking and drinking; the motto "And this gospel of the kingdom will be preached throughout the whole world, as a testimony to all nations" hangs above the main door, excluding the catastrophic conclusion: "And then the end will come."

The Bakkers' empire and vacation resort, Heritage USA (sold in July 1990, along with the ministry), is between North and South Carolina; Jerry Falwell is in Lynchburg, Virginia; Jimmy Swaggart, in Baton Rouge, Louisiana; and Oral Roberts, in Tulsa, Oklahoma. Evangelical TV is located in the South and the Southwest. For a while, the news shifted to the South— perhaps a last stand for regionalism.

The sexual-financial scandals "toppled two television ministries and tarnished others." Jimmy Swaggart lost "80% of his 2.2 million viewers, according to Arbitron," and Oral Roberts, 50 percent of his audience of 1.1 million. Falwell has decided that television is "no longer a priority." The attendance at a 1991 Jim and Tammy Ministries (in Orlando, Florida) was 150, down from the 6,000 on Sundays at Heritage USA. Tammy Faye's New Covenant Church is in a former Tupperware factory. Other ministries have sprung up in vacant malls, banks, and fast-food franchises. Like real estate, the electronic ministries have experienced a severe recession. This collapse of the national or regional electronic church has been accompanied by the rise of local "superchurches," which have membership of 5,000 to 20,000.[69]

While on the surface a sexual then a religious scandal of fraud and tax evasion, the story involved Tammy Faye's addiction to drugs and shopping and the Bakkers' magnificent obsession with costly possessions, sumptuous residences, and automobiles. The Bakkers were not living the religious vow of poverty; they had not repudiated worldly and bodily comforts. The media trial was an inquisition of their possessions and their emotive bodies, finding them guilty of greed, excess, and bad taste.

The Bakkers were tabloid fare which made it to the nightly news; a personal catastrophe was transformed into a media scandal, created and uncovered by gossip. The gossip about their private lives, initiated by Jim's illicit sex with Jessica Hahn and Tammy Faye's drug addiction, fueled the story and the legal machinery: before the gossip, the FCC had dropped an investigation into misallocation of viewer donations; slightly later, the IRS also found no cause for legal action against their tax-exempt status as a religious institution.

The couple became fair media game with the revelation in March 1987 on their PTL ("Praise the Lord," or "People That Love") TV program, *The Jim and Tammy Show*, that Tammy had been addicted to "over-the-counter" allergy and cold medications and had checked into the Betty Ford Center, which was near their home in Palm Springs. Only much later did she acknowledge her alcohol addiction. Tammy Faye wept and nodded, eventually admitting that she was also hooked on Valium, which she took to ease her fear of appearing on television. Her extreme emotions were symptoms of drug withdrawal, which the press failed to note.

Newsweek, with such digs as "his often teary eyed wife, Tammy" (28) in a column entitled "Paying the Wages of Sin," reported in March that the entire family had checked into a "California therapy center."[70] That same week, *Time* referred to her weeping through "enormous fly-whisk lashes" (62). Shortly after her on-the-air confession came the revelations of Jim's sexual tryst with Jessica Hahn during one afternoon in 1980, for which he paid her hush money. By April 6, 1987, the story became a lead in the "National Affairs" (no pun intended) section, titled "God and Money," which included reportage on the other ministries, crediting the *Charlotte Observer* with breaking the story, which eventually won a Pulitzer, with the reporter called on as an expert witness during the trial coverage. Tammy and Jim were depicted as ordinary people who indulged in personal confession and testimonial on their TV show: "College sweethearts, they worked their way up from a back-road tent show to a slot on Pat Robertson's *700 Club*" (18). The April 6 *Newsweek* was prescient: "Both sides hinted at further sex stories, but money and power were perhaps more important" (18). *Time*'s April 6 story, yet another cover, "TV's Unholy Row," accused the religious ministry of "being more concerned with bucks than Bibles."

Because the initial drama was cast by Bakker as an attempt by rivals to take over PTL, stories included Jimmy Swaggart (and his strange motel encounters with a prostitute) and Oral Roberts. After Bakker's temporary resignation, Jerry Falwell took over the television ministry. Other, smaller scandals kept popping up: Tammy's attraction to an old-flame singer, the marriage of their eighteen-year-old daughter to a lifeguard, and allegations of Jim's homosexuality. Each charge was tabloid *and* mainstream front-page news. *Time, Newsweek, People,* and the *National Enquirer* ran simultaneous stories.

In fact, the most grotesque image of Tammy Faye was on the cover of *Newsweek*; it beat out the *Weekly World News*, a black-and-white tabloid, for bad taste: "See Tammy Faye without Makeup": "Tammy Faye's bizarre makeup and loud wardrobe have made her the born-again laughing stock of the smart set" (figs. 14, 16). (She was a joke for the "smart set" but not to her followers.) Adrian Arpel, "Big Apple cosmetic consultant": "To me, the most obvious thing is the woman's exaggeration. Everything is big. . . . The enormous shoulder pads are overkill. And her dresses often look too big, too much, too fabulous. "[71] The number of mascara jokes and parodies of her emotional excesses are infinite, still late-night fare.

People's story on May 18, 1987, reported that Tammy Faye wanted to be "the Dolly Parton of TV evangelists—and unbeknownst to viewers had her breasts surgically enlarged." "I don't care how old you get. . . . I think a woman . . . ought to dress sexy and keep herself exciting" (81). The magazine quoted friends who analyzed her shopping addiction: "Even when

Figure 16

they were starving and there wasn't any money, she'd go to K-Mart and fill up a cart" (85). The conclusion psychoanalyzed her: "Tammy Faye had always been an emotional pressure cooker. . . . She was plagued by hives. She took Valium because of a fear of flying." She is the hysteric or addict as joke, her body a mass of symptoms to be ridiculed. The Bakkers' now-famous appearance on Ted Koppel's *Nightline* (a trailer for the April 1990 anniversary show) was reported in the June 8 *Time* and echoed by *Newsweek*: "Jim reported that Tammy had been shopping ever since, visiting at least two flea markets per week" (72). The same week *People's* headline was "Sapped by Wretched Excess, PTL Puts the Bakkers' Kitsch on the Block." They were guilty of the ultimate crime: bad taste. The Bible was used to bludgeon them: "Lay not up for yourselves treasures upon earth" (June 9, 40).

This auction reminded me of the Warhol auction, which sold items purchased during his habituation of flea markets and constant shopping. This, however, was "the Christian sale of the century," with luxuries such as an "air-conditioned doghouse" that was "as damning for the Bakkers as her shoe collection was for Imelda Marcos" (42). The similarities between the media coverage of these two women are quite uncanny. For women, shopping, their domestic work as consumers, can also be used against them. For Tammy, wretched excess was a sin; for Andy, it was art. In *People's* coverage of the auction, even the participants are mocked: "Kathy, 42—a Tammy Faye look-alike in two tone lipstick and abundant eye shadow" (43)—bought Tammy's desk. The saga became *Dynasty*: "a serial of sex, cash and power . . . a lurid . . . TV mini-series," an apt description of life now imitating television.

Jessica Hahn joined forces with *Playboy*, uttering her immortal words in *People* in October, "I am not a bimbo." She praised Ted Koppel, "who really encouraged me a lot. . . . He had more wisdom than all these so-called preachers put together."[72] Hahn's story is one of being subservient to men, of being the victim rescued by Hefner, then Koppel. Hefner was "a wise man in whom she could place her trust. . . . Hefner has more wisdom and understanding . . ." (36).

The story embodied every tabloid topic except a UFO sighting and deformity; it grew from drugs, sex, and bad fashion to economics and fraud; it moved from the tabloids and TV to the courts, from gossip and scandal to law. The downfall of PTL was a hyped media event which played daily for two and a half years, repeating the same list of tasteless offenses until the newspaper headlines of October 5, 1989: "Bakker guilty on all counts. . . . TV evangelist Jim Bakker was convicted Thursday of fleecing his followers of $3.7 million so that he could surround himself with everything from Rolls-Royces to gold-plated swan-shaped bathroom fixtures." His real crime was living "in high style, buying fancy cars, lavish homes, Rolex watches, diamonds, an air-conditioned doghouse and furnishings ranging from gigantic walk-in closets to motorized bedroom drapes."[73] The consumer crimes had become a litany as familiar as Tammy's eyelashes in a media blitz of righteous, condescending, often vituperative castigation which reveled in *and* trashed their consumerism. The tone of the mainstream press was the righteous "not-me" of anti-identification (so constant to television news coverage and catastrophe) as well as gossip.

While mainstream gossip cherishes rich and famous celebrities, with Barbara Walters visiting their lush homes and caressing their impressionist paintings and automobile collections in prime time (one seal of legitimacy for tabloid fare, increasingly crossing over into news), there is a fine line of style and class which cannot be crossed. Like Imelda Marcos, the darling of *Women's Wear Daily* in the 1960s, friend to the Rockefellers and Whitneys, the Bakkers had stepped over that invisible class boundary into a place where excess (emotions and bad taste) becomes criminal. The 1989/90 Trump gossip extravaganza also involved megabucks and consumer excess. However, the class allegiance was more fashionable, aligned with a "higher" social echelon, including *Vogue*, hence admired for (her) high style and (his) good business acumen (which took a nosedive in July 1990). (For the Bakkers, exactly the opposite applies. Tammy Faye shopped at K-Mart or Target rather than Nieman-Marcus.) Donald and Ivana each had their own gossip-columnist advocate in this ménage-a-trois scenario with its rising star, Marla Maples, who appeared on *Designing Women* in fall 1991.

Maples capitalized on her gossip status by appearing on *Primetime* in 1990, interviewed by the prestigious Diane Sawyer for huge ratings, recapitulating Barbara Walter's respectful and empathetic interview with Donna Rice in 1987 (another ratings blockbuster), who refused to tell whether or not she had had sex with Gary Hart, a nonsecret which everyone knew. In a hushed voice, midway through the program just prior to a commercial break, Barbara paused, took a deep, meaningful breath, and asked the big question. Cut to Donna. Break to commercial. After the return, Barbara respected her decorous demurral. Good girls don't kiss and tell. Unlike both these southern, educated, middle-class, soft-spoken coeds/models in love (the college sweetheart/cheerleader as mistress), Hahn, only a church secretary, squealed, named, accused, and described, relentlessly. Like Tammy Faye, she talked too much, overstepping the bounds of propriety. All these women (we'll see about Marla) are leftovers, abandoned along the way by their lover-husbands (who dutifully return to their forgiving wives) and by the media. Women are the detritus of gossip.

The transformation of scandal into joke for late-night comics such as the Church Lady, Johnny Carson, Jay Leno, and Joan Rivers suggests the kinship between gossip and jokes. Like the joke, gossip has a two-way, Janus-faced nature where fascination can, quite unpredictably, sour to revilement. This has happened to Roseanne Barr and Imelda Marcos. The reviled can also be rehabilitated or saved, particularly if they are men. In 1990 Rob Lowe was the guest host on *Saturday Night Live*, admonished and absolved by Dana Carvey as the Church Lady. Lowe's scandal of sex, lies, and videotape suggests that sex is not as scandalous as it used to be, even between underage women and naked actors campaigning for the Democratic Party.

For women, absolution is harder to come by. Although Tammy Faye was not even charged, however innocent she was of any legal crime, she was found guilty of being grotesque and emotionally excessive in a media trial of her body—her gestures, her masquerade, and her emotions. Rationality had a field day with bodily affect, transformed into a joke. In contrast to *Oprah*, women's addictions were not taken seriously. Rather than her confessions being inspirational, Tammy Faye in her suffering became a laughingstock. Whereas Oprah successfully linked materiality and spirituality, the Bakkers' possessions proved their bad faith. (For New Age fundamentalism, material plenty is the result of spirituality.)

The initial lawyer matched their publicity stature: Melvin Belli, the litigant in other media events—the trial of Jack Ruby and the victims of Bhopal. On June 28, 1989 (1J), *The Milwaukee Journal* summed it up: "Indeed, for all its soap opera elements—diamonds, minks, Mercedes, sex, sin and betrayal—the saga of the Bakkers is no mere comic romp involving a fallen preacher's sexual conduct or his flashy wife's penchant for heavy makeup and K-Mart shopping sprees. . . . The meteoric rise and sudden collapse of the PTL may turn out to be one of the biggest frauds in the history of American religion." Or, one of the biggest television frauds, comparable to the network quiz show scandals in the 1950s which revealed that contestants, like the college professor Charles Van Doren, had been coached, the contests rigged. Paralleling the response to those media events in the 1950s, the Bakkers' audience was nonplussed. Until Jim's imprisonment, there was little decline in the number of their avid supporters after the revelations.

The religious scam involved selling leisure, or vacation time, in the Heritage Grand Hotel. Heritage USA, called a Christian Disneyland by Swaggart, is "the third most popular theme park in the country (after the two Disney operations). It drew more than 6 million people last year to its 500 room hotel, 2,500 seat church, five-acre water park, and mock gable-fronted, Main Street USA, an enclosed mall with 25 stores and a 650 seat cafeteria" (*Time*, April 6, 1987, 62). The victims were members of the TV audience who had bought shares in Heritage or sent their money to support the ministry, not the Bakkers. That the ministry and the Bakkers were inseparable was rarely noted. That ministers, even television ones, should live modestly, if not poorly, was a presupposition for the mainstream press.

Along with shopping/consumerism, television, tourism, and leisure (and the fandom of their followers) have been added to their offenses—virtually covering the field of cultural studies. The linkage of consumer culture and the new fundamentalism is a precise illustration of the arguments of Lawrence Grossberg in *It's a Sin*, to which I will return.[74] Just as its power was being proclaimed by cultural critics, religious fundamentalism unraveled and left the media spotlight, suggesting that popular culture outruns even its best critics.

The Bakker case was a trial by middle to slightly liberal America of the southern right, a media lynching tainted by class (regional, educational, and sexual) bias, a sophisticated laugh at an old-style belief in God (precisely when "spirituality" of all sorts is again on the trendy rise), a vilification justified only in the end by the legal finding of fraud. While sex and religion were the titillating trigger and pathetic scandal (along with the hush money paid to Hahn, Spacks's prostitution metaphor taken literally), these were surface symptoms of the larger accusations of spiritual consumerism, emotional fraud, and television audiences.

The scandal was a battle for the TV audience and profits of syndicated programs. Given the audiences for religious TV shows, the media trial by tribunals such as *Time*, with its corporate ties to cable and broadcasting through Time-Warner, a *huge* oligopoly, was a claim by legitimate TV for audiences, a stance against religious syndication, which is outside the purview and domain of official TV. A University of Pennsylvania study in 1984 concluded that 13.3 million people were regular viewers of religious TV, with ministries on 221 TV stations vying for donations (*Newsweek*, April 6, 1987, 18). Virtually every mainstream cover story and secondary story included obsessively repeated data on television holdings and audience figures. Given the corporate interconnections between publishing and TV, this is not surprising.

In *Time's* cover story, the audience figures and TV are what really count. "The heart of the operation is the PTL cable network, a satellite network, which reaches 13.5 million households over 171 (also stated as 178) stations." Jerry Falwell heads an "empire that generates 100 million a year in revenues and employs 2,000 people," with "sermons over 350 TV stations to 438,000 households and via the Liberty Broadcasting Network to 1.5 million cable-TV subscribers." Oral Roberts's "syndicated 30 minute program, carried by 210 stations, reaches some 1.1 million people, but is dropping off" (April 6, 62-63).

In August, *Time* featured another story which detailed the TV evangelism empire, charting a decline in viewers, which equates with money. Unlike the audience for commercial TV, viewers pay to watch religious TV, sending in donations directly. *Time* analyzed the problem as one of "far flung real estate and broadcast empires," with "holdings dominated by a single, dynamic individual." Then follows yet another list of assets and net worth of each of the ministries and an analysis of business methods which are not efficient, not conservative, not proper. After consumer excess and bad taste comes bad business management, a "helter-skelter organization run by an insecure, often dictatorial man who . . . didn't know how to balance his own checkbook" (51). *Time* concludes with this indictment: "All those excesses, however, paled beside PTL's underlying corporate style." Lifestyle is what counts, and the Bakkers had failed "corporate style." Jim is doing time for being a bad businessman.

One journal's coverage was different, taking the press to task, reminding them that adultery is a serious offense for some people who take Christianity seriously. This, of course, was William Buckley in the *National Review* (May 8, 1987). Analysis of another kind also came from an unexpected source. In the December 21, 1989, issue of the *New York Review of Books*, Garry Wills takes on three books about the Bakkers, along with an analysis of an "evangelical subculture," reminding us that subcultures have also been right-wing, no matter how the term has been inflected in cultural studies.

After an interesting history of religious and erotic ecstasy, Wills acknowledges the relations between emotion and evangelicalism, "a collection of superstars and their followers," pointing to a long history of bodily affect: "People who find television's preachers overemotional do not remember how Billy Sunday would wrestle with the Devil for hours in front of the masses. . . .The emotions were summoned, wrought upon, dwelt on. . . . The body responded in agony to its inner renewal, swooning, 'quaking.' . . . Once labored up, these feelings could turn erotic" (23). He reads the body and affect differently.

Wills also reminds us that the preacher is "not authorized by some distant hierarchy." Identification is with the person rather than a sectarian position. "He stands or falls by the approval of his immediate 'flock'" (24). Thus, the preacher must embody the emotions and be an individual, outside institutional support. He argues via Billy Graham: "If even he feels the union of physical and spiritual power in his moments of psychic control over masses of people, we can imagine the strain on a Jim Bakker, swept from obscurity and poverty to celebrity as a holy superstar." Along with explicating the experience of religious ecstasy, a bodily event which is not outside the sexual, he also understands forgiveness: "It astounds nonbelievers to see Christians forgive and receive back . . . straying ministers like Jimmy Swaggart. The secular press tends to treat them like freaks, unaccountable extravagances to an underculture" (26).

Wills corectly cites class bias in *Penthouse's* coverage of Swaggart's prostitute, noting that this woman's sin "was not sex. . . . Her main offense was being poor. Her surroundings were not the affluent ski resort, the healthy recreation spot . . . but a shabby hotel room. A *class* difference was emphasized" (26). He argues that Swaggart committed another kind of sin, that of "bad taste. . . . He punctured the [*Penthouse*] dream." A comparable fate befell Jessica Hahn, transformed through plastic surgery and fashion into an airbrushed subject for *Playboy*. "She was lifted out of the sphere of Jim Bakker's cruder lust, into the refined atmosphere of Hefnerism, [making it easier to understand] why Jimmy Swaggart's people would rather have their preacher with his sin than his accusers with their sinlessness."

As defamation law dictated, the Bakkers were fair game. They were liable and had to pay by relinquishing their possessions and television ministry. The end had come for Jim and Tammy Faye Bakker—that is, until their made-for-TV movie.

X

◆

Theorizing Affect

During the 60s . . . people forgot what emotions
were supposed to be. And I don't think they've
ever remembered. I think that once you see
emotions from a certain angle you can never
think of them as real again.

—Andy Warhol,
The Philosophy of Andy Warhol, p. 27

It's a Sin

It's a Sin, Lawrence Grossberg's "state" of cultural studies, parallels the media critique of the Bakkers; both "address the hegemonic challenge of the New Right and the close relationship between that challenge and the terrain of the popular." Like the journalists who find incomprehensible followers' continuing admiration of their fallen preacher, Grossberg is bewildered by affect (18). The *National Enquirer* and the Bakkers configure two aspects of the "American New Right": "the economic neo-liberals who are absolutely committed to the free play of market forces . . . [and] the moral traditionalists . . . the most successful populist group having combined the techniques of televangelism and direct mail appeals" (29). (The third consists of neoconservatives recapturing " 'traditional' values: Three projects, three enemies—state regulation, the anti-christ, and communism," with the latter losing efficacy as the socialist Eastern Bloc turned against communism.)

For Grossberg, the "American New Right" is "not elitist." It is "imbricated within popular taste as much as its audience." True enough for the PTL ministry with its flashy packaging of Christian entertainment and vacations at Heritage USA. Where I diverge from Grossberg's impassioned analysis is with respect to his bipolarity between the ideological and the affective (31), along with his use of metaphors drawn from the military and Western, neocolonial expansion (the "frontier" an inverted echo of Kennedy's "new frontier"). "The crisis . . . according to the New Right, is neither economic nor ideological but rather, affective. It is a crisis of our lack of passion."

While it is not his intent, Grossberg makes an argument for ideology against affect; he accepts Jürgen Habermas's schematic separation between realms and spaces (the state apparatus, market forces, the public sphere, the private domain), arguing that the New Right "operates in the conjuncture of economics and popular culture rather than that of economics and the state. The latter demands an ideological struggle by which politics can lead culture. The former demands a popular struggle by which culture can lead politics" (32). That culture is leading politics (or that there is no difference) is no small insight, yet perhaps a simplification.

The traditional linkage of rationality, the "ideological," with men and thought, and the affective with women and the body (here a divide between the left and the right) suggests that this formulation needs to be questioned. The New Right is analyzed as emotionally empowering, as a series of affective investments (32). "The New Right has constructed its own DMZ with the national popular . . . a frontier which has been constructed elsewhere, through a redistribution of the cultural sites of our affective investment." The "frontier" is the "gap between affect and ideology . . . an unbridgeable chiasma which leaves us standing on the border of our affective relations, unable to anchor ourselves in ideology." In this analysis, based on binarism rather than a logic of contradiction, the left is outside affect, missing the boat, wondering where ideology has gone, incapable of "making sense" of affective experiences and putting "faith in our ideological constructions." This confusing inverse—of the "sense" of emotions and the "faith" of rationality—is promising.

Grossberg's unease is anxious and symptomatic of loss, of the '60s left, its thunder and passion stolen by the new fundamentalists, preachers and presidents alike, old-style religion transformed by TV, New Age therapies, and franchise economics into "lifestyle" and "spirituality." What exists for Grossberg as affect is reminiscence, the nostalgia (contained in his metaphors) for the 1960s and early 1970s, of Vietnam, the counterculture, and rock, an era when boys were men and politics were visibly divided into left and right.

Memory would remind us that only protest *techniques* were ripped off by the right. Many of the issues, including ecology, women's equality, the threat of war, and racial equality, remain as serious as ever. I would also remember that faith and love are not indigenous to the right but were also central to segments of the counterculture: mysticism and Eastern religions were practiced by 1960s artists, along with flower children, and the civil rights movement was guided by black fundamentalist preachers and carried on in churches. With New Age faith (called spirituality) linked to the good life of possessions, fundamentalist religion (like the many southern democrats who voted for Reagan) has moved to the political right, embracing the fruits as much as the values of conservative capitalism.

If the affective is so effective, as it proved to be for the left not so long ago, why not reexamine our premises regarding emotions, linked to women's bodies and bad faith as they are? I, like other women, would look for another "elsewhere," perhaps a theory of affect, its relationship to the body. I see a logic of contradiction superimposed over an inversion of issues (for example, in the abortion debate) rather than a bewildering enemy, the New Right.

Along with theorizing affect and the body (one way of revising hysteria), I would scrutinize the charismatics of faith, at the base not only of fundamentalist and New Age religions but of therapies based on the 12 Steps of AA, published in 1939; spirituality of all sorts is premise and afteraffect of many cultural productions not aligned with the New Right. As one brief example: When addicts enter treatment at Hazelden, the premier program in Minnesota on which other centers, among them the Betty Ford Center, are modeled, they learn to express their emotions and then to *properly* identify their feelings. Virtually all of them, but particularly men, find this initially silly and trite, then impossible, not knowing whether they are happy or sad, pretending to be OK but in a torment of free-flowing anxiety, unnameable fear, resentment, and anger. Mind and body, intellect and affect, have been severed. The divided subject of Lacan has become an unbearable insanity.

Breaking through the mask of pretense and the protective defense of the intellect—called denial—is taking the first step, the most difficult stage of early recovery. The naming and specifying of emotions is accompanied by a change in thought processes and the restoration of personal ethics. The long process of recovery begins on the affective and experiential level, where it remains. One cannot think one's way into sobriety and abstinence—after all, rationality produced the logic of denial. Laughing at Tammy Faye was laughing at an addict at the most painful and confusing time—pre- and early recovery, a mass of inappropriate, self-destructive behavior and displaced symptoms. Addicts hooked on tranquilizers are self-pitying and weepy as the result of miniature withdrawals; her compulsive shopping is a painful rather than comic obsession.

Like mechanisms of addiction and obsessive compulsions, popular culture might not be directly and overtly aligned with affect, as is so commonly assumed. Conversely, it might represent a negation or a denial, operating a displacement of emotions, containing rather than embodying them. In many ways, TV is a training manual for controlling and repressing emotions. The anchor during catastrophe coverage is evaluated according to a lack of emotions in times of travail. On local news, affect is represented by ordinary people, frequently women, and rationality by officials, usually men. In coverage of local murders or fires in Milwaukee, African-American women are depicted as hysterically crazed or dazed by grief; African-American men are linked to drug-related crime. Like poverty, affect has a racist dimension. For many entertainment programs, emotions are character flaws or narrative problems, like women, which need a cure or a solution, that of rationality, which Jessica Fletcher on *Murder, She Wrote* so readily provides. On this series, feuding family members kill each other off with alarming regularity. No one cares. No one mourns. We want mystery; affect might slow the plot. Affect, other than laughter, is often linked to ineffectiveness, to waste, to excess, to weakness, to the lower class. Power is affectless, or where affect cannot be seen or heard. Nixon's fall was sealed by reports of his display of emotions. However, this too is changing for men: even the powerful Victor Newman on *The Young and the Restless* shed a few tears after learning of the marriage of his former wife (the ex-stripper, Nicki) to Jack Abbott, his arch-enemy. And contradiction functions here as well: TV preys on fear during catastrophe coverage, while informing us that we are safe, urging us not to feel but to behave rationally. Affect is represented as something to be surmounted. Or, as Warhol said, "The movies make emotions look so strong and real, whereas when things really do happen to you, it's like watching television—you don't feel anything" (*The Philosophy of Andy Warhol*, p. 100).

Grossberg's left resembles the logic of addiction: "It is a crisis, not of faith, but of the relation between faith and commonsense . . . as if one had to live two lives, one defined by the meanings . . . and the other defined by the affective sense . . . [which] is unrepresentable" (40). When qualities such as faith or affect are outside the purview of men, they, like woman for Freud, become "unrepresentable" rather than not understood. Faith unites meaning and affect for the believer, as a collective, group ethos does for the recovering addict.

With the unrepresentability of affect a highly debatable premise (just think of the gestural, emotive code of silent cinema), Grossberg postulates a taxonomy of "inauthenticity" which recapitulates contemporary theories from Baudrillard to Bakhtin. One might, however, read the "inauthentic" as having origins in women's issues, women's culture, and perhaps women's bodies as well as religion. What is on trial in the Bakker scandal, along with a belief in Jesus and the good life, is Tammy Faye's masquerade body and excessive emotions—Jim's as well. Neither faith nor the bodily affects its ecstasy produces can be real. Therefore, for Grossberg, they become "inauthentic." For late-night comics, they are a joke. For mainstream media, they are a fraud. Claiming rationality in all cases, liberals (men) decry the public display of private emotions. Like the feminine for Lacan, affects are deceits or flaws.[75]

The Bakkers were also found guilty of committing several of the seven deadly sins, the bad addictive emotions: pride, greed, and lust. If this is the case, then the political assessment of which side was most fundamentalist is up for grabs. The press might have been inadvertently aligned with Jimmy Swaggart's brand of hellfire and brimstone faith, an apt assessment given that his cohorts broke the story of Jessica Hahn.

Grossberg's ambitious essay does admit that ideology is taken up with differing intensities, that we are always more than a "knowing subject" (35). Acknowledging the linkage between thought and affect, and the merger and crossover of the private, the public, the market, and state apparati would open up his argument, as it has for feminism. Market forces and television have not only permeated daily life, altering the everyday, but they have accessioned politics, the state apparatus, so clearly apparent in an economy of deregulation. The separation between the market and the state is no longer discernible. Politicians making news announcements do so according to the broadcast schedules of television stations (where the former distinctions between commercial and public service time have legally vanished). As in the Bakker coverage, it is not simply apparent which side is left or right, liberal or conservative.

These formerly binary oppositions—so clearly visible and audible from the post–World War II period until the 1980s, the big, determining ideological choice after which other issues fell into place as in the domino theory—have, like the rest of cultural productions, been deregulated and differentiated. Within the shift from military wars to trade wars, it is trickier locating an enemy (unless it's Japan or, more unpredictably, Iraq). It's not just that the Soviet Union and communism are "'changing'" to embrace some version of democratic capitalism, or, as a *Time* magazine editorial declared, were only imaginary enemies necessary for fueling fear which drove the corporate and atomic machinery,[76] but the shift illustrates the breakdown of binarisms in general.

"We are not losing some grand hegemonic war to the nihilism of postmodernity, nor to the commodification of late capitalism, nor to the ideological conservatism of political ideologies. But we are losing a specific set of battles, and we do not know the consequences nor how to struggle against it" (33–34). The "we" needs to be specified and gendered. If the "we" is the liberal male left, indeed the war might be over.

However, as Julia Lesage points out, "homophobia and racism are deep structuring principles in Christian television" (14). And, "even more than with its resolute opposition to abortion, the right maintains consensus about the evils of homosexuality . . . a consensus about gayness as pollution. If we want to fight the right on gender issues, we have to speak out for an explicitly pro-homosexual position whenever the subject of AIDS is discussed" (17). Equally, however, she argues that "to analyze Christian television we must deal with real class issues."[77] Lesage provides issues with which to "struggle," revealing the biased oversight of criticism which presumes heterosexuality.

One battle, Jesse Helms versus the National Endowment for the Arts, is a binary clash between political ideologies—the right versus the left and heterosexuality versus homosexuality. The scandals, and consequent targets (Holly Hughes, Robert Mapplethorpe, for example) challenge the heterosexual presumption while representing an erotics of gay and lesbian culture. Sexual desire which varies from, and threatens, the heterosexual norm is shocking and, hence, condemned and censored. Sex is further complicated by class. As with defamation law, the issue is one of protection by First Amendment rights, deflected and denied by issues of state support. It is also a matter of money—for legal fees to pay for one's constitutional protection.

A Sexual Detour to *Twin Peaks*

Formerly, like psychoanalysts, scholars plumbed the depths of texts to reveal the sexual, including the construction of the desirous spectator. Sex was buried beneath the veneer of cultural artifacts, desire was in the unconscious, and we needed to deconstruct its mechanisms—emerging with unconscious disavowal, the holding of contradictory beliefs of creation/cancellation. Coincident with the emergence of sexuality (or heterosexuality) from the post–World War II period of nuclear families and conspiracy theory, into the manifest claims in the 1960s for sexual liberation, and via the mid-1970s to early 1980s intellectual obsession with sexuality, heterosexual desire has become the daily topic of tabloid and soap opera fare (*Days of Our Lives*, NBC, has one steamy scene, amidst looks of unveiled desire, after another), still fascinating (and overrated) but raising few eyebrows as divorce, affairs, living together, and "relationships" become commonplace, rarely events (like Gary Hart) that triggered shock or demanded decipherment. Sex has been displaced, from deep structure and the secret of identity to the surface (where Foucault argued it had been for centuries).

Foucault's assessment in *The History of Sexuality* has become prophecy and soap opera routine: rather than sex being repressed, it is an everyday or banal, or, in the case of AIDS, fatal, obsession (one reason why *Fatal Attraction* was, along with its antifeminism, a throwback. Another reading— as an enactment of the destructiveness of sexual addiction and the death drive of obsessions—is more illuminating). The AIDS crisis, which is a long-term catastrophe, has added loss and fear to the public sexual agenda, a deathly reality that has displaced desire, replacing it with anxiety, if not terror. While the linkage of sex with disease is historical, for example, syphilis, and legal, there is a crucial difference—of sexual preference. Within the 1990s context of conservatism (where sex is being reregulated, as a result of AIDS and GOP fundamentalism), theories of gay and lesbian erotics are shocking challenges to the ideology of the New Right. There is good (and moral) desire and bad (immoral) desire, with demarcated battle lines. This substantial argument aside, however, older theories of (heterosexual) desire clinging to a libidinal erotics of sex (and the unconscious) have limited value either for an analysis of these critical issues or for TV.

Popular culture has outrun even Foucault: lifestyle, not sex (which, linked to fear, has become a prohibition), is the key to identity. Rather than Freud's fetish—a mechanism which was combined in film theory with Marx's commodity fetish—cultural productions have more to do with affect than repressed libido and are aligned with women's presence rather than absence or lack. TV might be sexy. It is rarely sexual, unlike *Twin Peaks* (and daytime soaps).

Parodically, with overtones of performance art and avant-garde, *The Young and the Restless, Dynasty,* '50s television series, and *The Singing Detective* (of the late 1980s), amidst late 1950s/'60s fashion, styles, and conspiracy theory, *Twin Peaks* staged desire, a reprise of *Rebel without a Cause.* Idiosyncratic lust, criminality, drugs, and youthful rebellion erupt from the baroquely stylized northern small town of sophisticates and weird eccentrics. *Twin Peaks* is a *Big Sleep* for the 1990s, the shadow of film noir within the narrative conventions of serial television, with doses of sitcom weirdo neighbors thrown in for good measure, along with remnants of soap opera visual technique as Hitchcock aesthetics.

David Lynch's thrall with adolescence and palpating desire is the fascinating revival for TV of Lacanian desire as mysterious, excessive-to-grotesque parody. Like film noir, Lacan, and Freud, "woman," in this case Laura, is the mystery and question. And, she is guilty—of sex, desire, and drugs. Masculinity, in various guises, is desirous yet ineffective. Everyone is afflicted or addicted, whether to donuts, coffee, romance, sex, power, money, or real estate. Beneath the veneer of the family and kinky sex, along with addiction, are economic corruptions—from drug running to the lumber mill to the department store to the Great Northern hotel to One-Eyed Jacks, the house of prostitution.

The economic and sexual are linked to addiction—in the nuclear and extended family, which is the crazed community. On the surface, *Twin Peaks* resembles Cabot Cove. However, Agent Cooper (who wears an FBI jacket when in the woods) is a far cry from Jessica Fletcher. Scratch the surface of both small towns, however, and one finds perversion and corruption—here, abusive truck drivers, log ladies, curtain-obsessed wives, hysterical fathers, murderous sons, seductive daughters, and cripples, a vision of insanity and criminality, where dreams and psychic projections are clues, and denial is everywhere. Perhaps *Twin Peaks* is the TV remake of *The Cabinet of Dr. Caligari.*

Graham Reed's description of obsession (the content of the experience is beside the point), of which *Peaks* is the blackly comic version, is appropriate to describe its form. *Twin Peaks'* initial violence, the murder of a blonde prom queen and small-town daughter, triggered the enigma "Who Killed Laura Palmer?" After two episodes, this highly charged content and affect were transformed by TV soap opera/serial conventions of multiplying/ intersecting characters and temporal prolongation, and displaced into form and cognition. After the first episode, the murder (an action, a catastrophe), along with the characters' feelings of love, grief, pity, or shock (everyone wept copiously and grieved mightily on the initial two-hour broadcast), mattered little. At the same time, the identity of the killer became everything, creating then frustrating a rampant epistemophilia, the desire to know.

However, this exceptional TV aside, wherein Bakhtin meets an uncanny Freud, including its publicity and initial lack of commercials and resolution, the deep structure of most television is not the sexual, predicated on desire, Oedipus, the unconscious, and the revelation of the secret at the end. Rather, the sexual as the secret is only the beginning of other chains, only the tip of the iceberg. Like Jim Bakker and Jessica Hahn (a one-afternoon stand, years prior to its revelation), the sexual is an effect demanding deeper causes, more revelations and interpretations. Thus, sex has moved to the conscious, to anxiety, an experience of loss (often economic) rather than lack.

Fall from Grace and Narrative Absolution

Fall from Grace was the slick made-for-TV movie of the Bakkers, who had sold their story exclusively to NBC in 1987, prior to the chaos. The screenplay, written by Kevin Trevey, came in part from interviews with them during that period. The expensively produced film was directed by a woman, Karen Arthur, which might account for the revision of the caricatured representation of Tammy Faye, well-played by Bernadette Peters. In interviews with TV journalists, Arthur and Trevey claimed that they rewrote the initial script after uncovering lies during the trial, discrepancies which may or may not have been intentional. The film, which raises questions about Jim's guilt other than his bad business practices, was broadcast in late April 1990 during a ratings "sweeps" period—legit TV capitalizing on the Bakkers' gossip fame.

The film opens with biblical inscriptions, followed by a discreet but erotic primal scene: the hotel tryst with Jessica Hahn. Significantly, in contrast to the journalistic scandal, motive for actions is granted, in this instance, by Tammy Faye's threatened separation. Narrative transforms all the media events, just as characterization, or acting, transcends caricature. *Fall from Grace* is a sympathetic portrait indeed, representing the decline as a set of circumstances, careless inadvertencies, and addictions: Tammy Faye to drugs, with K-mart or Nieman-Marcus shopping a secondary manifestation; and Jim to work, buildings, and houses, along with an obsessive focus on irrelevant details.

Along with their rise to fame, fortune, and chaos, the premises of their ministry are detailed: this is a religion of celebration and joy rather than punishment, of material success rather than poverty, of lively gospel rather than sober hymns, of entertainment and devotion. This a television ministry, with ordinary and older people shown in audience cutaways to living rooms and hospitals as their loving flock. The worshippers are not dupes but believers. Religion, like faith, is taken respectfully.

Tammy Faye is sweetly intelligent, desirous of more time and attention from her husband, pushed off to the side of this man's world of God's business, and caught in the contradiction of being central to the ministry as a performer yet patronized, marginalized. She tries to be heard and is rejected, as Jim talks constantly into a dictaphone, like Agent Cooper on *Twin Peaks*. Like so many other women as wives, crucial and peripheral at the same time, she eventually takes her anger out on herself. Via fashion, makeup, and gesture, her body transforms, becoming slightly grotesque, a garish mask to cover up her pain. Her body gradually becomes hysterical, then desperately ill, and is rushed to the Betty Ford Clinic. Her innocence, good sense, and lack of interest in empire and fame emerge as her defining qualities.

Jim, on the other hand, loves but ignores his childlike wife; he leaves big decisions up to his cohorts, concentrating on incidentals, merging corporate and personal funds, all in the name of Jesus and destiny. He has an edifice complex, raising funds for Heritage USA and shifting monies around, his undoing. Along the way, he manifests the anxiety and self-pity of a workaholic, never taking a break. Thus, addiction is both social problem and personal behavior, an intriguing metaphor for contemporary culture.

While taxes are mentioned, the fall is attributed to their religious enemies, particularly Jimmy Swaggart, and betrayal by Jerry Falwell, the savior in wolf's clothing. Fraud is there but as inadvertent, unintentional. More centrally, however, this is a story of romance, of true love and its travails, of success from humble origins. In the last shot, they face the music (or press) together, in front of their Palm Springs home, bravely holding hands. Tammy's calm courage has enabled Jim to appear publicly after his humiliation and loss. She is the strong woman, now the Tammy of Wynette fame, standing by her man, recovered from her addiction. Sustained narrative has, unlike media gossip, come to their public rescue, rehabilitating the scandal by transforming their caricatured lives into empathetic story.

What Spacks fails to note about gossip as classical narrative is that it focuses on love and the couple, instantiating romance, marriage, and heterosexuality as the happy ending and quintessential social value and goal. In this case, however, we know better: Tammy went back to Betty Ford, and Jim went to jail. This means, of course, more publicity and perhaps a movie sequel. Perhaps tabloid gossip, like the outrageous *Twin Peaks* and the sweeter *Murder, She Wrote*, is on the other side of romance, presenting marriage and the family as desirable and weirdly abnormal and grotesque at the same time.

As with Richard Nixon in the 1990s (coincident with the serialization and publication of his memoirs) and Rob Lowe (upon the release of his 1989 film), both objects of gossip, popular culture (like religion) forgives and repatriates sinners who have been humbled and have openly confessed their sins. Rather than seeking God's forgiveness in private, an older form of absolution, Jim Bakker, like Nixon and Lowe, should have confessed to the press in public, seeking popular culture's mercy rather than claiming his innocence. Like the courts, popular culture has scant respect for secrets; paradoxically, it also depends on secrets, whose form generates an investigative, adversarial search for the content—called truth or reality—creating story. TV, linked to tabloid media, manufactures events (like Baby Jessica) through sheer repetition, piquing audience interest, creating experiences and affects which can then be transformed into commodities (movies) revised or open-ended enough to alter affect, thereby necessitating more publicity. Baby Jessica was a national event of primal fear, then an *Oprah Winfrey* episode on location, and finally a made-for-TV movie, an enclosed tactic like a snake devouring its tail. TV generates celebrities and events, which it then turns into story, or familial romance, ironically like Spacks's assessment of the virtues of gossip.

In *The Tourist: A New Theory of the Leisure Class*, MacCannell notes the centrality of affect within contemporary culture. The shift from work to leisure, from the commodity to the experience, is embedded in his central concept of "cultural production," which sees the world as a series of events which orchestrate groups, with instant replay on sports as a metaphor. The replay tells us what to look for, what to savor, framing "select bits" from the "stream of action" as "cultural experiences" (27). "The group does not produce the world view, the world view produces the group" (30), a group which is united by experience (what he calls the "model") and its affect (what he flatly calls the "influence"). (Think of self-help groups, or 12 Step groups.) His thesis is that "the commodity has become a means to an end," which he argues is an "immense accumulation of reflexive experiences which synthesize fiction and reality into a vast symbolism, a modern world" (23, 26). "Modernity is transforming labor into cultural productions attended by tourists or sightseers" (36), with leisure and culture "at a remove from the world of work and everyday life" (34). All this is a good definition of religious TV, including its group affects.

Like tourism or sightseeing, which it closely resembles, gossip is a "cultural production that almost magically generates capital continuously, often without consuming any energy for itself" (29). This analysis is akin to that of Alliez and Feher, and also recalls TV preachers' ability to raise millions of dollars for their projects, including forestalling their own deaths—the Oral Roberts ploy. As MacCannell argues: "The economics of cultural production is fundamentally different from that of industrial production. In the place of exploited labor, we find exploited leisure. Unlike industry, the important profits are not made in the production process, but by fringe entrepreneurs, businesses on the edge of actual production" (29). Heritage

USA was such a fringe, leisure enterprise. The "fringe entrepreneurs" of the gossip trade perch like Harpies on the edge of culture, particularly the film and television industries. At the same time, gossip has become a cultural production central to television, with the new fringe entrepreneurs—made-for-TV movies and scholars—on the edge of the burgeoning gossip trade.

Like Winfrey, Donahue, Spacks, and Grossberg, affect and experience are central to MacCannell's thesis. However, around contradiction there is divergence. The talk-show hosts endorse pluralism, finding friends and resistance everywhere, much like many scholars of cultural studies; Spacks and Grossberg posit binary oppositions, each locating enemies—for Spacks, popular media; for Grossberg, the New Right. Rather than contradiction, MacCannell flips or inverts Marxist premises, arguing through *differentiation*: "the origin of alternatives and the feeling of freedom . . . also the primary ground of the contradiction, conflict, violence, fragmentation" (11). In his reasoning, he follows Marx, who "*derived* his model of social class relations from his analysis of the value of commodities. As new species of commodities appear . . . and as the fundamental nature of the commodity changes," he argues that critics must "repeat Marx's deduction." For MacCannell, differentiation is systemic, "it operates independently and simultaneously throughout society."

Differentiation suggests why genre analyses of TV no longer cohere. While there is still a programming block of time and general set of conventions which define "soap opera," each serial is also marked by differentiation, with technique and form spilling over into primetime slots. (At the same time, differentiation has always been critical to capitalist production, combined with standardization.)

Yet, although I pushed differentiation myself, I must cautiously pause over celebrating it as a single answer to modernity. While the duality of class structure of "owners vs. workers" has been differentiated into lower/upper/middle variants of class, the new international binarism might be rich versus poor. While "sexual differentiation progresses beyond . . . biologically based binary opposition into . . . third, fourth, fifth and sixth sexes," suggestive of Roland Barthes's multiplicity or Foucault's dispersion of sexualities, for women, white and of color, difference, whether biological or social, operates as power. Thus, differentiation must be inflected by repetition, the return of the same *as* the same, and the contradictions of gender and race. The proliferation of gossip is one case of differentiation, across media boundaries, with a legal base in defamation law which is akin to the process of market deregulation.

Keeping Secrets

Gossip details trivia or it uncovers a shocking secret buried in one's past, like psychoanalysis: "*Oedipus passes through all three secrets*: the secret of the sphinx . . . the secret that weighs upon him as the infinite form of his own guilt; and finally the secret at Colonus that makes him inaccessible . . . he who has nothing left to hide."[78] After the latter stage—which Nixon seems to have reached (with Bakker on his way to Colonus), as signaled by *The Final Days,* an October 1989 TV movie of Nixon's demise, isolation, and emotional breakdown (also a moment of abject prayer), witnessed with amazed disgust by "Henry Kissinger"—culture bestows forgiveness, restoring the father in old age to sage status.

The journey from gossip to narrative, from sin to forgiveness, is, like a Greek festival of three tragedies and one comedy, a long-playing Oedipal drama, an inclusive process which doesn't end with Sophocles' first play (in a trilogy) as does cinema, suggesting yet another but different snug fit between Freud and TV. TV's enactment is different from cinema's youthful struggle; it is staged later, when Oedipus was older, blind, and humbled, with women no longer necessary as obstacles or side effects.

When women are gossip's subject, Freud is also ironically applicable: for Freud, women can never surmount, never complete or escape the Oedipal drama. Liz Taylor has constant relapses and crises, careening from health to death, from fat to thin, from man to man, from tabloid to tabloid, from recovery to addiction (which explains all her symptoms), and back again. Roseanne, Oprah, Tammy Faye, Imelda, and Leona exist within comparable crises, with Leona on her way to jail, a made-for-TV movie, and perhaps a feminist inversion of Oedipus, but I doubt it. Or, it would be just like a woman not to keep secrets, to tell it like it is, on the air to millions, like Roseanne and Oprah, unlike the riddling sphinx, thwarting epistemophelia (the desire to know) and narrative, transforming gossip's private secrets into public therapy, and defusing the power of gossip and psychoanalysis.

In its compulsive repetition of information and by the eruption of the past into the present, gossip's incarnation resembles the model of shock and the style of catastrophe coverage, another interruption of the normal by the abnormal driven by the compulsion to repeat. The journey of gossip to narrative resembles the stages of catastrophe coverage, from shock or grief to recovery or mourning. Because television is a series of indiscrete events, a flow, its texts, like serials, are played out over long periods of time and in many formats. Along with rerunning its history, television changes over time, is a long-term process, like addiction and recovery. Gossip also resembles the habits of addiction, which is dependent on keeping secrets and living in a perpetual crisis state which is denied by the addict.

Gossip's power is fueled by secrets which necessitate evasion or lies. The subject's fear of revelation or discovery—which is also at the very base of addictive social structures and akin to a Cold War, paronoiac mentality—intensifies the drama. The *form* or hint of secrecy triggers the thrill of epistemophilia, rarely satiated by the telling.

"The many intrigues of the KGB are about to become fodder for mini-series and movies of the week on American television" (*Wall Street Journal*, January 16, 1992, B2). Davis Entertainment will produce "30 selected case histories from the files of the Soviet Union's notorious secret police." The first story will be about how Moscow "got the secrets to the atomic bomb," starring Julius and Ethel Rosenberg. The stories will involve "top secret KGB accounts never before made public," an "entertaining opportunity to re-examine history," and the U.S. fifty-year quota of fear. Topics include attempted assassinations of Roosevelt, Stalin, and Churchill; the Cuban Missile Crisis and the U-2 affair; sightings of flying objects; and "famous women of the KGB." "We're mining gold." But no one will reveal the economic terms of the agreement. After all, "We're dealing with the world of secrecy. This is the KGB." We know the Cold War is over when it becomes a made-for-TV movie. What child of the fifties could have imagined a series?

Deleuze and Guattari's analysis of the secret links it to psychoanalysis. "The secret as content is superseded by a perception of the secret, which is no less secret than the secret." Like the joke, the secret is "a content that has hidden its form in . . . a simple container. . . . The secret is elevated from a finite content to the infinite form of secrecy," what they call "secrecy as an eminently virile paranoid form."[79] The finite content of Jessica Hahn was indeed elevated to an infinite, virile paranoia. As Foucault points out, secrets, for him the secret that is sex, are paradoxical because we talk about them constantly. Rather than sex being repressed, as Freud argues and many presume, we speak about it all the time. However, to Deleuze and Guattari's distinction between form and content, I would add Freud on obsession: "the sexual pleasure which is normally attached to the content of thought becomes shifted on to the act of thinking" (SE X, 245). Thus the form—which triggers and is fueled by epistemophilia, the desire to know (whether sex is the content or not)—is sexualized. Jacques Lacan's reading of Poe's "The Purloined Letter" describes (and enacts) this scenario (which in Lacan's exuberant language verges on lust). In Poe's tale, a letter, used to blackmail the Queen, circulates among the King, the Minister, and the detective. Lacan does not note that the Queen (duplicitous and guilty as women are in his eyes) is squeezed between their glances—without a viewpoint of her own. For Lacan what is significant is that the contents of the letter are never revealed to either the characters or the reader. Only the blackmailing letter (form of the secret) and its circulation matter. This resembles Graham Reed's assessment of obsession—"the content of the experience is beside the point" (21). Lacan's scenario is one of vision—yet the mechanism would, I think, apply to thought.

Paradoxically, the form which most directly operates the virile paranoia of secrecy, where "the secret is made into a structuring form," daytime soap operas, is the genre analyzed by feminists as close to women's daily domestic lives of fragmentation, disruption, affect, and family. On the 1990s daytime soaps, the fantasy and trappings of adolescent, heterosexual romance are lifelong illusions and addictions; the one and only relationship is destined, long-delayed but inevitable; having a man is the *only* obsessive meaning for women's lives, with sex the definition of female identity, retrograde Foucault. Women—enduring great travail, if not trauma—guard the secret of desire and the name of the father with fervor, legitimating the paternal law and the symbolic via biology: the identity of the real father. On *Days of Our Lives*, the evil Victor is now the real father of Beau Brady and countless new and old characters. While even the most powerful men, including corporate moguls and police officers, are ineffective (and talk about relationships), here women are the guardians of Oedipus, playing out and into dramas of paternity. While babies and maternity proliferate in the new boom, and while women's issues and bodies make headlines and scandal, the old-fashioned name of the father is what still counts.

> After the secret has been raised to the level of a form . . . an inevitable adventure befalls it. . . . The news travels fast that the secret of men is nothing, in truth, nothing at all. Oedipus, the phallus, castration. . . . That was the secret? It is enough to make women, children, lunatics, and molecules laugh.[80]

This might explain why gossip and scandal can so easily transform into jokes.

In his analysis of camp, Andrew Ross suggests to me another interpretation.[81] Gossip is often material for camp, and like "pop camp," gossip is soon "outdated, spent, obsolescent, or out of fashion," an ecology of production which, like Elvis, Marilyn, and Liz, paradoxically also recycles detritus, refusing obsolescence. Thus, like pop, gossip "contains messages about the *historical* production of the material conditions of taste" (151). Gossip, linked with bad taste, is enjoyed "only at the expense of others," a pleasure predicated on a "necrophilic economy . . . not only in its amorous resurrection of deceased cultural forms, but also in its capacity to promise immortality to the tastemaking intellect" (152). Ross astutely assesses that "bad taste" "tends to be the preserve of urban intellectuals . . . for whom the line between work and leisure time is occupationally indistinct, and is less regulated by the strict economic divide between production and consumption which governs the cultural tastes of lower middle-class and working class groups" (156). The class structure of gossip, in tandem with conditions of production, which has everything to do with power, might be, along with gender, its most revelatory feature.

Perhaps we should also take our cue from the Ashanti, a West African tribe for whom "gossiping and ridicule are considered serious breaches of etiquette and are publicly punished. If the offense is committed against a person of high status, the perpetrator either has his lips cut off or he is executed. [I would invert this class bias.] However, the Ashanti . . . hold a yearly ceremony during which time everyone is permitted to say anything about anybody"—which might describe the state of postmodern culture.[82]

PART IV

CALCULATING DIFFERENCE

The Body and Age

The Cultured Body

Scene I: As I walked around the Rodin Museum in Paris, a chateau bursting with triumphant statues of famous men like Balzac, chests thrown out and youthful, muscular bodies in athletic poses, male desire was palpable. The virility of production spilled out to the terraces, displaying more art including Rodin's towering gates. The pleasure and power of work, like sex, was

Figure 17

A. Rodin, *Celle qui fut la belle Heaulmière* (bronze, 50 x 30 x 26.5 cm, collection of the Musée Rodin, Paris, item S. 1148). Photo by Bruno Jarret, courtesy of the Musée Rodin.

everywhere. Unexpectedly, amidst all this lusty creation, I came upon *Celle qui fut la belle Heaulmière*, the famous striking, small statue of an old woman (Fig. 17), her shrunken breasts sagging away from her skeletal chest bones, her protruding stomach only folds of wrinkled skin. Her shoulders and neck were deeply bowed, her head and eyes downcast, her mouth and chin collapsed with time into a posture of calm acceptance. Her strength was apparent in her sinewy arms and hands. She was beautifully old. I was startled by her familiar aging body.

The film *Camille Claudel* revises the Rodin scenario, starring another artist, his young lover, played by Isabelle Adjani, and critiques paternalism as well as documenting the studio system of production.[1] The story of the young female protégée seduced and abandoned by the older male teacher is complicated by Claudel's self-destructive compulsions. Along with being exploited by the masculine art world (here, raw patriarchy), Claudel is destroyed by her addictions—alcohol and her obsessive desire for the married Rodin—sacrificing herself and demolishing her work in the process. However, as tortured and demented as Adjani/Claudel inevitably becomes, isolated within her sealed flat and finally committed to an asylum, the star never ages until the epilogue, and then only in "real" photographs. While Adjani might look unkempt or garish, her face remains unlined, beautiful, young.

Scene II: In a telling footnote to his essay "The 'Uncanny,' " Freud describes his experience on a train of "meeting one's own image unbidden and unexpected." As he was sitting in his compartment, the train jolted; he saw "an elderly gentleman in a dressing gown and a travelling cap." After jumping up, Freud realized "to my dismay that the intruder was . . . my own reflection in the looking-glass. . . . I can still recollect that I thoroughly disliked his appearance."[2] Freud failed to recognize himself, wondering whether his dislike of his double was "something uncanny" (248). Mary Ann Doane's analysis of this scene notes that Freud was having a late encounter with the Lacanian mirror stage.[3] What she fails to notice is that Freud's old age makes a substantial difference for his perception and our interpretation of this scene.

Freud knows that the mirror stage, akin to the experience of the uncanny, radically changes in old age: "From having been an assurance of immortality, it becomes the uncanny harbinger of death" (235). In the "earlier mental stage," the double "wore a more friendly aspect. The 'double' has become a thing of terror" (236). For Freud, then in his sixties and plagued by recurrent cancer of the mouth and surgeries, the child's mirror of "immortality" has become a portrait of Dorian Gray. His aging body-double mirrors his fear of death—along with involuntary repetition (the compulsion to repeat), the basis of his later work.

"The 'Uncanny,' " published in 1919, was completed while he was writing the first draft of *Beyond the Pleasure Principle*. Like the 1926 *Symptoms, Inhibitions and Anxiety* (which he wrote when he was seventy), "The 'Uncanny' " argues that every affect "is transformed, if it is repressed, into anxiety" (241). Thus, the *experience* of the uncanny (distinct from representation, an "uncanny" "we merely picture or read about") "can be traced back . . . to something familiar that has been repressed" (247). Freud's list of the frightening includes "female genitals," "the omnipotence of thoughts, man's attitude to death, involuntary repetition, and the castration complex" (243), defining traits of obsessive neurosis described in the 1909 Rat Man.[4] Sexual difference (and castration) aside for the moment, it is important to note that as Freud aged, his theory changed—from pleasure to fear, from desire to anxiety, from life to death, from father to whispered asides of mother.

Just as Lacan's mirror stage has been a perilous place for young women as representation and for mothers as subjects, it would be a nightmare for old women—a portrait of Dora Gray. Is not the mother *as* other—the mirror image granting identity—eventually the visual sign of the adult child's aging? As the silent gaze of the mother granted integration to the child, later it would mark bodily disintegration. If we agree with Lacan that "what determines me, at the most profound level, in the visible, is the gaze that is outside. It is through the gaze that I enter life and it is from the gaze that I receive its effects,"[5] then our "mental projection of the surface of the body" comes, at least in part, from the gaze of another or mother.

Thus, "mother" is a word both full and empty, she is everything yet absent. In Lacan's view, the old woman would be the flip side of the idealized woman, her aging the complement to, or later stage of, castration. In both scenes, she represents death. It would appear that Lacan's mirror stage, like Freud's "uncanny," reflects male rather than female protagonists. Like Alice, women must look in another mirror, perhaps that of personal experience, for answers.

As Kathleen Woodward so stylishly argues in *Aging and Its Discontents*: "We may conclude that sometime in middle age, age itself becomes the dominant preoccupation, subsuming the fear of sexual castration [which Freud equated with baldness and the falling out of teeth]."[6] While it is true that women, like our culture, are preoccupied if not obsessed with age, we have little to fear from castration. Thus, if Woodward is correct, for women the fear of age must replace something other than castration—perhaps the loss of the mother or separation from the daughter, or the failure to separate from the mother and become an independent adult. For many women, passed from father to other men, age is only a surface covering a dependent girl, unlike the little boy in Freud, unable to escape or surmount the Oedipal stage, a Freudian history coincident with family structures.[7]

Woodward sees age as a leveling, maybe even erasure, rather than a further instantiation, of sexual difference. For Woodward, cautious of biological determinism, old age assumes "more importance than any of the other differences which distinguish our bodies from others, including gender." Her call for sameness "in advanced old age" is powerful and compelling, yet a position with which I am uncomfortable. For her, it is "self-evident" and "obvious" that "women are more disadvantaged in old age in terms of social opportunities and resources than are men." Also "self-evident" is that "the sexual allure of women," an asset, "diminish[es] much more rapidly with age than does that of a man."[8]

For me, the social, political, and fictive institutions that have diminished women's opportunities and resources, along with self-esteem and self-image, are complex and baffling rather than clear and apparent. If this were not so, why would anyone in her right mind go along with them? Ferreting out the legal, familial, psychic, and biological inequities of women's lives and representations, both conscious and unconscious, has so far taken me a lifetime of contradiction, only to discover yet another interiorization of patriarchy's phantasmatic scenes of inequality. I question whether the issue of gender, along with race so determinant of economic and social power (including hugely discrepant social security payments in old age, along with the medical establishment's radically divergent attitudes toward men's and women's ailments), can be subordinated to the bodily leveling of age. Yet I admire a stance of sameness, the "difficult unity of inclusion" (Venturi) rather than the exclusion of difference.

Woodward's mirror stage of old age (which includes a complex reading of Freud's uncanny misrecognition) is in tune with Freud and is not, like my mirror, gendered: "Old age is a state in which the body is in opposition to the self and we are alienated from our bodies. . . . Our real selves, that is our youthful selves, are hidden inside our bodies."[9] "Alienation characterizes the mirror stage of old age. . . . If the infant holds his mirror image in an amorous gaze, the elderly person resists it. The narcissistic impulse remains . . . but it is directed against the mirror image" (60). While I live this inalienable scene, so luminously portrayed by Woodward, as destiny, social relations (and my personal, familial history) might be as or more determinant.

I have been trained to see myself as others see me, internalizing the sight and desire of others. I have learned to see women of the same age as older than men. I have learned that the female body is a problem which can be cured or altered—by makeup, fashion, dieting, and surgery. I have learned that youth is more beautiful than old age, particularly for women. Unlearning social conventions, many argued through biology, is not easy; feminism first involves an undoing. For many years, I believed that I was fat, with a huge, long nose and protruding Cro-Magnon forehead, although old photographs clearly document that I was tall, not at all fat, with rather a small face and head. I still believe my knees are fat, rather like an elephant's, and that my mouth is enormous. I am less obsessive about weight, yet I still mistake my thin reflection in a store window as coming from a mirror distortion—until someone else walks into the image as normal size. I have no idea how old I look. Second-stage feminism is replacing self-hatred with acceptance and self-regard.

(I was taught [but no longer believe] that to live without a man is to be alone, equivalent to being lonely, unattractive, old. I was taught that good mothers sacrifice themselves for their children, putting them before work, self, and relationships. Overcoming these bodily and social constraints which figure a lifestyle of martyred masochism has been no small task.)

It is precisely misrecognition, a real alienation effect, of woman divided against her inadequate self, of the body versus the social/psyche, that must be overcome. After all, the body is an image and a sack; it is a historical fiction or style as much as a reality. Certainly the body is neither self nor identity.

The Mother Tongue (a fearsome title) looks in another mirror, toward mother and women's experience. Susan Suleiman writes that "psychoanalysis is nothing if not a theory of childhood. . . . It locates . . . every . . . aspect of adult personality in the child the adult once was."[10] In the master narratives, particularly psychoanalysis, mothers are rarely the subjects of stories or the producers of discourse. They exist, when they do, as repressed memory, longing, or remorse. "The child's particular blind spot is an ability to have any realistic notion of the mother as an other subjectivity. . . . The child the adult continues to be cannot tolerate the mother's otherness."[11] Along with the mother's subjectivity, the child (for Freud, a male) also does not tolerate aging. Old women are relegated to the place of monstrosity or horror—the crone of the fairytale. For women, growing old is represented as tragic, pathetic, consisting of a series of losses.

And no wonder, given the Freudian abhorrence of growing old. "It is well known, and has been a matter for much complaint, that women often alter strangely in character after they have abandoned their genital functions [menopause]. They become quarrelsome, peevish and argumentative, petty and miserly. . . . Writers of comedy and satirists have in all ages launched their invectives against the 'old termagant.' . . . This metamorphosis corresponds . . . to obsessional neurosis."[12] I will return to obsessional neurosis later; the menopausal woman as obsessional is more than intriguing. (In another essay, Freud defines "menopause" as "the reaching of a certain age.")[13] "Metamorphosing" into an "old termagant" is not a pretty picture. I suspect, however, that this male interpretation has more to do with older women's expression of their anger—the increasing difficulty of repressing rage which might become a compulsion, or rage as the result of women's economic insecurity and enforced dependency.

As Lois Banner points out in "The Meaning of Menopause," the period in which Freud wrote these words was one of feminist activism, the age of the "new woman" (1890–1920) who was "not only a young woman."[14] This "renaissance of the middle aged" provided "new opportunities" for aging women "to go outside the confines of the home and family"; the negative "spinster" became the positive "bachelor woman." Women's appearance also changed: "at 50 the woman of today [1920] looks like her predecessor of 35 a generation ago" (9). (Are women "looking younger" every generation? Is looking younger looking thinner? Why is looking younger looking better?) Banner observes that the "pouter pigeon" fashion "resembled nothing so much as the sagging breasts of an aging woman without a foundation garment to support them," a busty style derived from "the figure types of aging women" (15), before the 1920s passion for a flat-chested thinness. Comparable to the 1980s (and Jane Fonda, Raquel Welch, Joan Collins, Cher, Tina Turner), "35 no longer became the nexus of midlife; rather 40 and 50 became the defining points of entry into 'middle age.' " Like history, conventions of age repeat themselves.

Regarding aging and the history of the women's movement, Banner notices that while feminist activists of the Progressive era were in large part aging women, in the 1960s this was not the case: "young women came to constitute the majority of the activist feminist force" (30). For these women, aging was not a relevant concern, at least not yet, or until now. In this, they imitated their older forebears who also largely ignored the issue of aging, as do most contemporary feminists. This avoidance of age makes Banner's and Woodward's work both unusual and exemplary. In contrast to Freud's bleak assessment of "women of a certain age," Banner argues that "women of achievement experienced their menopausal years as empowering and invigorating" (31).

Her rather bleak conclusion, however, is that while anthropological studies in other cultures demonstrate an increase in women's power and regard in old age, in the West, with its emphasis on appearance rather than achievement, the opposite is the case for aging women. Like the Hollywood star system (with fewer roles and lower salaries for female actresses each year), women in the U.S. shift from center frame in the child's mirror to a subservient place, off to the side, taking mother's place in the periphery. Yet for women (as Freud knew so well), that image of mother, elided with self, is relinquished, if at all, with great difficulty. Later in the mirror, the old daughter is alone, granting identity not to her children but to her self. The mirror now works in reverse: unlike the child for whom the mirror integrates a body imagined in pieces, the mirror of old age reflects a disintegrating, wrinkled, sagging body, skin separating from muscles and organs like the sack it is, hanging there in folds; it is outlined with an internalized image, a superimposition of youthful memory—of self and of mother who comes back to haunt us. Age is history; the aging body is the historical body. For Woodward, "the body is the permanent record of time" (48).

The Lover

One approach to the body is as memory and memory as embodied. My own memory of my mother is inextricable from palpable images of her thighs, her breasts, her skin. She is dressing for a party and is happy. I still have the grey cashmere sweater she wore that night, now more than thirty years ago. It is a tangible, tactile, precise image scene which forever inhabits her living person. I am not visibly in my story. I am without a direct image of my own body except in old photographs. I identified with Marguerite Duras's words: "When I was a child my mother's unhappiness took the place of dreams. My dreams were of my mother."[15]

"One day, I was already old" are the first words of *The Lover*. Duras's face is "ravaged": "It's scored with deep, dry wrinkles, the skin is cracked. . . . I have a face laid waste." She describes her "ageing" as "very sudden. I saw it spread over my features one by one, changing the relationship between them, making the eyes larger, the expression sadder, the mouth more final" (4–5). While Duras's body is old, her memory is not. Like memory, her body—and her mother's body—is image and story. As an astute aside (in a Rat Man footnote), Freud observes that consolidating childhood memories at a later period "involves a complicated process of remodelling, analogous in every way to the process by which a nation constructs legends about its early history." The "real historian" views the "past in light of the present," and sexualizes memories.[16] This opens up history to include experience, so pertinent for feminism.

"It's not like other bodies, it's not finished. . . . It's still without set form, continually coming into being, not only where it's visible but elsewhere too, stretching beyond sight, toward risk, toward death . . . as if it were grown-up, adult, and it's terribly intelligent" (99). Her sense of being a child in a grown-up body ("the final, decisive knowledge that their mother was a child" [39], or its earlier reverse, a grownup in a child's body, is akin to the uncanny and to my initial experience of aging—the little girl in the middle-aged woman, young and old, internal and external projection, simultaneous yet out of sync. This is the reverse of my kindergarten experience of boarding the city bus as an adult, often treated like the child I resembled but wasn't, at five.

Duras's poetic words resemble Bakhtin's carnivalesque body, which has maternal contours: "The grotesque body is the open, protruding, extended, secreting body, the body of becoming, process, and change." This is "a body in the act of becoming. It is never finished, never completed; it is continually built, created, and builds and creates another body . . . a double body in which one link joins the other, in which the life of one body is born from the death of the preceding, older one."[17] Mother is the life of one body, the body both desired and ignored by Freud. Duras forgets and thus can write: "I no longer have the scent of her skin, or in my eyes the color of her eyes. It's over. I don't remember. That's why I can write about her so easily now. . . . She's become something you write about" (28–29). Duras's identity, pleasure, and solution come from work, her profession—a cure Freud deemed was unavailable for "the unmarried woman, no longer young," a passage to which I will return.

Duras's book—which is also about desire—is a settling of accounts, of coming to terms with the daughter's separation from the mother. The unconscious breaks into the present, like history or a story. Duras: "There, suddenly, close to me was someone sitting in my mother's place who wasn't my mother, who looked like her but who had never been her. . . . There was a youthfulness about her features. . . . She was beautiful. . . . My terror didn't come from her, it came from the fact that that identity had disappeared. There was no longer anything there to inhabit her image" (85). The question of whether we allowed mother an identity, a subjectivity, in the first place is critical.

"Everything connected with this first mother-attachment has in analysis seemed to me so elusive, lost in a past so dim and shadowy, so hard to resuscitate, that it seemed as if it had undergone some specially inexorable repression."[18] While Duras brings Freud's "dim and shadowy past" into focus, intertwining her memory of her mother with an internalized image of herself as a girl, she does not drop the heterosexual imperative of Freud's reading—in which the daughter separates from the mother in order to pass onto men. For Duras, this involves a claim of age for sexuality, for desire. Yet hers is an uneasy and unsatisfying passage. "My memory of men is never lit up and illuminated like my memory of women" (66). "The shapes of men's bodies are miserly, internalized" (72). And if the transference to men is not the singular happy ending, then the separation from mother would be another story (in fact, the feature film rather than the prologue)— one of subjectivity, of identity, of adulthood rather than perennial childhood, a mature and life-granting scenario which would embrace *and* separate from the mother. Perhaps then the image of the self in old age would no longer be haunted or made inadequate by the memory of the little girl. We would live in the present *and* not forget the past. For women, this would be collective, loving autonomy.

The search for mother involves revising the Freudian scenario by inscribing and remodeling memories of female subjectivity, constructing other "legends about our early history" in order not to repeat or internalize diminished accounts which lead to our impoverishment and dependency in middle and old age. One giant step is telling the tale from the old or middle-aged daughter's point of view.

All this illustrates how difficult understanding our relation to our mothers becomes when we are mothers ourselves, or when we are old but they are older, or when they are dead and we are alive. Like aging, mother is a historical process that accumulates memory, which is radically revised over time and with knowledge. (Death, like father, is seen as a climactic event rather than process; having children has recently been emphasized as event, as birth, a one-time experience that women cannot afford to miss rather than a lifelong process.) The memories told by my mother and my grandmother recede further in time, as if they were playing their lives in reverse. With each vivid telling, the details change, becoming clearer, remodeling family and personal history. As experience and memory transform into story, the pain, anger, and confusion of earlier renderings become softened and focused. Remembering their stories grants meaning to their histories and coherence to their memories, keeping them alive, their lives turned into fable and heroic survival.

My grandmother, who began shopping for clothes when she was more than eighty, urges my mother to dye her grey/white hair black. The daughter *as other* testifies to the mother's *external* age, which is not the same as her internal projection, and which she can no longer see clearly in the mirror. For women, the other is a blend of self and mother and daughter; the other is very familiar. As the body changes radically with age, its unfamiliarity becomes an uncanny *experience*, not something "read about," which is why younger women rarely address this difference. I see my grandmother's wizened, tiny body, shrunken with ninety-eight years of aging. It is a body which labored mightily—on a dairy farm in northern Wisconsin, birthing twelve children around a woodburning stove, hand-milking, canning, baking, cleaning, steadily from 4 A.M. to 8 P.M. The only respite was for prayer, her pleasure in devotion, the joy of her faith in God.

Her cat-quick mind's eye and words remember the cold death of her baby from pneumonia, when she was a very young woman, as if it were yesterday. Her voice, like her laugh, is the same, as she singsongedly calls me Patty, remembering the hot August day this city girl cleaned out the chicken coop, with the chickens on their perch above doing what it is chickens constantly do. Or my attempts to befriend dairy cows, like Buster Keaton and Brown Eyes in *Go West*. Or, in my best tomboy fashion of reeking jeans and men's flannel shirt, driving a tractor and raking hay with the other farmers (instead of cooking with the women) during the summer threshing when I was eleven.

While the words are clear, her eyes are slightly fuzzy. With the gradual loss of the eyes' ability to focus, personal age can have a soft-focus, gradual quality, like the vaseline/gauze lens favored by female movie stars. We would not see ourselves as others did. With contact lenses, optical mirrors, and high-intensity lighting, our bodies' changes are clearly visible and magnified. I had imagined doing my mother a favor by buying her a fancy lighted magnifying mirror for eye makeup. She took one look at her huge face and screamed with shock or horror. Because she wears trifocals, she had not seen her face in such clear and direct focus for years. I kept the mirror. There, as in my memory and history, I am framed by my mother and my daughter, both of whom I recognize as myself. With my son, who, like my daughter, looks like me, the story is slightly different.

Not a Jealous Bone

Cecelia Condit's videotape *Not a Jealous Bone* is a jarring and poignant narrative of memory—an encounter of an old woman, Sophie, eighty-two, wrinkled, very heavy, made-up, not apparently beautiful, with a younger, glamorous image, a pretty woman who is frail and sickly. Sophie is looking for her mother, recovering her history while living her daily life in the menacing city streets—perilous places for the aged. The aging or grotesque body meets the youthful or classical body. Memory merges and collides with history. Extreme closeups of fingers, breasts, mouths, false teeth, skin, eyes, and faces, in glimpses of undressing or masquerade, scrutinize and aestheticize the bodies of both women, the body parts as emblems of the passage of time. The body is the sack of skin that it is, merely the surface of the person inside—the guardian of memory who retains continuity and remains ageless.

At surreal moments, little children wearing garish old-people's masks are intercut, suggesting that we age from the moment that we are born, that dying has always been a part of life rather than a big event, that it can happen at any time. The past breaks into Sophie's search for her mother, remembered as young, as self; Super 8mm film and old photographic albums of childhood are reminiscences and clues to identity, mementos of personal history. Another version of memory is intercut in documentary clips of a mother and daughter in a home for the aged; they have lived together for years. The eighty-year-old daughter has Alzheimer's disease, confusing "homely" with "lonely," not recognizing the date or the year. This memory loss prevents women from remembering or telling their stories, their lives repeating childhood or taking on another identity, one removed from family history, which they cannot remember.

The tape is a journey, for Sophie and women in the audience, covering in just a few minutes the topics overlooked in volumes of Freud: mothers, aging, memory, daughters. While the central section involves the positive binarism of youth/age and the comparison between bodies, it is complicated by a frame structure on the visual and aural tracks. The opening scene is at the beach; Sophie's age, rolls of fat, and awkwardness set her apart from the slim, tanned, young bodies that surround her. In the Super 8 footage, she falls down, like a child, often a metaphor of old age. After her successful separation from the hold of the past (and the unconscious)—including the idealization of youth, the negative internalization of mother, and the fear of death, thereby overcoming envy and repressed anger—Sophie returns to the beach, dancing triumphantly to rock and roll, now an adult, a stage Freud's subject rarely reaches, increasingly plagued by fears as he is. The videotape is an unsettling, tender, and finally optimistic projection of our future in age and adulthood.

The title, *Not a Jealous Bone*, the phrase of an ironic cliché applied to women (and perhaps the ominous fairytale line "Give me my bone!") which becomes a visual metaphor and a literal conclusion, is also slightly inaccurate. Rather than the triadic form of jealousy, the tape analyzes the dyadic play of envy (analyzed by Melanie Klein), which has more to do with mother/daughter relationships and aging than the triadic Oedipus, whether positive or negative, pre- or post-. Envy of another, or mother, for women is the mechanism that must be surmounted; and, unless the outcome is something other than hatred, envy will only be turned against the self, dividing women against themselves and others. After Sophie's discovery and acceptance of herself—silencing the negative voices within which tell women they are lacking (too old, too fat, too stupid, too lazy) by outrunning envy—she sheds the stranglehold of the past (and childhood) and dons a fancy formal gown. She is all dressed up, for life, with somewhere to go. One is never too old to change or to grow up.

As Condit (a twin) worked on the tape, the narrative changed drastically, suggesting the stakes and risks of the struggle for women to understand and reenvision (never mind remember) the mother-daughter relationship. Throughout Condit's childhood, her mother had a series of surgeries, ranging from innumerable intestinal repairs and rearrangements to strokes and brain surgery. Because she was hospitalized and absent for long periods of time, Condit frequently believed her mother was dead. That she (I mean mother, but equally applicable to the child) survived these tortures is miraculous and almost horrifying. When Condit describes this carnal scene, it's with a Rembrandt directness of *The Anatomy Lesson*, embellished by Breughel—both a clinical and a magical rendering. In emulation of *Discipline and Punish*, a feminist could begin a book detailing Lloyd's (mom's) medical history, a real torture scene. The carnival of surgery conceals the daughter's fear, guilt, and anger. Thus, the subtle confusion about who *is* the mother (and who is the child), whether she is alive or dead, in the present or in the past, is deeply autobiographical for many women who have had difficulty loving *and* separating from mother and forging self-identity.

In the first version, the eighty-two-year-old daughter killed the young mother with a huge femur bone (from the fairytale line "Give me my bone!" not *2001*), followed by a dancing celebration and a joyous song. Mom is dead! Long live Electra. In the second edit, the young mother lived; however, this got no one anywhere. Furthermore, this upbeat conclusion would have necessitated dropping an entire song and performance which had been taped, "Tough Luck Tom" (Condit's mother is named "Lloyd"), a catchy tune which contains these lyrics: "You are dead and I am still alive." Thus, keeping the mother alive made no therapeutic or narrative sense, and it would have been too costly—economically and psychically. In the third version, mother dies of "natural causes," presumably a heart attack—perhaps a cop-out, but one Condit could live with. In the fourth version, the mother-daughter relationship is there but displaced. "Tom" has been changed to "Mom." The older woman is faced with youth, not a real mother, who dies in the struggle for the bone of life. During this time, involving her father's heart attack and a forced togetherness, Condit had reconciled with her mother, talking with her intimately, for the first time recognizing her mother's subjectivity. She was only human, after all. Condit feared her, and death, no longer. At least, this is my amateur analysis.[19]

The old daughter's search for and separation from her mother involves love and longing, deep emotions embodied in the five songs which orchestrate the tape, a musical scored by Steven Marcus. The lyrics, written by Condit, portray both the dilemmas of age and the poignancy of memory, both linked to mother. Although most of the numbers are over the scenes rather than performed directly, they belong to Sophie and to women in the audience, who have strong empathy with this tape. Mother is a refrain, a thread of Ariadne, leading us through, haunting the work and our memory of it. The third number: "Have you seen my mother, I can't find her anywhere; I'm so old I should not care. . . . She was often kind but she had a darker side and it etched itself on my mind"; or, the second number, which repeats, "Mother, Mother, I'm so lonely for you, Mother, Mother, How is dying, Mother, Mother, I'm afraid of dying, Mother, Mother." Or the fourth song, "Little crimes here and there, murders everywhere, Life's a strange affair, When I feel old, the world is ice cold. . . . I see faces that I know, though they died long ago, I move slow, everywhere I go and now I have nowhere to go," with nowhere repeated as a refrain.

While the three middle numbers are about mother and loss, the first and last songs are upbeat; the daughter has made peace with mother and age. "Maybe when I'm 102, I'll have a lift and look like new. . . . If my mother could see me now, she wouldn't know me anyhow. There's so little left to show of what I looked like years ago. When your body falls apart, remember that it's just a start. It doesn't matter what you're taught, it's never you who will grow old. I'm the same at 82 as I was at 32." The last song is upbeat, "Tough Luck, Mom," with "You are dead but I am still alive. Don't let being dead go to your head, I am old but you are dead."

What Freud cannot state, Condit portrays: The fear of death has everything to do with mother, with the failure to come to terms with that position of subjectivity and identity and meaning—in reality and as mother's voice has been internalized, unconsciously. Sophie confronts her mother and youth, separating from both illusions, escaping the confinement of fear. She becomes an adult rather than repeating childish fears. Death is no longer something to fear but something to accept, like mother. Condit takes Freud's images and fear of the "uncanny" (linked to death and castration) to different ends. His symbols of death and decay signal women's acceptance of aging and adulthood.

This discussion has emerged from serious thought or theory applied to important, historical culture or art, as opposed to popular, immediate culture. Ironically, television represents and enters domestic spaces, which, as we know, are filled with aging mothers—from the beginning, speaking subjects, often stars, on TV. Many feminists, however, are leery of noticing, let alone celebrating, this fact of daily life.

The Disciplined Body

Adrienne Rich's 1979 foreword to *On Lies, Secrets, and Silence* figures television, "a pale, wavering shimmer, emitting incessant noise," as the opiate of women's culture.[20] Her metaphor is an oblong drunk, and its female audience is addicted, domestically submissive, economically dependent. Rich accuses television of breeding "passivity, docility, flickering concentration" (12), and violence by replacing language. "To conjure with the passive culture and adapt to its rules is to degrade and deny the fullness of our meaning" (14). Against "the radical passivity of men" (13), or electronic culture, she advocates folk or verbal culture—"recitation, reading aloud, memorization of poetry" (12).

Rich's Cassandrad is coincident with 1970s binarisms of active/passive, women/men, counterculture/commercial culture. In her scenario, women must avoid, and the critic ignore, TV—even "to conjure . . . is to degrade and deny." While I am sympathetic with her call for women's culture, several things are wrong with dismissal as a strategy for the 1990s—including the fantasy of escaping television representation, which from the beginning has addressed women as subjects (albeit zany wives and crazy mothers) and rearranged everyday life. Television is an apparatus and enunciation of familialism contouring women's daily lives.

Rich's metaphor of addiction also points to obsessional neurosis and to the antidrug campaign of the late 1980s and 1990s. Paradoxically, while TV, with the U.S. government, and celebrities crusade against drug use, with emotional ads for local drug treatment centers (a style parodied by NBC in a July 1990 promo for a sitcom, *Sister Kate*, which promised "treatment" for people without laughter), commercials for other products embody rituals of obsessive-compulsive neurosis, one model of postmodern subjectivity which snugly fits the TV text, and a construct I will elaborate further.

In a brief synopsis, television embodies the contradictions of women's lives—rather than an "either/or" logic, one of "both/and" (the oxymoronic "working mother")—an inclusive logic of creation/cancellation in which mimicry and simulation are stolid cornerstones rather than lofty theoretical embellishments. The cultural logic of television imitates the "diphasic" quality of obsessional neurosis, what Freud calls in *Inhibitions, Symptoms and Anxiety* (1926) "the power of ambivalence": "one action is cancelled out by a second, so that it is as though neither action had taken place, whereas, in reality, both have."[21]

Like Freud's double-dealing joke, TV's enunciation is two-faced, addressing gendered subjects, often both sexes at the same time. The effect, however, is "as though neither action had taken place, whereas, in reality, both have." Thus, it is complexly easy, after arduous labor, to produce contradictions about TV, often shamelessly blatant about its equivocations—particularly regarding gender. Speaking overtly with a forked tongue to males and females in the audience, TV is just not as seamless as cinema. And unlike the early history of film and contemporary theory, TV is determined by aural as much as visual codes, a substantial difference.

Television—embodying contradictions and erasing boundaries between media and spaces—is obsessed with speaking bodies. Like its assertion/diffusion of political positions on news and talk shows, TV's version of the body includes every body—the docile, measured, subjected body of Foucault; the grotesque, transforming body of Bakhtin; the simulated, disguised body of Baudrillard; the sexual body of Freud; and even the desirous, masquerade body of Lacan (albeit rarely the latter).

Foucault's docile, subjected body is TV's subject, at home and onscreen (or working out): "The human body was entering a machinery of power that explores it, breaks it down and rearranges it."[22] Discipline required a realignment of space, emphasizing separation via enclosures and partitions rather than collectivities—like TV sets in individual homes,[23] or the mise-en-scène of situation comedy and local and national news, anchored in bland noplace. Like TV's miniaturizing and divisions of space, discipline parceled time into rigid series, hierarchized, segmented, predictable—the metronome of TV continuity time as minuscule normalcy.

Foucault outlines procedures for subjecting bodies, dated from the end of the seventeenth century and drawn from the military and pedagogy: "The individual body becomes an element that may be placed, moved . . . a fragment of mobile space . . . in order to obtain an efficient machine. . . . The body is constituted as part of a multi-segmentary machine [which] requires a precise system of command."[24] Members of aerobics classes move in tandem with the instructor, imitating confined, inward-turning movements, isolating muscles rather than working them together, as Margaret Morse has assessed.[25] Aerobics involves series, repetition, and imitative discipline meted out in imperative commands. "Divide duration into successive or parallel segments, each of which must end at a specific time" (Foucault, 157). We mimic, count, and repeat during aerobics and are told that we have only four left.

To paraphrase Foucault and the costly revival of Spartanism by Vic Tanney (now Bally's): Exercise involves techniques which impose on the body repetitive and different tasks which are graduated. Think of high-, low-, and intermediate-impact aerobics, graduated weights on the elaborate machines, color-coded as to normality, divided into male and female scales of strength—a coercion and isolation of body parts.

Upon entering programs, instructors measure the body, a standard against which the tightened future of weight loss is assessed. Nautilus, Kaiser, and Eagle machines distinguish and exercise our individual muscles, one at a time, in clubs of rigid dress codes and expensive memberships (a combination of the military school, country club, and public bath). Our separate bodies, visible amidst other bodies but never touching, are interchangeable with machines. Our sweaty labor is a leisure version of assembly-line production, with a twist—we pay for our workout rather than being paid for our work. Thus, the tenets of Fordism and Taylorism have been taken into leisure, while at work, conditions of production are rarely Fordist or Taylorist. Now that labor in a postindustrial age doesn't often require them, particularly for men and hard labor, muscles have become desirable—something else we don't need but want.

In "Artemis Aging," Morse sees exercise as *"holding off* aging and, by implication, *holding onto* a social position. . . . To be old, tired, or unattractive is to be vulnerable to a kind of culture extinction before death."[26] Morse sees exercise as "a ritual of passage for women of middle age and a new commodity in commercial beauty culture" (22). (At my gym, the women are mainly young rather than middle-aged.) She notes the paradoxes and contradictions: "dieting shrinks the body and its power," while "exercise prepares" an active, "freely moving subjectivity." (Women combine dieting with exercise—cancellation/creation.) "Femininity is no longer proposed as nature, but is read as cultural, as work," yet a femininity for Morse in which women are alienated from their bodies, which are not sanctuaries but automatons.

Aerobics is also a $1 billion market, which some analysts say is a "boom which has come and gone," undone by stair-climbing machines, rollerblading, and other fads. Others argue that aerobics will adapt. Experimental instructors are "reggae-ing, tai-chi-ing, hip hop-ing, and even praying to lure aging baby boomers back into the fold." Reebok will invest millions to promote a new gimmick, as yet undiscovered. Simulated skating motions on linoleum in stocking feet looked promising but was abandoned for obvious reasons. Meditation is in the running, as are mythological rituals such as "Around the Fire and the Earth"—grunting to African drumbeats and thereby getting in touch with spirits. Body and Soul Ministries teaches nondenominational, Jesus aerobics. At the moment, spiritualism and multiculturalism are favored. Ethnic beats like Salsarobics are contenders, although step aerobics may already be the winner.[27]

Judith Williamson suggests that this new image of the female body, advocated by fashion magazines and Jane Fonda workout tapes, is masculine: "The desirable shape held out through fashion photos and adverts has been that of a lean, tall, flat-tummied boy—leggy, tight bummed, curveless."[28] Woman's imaginary bodily ideal "that we inevitably compare ourselves with (to be found lacking!)" is masculine, "an imaginary with which we do more than identify: we attempt to incorporate it" (Morse, 33). To derail this new boyish (or girlish, prepubescent) ideal means revising the values attached to "fat, to aging" (Morse, 43). Yet differentiation has also occurred. Madonna's first incarnation as Monroe has been taken to the gym, flesh transformed into taut, lean muscles.

The female body is a construct with a history of imitation and return, like fashion: from the heavy-breasted pouter-pigeon of 1900, to the flat-chested flapper of the 1920s, to the leggy pinup of Alberto Vargas from the late

1920s through the 1950s (in *Esquire* and then *Playboy*) and the big-breasted Monroe ideal. In the 1960s, skinny returned, in the persons of Audrey Hepburn and Twiggy, a fleshless ideal developing into anorexia or into the worked-out, taut, muscular body of the 1990s. Fat has not been fashionable for years, although large breasts are once again "in"—another contradiction for women. Breasts disappear in the dieted and/or worked-out body, transformed into flat-chested muscle. The 1990 image of the muscular and big-boobed body involves cancellation/creation, the latter often by surgical implants. Jane Fonda, like so many other women, has had her breasts enlarged—the style of the late 1980s/1990s.

The 1990 ideal might be more classical, like the Venus de Milo and other Greek models—or like Bev Francis, the Australian weightlifter in *Pumping Iron II: The Women*. Many women are "bulking up," developing larger bodies, a muscular look which may also have been inspired by Arnold Schwarzenegger. This film about competitive women bodybuilders has a fascinating debate about standards of femininity, with doddering old male judges setting the rules, in the end preferring the Rachel MacLeish slim ("female") version. Big, strong women trigger male fear, linking bodybuilders and lesbians. *Pumping Iron II* goes to almost comic lengths to establish each competitor's heterosexuality. This is a tactic of conscious disavowal: Look at all these amazingly strong women working together, touching; see their male-trainer husbands in their bedrooms. The film's racism is even more insidious than its heterosexist terror. While cast as a battle between MacLeish and Francis, the competition is won by a black woman. Her victory is a real documentary anticlimax for the film's narrative drama. While the white competitors are frequently shown together in groups, the black bodybuilder was usually isolated, alone, "separate but equal" reinforced in the mise-en-scène and editing.

Cutting through all varieties of physique is a loathing for fat, for excess. (The judges deemed that Francis weighed too much.) "By 1988, diet clinics were a $10-billion-a-year industry, and hospital-sponsored programs generated $5.5 billion more, says Market Data Enterprises." "The money isn't in people who are medically at risk, the money is in the cosmetically obese, with 20 to 30 pounds to lose."[29] As Lily Tomlin quips, "I have lost the same twenty pounds so many times that my cellulite is experiencing deja vu."[30] The day Oprah broadcast her eighty-pound weight loss in 1989, the formula diet company received a "million telephone calls" (6E). Dieting, of course, not only is comic or profitable; it can also be a deathly obsession, anorexia or bulimia.

Regarding drag, or transvestism, Williamson wonders why "female body characteristics are supposedly funny, while male ones patently aren't?" (48). Women's lack of power and inferior status are her answers and her explanation for why "the 'silliest,' least valued shape for either men *or* women, is 'womanly' " (50). As she reminds us, "To play with the language of gender is not to escape it, merely to detach it from the sex of the 'wearer' " (54).

In 1991, girdles, abandoned with sighs of relief in the 1960s, are making a comeback—redesigned, recalibrated: differentiated. The corseted return is attributed to the new short, tight fashions and the aging (read "female") of the populace. "A little jiggle was fine when baggier styles hid all sins. But today, the body-hugging spandex dress is the rage and it is unforgiving when it comes to imperfection."[31] "Sins" and "imperfection" apply only to female bodies, held to more rigorous standards than those of men. Men can protrude, bulge, and sag with little or no guilt. The out-of-shape female body produces shame.

"An aging population has begun the long, slow surrender to flab. . . . Women of a certain age really could use some real support." (It would be nice if "support" would come in the form of money and power rather than spandex.) Although one brief male example is dropped in—Under Wares sells girdles to men, called a "man's support article," a "Manshape" garment—the massive presumption is that the aging, imperfect body is resolutely female. The codpiece, unlike padded bras and buttocks, is not, as far as I know, making a fashionable return. Nor is it being differentiated. Unlike the measurements of women's breasts, and female genitals, sized for diaphragms, penis size is sacred and remains a secret, except for Madonna, who remarks on the size of men's "units."

Sales of "body shapers," aka girdles or "foundations," have increased 7 percent since 1989. Bloomingdale's reported a jump of 35 percent (from December 1990 to May 1991) in the sales of stretch half-slips with sewn-in panties, called Hip Slip and Under Wonder. In a great paradox, spandex, the fiber used in making girdles, is responsible for their return. Spandex has blended into high fashion—which is imitating exercise clothing or the garb of women working the streets, the prostitution trade—necessitating the return of the girdle.

The return of breasts, along with the increase in the average U.S. bust size from a 34B to a 36C (amazing!), is another explanation. (I wonder if a similar increase has occurred for men. Will penile implants be as popular as breast implants?) After the 1960s, we either wore "no-bras" or no bras. Now, old-fashioned, push-up contraptions of wire and black lace have returned, along with molded cups. Post-Madonna, and as a result of clothes designed for sports, underwear has become outerwear, or the bodily private and intimate has, like everything else, including talk, gone public, been Donahued or Oprahsized. There is another difference, along with the sexual, from antediluvian private garments which stretched "only one way—horizontally." Playtex has differentiated and cleverly renamed its products: "The End" and "Subtract." However, my healthy favorite is Appel, which "gives active women the choice of the running bra, the action bra, the racquet bra [the RACQUET bra?] and—new this fall—the golf bra [!], which gives a woman "the freedom to take her golf swing while her bra stays in place," says Norman Katz, chairman of I. Appel. With differentiation comes specialization. Girdles taper hips, thighs, or abdomens. The biggest seller is the "Thigh Slimmer," stretch shorts with side panels that "compress thunder thighs." The Aubergine "flattens the tummy but not the buttocks." Many wearers let these garments show beneath shorts—the Madonna effect, which combines lingerie with exercise clothes and sex with working out. As with Madonna looking like Marilyn Monroe, this is the return of the 1950s—differentiated—worked-out, taut, and muscular.

Helen Gurley Brown, "paper-thin" editor of *Cosmopolitan*, says she won't be wearing a girdle, although she "applauds other women for trying to fix their bodies with a girdle." Eva Gabor says that "you must suffer for everything. . . . You can't be comfortable if you want to look smashing." These double-whammies of "look good/feel bad" have been psychically and physically uncomfortable for years. I remember my history as a tomboy and a fat girl (actually a memory that was imaginary, not real; I *felt* fat and, despite photos to the contrary, remember myself as fat). After leaving the house for school wearing a girdle that cut off virtually all circulation to my legs, I would sneak into a filling-station bathroom, take off the torturous contraption, breathe an exquisite sigh at the pleasure of release, and stuff the hideous thing into my pocket. For big dances, I would squeeze my body into a corset and from there into a too-small-waisted dress. During one pre-prom dinner, I sneezed and, to my everlasting chagrin, split the entire side seam of my red taffeta gown (a *Jezebel* tribute). I thank God for the women's movement of the 1960s, which, among many political issues, included a campaign for the health and comfort of the female body, along with acceptance of our various shapes, sizes, and selves. Under the 1980s and 1990s regime of health and exercise, these gains, like fat, have partially vanished from contemporary styles. The return of the pencil-thin Audrey Hepburn—like other celebrated women of my past who had anexoric bodies which I failed to notice—in spite of the addition of muscles and breasts, is not a good sign of the times.

TV both traverses *and* maintains Habermas's and Foucault's divide between the public sphere and the private home, representing and entering governmental agencies and domestic bedrooms with undecorous aplomb—the former filled with business-suited men and the latter with aging mothers. While this is a significant gain for maternal difference, TV's bodily codes adhere to sexual difference and a fundamentalist propriety, particularly when it comes to the ideology of age and gender. The political distance between Lucille Ball's portrayal of a bag lady on a made-for-TV movie, *Stone Pillow*, and the visual disturbance of encountering real street people in public places, uncontained like mad people in the seventeenth century—a modern eruption from the private spaces hiding the poor and aging—is not insignificant.

Although Ball played old and her hair and lips were not flaming red, it was this sweet and savvy character's independent choice, after all, to remain outside. The sweet and crazy old bag lady returned on the premiere of Jane Pauley's *Real People* (summer 1990), located by her daughter in a search for her mother and her identity. Accompanied by NBC cameras, the daughter tracked her mother to New York, a park bench, and finally a shelter for the homeless, where they were reunited. Photographs of the old woman's suburban past as a young, beautiful prom queen, then a wife and glamorous New York showgirl, with remembrances by her brother of her incarcerations in asylums, suggest that her fate could befall anyone: now she was toothless, fat, scraggly-haired. "The homeless old bag lady embodies the worst fears for the future of even successful women. Oddly enough, considering that a bag lady may not eat regularly, in our imagination she is " 'fat' " (Morse, 21). Although her "real" mother died two weeks after the reunion, for the daughter, finding her mother, even as a toothless bag lady, was a happy completion rather than a tragic loss.

If the Salvation Army cannot contain the poor and aging, then TV will defuse social, economic issues (which link women, insanity, and the family as did this story) by transforming them into either Lucy or *Real People*. In the divisions between daytime and primetime, entertainment and news, the aberrant and the normal (and homosexuality and heterosexuality), taxonomies emblematic of private/public spaces, TV enacts institutional containment—reminiscent of Foucault's definition of the disciplinary society.

Along with poverty and insanity, TV also mediates death, "grief on the go." A funeral parlor at Gatling's Funeral Home on Chicago's South Side has added a drive-through service with video cameras, monitors, and a sound system. "Visitors pay their respects, sign the funeral register and view the remains of the loved one round the clock without ever leaving the car." Mourners request a particular dead body on a speakerphone (as at McDonalds—imagine confusing the two places!), then drive to a viewing area where "a head shot of the loved one in a coffin instantly appears on a 25 inch screen." While the picture lasts only three seconds, the button can be pushed over and over, until pressure from the next car urges the grief-stricken to drive away. All this because mourners no longer have *time* to come in, and don't want to *wait*.

Another version of video and death is the "Tribute" video hawked by the National Music Service, a Spokane, Washington, company that "provides recorded music" to funeral homes. "I first thought about it when John F. Kennedy was assassinated. . . . Why can't a tribute to be paid to us normal peons rather than just reserved for heads of state? Do not our families love us as much as JFK was loved?" The "Tributes" intercut photographs and still "nature" images, all edited to tunes from the music service's 2,500-title library. Friends of Amanda Blake, Miss Kitty on *Gunsmoke*, "bought a Tribute video that was played on a huge TV monitor at her Aug. 24 memorial service in Sacramento, Calif."[32]

The inversion of this final, sanctified, whole image of the dead body or "loved one" is the cut-up body, the body of live TV surgery. "Relatives can get a close look at a loved one's surgery." In Oshkosh, Wisconsin, Bernice Hoke "gazed intently at a television screen a few feet in front of her as a surgeon made an incision in her aunt's eye." Although this sounds like the real remake of *Un Chien Andalou*, Bernice's response was, "Well, isn't that interesting," and "Isn't that beautiful." The Doctors SurgiCenter bought $10,000 worth of video equipment and has gone into business; along with closed-circuit monitoring, they sell videos of the surgery "which can be watched at home later and shown to other family members or friends." (What a great night! Let's invite the neighbors to see our new tape!)

Not all the doctors at the center are so enthused about these video visions: "They don't like the feeling of people watching over their shoulders" (or, more likely, they fear a malpractice suit). Rose Olsen, who watched her seventy-five-year-old husband receive a lens implant, "became a little queasy. . . . 'It gets to you a bit when it is your loved one.' " However, she enjoyed "every bit" of his second procedure. " 'It takes the scariness away,' she said of seeing the operation live."[33]

"A Philadelphia woman who underwent back surgery on live TV" did it to help others. This surgery to correct curvature of her spine, making her taller than her 5'9" frame, was shown on public TV. It received a "6.9 rating and an 11% share" against *Kate & Allie, Alf*, and *MacGyver*.[34] Like the all-travel channel, there will soon be a surgery channel, one not just closed-circuited to doctors. In many ways, TV is breaking down privacy, secrecy, and professional preserves.

Like increments of time, the mainly white body (although the network coverage of the 1988 Olympics, at which the nation/U.S. was represented by black athletes, necessitated special commercials with black actors, which in turn has led to increased representation of African-Americans) is anatomically seriated via extreme closeups and gendered—at a glance. If the body suggests "deviant" readings, as did Bev Francis in *Pumping Iron II*, other systems constrain it. Deviance depends on a norm or major premise, heterosexuality, and a point of view: deviant for whom? The concept of "passing" can thus trigger paranoia or revelation, as in the case of Malcolm Forbes. As Foucault argued, and thirty-second grief demonstrates, paradoxically, tactics which individualized and privatized the body also subjected it.

The TV homebody is surveyed, examined, and tested by the Nielsen ratings and reception theorists alike. The Birmingham School analyzed the audience more than representation; data produced a resistant homebody which was not so disciplined. Some scholars took this to be a transgressive body, like Hulk Hogan, a subcultural body of "the people" which can be spoken for by the intellectual. Others, like David Morley's *Family Television*, deduced from on-locale interviews with "actual viewers" an account of familial watching strangely akin to Madison Avenue: men watched sports and women soaps; men viewed silently while women talked. The move from Foucault to Bakhtin (like U.S. foreign policy during the late 1980s, from Europe to the Soviet Union) was a predictable one. Baudrillard's conception of the mass as fascinated rather than convinced by TV was also compatible, although his cynical stance regarding popular culture would prove politically troublesome to a celebratory pluralist position.

XI

◆

Obsessive Subjects
Renifleurs

Unlike representations of the ideal, visual (youthful, female, and white) body in cinema (although this classical ideal is invoked and hovers over), television also represents and addresses a flawed, tactile, pre-exhibitionist body, with commercials predicated on smell, taste, and touch speaking about the most intimate bodily functions—hunger and thirst in commercials for prepackaged *fast* food, epitomized by the burger, cola, and beer wars; smell *as*/and cleanliness via cleaners, deodorants, and perfumes for every orifice, limb, and apparel of the body, each niche of the household; excretion in ads for diapers, hemorrhoids, constipation, diarrhea, menstruation, incontinence; pain in aspirin, arthritis, menstrual products; and everyday favorites, indigestion, insomnia, colds, flu, hay fever, allergies, and headaches. Age, menopause, PMS, and weight are all afflictions which can be cured by products recommended by pharmacists or middle-aged sufferers.

Commercials, based on discomfort and regression (sometimes literally, as men with colds become whining little boys; eating Grape Nuts also can trigger instant, snotty male regression), uncannily resemble Freud's "obsessional neuroses symptoms," which "tend to repetition and waste of time, attached to activities like sleep, washing, dressing, and walking about," and which "prevent associations and connections of thoughts by isolating, removing the possibility of contact, predicated on the taboo against touching."[35] TV's hungry, odorous, inadequate yet eternally optimistic body in pain is overweight, out of shape, wrinkled. It is an aging body inscribed in generational differences spanning a spectrum of age which includes childhood.

In one interpretation this could be the Bakhtinian body, which resembles the maternal body or the pumped-up, cyborgian body, and television's flow, which has an indiscrete, transformative quality. Unlike the Freudian body, the TV text (and audience) can be imagined as an indivisible body without inner/outer, self/other polarities in which the exterior is inauthentic, merely a cover-up; it is a body of doubled surfaces rather than inner recesses which need to be analyzed, explained. But this is not the whole story. For what is crucial for the TV body in pain is that it can be altered and fixed, particularly by medication, including aging creams and weight-loss products. Rather than the celebratory Bakhtinian body, this is an inadequate body, too fat, too old. This is also the body of addiction, caught in obsessive compulsions.

This model of subjectivity differs substantially from both film theory and Fredric Jameson's postmodern schizophrenic, an amnesiac who has lost history and memory through the "transformation of reality into images, the fragmentation of time into a series of perpetual presents."[36] Collapsing "the media" into the schizophrenic subject, Jameson argues the "disappearance of a sense of history, the way in which our entire contemporary social system has little by little begun to lose its capacity to retain its own past" (125). "Schizophrenic experience" consists of "isolated, disconnected, discontinuous material signifiers which fail to link up into a coherent sequence. The schizophrenic thus does not know personal identity in our sense" (119). For me, schizophrenia, known in the shrink trade as a cognitive rather than affective disorder, is a limited model for the TV text/audience (although it has its moments, for example, *Twin Peaks*).

Jameson's schizophrenic is also not the schizo of Deleuze and Guattari. For them, the schizo position is on the periphery, "opposed to the paranoid position of the mass subject [which is akin to Jameson's and Baudrillard's models], with all the identifications of the individual with the group, the group with the leader, and the leader with the group."[37]

"On a wider scale, if a paranoiac delusion is a caricature of philosophy [Baudrillard], and hysteria a caricature of a work of art [1970s film theory], then obsessionality figures likewise with regard to religion" [fundamentalism, the New Right, and TV] (Mahony 170). By 1931, Freud distinguished three libidinal types, "the erotic, the narcissistic, and the obsessional" (173), traits which can be intermixed, providing recombinant subjectivities for the TV-audience encounter.

Comparable to television commercials obsessed with the digestive/excremental tract, including bran cereals and the new campaign for Metamucil called "fiber therapy," and the emergence of AIDS and vindictive homophobia, Rat Man contains a primal, recurrent scene of excremental torture in which trapped rats eat their way through a man's anus and intestines, an image more excruciating than Foucault's painful citation of a torturous quartering of the body which opens *Discipline and Punish*. Unlike Foucault, however, who, in the name of history, brazenly elaborates and perversely elongates the spectacle of dismemberment (to elicit confession), Freud anxiously embeds Lanzer's rat nightmare in a fragmented scene concealed in dialogue taken from personal observations recorded in notes of the sessions (which lasted only three months). Freud is uncomfortable with this scene, interrupting with reassurances rather than listening. Here is a condensed and hence more violent version:

After Lanzer began his tale by describing the loss of his glasses, " 'the captain told me he had read of a specially horrible punishment used in the East. . . . ' He begged me to spare him the recital of the details. . . . I assured him that I myself had no taste whatever for cruelty, and certainly had no desire to torment him." The enactment and repression of the homosexuality of the exchange are not without interest. After Freud's assurance, Lanzer continues, with descriptive interruptions by Freud, almost stage directions for this analytic scene: "The criminal was tied up. . . . A pot was turned upside down on his buttocks. . . . Some *rats* were put into it . . . and they . . . *bored their way in*. . . . ' Into his anus, I helped him out" (SE X, 166). These thoughts were "entirely foreign and repugnant" to both Lanzer and Freud (SE X, 167).

"The Father Complex and the Solution of the Rat Idea" is a Freudian subtitle which says it all. Eventually the analysis will be run back through Oedipus, avoiding homosexuality yet analyzing obsessional neurosis as a fixation to sadistic anal eroticism (in 1913 in "The Disposition to Obsessional Neurosis" [Mahony, 158]). Although "the idea of punishment carried out by means of rats had acted as a stimulus to a number of his instincts and had called up a whole quantity of recollections," Freud runs it back to infantile sexuality.

Crucial for my purposes, Freud also *equates rats with money*, "the whole complex of money interests which centred round his father's legacy to him" (SE X, 213). The linkage between obsession and money (the swerve of desire from sex to economics and to anxiety) is important, at least for me. (Like obsession, money lacks a material base, and is increasingly less tangible in electronic stock markets.) After this profitable assessment, rats are then unfortunately linked to disease, syphilis (it could be AIDS), the penis, "the rat as the male organ of sex." Finally, after discussing with some revulsion "intercourse *per anum*" suggested by the rat tale, rats are connected to children. "When we reached the solution that has been described above, the patient's rat delirium disappeared" (SE X, 220).[38] This tepid "solution" suggests that this case needs to be reopened.

Mahony's most enticing reconstruction/critique concerns the place of "mother"— observations not taken to feminist argument: "The relatively pallid picture of the Rat Man's mother and the full-bodied picture of his father fit the lopsided pattern in Freud's descriptions of both Dora's and Little Hans's parents" (35). Mahony reiterates an early challenge issued by Rank: "All factors clearly point to the patient's love for his mother," who was miserly, compulsively neat, controlling, and, for Mahony, "dangerously seductive and phallic" (36).

Near the conclusion of this case, Freud *very briefly* discusses the epistemophilic instinct (rarely mentioned in other texts and, in fact, never elaborated), connecting looking and knowing, scopophilia and epistemophilia —the latter more applicable to TV than scopophilia, a primary mechanism (and a perverted one at that) beneath feminist film theory. In epistemophilia, "the thought process itself becomes sexualized, for the sexual pleasure which is normally attached to the content of thought becomes shifted on to the act of thinking itself, and the satisfaction derived from reaching the conclusion of a line of thought is experienced as a *sexual* satisfaction" (SE X, 245)—an epistemophilic satisfaction excessively thwarted by the "concluding" episode of *Twin Peaks* in May 1990. Epistemophilia transforms actions into the pleasure (or displeasure) of thoughts, a pleasure then derived not from the content of thoughts but from the process of thinking, perhaps preventing action, a formidable procrastination.

One major and, I would assert, defining pleasure of television is derived from various forms (processes analogous to thinking) more than their content—the *process* of daytime soaps, the *process* of catastrophe, the *process* of sitcoms. Familiarity (and predictability) along with innumerable *conclusions* (within and between programs) of thousands of lines of thought (the tiny but resolute satiations of promos, newsbreaks, commercials, summations, trailers, logos, to say nothing of program conventions), on TV breeds not contempt but high ratings and longevity, like Johnny Carson. (Why does Carson conclude the monologue by pantomiming golf?) Critics looking at content and theme throw up their hands in dismay at the trash on TV, never realizing that the knowledgeable TV viewer is dealing with form, is experiencing pleasure of another kind, one which is learned, paradoxically enough, from TV.

Or, like racial, sexual, and ethnic differences, epistemophilia sells, has become marketable. Estee Lauder—under the tutelage of the young, stylish exec Robyn Burns, formerly of Calvin Klein and Obsession fame— began its campaign in May 1991 for its new perfume, Knowing, which could be marketed as a scent for the intelligent "renifleur." Burns must have read Freud on "obsession"—which has everything to do with thought, with the desire to know, with epistemophilia, not scopophilia.

As almost an afterthought, Freud abruptly throws out a metaphor of subjectivity—the renifleur: "more susceptible to sensations of smell than most people . . . a tendency to taking pleasure in smell, which has become extinct since childhood, may play a part in the genesis of neurosis" (SE X, 247). Freud then connects smell to sex, and the rest is forgotten history.

The number of TV commercials devoted to odor prevention, necessitating new zones and sources of smell, sketch a model of the TV homebody as "renifleur." If I could only uncover another bodily odor zone (feet, under-arms, genitals, and mouths have already been spoken for), I could make millions! Eye odor? Knee sweat? I've got it! Either under-breast or under-chin (perhaps back-of-knee).

Renifleurism is also big business. The battle between Estee Lauder and Calvin Klein is between "the family owned House of Lauder," a $2.5 billion enterprise, versus Unilever Group, an Anglo-Dutch company which bought Klein in 1989 and also owns Elizabeth Arden, which is marketing Liz Taylor's perfume, White Diamonds. Klein's new fragrance is Escape; Lauder's is Spellbound; both are "floral bouquets with spicy un-dertones. Even the bottles were created by the same designer." What makes this high drama is Burns's presence at the top and the fact that "sales are flat." With over "500 fragrances on the market and another 22 scents" being introduced in 1991, Christmas competition—the big season, ac-counting for "over 40% of perfume sales"—will be intense. Robyn Burns's campaign was inspired by *Ghost* and *Pretty Woman*, the high profits garnered by romance.[39]

In *Inhibitions, Symptoms and Anxiety*, a text which returns seventeen years later (inflected by World War I and shell shock) to the concerns of Rat Man, Freud traces the origin of anxiety back to "missing someone who is loved and longed for," with anxiety a "situation of non-satisfaction in which the amounts of stimulation rise to an unpleasurable height without its being possible for them to be mastered . . . or discharged." In relation to the im-perfect body addressed by TV commercials, TV preys on/creates nonsatis-faction. Like the rest of Freud, sexual difference circulates. "It is precisely in women that the danger-situation of loss of object seems to have re-mained the most effective." Women's "loss" of youth as if it were a tangible object (not a time), measured by our faces and bodies, rather than a gain of wisdom and influence over time, is a manufactured fear that verges on a national obsessive-compulsion.

Women's Bodies

While television does directly address women, in commercials perhaps more than men, granting us subjectivity—no small step for humankind—it urges relentless, microscopic self-scrutiny and physical transformation. Pi-erre Janet's 1903 taxonomy of shame is applicable to TV commercials and women: self-shame, shame of one's body, and hypochondria. Graham Reed updates Janet's list to include shame of self (social abilities); shame of self (moral and characterological); shame of one's physique; hypochondri-acal; death, dirt and contamination; and possible harm to oneself and pos-sible harm to others (Reed, 27–32).

While Janet and Reed fail to note sexual difference, Freud's assessment does not. The obsessive subject, a female subject(!), has two "different outlooks upon life." "She puts forward the first of them (easy going and lively) as her official ego, while in fact she is dominated by the second (gloomy and ascetic)." Although Freud is, as usual, negative when speaking of women, "she" becomes a subject. Behind the latter gloom and asceticism are "ancient and long-repressed wishful impulses." (See their emergence, and the accompanying male fear, in *Thelma and Louise*.) "Long-repressed" resembles Freud's anatomy of "humour," predicated on rage. On the way to the gallows, as in many women's lives, rather than directing anger outward, the subject takes anger inward—finding herself inadequate. Rather than railing against social conditions, TV urges us to change our bodies, our clothes, our lifestyles. By preying on shame, it catches the victim in a contradictory logic in which she assumes the blame—a double whammy which orchestrates many women's lives.

On TV, the female body in disarray is in need of infinitely more repair and more products than the male body. (Address reveals demography, a female audience, along with very old-fashioned divisions of labor: women clean, cook, and shop more than men.) It is significant that hair products for balding, a man's dilemma, have only recently been advertised, allusively so by Upjohn, the drug manufacturer, on network TV; they appear mainly in late-night commercials/testimonials, after the faith healers, nuns, and failed game shows, intimating that loss of hair is neither flaw nor problem, like the rest of the male body. As Woodward has pointed out, for Freud in "The Dream-Work," baldness, along with "hair-cutting, falling out of teeth and decapitation," represents castration rather than aging.

And, speaking of Freud's favorite topic, while TV men have bad breath and underarm odors which cause double-take recoils, there unfortunately are few products which will improve their genitals, in contrast to women and "feminine protection"—a phrase undoubtedly turned by a Madison Avenue man, which gives virginal pause. However, this is changing. Ex-stars (Chad Everett) hawk products (penile implants) in thirty-minute "informercials"—commercials which are a cross between talk shows and testimonials.

Vaginas have become big business for a corporate battle right out of *Oedipus*.[40] After the Food and Drug Administration approved the over-the-counter sale of medications for female yeast infections in November 1990, the competition between Johnson & Johnson, which previously had over 80 percent of the prescription market, and Schering-Plough Corporation, which had a paltry 8 percent, began. David Collins, after spending twenty-six years at Johnson & Johnson (including the two Tylenol poisoning incidents), "masterminded" the yeast infection campaign for Schering. As *The Wall Street Journal* unwittingly remarked about this vaginal corporate assault, "The prize is huge. Analysts say manufacturers' sales . . . could top $400 million by 1995. This is a brand new consumer market, and it's going to be big. . . . This is a serious battle" (A9). Exactly what "it" is and "this" means are up for grabs.

Suffice it to say that vaginas, particularly those with yeast infections, mean money, and, for Collins, power and revenge (J & J had passed him over for the top slot). All the soldiers with their eyes on the prize (worth "150 million for the first year of sales") are men. Another irony is that women will pay more—the cost of over-the-counter drugs is not paid by insurance.

None of this high Oedipal drama would have been possible without women. As a result of FDA approval, Schering-Plough's Gyne-Lotrimin had a three-month lead time (an advantage which might make the difference) on Johnson & Johnson's Monistat 7. Schering had swayed the FDA with an unsettling yet not surprising study in which women correctly diagnosed their yeast infections 72 percent of the time—a higher accuracy rate than that of the physicians they visited. Within five weeks of approval, they were shipping Gyne-Lotrimin to stores via overnight mail. "Because the two products are so similar," the two companies are "emphasizing marketing over medicine," with estimates of $100 million spent to "woo women during the rollout." (Last year, J & J spent $90 million advertising Tylenol.) "It's going to be a mega-battle."

The high-stakes maneuvering for women's bodies is being fought in the "pages of consumer magazines and on network television," but also in doctors' offices. One of the reasons that Johnson & Johnson had cornered the prescription market was their targeted selling to doctors. For this campaign, Schering has hired a "220-person outside sales force to ply physicians with free samples and cajole them into mentioning the brand to their patients." The company will also advertise on Whittle Communications' Special Reports Network, which reaches "about 20,000 doctors' offices"—an example of direct or special-interest advertising (and a specialized TV service which links television and waiting, already in supermarkets and coming soon to other places where people wait in line). However, 70 percent of Schering's "marketing dollars" will be directed at consumers.

One ad campaign presents female gynecologists who have had yeast infections commiserating with sufferers and proclaiming that "relief is now available." These ads for the euphemistically labeled "personal care products" can be aired on the networks only during daytime programming and after 9 P.M. In a debated, daring first for television, the word "vaginal" is used twice. "We wanted to be straightforward. . . . Women are ready to hear it." *Women* are ready to hear "vagina"? Are men ready to hear "penis"? Why are there no "personal care products" for that appendage?

One can imagine David Collins, the Norman Schwarzkopf of vaginal campaigns, standing beside his graphs and charts, wielding a pointer and deploying his weapons and troops against the silent enemy, Johnson & Johnson. The female body as a site of battle has a famous history—the battle of the bulge.

A regimen of reconstruction by dieting and working out, plastic (euphemistically, cosmetic) surgery, masquerade, or "makeovers" is urged on inadequate bodies in need of overhaul. The propagation of wares, like channels and programs, operates, if we want to be fancy, paradigmatically as well as syntagmatically: like women's clothing, makeup is layered, with daytime and nighttime versions, necessitating at least two eyeliners and three shades of seasonal eyeshadows (in 100 colors, by countless manufacturers), smoothed over an eye-wrinkle cream; combined with various colors of mascara, this adds up to the purchase of a minimum seven products. Lips follow suit: cream, lipstick, lip liner, then a gloss total four products. The same accumulation is true for current hairstyles; after shampoo, equalizer, conditioner or rinse, and color toner, a mousse is applied, followed by either gel or gallons of hairspray. When aging cream, moisturizer, foundation base, powder, shading stick for bags, and blush-on are tallied, twenty-two products are washed down the drain with every daily shower and early evening bath. The estimate of this costly masquerade, designed to appear "natural" (with invisible mascara the most recent absurdity), does not calculate the variety of colors or the concealed lotions, deodorants (for women, at least three body zones, not counting the mouth), oils, and perfume, or the ephemeral fact of twice-daily reapplication and touch-up.

The genius of capital here is creating not only new looks but also new problems and spaces for our relatively small faces, which need new products—the brilliance of differentiation, what Hilary Radner, after Deleuze and Guattari, calls "deterritorialization and reterritorialization."[41] "The defining instance of making up is not representation but exchange, here exchange of capital. It is crucial to spend money on makeup . . . pleasurable precisely because it is excessive, without any 'real' purpose." In *The Theory of the Leisure Class,* Thorstein Veblen provided the classic capitalist maxim: the more something costs, the more it will be valued. (This was pre–discount store, pre-Loehmann's, which is a different kind of libidinal exchange.) "The results of this process are usually imperceptible to anyone but the practitioner herself. . . . It is this investment that makes the process signify differently, through an economy that is not grounded in rational equivalence." I suspect, in contrast, that for "the practitioner" the process is "imperceptible." Marketers understand this investment clearly. "The money sign" regulates "a flow of figuration without representation" (311). Thus, money works.

Women's work (and leisure, which includes working out) is shopping (not in one store but many, selecting among not three lipsticks but a thousand) and the preparation of their bodies and their homes for the party and public life (women with careers perform the same rituals, only faster); on television, men just show up. Like the network division between entertainment and news, women are linked with affairs of the body, including time-consuming consumption, while men deal with affairs of state. Television is a how-to training manual for exhibitionism, a medium of passage, with stars like Cher moving on to the big-time of cinema, and older performers like Lucille Ball, Mary Tyler Moore, Bea Arthur, and Angela Lansbury returning from Broadway and the movies, older and wiser.

(Shopping can be heavy, repetitive labor, carried on in supermarket warehouses, or it can be mothering—my mother still buys all my father's clothes. For Benjamin, thinking of Baudelaire, shopping [although he and his disciples never label it as such, the shopper becoming the fancier "flaneur"] was an experience of public shock and private desire—an illicit, desirous adventure with mass culture wares equated with prostitutes. For me, shopping is rarely akin to Benjamin's pleasure, although I do experience the rush of discount and markdowns. Along with physical labor, shopping is one cover-up for the anxiety of loss, separation, or fear of inadequacy; it can become an addiction like food.)

At the same time that TV etches an inadequate female body, an image of the classical body of Freud—irreparably divided by age and sex—haunts television and our lives. Thus, sleek, glamorous models sell cosmetics and other female products, with a twist—for their own and our own pleasure, the "I'm worth it" gambit. In an analysis of post-1970 ad campaigns for makeup, Radner labels this an "effect of pleasure" in which "the feminine is situated as a subject of her own pleasure" (314). This could also be the dyad of envy rather than the triad of jealousy. For Radner, this is a historical change from the "domestically oriented woman to a woman who sought to please herself. Femininity was no longer exclusively defined through the representation of male desire" (302)—at least not male *sexual* desire. (Conversely, it might represent women's internalization of themselves as male fantasies.)

Quoting the writings of female ad execs, Radner argues that this image of women is not for male consumption. At the same time, Radner is aware that "the dominant economy predicated on feminine narcissism as a reconstitution and objectification of the male look has not been replaced; rather the two exist alongside each other. This new libidinal economy would be one of affect [also called "figuration" (314)] rather than representation (as in an oedipalized regime)" (305). She posits a "new libidinal economy that conflates the two seemingly contradictory demands of femininity and autonomy" (304). Her analysis uncannily fits my Freudian model of contradiction which also has a TV twist. In contrast to the Marxist analysis of the commodity fetish, which depends on a covert operation which severs the worker from the product (and from affect, it might be argued), postmodern capital brazenly announces what was formerly concealed, like Linda Evans and Cybill Shepherd proclaiming rather than denying their use of hair-color products. However, I do not agree with Radner that this is new or a necessarily good thing. Because we know we're being ripped off doesn't change things. It is denial.

Radner links makeup to capital: "It is her credit rating and available credit line that she announces," with "capital" opening up "moments of personal resistance as pleasure" (314). Herein lies the problem: She plays into *his desire for her money*. Within the pleasure regime of the *declared* commodity fetish, the economy, or money, has replaced alienated work and sex as the mechanism of desire. The postmodern subject might no longer be primarily divided by language or sexual difference but by money, with economics replacing linguistics (and sexuality) as the new theoretical foundation for cultural analysis.

If we calculated differently, by the pound and gallon rather than quarter-ounces and grams, the cost of makeup would be apparently astronomical and nonsensical: one and one-fourth ounces of Germaine Monteil's Infusion, a "triple action firmer," costs $40, with one pound costing more than $500, a shocking expenditure. We should be cautious of pleasures which objectify, which depend on our remaining objects: in gossip, spoken for and about; in cosmetics, half-subject/half–visual object. Thus, while I understand and live Spacks's and Radner's mutual claims, I question either their empowering or resistant potential.

Lily Tomlin as the upper-class, bored, but acutely fashionable Kate says while waiting for the hairstylist, Anouk, to undo the harm done by Bucci the Arrogant: "This side ends well above the left ear, and this side ends, as you can see, at the collarbone. . . . There were people in the streets actually staring at my haircut. People who normally would be intimidated. . . . I am *sick* of being the victim of trends I reflect but don't even understand."

XII

♦

Aging Bodies

The sexing of the shopping, consuming body as female, as Tammy Faye Bakker – Imelda Marcos (or Roseanne Barr, Zsa Zsa Gabor, and Leona Helmsley) excess (concealing real social and political problems), is linked to the grostesque body and opposed to the classical body, which is monumental, static, closed, sleek, and quiet. While women's work is consumption, this labor must not show, like Marx's commodity fetish. As I stated, a sanctified image of the classical body haunts television and inhabits our bathroom mirrors: in U.S. culture, the ideal body, although historically inflected by physical fashions of height, weight, and anatomical emphases (breasts in the '50s, buttocks in the '80s; short legs in the '20s, elongated in the '40s) in one regard never changes—it is a youthful, thin body, airbrushed of blemishes, lines, and wrinkles.

Like psychoanalysis itself, which is a doggedly relentless theory of childhood, the desirable, sexual body of Freud is a young body. As Woodward has written: "When Freud theorized that the ego 'may thus be regarded as a mental projection of the surface of the body,' he imagined the body as smooth, unwrinkled, as, in short, young."[42] The classical body is young, the grotesque body is old. To quote Susan Stewart's *On Longing*, the youthful body exists within an "illusion of stasis, an illusion that the body does not change. . . . [It] implicitly denies the possibility of death" (3).

Thus the Freudian body is irreparably divided, biologically by sex and chronologically by age. Transvestism conceals or reverses the first difference (sexual difference), masquerade the second; surgery can alter both. Bakhtin celebrates as transgressive what Freud represses as repugnant. For Freud, dependent on vision and hearing, in contrast to Bakhtin's invocation of other senses and bodily functions, processes are terrifying; death (an event) was preferable to aging (a process): "I have one quite secret prayer: that I be spared any wasting away and crippling of my ability to work because of physical deterioration."[43] Freud would rather die than grow old.

I repeat: Freud's theory of childhood and memory is applicable to masquerade, cosmetic surgery, and television programming. TV reruns and remakes Freud's "repetition compulsion": "Theoretically, every earlier state of content could thus be restored to memory again even if its elements have long ago exchanged all their original connections for more recent ones."[44] For Freud, like Newton, Darwin, and reruns of "I Love Lucy," time is "embedded in our embryonic beings . . . in which every experience leaves a trace." (The paradox of plastic surgery is the erasure of traces and the restoration of an imaginary earlier state—what Woodward calls "a longing for continuity" [24].)

Television is a medium of remembrance rather than memory: "The function of remembrance," Reik writes, "is the protection of impressions; memory aims at their disintegration. Remembrance is essentially conservative, memory is destructive.'"[45] Makeup becomes remembrance; plastic surgery would be conservative destruction. Both are uncanny doublings for aging women, the "sense that one's body is not one's own" (Woodward, 23).

TV's very corporeal enunciation is rarely destructive—as a fully Bakhtinian dialogic would have it. The invocation of carnival, resistant bodies in celebratory models of transgression and pluralism (like the advocation of every shocking topic and position by Oprah, Phil, Geraldo, and Sally Jessy, the quintessence of "diphasic ambivalence"), is a very different story from my tale of contradiction and anxiety. Paralleling TV's temporal effects, anxiety about one's body (and choices, the time-consuming, paralyzing conundrum of discerning proclaimed yet infinitesimal difference among apparent samenesses, a version of the shell game played by Procter and Gamble and presidential candidates alike) is television's conservative affect.

Television is a machine capitalizing on (fear of) the passage of time—as aging and death. Like sponsors, for whom time is money, we can also buy or stop time. If this is so, and if women are a focus, then, as I argued via catastrophe, we might consider shifting our analysis from theories of pleasure to include theories of unpleasure (and paradoxically, from constructs of work to models of leisure as work), away from desire and toward anxiety.[46] The theoretical move is thus away from sexuality and toward economics, with money and appearances as the key to identity, away from inner recesses and toward surfaces, an overt rather than covert operation.

On the side of remembrance and conservation, TV visually charts the passage of embryonic, Darwinian time as aging. Chronological age, assessed at a glance like sex, is television's and the nation's gendered obsession. Dates are minutely specified—in the detailing, in virtually every newspaper story, of the age of the subject, a number which halts the story's progress as we stop to calculate "self-other" ("Jane Fonda, 50, fell off her bicycle in Toronto"); in the string of birthdays on *Entertainment Tonight*, gossip disguised as congratulations or celebration; on Willard Scott's weather segment on *Today*, which features photographs of local centennials—100-year-olds, all dressed up on their birthdays, often in hospital beds, representing age, like the weather, as a natural, local event.

Age, a variable dependent on height, weight, masquerade, money, and generation, is a statistical "calculus of difference" (Woodward, 1) against which we are measured, and an internalized bodily calculus against which we narcissistically measure ourselves in relation to others. Like sex, age is mistaken for *only* biology, illness (or lack of effort and poverty). Like sexual difference, age is related to economics and power. As women age, they move to the margins of power. For men, the inverse is true.

This narcissistic self-other calibration is different for men and women. As Virginia Woolf, then in her fifties, wrote with insistent irony in *Three Guineas*, "We have been trained differently from you. We see the same world but we see it through different eyes."[47] Women have internalized a social drama of vision, what John Berger called "seeing ourselves being seen." (To reject this "radical passivity," to see oneself as only the seer, the observer, rather than the seen, the observed, is extraordinarily empowering, suggesting that our theories, and our perceptions, can ensnare us in the victim position as much as, if not more than, the real world.) Along with this double vision, I see myself seeing—my gaze projected and introjected simultaneously, a superimposition in which I can see myself only comparatively, through you, often another woman. (Again, to replace an envious gaze with a noncomparative narcissistic glance which does not negatively rebound is also empowering.)

This "autoscopy" (Woodward, 17) can be a complex and unsettling process which resembles Freud's assessment in *Mourning and Melancholia* of displacing libido from an object and withdrawing it into the ego, resulting in "an identification of the ego with the abandoned object. Thus the shadow of the object fell upon the ego . . . judged . . . as an object, the forsaken object. . . . An object-loss was transformed into an ego-loss."[48] Youth is represented as a lost object rather than a process or a passage. One can imagine an acceleration of this with age, portrayed as a series of losses rather than achievements, gains, or successes for women. An abnormal modeling of ego or self as an object, often of contempt, rather than a subject can be the rageful result. "This substitution of identification for object-love is an important mechanism in the narcissistic affections"[49] says much about the logic of enduring plastic surgery, and a great deal about the fears of aging, in which we imagine that we become "the forsaken object." This irrational fear is expressed in women's terror of living alone, i.e., without a man—for many women, an unspeakable, unforeseeable nightmare. The fear is supported by social reality, as older men desert their wives for younger ones.

On a more trivial plane: Every time Mary Tyler Moore is on television in her decade-by-decade returns, I anxiously await a slow, scrutinizing closeup to reveal the uncanny effects of plastic surgery, which has widened her eyes and mouth. I cannot relax until this very privileged view is granted. The moment did not come on her last series, which was canceled. I measure the new, older Mary against the old, younger Laura Petrie, the girl/wife of the '60s, happily at home in her capri pants in New Rochelle, or I compare her to the 1970 TV producer Mary, unembarrassed by being in her thirties, where she apparently wants to remain, unexamined. When Ann Guilbert, her neighbor in New Rochelle, appeared on *The Fanelli Boys* as a woman old enough to be a grandmother, I wondered if Mary would ever have grey hair—in effect, act her age, as Shirley McLaine does so brilliantly at the end of *Postcards from the Edge*, a portrayal of *knowing* and funny narcissism. I contrasted the diffuse, vaselined, fill lighting on Cybill Shepherd's moonlit face against the harsher treatment of Bruce Willis in *Moonlighting*. I cannot believe that Connie Chung has nary a bag nor a wrinkle at her middle age(!), which, of course, we know, as she determinedly works on pregnancy, trying to beat her biological clock. Bea Arthur on *The Golden Girls* looks younger than she did on *Maude*, more than fifteen years earlier. All three stars of this series look younger (more fashionable, thinner) every season. Arthur (given the last putdown, reaction shot as was Lucy) has a strangely expressionless, deadpan face. The fascination with Estelle Getty's real age—she is younger than her mother-character and the three other women—reverses the tabloid saga of being older but looking younger; gossip marvels at her "real" age, which she is reluctant to divulge in order to protect the vanity called age of the other actresses. Gossip outside the series, in which men are good for only one thing, maybe two if you count the ex-husband jokes, contains all this comic liberation—Arthur is old and abandoned by her husband.

Granting us the telltale closeup is a form of suspense, satiation/ frustration, operative not merely on quality TV or TV movies resonant of cinematic structures but on talk shows as well. Carson and Letterman, like most primetime programs, rely on medium to long shots of short duration with careful fill lighting, continually cutting away from faces to other distractions (reactions serve *as* welcome distractions), never giving enough visual information, staying politely on the surface with superficial, verbal banter, discussing whatever catches their quick attention, a scripted spontaneity of triviality. In his opening monologue, the boyish Dave will adolescently rebel and walk into an extreme closeup, disobeying his mark and transgressing primetime visual decorum. What a rebellious rascal, breaking all the rules! While Dave was astonished by Cher's leathered, tattooed, peak-a-boo body and Bob Mackie costume on the reunion show with Sonny, I couldn't see enough. In keeping with TV's decorous primetime conventions, which refuse to stare, she carried a cover-up coat. Although she is on television commercials adorned in SM outfits, conversationally urging us as close friends to work out along with her, we can see more of her in her films, but not enough. We need daytime TV, the supermarket tabloids, and *Ms.* for a closer look. One moment on Carson in 1990 was revelatory: a guest comic wanted to direct a portion of the show; he called for alternate camera shots which appeared; then, on a cut to Carson, he called for a closer shot, which was shown for a split second until Johnny censored it and abruptly canceled the game. The camera had crossed over an invisible line.

When Suzanne Pleshette returned in a TV female melodrama in 1987 after a long absence (and fifteen-year daily presence as Emily via reruns of *Newhart*, a character and voice who concluded the brilliant last episode of the new and canceled *Bob Newhart* show), I saw her face in closeup along with her would-be younger murderer. Shot—reverse shot. She was, indeed, in this intercut closeup, too old for him and hence needed to be punished for her lustful desire. In this female remake of *Fatal Attraction*, her crime, and the film's taboo, is her age rather than adultery. When female stars appear on primetime TV melodramas without makeup—for example, Natalie Wood in *Crackers* and, recently, Meredith Baxter Birney in *Winnie*— the naked lack becomes the standard of quality. They are hailed as courageous and "real" actresses, their performances as moving and "heroic." Another reading of these two films reveals that to be without makeup is to play insane or retarded.

In the 1980s and 1990s, the absence of makeup is a sign of poverty or insanity, whereas in the '60s, it meant left, protest politics or that the woman was an intellectual—a nonmasquerade signifying assertive courage or brains, still true today. A consummate act of bravery for many women, including me, is to leave their homes without makeup. The latest biography of the Duchess of Windsor, whose dedicated life's work was shopping, reports that only her personal maid ever saw her without her face on. From the costly masquerade of the '80s and '90s, the truly radical makeup politics of the women's movement of the late '60s and '70s is apparent.

However, this is primetime television—on daytime not only will we get the desired closeup, but we can linger on soap-opera faces in a system hinged on extreme closeups, regularly intercut, often *concluding* scenes—a *satiating* resolution of an order of masquerade more critical than the narrative irresolution usually argued and claimed for this story-editing pattern. For example, Jeremy Butler writes that soap opera's "audial and visual style" preserves rather than resolves enigmas.[50] Sandy Flitterman-Lewis claims that soap opera has "openness, multiplicity, and plurality as its aims," with vision "dispersed, fragmentary, amplified."[51]

Contrary to this accepted reading of dispersion, nonclosure, and multiplicity (akin to high modernism), I suggest that these are moments of resolute closure of a higher order—of *identification* (primary rather than secondary), of masquerade rather than story, of affect rather than effect (replacing Radner's affect-representation distinction). Rather than story logic, these shots, dramatized by deliberate track-ins or zooms, are located along the self-other, internal axis of vision—a very different, temporal structuration of the gaze, one not necessarily bound to narrative, and one which has more to do with extraneous gossip and fashion. It is a doubled look at women, by women.

Along with the face shot and the slow zoom to the closeup, another convention peculiar to soap operas supports this analysis. I will call this peculiar shot the line-up or two-face shot. This is a conversational (or argumentative) shot which, in cinema, would be handled by shot-reverse shot, a medium two-shot, or characters moving within the mise en scène. Here, however, one character stands closer to the camera with her back to the other. Both actors face frontally; both are in focus; they talk to each other in a single take but cannot see each other's faces. (This is an old stage tactic, upstaging.) We see the reaction and the action in a single take. There are variations on this staple shot—including movement of the actors to face each other, or pulling focus, changing from one character to another. The scene closes on the character who will make the next narrative move, the one who knows something the other character doesn't. Character knowledge, or suspicion, is the key to the "flow" of soap story.

This self-other autoscopy calls for women to meticulously scrutinize other women and then turn this glance back on themselves. In these moments of satiation/closure, we get the answers we want about wrinkles, bags, and makeup. *Days of Our Lives* (NBC) is a how-to manual for eye makeup glamorization. We see the "before" when young actresses are introduced, and the "after" as they are transformed by romantic love into leads, sophisticates, via makeup and hairstyle. If the masquerade is not successful, they usually leave the show. As in cinema, men have completely different codes and standards. Lines represent character, which they have earned. I have not been trained to microscopically dissect men with either narcissistic or masochistic glances. In this calculation, men have nothing to do with me. For me, the "other" is another woman, or as melodrama would have it, the infamous "other" woman (a two-way structure of envy rather than the triad of jealousy, another story). As I age, this other can also be my historical self as memory. The face in the mirror grows old, first as a stranger, than as a friend.

Age can be both obsession and contradiction, a secret, like sex, which gossip refuses to let us keep—not to tell is a sign of vanity, false pride, dishonesty. The downfall of Gary Hart began, and perhaps ended, when he lied about his age, setting off a calamity of further secrets. After a "certain age," women who proudly tell elicit amazed disavowal: But you don't look fifty! We can be older, but we must not be as old as we are. Women measure themselves and each other across a chasm, a ten-year or greater discontinuity between the real and appearance, a gap literalized by reruns.

When I first began to study Lucy, I was impressed that she was thirty-eight when preparations began and forty in the first season of broadcast; a forty-year-old female star was unusual by U.S. standards, particularly a star constantly upstaging her husband, desirous of a job, and railing against housewifery by performing in a man's world of physical comedy.

However, Lucy didn't play forty, nor did the diffuse lighting which erased any wrinkles or bags—further concealed by her caricature trademark eyes, hennaed hair, and lips. That Karl Freund's (the German Expressionist cinematographer) tour de force lighting achievement might have been to enable stage movement without revealing wrinkles has not been noted. (In cinema, female stars are carefully lighted and cannot move outside a delineated space. In one disconcerting moment during the ice floe sequence in Griffith's *Way Down East*, Lillian Gish is shot outside. In this scene, unlike the controlled studio shots, she looks disconcertingly OLD—thirty.) Lucy's age was further determined by her playing opposite Ethel, her contrast in weight and fashion. Vivian Vance was, in fact, one year younger than Lucy. So that she could play the older woman and serve as the butt of Fred's numerous weight jokes, her contract stipulated that she retain twenty extra pounds and wear frumpy housedresses—terms she carefully renegotiated before accepting the next Lucy series.

But this is nothing compared to the gender discrepancy: Fred was sixty-four when the series began—short, fat, and unattractive, with a drinking problem. No matter. Considering the very substantial girth of Mr. Grant (Ed Asner), the number of Rhoda fat jokes on the *Mary Tyler Moore Show* is more staggering than Mr. Grant's waist. We have internalized yet another division of the sexes: we "measure age by a calculus of difference" between bodies of the same sex—less rigorous mathematical standards for men do not apply to women. While gossip hailed the miracle of Linda Evans's preservation by proclaiming her real age, and treated Joan Collins's fifty-year-old body as a miracle of petrification or historical preservation, the truly old Blake Carrington, the mannered, bad actor John Forsythe, doddered around *Dynasty* trying to act powerful and sexual but showing signs of senility. He was truly old, but gossip and the series refused to notice. As he feebly pawed Crystal in simulations of passion, incest was the logical, visual explanation. Why would Alexis desire him anyway? They might have been mothers, but he was a great-grandfather.

Another example of fashionable motherhood is Claire on the Bill Cosby show. This glamorous attorney is superwoman—witty mother of four, sexy wife to Cliff, on-guard, radical feminist, friend to her extended family, plus, we presume, although we rarely see this, a successful attorney. In contrast to the boredom of parenting and the tedium of children on Lucy or Dick Van Dyke, she plays mother and mother plays funny. The interesting moments happen with the children rather than after they have been banished to their offstage rooms. No matter; the gender differential is still powerfully operative. The mate of this gorgeous young woman has a substantial paunch and re-creates, for her motherly pleasure, athletic tales of his adolescence, which he passes on to his son. In fact, Cliff the child is almost old enough to be her father. Mom—svelte, seductive, young—is discernible as mother by height and a steely glance capable of stern disapproval. Cliff—although clearly marked as star—also toes the line and cowers under her disapproval. Height, here, is a sign of age. It would seem that taller women, like fatter women, can be construed as older women.

To unpack this gender differential, imagine a fifty-year-old 160-pound woman with a big nose who impersonates little girls and remembers high school dances, in long detail. Now, marry her to an intelligent, funny, sensual, younger, muscular and handsome physicist—say Jimmy Smits from *L.A. Law*. The magnitude of this impossibility suggests how deeply the ideology of gender is ingrained. (In the film *Tucker*, the inventor is played by an actor who resembles him; his wife, on the other hand, in the "documentary" footage is middle-aged and relatively heavy; she returns in the film as skinny and twenty-three.)

Age is a contradiction and identification which elucidates television's double-whammy tactic of liberation/containment—a real critical dilemma of life and TV which for me no modern theory can encompass, to say nothing of resolve. Women can now be middle-aged, a privilege accorded to men for years; *however, women must not look it*—yet another double bind or simulation—*chronology disavowal*. For women, to look younger than they are is to look good. It is telling that Baudrillard was first picked up in the U.S. by female critics (Pamela Falkenberg and Mimi White)—who have always understood contradiction and practiced simulation (like the colonized, for survival) in very complex (often self-destructive) ways—including makeup and costume, playing Daddy's girl, granting competence to their husbands, or more confusing roles as in the paradox of "the freedom to remain at home" and serve children and husbands. The late 1980s ad campaign for Oil of Olay is exquisite TV theory: after stating the advantages of being forty, the woman concludes with the reversal tag line (like the structure of so many situation comedies): "I might be forty, but I'll fight it all the way."

In a massive study of television characters, George Gerbner and his research associates argue that "age is a strong determinant of who appears most and gains most on television. . . . [TV] grossly under-represents both young and old people. More than half of TV's dramatic population is between 25 and 45. . . . Those over 65, comprising about 11 percent of the U.S. population, make up 2.3 percent of the fictional population. . . . [This] does appear to reflect the distribution of consumer income by age. Television's prime-time population may well be seen as a mirror of the prime demographic market."[52]

While "men outnumber women about three to one, women outnumber men among characters in their early twenties, when their function as romantic partners is supposed to peak, but then their numbers fall to 4 or 5

times below the number of men as their usefulness in the world of television declines." While one-third of women are "in the 25 to 34 age bracket,
men are the most concentrated, also one-third of their numbers, in the 35
to 44 bracket. The character population is structured to provide a relative
abundance of younger women for older men, but no such abundance of
younger men for older women" (40). "Women on television 'age' faster
than men. As women age, they are cast for roles that decrease their romantic possibilities" (42). "Among characters 65 and over, 28 percent of the
men still play settled adult roles and 72 percent are cast as old, but 90 percent of women of the same chronological age are cast as old" (43). "The
percent of successful men increases with age, but as women age, the percent who are successful see-saws and then drops to 16 percent. In fact,
more older women are unsuccessful than are successful. We do not find
this for any other group" (43). The conclusion—"the distributions do not
change much from year to year; the age structure of the world of television
is a stable one"—is not heartening. (The study also demonstrated that this
is not a "youth culture," as so massively presumed.)

Even more disheartening is the realization that conscious conventions of
chronological difference reiterate unconscious Freudian desires and taboos:
Men's desire for their mothers and women's desires to possess their sons
are unconscious prohibitions restaged in the spectacle of the older woman
with the younger men—a sensational topic on Phil and Oprah. This rare
scenario is not readily accepted, as is the operative and sanctioned
reverse—the older man and the younger woman. For, within the Freudian
scenario, it is proper that the girl pass on to her father, often elided with
husband. Thus, men traverse or can cross the generational divide, while
women are rigidly held to their prescribed, chronological role and place.
Men are generationally mobile, even without mask or disguise, and thus
appear to be younger. Women are fixed within a dated schema of generation. (Cher, realizing overtly that power more than sex is involved in this
restriction and more respectably than, for example, Joan Collins, exists as a
challenge to the decorum of chronology—although her "looks" belie her
age as her costume denies "mother" and thus sanction her actions—living
with a twenty-three-year-old man, then a thirty-year-old rocker.)

A sad reprise of generational difference is heard in Freud's "Anxiety and
Instinctual Life": "I once succeeded in freeing an unmarried women, no
longer young, from the complex of symptoms which . . . had excluded her
from any participation in life. She . . . plunged into eager activity, in order
to develop her by no means small talent and to snatch a little recognition,
enjoyment, and success *late though the moment was* [my emphasis]. But every one of her attempts ended either with people letting her know or with
herself recognizing that she was too old to accomplish anything in that
field."[53] Social conditions are mistaken for symptoms, as Freud continues
his tale—remade as *"I Love Lucy."* Rather than relapse, she, the "unmarried woman, no longer young," had continual accidents "till at last she

made up her mind to resign her attempts and the whole agitation came to an end." Her resignation, like Lucy's, is Freud's success, the happy ending, and women's tragedy. In spite of her talents, she was "too old"; narcissistic rage was the result.

In gallows humor, the prisoner makes a joke on the way to the hanging; likewise, women's anger against social conditions is turned inward, inflicted on their bodies: "She fell down and sprained her ankle or hurt her knee or she injured her hand." Later, there are "sore throats, rheumatic swellings" (109). Thus Freud links masochism with femininity, when aggressiveness "may not be able to find satisfaction in the external world because it comes up against real obstacles," triggering "the compulsion to repeat." Again, I think of Lucy's weekly *physical struggle* to escape the confines of '50s policies of containment of women in marriage and domesticity by getting a job, and of her ending up instead in the suburbs of Connecticut, away from New York City and work, wearing Pendleton country garb rather than the Lois Jensen high fashion of earlier years with Fred and Ethel raising chickens while Ricky now owns his own Club Babaloo. However, unlike the other "woman, no longer young," Lucy never resigned herself to domesticity, and returned in new series, reaping tributes and accolades for her role in television history and comedy until her death in 1989. For Freud, there is "no doubt about the origin of this unconscious need for punishment." While he labels it "guilt" (so determinant in many women's lives), the "real obstacles," are, of course, sexism, racism, and ageism. For women, there is radical doubt about Freud's analysis and conclusion. Like Lucy, eventually the owner of Desilu, ultimately the victor who got the last laugh, I cannot agree with Freud, who thought that the "unmarried woman, no longer young" was too old to be of any use.

Masquerade and cosmetic surgery work against the numerical declaration. The aging body is the historical body, which might be vanishing along with wrinkles and grey hair. Given the uninsured cost of plastic surgery, "looking old" might become just another disadvantage of being poor, as being fat is seen today as a sign of weakness and failure, the lack of control also attributed to alcoholism. Cosmetic companies are capitalizing on this manufactured fear, as women buy expensive products to erase time and character lines which we have arduously earned. As one critic asks, "Have we seen the last of the great, ancient faces?"[54] reminding us of photographs of Einstein, Duras, and Collette. And, when the cost of masquerade is calculated, keeping up appearances is an exhausting and unimaginably profitable business.

The Young and the Restless

On this CBS soap opera, one of the dynasty families, the Abbotts, owns Jabot cosmetics, which introduced a men's line. The titular head of this familial empire of glamor and scandal-sheet gossip, John Abbott, married a young woman with AIDS—talk about displacement of social issues! Before her death a couple of seasons ago, his shy, sweet young bride revealed her disease to the family at the wedding-reception dinner. Amazing! But John Abbott is not your average CEO/patriarch: five years ago, he returned from a vacation and acknowledged that he had had his eyes lifted. He looked ten years younger. Other denizens of steely, seductive corporate power include the penetrating starer and romantic lover Victor Newman (whose unauthorized biography was published and picked up by TV gossip)—hideously wealthy, dedicated to his little girl, romancing other up-and-coming blondes young enough to be his daughters, and determined to best his nemesis, Jack Abbott, an officer of Jabot and son of John.

However, the reigning grande dame and one of my favorite old women on TV is Catherine Chancellor, the indomitable Mrs. Chancellor, Kay to some of her close friends, improbably including Nicki the former stripper, ex-wife of Victor, and present wife of Jack Abbott. Kay's ravaged, regal face, pursued like no other old TV face by the camera's relentless zooms, tracking shots, and final-scene closeups, is rigidly and deeply lined, as well as very made-up. This actress of the classically trained and mannered school plots, broods, and suffers (and fell in love and married, was divorced and remarried the same man, Rex Sterling), dressed in formal gowns, stylish suits, and glittering jewels at all times of the day, adorned for the ball or corporate suite, yet staying at home, in the Chancellor mansion. She battled alcohol years ago on the show.

She fought polished tooth and manicured nail for her aristocratic, wealthy husband, Phillip, only to lose him to the young, conniving Jill, her former sobriety keeper when she was a practicing alcoholic. She then battled her younger nemesis again, for custody of Phillip's bastard son with Jill, named, of course, Phillip. In order to possess the son, she was willing to play grandmother. But more remarkable, Kay joined forces with Jill on the show to protect her son (presumably the father of an illicit child—the grandson) from the social-climbing young mother, Nina (who until recently wore virtually no makeup, a sign of her lack of class, money, and beauty)—claiming divided rights to her grandson (named, of course, Phillip Chancellor).

After Phillip died of an alcohol-related auto accident, Kay, now a grandmother, remarried, becoming Mrs. Rex Sterling. She was kidnapped in the 1989/90 season, and an impersonator was substituted in order to steal her fortune. This grande dame was granted the penultimate soap-star turn of playing not two but three characters: her impersonator and lookalike, the working-class, gritty, tough-talking waitress named Marge, who wore a waitress costume, had dull brown hair, chewed gum, slung hash, drank beer, chainsmoked, and had bad grammar, a nasal tone, a coarse laugh, a loud voice, and tough language and gestures; the imprisoned, unmade-up Kay, with unkempt hair, slacks, and virtually no change of clothes; and

Marge impersonating the glamorous Catherine. The noisy Marge gradually became quieter, hence classier.

As with Roseanne and, to a degree, Lucy, noise suggests a lack of femininity, along with crudeness. Perhaps women's assertion, aggressiveness, and wit have been socially mistaken for noise, and silenced. Perhaps women should expand the range of their intonation and acoustic space and make an aural, as well as visual, spectacle of themselves. What is apparent is that women are being seen but not heard—living examples of the admonishment given to young children.

Like *Pygmalion*, Marge was vocally coached and taught Catherine's history and upper-class, refined manners. Her biggest hurdle, the sacrifice which almost caused her to abandon the hoax, was that because Catherine was a recovering alcoholic, Marge had to stop smoking and drinking beer (which were presumed as lower-class giveaways). However, the lure and reward was that the lusty Marge would be able to have sex with Rex Sterling, Catherine's husband, a handsome, reformed con artist. Another obstacle was Catherine's skill as a horsewoman—an upper-class pursuit which was frightening and foreign to the tough hash-slinger, Marge. The funniest delay in the scam was Catherine's emergency appendectomy on the day of the switch, necessitating that Marge have unnecessary surgery. For her masochistic suffering while being held captive by Morey Amsterdam, for playing Kay without makeup, cooped up for months with her maid, Esther, for impersonating Marge's untrained vocal intonation, and for wearing garish blue eye shadow, Jeanne Cooper won the 1989 soap opera actress of the year award, to thundering applause. (Playing doubles or triples [manic-depressives or schizophrenics] of opposite natures, or multiple personalities, along with enduring unimaginable physical travails, as Victoria Buchanan, aka Erica Slezak, has on *One Life to Live*, is the ultimate sign of soap-star status and high audience approval. Judith Light endured so much agony on this soap that she became the co-star of a primetime sitcom. For women, portraying a range of affect [which can also be excessive, a joke] is the mark of a great actress.)

During the physical and vocal makeover, we learned the intimate details of Catherine's daily life: that no one ever saw her without makeup, which she wore to bed; that she loved glamorous lingerie, taking long baths, and anointing her body with expensive oils; that she wore real jewelry, constantly; that, like Mary Fisher, she read books rather than watching TV (another painful sacrifice for Marge); and, most pertinent for Marge, that she and Rex had sex at least four times per week. While all the other young women on this program are "naturally" glamorous and beautiful, the old, rich, and glamorous Catherine is manufactured—a masquerade woman.

Marge slept with Rex Sterling and passed the impersonation test. While Kay was held prisoner in a cabin guarded by Morey Amsterdam—reprising his repartee on the *Dick Van Dyke Show* with a sinister, cello-playing twist— and his female cohort, Marge/Kay obtained a divorce. And, infamy of infamy, Jill, the arch-manipulator, seduced Rex Sterling. Kay finally escaped her captors and returned to fight for her husband against her nemesis, Jill. Shortly thereafter, Rex became infatuated with a young, blonde personals columnist and TV personality, Lianna Love. Lianna refused to have sex with Rex; we thought something dreadful and deep, like frigidity or hysteria or trauma or all of the above, might emerge. Fortunately, in the summer of 1991, Lianna was artificially inseminated, thanks to Rex, lightheartedly confessing that while she very much wanted a child, sex was of little interest to her. Soaps can be surprisingly radical. At the same time, Kay wooed and won Rex over with friendship as they organized a charity ball together. I await each and every extreme closeup of her brooding, plotting (recently, playful and knowing), old, and beautiful face.

This intrepid woman, the survivor of TV series reruns, now famous as the mother of Corbin Bernsen (who plays Arnie, the divorce lawyer on *L.A. Law*), has confessed her real battle with alcoholism, as has, of all people, Jess Walton, who plays the newer Jill Abbott (she married John Abbott). The fact that in real life both Jill and Catherine are recovering alcoholics explains why the depiction of the disease and recovery (which included a detailed account of Phillip's losing struggle—he died in a drunk-driving accident) is more accurate than on most programs. In the October 18, 1988, issue of *Soap Opera Digest*, the arch-enemies are united in a feature, "Real-Life Triumphs over Drugs and Alcohol," with Walton and Cooper together on the cover.[55] "These courageous actresses recount how they conquered their addictions."

Walton's analysis of the disease, its symptoms, and its progression is sophisticated. As she says, "This is a disease of denial, so you've got your own mind fighting the fact that there's anything wrong" (111). The steps she took toward recovery are those of a 12 Step program, granting her eight years of sobriety. Cooper follows suit, discussing her treatment program. As at AA meetings, both women tell their stories, sharing their "experience, strength, and hope" in order to help other alcoholics. That gossip is a profitable sidelight of soap operas, with digests specifically devoted to daytime stars and story recaps and predictions, is critical, giving us tidbits of identity while at the same time eliding the differences between real life and soap characters.

Sometimes TV realizes Baudrillard's nostalgia for a real, a referent—via gossip and catastrophes, live broadcasts of death events. Sometimes, as with Freud's uncanny, this real is an archaic, violent, predisciplinary body, the body in process à la Bakhtin. One has to wonder where the tenets of the historical avant-garde are practiced today—when we see it, performance art might be the answer; when we think about it, perhaps TV. In yet another of television's many collapses of fiction with the real (a landmark being Lucy's real afternoon C-section, timed to coincide with the Monday night broadcast of little Ricky's birth), Kay (I am her friend and fan) was going to have real plastic surgery—a full face and neck lift. A real cosmetic surgeon became a character on the program—they fell in love, and we imagined Kay with, at last, a husband. This was not to be; he already had a profession.

Toned down and sanctified by classical music playing softly in the oper-ating-room background but intensified with microscopic closeups and lo-cation realism of little fill sound, Kay had a facelift (a rhytidectomy) on TV (at least we didn't watch Lucy's C-section). The body as a sack of skin be-came literal as we watched the surface of Kay's face—detailed closeups of her bleeding skin being cut, pulled back, stretched, then sutured. (Because patients are conscious but drugged during this procedure, this treatment of the character as a surgical object is remarkable.)

Cuts back to the narrative were moments of supreme relief from this close-up, high-anxiety medical tension. (I taped these segments, stopping and looking away as if I were watching a movie with extreme violence, thus breaking the identificatory intensity of *cause-affect*.) This was indeed an assault on the face, an attack on faciality (open to a Deleuze-Guattari take), comparable to the slashing of the eye in the opening twelve shots of *Un Chien Andalou*. In contrast to John Abbott's off-story and -screen oper-ation, we subsequently watched Kay's bruised face, swathed in huge ban-dages, heal on TV. As always, we inspected her in lingering closeups and assessed the success. Did she look better? Younger? (Is to look younger to look better?) According to the soap opera digests, she was dissatisfied. I agree with her. While she looked less tired and healthier, she still looked old. The audience wanted her to look young, as she does on TV reruns of various series in which she guest-starred.

In April 1991, standing in front of a gilded mirror, reflected in a medium-close shot with Rex, Kay was forlorn: "In spite of creams, makeup, tucks here and there, time is passing. I find that a bit depressing." What is ex-traordinary about this scene, another purloined-letter ploy, a moment as clear as the nose on one's face, is that exactly like Kay's, Rex's face has wrin-kles, bags, and skin pouches. Yet no one notices. His age is neither a prob-lem nor a tragedy as he blithely dates women half his age. Vision, that much-vaunted sense, linked to the real, conceals as much as it reveals. Not to see something right in front of our eyes suggests how powerful are the conventions of chronological difference.

The surgery episodes were timed with a *Today Show* debate about the eth-ics and propriety of cosmetic surgeons' advertising on TV and included TV soft-focus commercials by a Milwaukee surgeon, urging us to remove the marks of history. His brochure, *facial facts*, is a surgical bill of cosmetic rights: "We firmly believe that every individual has the right to feel good about themselves and their appearance. Ultimately, their physical appear-ance should be a mirror image of the person inside, accurately reflecting the way they feel about themselves. . . . It is our goal to help you look as good as you feel."[56] Appearance is tied to the correlation between feeling and looking, with self-image determined by appearance. Good Lacanian theory. In the desire to "eliminate evidence of aging," surgery is also tied to revisionist history and aesthetics: "A rhytidectomy is aesthetic surgery."

For Catherine Chancellor, her masquerade of makeup can also point to "the longing for continuity" of the subject. Our masks, our makeup, are often the same for years. As I age, my vision is doubled by a youthful image which I trace on my face with makeup. I have been dutifully applying black eyeliner since I was eighteen—the wrinkles and creases, plus failing vision, my eyes grotesque in a magnifying mirror, make this cover-up difficult. With an aging face, subtlety of makeup vanishes. A garish exaggerated mask, applied by habit but obscured by vision, hovers over as a reminder that we want to be someone we no longer are.

Cosmetic (from the Greek, "kosmein," to decorate) surgery is distinguished from masking. Woodward: "For at its extreme, cosmetic surgery— which is in the Lacanian sense the desire for the lost object . . . youth . . . can never restore what has been . . . lost" (23). Equally, surgery eradicates what has been gained and learned—the traces of history, one's subjectivity, knowledge and wisdom, resulting in "the uncanny sense that one's body is not one's own." It's as if the projected look of identification had been carved on the face, no longer imaginary but real, while the real face had been irretrievably erased.

The Life and Loves of a She-Devil

The 1986 four-part British television series (coproduced by the BBC, Arts and Entertainment Network, and Seve Network Australia) of Fay Weldon's novel *The Life and Loves of a She-Devil* ghoulishly enacts a sexual, economic, and surgical vendetta. It is also an intriguing commentary on reception, one which calls conventions of beauty into play. The abandoned housewife first directs her rage outward, finally turning it on her own body. (The U.S. Susan Seidelman film reprise, *She-Devil*, starring Meryl Streep and Roseanne Barr, ignores several sexual encounters and the entire last episode.) Julie Wallace plays Ruth, the tall, heavy, muscular, ungainly wife with facial hair who loses her bland-to-wimpy accountant husband to the successful, rich, wispy-thin, blonde-haired writer of romance novels Mary Fisher (Patricia Hodge), the perfect superwoman hostess/writer/lover. Closeups chart the difference between the grotesque, overweight housewife, obsequiously serving her husband and children, and the classical single woman, the object of adoration. Ruth is represented as ugly, as asexual, as masculine, while Mary is beautiful, desirable, feminine. Ruth vows revenge—on Mary Fisher and patriarchal institutions, taking the law, medicine, business, the family, and her body into her own hands. Ruth, like Sarah in the Old Testament, becomes a she-devil, challenging the ultimate patriarch, God, including remaking her own bodily image and thus defying biology, which, despite assertions to the contrary, matters.

The trenchant critique of romance (elided with the male logic of patriarchy rather than women, as recent feminism has claimed) reveals the genre's collusion with structures which serve men and their fantasies. Ruth's voiceover, which is omniscient, God-like, immediately warns us: "Mary Fisher lives in a high tower on the edge of the sea. She writes . . . about the nature of love. She tells lies to herself and to the world. I hate Mary Fisher." Mary inhabits a fantasy world which serves masculinity. She lives with the accouterments of romance: in an isolated, windswept castle with a handsome male servant, drinking champagne and quietly writing her best-sellers, adorned in glistening lounging outfits or gowns, and driving luxury cars. The only sound is classical music amidst quiet conversations of love. Her life is serene, soft, and pastel, as is her work. As she says on a TV interview for her sixth best-seller, "I can do without the essentials as long as I have the luxuries." Mary Fisher is dedicated to the belief and logic of love, which can solve and survive any problem.

Ruth lives in noisy, cramped suburbia. She cooks, eats, cleans, raises two children, and tends her husband until Mary Fisher seduces him at a cocktail party while "Some Enchanted Evening" plays in the background. Bobbo the boring accountant, a real passive-aggressive, confides to Mary that Ruth is a giant mouse, that he felt sorry for her, that his was a marriage of pity in which Ruth had become dependent on him. The subtle inversions and deceits of patriarchy that rule women's conscious and unconscious lives continue to astonish me—one ruse is the noble, innocent, self-sacrificing husband. In her prescient voiceover, Ruth asks, "How do ugly women survive? We wait for old age to equalize all things."

Within the structure of ironic parallels or inversions, Bobbo discusses Mary with Ruth—Mary doesn't have any real friends; she likes theater rather than TV; for her, everything is delicate, a "ripple of conversation." Bobbo the dull and boring then administers a double-standard whammy that women have heard and endured for centuries: "I love you, Ruth, but I'm not in love. . . . But I don't love Mary the way I love you." After this old and weary ploy claiming that "true love isn't possessive," he has grunting sex with a pained, enduring Ruth. We see her dazed, wifely, unattractive face, then a shot of her lying on her side, quietly crying. Bobbo, of course, is oblivious, smug in his narcissistic tumescence. Later, Ruth will look in the mirror in a lingering closeup which reveals her huge mole and facial hairs: "I must not embarrass him."

However, after staring at herself, she discovers that she hates Mary Fisher and that she has "fallen out of love with Bobbo." Ruth has broken the bonds of romantic delusion. After Bobbo, in the midst of his hot affair with Mary, blames everything on Ruth, informing her that he is leaving and that she should sell the home, Ruth takes her life into her own hands. In an extraordinary scene, she sends the kids to McDonald's, turns on all the domestic appliances, spreads gasoline around, and blows up the family home. It is a splendid moment.

Ruth then enacts a brilliant social logic, with, however, a twist: she wants Bobbo back, "but on my own terms, oh sweet vengeance." Her first clever strategy consists of inflicting the children on the blissful couple in their luxurious castle by the sea. Shortly after this nightmare of mess, noise, and unruly fighting, she frees Mary's mother from a Valium-wielding old folks' home, sending the drunken lush to further disrupt the romance and Mary's work—the writing of romance. While Mary Fisher lives the clichés of true love enduring anything, embodying the logic of romance she writes, Bobbo's commitment disintegrates under the pressures of daily life and domestic chaos. As the She-Devil says, "Mary Fisher created a dream of love. But I live in reality and love cannot survive reality." The form continues the parallel editing between the two lives, with Mary spewing forth clichés, "wishes can be fulfilled," while her life chaotically disintegrates, and Ruth dealing with reality and achieving economic and personal success. Their fortunes have been reversed. Next will come their bodies.

Ruth's parallel scenario is more disconcerting and less predictable and, in a deeply ironic way, also the result of patriarchy, or capitalism: Ruth's desire to become the sexual object, knowingly, a subject with the power to turn patriarchal logic back on itself and, perhaps, herself. She adopts various masquerades and names, playing various roles accorded to women, fashioning a new identity for her outward appearance. First, adorned in a loud, garish outfit, including a blonde wig, sling pumps, and brazen makeup, she has a brief fling with a traveling salesman in a motel. As an attendant in the old folks' home, with a tailored, more refined "look," she has a lesbian love affair with a coworker. In her climb to economic independence and success, the She-Devil then studies accounting, Bobbo's business, and forms her own employment agency, with her lesbian lover: "We shall provide work for women whose talents have been spent on children, on domesticity. We shall liberate women from love." Ruth has learned to "dress for success," tastefully adorned in fashionable beige suits, and inhabiting a high-style, high-tech office with many employees. Like Marge/Kay, she is quiet, restrained, her gestures measured and subtle, as are her posture and walk polished, dignified, purposeful. With the right clothes, hairstyle, and makeup, her body has changed; it is now a successful, powerful body. So far, so good for feminist viewers.

Meanwhile, Mary's career, like her fashion, is in decline, and her environment is noisier, messier, suggesting that for women, success and marriage are not compatible, in fact are at odds. Because Bobbo has urged Mary to write more realistically rather than her fantasy pop culture, she receives her first rejection letter. "I am not Emma Bovary," she claims while worrying whether Bobbo will ever leave her. Like Emma Bovary, stripped of her former premarital and false power over Bobbo, caught in the contradictions of romance, the increasingly miserable Mary becomes the abandoned lover while Bobbo goes out with younger women. The argument, like the body, has radically altered: Mary is still beautiful, yet just as undesirable and pathetic as Ruth, coded as dependent, available, and hence unattractive. The terrain has shifted from the body, and biology, to social institutions, including beauty culture (a mesh of economics, historical conventions, and unconscious aesthetics), which seduce and abandon women. The VO intrudes: "Mary Fisher: You thought that love could create a heaven on earth, but love can only create a hell. I shall teach you that lesson."

It is significant that Ruth controls the voice, the gaze, and the story, that the point of view is from the grotesque rather than the classical body. Equally critical is that the series scrutinizes, in closeup, an unattractive woman, forcing us to come to terms with our visual prejudice if not slight revulsion. Their bodies are given as biological and remade by masquerade, gesture, social position, and finally surgery, raising the question of whether surgery is a biological or social practice. To tamper with biology is to challenge destiny, with the greatest familial crisis being the confusion at birth of sexual identity. Sex-change operations cause comparable queasiness. At the same time, we know (and have fought for the concept) that gender, like heterosexuality, is not biological but a social construction. Comparable to the structure wherein declared oppositions (classical versus grotesque, self-other, beautiful-ugly, lover-wife) are stated as givens, then overturned as argument, Weldon has grafted a third entity, a social biology wherein neither term is fixed or immutable.

Coincident with the critique of romance and gender, the law comes under siege. Ruth becomes the maid for a sadomasochistic judge trying Bobbo's legal case (Ruth had pulled an accounting scam, transferring Bobbo's accounts to her Swiss bank account, becoming rich in the process and bankrupting Mary, as well as turning Bobbo into a criminal). Ruth makes a contract with the judge's masochistic desires, becoming his torturer after turning him on with her impeccable legal logic that Bobbo should be incarcerated for a longer period of time. The ante of the critique is being upped to include a perverse legal system and a corrupt, misbehaving judge, whom Ruth easily manipulates by pulling the childish strings of his male sexual desire. Unlike romance, sex has nothing to do with love, but everything to do with male narcissism and corruption. However, sex can be used against patriarchy; women can play the game of male desire, perversely so. Foucault's *Discipline and Punish: The Birth of the Prison* and *The History of Sexuality*, echoing and inverted texts, are combined and re-created. Romance (the family) and the law will soon be followed by the church and medicine as corrupt practices.

While Bobbo is in prison, Mary continues to act according to the dictates of romance, dutifully selling her possessions to pay for his legal counsel. The scenario continues to reverse itself, with Mary now looking into the mirror: "Bobbo, forgive me. I feel so guilty," about Bobbo's sleeping with younger women. Bobbo again has wielded the illogic of patriarchy, one of denial and reversal: his "affairs didn't matter." While Ruth has mastered this logic, using it against its perpetrators with a vengeance (writing a new narrative in the process), bribing the young woman and setting up the predictable affair, bankrupting and imprisoning her husband, Mary is caught with an insane and self-destructive logic, one of romance or addiction—to sex, relationships, fantasy, in short, to love. Romance demands female martyrdom, self-sacrifice. "You celebrated love and now it is destroying you."

After the tryst with the wife-tormenting Sadean judge, Ruth then seduces a priest for whom she is impersonating a voluptuous maid; his religious ecstasy becomes raw lust and an unnerving critique of Catholicism. The drunken priest is inflicted on Mary Fisher, who has an affair with him—her ultimate decline and Weldon's most licentious depiction of sex/love as patriarchy. When even the repulsive priest is leaving her, Mary Fisher says, "I'm not in love anymore . . . not even with love." The priest replies, "Even when you're suicidal, you're romantic." During a gusting, violent storm, the wrath of the she-devil, Mary is sucked out of the house and found dead on the shore—a bit too gruesome, too violent, for many viewers who preclude violence as a female strategy. Identification is not merely enabling or a given, it becomes a political question; it is a process which is continually overturned and thrown back on the viewer, accounting for unease if not confusion.

Just prior to the sequence with the priest, midway through the third episode, my feminist students applauded the radical tale. However, as with Mary's inevitable death (addiction of any sort leads to death), Weldon's story takes its logic to a relentless conclusion. So far, Ruth's rage has been directed outward, against Bobbo and Mary as exemplars of patriarchal logic and romance. Now the blonde ideal, the imaginary signifier, is internalized. In the ultimate challenge, Ruth will "defy my maker and remake myself." As Holly, Ruth has jawbone surgery; shots of the doctor's instruments of torture and mutilation and photographs describe the medical scene and the disciplinary regime of cosmetic surgery—not just a matter of choice or economics. As always, the point of view belongs to Ruth, the body of the patient usually seen by the gaze of the doctors; this reverse becomes a critique of medicine.

The last segment takes place in the U.S., just prior to the return to the castle. As Marlena, Ruth flies to a plush medical spa in California for a massive series of plastic surgeries, including taking six inches off her legs, a process which will be excruciating and possibly crippling. The ideal woman, Mary Fisher, is represented by huge blowups in the doctors' examination room. As the doctors quietly say, Ruth will be old inside but, reiterating the logic of late capitalism so applicable to plastic surgery, "age is what the onlooker sees, not what the looked upon feels." Age, here, is a matter of surfaces, of appearing rather than feeling, of impressions rather than identity. Youth is a commodity which can be purchased, like identities or lifestyles. The doctor, whether Pygmalion or Frankenstein, is gleeful about the prospect for a complete bodily makeover, suggesting that they tighten the vagina.

After painful surgeries, Ruth partially becomes Mary, with Ruth's voice. Recovery fuses the two women, linking voice and body which previously had been separated, the feminist or Kleinian version of Freud's "uncanny." Ruth moves into Mary's house, with the male servant and Bobbo watching: "Are you jealous Bobbo? I was jealous of you. I thought it was a matter of male and female but it isn't. . . . It's power, merely a matter of power. I have all and you have none." I think Foucault would agree with power as an interpretation, although he would not have imagined it the domain of the excessive female controlling the terms of her own spectacle. In the end, she is grotesque in another way, disguised as the classical ideal, yet one with power, which in the hands of women is more unsettling than beauty.

One interpretation is that Ruth's vengeance is complete, as with Medea's killing of her children. Another would suggest that Ruth's rage against social systems has soured to envy of another woman and been negatively turned against herself; to become the envied other, the self is mutilated and the other destroyed. Or surgery has transformed the dictates of biology as destiny. While Ruth's manipulation of the narrative turned sex against patriarchal institutions—Mary and Bobbo, the judge, and finally the priest, ripping love and sex apart, the duo which romance resolutely holds together—the ideal classical female is another of its conventions, albeit here a masquerade. The preferred ending for many feminists would be the lesbian relationship and the business success—a utopian solution outside the confines of patriarchal logic.

The transformation of bodies and roles, enabled by spectatorial looks and identifications across a spectrum of gender identity ranging from masculinity to femininity, is complicated at the end by the gradual merging of bodies and the conclusive linking of the two identities, Mary and Ruth— one as body, the other as voice. Furthermore, while Bobbo is the excuse (as initially are the children), Ruth's desired object is the classical body of Mary Fisher, her other more than Bobbo, involving a female drama of dyadic envy and eventual incorporation more than a triad of jealousy. This is a Kleinian more than a Freudian scenario. More complex is the complicity of the spectatrix, measuring herself against others—misrecognizing herself as Mary, looking away from Ruth, looking with disapproval on Ruth/Mary.

Paradoxically, while many feminists critics, including Tania Modleski, Janice Radway, Rosaline Coward, Helen Taylor, and Ann Barr Snitow, have brilliantly analyzed romance (a debate which became an intellectual battleground over method, the merits of inscribed or real audiences), the presumption has been that romance, consumed by female audiences as is the *National Enquirer*, involves female fantasy. Perhaps as with gossip, this series switches that assumption, portraying romance as a male fantasy which has been internalized by women. Romance is a contradiction that serves capital and Bobbo. When dissected by Ruth, the feminist critic, romance returns as an economic and personal nightmare. The series suggests that even feminists have unconsciously internalized romance scenarios, the very basis (not a subtext, pretext, or subgenre, whether patronized or consumed) of patriarchal institutions such as the law, the church, medicine, and the family. Romance might be the great delusion which enables these institutions to survive. Paradoxically, it is a delusion that prevents women from working, including the destruction of Mary Fisher's career.

The film remake of this television series stopped after the first three parts, before the surgical and shocking bodily remake. On the less troubling surface, it is more politically correct. But the film is also very different from the series. Barr as Ruth is having a makeover in the opening scene, excited about the party that evening. She looks great, although not as great as Meryl Streep. Ruth is represented as a suburban reader of romance novels, including those of Mary Fisher. In Ruth's voiceover, thin is Fisher's greatest difference. The film literalizes what was apparent, and complicated, in the novel and the series. Equally, it is structured around Bob's list of assets, a list which is frequently intercut: home, family, career, freedom. Ruth takes them all away. However, there is no kinky sex with the various representatives of patriarchy—the judge and the priest. Because she looked good in the beginning, there is no makeover. In fact, Barr's appearance goes slightly downhill. She has no plastic surgery, and Mary lives to write another best-seller.

In the film's happy but sappy end, Ruth brings the children to visit Bob in prison, a reformed male concerned about cooking. Mary Fisher is interviewed by Sally Jessy Raphael and is receiving fabulous reviews for her now-serious book. The end, a reprise of scenes from Yvonne Rainer's *The Man Who Envied Women*, has shots of women walking down crowded city streets, to the tune of Elvis singing "You're the devil in disguise" (triggering memories of *Scorpio Rising*), a song and lyric which segues into another rock-and-roll tune, "You Can Have Him, I Don't Want Him." In the guise of the liberated woman, the film contains the radical critique of the body, masquerade, romance, and aspects of feminism.

Real life, or gossip, has re-created this TV series surgical scenario, albeit not so directly or apparently ghoulishly. After Tom Hayden reportedly left Jane Fonda for a younger woman, Fonda had breast implants and a facelift, emerging coupled with a new and powerful beau, Ted Turner, and appearing on talk shows as glamorously youthful. Ivana Trump's plastic surgery was widely reported after Donald's affair with Marla Maples, a much younger woman. Now Ivana, on the cover of *Vogue*, is dating others and perhaps winning Donald back, as Ruth did Bobbo. Both already beautiful women transformed themselves into the younger women their husbands desired, becoming, like Ruth, that ideal. Critical for cosmetic surgery—the *perfect* and painful commodity fetish—and in contrast to *The Life and Loves of a She-Devil*, we (usually) see only the finished product, not the conditions of labor. Unlike Marx's model, however, the body of plastic surgery is only partially alienated from the product, a new and improved body, the uncanny experience of seeing oneself as a younger stranger—the inverse of Freud's train ride.

The *National Examiner* of December 29, 1987, told us "How to Look 30 at 50," which both Jane and Ivana have accomplished. Along with surgery, the article recommends smiling, reading current affairs, dieting, exercise, hormonal skin sprays, and new makeup, hairstyle, and wardrobe as antidotes for aging. "The first step is to realize that the theory of growing old gracefully is outdated" (14). The flip side of Liz, Joan Collins, Jane, and Diana Ross's fifty-year preservation as thirty is "MOM, 51, HASN'T AGED SINCE 18!" a headline in the *Weekly World News*. "The object of all this scientific scrutiny is an ordinary wife and mother from Copenhagen, Denmark. . . . At first I was pleased by the fact that I looked so much younger than other women my age. . . . But as the years passed and I looked and felt so young, I thought perhaps I had some rare disease." Here youth is an illness, a spectacle, which, if doctors can locate the gene, "might be able to eradicate aging and its problems altogether." Biology will then rewrite history.

This story of August 1987 had a sequel in January 1989: "COUPLE, 70, HASN'T AGED IN 35 YEARS." Again, "Dr. Jensen said the couple walked into his clinic after reading about Elsa Hove, the 52 year-old grandmother." Anders and Ola Stampe "avoid alcohol and exercise." "We spend most of our time watching TV or talking on the phone. We think that taking it easy keeps us from getting old. My friends are wrinkled . . . and jealous." "Dr. Jensen is looking for the hidden gene that could help us stay young" (5). Other regular tabloid headlines include quasi-surgical solutions: "AMAZING FAT GUN FACELIFT Makes You Look 20 Yrs Younger" (*National Examiner*, November 10, 1987), or "AMAZING $3 FACE CREAM TAKES 20 YRS OFF YOUR AGE" (May 10, 1988).

Like age, surgery is no longer an acceptable secret. *Spy* published a detailed chart of celebrities' plastic surgeries, listing each type, often with before and after pictures—for example, Morgan Fairchild wearing a low-cut evening gown before and after breast implants. No wonder Angela Lansbury revealed her history of plastic surgery in the April 1989 *McCall's*, including her recent eyelifts and neck tucks. (Facelift [rhytidectomy], 1966; eyelifts, 1969; neck and chin redone, 1976, 1986; neck tuck, twenty-pound weight loss, 1989.) Age and surgery are intertwined: we can *be* fifty but we must not look it. Women must consume, constantly, but consumption must not show—with the media attack on fat as the most blatant example of this contradiction. Roseanne Barr, now under mainstream and tabloid attack, and Barbara Bush, emblem of media praise, are the negative and positive challenges to this argument.

Joan Rivers and Phyllis Diller are living TV examples of uncanny bodies,

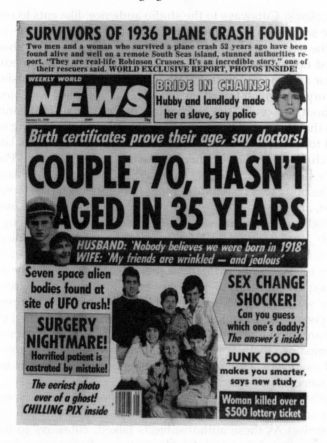

taking the source of their comedy, their loathed female bodies which never dated, and transforming them initially into jokes, and later into their ideal via massive, constant surgery—the verbal dissection became a surgical dissection. The comic female body wanted to be a desirable, classical body, Freud's sexual body, a young body. Adorned in makeup and high fashion, Diller and Rivers are perfect examples of "the child in the adult" not being able to tolerate aging. "Oh, grow up!" Rivers's famous putdown, is self-diagnosis. Like the woman (Catherine Helmond) of the disintegrating plastic-surgery face in *Brazil*, the horror of mutilating the body permeates these scenarios, woman's vanity as joke or monstrosity—the uncanny feeling that one's body is not one's own, a literalization of autoscopy.

In a reprise of *The Young and the Restless*, a May 1990 episode of *Donahue* was devoted to a real facelift. While male medical experts were in the studio, along with a queasy audience and a brave Phil, the monitors showed a live, female facelift in detailed closeups which uncannily resembled Catherine Chancellor's. Cutaways to the studio audience, like cuts to other story lines in the soap, were welcome respites from the painful scene—a violent attack on the face. In keeping with the format of *Donahue*, this shocker was represented not as the sensationalism it was but rather as an educational program for audience edification rather than displeasure. Focusing relentlessly on surgery, which forced me to look away, was like watching slasher films, without, however, the mechanism of disavowal. Phil continued to remind us that this was a real operation, in real time, something which we all needed to watch so that we could make informed decisions later.

On March 30, 1989, *Geraldo* aired a plastic surgery exposé: "Plastic surgery horror stories are the focus . . . of 'When the Search for Beauty Turns Ugly.' " The body was taxonomized into four surgical types: face, liposuction, breast, and nose, with inserts of anonymous testimony of eyelids that were too tight, of eyes that wouldn't close. Statistics of famous patients were cited: Joan Rivers's twelve-plus makeovers, Phyllis Diller's entire body, Carol Burnett's jaw, face, and eyes, and Liz Taylor's chin and eyes. The victims onstage were ordinary women, like 90 percent of the audience, while the experts in the audience were men, including a congressman investigating surgery beamed in via satellite. The women represented the body and personal experience, the men, knowledge and trained expertise. Each woman embodied a particular surgical error; their bodies were objects, accompanied by their verbal reconstruction. Men were professionals, addressed as Doctor, Congressman, Professor, while women were only their first names.

The "Father of Liposuction," along with practitioners and authors of new books on plastic surgery, hawked their wares and all-knowing professional expertise. As these author/subjects talked, cutaways to the female objects demonstrated their points. Also in the audience was a happy male patient, unlike the distraught and angry women onstage—another "plastic surgery junkie" who was randily proud of his youthful appearance (he looked at least sixty), a patient of Dr. Newman who had undergone seven procedures, a living advert. Ironically, the program that detailed failures included ads for a Milwaukee plastic surgery clinic. One woman informed us about what is called the "Command Trust Network," a national hotline for women who have had problems with plastic surgery. All agreed there was no medical or legal recourse. The show hawked doctors, books, and surgery, the domain of men, while supposedly commiserating with female victims. Like so many episodes, this was also a tale of addiction: all of the women had had multiple procedures.

Murder, She Wrote

The logic of TV has it both ways with its inclusive/cancelling logic of contradiction. I can make the opposite argument—both/and rather than either/

or. To restate TV's "diphasic quality": "an action which carries out a certain injunction is immediately succeeded by another action which stops or undoes the first one . . . as if neither action had taken place," the last parenthetical clause forcibly explaining why gender is rarely analyzed by TV scholars.

Unlike cinema and Freud, who would rather have died than grow old, TV has always allowed women to be middle-aged and mothers. Gracie Allen, derailing the laws and syntax of patriarchal language, was well into her forties during her series, with her real son, Ronnie, playing a college student at USC. Middle-aged mothers have always been center-stage in U.S. situation comedy. In her seventies, Lucille Ball returned in yet another series, as a grandmother. *The Golden Girls* is a big hit; women's desire and friendship predominate, with men good for only two things, one being ex-husband jokes. Now in constant reruns, *Cagney and Lacey* stride the streets of New York together, confidently, tough but idiosyncratic and sensitive women. For years, *Dynasty* and *Dallas* depicted powerful, over-forty women, mothers who dated handsome, young, but powerful men, while Angela Lansbury rules the mysterious roost of aging, out-of-work, TV-rerun celebrities on *Murder, She Wrote.*

In this Sunday-night series, the jogging, jowly Jessica Fletcher, the famous writer of best-selling mysteries, is hefty, with bags, sags, wrinkles (albeit fewer in 1990 after surgery), wit, and intelligence. Humble as mom's apple pie and sharp as a motherly tack, she is also clearly superior—the respected star of Broadway musicals who here plays a mystery writer (and appears, outside the series, as the host of prestigious award tributes in New York) surrounded by TV history, former stars, now content to play second fiddle, whom this series remembers and employs. We measure these many guests against the last time we saw them, as at a high school or college reunion, which the programs resemble—assemblages of people with little in common other than being vaguely familiar as other characters whom we try to remember and identify from our past by providing an old context of memory—not our own but of TV. The former stars are more humble here, like the captain of the football team returning as a bill collector, growing shorter with the years.

Shortly after Jessica meets many of the visiting stars, they die and return to TV heaven in reruns—the series as a graveyard of TV history. The show is grisly, with casual, predictable murders (which no one mourns) by Jack Carter, Martin Landau, or Lynda Day George. Death, like celebrity, is evanescent, transient, insignificant, not nearly as tragic as not working. Death triggers little affect. *Better Health,* which rates TV programs according to their healthy lifestyles, ranks this program highly because Jessica bicycles and jogs through her quaint Maine seacoast fishing village, hustling to scenes of the numerous crimes.

While Jessica/Angela is clearly positioned as a world-famous author/sleuth, a very independent woman quite content to remain at home, working in Cabot Cove, she is also an inveterate globetrotter, with famous friends and relatives whom she rescues around the world. Thus, she has both the security of being a small-town local, and the fantasy of the retiree as professional, capable tourist—tourism as beneficial, adventurous leisure. Each episode proves Jessica's real sleuthing skills and becomes material for her next best-seller; she can deal with the real as well as its fiction.

Each program has a three-tiered introduction: a preview/trailer presents that week's enigma; then a Lansbury montage follows, with shots of her typewriter, manuscript, running, bicycling, her name and the series title, with an inserted sponsor; after the title—for example, "Who Threw the Barbitals in Mrs. Fletcher's Chowder?"—the third segment is the beginning of the episode, with credits of the guest stars and the production staff superimposed over the story. That Lansbury has her own clearly demarcated credits and theme song separates her from the other mortal actors.

As an example of the program structure, Kristy McNichol, for some unknown reason, was touring with a rodeo in Saskatchewan, in love with a rider. At the request of her mother, Aunt Jess stops cleaning her kitchen oven and travels to Canada to "stand in for your mother, but I'm not here to tell you how to run your life." This very capable woman, quite content to live alone and write, who does her own housework, will drop anything for a friend. She is also a great sport—the Auntie Mame of our dreams. At the local country bar, she is not only adorned in western garb, but she dances with the boys and graciously "tosses back a few beers" from pitchers. All the guest stars gradually enter the bar in the central, collective, presumably celebratory scene that occurs before the crime; there is a fight—underneath domesticity lurks violence, here including drunkenness and wife beating.

Jess, always on visual and auditory alert, sees and hears all from her privileged vantage point at the center of the series' panopticon. Inevitably, in a weekly giveaway shot, she will look quizzical and then shrug off her puzzlement, a moment or shot which will return to her as memory and as the key to the murder enigma—which she repeats verbally for us. In one construction, this is power; in another, she is a busybody, overhearing conversations, butting in when not invited, solving problems which are of no concern to her. However, her star status, fame, and successful detection curtail this reading.

Next follows the predictable, foreshadowed murder about which no one cares—the more we learn about the dead, the more loathsome they become. Jess then links up with the official investigator (a Canadian mountie in this episode) but always solves the case herself. She is the best detective, the quintessential logician, the most observant—like her forebear, Agatha Christie, updated via Dorothy Sayers. Sometimes the unmarried detective, often an inept bumbler, and always male, is interested in her; she does not reciprocate his desire—perhaps because he is not as intelligent or powerful as she is. Work, not sex, is the wellspring of her desire and the source of her pleasure. Jessica doesn't need or want a man, although the repeated references to her dead husband and their high romance are the true-love sanction for her independence. (Also, is this what we expect from a widow of more than fifty?) At the end of each episode, she solves the mystery *and* the personal dilemma that went with it. Solving crimes is helping friends and fodder for her next best-seller; the personal and professional overlap for this woman who takes pleasure in her work, and in her solitude.

More remarkable, however, is what I can only call a TV critique of the heterosexual couple and the family—resembling Barthes's description of domesticity as an endless, nagging argument which can stop only with violence.[57] While Jessica's world consists of a series of multiple couples, often with deceitful older children, they are unpleasant if not miserable partners and families—bickering, unfaithful, disloyal, larcenous, and frequently murderous. For example, in the chowder episode, Amos, the sheriff (Tom Bosley), is visited by his sister, Vinnie (Anne Meara), who has left her husband, Elmo. Elmo and his horrid, rude family travel to Cabot Cove to bring back Vinnie. At a dinner party at Jessica's, Elmo the ugly is drugged to death. No one cares.

These awful people who insulted the food and each other play out domestic squabbles more violent than murder. As we learn during the investigation, the marriage was even worse than it initially appeared—Elmo was a drug addict, a manic-depressive who beat his wife. As horrendous as all this might appear, the affects are canceled. Benjamin's distinction between memory as destructive and remembrance as conservative aptly describes the affects which finally preserve, conserve "the family"—Jessica's extended family.

In contrast to marital strife, Jessica's self-contained life is harmonious and exciting. During this episode's family squabble, Jessica is trying to finish her book, constantly being interrupted at home by either the sheriff and his problems, or the doctor (the other Cabot Cove regular, played until 1990 by William Windom)—at one point, she imitates an answering machine to preserve her privacy. Amos and Seth, like Cabot Cove, serve as her jovial, extended sexless family. However, she can say no, which she does in this episode; she can preserve time for her own work: she agrees to have the central dinner party (actually a nightmare—everyone criticizes the food and falls asleep during the soup course; one guest dies after eating her famous fish chowder) after she has finished her novel. While it is always a struggle against her helpful nature, her work comes first. As a concluding aside: a deputy female sheriff who won't make coffee or type, who rides a motorcycle and arrives, competently, in the nick of time, was introduced on this episode. The tongue-in-cheek parody of feminist exaggeration, including the almost comic sheriff and doctor, tones down and contains the social commentary, as does the narrative trajectory of solving crimes.

Gossip occupies a central role on the series, cleverly playing out the similarity between gossip and detection, the sheer pleasure of pursuing a rumor, scandal, or crime, the satiation of uncovering the truth of a person or whodunit, Jessica's genre. On many syndicated programs, crime becomes a legitimation, an excuse, for gossip and sensation, with the reporting of a crime or turning in of a criminal strangely equated with gossiping. In addition, behind domestic crime is family gossip—secrets, skeletons in upper-middle-class closets, which often have to do with abuse and addiction, covered up by the middle class but being revealed by Oprah, Phil, and Jessica.

On the December 17, 1989, episode, suggesting, as one character remarks, a Jacqueline Susann novel, the concerns are the inflated economy and the real-estate market, political scandal, and small-town versus city values. East Coast land speculators are buying houses in Cabot Cove for extraordinary and inflated prices—weekenders for Boston commuters. Eve Simpson, a sporadic regular and real-estate agent, is on the developmental bandwagon, urging Jessica to sell her house, an offer which, of course, she refuses. The program addresses very real issues by pitting the old versus the new, with Jessica and the good folk, mainly bumbling but good-hearted men, representing the old, small-town values—including the acceptance and function of gossip. Because they are seen through Jess's virtuous eyes, all the regulars are good and asexual, tolerated and enjoyed.

The beauty parlor is the scene of local information, with episodes frequently showing a group of townies, older Hollywood stars such as Ruth Roman (the hairstylist and owner) and older TV performers, sitting under the dryers and gossiping, as in *Steel Magnolias'* gathering of idiosyncratic friends and gossipers. Into the shop comes Annie May, a sweet-talkin' redhead from Wyoming who later will accuse the town's mayor, Sam Booth, of being the father of her four children. The women love the story, literally perking up their lotioned ears. Because this election is all about the new zoning rights (for a commuter airport, along with new ocean developments, which Sam, who is the swing vote, opposes, thereby always keeping everything the same; like TV, the show opposes change of any sort), this scandal is a political issue.

Eve Simpson, invoking women's issues and strengths, decides to run, after first encouraging Jessica (who would have the "good sense to keep her trap shut and has no history of philandering") who refuses because she has just "finished two books in a row." Jessica, who pivots between the male and female characters, who rarely interact, does not support Eve; rather, she supports Sam by solving the mystery—the murder of the red-haired accuser. Jessica is exceptional, a message which the programs repeat again and again. The other women are types, excessive and rather silly. What is significant, other than her logical and perfect nature, is her ordinariness—when the men visit her home, she is in the kitchen cooking. When the women visit her, she is cleaning woodwork.

Along the way, Seth, her doctor friend, is accused of being "an old gossip," which he is, and the red-haired interloper is murdered in her hotel room. The key to solving the crime is contained in two conversations with

Jessica—including the beauticians' revelation that "the color job on her hair is New York; that's no Casper, Wyoming, color job." Typically, the happy, middle-to-upper-class couple, so together on the surface, is a hotbed of seething discord. The guilty couple are weekenders from Boston, with the wife committing a constant offense throughout the program— complaining, actually whining, about the people in Cabot Cove. The suave husband is interested in developing the town, but uncomplaining. First, the husband is accused of murdering the woman pretending to be Sam's wife. But finally, after discovering that he is a philanderer, Jessica accuses the wife, who slips up, a slip noticed by the ever-alert Jess. "I killed her, the same way I wanted to kill all the other women he humiliated me with." Beneath the surface of the heterosexual couple is murderous larceny, and usually one form or another of addiction—drugs, alcohol, or relationships.

While Jessica is exceptional, strong, independent, relishing her work, freedom, and privacy, also handling fame with humility and disaffect, the program is finally conservative for women. Jessica is only rivaled but never matched by men, her usual companions, although she travels everywhere to see good female friends and is represented as one of the girls who also goes to the beauty parlor. The program only flirts with feminism; the candidacy of Eve Simpson is a joke, as we hear she received only sixteen votes, while Jessica the healthy is jogging with Seth, as she was in the beginning. While Jessica is on the alert for gossip, she is not, like the other women or Seth, the doctor who should retain confidentiality, represented as a gossip—only a professional who cleans, cooks, cares, writes, and solves crimes. To be a gossip, for both men and women, the program says, concerns small-town values and is bad but pleasurable and necessary. Without gossip, this program would not exist—like the novels Spacks analyzes, it fuels the narrative, granting us major clues. Gossip and scandal are at the very basis of the detective story.

The series represents old age as pleasurable and idiosyncratic, and older women, and men, as independent, surrounded by a stable and supportive community, an extended family without economic woes, illness, loneliness, and boredom. The program is indeed a fantasy of old age, wherein the younger nuclear family is not healthy. At the same time, it is a fantasy of small-town life as a secure collectivity.

Rosalind Coward and Linda Semple trace the revival of detective fiction written by women and analyze women's history of crime writing, noting an overlooked fact: that women have always excelled at this genre.[58] Along with revising the history of authorship, they challenge the inherent conservatism of the genre, particularly its presumed reconstitution of a "hierarchical, establishment world and a faith in traditional authority" (49). For them, "the outcome . . . is often secondary to . . . the unfolding of the crime, with the revelation of who done it [as] perfunctory . . . hardly adequate to the complex . . . interactions which preceded it" (51). The "final convention" cited as conservatism is the "closed circle of suspects" (52).

Rather than a limitation, Coward and Semple argue that in detective tales written by women, this tactic exemplifies a "complexity and richness of characterisation; the relationships between women . . . [are] deep, often passionate . . . [extending] the notion of community" (53). The detective form "raise[s] and explore[s] issues affecting women"; "women's concerns, far from being alien to this genre, are often the very stuff of the crime novel." While the form tends "towards tradition and repetition" and "individualism and faith in authority," nevertheless "there is nothing necessarily conservative in the form" (54). Hence, the form "can be used specifically for radical ends."

In Amanda Cross's *Sweet Death, Kind Death,* the middle-aged scholar/detective Professor Kate Fansler is investigating the death of an older woman and scholar, Patrice Umphelby, who had been writing on aging before her murder. The interpretation of women and age (by Carolyn Heilbrun) as told by Patrice's diary is enlightening and empowering. "Whenever I read the story or autobiography of an older woman . . . she writes only to go back to her youth; she abandons age, experience, wisdom, to search the past, usually for romance, always for the beginnings in childhood. . . . The story of age, of maturity before infirmity, before meaningless old age, has never been told. Except perhaps by Shakespeare. . . . Surely I cannot be the only woman in her fifties who lives in the present alone." Her mentor is Virginia Woolf, her distinction between moments of nonbeing (housework, party chatter) and being or intensity. Both are valued.[59]

After solving the mystery of Patrice's death, Kate discovers the meaning of her life, the value of age: "She began to see that many women's lives . . . [begin] just when it was all supposed to be over. A life wholly apart from youthful sexual attractions and domestic services." (202) The murderer, a competing male scholar, had been arguing that older age was a depressing time for women.

While the far-from-radical *Murder, She Wrote* is produced by an all-male group, and charges of deep conservatism can be leveled against Jessica's wardrobe, these revisions are applicable. Like the detectives of earlier writers, for example, Ngaio Marsh, Agatha Christie, and Dorothy L. Sayers, Jessica is "upper-class, often intimate with the police but also literate and well-educated." She is a "god-like figure whose intellectual power . . . with . . . deductive reasoning . . . was often understood to be decidedly male." However, like these literary sleuths, sometimes old and frail, she is distinctly female.

Like Agatha Christie, *Murder, She Wrote* represents the "police as bumbling and inefficient, much more likely to get it wrong than right." While the series is neither written, produced, nor directed by women, it is tailored to the star, Lansbury, and the character, Jessica, inscribing female authorship in its very title, thus (dis)placing it within the tradition of female detective writing. The series embodies a collective community and maintains a healthy ambivalence about law and order, upheld but almost as an afterthought or a parody. An even stronger affinity is the linkage of the genre to middle-aged women, a history that has been ignored, as the genre was disparaged.

Paralleling the similarity between the female sleuth's detecting and the process of reading detective fiction, the viewer pits her wits against the genre's conventions and Jessica. "One of the pleasures of the unfolding narrative is whether the reader will be able to solve the mystery before the detective" (50). Predicting TV, in the U.S. against the clock, is one of its great pleasures. We learn the conventions and set-up in the initial episodes, with subsequent renderings formulaic variations. On this show, an incidental, in-passing moment contains the critical clue to the murderer's identity; on soap operas, conjoined, meaningful looks, a version of shot–reverse shot, between "uninterested" couples mean everything, including future sex; for sitcoms, the two-part story, plus the clock, determines the last three- to four-minute resolution. We know the various rules of the conventional game and play along. How unusual to be led by an intelligent, assertive woman, and a middle-aged one at that!

According mothers and fifty-year-plus female characters central roles and careers is not insignificant. In contrast to the duality of cinema's representation as either young or old (and holding stars to that determination, for example, Mary Pickford, Greta Garbo, Mickey Rooney, Buster Keaton), a spectrum of age and generational difference exists on television.

PART V

REGIME OF DOMICULTURE

Women and Situation Comedy

Since we said "I do," there are so many things
we don't.

— Lucy Ricardo

This is a battle between two different ways of
life — men and women.
The battle of the sexes!?
Sex has nothing to do with it.

— Gracie Allen and Blanche Morton

During the late 1940s and '50s, television, linked to or owned by the major radio networks in the U.S., recycled radio's stars, formats, and times through little proscenium screens, filling up the day. Vaudeville and movies fed both these voracious domestic media, each reliant on sound, and each influential in the rapidly developing suburbs. With a commercial collage of quiz, news, music, variety, wrestling/boxing, fashion/cooking, and comedy shows, both media were relatively irreverent toward well-fashioned narrative and worshipful of audiences and sponsors. TV was then (and continues to be) an ecology, a repetition and recycling through the years, and a family affair, in the 1950s conducted collectively in the living room, the dial dominated by Dad. A TV set was a status symbol, a rooftop economic declaration, and an invitation to other couples to watch. The agenda was familialism. Or as George Burns put it: "There are more husbands and wives on television than at home watching."

Coincident with the massive licensing of broadcast air and time, women were being urged to leave the city, work force, and salaries; move to the suburbs, leisure, and tranquility; raise children; and placate commuting, overworked husbands for free. In reality, of course, not all women did so. Most women over thirty-five remained in the paid work force; when allowed, instead of building battleships, they took other jobs. That TV, and particularly situation comedies, would, like radio, both serve and support the new, imaginary blissful domesticity of a ranch-style house, a backyard barbecue, a tree, and a bath and a half, seems logical — it is, of course, historical. "Containment" was not only a defensive military strategy developed as U.S. foreign policy in the 1950s, it was practiced on the domestic front as well, and it was aimed at excluding women from the work force and keeping them in the home. For Andrew Ross in *No Respect*, "This mechanism of containment is a process of identification, not an act of annexation. It results in the formation of new audiences, new cultural identities . . . not in . . . homogenizing of . . . cultural production and consumption."[1] For women, however, containment was a double whammy—identification *and* (by or with) annexation. The "New Traditionalist," fashionably dressed to stay at home as were Gracie and Lucy, is a revision of an earlier campaign, a "situation" which occurs when jobs are fewer and too many men are unemployed. For women in the 1950s, consumption for the family home became a full-time, unpaid job. "*I Love Lucy*" brilliantly documents this process of "upward mobility," with Lucy always aware that her talents might be wasted on full-time housewifery.[2]

The self-sufficient/contained family home—the locus of situation comedy—is a haven for consumer durables and services, along with marriage. The "household" is the setting for the neo-Fordist regime: domiculture.[3] For example, the introduction of TV (a piece of furniture and entertainment) into the home in the late 1940s and 1950s was accompanied by redecorating or the construction of a rec or family room. As Lynn Spigel demonstrates, it was a marketing campaign addressed to women, urged to alter predetermined spaces. The campaign was contradictory: TV was disruptive and hence demanded spatial change, but it would bring the family together.[4] In the beginning, there was one set per family, in a central viewing space. Now, TVs sit in many rooms of the house, watched by individual family members while babies are monitored by closed-circuit surveillance cameras. TV is not only a stationary piece of furniture but a mobile appliance. It can be bought as a series of components and then hooked up to other high-voltage electronic durables—VCRs, computers, and stereo systems. With men now included in on the purchase, the latest redecorating phase is designing costly "entertainment centers." The electronic expansion capacity might be endless.

To argue that television was and is a powerful machinery of familial containment of women is hardly original. Yet, the disparagement of situation comedy suggests that more is going on in these twenty-four minutes than meets the eye. Because this form has been dominated by middle-aged women, often mothers, its lowly stature might be a symptom of disrespect for, particularly, housewives (the least regarded and the most crucial job). Yet, this cultural disrespect is promising, especially for women of a certain age. The history of sitcom women is my history—one of contradiction.

XIII

◆

Gracie

In fifteen-minute segments, broadcast live three times a week in 1949, Gertrude Berg—writer, producer, and star—disguised herself as Molly Goldberg, the quintessential Jewish mother, a mélange of chicken soup malaprops, and advice. Leaning out of her window, she would intimately confess to us: "If Mr. Goldberg did not drink Sanka decaffeinated coffee, I don't know what I would do—I don't even know if we'd still have a marriage. . . . Just try it once, and that's what I'm telling you." The program and its popularity were emblematic of the subsequent televised avalanche of situation comedies, a direct descendant of radio, vaudeville's "husband and wife" sketches (which continued in variety shows or "vaudeo"), music hall, and commedia del'arte's stereotypical scenes and characters. The elision of program and star with sponsor was another version of television's corporate coupling/ownership.

In the 1950/51 season, the *George Burns and Gracie Allen Show* (on the air Wednesdays until June 11, 1958, when Gracie left the show) debuted, continuing and altering this tradition. Sponsored by Carnation and B. F. Goodrich, the program was broadcast live from New York for two years before following the economically successful precedent of *"I Love Lucy"* and moving to Los Angeles and film. There, shot with two cameras (a three-camera format was used for *Lucy*), *Burns and Allen* was filmed and *then* shown to an audience for the recording of laughter, which, to a degree, determined the editing: if the joke got a laugh, the reaction shot would most likely be used (eliding the at-home spectator with the bewildered character); if not, the camera stayed on the joker and followed his or her exit. "Canned" laughter was also added, both strategies simulating the presence of a live audience beyond the screen's range of the unseen yet heard fourth wall. The addition of laughter was, according to Freud, a signal of conclusion, a critical component of jokes and the comic.

Burns and Allen funneled their 1926 marriage, vaudeville, radio, and film routines and characters/stars into an upper-middle-class situation comedy format and style—a historical agglutination suggesting that what is monolithically termed popular culture is a process: a collection of discourses, scenes, or turns recycled from various media and contextualized within historical moments. Despite its similarity to the Molly Goldberg type of program, this show represented a new version of the happily married couple, featuring the zany, fashionable Gracie of bewildering sequiturs (different from non sequiturs) and the relaxed, dapper George of oneliners and wisecracks. They lived in suburban, affluent Beverly Hills; their TV home was meticulously neat and spacious—two stories with a large entrance, big living and dining rooms, and kitchen, with many windows, and surrounded by patios, porches, and landscaping. There was a TV set in the upstairs bedroom and another in George's den/office above the garage, his place of escape and surveillance: his TV set was a closed-circuit monitor of the house and Gracie.

Gracie was certainly unlike TV's nurturing yet domineering mothers who dwelled in city apartments. Yet, she was familiarly different as "Gracie." Derailing the laws and syntax of language and logic, her technique was a referral back to either the nearest or the unexpected referent as a comic turn on the arbitrary and conventional authority of speech. It is important to emphasize that Gracie took grammar literally, and hence was rigorously logical; it was language and its learned conventions which were arbitrary, vague, and confusing, not Gracie, who did not play by conventional rules. And, just when her friends and we caught on and agreed or got it, Gracie would break her own rules. She baffled all the male and most of the female characters, concocting improbable stories and schemes that were invariably true or "logical" in amazing circumlocutions which became that week's story. Significantly, unlike Lucy's outlandish exploits and explanations— usually wide-eyed, deliberate lies—Gracie's inadvertent implausibilities were successful. (The enigmatic quality of Gracie Allen, her consistent characterization *as* Gracie, triggers a desire to know what she "was really like," as the best-selling status of books by George Burns suggests.)

The casual narratives of each week's program were used merely as continuity for vaudeville routines and everyday life; the story existed primarily to be mocked by George, particularly in his monologues, voiceover commentary about Gracie, marriage, events, or the week's story. The scenario was usually as follows: an ordinary event—shopping, going to the movies, wanting a new lamp—would be misinterpreted and then complicated by

Gracie, who would then connect a second, random event to the first. For example, their college son, Ronnie, needed a story for the USC newspaper; Blanche Morton, Gracie's next-door neighbor, ally in the battle between the sexes, and confidante, wanted new dishes. Linking these two unrelated co-incidences, Gracie contrived a fake theft of Ronnie's wealthy friend's car. When the car was found in the Mortons' garage, Blanche's husband was so relieved not to have to pay for this "new" car, which he believed Blanche had bought, that he gladly bought the plates; and Ronnie scooped the story of the theft.

Adding to the shaggy-dog quality of these plots of the everyday were the many bewildered characters (frequently the postman) who would drop by the house, or strangers encountered in public places, who would then be involved by Gracie. The more unrelated the character or innocent by-stander to the plot, the better; a large measure of Gracie's comedy depended on other characters' astonishment. Her naive, friendly (non) sequi-turs rendered them speechless, reluctantly agreeing, finally reduced to staring in stunned or amazed reaction shots. (This is diametrically opposite what occurs in *"I Love Lucy,"* where Lucy is invariably given the last word or look, the editing (particularly of reactions) indicating that different mechanisms of identification and spectator positioning are operative in each show.) Then, winking at us, George would either join in the linguistic mayhem or sort things out. Ironically, his intervention was not for our un-derstanding but for the confused, speechless characters; his Aristotelian analyses of Gracie's behavior and illogic left bystanders doubly amazed while repeating what we had just witnessed.

Garbed in dressy fifties fashion, set in an upper-middle-class milieu of dens, patios, and two-car garages, constantly arranging flowers or making and serving coffee but not sense, Gracie equivocally escaped order. Despite being burdened by all the clichés applied to women—childlike, illogical, crazy, nonsensical, with their own peculiar bio-logic and patronized (and infantilized) accordingly—in certain ways, she was out of (or beyond) men's control. Unlike the ever-loyal and bewildered Harry VonZell, this se-ries and the story's announcer, and other characters in the narrative sketches, neither she nor her neighbor and best friend, Blanche (who loved and understood Gracie), revered George or was intimidated by his clever-ness; in fact, Gracie rarely paid attention to him or any authority figure. She unmade decorum, she unraveled patriarchal laws, illustrating Jean Baudrillard's assertion through Freud: "the witticism, which is a transgres-sive reversal of discourse, does not act on the basis of another code as such; it works through the instantaneous deconstruction of the dominant discur-sive code. It volatizes the category of the code, and that of the message."[5] The "dominant discursive code" of patriarchy tried, through benevolent George, to contain Gracie's volatilization, her literal deconstruction of speech, and her tall tales of family. Whether or not the system or she suc-ceeded can be answered either way, depending on where the analyst is politically sitting—with George in his den, or at home, with women. (And George would side with the women anyway.)

Gracie's forte was the shaggy-dog story—either as verbal riff or as the very substance of the narrative: The first use led to illogical nonsense, a way of thinking definitive of Gracie's comedy, frequently about her wacky relatives, whom we never saw; the second led to instigation *and* resolution of the week's episode. Furthermore, for the story (which often depended upon Gracie's lack of credibility and sense), the shaggy-dog event would always prove to be "true." Thus, many episodes are about how to tell and prove a claim or story. (It would take just a slight shift to turn Gracie's and women's lack of credibility, their lack of believability, to frustration and rage. If no one is believing or listening, then women might just as well speak nonsense.) Take, for example, the following episode. The scene is Gracie's sunny, ruffle-curtained kitchen, with a center-placed table, an auto-replenishing coffeepot, and numerous exits. The initial situation is explicated in the dialogue:

> Gracie: Thanks for driving me home, Dave.
> Dave: As long as I towed your car in, I didn't mind at all, Mrs. Burns.
> Gracie: There's some coffee on the stove. Would you like some? . . .
> Dave: I've been wondering, Mrs. Burns. How are you going to explain this little repair job to your husband?
> Gracie: I'll just tell him what happened. I went shopping and bought a blouse and on my way home I stopped to watch them put up the tents and this elephant came along and sat on my fender and smashed it.
> Dave: He'll never believe it.
> Gracie: Of course he will. He knows a fender isn't strong enough to hold up an elephant. George is smarter than you think he is.[6]

To prove her story (that she went shopping) to George, Gracie will show him the blouse! Her idiosyncratic but sensible cause-effect connections have nothing (or everything) to do with physics or the arbitrary conventions of language or common sense. In many ways, her style of speech is uncommonly funny because it is ahistorical, ignoring the speaker and the situation while obeying the rules of language. Like Chico Marx, she takes language literally; unlike Chico, she is unaware of her effect on other characters.[7] Gracie delivers her deadpan lines without reaction or expectation, obliviously using the same expressive tone no matter what the terms of the discursive contract—which she ultimately reconstructs anyway.

The rest of this episode consists of retelling the story—first to Blanche, who then tells her husband, Harry; then to the insurance salesman, Prescott; and simultaneously to Harry VonZell and Stebbins, the circus man. George, basically a solo narrative entrepreneur, keeps breaking and entering Gracie's dilemma of credibility with comments over: "All I wanted was a little proof," observations on life, and ironic maxims about marriage:

"Married people don't have to lie to each other. We've got lawyers and friends to do that for us." Gracie turns everyone into a straight man. For example, Prescott says: "I keep coming back to the big top and the sawdust. It's really gotten under my skin." Scrutinizing his face, Gracie replies, "Oh, you must have large pores." Neither figures of speech nor clichés are safe when Gracie is around. The second complication of this meager plot is added offhandedly by George in voiceover: "I don't know what happened to our car, but Gracie had our insurance canceled." He then bribes her with a promise of a mink coat for the "true" story, which, of course, she has already told him.

The show culminates in a final courtroom scene, with all of the participants sitting in the Burnses' living room validating the truth of Gracie's initial story, which is confirmed by Dave, the "seeing is believing" mechanic. The truth of male vision verifying Gracie's words is endlessly repeated, in the series and in this program: Dave: "If I hadn't come down to the circus grounds to tow away your car, I wouldn't have believed it myself." During the last scene, he reiterates: "If I hadn't seen it with my own eyes, I wouldn't have believed it myself." During this conclusive trial, presided over by George, a new character, Duffy Edwards, the furrier, enters with Gracie's newly won fur coat and, to George, summarizes the show: "I always watch your show. I knew you were going to lose."

Unlike Lucy, Gracie always wins in the narrative. Her victory is a quasi-validation of her credibility, *verified weekly*, and demonstrates the success of her crazy strategies. Gracie's schemes also bring George and Gracie from their separate realms of the house; thereby, her antics sustain the story and maintain marriage. The resolution of the two-strand plot is the uniting of the couple. The story's conclusion of togetherness is followed by an epilogue: a vaudeville routine initially performed on a curtained proscenium stage, then from their Beverly Hills vine-covered porch. After they had performed directly for us, George would issue the imperative "Say goodnight, Gracie"—sealing her status as a child.

However, other codes are also operative: in the above episode, George is center-framed in the mise-en-scène and by the moving camera which follows him; he is taller than all the other characters (who are seated); he has access to the audience via his direct looks at the camera and verbal asides, in addition to interspersed standup monologues. He nods knowingly, with sidelong collusive glances at us (or perhaps husbands everywhere). In the end, Gracie is frame left. She wins the narrative and the mink coat but loses central screen space; perhaps most important, along with having no credibility of speech, she never was in possession of "the look." (Her gaze is not tied to interpreting and knowing—or "normal" interpretation and Gracie's interpretation of events are two different things; we don't see things from her point of view, and thus don't ever really know her.) Roland Barthes, placing power firmly in language, asks: "Where is speech? In locution? In listening? In the returns of the one and the other? The problem is

not to abolish the distinctions in functions . . . but to protect the instability
. . . the giddying whirl of the positions of speech."[8]

The whirls are giddying; yet George Burns, the dapper entertainer as
Hollywood gossip, TV critic, political commentator, female psychologist,
and golf partner of CBS president William Paley, presides over the show
with benign resignation, a wry smile, and narrative logic firmly grounded
in bemused knowledge of the frothy status of the situation, comedy, and
television. Throughout each program, Gracie is blatantly dominated not
only by George's looks at the camera and his direct monologues to a TV
audience, but also by his view of the program from the TV set in his den
and his figure matted or superimposed over the background action as his
voiceover (and body) comment on marriage, Gracie, her relatives, movie
stars, show business, and that week's story.

In his analysis of Freud's *Jokes and Their Relation to the Unconscious*, Samuel Weber suggests an intriguing reading of the *Aufsitzer*, or the Shaggy
Dog jokes—nonsense jokes which create the expectation of a joke, causing
one to search for concealed meaning. "But one finds none, they really are
nonsense," writes Freud. Weber argues that the expectation consists in the
desire "to make sense of the enigmatic assertion with which the joke begins. . . . Such jokes 'play' games with the desire of the listener. . . . By
rousing this 'expectation' and then leaving it unsatisfied . . . such jokes
function in a manner very reminiscent of the discourse of the analyst, who
refuses to engage in a meaningful dialogue with the analysand."[9] It is difficult to apply Weber's insight to Gracie, to compare *her* rather than George
to the analyst. After all, it is George with whom the listener is in collusion;
it is George who hears and sees Gracie from his tolerant, bemused, central
vantage point. It is as if he occupies the central tower in the panopticon, or
the analyst's chair behind the couch, unseen, with all scenes visible to his
gaze. Because the *Aufsitzer* doesn't conclude, the laugh track is not tied to
Gracie but to other characters' *reaction* to her. Gracie has few reaction shots,
and indeed few reactions to anyone or anything other than a nonplussed
stoicism; she is indeed self-contained. (Laugh tracks involve a rigorous redundancy of visual and aural editing and punctuation.)

As Weber writes, these jokes are "come-ons," taking us for a ride. "For
at the end of the road all we find is nonsense: 'They really are nonsense,'
Freud states, thus seeking to reassure us, and himself as well" (114). Perhaps *Burns and Allen* could be read as a massive male reassurance that women's lives are indeed nonsense. The *Aufsitzer* is a joke played on the expectation of a joke, and is clearly a complicated matter—in the case of
Gracie Allen, it is a refusal of conventional meaning gleefully accepted and
encouraged as rebellion by Blanche Morton and contained for the audience
by the omniscience of George, who narcissistically strives, as super/ego, to
"unify, bind . . . and situate [himself] as a self-contained subject" (116).

Nor should we be misled by the fact that George is the straight man and thus seems to occupy a slightly inferior position, which he describes as follows:

> For the benefit of those who have never seen me, I am what is known in the business as a straight man. If you don't know what a straight man does, I'll tell you. The comedian gets a laugh. Then I look at the comedian. Then I look at the audience—like this. . . . That is known as a pause. . . .
>
> Another duty of a straight man is to repeat what the comedian says. If Gracie should say, "A funny thing happened on the streetcar today," then I say, "A funny thing happened on the streetcar today?" and naturally her answer gets a scream. Then, I throw in one of my famous pauses. . . .

But George (unlike Ricky) was never *just* a straight man; the monologue continues.

> I've been a straight man for so many years that from force of habit I repeat everything. I went out fishing with a fellow the other day and he fell overboard. He yelled "Help! Help!" So I said, "Help? Help?" And while I was waiting for him to get his laugh, he drowned.

This gag defines quite precisely George's actions, as well as indicating their vaudeville origins. (Current sitcoms draw on television and tabloid history rather than vaudeville.) Inevitably, he got the last and controlling look or laugh. Containment operated through laughter—a release which might have held women in their place rather than "liberating" them in the way Freud says jokes liberate their tellers and auditors. As radical as the nonsense joke might be (when it comes from the mouth of the male), it is different, like the rest of life, for the female speaker. The audience, too, is measured and contained by George, whom both the camera and editing follow: the husband as TV critic, solo standup comic, female psychologist, and tolerant parent/performer. Yet, in contrast to most situation comedies, it was clear that George depended on Gracie, who worked in both the series' imaginary act and the programs' narratives. On talk shows today, the old and dapper George gives Gracie all the credit. Thus, the contradiction of the program and the double bind of the female spectator and comedian—women as both subject and object of the comedy rather than the mere objects that they are in the Freudian paradigm of jokes—are dilemmas which, for me, no modern critical model can resolve.

XIV

◆

Lucy

In its original version, "*I Love Lucy*" debuted Monday, October 15, 1951, at 8:00 P.M. (It ran until May 6, 1957.) The means of filming involved the simultaneous use of three 35mm cameras with ten-minute magazines (the discontinuous stop-and-start method) for a live audience in a converted sound stage. The mise-en-scène was of minimal sets—kitchen right, bedroom left, central living room—and uniform lighting, "invented" by the German Expressionist cameraman Karl Freund. The method, attributed to Desi Arnaz, was and continues to be hailed as a technological rather than economic innovation; and, indeed, this style and apparatus set the pattern of three cameras, a live audience and laugh track, and a filmed/edited product. Under the rubric "Desilu" (his name first, the name of their ranch in the valley, eventually a corporate studio logo), they owned a tangible product (after sacrificing salaries for ownership) which could be corrected by postproduction editing, unlike live broadcasts or the low-resolution kinescopes (filmed from the TV screen).[10] The postproduction schedule was from six to eight weeks. Each episode was edited on a Moviola, producing a master print which included opticals such as wipes, fades, and dissolves. Prints were sent to CBS outlets prior to air date. There were thirty-nine episodes per season. And unlike the two-camera setup without an audience (which accounts for *Burns and Allen*'s [his name first] multiple sets and scene changes), this system seemed to encode presence and the status of live performance.

Perhaps most important, the standardization of product and broadcast times was achieved. The system was economically brilliant, if (visually) artistically retrograde—a profitable hybrid of nineteenth-century staging techniques and B-movie continuity style and abbreviated conventions, necessitating, for example, the center-frame, frontal, uniformly lighted mise-en-scène. Desilu went on to make hundreds of hours of programming, employing the same system in their own studio empire, purchased, through the presumed economic savvy of Arnaz, the independent producer/entrepreneur, with the profits from the first series. In 1954, Arnaz produced, for example, *December Bride, Make Room for Daddy, The Ray Bolger Show,* and later *The Untouchables,* totaling some 229 half-hour shows.[11] The three-camera format, the central living room and women's place within the home, the studio audience, frontal staging, and the laugh track—tied to reactions—have become an institutionalized, familiar style which has endured, with minor stylistic revisions, for forty years. The major locale was the family dwelling (with forays to workplaces), significant in that situation means, among other things, "a place of employment"—so true for female stars and viewers.

Held to the domesticity of situation comedy's conventions, Lucy Ricardo was barely in control, constantly attempting to escape domesticity—her "situation"—always trying to get into show business by getting into Ricky's "act," narratively fouling it up, but brilliantly and comically performing in it. Lucy endured marriage and housewifery by transforming them into vaudeville: costumed performances and rehearsals which made staying home (a lack of choice and economic power) frustrating, yet tolerable. Her dissatisfaction, expressed as her desire for a job, show business, and stardom, was concealed by the happy-ended resolutions of hug/kiss (sometimes tagged with the line "Now we're even")/applause/titles/theme song, over the famous heart logo. Her discontent and ambition, literally and weekly stated, were the show's working premises, its contradictions massively covered up by our sheer pleasure in her performances, her "real" stardom and brilliance. The series typified the both/and logic and the paradox of women and comedy (and work)—the female performer/spectator caught somewhere between narrative and spectacle, always having two effortless jobs, historically held as a simulation between the real and the model. The serious contradictions of women's lives were blatantly there, often spoken, but covered up by laughter and by Lucy's childish antics.

(In a sociological study [1991], Andrea Press interviewed groups of women regarding their responses to situation comedies. She discovered that working-class women's response to Lucy was a negative one, perceiving Lucy's antics as mere zaniness. Working-class women's responses were immediate, predicated on "the real." On the contrary, white, middle-class women could separate Lucy the character from Ball the comic performer, responding to her with respect. In other words, middle-class women could have a double understanding. For this study, the maintenance of contradictory belief depended on class. Women with more education and more money could deny/disavow; working-class women could not. While addressing the important issues of class, the determinism of the finding is troubling. At the same time, it is positive, suggesting that knowledge enables us to perceive the contradictions in which we are held.)[12]

On a more general level, the series dramatized the social phenomenon of "upward mobility." One version is embedded in Raymond Williams's analysis of the function of "consumer durables": "Socially this complex is characterized" by a paradox of (1) upward "mobility" and (2) the "apparently self-sufficient family home."[13] For Williams, there is as yet "no satisfactory name" for this "paradoxical" tendency of "modern urban industrial living," a technology which is both "mobile and home-centered," the phenomenon he describes as *"mobile privatisation"* (26). Williams places "broadcasting institutions" as the resolutions of these contradictory pressures: consumer durables improved small homes for families, which then needed new forms of contact, services which TV, like radio, provided. Consumer durables also covered up the contradictions in marriage and domestic labor. (Electric appliances were supposed to make housework easier and faster, along with providing cheaper entertainment at home. Arguing "the freedom to stay at home" or the virtue of saving money, audiences could accept the infinitely lower resolution and bad sound of television when compared to movies. Purchase and debt still hold marriages together.)

Lucy and Ethel crave dishwashers, freezers, and other domestic appliances, as well as clothing. Shopping for these two close friends is a pleasure, a rebellion, and an occupation—they always run the risk of spending too much and being chastised. Their lack of economic independence is a given, a source of comedy and plot, yet a frustrating one familiar to many women in the 1990s as well as the 1950s. "Pioneer Women" involves a bet on whether Lucy and Ethel can go without modern conveniences; the episode is also a parody on baking, the reality of women's work, which Lucy transforms into a comic routine. ("Job Switching" poignantly exemplifies women's economic subservience and the difficulties of housework, at which Fred and Ricky fail miserably. Housework is gender-determined.) In "Oil Wells," broadcast February 15, 1954, the Ricardos and the Mertzes buy Texas oil stock; then come the fur coats and "custom-built periwinkle blue Cadillacs." As always, Lucy's scheme is initially right, hailed, and finally wrong; she loses the money in the end after a great performance with a microphone in her pant leg. Their dreams of wealth vanish. Situation comedy is destined to be middle-class. In "Ricky Loses His Temper," the bet is on that Lucy cannot refrain from buying. She can't, but neither can Ricky keep his temper. Again, they are "even." It should be noted that while she was the emblematic 1950s consumer, Lucy (like Buster Keaton's one-reelers) also gleefully and offhandedly trashed possessions, suggesting their irrelevance and the risk of her endeavors.

The Ricardos' upward mobility is apparent throughout the series, including the early move to an apartment with a window. In fact, the series neatly coincides with newly introduced products and advertising campaigns in picture magazines such as *Look*. In the twenty-seven episodes devoted to the California sojourn (where the series originated, although it claimed New York as its setting)—Ricky's stint at becoming a famous movie star—aired during the 1955-56 season, Ricky buys a car (for all the bad women-driver jokes that the series had so far avoided). In ad campaigns increasingly pitched to women, the family car was the big consumer item, along with the family home. Family travel and vacations (by car, and a bit later by plane) were increasingly advertised. In 1954, Chrysler (which then sold the following models: Plymouth, Dodge, Desoto, Chrysler, and Imperial) called their campaign "The Forward Look," a campaign linked to women and high fashion: "7 top fashion designers find Chrysler Corporation's 1955 cars a stimulating new concept of good design." Six women designers (Anne Fogarty, Pauline Trigere, and Lily Dache, for example) are adorned in formal finery, leaning against a Chrysler (*Look*, November 20, 1954). In all the ads for "The Forward Look," women were featured as drivers, the "you" of the copy apparently addressed to women through style and fashion. Pontiac ads that same season were careful to include women drivers. Two episodes of *Lucy* are devoted to the purchase of an automobile (which Lucy will then predictably crash).

Now the couples, constantly together, are mobile and drive cross-country. In the Hollywood episodes, they stay in a luxurious hotel suite and concoct schemes to meet movie stars, which are wildly successful. In May 1956, "Lucy Goes to Monte Carlo" (and makes, then loses, piles of money), and after seventeen episodes devoted to Europe, she returns to New York, carrying her cheese "baby" on the plane. In November 1956, they're "Off to Florida" and "Deep Sea Fishing" (with another bet between women and men, wives versus husbands, the battle of the sexes which has nothing to do with sex, over who will catch the biggest tuna). In December that year, "The Ricardos Visit Cuba."

Finally, the ultimate 1950s seal of upward mobility—the move to suburban Connecticut, with the Mertzes as entrepreneurial chicken farmers (they also try some other small-time business schemes, which fail). This enterprise, "Lucy Does the Tango," resulted in the longest laugh on the series—Lucy doing the tango with Ricky (who apparently *wants* her in his act!), with dozens of eggs stuffed in her clothing. After a long dance routine, they finally collide, and the audience breaks up. The scene builds on that laugh when Ethel is slammed by a swinging door, squishing her concealed eggs. One episode is devoted to Lucy's redecorating; she spends too much money on furniture because she is afraid to let the decorator know she, and Ricky, can't afford to spend so much. (In many ways, one had to live through the 1950s to understand its middle-class eccentricities and the real debilitating paradoxes for women: I could not tell my friends that my mother worked; her professionalism might have challenged my father's economic capabilities or jeopardized his job. Pretense of all sorts, including the very familiar "keeping up with the Joneses," was widespread, very real, more painful than parodic.)

At the same time, Ricky has moved from performer, to manager, to movie star, to owner of the Club Babaloo. Lucy has also been working: "Little Ricky Gets a Dog, "Little Ricky Plays the Drums," and everyone goes to "Little Ricky's School Pageant." It goes without saying that the latter are among the least interesting episodes. (As children are turned into consumers, their TV characters become more prominent and interesting, for example, the portrayal of children on *Cosby*. Each child is decked out in amazingly expensive kid fashion. As children demonstrate their consumer prowess, their numbers on sitcoms directly increase, although there was always "the Beaver.")

Outside the fiction (which was always elided with the real, particularly the Arnazes' marriage), Desilu purchased RKO, Lucy's former studio. In addition to their seven-acre, nine-stage lot, purchased in 1953, they now owned RKO's fifteen-stage, fourteen-acre Hollywood lot as well as RKO's Culver City Studio of eleven stages. Desilu, consisting of thirty-five movie stages, a forty-acre backlot, and offices, along with the Motion Picture Center, was bigger than MGM or Fox. Charles Higham called it "the biggest production facility on earth."[14] Along this corporate way, in the best entrepreneurial fashion, they crossed media boundaries, staging the series live in Las Vegas and releasing combined episodes on film for movie showings. They "tied in" with the American Export Lines, in return for a plug on the European voyage, and General Motors, for a car plug on the California trip. The lucrative sponsorship/linkage with Phillip Morris is apparent in almost every episode; Lucy and Ricky frequently smoke or handle cigarettes. In the famous "Lucy Makes a TV Commercial," Lucy imitates the Phillip Morris boy in the TV set which she has trashed.[15]

In the best Walt Disney fashion, hundreds of Lucy products were manufactured: Lucy and Little Ricky dolls, Lucy bedroom suites, Lucille Ball dresses, Desi Arnaz smoking jackets (then very much out of style), he-and-she pajamas, Desi Denims, Lucy Lingerie. There was a syndicated comic strip for King Features from December 8, 1952, to May 30, 1955, records, Dell comic books, and *"I Love Lucy"* one-act plays for amateur theatrical groups. However, in an intrusion of the real, after a season of one-hour shows with famous guest stars, the couple separated and then divorced. Rather than bringing the couple together, which Lucy commentators never cease to repeat was the virtual reason for the program (Lucy's stymied, flat film career might be as significant), upward mobility led them apart, along with gossip's (and a TV movie's) later reports of Desi's drinking and infidelity and Lucy's "workaholism" and demanding perfection. The "real," incorporated into the series, was carefully managed until much later, after Lucy's death. After the divorce, Lucille Ball bought Desi Arnaz out and continued on in a successful single-parent series. In the 1980s, she began a new sitcom, as a grandmother, which was soon canceled. In *Stone Pillow*, a TV movie, she played the lead bag lady. Just prior to and after her death, she was hailed as an entertaining genius.

Along with the consumption of consumer durables and upward mobility, the series portrayed irrevocable, stereotypical differences between men and women. Fred is cheap, Ethel eats too much, Ricky loses his temper, and Lucy plots and shops. Like George Burns, Fred is a 1950s expert on female psychology, with constant commentary on women and marriage. In "Oil Wells," he labels Lucy and Ethel "the snooper patrol," followed by "Nosiness is just part of a woman's charm, like hanging stockings in the bathroom and nagging." In "Job Switching," Fred divides the world sexually into "earners and spenders." Ethel gets almost equal time for her "men" and "husband" jokes. At least TV, unlike the movies, presumed that women occupied other subject positions, with different identifications possible. This double-directed strategy was also apparent in the gender base of 1950s television, with sports and news shows for men, cooking and fashion shows for women, and "kidvid" for children, differences which "family shows" elided. However, while acknowledging women's existence, U.S. television scheduled few daytime programs for women. As Jack Gould, the TV critic for the *New York Times,* wrote: "The idea of a nation of housewives sitting mute before the video screen when they should be tidying up the premises or preparing the formula is not something to be grasped hurriedly."[16] Neither is Gould's remark easily grasped.

The series is a compendium of references to 1950s popular culture. Fifties fashion of full skirts and crinolines, tight waists, capri pant outfits, casual and formal aprons, and hats was seriously acknowledged in episodes devoted to designer clothing, parodied, as are many upper-class forms, including ballet and *House Beautiful*, in "Lucy Gets a Paris Gown." Her style was glamorized in 1953 with the hiring of award-winning Elois Jensen as costumer. Max Factor's brother-in-law was Lucy's constant makeup man, taking her age down from more than forty to the program's stated twenty-nine—a process aided by Freund's diffused lighting and the presence of Ethel, beside whom Lucy looked younger and more glamorous. Her trademark, along with her huge, false-eyelashed eyes, was, of course, her strawberry or hennaed hair, clearly not natural and a source of endless jokes.[17]

Additional references include the Kinsey report, Joe DiMaggio, and Marilyn Monroe. "Second Honeymoon," broadcast in January 1956, reenacts the scenario of *Gentlemen Prefer Blonds*, with Lucy as Lorelei and Kenny as the young boy, Spofford; they restage the scene where Monroe gets stuck in a porthole. (As anecdote has it, Lucy's impersonation of Monroe on another episode amazed passersby.) The show's brilliant writers, Marilyn Pugh, Jess Oppenheimer (the producer), and Bob Carroll, admitted to combing films for stories and bits. Lucy imitated Katharine Hepburn and Tallulah Bankhead. "Lucy's Italian Movie," which contains the grape-stomping sequence, dissects 1950s art films, specifically Italian neorealism: An Italian director, Vittorio Fellipe, approaches Lucy (the couples are vacationing in Italy) with the question, "Have you ever considered acting?" Huge laugh. Lucy, imagining herself as Anna Magnani, dresses as an earthy, disheveled peasant in order to gather "local color" and prepare for her part in the film *Bitter Grapes*; her hilarious sequence with the female peasant in the wine vat *is* the film, including subtitles, which in the end she doesn't make. As usual, she broke her promise to Ricky, disobeyed, is purple from the grape catfight in the vat, and must be narratively punished or contained.

Although not as reflexive as *Burns and Allen* (the forebear of Gary Shandling), the series also alluded to television. One example—the consummate testimony to Lucy's ability to endlessly vary a bit—is "Lucy Does a TV Commercial." The episode is predicated on the pretense of the live while acknowledging that *Lucy* is not live—it only pretends to be. The "real" Lucy stages a commercial in her living room, dressed as the Phillip Morris guy in the now-trashed TV set. Ricky tries to change the channel. Later, in the television studio of Ricky's show, Lucy rehearses for Vitametavegamin, a health product with a high dosage of alcohol, becoming drunker with each runthrough. (She is as brilliant as Chaplin.) Fade. Ricky is broadcasting *his* live show; the delightfully drunk Lucy walks onstage, upstaging Ricky and disrupting his act.

During the Hollywood episodes, she imitates star behavior—wearing dark glasses and scarves, carrying a long cigarette holder, and walking with an affected, hip-swinging gait. She sits on drugstore stools waiting to be discovered and tells stories about overnight fame. Like the audience, Lucy is starstruck, the consummate fan who will do anything to get star mementos, including a huge block of cement from Grauman's Chinese Theater with John Wayne's footprints in it. Being a star, viewed as an effortless and pleasurable job, is the show's ultimate fantasy and narrative gimmick. In "The Ballet," Lucy says: "Here I am with all this talent bottled up inside me and you're always sitting on the cork. . . . I'm going to get into that show or my name is not Lucy Ricardo." She goes on work and hunger strikes to get either clothes or a shot at a job performing. In order to work, she will lie, cheat, and even blackmail Ricky. In "Don Juan Is Shelved," Lucy tries to steal Ricky's big screen test by upstaging him. She is strapped to a couch, which doesn't stop her; finally, she pulls off Ricky's pants. In "Lucy's Fake Illness," she and Ethel are sitting in the kitchen, the scene of so many openings. Lucy is reading a psychology book: "I'm learning to act abnormal." Already by air date, January 1952, this bit receives laughter. After she decides to have amnesia, she says: "Ricky has kept me from becoming a famous actress."

Like Gracie, Lucy was a comic clown, a fashion model, and a "typical female": she was stylishly dressed, with extravagant tastes for hats; she loved gossip and was prey to jealousy; she was zany, without inhibition—

the child whom the husband or father, Ricky, tried to control. His noble tolerance was particularly evident in the Hollywood episodes. All the stars—Rock Hudson, Richard Widmark, John Wayne, and Dore Schary, the producer—know about Lucy's wild antics and empathize with Ricky and presumably tolerant husbands everywhere.

As was the case with the *George Burns and Gracie Allen Show,* the entire series was biographically linked to the marriage of the two stars. Lucille Ball, movie star, and her husband Desi Arnaz, Cuban bandleader, became disguised as Lucy and Ricky Ricardo; their friends appeared on programs as bit players or as "themselves." At the end of "Harpo Marx," in which Lucy and Harpo re-create the famous mirror scene of *Duck Soup* (with Lucy wearing a Harpo wig and baggy coat, as earlier in the episode she dressed as Clark Gable, Gary Cooper, and Jimmy Durante), the voiceover announcer said: "Harpo Marx played himself." Image/person/star are totally merged as "himself"; the real is a replayed image, a scene, a simulation— what Baudrillard calls the "hyperreal." The most extraordinary or bizarre example of the elision of "fact" and fiction, or the "real" with the simulation, was Lucy's hyperreal pregnancy. In 1952, with scripts supervised by a minister, a priest, and a rabbi, seven episodes were devoted to Lucy's TV and real pregnancy (without ever mentioning the word, except in Spanish). The first episode was aired in December, timed in accordance with Lucy's scheduled caesarean delivery date of Monday, January 19, 1953. Lucy's real baby, Desi, Jr., was electronically delivered, after a seven-week TV gestation, on January 19 at 8:00 P.M. as Little Ricky, while 44 million Americans watched. (Only 29 million tuned in to Eisenhower's swearing-in ceremony. We liked Ike. We loved Lucy.) Like all the episodes in this series, this one was given a children's book title, "Lucy Goes to the Hospital."[18]

But if the "real" domestic and familial details of the stars' lives (including the state of their marriage and Desi's reputation as a producer) were so oddly mixed up with the fiction, perhaps the supreme fiction of the series what that Lucy was not star material and hence needed to be confined to domesticity. Thus, the weekly plot concerned her thwarted attempts to break out of the home and into show business. Unlike Gracie's implausible connections and overt machinations, all of Lucy's schemes failed, even if failure necessitated an instant and gratuitous reversal in the end. Lucy was the rebellious child whom the husband/father Ricky endured, understood, loved, and even punished, as, for example, when he spanked for for her continual disobedience.

However, if Lucy's plots for ambition and fame *narratively* failed, with the result that she was held, often gratefully, to domesticity (and Ricky was therefore right), *performatively* they succeeded. In the elemental, repetitive narrative, Lucy never got what she wanted: a job and recognition. Weekly, for six years, she accepted domesticity, only to try to escape the next week. During each program, she not only succeeded but demolished Ricky's act, upstaging every other performer, including Orson Welles, and got exactly what she and the television audience wanted: Lucy the star, performing off-key, crazy, perfectly executed vaudeville turns—physical comedy as few women (particularly beautiful ones, formerly Goldwyn girls, with gorgeous legs and face) have ever done.

The typical movement of this series involves Lucy performing for us, at home, the role that the narrative forbids her. She can never be a "real" public performer, except for us: she must narratively remain a housewife. In the episode entitled "The Ballet," for example, Ricky needs a ballerina and a burlesque clown for his nightclub act; Lucy pleads with him to use her. Of course he refuses. Lucy trains as a ballet dancer in one of her characteristic performances: resplendent in a frothy tutu, she eagerly and maniacally imitates the dancer performing ballet movements, which she then transforms through automatic, exaggerated repetition into a Charleston. Whenever Lucy is confident that she has learned something new, no matter how difficult, she gets carried away. (To a degree, these moments recall Chaplin's bodily transformation into an automaton of repetitive motions.) These are the great comic scenes, occurring after the narrative setup: pure performances during which the other characters show absolutely no reaction.

This is the first "story" line, before the mid-program "heart break"— "curtains" as halves of a heart lovingly open/close, or frame and divide each episode. Then, the second: Lucy will now train to be a burlesque comic. Her baggy-pants clown/teacher, an old vaudevillian partner of Fred, arrives at their apartment with a bit for two men. Lucy says, "Just pretend I'm a man." He tells his melodramatic tale of woe about Martha and betrayal; Lucy becomes involved, says the Pavlovian name, Martha, and is hit with a pig bladder, sprayed with seltzer water, and finally, gets a pie in the face. The scene ends with Lucy saying, "Next time, you're going to be the one with the kind face"—in other words, the victim of the sketch. By assuming the mantle of male clothing and slapstick in the "Slowly I Turned" routine, she will become the perpetrator. Lucy never could be the straight woman. (Like the bet between men and women, turning the tables, or getting even, is another story gambit. Here, Lucy demonstrates her mastery of physical comedy, burlesque, and vaudeville, historically a male domain. In a style which she made her own, there are overtones of Keaton and Chaplin.)

Then, as in all the episodes, in this one more literally than most, the two stories are condensed in a final, onstage performance. At his nightclub, Ricky is romantically singing "Martha" in Spanish. Ethel calls Lucy to inform her that Ricky needs someone in his act. She dresses up as the burlesque clown (not the needed dancer) and steps onstage with her wrong props. When Ricky sings his refrain, the word "Martha" is now her Pavlovian cue: she beats the male ballet dancers with the pig bladder, squirts the female ballerina with seltzer water, and, in a conclusion which uses up all the previous setups, slams a pie in the singing face of tuxedoed, romantic crooner Ricky. The Saudi Arabian government noticed the gentle subversion of this series, banning it because Lucy dominated her husband.

This episode, like so many others, is a rehearsal for a performance, involving in the end a comical, public upstaging of (or getting even with) Ricky. We are simultaneously backstage and out front, in the audience, waiting for the surprise and pleasure of Lucy's performance and Ricky's stoic, albeit frustrated, endurance; thus, expectation is connected not to narrative but to anticipation of the comic—a performative, or proairetic, expectation.

An exemplary instance of Lucy's upstaging, or humiliation, of Ricky may be seen in the episode entitled "The Benefit," in which Ricky's attempts to be the comedian rather than the straight man are utterly foiled. In this episode, Lucy, along with the audience, discovers that Ricky has re-edited their benefit duo, taking all the punchlines for himself. Fade. Onstage, in identical costumes of men's suits, straw hats, and canes, Ricky and Lucy perform a soft-shoe sketch. Ricky stops, taps his cane, and waits for Lucy to be the "straight man." Of course, she won't comply. While Ricky sings "Under the Bamboo Tree" about marriage and happiness, Lucy, with camera closeups as her loyal accomplice in the reaction shots, outrageously steals all of his lines, smirking and using every upstaging method in the show-biz book. Applause, exit; the heart, this time as a literal curtain, closes. Lucy gets the last word and the last laugh during this ironic "turn" on the lyrics of the romantic song.

It is interesting to compare Ricky, the would-be comedian forced by his partner/wife to be the straight man, to George, the "straight man" who always gets the final, controlling laugh. That Ricky can be so constantly upstaged and so readily disobeyed is not insignificant, for with his Cuban accent (constantly mimicked by Lucy), he does not fully possess language, and is not properly symbolic as is George, the joker or wielder of authoritatively funny speech. The program's reliance on physical rather than verbal comedy, with Lucy and Ethel as the lead performers, constitutes another exclusion of Ricky. Unlike George, who stays at home, Ricky is not given equal, let alone superior, time. He constantly leaves the story, and his departure for work becomes the cue for comic mayhem and audience pleasure. The comedy cannot begin until he leaves. Although he is "tall, dark, and handsome," not the usual slapstick type, his representation as the Latin lover/bandleader/crooner and slapstick foil for Lucy's pies in the face suggests that Lucy's resistance to patriarchy might be more palatable because it is mediated by a subtle racism which views Ricky as inferior.

At the same time, Ricky is clearly the father figure, albeit a funny one. A sample of his responses: in the TV commercial episode, "I don't care if you talk to me, just give me my breakfast." In "Lucy Plays Cupid," aired in January 1952, Ricky is at the breakfast table, talking about marriage, men, and Lucy's scheme to arrange a date for another woman. He threatens

Lucy, "If you're gonna act like a child . . . ," followed by a spanking, then a fade. Fortunately for the series, Lucy always disobeys. In "The Adagio" (December 1957), Ricky repeats the inevitable "I'll teach her a lesson she'll never forget." In "The Saxophone," he best summarizes his position:

> Ricky: When I go on the road, I want you to stay home and be a good little girl.
> Lucy: Well, I'll stay home.
> Ricky: What do you mean by that?
> Lucy: Oh, nothing . . . [sauntering away, swinging her key chain, wearing her man's zoot suit—for her audition]

Typically, Ricky says: "No funny business." Lucy promises. Door closes. Lucy: "Let's go, Ethel." That Ricky could be so readily disobeyed is not insignificant. That marriage was a series of one-upwomanships within a structure of domination/subordination, that independence involved disobedience and deceit, should not go unremarked, covered up by laughter as these inequities were. At the same time, this very structure of marriage was the comic premise.

In "Vacation from Marriage," the underside of situation comedy's reiteration of the same is briefly revealed. Lucy, with Ethel in the kitchen, is talking about the boredom and routine of marriage. "It isn't funny, Ethel, it's tragic." The rest of this show and the series make marriage funny and adventurous. Week after week, the show keeps Lucy happily in her confined, domestic sitcom place after a twenty-three-minute tour de force struggle to escape. That neither audiences nor critics noticed Lucy's feminist strain is curious, suggesting that comedy is a powerful and unexamined weapon of subjugation, escape, and survival. The most famous episode, "Job Switching," in which Lucy and Ethel sit at an assembly line making chocolates at Kramer's Candy Kitchen, a brilliant staging of comedy, is also a commentary on women and work. The double plot—women at work in uniforms and men at home cooking in aprons—is a bet and a role reversal. Lucy and Ethel, like Siamese twins moving and responding as one, interview for a job at the Acme Employment Agency with A. Snodgrass: "What do you do?" Lucy: "What kind of jobs do you have open?" Snodgrass: "What do you do?" Lucy: "What kind of jobs do you have open?" This bit repeats. Snodgrass suggests another rhetorical method; Lucy agrees and asks: "What do you do?" He in turn asks: "What kind of jobs do you have open?" Finally, as always, Lucy wins, and he asks whether they are (of course) stenographers; then he reads a list, including candymakers.

Housewives, on this program and in the series, can't *do* anything except housework, which isn't taken seriously; and while Lucy and Ethel are great comedians on the assembly line, they can't handle the system when it speeds up. Wearing a hat, Lucy, with Ethel beside her, as always receiving fewer shots, imitates the female candymaker, thinks she's got it, makes a mess of things, and with a child's pleasure of playing in messes of chocolate, gets into a candy fight with her coworker before the fade. Comically she makes it; narratively she fails, losing her job and returning home to clean up the kitchen, which Ricky has demolished with his rice and chicken. "Now we're even." At the end of "The Ballet," her return home is met with a bucket of water dumped on her head, rigged over the doorway by Ricky. She smiles, "Now we're even." But women were not then, and are not now, even. And Gracie Allen was right: sex has nothing to do with the battle between the sexes.

In most of the programs' endings, the narrative policy was one of twofold containment: every week for seven years, Lucy was always wrong and duly apologetic; and while repeating discontent, her masquerades and escapades made Monday nights and marriage pleasurable. Allen, on the same network, untied legal language and the power polarities implicit in its command; Ball took over the male domain of physical comedy, revising history, with few imitators. Both unmade "meaning" and overturned patriarchal assumptions, stealing the show in the process; yet neither escaped confinement and the tolerance of kindly fathers. "That's entertainment!"— for women a massive yet benevolent containment.

XV

◆

Jokes and Their Relation to TV

As theorists of historiography have argued, discourses of "truth" and the "real" move through a cause-effect, narrative chronology to a resolute closure without gaps or discontinuities. There is something at stake in this strategy, and it is related to power and authority. Narrative embodies a political determinism in which women find a subordinate place, often to their surprise.[19] But narrative in situation comedy is only the merest overlay, perhaps an excuse. As George Burns said, "more plot than a variety show and not as much as a wrestling match." This implausible, sparse "situation" exemplifies—in its obsessive repetition of the domestic regime, of marital bliss as crazy "scenes," bets, deceits, and competitive squabbles—a social plaint, if not a politics.

Situation comedy, with "gaps" of performance and discontinuities, *uses* narrative, offhandedly. There is no deep and meaningful enigma and little mystery or suspense. The hermeneutic code is not replete with expectation, not in need of decipherment, not ensnaring us, not lying to us. That is what the characters say and do—the dominance of the proairetic. Comparison and expectation of pleasurable performance, the workings of the comic and humor, rather than narrative suspense are currencies of audience exchange. Perhaps this system might challenge "narrative's relation to a legal system";[20] certainly narrative is not viewed as sacred or authoritative any more than husbands are. It is necessary but not equal to performance. In trying to determine how comedy works to contain women and how successfully it does so, theories of narrative are thus of little help.

In Freud's study of jokes, particularly tendentious or obscene jokes, he assigns woman to the place of object between two male subjects. However, as I will argue regarding Roseanne Barr, there must be a difference when women become the joke-tellers. Also, given that the process between spectator/auditor and joker is, according to Freud, a mutually timed, momentary slippage into the unconscious, one wonders what occurs when that "unconscious" is labeled "female"—without essentialist or biological simplifications, but with historical and cultural specificity in mind. Yet, while the "joke" constitutes the majority of Freud's study, and while the joke is, for Freud, a more complicated process than is the comic, its structure is not directly applicable (except for the key place of the auditor and laughter as completion) to the structure of either of these television series (with the crucial exception of George Burns, for whom Freudian joke analysis works perfectly), possibly because the joke *is* such a historically strong male preserve—which Barr, along with other standup women, cracked in the 1980s. (The joke is a great model for TV reception.)

Unlike the three-way dealings of jokes, the "comic" for Freud is a two-person/two-way process; it is not gender-defined, and it derives from the relations of human beings "to the often over-powerful external world."[21] We experience a pleasurable empathy with the person who is pitted against this harsh world, whereas if we were actually in the situation, "we should be conscious only of distressing feelings" (197). (Freud emphasizes that we do not feel superiority to the person in the "situation.") We laugh at Lucy's comic moments, yet I wonder whether women might not also have experienced a certain amount of distress, particularly given the constraints of the 1950s and the constant subtle and not-so-subtle attempts to confine women to the home.

Freud notes that "persons become comic as a result of human dependence on external events, particularly on social factors" (199). Lucy is caught in her economic subservience to Ricky, as well as in the social mores of the '50s, a decade which covertly tried to reduce women to the status of dependent children. Lucy and Gracie are continually referred to as children; the women are "helpless" or economically dependent on males, particularly Lucy and Ethel, who do not have real (money-earning) jobs as Gracie does. Thus it is interesting to note that what Freud calls the "comic of situation is mostly based on embarrassments in which we rediscover the child's helplessness" (226) (one thinks perhaps of Lucy's exaggerated crying when she is frustrated or thwarted in her desires). Of course, Freud's term "comic of situation" becomes a form—situation comedy—a set of conventions millions of people know.

Moreover, just as one rediscovers the helplessness of children in the comic of situation, so too the pleasure it affords is compared by Freud to a child's pleasure in repetition of the same story. Each situation comedy end-lessly repeats its mise-en-scène, characters, and story; this pleasure, like the pleasure derived from most television, must depend, to a degree, on weekly forgetting, as well as on repetition of the intimately familiar and constant conclusions. Freud concludes his meandering thoughts on the comic and its infantile sources with: "I am unable to decide whether deg-radation to being a child is only a special case of comic degradation, or whether everything comic is based fundamentally on degradation to being a child" (227). "Degradation" is the crucial word here. Featuring the pe-rennially disobedient and rebelliously inventive child, "I Love Lucy" hovers somewhere between the comic of situation and what Freud calls the "comic of movement" and "character"; or better, the situation (the external world) is the problem which necessitates the comic of movement, of which Lucy is the master. (The comic of movement, like the comic of mimicry, is derived from comparison, which becomes intriguing when the comedian is a woman. Comparison, not recollection, also defines comedy's infantile sources, apparent in the adolescent characters Buster Keaton played and the childlike innocence of Charlie Chaplin.) Both the comic of character and the comic of movement concealed, as sitcom does, the home as women's workplace, the laugh tracks covering up the reality of women's work. It was there, right in front of our eyes, but we rarely noticed: creation/cancellation.

While an analysis of Freud's typology of comedy would be interesting, particularly for Lucy, an appendage ten pages before the end of *Jokes and Their Relation to the Unconscious*, and a later, brief essay by Freud entitled "Humour" intrigue me more. Freud's analysis of humor—epitomized by gallows jokes, the clever, exalted diversions of the condemned victim just before the hanging—as a category distinct from either the joke or the comic better explains the female victim (both subject and object, both performer and spectator), her place in the internal and external conditions of *Lucy*'s production. Endlessly repeating that she wanted to work outside the home, to perform, Lucy used humor as "a means of obtaining pleasure in spite of the distressing affects that interfere with it." It acted precisely as a "substitute" for these affects (228). Humor was a "substitute" produced "at the cost of anger—instead of getting angry" (231).

As Freud observes, "the person who is the victim of the injury, pain . . . might obtain *humorous* pleasure, while the unconcerned person laughs from *comic* pleasure" (228). Laugh tracks (comparable to "the audience"), which appear to be genderless, might have concealed the different re-sponses. Perhaps in relation to husband-and-wife sketches and audiences, the sexes split right down the middle, alternating comic with humorous pleasure, depending on one's view of who the victim is; this invocation of different pleasures suggests a complexity of shifting identifications amidst gendered, historical audiences. (The series tries to direct us to Ricky's po-sition as the victim of Lucy's ploys—for example, all the Hollywood, male guest stars empathize with Ricky. Yet these moments are brief in comparison to Lucy's scheme and performance time. Rarely, with the exception of Ethel and infrequently Fred, are secondary characters on Lucy's side.)

Trying to revive Lucy for feminism (although younger scholars have recently questioned my interpretation),[22] I have suggested that throughout the overall series and in the narrative structure of each episode, she is the victim, confined to domesticity and outward compliance with patriarchy and consumer capitalism's 1950s contradictory mandates. Yet this series is complex; Ricky is often the immediate victim of Lucy, a role more easily accepted because of his Cuban rather than Anglo-Saxon heritage. Given this perhaps critical qualification, Lucy is, finally, rebelliously incarcerated within situation comedy's domestic regime and mise-en-scène, acutely frustrated, trying to escape via the "comic of movement," while cheerfully cracking jokes along the way to her own unmasking or capture. She also became the star she wanted to (and couldn't) be.

Importantly, humorous pleasure comes from "an economy in expenditure upon feeling" rather than the usual lifting of inhibitions that is the source of pleasure in jokes—not a slight distinction, suggesting a displacement of affect or emotion, which I argued earlier might be one critical effect of television, a medium so reliant on comedy. In contrast to the supposedly "liberating" function of jokes, humorous pleasure "saves" feeling because the reality of the situation is too painful. As Lucy poignantly declared to Ethel: "It's not funny, Ethel. It's tragic." Or as Freud states: "The situation is dominated by the emotion that is to be avoided, which is of an unpleasurable character." In *"I Love Lucy,"* the avoided emotion, the "unconquered emotions submitted to the control of humor" (235), is anger at the weekly frustration of Lucy's desire to escape the confinement of domesticity. Her desire is caricatured by her unrealistic dreams of instant stardom in the face of her narrative lack of talent—her wretched, off-key singing, mugging facial exaggerations, and out-of-step dancing. Her *lack* of talent is paradoxically both the source of pleasure and the narrative necessity for housewifery. Using strategies of humorous displacement (the "highest of defensive processes," says Freud—a phrase that takes on interesting connotations in light of 1950s containment policies) and the comic, both of which are "impossible under the glare of conscious attention" (233), situation comedy avoids the unpleasant effects of its own situations (a logic of creation/cancellation). The situation of Lucy was replicated by the female spectator, whether working as a wife or in another "job," moving between comic and humorous pleasure, from spectator to victim, in tandem with Lucy.

In his later essay, Freud elevates humor to noble, heroic status. For Freud, humor is "fine . . . elevating . . . the triumph of narcissism, the ego's victorious assertion of its own invulnerability. It refuses to be hurt . . . or to be compelled to suffer. It insists that it is impervious to wounds dealt by the outside world, in fact that these are merely occasions for affording it pleasure. Humour is not resigned, it is rebellious. It signifies the triumph of not only the ego but the pleasure principle. . . . It [repudiates] the possibility of suffering . . . all without quitting the ground of mental sanity. . . . It is a rare and precious gift."[23] For Lucy, Ethel, Gracie, and their audiences, humor was "a rare and precious gift." Given the repressive contradictions of the 1950s, humor might have been women's weapon and tactic of survival, ensuring sanity, the triumph of the ego, and pleasure; after all, Gracie and Lucy were narcissistically rebellious, refusing "to be hurt." Lucy's crying, "puddling up," is always fake, and therefore funny. Her reactions—"credentials" (a mouth open, "how dare you"), "foiled again," "light bulb" (a brainstorm), and "spider" (a curled upper lip plus a guttural sound labeled "gobloots")—were predictable, short-handed in later scripts (Andrews, 121).

On the other hand, comedy replaced anger, if not rage, with pleasure. The double bind of the female spectator/auditor and the female performer is replicated by the structure of the programs—the shifts between narrative and comic spectacle, the latter being contained by the resolute closure of the former—and the response of the spectator/auditor is split between comic and humorous pleasure, between denial of emotion by humor and the sheer pleasure of laughter provided by the comic of movement and situation of Lucy's performances. Whether heroic or not, this pleasure/ provoking cover-up/acknowledgment is not a laughing but a complex matter, posing the difficult problems of women's simulated liberation through containment.

Roseanne

Roseanne might be the dark side of *Lucy*, those moments when she disguised herself as an uncouth, unkempt, tough-talking character or hillbilly. While to have a messy house, let alone sassy children, was too great a felony on 1950s TV, Lucy would have enjoyed Roseanne's complaints about housewifery. Roseanne would have been Ricky's worst nightmare, although she would not have humiliated him in public or continually lied to him as Lucy did. Like Roseanne, Lucy had no skills and thus couldn't hold a job, although both women knew they were talented. Like Ball, Barr is in control of her working conditions; unlike Barr, Ball stayed out of the tabloids.

The October 1988 premiere of *Roseanne*, a situation comedy build around Barr's standup act as the disgruntled, sardonic housewife/feminist, was a remarkable take on the genre, demonstrating its malleable and consistent form. The astonishingly popular series functions both within and against the forty-year-old conventions of sitcom. Critically, Barr is unabashedly to proudly fat (with few stated regrets for her thin past), with a deadpan, strident voice which inevitably gets the last word or putdown. She is not zany, like Lucy and Gracie, nor is she the ideal middle-class mother of TV history and reruns, as the first promos ironically announced: "She's Donna Reed, June Cleaver, and Harriet Nelson . . . rolled into one. Finally a real mother comes to TV."

Against this thin, quiet, decorous, uncomplaining 1950s ideal, Roseanne wields acerbic one-liners (labeled whining, grating) with a deadpan, stoic face which cannot be fooled or cajoled (called inept to bad acting), in a body unconcerned about weight or high fashion (labeled uncontrollably fat). She is noisy and lumpy rather than acquiescent and sleek (although this is changing). She is never silenced, and often she is not nice—capital offenses for women. The very contours of the character—previously successful in a man's intensely competitive world of standup nightclubs and TV talk-show stints (as Lucy was brilliantly adept in the male-dominated world of vaudeville/physical comedy)—are the objects of attack.

Barr calls herself a "gynanarchist," with such lines as "I figure when my husband comes home from work, if the kids are still alive, then I've done my job."[24] Or that she will clean house when Sears sells a riding vacuum cleaner. Like Kate Millett, she was placed by her family in "a nuthouse" (108). She married Bill, lived in a trailer, and had three children ("I breed well in captivity") while she gained weight. Her sisters visited her and became involved with a women's bookstore. "I sat in the back room and read for two years." She became angry with her husband and lost 100 pounds; without even a high-school degree, she got a job as a cocktail waitress, which led to laughing customers and her decision to be a standup comedian (205). As her personal story goes, 1981 was the date of her first comedy-club appearance, a five-minute rebuttal of the male comics.[25]

"I realized that I had to create a whole new kind of comedy called "funny womanness,' "—women's experiences which are funny to men *and* women (However, "funny womanness" was not new.) (*Ms.*, 108). Her targets are husbands and children, mothers-wives talking back. To a suggestion that they take a family vacation: "Not without a court order!" Or, "I'm the mother they never had" (*Vogue*, 336). That her standup act was successful was demonstrated by the sale of her book, in October 1987, before *Roseanne*. Based on an HBO special and clippings, Doubleday paid $250,000, hoping for an Erma Bombeck of the 1990s.[26] In 1988, after only seven years doing standup, she became a star and a cover girl. In October 9, 1989, *People*, coincident with the publication of her book, featured her recent history, her new life after success: "I lost my marriage, my children got very messed up. Then in a three-month period I ended up with a new man, a new daughter, a new house. But I almost died. It was just so insane" (85).

Kathleen Rowe argues the "ambivalence" of *Roseanne* predicated on models of vision. Drawing on a history of "unruly" women and Nancy Henley's *Body Politics*, she writes that "women who are too fat or move too loosely appropriate too much space, and 'femininity is gauged by how little space women take up.' "[27] The contested space of the small family bungalow is crowded by overstuffed furniture, trinkets, junk mail, kid debris, and Roseanne's (and Dan's) hefty body, which "sprawls, slouches, flops on furniture" (Rowe, 9). Henley notes that bodily habits connoting "loose-ness" (like belching and nose-picking, Roseanne's mocking teases) are "generally not open to women . . . as an avenue of revolt," a "peculiarly male type of . . . hostility toward authority. If it [looseness] should ever come into women's repertoire, however, it will carry great power, since it directly undermines the sacredness of women's bodies, a cornerstone of their suppression; and it will consequently command greater retaliation."[28] While this is an acute analysis, I wonder how powerful this loose or exces-sive body would be without verbal wit; it could be an embarrassed, inade-quate rather than rebellious body. "Looseness" is a matter of class and bodily manners, with little girls trained how to sit properly and be ladylike, which Roseanne rarely does. Class pretensions, in turn, are undercut by wit and laughter.

What is really scandalous about Roseanne, however, along with her non-chalance about weight and eating, is her overt feminism or "funny-wom-anness," delivered with an offhanded, casual but piercing tongue. Draw-ing directly on Barr's 1989 autobiography, Rowe writes that Roseanne "built her act and her success on an exposure of the 'tropes of femininity' (. . . 'true womanhood,' the perfect wife and mother) by cultivating the op-posite (an image of the unruly mother)," parodying the lifestyle urged upon women by Marabel Morgan, which "taught women to manipulate men by becoming domestic goddesses" (8). More likely, Roseanne's scan-dal was gaining so much power, fame, and money (so fast) from feminist comedy. The contradictions of women's daily lives, drawn from personal experience and popular culture, are not supposed to be so profitable, so entertaining, so highly rated. Nor is the perpetrator supposed to be so un-compromising and unconcerned about making such a public spectacle of herself, divorcing, cavorting, remarrying, singing off-key, and mooning at football games. Neither is she to be so uneducated and so fat. At the same time, this popular reception, ambivalent or not, also gives pause, suggest-ing a double-whammy containment endemic to sitcom and U.S. TV: while domesticity, romance, and femininity are critiqued, marriage, along with motherhood, is upheld—on and off the show.

While I prefer contradiction, Rowe points to Roseanne's "ambivalence": "Because female unruliness carries a strongly ambivalent charge, Rose-anne's use of it both intensifies and undermines her popularity. Perhaps her greatest unruliness lies in the presentation of herself as *author* rather than actor, and, indeed, as author of a self over which she claims control. Her insistence on her 'authority' to create and control the meaning of *Roseanne* is an unruly act *par excellence*, triggering derision or dismissal" (3). As in her relation with Dan, her sitcom husband, and her place within the joke, this unruly woman is on top, in a social structure which imagines and economically locates her on the bottom.

The question of Roseanne as an author is debatable, and was literalized on a late 1990 episode, a season of job losses. When she was in high school, she kept a daily diary and always wanted to be a writer. Presumably in her real life, she wrote poetry and fancied herself a writer. As with Gracie and Lucy, it is difficult to separate life from the series. In contrast to Gracie and Lucy, who claimed to be unlike their zany characters, Roseanne collapses character, person, and star. On this episode, she now imagines her life and talent passing her by, spent on motherhood and menial jobs. After Dan builds her "a room of her own" in the basement, she sits at her desk, trying but unable to write the great novel. However, like the tagged resolutions of sitcom, the ending unites contradictions—here, mother and writer, domesticity and career. After resigning herself to the loss of her dream, she tells a bedtime story to her son, who is an astute critic and praises her creativity. The scene cuts back, late at night, to Roseane, hunched alongside her now-sleeping son, pencil and paper in hand, *writing* her children's story. Yes, a compromise fantasy, but what a great source of comedy—the arch-to-insolent Roseanne as an author of children's books!—the sitcom version of *Murder, She Wrote.*

For Rowe, along with authorship, the overt sign of Roseanne's unruliness is her weight: "Excessive fatness carries associations with excessive willfulness and excessive speech." She is a "fat text." Like Bakhtin's model of carnival, the unruly woman both upholds traditional structures and "sanctions political disobedience." "She evokes not only delight but disgust and fear," with a place in the spectacle that, like carnival, is "not one of weakness." This is a strategy recommended by Mary Russo, following Luce Irigaray and Bakhtin—fashioning oneself as the subject, not the object, of the spectacle, being a knowing rather than unwitting female spectacle. However, being the spectacle can go either way, as Tammy Faye so aptly illustrates, turning women into jokes as well as jokesters. (Barr: "I'm a major food-and-cigarette addict.")

Thus, I think Rowe gives too much resistance (which might be repulsion) and unruliness to visual spectacle alone, particularly for TV, a very aural medium. The joke is Roseanne's ultimate weapon, a verbal assault which includes her intonation and grammar. For Bakhtin, intonation was as important as the body. For Roseanne, jokes deem her clever, wise, and always the winner, since no one one-ups her remarks. Like the joke, historically told by a male jokester to a male auditor who laughs his quota off, often at the expense of women, Roseanne is aggressive, sometimes hostile. The Freudian tables are turned. The joke is on authority (men and children), a challenging inverse of the poles of domination and subordination. In these jokes, unlike those of Joan Rivers and Freud, women and their bodies are not the problem. For Roseanne, patriarchal institutions, particularly masculinity but including middle-class pretensions both male and female, are the problem, the objects and targets of her jokes. Thus, the series radically revises Freud's structure of the joke by shifting its second-person object, usually a woman, replacing her with patriarchal social structures.

This is no small gain for women and comedy, although it has been years in the making.

I will briefly reiterate Freud's structure of the joke—a detour of tedium no worse than the endless bad jokes Freud relates. While Roseanne claims authorship of a character drawn from her life, jokes are usually authorless. Like gossip, jokes are historical and without clear origin, retaining a certain anonymity. Yet, at this historical juncture of female comedy, Barr's jokes seem almost uniquely her own. For me, the triadic structure of the joke, an aural register, is more applicable to TV than a dyadic visual model for several reasons: (1) the terrain of auditory pleasure and its sources in an amalgam from unconscious to conscious processes; (2) the necessity for a listener, Freud's "third person," who completes the joking process; (3) the signal role of laughter as a discharge documenting the joke's existence as a joke, as well as (4) the pleasure of completion and closure.[29]

Freud locates the joke's work and its sources of pleasure in relation to (1) the technique (an envelope, a container), (2) the play of words and sounds, and (3) the lifting of inhibitions—in a join, or a brief, mutual, disparately timed slippage into the unconscious, between the first-person maker and the third-person listener (the TV audience or sitcom sound track). Jokes *work* by "consciously giving free play to unconscious modes of thought" (204) which have, through acculturation, been rejected as faulty. Mothers are not supposed to insult their children. Like anxiety, jokes work consciously. Thus, Roseanne has at least three jobs, one of which is joking. The joke is a process and is temporal in its passage, finally dependent on intelligibility. Jokes have both a retroactive and an anticipatory narrative movement in time.

Like dreams, jokes work through condensation, a play with words and sounds, and displacement, "a diversion of the train of thought" (51). Both techniques secure pleasure from regression *and* lack of criticism, making the joke both rebellious and safe, like Bakhtin's model of carnival, unofficial culture, and the contradictions of sitcom. The joke's "technique" is a concealment enabling the hearer's delight in getting it and the jokester's pleasure in making it: "The thought seeks to wrap itself in a joke because in that way it recommends itself to our attention. . . . This wrapping bribes our powers of criticism and confuses them" (132). Sitcom is one technique of bribery, a defusing mechanism. The technique circumvents censorship and analysis in a double move: the rules of the joke's games are the butt of the joke as well as the source of pleasure. Thus, we laugh, often, at ourselves, at our own values. Pleasure circulates through the third person, the TV auditor, more than the characters within the program, who often react not at all or with bewilderment or outrage.

Thus, the spectator/auditor is in direct identificatory collusion with the star maker—we identify with lifted inhibitions and sound. Freud's very definition of the joking process (as distinguished from the comic) depends on its telling. "The psychical process of constructing a joke seems not to be completed when the joke occurs" (144). The need to tell is connected with the laughter produced. The critical function of laughter from the third person, absent from the event but there on the laugh track or from a live studio audience, is performed by the spectator/auditor who "laughs his quota off" (144). Pleasure paid for with laughter (and high ratings) signals the joke's completion.

"A joke is thus a double-dealing rascal who serves two masters at once (the Janus-like, two-way-facing character of jokes). . . . Everything in jokes that is aimed at gaining pleasure is calculated with an eye to the third person [TV's obsession with ratings and audiences], as though there were internal and unsurmountable obstacles to it in the first person. And this gives us a full impression of how indispensable this third person is for the completion of the joking process" (155). That completion is also indispensable for sitcom is demonstrated by the presence of studio audiences and the addition of laugh tracks from *"I Love Lucy"* on. This rascal joke has historically served two masters: the male teller and the male auditor. By necessity, auditory pleasure must be different when the teller and auditor are female, with the second-person object male authority rather than women.

The term "bribe" reappears in Freud's description of tendentious jokes: "obscene jokes, serving the purpose of exposure," "hostile jokes, serving the purpose of aggressiveness and satire," and "cynical jokes," usually attacking marriage and dealing with "the personal claim for sexual freedom, the pleasure of lifting inhibitions by bringing into prominence sexual facts and relations by speech" (97). It is here that Freud puts women in their historical place, as objects, dispossessed of language—the very speech necessary for making a joke and, reciprocally, understanding it. Tendentious jokes make possible the lifting of an obstacle, and the obstacle is "nothing other than women's incapacity to tolerate undisguised sexuality, an incapacity correspondingly increased with a rise in education and social level" (101). (This cultural difference recalls Freud's distinction between hysterics and neurotics.) It is on the terrain of the tendentious joke that Roseanne takes her radical stand, which might somehow be connected to the character's "education and social level."

Roseanne makes cynical, obscene, and hostile jokes against her obstacles: male authority, men's behavior, middle-class pretension, and the unequal division of familial labor. Paradoxically, one of her obstacles is comparable to Freud's—middle-class female decorum, with Freud's middle-class bias reiterating that of TV. Yet the differences are more glaring than the similarity: for Freud, verbal and auditory pleasure circulate through an unconscious labeled male; for Roseanne, this unconscious is female, brought to the surface. For Freud, marriage is a female institution of male entrapment. For Roseanne, exactly the opposite is the case.

In contrast to the illogical Gracie, Roseane is supreme logical; unlike Lucy with her crazy schemes, Roseanne is coolly rational. Yet, her intonation, her verbal style, is as distinct and perhaps as insistently irritating as that of her female forebears. Within the realm of joking, a verbal genre, Roseanne's voice is as rebellious as her double negatives, breaking the vocal conventions of femininity along with the rules of grammar. Henley suggests that "masculinity and toughness" are traits of nasal speech, wherein gentlemen and women have "non-nasal, or oral, speech" (75). Roseanne's insinuating intonation, her slow nasality, delivery, and caustic timing, is assertive, coupled with an openness and sweet directness that catch auditors off guard. Like her voice, body, and authority (including authorship of her program, autobiography, and standup act), Roseanne's actions fly in the face of feminine definition and propriety. Critics label her an untrained actor and an uncontrollable person. It would be another story if Roseanne's persona, drawn from life and standup comedy, were not so unimaginably profitable, if she were the underdog rather than the ratings top banana. Women's power can be used against them.

The series paradoxically undermines white middle-class familialism, the very basis of Freud and television programming, *and* adheres to the stylistic conventions of sitcom, the most rigorous of which is that the couple and the family stay together, briefly happy at each week's end. The irony is that, like Lucy and like the joke, the domestic critique is also the enabling premise (familialism is a problem, but marriage to Dan, along with parenthood, is a good if compromised thing). Thus, the contradiction cannot be resolved; it is the ultimate comic situation enabling laughter, ratings, and reruns. If the critique were carried to its logical conclusion (as it was by Lucy's and Desi's divorce), then the marriage, like the series and the family, would end before the profitable five-year run and syndication sale.

Equally threatening to the middle-class historical bias of TV, particularly sitcom, is Barr's staunch allegiance to the working class, which is ordinary rather than heroic, sensible rather than ridiculous, wherein family and marriage are central, albeit difficult. The unmarried status of Jackie, her sister, is, for example, a partial dilemma, not necessarily a good thing. After divorcing one husband in her real life, setting off a tabloid field day, Roseanne immediately married another amidst tales of hotel food, sexual excess, and their mutual recovery from addiction. Barr's bodily and social rebellion is also related to class—the upper-class body is not loose but impeccable. Her takes on marriage and the body (including the anti-romance of motherhood) suggest Roseanne's serious disagreements with aspects of the women's movement. Along with Marabel Morgan's "domestic goddess," woman's liberation into superwoman is overtly challenged. Roseanne's arch enemy would be the "new traditionalist."

The opening credits of the first episode roll over a tracking shot around the kitchen table, the central room of the series, revealing a mise-en-scène of disorder, with dishes stacked in the sink, open cupboards, and a cluttered table of food cartons—a messy rather than perfect house. Roseanne is neither discreetly tasteful nor an obsessive housekeeper. Cooking is not a comic routine of physical skill but an everyday plaint, funny monotony.

The appliances are old and broken, with a back-porch storage room containing a washer and dryer and boxes of stacked junk. Consumer durables are broken and used rather than coveted and purchased as in *Lucy*. Off to the left is the haphazard living room of clutter, discount warehouse furniture glopped around a big television set. The style is brown tweed Barcalounger. The upstairs bedrooms for this family of five are filled to bursting. Along with domestic disarray, clutter, and bad taste, other differences are immediately apparent in the credit sequence: the clothing fashion is K-Mart or Montgomery Ward's—Roseanne and her husband wear jeans and baggy, untucked shirts and lean their elbows and bodies on the table. Significantly, women receive the majority of production credits: Gayle Maffeo and Laurie Gelman are the first, with Marilyn Loncar cited at the end as the executive in charge; the first episode was directed by a woman, Ellen Falcon.

While the staff has fluctuated, and there are credited writers, it is argued that Barr is the author not only of her character but of the situation. Whether creator or not, she is a significant power behind the series. That a woman is in the unique TV position of being author, creator, and star might be one powerful reason for the tabloid gossip about her aggressive demands and antics on the set. According to her initial male producer, who was since fired, she is difficult and temperamental. Apparently, like her TV character, and unlike Donna, June, and Harriet, she is just not as nice and malleable as mothers and women are supposed to be. Like her autobiography, an interview in *People* has a rejoinder to Matt Williams, her former producer and source of tabloid headlines: "He compiled a list of every offensive thing I did. And I do offensive things. . . . That's who I am. That's my act" (86). (Most addicts are obnoxious right before recovery.) She asserts that Williams wanted the show to be from the little boy's point of view.

Barr represents this as a struggle for power and integrity. "I was seeing a male point of view coming out of women's mouths on TV, particularly around families. . . . The fathers did the major caretaking and nurturing; the mothers just were there and came in and out" (85–86). Williams is then accused of sanitizing Roseanne's life and act, and stealing creative credit along the way. "I didn't know until I saw the pilot that only his name was on it [as the show's creator]. They had told me it was a collaboration. I freaked. I fired my lawyers. Fired my agents. Everybody. . . . I asked the producers to fire Matt" (86). "There was no support for me anywhere. . . . When I threatened to quit, that's when they fired Matt. Or 'removed him from the creative process,' but he still has a 'created by' credit on the show. Two weeks after Matt left, the show went to No. 1" (90). In many ways, Barr is her own best critic. (However, she was also out of control, perhaps bottoming out.) The credits conclude with Roseanne, in mid-shot, laughing a last high-pitched laugh all the way to the bank, as her series beat out even *Cosby* in the ratings, and she gained authority.

In her case study of *Roseanne*, which involved "on-the-set" observation,

Judine Mayerle paints another, less public portrait of the tabloid feud and the show's conditions of production.[30] For Mayerle, *Roseanne* "reflects the growing influence of women in the production of primetime television programming, with women in such key positions as executive producer, producer, director, and writers for the series. Finally, although the multiple-camera video production of *Roseanne* is typical of contemporary situation comedy, the unusual production culture created by the often conflictive personalities of its production staff and ensemble cast has a significant effect on the overall tone of the series" (71). After documenting the Carsey-Werner Company, the independent company founded by Marcy Carsey and Tom Werner in 1981 (which later produced *Cosby* and *A Different World*), she discusses the role of Matt Williams in developing *Roseanne*—a concept which drew on his Midwest past, where he interviewed fifty women. Her story is that Williams had developed his concept independently of Carsey and Werner's discussion with Barr.

After giving due credit to Williams, Mayerle repeatedly points to conflict on the set—all of which revolves around Barr: "It is evident that the creative conflict . . . will . . . build throughout the week and affect not only the ensemble players, but the production staff and writers as well" (75). "The conflict between director [Ellen Falcon] and star" eventually compelled Falcon to leave the series (76). "The insults and disagreements found in virtually every episode of *Roseanne* have their origins as much in the production culture of the series as in the scripts." For Mayerle, the insults and disagreements "can turn harsh and abrasive." Often Barr does not know her lines, which slows down rehearsal and requires the other leads, John Goodman (as her husband, Dan Conner) and Laurie Metcalf (her sister), to "keep Barr on an even keel." This "horseplay" in rehearsal can "spill over into performance" (77), and at the same time, it is a "dissipation of creative energy" apparent in episodes of "uneven comedic pace" (79). At times, Barr is described as rude, temperamental, given to "emotional interruptions." Along with Williams and Falcon, Gayle Maffeo, the producer, also left the series at the end of the first season. (Crisis and chaos describe the logic of addiction.)

Mayerle attributes the immediate success of the show partially to the six-month strike (March to August 1988) by the writers' guild. Because *Roseanne*, ironically enough, was a nonunion show (an intriguing paradox given its blue-collar ethos), and Carsey-Werner a nonunion company, it gained an advantage over other series, which had been shut down (84). *Roseanne* went into production ahead of most other series for 1988-89 (87). The paradox of a working-class series gaining because it is produced by a nonunion company abounds in that the show is produced on the CBS/MTM lot in Studio City, "which historically is a union lot" (87). The show was not effected by the Teamsters' strike in October 1988, as were other shows which had difficulty with transportation.

The first episode begins with the nightmare called breakfast and three children leaving for school, moving to Wellman Plastics and the assembly line, where Roseanne works, then to a meeting with her daughter's history teacher, and finally home to dinner—a day in the life of a working-class mother with minimal formal education, three children, a husband who was her high-school sweetheart, and little money. Along the way is an ongoing feminist critique of divisions of labor, at work and at home—a comic situation which includes a real fight, bickering, interruption, and shouting.

If the containment of the liberation called comedy were lifted off, the series, like *Murder, She Wrote*, would resemble Barthes's assessment of familialism: "He has always regarded the (domestic) 'scene' as a pure experience of violence. . . . The scene always inspires *fear*, as though he were a child panic stricken by his parents' quarrels. . . . Scenes . . . lay bare the cancer of language. Language is impotent to close language. . . . The retorts engender one another, without any possible conclusion, save that of murder."[31] I will return to this underside of situation comedy later.

During the breakfast scene, the children fight with each other and make demands on Roseanne: "I got a knot in my shoe." "Wear loafers." The kitchen-sink debate ensues—Roseanne asks her husband not to plunge it, once again, but to fix it. He reluctantly agrees. Then one daughter requests a new book bag, the other that Roseanne visit her history teacher. When she asks Dan to take on one of these tasks, he barters with the sink repair. Roseanne reluctantly agrees to get off work early and visit school—after complaining that "I got a lot to do." Darlene: "What do you want me to do? Throw myself off a bridge?" "Yeah, and take your brother and sister, too." After they have left: "Quick, change the locks." The episode consists of the irritating stuff of daily life—the couple bickers about crumbs on the butter or jelly in the peanut-butter jar.

Lucy endured the boredom and demanding routine of housewifery by transforming it into physical comedy; Roseane endures by turning domesticity into wit. Even the children are not sacrosanct—one of the critical differences between sitcoms of the 1950s and 1990s. Like Gracie, Lucy schemed behind Ricky's back, while Roseanne's is a frontal assault. Both women complained weekly about women's daily lives, turning contradiction and perhaps rage into comedy.

Like Lucy, Roseanne repeats her real discontent: "I'll do everything else, like I always do. . . . I'll get off work, rearrange my schedule, but I don't mind." Her ironic tag line is a serious joke. Briefly the underside is revealed: Dan: "Are you ever sorry we got married?" "Are you? Then, I'm not neither." The pause, like her bad grammar ("Don't spill the milk, neither"), says or buries everything. This working-class woman saves coupons, uses double negatives and real sugar, serves food from cartons rather than dishes, and states what TV mothers and women usually repress—raising children is disrupted, fragmented work, with the majority of the tasks falling on women's shoulders. Women have two full-time jobs which often collide. In each, they are underpaid and unappreciated.

At Wellman Plastics (where she initially worked, along with her sister and other female friends), her young and rigid male boss, in answer to her request to leave early, replies with a sports team metaphor. Roseanne, who stands up to male authority by questioning logic, is intolerantly bored and answers with a quilting-bee example. He doesn't understand her feminist retort to his male metaphor. In a wonderful scene with the other women during a coffee break, she undercuts sports talk: "The only thing that's more exciting is when Dan talks about hydraulic jacks and snow tires." Holding a doughnut as her model, she asserts that "a good man don't just happen. . . . They have to be created by us women. A guy is a lump, like this doughnut. Gotta git rid of all this stuff his mom did to him. Then you gotta get rid of all the macho crap from the beer commercials. . . . And then, there's my personal favorite, the male ego." On this line, she pops the now-mutilated doughnut into her mouth and chews, grinning, like a Cheshire cat.

Not only gender inequities are under siege, but class differences as well. Labor is good but not brilliant, management inept to wimpy. When Roseanne and Dan go out, it is to the neighborhood bar for a pitcher of beer and pool. Jackie's new job is as a policewoman, and she dates working-class men. Middle-class values and postures are lampooned in scenes which paradoxically reveal Roseanne's palpable unease and discomfort. When they eat in middle-class restaurants, a source of yuppie cuisine/waiter jokes, their bodies and manners look out of place, as if they don't belong. These moments are deeply unsettling because they palpably literalize class difference. Parody can also be double-edged, the target turning on the shooter.

Roseanne's encounter with the young, thin history teacher—and pop psychology—is a collision between a middle-class yuppie and the working class. A funny long shot illustrates that Roseanne is too fat to fit into the student desk. The dialogue and reverse shot encounter: "Darlene has been demonstrating behavioral problems." "What does that mean?" "She has been barking in class." "Did you ask her to stop?" "Yes." "Did she?" "Yes." "Then, what's the problem?" Roseanne's logic, like her practicality and everyday wisdom, is impeccable. The teacher then asks whether Roseanne has a "special" relationship with her daughter. Roseanne says that it's "typical" (a key to the situations of the series which are ordinary rather than extraordinary). In response to the query about spending time with her daughter (Barr archly intones: "You mean, *quality* time?"), Roseanne says that she works and is raising three children and has no free time. The teacher then sees that as the problem. Roseanne: "The problem seems to be that there is no problem." Cut to a long shot of the encounter. Fade.

In several episodes, Roseanne has disconcerting exchanges with middle-class women—a cosmetics saleswoman, office secretaries, and an upper-class patron of the beauty salon—which are class clashes. Roseanne might look like the underdog, yet middle-class pretensions are the object of ridicule. At the same time, the poles of power are clear—social and economic power are not within Roseanne's grasp. Employment is a deadly serious issue. In the second season, Roseanne unpredictably loses her job after leading a walkout and refusing a lower, compromise salary plus higher piecemeal quotas. She has difficulty finding another position and fails a secretarial test because of her lack of computer skills. In this episode, her friends, like the viewers, are so positive she got the job that they throw her a celebration party. She didn't, and goes back to telephone solicitation. Capable and highly intelligent as she is, she is untrained, uneducated. In the 1990 season, Roseanne was working as a shampooer in Crystal's beauty parlor, an unlikely place for this woman so unconcerned about vanity.

Along with the scarcity of jobs and the difficulty of finding work—very real issues in 1990—money is not plentiful, another series concern. For Dan and Roseanne, the monthly payment of the bills demands juggling. As with Lucy, who was unqualified for virtually any job, including candy-maker, finding a job is a constant pursuit, leading to repeated failures. The difference, one of class and money, is that the Ricardos didn't depend on two salaries, and that Ricky climbed the success ladder while Dan, a sporadic contractor, keeps slipping off. However, both talented women's official lack of training and work, one source of discontent, keeps them economically dependent on marriage—the monetary bind of many women.

The fourth scene of the first episode returns to the kitchen. Interrupted by the ever-present, elongated whine familiar to every U.S. mother, MMMMOOOOOOMMMMMMM, wavering up and down the tonal scale, grating on the ears, always demanding time and action NOW!, Roseanne resumes the kitchen-sink repair fight with Dan. This escalation is serious, not interrupted by laughs or jokes: "I put in eight hours at the factory and then come home and put in eight more hours. You don't do nothin'. . . . " Dan: "What's the point?" Roseanne: "There's no point." Pause. "The point is that you think this is a magic kingdom—poof, the laundry is done—poof, the dinner is made—while you just sit on your throne." An arbitrary convention of situation comedy stops this argument—momentarily for this episode. Darlene cuts her finger; the couple come together to bandage it, with a fantasy of the demolition derby, another class-bound entertainment, to distract their daughter from her pain. After the domestic crisis is over, there is silence. Intercut shots of the couple, looking resigned, a quick touch of hands, and Roseanne moves to the stove. Fade. However, the premise of the series—women's work *for* husbands, children, and the factory—has been established.

A working-class woman, a writer/performer knowledgeable about the conditions of familial and factory labor, has been installed at the center as a sitcom, now movie, star. Roseanne talks back, to her bosses, her husband, and her children. At the same time, she is a good friend and wife, a mother who listens carefully, particularly to her children, and accepts Dan, foibles and all. Her wisdom and dead-on logic about the contradictions of women's daily lives are, as previously stated, no small gain for comedy. Roseanne's snappy wisecracks hark back to *The Honeymooners*, with Alice Cramden's nasally intoned putdowns of Ralph. Like motherhood, wifery is neither seamless nor blissful; however, for these sitcom women, there are no better options.

Like Lucy, Roseanne makes her plaint on a weekly basis, covered up by the tag-line epilogue: after the bandage crisis, this episode concludes with a brief scene in the garage—Dan's space. He is building a boat, his fantasy, on which they will "sail in the Caribbean after they retire." In spite of his sporadic work habits, he is basically a sweet and helpful fellow, a liberated man who respects his wife, whom he has loved since high school. Their relationship pushes sitcom in a sexual direction missing from *Lucy*: She: "You're turning me on. . . . Let's do it." He: "What about the kitchen sink?" She: "Anywhere you want." The end credits roll after the familial resolution.

Female friendship is valued by all the women on *Roseanne*, and respected by Dan. Particularly complex is the close, loving, and squabbling relationship between Roseane and Jackie, her sister, a postmodern reprise of Ethel and Lucy, replete with all the dilemmas of older/younger siblings. Their parents are far from ideal. Roseanne's women friends receive equal and quality time. Unlike Ricky, Dan has a central, domestic role and presence, sharing in childcare and discipline, and comprehending Roseanne's feelings. In fact, rather than Dan enacting the domineering husband role, in control of the purse strings, either treating his wife like a child or escaping to work, Roseanne is clearly in charge of the house and the relationship.

Rowe's "unruly woman" points to the ambivalence of reception, "snubbed by the Emmies, condescended to by media critics and trashed by the tabloids (never mind the establishment press)." She argues that our pleasure comes from "economy or wit by which the show brings together two discourses on family life: one based on traditional liberalism and the other on feminism and social class." Her argument is that "Roseanne uses a 'semiotics of the unruly' to expose the gap she sees between the ideals of the New Left and the Women's Movement of the late 60s and early 70s . . . and the realities of working class family life two decades later." What partially undermines this analysis is Roseanne's need for a man and marriage —in life and in the series.

Who's the Boss?

Roseanne was, until fall 1991, preceded on Tuesday nights on ABC by another well-established sitcom, already in reruns, *Who's the Boss*—another version of the family and class dependent on role reversal. In this postmodern extended couple, Tony Danza plays Tony, the sexy Italian working-class housekeeper for a successful and glamorous businesswoman, Angela Bauer, played by Judith Light. She works in New York, now at her own high-powered Manhattan ad agency, has influential male friends, drives a Jaguar, wears high fashion, and commutes to her cushy country house/ estate in the wealthy Connecticut suburbs. She has a young son, and Tony a teenage daughter, Samantha (Sam). Catherine Helmond, Angela's mother, is the sex-crazed, older, glamorous Mona, who lives in the carriage house. She is unrepressed, unlike her daughter, of whose inhibitions she continually makes fun. Here, the mother-daughter roles are inverted in a playful relationship.

Initially, the series hinged on whether or not Tony and Angela would have sex—they have not so far, but do indeed love each other and became engaged in 1991. Along with romance, the show is predicated on the dilemmas of parenting, with a version of the sensitive, liberated father who does domestic duty better than Angela, whose bad cooking is a constant joke. Significantly, Tony is attending college in order to get a better job, which might end the first premise of the series. During the 1990 season, the emphasis shifted back to their relationship, including the season's cliffhanger—Tony's affair with another student.

The class differences between these two series are quite extraordinary—including Angela's high style, the concern with upward mobility and suburban social pressure on, particularly, Samantha, the savoir faire of Mona and her casual attitude toward sex that is the preserve of the upper class, the Jaguar and the country house with the huge stone fireplace—to say nothing of Angela's being able to pay a full-time housekeeper! Everyone on the show, but particularly Sam, is careful not to hurt or insult Tony—the possessor of real values but little money—who is so sexy, funny, and toughly Italian that he can never be misconstrued as less than masculine. Various episodes, however, challenge his economic ability—Sam and the car, Sam and expensive boots and a modeling job, cautious of the fact that he does not have as much money as Angela. The equality between the two characters might be the result of this monetary inequality: his low economic and professional status and her executive achievements and economic power.

Angela Bauer has the professional job and economic freedom Lucy always wanted. She has the liberation from domestic chores and childcare that Roseanne would covet. She is the single, professional, middle-aged mother who is successful rather than exhausted, harassed, and harried. In many ways, this series, not taken seriously by anyone, might indeed be a middle-class female fantasy rather than contradiction. Angela has the best of both worlds without being trapped in either. At the same time, *Who's the Boss* represents the version of white middle-class feminism that *Roseanne* works against. Imagine an encounter between these two characters!—the sitcom version of Barr's meeting with Meryl Streep in *She-Devil*.

Murphy Brown

Murphy Brown could be Lucy's ego-ideal, although Murphy's political liberalism might have bothered Ball, who professed a rather conservative politics. Both Ball and Candice Bergen had film histories as beautiful women, although Ball's film characters were tougher, sassier, and brassier. Murphy, or "Murph," is a big network star, a news anchor who makes a huge salary and is constantly recognized, has economic independence, never cooks or cleans, and expresses her irritability (verging on anger) with the people around her. Her string of nutsy secretaries drives her nuts. She wears the latest Donna Karan fashion of tailored blazers, skirts, or slacks. Her "working-girl" wardrobe is smashing, and very expensive. Beneath her mean-spiritedness, which plays wicked pranks and delights in practical jokes, she has an irascible heart of gold. Murph is an independent woman, beholden to no one, including her parents, and dedicated to her work. In fact, she comes close to being one of the boys. However, she is too independent and self-sufficient to be a man. As she repeatedly states, her work is her life, the source of her pleasure; her home (which Eldon, the charming painter/philosopher, will never finish painting) is a place to go at night when work is over. When she was briefly suspended, she stayed in bed, didn't shave her legs, and wore ugly flannel pajamas, momentarily becoming depressed. She rarely dates and spends weekends and holidays alone. When she does find the rare date, he eventually will be attracted to another woman—until the pregnancy episodes in 1991.

In fact, with the exception of her relationship with the FYI news team— Frank Fontana, investigative reporter; Jim Dial, stuffy, old-fashioned, ethical anchorman; Corky Sherwood, the former beauty queen and woman's reporter; and Miles Silverberg, the young, hesitant producer who fears and worships Murph—she has little social life and few friends, although she is the life of various parties. This forty-year-old fan of 1960s "girl group" rock and roll is a graduate of the Betty Ford Center; this former big drinker who, when drunk one night, "faxed her chest to the coast," is a recovering alcoholic who no longer drinks or smokes. She is a feisty liberal who protested the male membership of a local club and uncovers corporate waste and governmental corruption. Although she has no female friends other than Corky, who drives her crazy and who wants to be like her, Murphy comes close to being a feminist. Thus, I wondered why men like this series and this character so much. In many ways, Murphy is one of the boys, which also makes her a tough journalist. At the same time, she is smashingly beautiful. With her gorgeous physique, face, and designer style, Bergen is the opposite of Barr. More significant, Murphy's critique is (unlike Barr's, which is directed against men) of idiots everywhere, whether male or female. Murphy has made it in a man's world which she has made her own.

Critically, however, Murphy is not nice at all costs; she is direct, rude, and intensely competitive.

While surrounded by her TV family (with her mother, played by Colleen Dewhurst, and her remarried father also appearing), Murphy is a loner, with few dates and few friends—one way to survive the 1990s. Equally, her fame grants her power which few women have: famous politicians regularly contact her; thus, she gets away with social murder. Although in one episode she fancied having a baby with Frank as the surrogate father, Murphy was, until 1991, outside the nuclear family and delusions of romance. During a Christmas episode, she was saddled with three abandoned children, telling them bedtime stories about Haldeman and Ehrlichman. When they misbehaved at a restaurant, she shouted, "Stop throwing food, you rotten little Huns." As I wrote in 1990: "Whether she can stay there, happily unmarried and intensely productive without children, in the 1990s is open for speculation. Given alternative forms of 'parenting' and the conservativism of this era, anything (heaven forbid!) could happen."

And, already has. In May 1991, Murphy's activist ex-husband returned, as did her ex-lover, Jack Gold, the brash reporter. She dated both. One offered marriage, the other a relationship. One is a liberal, the other a neoconservative. Murphy was caught between a rock and a hard place. Worst of all, she might be/is pregnant: the series concluded with a pregnancy test, results to be/were announced in the fall 1991 season. She will become an unmarried mother—to the consternation of her co-workers. She must have slept with them during the commercials—except for her distracted and exhausted state, there was little sign of desire and sex.

That this series is the creation of a woman, Diane English (writer *and* executive producer), is not sheer coincidence. "I'm going to become my own studio. I want the profits and the control."[32] Linda Bloodworth-Thomason of *Designing Women* is treading a comparable creative/control path, as are other women entering television's "conditions of production." Both of these series provide their characters with an activist past in the 1960s-1970s, the inscription of the women's and protest movements. *Designing Women* literally incorporates women's issues, such as wife beating, into the story, revising the sitcom format. Jane Wagner inscribes women's history in her scripts for Lily Tomlin. Madelyn Pugh, one of the constant writers of *Lucy*, has an important place in the history of women in comedy. It is a history of contradiction that belongs to all middle-aged, smart women.

PART VI

COUNTERCULTURES

Women's Economies

A middle-aged sociologist straightfacedly announced the results of a government study on the CBS morning news show (December 1988): the married are healthier than the unmarried. Marriage prevents flu (although not colds), certain forms of cancer, and heart disease. Divorced (and never-married) women are prone to significantly more household accidents because they attempt tasks for which men are qualified, risking the danger of electro-shock from light-bulb changing. (In the many routines of *"I Love Lucy"* in which Lucy and Ethel used and demolished household technologies such as toasters, ovens, and TV sets for comedy, domesticity was indeed a risky, and parodied, business.)

The marshaling of statistics by the U.S. government arguing the bodily and mental health of the marital state is only one way familialism and the couple are in demand and fashion in the U.S. in the 1990s. The New Paradigm Society consists of conservatives and liberals, mainly men, discussing solutions to the nation's problems over dinner in Washington. One participant, E. J. Dionne, Jr., in *Why Americans Hate Politics*, extols the old virtues of self-reliance, family, and work as a compromise between the two parties. Around these values, he advocates a new "politics of the center."[1] It would appear that the *imaginary* of the family—and individualism—has emerged almost unscathed from the 1960s collective assault.

What is left of the counterculture protest is memory, an obsession with youth, with staying fit and looking young. The bodily and mental health movements—exercise, food, and therapy—are lifestyles which promise to improve the familial everyday by rigorously orchestrating leisure time, making it productive. The historical trajectory transforming the family from a producing into a consuming unit has been realized, in spite of countercultural efforts to reverse this trend.

Susan Strasser analyzes the producer-consumer pendulum as a combinatory of public and private, and gives it a turn-of-the-century date: "Household routines involved making fewer things and purchasing more; consumption became a major part of the work of the household. Formerly *customers*, purchasing the objects of daily life from familiar craftspeople and storekeepers, Americans became consumers . . . who [understood] less about how things were made, how they worked, how they could be fixed," the latter ignorances a key to the need for services.[2]

(As a brief aside: This analysis is complicated by a change in the system of production. For example, my old Sunbeam toaster could be repaired because it consisted of separate, mechanically assembled parts. My new Sunbeam, which looks *exactly* like the old, cannot because in the unit/component system, the parts are welded together; therefore, separate parts are no longer manufactured for repair. My GE repairman informed me that rather than repair my washing machine's motor, it would be cheaper to buy a new machine. Replaceable, standardized component parts, measured and gauged by a Bureau of Standards at the turn of the century, are no longer either cheap or available. However, as might be expected in the revival of pre-Fordism, the old system of assemblage has returned in 1991, expensive and ecological. Very soon, a designer line of appliances with replaceable and biodegradable parts will be available. Taking a step back in history is not cheap.)

XVI

◆

Women's Spaces/Women's Work

Strasser's history of mass marketing and Susan Porter Benson's history of the department store document the shift from producer to consumer, dating it much earlier (1910-1920) than the post–World War II period argued by neoclassicism and Alliez and Feher (detailed in Part I).[3] This divergence is due to the focus on what is missing in liberal-Marxist *and* in neoclassical economics: women. Benson tells the story from women's point of view. Benson asserts that in order to understand the workplace dynamics of service industries in general, a central place must be granted to "the ambiguities and subtle dynamics of class and gender" (288), to which I will add race. Fordism and neo-Fordism "sought the relatively cheap and supposedly docile labor of women—who were and are often black and Hispanic. Simultaneously, women at the other end of the economic spectrum flocked to colleges and universities" (177–78).

In order to reduce labor costs, women, then and now, were paid less than men. Women's low wages were not accidental but calculated (182). Like McDonald's, department stores focused on two groups, "students and married women," who would work cheap (185). "Managers assumed that both were docile employees: their primary identities lay elsewhere" (186). The use of "supposedly docile" and "assumed" gives credit to women, thereby complicating the usual accounts of exploitation. The notion of "primary identity" or divided loyalty is a tug of war pulling women in two directions—toward family, away from work. For many women, this has transformed the pleasures of work into guilt.

Benson's history depicts a women's space more complex than that of private/public spheres; her analysis is an exemplum of contradiction, focusing on the saleswoman—her own best customer. Stores "appealed" to "frugality" and "desire for status and luxury," a "both/and" logic which women have negotiated for centuries (21). Saleswomen were "both sellers and buyers, workers and consumers" (239), in the workplace seeing themselves as "working class, cajoled by the rewards of mass consumption to see themselves as middle-class" (271). "The combination of a need to be well dressed and a limited income" could exhaust their resources (194). The simplicity of a domination/subordination model (an either/or logic) is unraveled by inscribing women's experience: "The lessons of department-store selling, then, surpassed simple precepts about women's subordination to men and included validation for female values and competence, bolstering women's confidence and self-esteem" (289). In other words, there were gains along with losses.

Managers' "definition of selling skills rewarded women for being women, gave exchange value to their culture" (with the saleswomen serving as hostesses in stores increasingly designed like homes) (130–31). At the same time, pay was low, selling was scorned, and the job was dead-end: "Scorn for selling went hand in hand with a low opinion of those who sold" (156). Another double whammy was that salespeople were to be both "deferential and authoritative"—the central contradiction of women's lives in general. This is a no-win, and deeply familiar, logic (often buried in women's unconscious rather than conscious experience—which explains women's complicity). This history keeps repeating itself, differentiated. No matter what their training, salespeople failed to ever satisfy managers. Saleswomen emulated the middle class, yet failed to gain the social or economic powers of that class. While "in the formal hierarchy of the store saleswomen were near the bottom in pay and authority, they in fact wielded enormous influence over the daily operations of the store" (289). They were everything *and* nothing.

Particularly significant is the fact that department stores (1) did not adopt Taylorist principles or self-service but rather a method of intricate sales (which is returning in a test store of Wal-Mart, the profitable chain of discount stores) (4); (2) provided a service and did not produce products; (3) involved a triangulation between saleswomen, managers, and customers; (4) blurred "the line between consumption and recreation, life on and off the job" (7); and (5) functioned so that "social interaction replaced production as the essence of the work process" (10). In other words, what neoclassical economists have recently discovered as post-Fordism is *much* older, linked to women's culture, which ironically and unwittingly becomes the model for contemporary culture.

The department store was different from the general store and the specialized shop. Diversification rather than specialization was the key—with "diversified stores" relying on impulse buying (15). Unlike the film studios, which adopted both specialization and differentiation, vertically integrated monopolies did not arise, and the branch or franchise store was also rare—until the buying spree of the 1980s, when international moguls bought up prestige retail stores such as I. Magnin and Saks Fifth Avenue, only to see their profits plunge, losing out to K-Mart and Wal-Mart in the late 1980s, whose profits rose during the recession. Prior to World War II, the stores did not rely on national brands, retaining localism.

Like the major film studios during the era of picture-palace splendor, stores sold an array of pleasures and services in addition to products: luxurious restrooms, air conditioning, babysitting, workout facilities, hairstyling salons, and restaurants. The store, like the motion-picture palace, and later the shopping mall, was a space of congregation. It was a place that instilled middle-class values—tasteful decorating, entertaining, and fashion, "dynamic museums . . . attuned to style and propriety" (22). The store did not sell what the manufacturer produced but was an agent for the consumer, creating an "atmosphere for selling that would encourage consumption" (36). One means of incentive was offering credit as a service (75). After World War II, the charge account, like credit cards later, initially granted only to the wealthy, became available to many customers.

Benson seriously challenges accepted economic accounts, along with the veracity (or explanatory power) of any history, particularly of business, which precludes women. It is ironic that one of the last bastions to be cracked by women is the upper echelon of the corporate world, along with professorships in the business schools of universities. If IBM had looked to women, it would have realized the differences between retail and discount shopping much earlier—even Compaq's discounting came decades after women had discovered the new pleasures of Loehmann's, a designer discount store which specializes only in women's clothing; this is no-return self-service without frills, decor, changing rooms, or credit.

(When it comes to business, the double-standard is not a laughing matter. Workshops on comedy and humor, along with videotapes by producers such as John Cleese on corporate humor, are popular—more so as pressure builds. "For women, though, getting onto the new corporate laugh track can be a little sticky." For women, being "lighthearted" has been seen as being "lightweight." One professor tested techniques in Rochester and discovered that men were more likely than women to use kidding as "an influence tactic. . . . Women are beginning to recognize" that humor is essential.[4] Where has this guy been for the past fifty years? The history of funny women on television suggests that the joke is on him.)

Rather than merely a place of exploitation of cheap labor by women with a weakness for consumer items, Benson presents an empirical analysis that represents the department store as a public space for women which expressed "the saleswoman's three identities—worker, woman, and customer." In this new space, "gender characteristics and conduct were a matter of daily struggle" (9).

Benson's account is not a celebration of the quandaries and pleasures of shopping in luxurious surrounds; neither is it a tale of female gullibility manipulated by management. Rather, the analysis, written from women's viewpoint, details the contradictions of working women. For women, the shift from producer to consumer involved a serious "tradeoff": homemade, formerly women's work and skills, became devalued, a reproach (76). I remember pitying my grandparents, who had to eat only homemade bread, jams, ice cream and butter, or peaches, raspberries, and apples that had been hand-picked and canned at home. Homemade was a sign of lower economic status. Homemade returned in the late 1960s and 1970s as a countercultural, do-it-yourself, ecological move. In the 1980s, homemade became an expensive commodity and a sign of good taste.

Along with the reproach against homemade, "women as consumers in department stores had a power out of all proportion to their power in the society as a whole" (94). Consuming and good housekeeping linked up. Consumption, which was linked to anxiety, was both a problem and a cure (79). Shopping was suggested as a "cure for neurasthenia"; shopping became part of "the new therapeutic ethic" (17). Fashion, which unsettled the predictability of purchase, "injected a new note of uncertainty." However, in spite of the fact that the stores trained consumers and were key players in the shift from production to consumption, managers never could understand "the difficulties of integrating women's culture with business culture" (167). This, of course, accounts for the presumed lack of humor attributed to businesswomen—who might not find their situation particularly funny.

Susan Strasser's history of housework, *Never Done*, is the flip side or companion volume to her rendering of the corporate sphere of marketing, *Satisfaction Guaranteed*.[5] Like Benson, she takes her history back further than men's, to the turn of the century rather than the late 1940s. The issues women faced in the early 1900s, and earlier, return, like clockwork, every twenty years. The dispute or conundrum over "women's profession," to work inside or outside the home or both, has endured, in various guises, for over one hundred years. (No wonder reruns of *"I Love Lucy"*—which stage this dilemma—have been on the air, often four times per day, for forty years.) *Never Done* charts this history and its return—the ongoing debates over domestic space and women's work: "In a society where most people distinguish between 'life' and 'work,' women who supervise their own work at home do not seem to be 'working' " (4). As a result, women's work and lives are both devalued. Because economics in the U.S. depend on the household, this disdain is paradoxical, and the domain contradictory—everything and nothing, a logic also applied to women.

Another paradox is that, with the exception of microwave ovens (introduced to the mass market in the early 1970s), our domestic appliances (and arrangements) are also a hundred years old. There has been little innovation—of either thought or materials—regarding domestic labor, just a recycling of the same arguments and products. At the same time, women's household history has been consistent: from production to consumption, from collective activities to solitary actions, from social life to private life and isolation (which necessitates group therapy).

Just as Benson's picture of the space of the department store does not fit into the "ideology of separate spheres," so Strasser disputes this received notion. The "idea could not endure because the spheres were not separate. . . . The qualities that defined the ideal wife—dependence, gentleness, emotionality—destroyed the ideal mother, who performed heavy housework duties and prepared children for the demands of the outside world" (183). This is a both/and logic of creation/cancellation. While the separate spheres' "reality"—the focus on consumption and motherhood—faded "more than a century ago," the presumption comes back to haunt us as the Feminine Mystique or the New Traditionalist. For Strasser, illustrated by department stores, the presumed separate spheres are inextricably merged—creating what Raymond Williams has called the paradox of mobile privatization. Consumption was "established as the new task of the private sphere, now completely dominated by the public" (243). The "domestic market" is the main target of manufacturers, with infinite products and services created for the household economy. Fear was a big appeal early on—"sneaker smell, paralyzed pores, vacation knees, underarm offense, and ashtray breath" are just a few (253).

Strasser traces the history of domestic reformers. Melusina Fay Peirce perceived "the profound contradiction between the increasingly social aspect of men's work in production and the privatism of women's work in the home" (199). She advocated removing work from the home into collective spaces. Christine Frederick, and the discipline of home economics which trained women how to be good consumers, applied the principles of Taylorism, particularly standardization, to the home between 1910 and the 1920s. However, Taylor's key ingredient, the profit motive, was disdained. Wives and mothers worked for love, not for money. Ironically, around the same time (1910), advertising began to equate money with love and sex appeal. The enemy for Frederick was the career woman who loathed housework, which Frederick saw as a noble profession—an either/or logic.

Charlotte Gilman Perkins challenged the value or progress of the individual woman in the private home, advocating that housework become industrialized, specialized, with divisions of labor and profit incentives. Perkins took capitalism as a given. "Women must utilize the best features of capitalism—like organization and the division of labor—for their own advancement" and for social change (220). Domestic labor was not a type of work but a stage in evolution: "All industries were once 'domestic' . . . performed at home and in the interests of the family." The problem was the nature of the work done privately—"the solution was to remove it from the home" (221). Gilman believed that sexual equality could come only when "men stopped supporting women, the over-developed sexual prisoners of a parasitic economic relationship." For this to occur, women must "follow men out of the house" and into the realm of social production. "Perkins was a first-rate prophet."

She "envisioned kitchenless houses," with families eating at places that cooked food according to the "principles of division of labor and economies of scale." Ironically, McDonald's, Taco Bell, Pizza Hut, and KFC have realized this feminist goal, with a profiteering twist. The historical swing of ideas from the radical left to the market—capitalism's ability to incorporate—makes the analysis of culture tricky business.

XVII

◆

Family Therapy

Like the paradoxical status of historical women in the workplace, whether TV studio, factory, office, or household, the desirable family has been and continues to be, at least for me, a conundrum: we must go outside its warm embrace for advice and solace from professionals in order to create a happy family. In an extraordinary contradiction, the family is constituted, at the same time, as desirable and "dysfunctional" (the new therapy term, along with "co-dependency"). Therapy reveals the dysfunction which necessitates therapy to reconstitute the family differently; antagonism turns to togetherness, quality time, or the ultimate goal, "separation" from the family. Thus, "the family" is problem and goal; the cure is therapy.

Not surprisingly, Erica Jong and Linda Yellen are writing a daytime soap, *The Women's Group*, for Aaron Spelling (of *Dynasty* and *Beverly Hills 90201* fame). This soap, about "real women coping with problems in today's world," will "follow the lives of seven women who are members of a self-help group," ranging in age from the teens to the fifties.[6] Jong says that she wanted a "durable" premise "that could go for years," just like the circuit of recovery and therapy, which is endless. For example, alcoholism is a "family disease"; after the addict, family members enter the circuit of therapy, including "family programs" at treatment centers. Adult Children of Alcoholics (ACOA) and Alanon are familial capillaries of AA (a very good thing which is anonymous). Not surprisingly, therapy has become a profitable, entrepreneurial service industry, frequently capitalizing on the principles of Alcoholics Anonymous, which is free. Predictably, this therapy (a very good thing) is tied to the middle-class insured, avoiding the uninsured.

The cultural production of obsession necessitates goods and services to lessen fear and anxiety. Time is a resource "productively" spent in therapy, uncovering issues which necessitate more services, like exercise or group counseling, and products, like self-help books. Information, and time spent, will cure addiction and anxiety.

Roby Rajan calls these "perverse" markets that "sell the non-consumption" of commodities, "markets in which consumers pay *not* to consume liquor, cigarettes, gambling, food, sex, drugs, consumer credit, etcetera. Annual outlays in anti-consumption markets in the U.S. have been estimated to be over 5 percent of personal consumption expenditures."[7] "The boom in the mental health industry" suggests that "by constructing the market for psychopathology as a market like any other . . . economics . . . effaces . . . any active role it might play in the production of the pathologies." Rajan asserts that "carcinogens in the environment, and pathologies in the self are created by the econologic." Toxicity and pathology, rather than being waste products (waste disposal is another booming industry), are fuel for reproduction, treatable by technology and therapy. Except for the family, all institutions are acquitted of any role in production.

Rajan calls these the "negative values" of the Gross National Product, the measure of a nation's output, which includes criminal services such as lawyers, penitentiaries, and police. The GNP also includes services which have shifted from the household to the market, such as daycare, food preparation, care of the aging, sick, and indigent, and cosmetic and physical care of the body. Because Rajan doesn't notice sexual difference, he infers that all these changes are negative, or perverse. Within his model, women still do not count.

(Fred Block's model is less polemical. For him, in "postindustrial development," the distinction between production and consumption no longer holds.[8] Instead, in education, medicine, drug counseling, travel, and physical fitness, there is the practice of "productive consumption." "If it is possible for people to combine consumption and investment in the same activity, then, even without capital savings, it is possible to consume more today *and* have more tomorrow" [177]. As with no-cal food, we can have our cake and eat it.)

As Dolores Hayden argues, "Both neo-classical economists and Marxist economists have over-emphasized wage work and rejected household work in their definitions of economic productivity, economic growth, and national product. These faulty definitions can be traced to the nineteenth-century doctrine of separate spheres for men and women."[9] For neoclassicists, for example, "housing construction" is a "key sector of production, crucial to stimulating the entire economy . . . maximizing consumption of cars, appliances, and furnishings." "Within socialist economics . . . housing construction is seen as resource consumption." "What both calculations . . . miss is the essential nature of home as a domestic workplace" (146). Hayden cites a 1979 United Nations report that showed that women "perform two-thirds of the world's work hours, counting both paid and unpaid labor. They receive one-tenth of the world's wages. And they own one one-hundredth of the world's property." In the U.S., women work twentyone more hours per week than men (147). These startling figures, along with women's higher grades and more advanced degrees, unsettle both neoclassical and Marxist accounts.

Like Benson and Strasser, Hayden also dates her account earlier—to the measurement of economic productivity in 1920: "Both production and reproduction were restructured around the concept of the single-family detached home." Women's place was "explicitly in the home." "Economists decided to exclude all household work for which no wage was paid." As William Gauger said, "Let's face it. If household work had traditionally been a man's job, it would always have been included in the GNP" (149). Thus, economists consciously decided to exclude women's work from the GNP, literally putting "female labor-force data and female political participation aside," banking on "mother-love" as priceless and on "family" wages for men. "They couldn't have made a more serious error. . . . Throughout the last half century the greatest visible economic gains have occurred in the expansion of consumer goods and services, exactly those which replace women's unpaid labor in the home and are the most impossible to calculate under the present system. Thus no one has known the real state of the American economy for decades." It is critical to remember that housewives "are ineligible for Social Security and for health and disability benefits given paid workers" (151).

This system of ignoring women's work extends to transportation—more female workers than male use public transportation, while transportation planning has supported the automobile industry. One out of seven American workers earns a living related to highways or cars—most are male. "It could be argued that car culture in the United States represents economic development for male workers as well as convenience for male consumers. . . . 3/4 of the miles driven in the U.S.A. are driven by men, and while men make the majority of their auto trips as drivers, women make the majority as passengers." Suburban women drivers provide the transit service which planners have not offered (153).

"The family" is a full-time, nonpaying job which necessitates outside expertise to maintain and improve it—the richer the family, the more services it requires. As I argued in the first chapter, the shift of the U.S. economy from producing products to providing services is interlocked with the imaginary of the family—a market for advanced consumer durables. Heidi Hartman, an economist, defines the current economic situation in the U.S. as a "capitalist mode of production harnessed to a pre-capitalist, patriarchal structure of reproduction" (147). The "labor of love" of domestic work becomes a "low-paying job outside the home"; "jobs requiring many of the traditional 'womanly' skills of homemaking have been rated as unskilled work" (148).

The family, splintering or changing in reality, is the target for our mental health *and* national economic growth, with the economy, like marriage, increasingly described by bodily metaphors of health or illness. Reminiscent of the 1950s and the postwar move to suburbia, which also saw a boom in self-help philosophies including Dr. Spock and pop Freud, there are two kinds of public or media *Baby Booms*: college-educated, professional white women, under the mandate of a ticking biological clock, are being urged to have babies and leave the work force before "it's too late"; and uneducated, unmarried black teenagers are bearing children too early and dropping out of high school in unprecedented numbers. Rather than "family," the construct must be pluralized. In any version, with the shift from production to consumption (as a full-time job), *families* have become costly enterprises, demanding two or more incomes.

Upscale parents are frenetically fast-tracking their children. "Parenting nowadays has become as frenzied a job as many management positions." Kid activities have "exploded" in numbers, and "fasttrack parents don't seem to be able to just say 'no.' " Parents are "fully involved" in "helping their children achieve their full potential." The cost is, predictably, high anxiety: "Everybody's in such a hurry, and adults end up transferring the anxiety they feel to their children." Shuttling from one activity to the next, parents have no free time (many mothers never did.) "New fathers . . . face more stress than ever," just like women. "Society expects that fathers be more involved. . . . There's a lot of anxiety associated with fatherhood now." At last—equality.

However, there is still a big difference. "Working women with children are more than twice as likely as men to feel constant stress," with 40 percent of women feeling "trapped by their daily routine." "The stress of balancing personal and professional lives" is so great that (herein is the quintessential rub) women consider cutting back on their hours or quit their jobs.[10]

After therapy, childcare, health, fashion, and fitness, statisticians are trying to predict the next trend for the boomers—"the largest generation in American history, born between the end of World War II and 1964, with 76 million members who have wreaked havoc with American culture, confounding demographers with their size, affluence, education, politics and feminism." I love "feminism" confounding demographers—the old denial ploy. The many factors that make demographers anxious (in addition to feminists) read like a summary of this book: "They are the first TV and atomic generation; they lost a president to assassination; they took drugs; they forced a president to resign in disgrace; women got jobs; they had children very late."

However, for marketers the significant problem is that "they have the power to make their new behavior the norm almost overnight." Trends anticipated for the future cluster around aging and money. Boomers "will fight aging like no generation before." Plastic surgery will triple. "The look: a relatively small nose, no wrinkles. . . . Menopause is on the horizon." There are already menopausal products and new research. The biggest debate about the boomers is "whether they will buy with abandon . . . or settle down to saving."[11] Or both.

However, the immaturity of the boomers has become a national dilemma, according to *Time*'s cover story for August 12, 1991, a problem attributed to metaphorical addiction. The U.S. has become a nation of "Busybodies & Crybabies"—either the need to "regiment others" or to blame "everyone except himself" (14–15). "Each trait has about it the immobility of addiction." "Victims become addicted to being victims" (a double-whammy logic applied to women, rarely understood by white men, particularly U.S. senators). "The spectacle of the two moral defectives" is "evidence that America is not entirely a society of grownups" (15). Lance Morrow, the author, often refers to addiction in his feature stories, using it literally and figuratively. However, he gets it wrong, including denying the evidence that Ted Kennedy's behavior is typical for a drunk, no different from millions of others with the same disease of alcoholism—deadly, self-destructive.

Outside the costly individualism and familialism is noise—the homeless, welfare recipients, in effect, the poor, a class which is increasingly female, increasingly black. When headed by poor teenagers or middle-aged divorced women, families become downwardly, rather than upwardly, mobile. Indeed, downward mobility might be the 1990s inverse echo of the 1950s.

"And now for the fun years" is *Time*'s cover portrait of the new aging—pun intended (February 22, 1988). "America is finding a new way to grow old," a time of curiosity, energy, and athletic pursuits. "But with these come other, less cheering images . . . the elderly poor, most of them widows, many of them black." "Nearly a third of elderly blacks live on less than $5,300 a year. Among black women living alone, the figure is 55%" (69).

Revising the Counterculture

Throughout the 1980s and into the 1990s, television revised the liberal, counterculture critique of the family (and the state), containing the radicalism of the 1960s and early 1970s via parody and nostalgia for a lost, noble youth. Television writer-producers (mainly men) in essence wrote a revisionist history of late-boomers, forgetting the radicalism of 1960s politics and jumping back not to adolescence but to childhood. This nostalgia for the good old days of the 1940s and 1950s emerged with the War in Iraq and became full-blown in the 1991 season, for example, *Brooklyn Bridge*, *Homefront*, and *I'll Fly Away*.

Protest—including civil rights, women's rights, the Vietnam War, and ecology—became funny. On *Family Ties*, Steven and Elise Keaton were lovey-dovey parents, formerly Berkeley war protesters, seen in flashback wearing hippie, flower-children clothes, looking very silly. What was an unimaginable nightmare then, a Reagan presidency, was the program's central joke (and reassurance) via the star of the show, Alex, the adorable, funny, conservative son (and famous movie star Michael J. Fox) whose idol, then a joke, was Richard Nixon (a portent of his 1990 absolution). A cliché of reversal (What if our children rebelled against us and became ad execs and Republicans?) twenty years ago became a top-ten weekly situation comedy—a series with inventive "situations," elegantly clever scripts of one-liners, and perfectly gauged comic timing. The political effects of this series, to me, were astonishing yet not noted.

On a peculiar episode of *Murder, She Wrote*, Jessica locates the missing son of a dying wealthy man, or at least so she thinks. He had attended the 1968 Democratic National Convention, was hit on the head, and has had amnesia ever since. It turns out that he is the real thing, is reunited with his family, and inherits a bundle. The protester has been richly rewarded for returning to the family's bosom, happily married. As I stated earlier, Murphy Brown has a protest past. All of this might suggest the age and generation of TV's current crop of writers. A protest history lends credibility to the characters; it is deep nostalgia for an era when pleasure was political and boys were men.

The ennui-laden *thirtysomething* documented the hippie-turned-handsome-yuppie family (Michael and Hope), surrounded by remnants of a discarded, outmoded past, living (and redecorating) the suburban, big old home life filled with work on personal relationships and the everyday, proclaiming the quintessential virtue of the nuclear, central couple relentlessly focusing on their pivotal fetish, the baby girl. Hope, the mother, preferred staying home and looking at her child, and Michael, the husband, was sensitive and involved with the star of the series, domesticity. (That is, until the 1989/90 season—Hope was pregnant again, and Michael was finally a successful ad exec. Domesticity, like the house and the suburbs, lost to work, the ad agency, and Michael's now-plush offices in a loft/warehouse in the city.) Sex was excellent (it became less so as Michael worked more). Their past dropped by, embodied as the single, artistic longhair and the single, neurotic female; for them, sex was not great.

Unlike the upwardly mobile central and married couple, these dissatisfied friends/dinosaurs failed to make the successful transition into the familial, corporate materialism of the 1980s and 1990s. Like the loyal, secondary, but inferior characters they were, they visited and relived their shared protest past as the good old days; no matter how many forays these misfits made, they could not break into the secure stronghold of the united couple now sealed off as "nuclear" family via many meaningful glances and long, bated pauses. Sometimes, as with Gary, they died. The with-it, revisionist message is clear: the past was childish, unproductive, unhappy. Grow up. Adapt. Get married and pregnant. Buy an old house. Get a real job. Cut your hair.

What was startling was not the intricate conscription and defusing of the student protest movement via memory, but the current recuperation of this blatant content. *Family Ties* was hailed because of the "liberal" producer Goldberg, who demanded a daycare facility on the set (a good, feminist thing) and stumped the Maine primary elections for childcare programs, including "maternity" leave for fathers. *Thirtysomething* was praised by critics for its timely relevance, its innovative, "radical," "hip-slick-'n'-cool" style. *Thirtysomething*'s 1989/1990 shift, from a local ad agency owned by two old pals to a profitable, manipulative, cynical ad agency and the realm of corporate negotiations and hostile takeovers by multinational firms, with Michael rising to star ad-man status, huge salary, and unfathomable power, was predictable. What was surprising was the accompanying boredom of domesticity. The office was intrigue, power, drama, and high anxiety. The home, formerly a locus of desire, became just a place to go after the thrill of work. That is, until Hope discovered homelessness and began to volunteer at a shelter in May 1991. Michael: "I'm not one of the bad guys." The always self-righteous Hope: "Are you sure?" In the end, the home represented middle-class, liberal guilt. In many ways, this series was a history of attitude, or lifestyles.

Another trend beginning in the 1990s was the takeover of situation comedy by male 1960s memory, the era of the male adolescent on *Doogie Howser*, *The Wonder Years*, and perhaps *Growing Pains*, along with the continuing spate of sitcoms about single men raising children, particularly young girls. Dads raising daughters made serious inroads into a genre that has been dominated by mothers: a college football coach/father on *Coach* and a conservative Marine/father on *Major Dad* (September 1989). While the women in the lives of these two middle-aged, balding, athletic, and macho but funny types are professionals, presumably strong, independent journalists and writers representing the women's movement (including liberal politics on *Major Dad*), they are peripheral. The point of view is from the central male jock character—it is a conservative view. Both women circle around the central male's life; neither receives comparable time or story.

Since the War in the Gulf, *Major Dad* has shoved the young, independent, and feisty mother of three daughters, Polly Cooper, to the margins. More time is spent in the military workplace away from the home—initially a central locus of the series. When the show moved to a new base, funny work cohorts were added, including a lusting female caricature right out of a Bob Cummings 1950s sitcom. More surprising, as James Castonguay has shown, the series shifted into high military gear, with episodes directly coinciding with events in the Gulf War; Major Dad, or Mac, aka John MacGillis, applied for active duty in Saudi Arabia, after fighting in a Latin American "incursion" in an earlier episode; Dan Quayle appeared on the show, and references to General Schwarzkopf abounded. Gerald McRaney wore his Marine fatigues on tribute shows for returning soldiers in 1991.

As the military references increased, Polly became less concerned with her career as a journalist—that is, when the plot addressed her at all. Mac, now her boss and censor (she works for the paper on the base), is increasingly taking over parenting duties for her three girls. A sitcom with a Marine as the attractive-to-sexy lead playing an understanding father, a series endorsing military actions which, unlike *Sergeant Bilko*, for example, are taken seriously and emotively, suggests that the swerve from the left to the right, from anti-war to pro-military, is complete. The 1990s have returned to the 1950s. Am I living my life over? Sometimes I wonder.

XVIII

◆

The Search for Signs of Intelligent Life

Television, the counterculture, the women's movement, and families are represented in another way in *The Search for Signs of Intelligent Life in the Universe*, the 1986 Broadway show written by Jane Wagner and starring Lily Tomlin.[12] The star/narrator is a bag lady, Trudy. As a result of shock treatment which "gave me new electrical circuitry," this acute observer of popular culture has a "built-in Betamax in my head. Records anything. It's like somebody's using my brain to dial-switch through humanity. I pick up signals that seem to transmit snatches of people's lives."

Trudy tours her "space chums" (whom she received or picked up on her umbrella hat, a satellite dish/antenna) through a history of U.S. women's culture, particularly the women's movement. "My space chums say they're learning so much about us since they've begun to time-share my trances. They said to me, 'Trudy, the human mind is s-o-o strange.' I told 'em, 'That's nothin compared to the human genitals.' " Trudy switches channels; she is the remote-control viewer of the *mystery*, not meaning, of women's lives. Wagner's parody, performed by Tomlin, of the pop-psychology and self-help movements, like the critique of popular culture, is exquisite theory and powerful politics.

For Trudy, there is no separation between art and popular culture as she ponders recurring dilemmas of philosophy—the nature of art, reality, and the meaning of space and time. "This is soup and this is art. Art. Soup. Soup. Art." Or, "I got the kind of madness Socrates talked about. A divine release of the soul from the yoke of custom and convention." Unlike Baudrillard and TV news anchors, Trudy refuses to be intimidated by reality: "After all, what is reality anyway? Nothing but a collective hunch. . . . I made some studies, and reality is the leading cause of stress amongst those in touch with it. I can take it in small doses, but as a lifestyle, I found it too confining."

Trudy tunes in Tomlin's other female characters, who emblematize aspects of feminism and the women's movement. Women's lives, constructed by conversations and diary excerpts, are read historically through popular culture—including the protest, women's, ecology, and self-help movements of the 1970s. The show is, for me, the writing and performance of women's history—collective history which is familiar. The format is a string of sketches with recurrent characters to which Trudy returns. Trudy—"Did you know what most distinguishes us humans from lower animals is our desire to take drugs?"—dial-switches between characters: the uptight, perfectionist homemaker Judith Beasley ("To me, the term 'sexual freedom' meant freedom from having to have sex"); the anxious, pensive Lily ("I worry that Andy Warhol may be right—and everyone will be famous for fifteen minutes. How will there ever be room for us all at Betty Ford's? I worry if peanut oil comes from peanuts and olive oil comes from olives, where *does* baby oil come from?"); the earnest airhead Chrissy, attending the Phobia Institute and aerobics classes ("All my life I've wanted to *be* somebody. But I see now I should have been more specific." "I am creative but I lack the talent to go with it"); the sensitive Paul, concerned about male bonding and his psychic powers; upper-class, trendy, bored Kate ("As a little girl I dreamed of being a concert violinist. What a tragedy if my dream had come true"); the prostitutes Tina and Brandy; the punk Agnus Angst; and the druggy, politically concerned Tina.

Sexual difference is a given, a shared rather than divisive premise (including the uncanny impersonation of Paul). The operative differences are class, education, experience, language, and history. Difference is neither a joke, as it was for Fred Mertz and George Burns, nor a standard against which women are measured and historically fail, as it was for Sigmund Freud, nor a tactic of marketing (diversification), as it is for Procter and Gamble, but differences are the conscious production of knowledge and pleasure. In fact, differences have become sameness. That Lyn has lived through a period comparable to Wagner's, Tomlin's, and my life locates this tale in middle age.

Trudy, the homeless bag lady on the streets ("I forget things. . . . The other day, I forgot where I put my house keys—looked everywhere, then I remembered I don't have a house"), is what we avoid seeing, never mind hearing, as we look away and are repulsed by old age and poverty, ours and others. Because she hears voices, including aliens from another planet and Howard at Howard Johnson's, and talks to herself, she is perceived as crazy. Yet she demands that people see her, look at her, realize her intelligence, which as assembled audience, now captive rather than hurried passersby on the street, we must do. The outcast is everywoman, prophet and sage, the unifying thread of all the characters' lives.

The entire performance is akin to flipping through TV channels, picking up bits and pieces of diverse lives, overhearing intimate conversations and gossip. As on TV, the characters share private experiences in public, with strangers, providing companionship—for the homeless Trudy and for the TV audience. "Laugh tracks: I gave TV sitcoms the idea for canned laughter. I got the idea, one day I heard voices and no one was there."

The disembodied voice of TV intrudes on the performance: "To boldly go where no punk has gone before. Suburbia." Or, "And these are the days of our lives." The performance, like television, is a generational dialogue of women that cuts across class differences, denying hierarchy and acknowledging age. Agnus: "I don't mind that there's no more avant-garde, but my mom took it pretty hard." And "I don't mind it when I first came into this world Elvis was already fat." For Wagner, women's issues and daily lives are inextricable from popular culture which links us together. The most deprived woman is the wisest: "When a man gets hanged, he has an erection. When a woman gets hanged, the last thing on her mind is sex." "I personally think we developed language because of our deep inner need to complain."

The last part of the show is a conversation among Lyn, Marge, and Edie, with excerpts from Lyn's journal detailing her involvement in the women's movement in the 1970s—the vast political divergences between then and now: "Oh, Edie . . . it's hard to be politically conscious and upwardly mobile at the same time." Lyn's story moves from the women's movement, Bob/marriage/motherhood, to single-parenthood, divorce, and unemployment. At the divorce garage sale, Lyn keeps the autographed old copy of *Ms.* and throws out the flotation tank and the "Whales Save Us" T-shirt. Popular culture does devour and deflate even the most serious of concerns. "You're sure, Doctor? Pre*men*strual syndrome? . . . I'm getting divorced. My mother's getting divorced. I'm raising twin boys. I have a lot of job pressure—I've got to find one. The ERA didn't pass. . . . And you *think* it's my *period* and *not* my life?"

Trudy is the aging receiver of television, but hardly passive, as Adrienne Rich argues. However, socially and politically, the bag lady, the old woman, the frightening crone of fairytales, is the most marginal character —crazy and homeless, a real 1990s social problem, a comic representation, like Lyn's potential new poverty, of women's current economics, which are not funny. The monologue unravels the contradictions of women's history by looking at everyday life, defined by popular culture. Wagner's witty reversals also revel in the pleasures and power of language—truly a "dream of a common language," an illustration of what Venturi calls "complexity and contradiction," the "difficult unity of inclusion."

While the recuperation of the noble dreams (and, in retrospect, naive remedies soured to fads) of the women's movement is charted, with Lyn being conscripted into the heterosexual couple and motherhood, now without a job and divorced, bewildered about how she got here after the struggles and aspirations, Tomlin's is a tour-de-force success story— the move of Mary Jean Tomlin from a working-class neighborhood in Detroit to *Laugh-In*, TV shows, films, then Broadway and critical acclaim as the female standup in a show written by a woman—Jane Wagner. Their comedy, born from friendship, experience, and popular culture (or women's daily lives), is performed by a chameleon body capable of minute, astonishing transformation into multiple selves—differences within and among women, and even men. Yet Tomlin holds something back; she is not fully accessible, not available, not on display, but existing as a challenge signaled by a Cheshire cat smile and the recesses behind her eyes. Hers is comedy of the body, including inflection, intonation, as well as language. Yet, Tomlin the person (and her desire) is elsewhere, outside the prescription of the heterosexual couple, working with Wagner in small storefront theaters, perhaps on another comic treatise for, by, and about women.

Wagner's brilliant comedy is not at the expense, the cost of women's rage, like Lucy, nor is it directed against women's bodies, like Sally Rogers (on *The Dick Van Dyke Show* in the 1960s), Phyllis Diller, or Joan Rivers, predicated on guilt or shame in which the joke is often on us. Like Tomlin, we embody differences and can identify with *all* her characters, whom we deeply respect. To laugh with and for women is not the same as laughing at them. In Wagner's scenario, unlike Freud's, we are never too old. At the same time—although disagreeing with Rich's polarities and opposition to mass culture, preferring instead to conjure with the contradictions of everyday life—Wagner's text and Tomlin's performance of the history of feminism from the 1970s through the 1980s reposes Rich's argument for women's culture. For, when told from women's points of view, the story is not the same.

Epilogue: The Condensed Version

I have tried to paint a contradictory portrait of U.S. TV culture around time, the body, and anxiety—drawn from Freud's texts on obsession and from contemporary cultural artifacts (including economics). I have suggested that these new cultural figurations are revisions of older forms of women's culture—perhaps one reason for the increase of anxiety. The fragmented, disrupted flow of news, entertainment, and commercials is smoothly held together by rigorous conventions of time. U.S. network television apportions the present, reruns history, and anxiously awaits the future, which might promise a natural, technological, or political catastrophe—a precious and noble time during which commerce is suspended and life hangs in the balance. If a program begins off the half-hour, either a catastrophe or a political event has occurred. That narrative, regular programming has resumed assures us that the catastrophe was not in the U.S. When narrative stops, history is being made, usually by men.

The hours, days, and television seasons are seriated, scheduled, and traded in ten-second increments modeled on the industrial work week—daytime, primetime, late-night, or weekend. TV's expenditure of time, unlike cinema's tallies of box-office attendance, is what counts. Our time is money. Time is a hierarchical, gendered commodity capitalizing on leisure, metronomically meted out according to the principles of Taylorism and Fordism, developed in the early 1900s for mass cultural and industrial spheres of U.S. life. However, whereas those assembly-line principles of standardization, specialization, and efficient time management clearly separated, for men at least, work from leisure, the public from the private, the job from the home, television, along with other artifacts and services of everyday life, has erased the borders and distinctions between work and leisure, the workplace and domestic space, the public and the private—distinctions which served men, who could exchange time for work and preserve free time.

Families and homes are being professionalized, differentiated. Leisure involves a great deal of arduous and efficient work construed as pleasure. This new domestic professionalism is primarily the task of women, now being urged out of their professions and back to the family and child-bearing/raising—where designer costs are soaring. Like products, the family has been diversified, with each family member targeted for costly consumer items. For example, in the 1950s, television sets were marketed as family purchases, one per home, and located in a central family space or room, with the dial dominated by Dad. Now television sets hold sway in several rooms of the house, including children's bedrooms, kitchens, and bathrooms. Television's version of "the family"—of pro news teams, situation comedy, network stars, late-night talk shows, morning news—and its gendered address to men and women are key areas of contradiction.

Along with selling public time to private homes, TV quantifies the body, collectively imagined by the networks as the audience, now splintering into smaller fractions. In contrast to representations of the ideal, visual, youthful, female body in cinema, television represents and addresses a flawed, tactile, middle-aged body, often in pain, with commercials predicated on smell, taste, and touch speaking about such intimate bodily functions as constipation ("irregularity") or nausea ("a Maalox moment"), using temporality to define problems. The female body, along with her family home, is in need of infinitely more repair and work than the male body.

Television's stylistic conventions of time—successive, simultaneous, or radically disruptive; Newtonian, Darwinian, or Einsteinian—are exemplified in three versions of time posited in relation to the body: catastrophe, scandal/gossip, and age. TV's successive "flow" of narrative, whether news or entertainment, is disrupted by catastrophe coverage, is measured by aging stars in simultaneous reruns and remakes, and is made shockingly trivial and anecdotal by scandal and gossip. Focusing on these discourses cuts through the usual distinctions used to describe television representation, usually genres or news versus entertainment.

In addition, because catastrophe, age, and gossip are predicated on structures of time, they are intertwined with historiography. Catastrophe fears and addresses the future, gossip the past, and aging the present, while longing for the past. Television has altered our writing and perception of history, which also has no boundaries. The past is always there or imagined as retrievable—like fashion, decades keep returning. The National Association for the Advancement of Time (NAFTAT) has promised to "end the 1960s in your lifetime." Their slogan is, "Let's make nostalgia a thing of the past."

The logic of franchise culture and television is one of contradiction; because the logic is overt rather than concealed, it can be witnessed. Thus, Tomlin, Leno, and Barr can turn cultural capital into jokes. Like the joke, the forked-tongue logic can go both ways: toward cancellation and toward critique. Wagner and Tomlin choose the latter.

I will close with one of Trudy's brilliant insights, with which I opened, an epigram emblematic of the current expansion of capitalism: "I said, 'Mr. Nabisco, sir! You could be the first to sell the concept of munching to the Third World. We got an untapped market here! These countries got millions and millions of people don't even know where their next meal is comin' from. So the idea of eatin' between meals is somethin' just never occurred to 'em!'"

Or as Lyn says, regarding women: "And you *think* it's my *period* and *not* my life!"

By Dae Mellencamp, 1990.
Figure 18

Notes

◆

Part I: Packaging the Difference

1. Jane Wagner, *The Search for Signs of Intelligent Life in the Universe* (New York: Harper and Row, 1987).

2. Robert Venturi, *Complexity and Contradiction in Architecture* (New York: MOMA and Doubleday, 1962), pp. 22-29.

3. Fredric Jameson, "Postmodernism and Consumer Society," in *The Anti-Aesthetic: Essays on Postmodern Culture*, ed. Hal Foster (Port Townsend, Wash.: Bay Press, 1983). In a familiar passage describing the schizophrenic subject of postmodernism (119), Jameson refers to this poor soul, condemned to fragmentation and the present tense, as "he or she."

4. Sigmund Freud, *The Complete Psychological Works of Sigmund Freud*, Vol. 20 (London: Hogarth, 1959), pp. 113, 119.

5. Morris's remarks were made during a videotaped session regarding women, the body, masquerade, and age (Milwaukee, 1989). She implied that stress levels appeared to be more intense in the U.S.

6. Lee Berton, "The CPA Jungle: Accounting Profession, Once a Staid Field, Is Torn by Incivility," *The Wall Street Journal*, July 24, 1991, pp. A1, A8.

7. Jane Mayer, "Krim's Tales: Hollywood Mystery: Woes at Orion Stayed Invisible for Years," *The Wall Street Journal*, October 16, 1991, pp. A1, A11.

8. Sigmund Freud, " 'Civilized' Sexual Morality and Modern Nervousness" (1908), in *Sexuality and the Psychology of Love*, ed. Philip Rieff (New York: Macmillan Publishing Co., 1963), p. 23. For an elaboration of neurasthenia, see Patricia Mellencamp, "Female Bodies and Women's Pastimes, 1890-1920," *East-West Film Journal*, December-January 1991/1992.

9. T. J. Jackson Lears, "A Psychic Crisis: Neurasthenia and the Emergence of a Therapeutic World View," in *No Place of Grace: Antimodernism and the Transformation of American Culture, 1880-1920* (New York: Pantheon Books, 1981), p. 56; in tracing the origins of contemporary therapeutic culture back to the nineteenth century (and further), Lears argues that "the therapeutic world view was less a formal regime than a way of life embraced by people sometimes only dimly aware of psychiatry." For him (unlike Christopher Lasch and Philip Rieff, the subjects he is debating), the "neurasthenia epidemic epitomized the crisis of cultural authority"—an undermining of "individual autonomy." "Antimodernism" was "a reaction against that helpless feeling" by "recovering intense experience" through a combination of "therapies of abundance" and "corporate liberal social engineering"; antimodernism "contained a vein of deep religious longing" (57-58). One means of escape was through "feminization," the cultivation of "emotional spontaneity, creativity, responsiveness, and nurturance," a release into "passivity" (250). Needless to say, this revival of "feminization" has been critiqued.

10. The books by George Miller Beard I have read are not called *American*

Nervousness. Their titles, in their original volumes, are *A Practical Treatise on Nervous Exhaustion (Neurasthenia): Its Symptoms, Nature, Sequences, Treatment* (1894), *Sexual Neurasthenia: Its Hygiene, Causes, Symptoms, and Treatment* (1898), and *Stimulants and Narcotics* (1871). What Lears fails to note is that for Beard, male impotence was a serious dilemma—perhaps accounting for Lears's dismissal of neurasthenia.

11. *The Milwaukee Journal,* December 5, 1990.

12. Many of these products were quoted from an article by Jacquelyn Gray, the fashion reporter for *The Milwaukee Journal,* May 10, 1991, p. G4. This newspaper has some of the best cultural critics, all women, writing social critique and commentary under the rubric "Lifestyle."

13. Douglas Gomery, "Hollywood and Television: The New Economics," paper written for (but not presented at) "Television: Industry, Audience, Representation," a conference I organized in Milwaukee, April 1987; in this essay, unlike his prior analyses of the film industry, Gomery focuses on products more than company, on the business of representation, if you will, rather than the strictly corporate structure. Arguing that television consists of more of the same, he writes, "Since the late 1950s Hollywood production companies have supplied the bulk of what we see on television, certainly the dominant entertainment programming." When the networks begin to produce more and more programming, this might change. However, "for now Hollywood continues to exert great and greater economic power." They have the programs "that the new (and old) television technologies want." The symbiotic relationship between television and movies is even more profitable: "In 1980 the Hollywood majors collected some twenty million dollars from world wide sales of video cassettes. In 1986 the figure topped three billion dollars, making home video the equal of theatrical box-office rental take in the U.S. By 1987 the figure was over seven billion." In essence, Gomery argues that the "new" technologies have enabled Hollywood to garner "even more power and profits," pointing to vertically integrated "movie-television company" monopolies: "Paramount and Warner Bros. today also jointly own a sizable chain of movie theatres. Rupert Murdoch . . . bought Hollywood's Twentieth Century Fox in 1985 and combined it with Metromedia's chain of six big-city independent television stations. Disney and Universal also own television stations."

Eileen R. Meehan, "Towards a Third Vision of an Information Society," in *Media, Culture and Society* (1984), pp. 257-71; Meehan contrasts the utopic with the dystopic visions of society predicated on new technologies and information, with an assessment of the corporate practice of deregulation. In this detailed analysis of tactics of the corporate players, she argues against a wild dispersity of product presumed by a proliferation of technologies.

14. Rosalind Coward, *Female Desires* (New York: Grove Press, 1985), p. 13. The sections in this book are journalistic excursions into popular artifacts, short pieces informed by theory and feminism.

15. Iurii M. Lotman, "The Poetics of Everyday Behavior in Eighteenth-Century Russian Culture," in *The Semiotics of Russian Cultural History,* ed. Alexander D. Nakhimovsky and Alice Stone Nakhimovsky (Ithaca and London: Cornell University Press, 1985), pp. 67-68.

16. This double stance underlies feminist criticism of contemporary culture; it is literally argued in the collection of essays by Teresa de Lauretis *Technologies of Gender* (Bloomington and Indianapolis: Indiana University Press, 1986).

17. Walter Benjamin, "Theses on the Philosophy of History," in *Illuminations* (New York: Schocken, 1969), p. 261. Benjamin writes that "fashion . . . is a tiger's leap into the past."

18. Patricia McLaughlin, "Call of the Wild," *The Milwaukee Journal,* February 11, 1990, p. 4G.

I. Differentiation

19. John Berger, *Ways of Seeing* (London: BBC and Penguin Books, 1972); in his analysis of publicity, which is *eventless* (a position which would, then, disagree with Dean MacCannell), Berger writes that publicity turns consumption into a "substitute for democracy" (149). Unlike Jameson's analysis of living in a perpetual present, Berger's analysis argues that we live not in the present but in a delayed, imaginary future; "for publicity the present is by definition insufficient" (144). Publicity uses the past to sell a future, making us discontent with ourselves in the present. This was a very prescient chapter, particularly its critique of the inadequacy of the present and the overriding desire for money. The book's comparison between oil painting and publicity to a degree covered up its status as cultural studies, placing it more within the art scene. Rather than being dated, these theses needed to be updated for the 1990s, although the passivity accorded to women needs revamping, a makeover. Women have not been merely objects of the gaze, there to be seen, but have been looking, and knowing, for centuries.

20. Patricia McLaughlin, "High Tide for Water Socks Washes Over U.S. Beaches," *The Milwaukee Journal*, August 5, 1990, pp. G1, G6. This funny Milwaukee writer asks where new shoes come from. Her answer: "Not from virtuoso shoe designers" but from their imitation of 200-year-old-images. Against this, she assesses that "truly new shoes seem to come not from the aesthetic side of things but from the functional."

21. *The Wall Street Journal*, September 18, 1991, p. B1.

22. *The Wall Street Journal*, July 29, 1991, p. A2.

23. *The Wall Street Journal*, September 18, 1991, p. B7.

24. Matthew Abbott, "Kentucky Fried Wants 500 Shops in South Pacific," *Financial Review* (Sydney, Australia), October 5, 1989; thanks to Meaghan Morris for sending this clipping.

25. "Colonel Sanders Gets a Spot near Mao," *The Milwaukee Journal*, November 13, 1987, p. A4.

26. "Parents Buying the Very Best for Baby," reprinted from *The San Francisco Chronicle* in *The Milwaukee Journal* sometime between 1987 and 1989.

27. *The Wall Street Journal*, June 25, 1991, p. B1.

28. Caryn James, "Pregnancy Fad Reflects, Blurs Reality," reprinted from the *New York Times* in *The Milwaukee Journal*, October 27, 1991, p. T13.

29. Frederick Winslow Taylor, *Shop Management* (New York and London: Harper and Brothers Publishers, 1912). As the foreword (an address to the graduating class of Purdue in 1905 by one Henry T. Towne, president of the Yale and Towne Manufacturing Company) says, "Industrial engineering . . . implies not merely the making of a given product, but . . . at the lowest cost consistent with the maintenance of the intended standard of quality" (p. 7). "The *dollar* is the final term" (p. 6). As Taylor writes: "The first of the four leading principles in management calls for a clearly defined and circumscribed task [time studies]. . . . The second principle calls for such conditions that the daily task can always be accomplished. . . . The third and fourth principles call for high pay in case the task is successfully done, and low pay in case of failure" (95). The analogy was a comparison between modern engineering and modern management, with modern management one of "high wages and low labor cost": "it assigns wages . . . which are uniformly fair." (Time studies were prerequisites for everything—the switch from piecework to continuous flow, with the continual reminder that these new methods would reward the worker properly and prevent strikes.) In fact, Taylor emphasizes *maximum* rather than minimum wages, correlating time studies with money, much like television, either networks or pay-per-view. As yet, however, there is little attempt to

sell "quality" time for more money. What should be noted is that higher pay for skill is usually applied to work performed by men; for women's work, such as sales clerk, the pay was low, often uniform. Models derived for production also did not apply for service, such as selling, not so easily conceptualized or measured, the very vagueness of women's work a political problem. McDonald's is Taylorism applied to product and service.

30. Jeffrey Trachtenberg, "Home Economics," *The Wall Street Journal*, September 17, 1991, pp. A1, A2.

31. *The Wall Street Journal*, October 8, 1991, pp. B1, B6.

32. Dana Milbank, *The Wall Street Journal*, June 24, 1991, p. B1.

33. Kathleen Deveny, "Segments of One," *The Wall Street Journal*, March 22, 1991, p. B4.

34. Richard Gibson, "Marketers' Mantra: Reap More with Less," *The Wall Street Journal*, March 22, 1991, pp. B1, B2.

35. Robert Johnson, "In the Chips," *The Wall Street Journal*, March 22, 1991, pp. B1, B2.

36. Richard Gibson, "Burger King Lets Diners Have It Weight Watchers' Way," *The Wall Street Journal*, July 18, 1991, p. B1.

37. *The Wall Street Journal*, July 1, 1991, p. B1.

38. Michael J. McCarthy, "Added Fizz," *The Wall Street Journal*, June 13, 1991, pp. A1, A12.

39. Laurie Grossman, *The Wall Street Journal*, September 17, 1991, p. A4.

40. Michael Miller, "Hot Lists," *The Wall Street Journal*, March 14, 1991, pp. A1, A12.

41. *The Wall Street Journal*, April 25, 1991, p. A1. "There are more than 100,000 cemeteries in the U.S. of which 5,000 to 7,500 are 'active'; each one of these has at least one interment a year."

42. *The Wall Street Journal*, April 11, 1991, p. B2.

43. *The Wall Street Journal*, April 25, 1991, p. A1.

44. Michael McCarthy, "Mind Probe," *The Wall Street Journal*, March 22, 1991, p. B3.

45. John B. Hinge, "Advertising," *The Wall Street Journal*, sometime in late summer or fall 1991.

II. Obsession

46. Lee Baer and Michael A. Jenike, "Introduction," in *Obsessive-Compulsive Disorders: Theory and Management*, ed. Michael A. Jenike, Lee Baer, and William E. Minichiello (Littleton, Mass.: PSG Publishing Company, 1986), p. 3; Stanley J. Rachman and Ray J. Hodgson, *Obsessions and Compulsions* (Englewood Cliffs, N.J.: Prentice-Hall, 1980), chapter 3. This book contains many detailed examples of the disorder, along with most researchers referring back to Rachman and Hodgson's work.

47. Variety *and* sameness govern the repetition of obsession—akin to the standardization and differentiation of Fordist production. What happens in OCD is that repetition takes over, spreading in time and space. The trouble with obsession is that it can't end; it is always inclusive, never enough.

48. Differentiation, is, of course, a very old tactic of manufacturing and sales, whereby products were differentiated from each other in order to sell. For Hollywood, one means of key differentiation has been the star system; genre is another; even auteurism was a means of differentiation—a Hitchcock or Ford stylistic touch. What differentiation, paradoxically, counts on is a basic sameness. What is interesting today is how we can be told something is different, or it can be the same by another name or box.

49. Graham Reed, *Obsessional Experience and Compulsive Behavior: A Cognitive-Structural Approach* (New York: Academic Press, 1985), p. 44.

50. Ibid., p. 46; ibid., pp. 50–51.

51. In "Behavior Therapy with Obsessive-Compulsives: From Theory to Treatment," E. B. Foa, G. S. Steketee, and B. J. Ozarow argue that "traditional psychotherapy has not proven effective in ameliorating obsessive-compulsive symptomatology" (p. 61); in *Obsessive-Compulsive Disorder: Psychological and Pharmacological Treatment*, ed. Matig Mavissakalian, Samuel M. Turner, and Larry Michelson (New York: Plenum Press, 1985). S. Jack Rachman, in "Overview of Clinical and Research Issues," writes that there is "little confidence in conventional treatment" (p. 29). The conclusion of Cawley, "that these disorders are unlikely to be helped by formal psychotherapy appears to be shared by a majority of writers, excluding . . . proponents of the psychoanalytic method" (p. 32); Martine Flament, M.S., and Judith L. Papoport, M.D., "Childhood Obsessive-Compulsive Disorder," in *Obsessive-Compulsive Disorder*, ed. Thomas R. Insel, M.D. (Washington, D.C.: American Psychiatric Press, 1984), p. 31. (Freud claimed a cure with the Rat Man.)

52. In Patrick Mahony, *Freud and the Rat Man* (New Haven and London: Yale University Press, 1986).

53. John C. Nemiah, M.D., "Foreword," in *Obsessive-Compulsive Disorder*, ed. Thomas R. Insel, M.D., p. ix.

54. Edna B. Foa, Ph.D., and Gail Steketee, M.S.W., "Behavioral Treatment of Obsessive-Compulsive Ritualizers," in Insel, p. 46; Foa, Steketee, and Ozarow, "Behavior Therapy with Obsessive-Compulsives," in Mavissakalian, Turner, and Michelson, pp. 49-51; this is an agreed-upon definition that varies slightly from behaviorist to behaviorist.

55. Insel, pp. 17, 18.

56. Baer and Jenike, "Introduction," p. 3; Jenike, p. 49. Rachman and Hodgson, "Psychotherapy of the Obsessional Patient," in *Obsessions and Compulsions*, pp. 113-24.

57. Rachman and Hodgson, "Cleaning and Checking Compulsions," in *Obsessions and Compulsions*, chapter 9.

58. Teri Agins, "Claiborne Unveils Its First Big Campaign," *The Wall Street Journal*, sometime in fall 1991, pp. B1, B4.

59. Rachman and Hodgson, p. 111.

60. Judith Williamson, *Consuming Passions: The Dynamics of Popular Culture* (London and New York: Marion Boyars, 1986), pp. 224–25.

61. Brent Bowers, "Enterprise," *The Wall Street Journal*, August 9, 1991, p. B1.

62. Rachman and Hodgson, p. 111.

63. Sasha Torres, "Melodrama, Masculinity, and the Family," *Camera Obscura* 19 (January 1989). For another instance of postfeminism—which means that women are no longer central to representation or that postfeminist critics are missing women's absence or secondary status in texts—see Elspeth Probyn's "New Traditionalism and Post-Feminism: TV Does the Home," *Screen* 31, no. 2 (Summer 1990). The discussion among feminist critics increasingly concerns sensitive men (the Robert Bly movement) or masculinity in crisis, the real concern of *thirtysomething*.

64. Reed, p. xiv.

65. Thomas R. Insel, M.D., "Obsessive-Compulsive Disorder: The Clinical Picture," in Insel, p. 13. There is an ongoing debate about the presence and importance of a precipitating event or incident.

66. Mahony, p. 166.

67. Benjamin, in *Illuminations*, p. 160.

68. Felix Guattari, *Molecular Revolution: Psychiatry and Politics* (New York and London: Penguin Books, 1984), p. 54.

69. Georg Simmel, trans., "Money and Modern Culture," in *Theory, Culture and Society* 8, no. 3 (1991). Simmel's *big* book, *The Philosophy of Money*, was published in 1900 and revised in 1907—just two years before Freud's study of the Rat Man and

obsession. Simmel's contemporaries compared the work of this sociologist, currently in revival, to Durkheim's *Division of Labor* and Marx's *Capital*.

70. Fred Block, *Postindustrial Possibilities: A Critique of Economic Discourse* (Los Angeles: University of California Press, 1990), p. 31.

III. Deregulation

71. Eric Alliez and Michel Feher, "The Luster of Capital," *Zone* 1/2 (1986). I have not quoted passages as directly as a good scholar might have but have summarized or appropriated their arguments, just as they have synthesized the arguments of neoclassical economics. Their analysis of the shift from product to service might be both too linear and chronological *and* dated too late. Alliez and Feher's lack of focus on issues of gender leads them into this oversight. Both Susan Porter Benson (*Counter Cultures: Saleswomen, Managers, and Customers in American Department Stores, 1890-1940* [Urbana and Chicago: University of Illinois Press, 1986]) and Susan Strasser (*Satisfaction Guaranteed: The Making of the American Mass Market* [New York: Pantheon Books, 1989]) date and historically document the shift from producer to consumer as occurring much earlier, from around 1910-1920, a shift which from the beginning, according to Benson in *Counter Cultures*, "sought the relatively cheap and supposedly docile labor of women" (185). "Managers assumed that . . . their primary identities lay elsewhere" (186). Benson asserts that in order to understand the workplace dynamics of service industries in general, a central place must be granted to "the ambiguities and subtle dynamics of class and gender" (288), overlooked by Alliez and Feher. In many ways, Alliez and Feher's argument is another example of taking women as a theoretical object beneath the presumably neutral model. The familiar for women comes back as the new and innovative for men.

72. This information came from my friend Scott Dean, who has opened six Subway franchises on Maui, hiring his friends and family to work (and vacation) in his profitable enterprises.

73. *The Wall Street Journal*, September 30, 1991, p. B1. Recent statistics (*The Wall Street Journal*, September 19, 1991, p. B1) state that 39% of self-employed workers are in service industries. The most popular is lodging, followed by beauty shops and car repair shops.

74. Ellen Graham, "McDonald's Pickle: He Began Fast Food but Gets No Credit," *The Wall Street Journal*, August 15, 1991, p. A1.

75. Eric Morgenthaler, "Mom's Best Cookies Revives Memories of a Happier Time," *The Wall Street Journal*, October 10, 1991, pp. A1, A5.

76. Janice Castro, "Staying Home Is Paying Off," *Time*, October 26, 1987, p. 112. Rather than just timely biographies of current celebrities, *Time* now jumps on cultural events, featuring issues of popular culture.

77. This, of course, is very complicated. Women might be working at home because they cannot afford daycare; it might be the result of all the new "studies" documenting children's constant need for their mothers, and the ill effects of daycare in the early years; or it might be the result of the few rewards of the workplace.

78. *The Milwaukee Journal*, August 5, 1990, p. T25; with the opening 1990 *Peaks* season, the marketing began. Adolescence and romance dominated the series, or better, lust and addiction, the flip side of the first two. Cancellation of the series (due to the ratings bottoming out) put a crimp in sales, to say the least.

79. Alexandra Peers, *The Wall Street Journal*, May 10, 1991, pp. C1, C10.

80. Alexandra Peers, *The Wall Street Journal*, October 4, 1991, p. C1.

81. Alexandra Peers, *The Wall Street Journal*, August 15, 1991, pp. C1, C12.

82. Francine Schwadel and Judith Valente, "Meat Loaf Years," *The Wall Street Journal*, September 3, 1991, pp. A1, A4.

83. Roby Rajan, " 'Rationality' and Other Pathologies: Economic Discourse as

Cultural Representation," unpublished manuscript (without page numbers), University of Wisconsin-Milwaukee, 1991.

84. "America Is Coming Home to Good Housekeeping," an ad in *The New York Times Magazine*, October 9, 1988, p. 19.

85. Freud, " 'Civilized' Sexual Morality and Modern Nervousness" (1908), p. 32.

86. *The Wall Street Journal*, August 8, 1991, p. B1.

87. *The Wall Street Journal*, August 5, 1991, p. B1; also discussed in Block's *Post-industrial Possibilities*.

88. As one of the stories goes, Bush's advisors lied to him, stating that the fish were not biting, in order to avoid yet another leisure activity, fishing in the rain, to demonstrate a U.S. macho lack of Carter panic to Saddam Hussein. The sight of officials determinedly vacationing demonstrated that vacations are not what they are cracked up to be.

89. Mary Pattison, *Principles of Domestic Engineering* (New York: Trow Press, 1915). Pattison set up an experimental station where she timed domestic tasks and organized domestic labor according to the principles of Taylor. Unfortunately, this home engineer agreed that women should not be paid for domestic labor, that it was of higher spiritual value than mere money. The arguments that convinced even professional home economists that money should not matter should be more carefully examined. The women who accepted and even endorsed them were not stupid.

90. *The Wall Street Journal*, March 5, 1991, p. A1.

91. *The Wall Street Journal*, April 23, 1991, A18.

92. Patrick Reilly, *The Wall Street Journal*, sometime in fall 1991.

93. These conventions, and their historical lineages, are arduously documented by David Bordwell, Janet Staiger, and Kristin Thompson in *The Classical Hollywood Cinema—Film Style and Mode of Production to 1960* (New York: Columbia University Press, 1985).

94. See Part II for further elaboration of Benjamin on information.

95. For a thorough history of the ratings, see Eileen Meehan, "Why We Don't Count: The Commodity Audience," in *Logics of Television*, ed. Patricia Mellencamp (Bloomington: Indiana University Press, 1990), pp. 117-37. Meehan argues that "ratings and the commodity audience are themselves manufactured. . . . And it is only the manufactured commodity audience, measured by commodity ratings, that counts" (132).

96. Thomas R. King, "See the Movie! Eat the Lunch Special!" *The Wall Street Journal*, June 4, 1991, pp. B1, B6.

97. *The Wall Street Journal*, September 6, 1991, B1.

98. For a detailed analysis of the new constellation of TV corporate technologies and players, see Meehan's "Conceptualizing Culture as Commodity: The Problem of Television," *Critical Studies in Mass Communications* 3 (1986): 454.

99. For an analysis of "guerrilla video," see my section on *The Machine That Killed Bad People* (the title taken from a Rossellini film); for a more thorough discussion, from which I lift these remarks, see my *Indiscretions: Avant-garde Film, Video, and Feminism* (Bloomington: Indiana University Press, 1990).

100. Victor E. Ferrall, Jr., "The Impact of Television Deregulation on Private and Public Interests," *Journal of Communication* 39, no. 1 (Winter 1989): 8. As the title declares, Ferrall sees private and public as separate spheres, although his history suggests, if not declares, their breakdown. Also, I wonder why what I will call social scientists have retained the importance of middle initials to declare proper authorship and authority, unlike the scholars in the humanities?

101. *The Wall Street Journal*, April 10, 1991, pp. A1, A8.

102. Daniel Pearl, *The Wall Street Journal*, June 18, 1991, p. B1; Laurie Grossman, *The Wall Street Journal*, June 21, 1991, p. B1.

103. *The Wall Street Journal*, September 23, 1991.

104. "The confusing key to the entire superstructure" was "the choice of biology and technology over philosophy and ideology"; *Indiscretions*, p. 69. Thus, their arguments resembled the technological determinism of many communication scholars today — that technology will alter social relations, and for the guerrillas, even the body itself, equated with technology. Many of these left-wing dreams have become corporate or right-wing realities, for example, fundamentalist television and the replacement of workers by robots.

Guerrillas also advocated an international media structure, one which would bypass nations and other boundaries, going past business and leaders directly to "the people." The new technologies of cable and satellite and cassettes would enable new political configurations. It just depended on who employed them. In many ways, international communications scholars are arguing this position, particularly regarding the use of video and television by indigenous peoples.

105. John Keller, "Telecommunications," *The Wall Street Journal*, October 4, 1991, pp. R1, R4.

106. Raymond Williams, in *Television: Technology and Cultural Form* (New York: Schocken Books, 1975), argues against technological determinism, the history of invention: "The effects of the technologies, whether direct or indirect, foreseen or unforeseen, are as it were the rest of history." The second kind argues *symptomatic* technologies "as *symptoms* of change of some other kind." He assesses that both of these debates which dominate our thinking about technology and society are "in the end sterile, because each position . . . has abstracted technology from society; both view research and development as 'self-generating' (13). "Each view can then be seen to depend on the isolation of technology. It is either a self-acting force which creates new ways of life, or it is a self-acting force which provides materials for new ways of life. These positions are so deeply established in modern social thought, that it is very difficult to think beyond them" (14).

107. Colleen Roach, "The U.S. Position in the New World Information and Communication Order," *Journal of Communication* 37, no. 4 (Autumn 1987): 38.

108. Douglas A. Boyd, "Third World Pirating of U.S. Films and Television Programs from Satellites," *Journal of Broadcasting and Electronic Media* 32, no. 2 (Spring 1988): 149.

109. Christine Ogan, "Media Imperialism and the Videocassette Recorder: The Case of Turkey," *Journal of Communication* 32, no. 2 (Spring 1988): 93.

110. *The Milwaukee Journal*, February 18, 1991, pp. A1, A9.

111. *The Milwaukee Journal*, March 5, 1989.

IV. Representing Difference(s)

112. Jacquelyn Gray, *The Milwaukee Journal*, April 21, 1991, pp. G1, G8.

113. Teri Agins, "Egad, Why Plaid?" *The Wall Street Journal*, September 6, 1991, p. A1.

114. Teri Agins, *The Wall Street Journal*, July 2, 1991, p. B1.

115. Marcus Brauchli, *The Wall Street Journal*, August 6, 1991, p. A9.

116. Philip A. Kalisch and Beatrice J. Kalisch, "Sex-Role Stereotyping of Nurses and Physicians in Prime-Time Television: A Dichotomy of Occupational Portrayals," *Sex Roles* 10, nos. 7/8 (1984): 534.

117. John F. Seggar, Jeffrey K. Hafen, and Helena Hannonen-Gladden, "Television's Portrayals of Minorities and Women in Drama and Comedy Drama, 1971-1980," *Journal of Broadcasting* 25, no. 3 (Summer 1981): 281.

118. Nancy Signorielli, "Marital Status in Television Drama: A Case of Reduced Options," *Journal of Broadcasting* 26, no. 2 (Spring 1982): 589.

119. Kalisch and Kalisch, p. 535.

120. Kay Kline Hodges, David A. Brandt, and Jeff Kline, "Competence, Guilt,

and Victimization: Sex Differences in Attribution of Causality in Television Dramas," *Sex Roles* 7, no. 5 (1981): 541. (Is Jeff related to Kay? If not, what happened?)

121. A. Chris Downs and Darryl C. Gowan, "Sex Differences in Reinforcement and Punishment in Prime-Time Television," *Sex Roles* 6, no. 5 (1980): 690–91.

122. Kalisch and Kalisch, p. 536.

123. Scholars from liberal arts and theory have difficulty in locating their theoretical object when it comes to television given the sheer amount of TV representation, and, I would argue, TV's downplay of authorship. This problem of definition is, of course, historical, and is changing as I write.

124. A short selection of the many other communication studies I examined included Tamar Zemach and Akiba A. Cohen, "Perception of Gender Equality of Television and in Social Reality," *Journal of Broadcasting and Electronic Media* 30, no. 4 (Fall 1986); Rita A. Atwood, Susan Brown Zahn, and Gail Webber, "Perception of the Traits of Women on Television," *Journal of Broadcasting and Electronic Media* 30, no. 1 (Winter 1986); John Turow, "Casting for TV Parts: The Anatomy of Social Typing," *Journal of Communication* 28, no. 4 (Autumn 1978); David H. Goff, Lynda Dysart Goff, and Sara Kay Lehrer, "Sex Role Portrayals of Selected Female Television Characters," *Journal of Broadcasting* 24, no. 4 (Fall 1980); Deborah Haskell, "The Depiction of Women in Leading Roles in Prime Time Television," *Journal of Broadcasting* 23, no. 2 (Spring 1979); Bradley S. Greenberg, Katrina W. Simmons, Linda Hogan, and Charles Atkin, "Three Seasons of Television Characters: A Demographic Analysis," *Journal of Broadcasting* 24, no. 1 (Winter 1980); Michael E. Pacanowsky and James A. Anderson, "Cop Talk and Media Use," *Journal of Broadcasting* 26, no. 4 (Fall 1982).

125. Strasser, *Satisfaction Guaranteed*, p. 155.

126. Richard Glover, *The Sydney Morning Herald*, October 7, 1989, p. 74; thanks again to Meaghan Morris for this gift.

127. Seggar, Hafen, and Hannonen-Gladden, p. 285.

128. *Window Dressing on the Set: Women and Minorities on Television*, United States Commission on Civil Rights (95th Congress, 1st Session, 1977), p. 48.

129. Michelle Wallace, *Invisibility Blues: From Pop to Theory* (London and New York: Verso, 1990).

130. Jacqueline Bobo and Ellen Seiter, "Black Feminism and Media Criticism: *The Women of Brewster Place*," *Screen* 32, no. 3 (Autumn 1991): 288.

131. Kalisch and Kalisch, p. 533.

132. Michel Foucault, "What Is an Author?" *Screen* 20, no. 1 (Spring 1979): 22. Foucault's precepts are inordinately appropriate to television. Rarely does the television text point "to this figure who is outside and precedes it"; in other words, rarely does TV point to an author (14). Regarding the cultural and literary need to assign individual authorship, Foucault equates this with the transcendental "theological affirmation of . . . sacred origin or a critical belief in its creative nature" (17). Perhaps because little television is believed to be creative, the need to locate authors is less. Rather than author, Foucault prefers "author function," which serves as a means of classification. He reminds us of history, one which pertains to gossip: "Speeches and books were assigned real authors . . . only when the author became subject to punishment . . . his discourse was considered transgressive." Discourse was not a thing, a product, or a possession, caught up in property values, but "an action"—reiterating the distinction of television as a service rather than a product, which is changing (increasingly as the networks become producers). Or texts circulated anonymously as epics or scientific theorems where "authentification no longer required reference to the individual who had produced them"; the role of the author disappeared as an index of truthfulness (like soap operas, or nighttime series, or the nightly news, or *60 Minutes*, with story aligned with star reporter, with, however, the name of the producer more recently writ large on the book page

behind them.) Against science, mythology, and the epic, "literary discourse was acceptable only if it carried an author's name" (21). Television fails this cultured test, unfortunately, a situation which might, like David Lynch and Steven Bochco, or Rod Serling, Gene Roddenberry, and Alfred Hitchcock before them, be changing. Citing Saint Jerome, the criteria of "author-functions" are (1) standard of quality; (2) field of conceptual coherence; (3) stylistic uniformity; and (4) definite historical figure, with the author constituting "a principle of unity" neutralizing "the contradictions that are found in a series of texts" (22). Because TV, a series of texts, so undervalues the author-function (on the level of representation, not on the level of corporation negotiation, e.g., Aaron Spelling), contradictions might not be neutralized. As if television were his unconscious "theoretical object," Foucault concludes that "we can easily imagine a culture where discourse would circulate without any need for an author. Discourse . . . would unfold in a pervasive anonymity. . . . New questions will be heard: 'Where does it come from; how is it circulated; who controls it,' 'What placements are determined for possible subjects?' " (29). One means of holding representation together, one means of defining our various texts, has been "the author." Missing this, TV has been difficult for many critics to conceptually grasp. At the same time, money authorizes television, its criticism a discourse of points, bucks, and ratings—a discourse of numbers not words, of charts, statistics, and graphs rather than sentences and paragraphs, TV somewhere between science and art, measurement and its failure.

133. *New York Times*, March 3, 1991, p. 29.

134. *The Milwaukee Journal*, March 25, 1990, p. 7D.

Part II: Beyond the Pleasure Principle of Television

1. William James, *Principles of Psychology* (New York: 1890), p. 239. The earlier reference is to Raymond Williams, *Television: Technology and Cultural Form* (New York: Schocken Books, 1975).

2. Susan Strasser, *Satisfaction Guaranteed: The Making of the American Mass Market* (New York: Pantheon Books, 1989), p. 6.

3. Janet Staiger has written extensively about Hollywood's mode of production. See, for example, "Blueprints for Feature Films: Hollywood's Continuity Scripts," in *The American Film Industry*, ed. Tino Balio (Madison: University of Wisconsin Press, 1985), pp. 173-94.

4. Sigmund Freud, *The Complete Psychological Works of Sigmund Freud*, Vol. VI (London: Hogarth Press, 1959), p. 274.

5. Walter Benjamin, "On Some Motifs in Baudelaire," in *Illuminations* (New York: Schocken, 1969), p. 158.

6. Ibid., p. 159.

7. Ibid., p. 158.

8. Ibid.

9. Ibid., p. 160.

10. Walter Benjamin, "Theses on the Philosophy of History," in *Illuminations*, p. 263. Obviously, this formulation is Hegelian.

11. Ibid.

12. Ibid., pp. 255, 261, 262 (collapsed together, in this order).

13. In Part III on gossip, Phil, Oprah, and Geraldo are discussed as exemplars of liberal pluralism. The discussion of "differentiation" begins in the first section and is picked up again in relation to Dean MacCannell's arguments.

14. Sports also cause network delays off the half-hour; this is an almost regular occurrence on CBS on Sunday evenings, pushing back *60 Minutes* (ironically enough), and hence the entire night's programming, to a frequently irregular scheduling. Along with sports, presidential addresses also cause off-hour tempo-

ralities. Because everything is so rigidly preprogrammed, there is no means of condensation to catch up, other than eliminating ID's, promos, or commercials—coded, profitable, and hence necessary ellipses for program sense and continuity; TV can only run late, or over; it is never early.

V. Shocking Thoughts

15. The resemblance of Baudrillard to the early catastrophists suggests an intellectual politics.

16. René Thom, *Structural Stability and Morphogenesis: An Outline of a General Theory of Models* (Reading, Mass.: W. A. Benjamin, 1975), p. 323. In *Catastrophe Theory* (New York: E. P. Dutton, 1978), Alexander Woodcock and Monte Davis trace the dates of the appearance of Thom's seven archetypal structures, from "ideas contained in his paper published in the 50s . . . the book draft was finished in 1966, with a six year delay in publishing" (16).

17. A. G. Wilson, *Catastrophe Theory and Bifurcation* (Berkeley and Los Angeles: University of California Press, 1975), p. 1. After Thom's book was published, there were hundreds of studies in countless areas using his models, including the work on urban retail structures by Wilson in *Aspects of Catastrophe Theory and Bifurcation* (Leeds: University of Leeds, 1979); in *Catastrophe Theory*, V. I. Arnold, a Soviet mathematician and a professor at the University of Moscow, scathingly critiqued its mass-media circulation, which I discuss a bit later.

18. Wilson, p. 5.

19. Thom, pp. 6, 251.

20. Ibid., p. 9.

21. Ibid., p. 290.

22. Woodcock and Davis, pp. 40, 4.

23. Freud, *The Complete Psychological Works*, Vol. XX, p. 109.

24. The feminist revision of film theory was predicated on vision (at the serious cost of sound, fully in cinema since 1928), with woman posited as the exhibitionist, the passive recipient of male desire, "the bearer not the maker of meaning," with the male in possession of both the story and the gaze, his place on film and in the audience an active one. While this schema became a powerful tool for analysis, regarding oneself as the seen rather than the seer is a disempowering personal model for women; to constantly see women as objects rather than as subjects, as others rather than as selves, over time is not beneficial—it involves narcissistic rage, that of turning oneself into an object, often an inadequate one (a theoretical inadequacy fueled by theories of women's infamous Lacanian "lack"). The model so *actively* employed by feminists about women in representation did not empower women in real life; in fact, it constantly pointed out what women were not. On a purely formal level of technique, the model of men looking at women needed to be complicated: men at men, women at women, women at men, and men at women, along with the gaze articulated as seeing (and not seeing), interpreting (and misinterpreting), and knowing (and not knowing). For film theory, only the last dyad of four and the first of six possibilities for the gaze, seeing, were emphasized, at, I would argue, the expense of female subjectivity, which women are still trying to reclaim, still, paradoxically, by arguing women's passivity in representation. Equally, positing women as the central objects of sexual desire concealed the historical fact that men have also been sexual objects, in addition to running the narrative show. Think of John Wayne in Ford's westerns, or Jimmy Stewart in Anthony Mann films, or Cary Grant in virtually all his movies (with the exception of *Blonde Venus*), or James Cagney. The resurgence of the male buddy film and Arnold Schwarzenegger would make no sense unless men were posited as the subject/object of audience sexual desire. In much contemporary cinema, women are no longer necessary excuses as they were historically. Now, men can be both subject and object, taking up all the

functions. Women should imagine themselves as the observer, not the observed, not the other, keeping the focus on female subjectivity. Like this film theory, which posits women as objects, which describes women as others, gossip also focuses on embodiments of the "other," a theoretical structure which also is not personally empowering for women. Thus, in both practices, we talk subjectively about ourselves as objects or others, a process of creation/cancellation, a double whammy which must take an unconscious psychic toll.

25. Madelon Sprengnether, *The Spectral Mother: Freud, Feminism, and Psychoanalysis* (Ithaca: Cornell University Press, 1990), p. 121.

26. Sonja Rein, "Whose Whip Is It?" unpublished graduate seminar paper, University of Wisconsin-Milwaukee, 1986/87.

VI. Disastrous Events

27. Stephen Kern, *The Culture of Time and Space, 1880–1918* (Cambridge, Mass.: Harvard University Press, 1983), p. 67. Going back more than one year later to check this quotation, I cringed slightly at how deeply this book had influenced the first pages of this section. I thought Kern's book was quite wonderful, assigned it to my students immediately upon its publication, and quoted it in talks, so my attraction was apparent. However, I had not realized how my thought process had been affected.

28. Walter Benjamin, "On Some Motifs in Baudelaire," p. 163. Film is Benjamin's theoretical object for his theory of the reception of modernity. Film, a newer medium, was as central as the poetry of Baudelaire in relation to the crowd. Systems of Fordist production serve as metaphors of reception. For example, "That which determines the rhythm of production on a conveyer belt is the basis of the rhythm of reception in the film" (175).

29. Ibid., p. 188; this potential of return transforms an object into a subject, a reciprocity that, as Proust writes, concerns "the world of emotions" which renders the truth of the experience. This reading, of the truth (of TV) established by an emotive aura, is an intriguing one, an *affective* ground for TV's "reality" *effect*.

30. Wolfgang Schievelbusch, *The Railway Journey: The Industrialization of Time and Space in the Nineteenth Century* (Berkeley: University of California Press, 1986), p. 167; his analysis connects Freud's model of shell shock with the military, taking it from there to technology. Stephen Kern moves from an analysis of time and space to technology.

31. Benjamin, p. 184.

32. Samuel Weber, *The Legend of Freud* (Minneapolis: University of Minnesota Press, 1982), p. 143.

33. Jean Baudrillard, *Simulations*, trans. Paul Foss, Paul Patton, and Philip Baitchman (New York: Semiotext[e]), 1983), p. 38. I deal with Baudrillard in more detail in *Indiscretions: Avant-Garde Film, Video, and Feminism*, where I first wrote about *Eternal Frame*, a section which I quote or repeat here in a shorter version.

34. Gilles Deleuze, "Plato and the Simulacrum," *October* 27 (1984): 47-56.

35. Other Ant Farm projects in the 1970s include "Cadillac Ranch" and *Media Burn*, an event in San Francisco in which a "customized dream car" drove through a flaming wall of television sets, an art event which was reviewed, to the TV journalists' condescending consternation, on local evening news. In the 1980s, Doug Hall, Chip Lord, and Jody Proctor were all "resident artists" at a local news station in Amarillo, Texas, impersonating news, weather, and sports announcers, learning how to be on-the-job reporters. One cannot be initially sure whether their local news is parodic or serious as clips from a tornado, then its destruction, become powerful and visual. The "Amarillo News Tapes" is a wonderful critique of the conventions of local news, as well as a portent of what local news could visually be. The local newsman is a willing accomplice of this critique of bland anchorspeak, of empty language filled with redundant images.

36. Patrick D. Morrow, "Those Sick Challenger Jokes," *Journal of Popular Culture* 20, no. 4, p. 179; other examples of these jokes are "Did you hear that Christa MacAuliffe has been nominated for the 1986 Mother of the Year Award?" "Of course, she only blew up once in front of her kids this year." "What does Christa MacAuliffe teach?" "English, but she's history now."

37. Dan Nimno and James E. Combs, *Nightly Horrors: Crisis Coverage by Television Network News* (Knoxville: University of Tennessee Press, 1985); see Mary Ann Doane, "Information, Crisis, Catastrophe," in *Logics of Television*, ed. Mellencamp, pp. 222-39.

38. Thomas Drabek, *System Responses to Disaster* (New York: Springer-Verlag, 1986), p. 6. He goes on to assert that "certain natural disasters can be compared to effects of man-made and technological disasters," presumably operating on the premise that technology has little to do with human intervention—a critical dilemma of *Challenger* which was explained by or blamed on human error or technological failure, which were frequently conflated. The confusion or the elision between the technological and the human here is more than intriguing.

39. *Behavior and Attitudes under Crisis Conditions: Selected Issues and Findings* (Washington, D.C.: Federal Emergency Management Agency). The problem of taxonomy reappears in *Natural Disasters: Acts of God or Acts of Man*, published by the International Institute for Environment and Development, which argues that when the ecology, the balance of nature, is destroyed, natural and manmade events can no longer be differentiated.

40. *Behavior and Attitudes*, p. 17.

41. Meaghan Morris, "Banality in Cultural Studies," in *Logics of Television: Essays in Cultural Criticism*, ed. Patricia Mellencamp (Bloomington: Indiana University Press, 1990), pp. 14-43. For a complicated reading of cultural studies, check out this influential essay, published in *Discourse* in a shorter version.

42. *Behavior and Attitudes*, a notion repeated throughout this federal publication. Their model is derived from "stress" studies not specifically influenced by Freud; rather, they are taken from U.S. psychology, tested by sociologists. Reading the lists of catastrophes, mentioned almost as asides in flat language, becomes parody, comparable to the nightly news, which casually refers to horrendous events, without emotion or poetry of thought or word. *One means of containing shock appears to be the deathly use of dull and boring language*, carefully measuring out intonation—the affect embodied in sounds, in words, in appearance, in gesture; or, in order to be either academic or official, the writer, like the TV anchor, must be "objective," in control, unemotional, bland, and expressionless. In many ways, this divide between affect and effect, between emotions and behavior (and thought), with the first term the lesser of the two, splits along gender lines, with catastrophic events, the big history-making moments, aligned with men and lack of emotion, and daily events, the trivial and ordinary, tied to women and the expression of affect. The divide also breaks down regarding control (or its absence, a bad thing) and concealing (or revealing, another rather bad thing) one's feelings. Women, of course, do the latter. Thus, most writers' models of disaster, like the weather on TV, level difference, dulling the landscape, turning tragedy into routine. The reason Prince's book is effective is that it is also affective—his language re-creates the scene rather than turning it into a list, a statistic, a distanced, impersonal event; his analysis, like Benjamin's, incorporates "personal experience" through the terrain of memory; equally, Prince's analysis encompasses many disciplines with the unusual commitment, not Marxist but close, that disaster can lead to change and that it cuts through class divisions, at least for a moment before they are erected again.

43. *Behavior and Attitudes*, p. 17 (I think).

44. *A Brief History of Panics* (New York: Knickerbocker Press, G. P. Putnam Sons), copyright in 1893 by De Courcy W. Thom (who "Englished and Edited" this French book), is uncannily applicable to journalists' assessments of Black Monday in 1987

and the drastic stock drop, replete with recession predictions, that accompanied the Iraq oil crisis, which included more reports from brokers than generals: for example, the symptoms of a panic (based on the silver standard!) are wonderful prosperity, rising prices of commodities, lowering of interest rates along with a rise in salaries, large numbers of discounts, loans, and banknotes, and decreasing deposits and reduced reserves, plus, critically, "growing luxurity leading to excessive expenditures." What he grandly but perhaps accurately observes is: "What must be noted is the reiteration and sequence of the same points under varying circumstances at all times, in all countries, and under all governments" (argued well before the Soviet revolution, which, of course, is reinstating a gold standard, hence making his statement absolutely correct). After analyzing panics in thirteen countries, he asserts that the only common cause is overtrading, so credit and money become scarce. The difference is the focus on banks rather than the new brokerage institutions, which are replacing banks as gold did silver. That economic panics are comparable to natural disasters is not without import for my model.

45. Samuel Henry Prince, *Catastrophe and Social Change* (New York: AMS Press, 1968 [Columbia University Press, 1920]), pp. 16-17. In chapter I:

> About midway in the last two years of war—to be exact December, 1917—a French munitioner heavily laden with trinitrotoluol, the most powerful of known explosives, reached Halifax from New York. . . . Suddenly an empty Belgian relief ship swept through the Narrows directly in her pathway. There was a confusion of signals; a few agonized maneuvers. The vessels collided; and the shock of their colliding shook the world!
> War came to America that morning. Two thousand slain, six thousand injured, ten thousand homeless, three hundred acres left a smoking waste. . . . Such was the appalling havoc of the greatest single explosion in the history of the world. It was an episode which baffles description. . . . It was all of a sudden—a single devastating blast; then the sound as of the crashing of a thousand chandeliers. Men and women cowered under the shower of debris and glass. . . . To some death was quick and merciful in its coming. Others were blinded, and staggered to and fro before they dropped. Still others with shattered limbs dragged themselves forth into the light—naked, blackened, unrecognizable shapes. They lay prone upon the streetside, under the shadow of the great death-cloud which still dropped soot and oil and water. It was truly a sight to make the angels weep. . . . It was an earthquake so violent that . . . the city shook as with palsy. The citadel trembled, the whole horizon seemed to move. . . . The mute record tells not of the falling roofs and collapsing walls which to many a victim brought death and burial at one and the same time. . . . It was a flood. . . . It was a fire or rather a riot of fires. . . . It was like the flight from Vesuvius of which Pliny the Younger writes. . . . And when the hegira was over . . . a succession of winter storms.

46. Ibid., p. 18.

47. Ibid., p. 46. The psychologists Prince uses for his behavioral model of shock and the ensuing emotions are William McDougall (*An Introduction to Social Psychology*, 1917), William James, M. Dide, a French psychologist who analyzed the hypnosis produced by shock, and several others writing between 1917 and 1920.

48. Prince, p. 60. After the initial shock and calamity, the community begins to reorganize. This protocracy arises initially from "the part of society which is most closely organized and disciplined in normality." Prince cites the militia as his example, mentioning not only the army's speed, its power, but "the attending psychological effects of orderly bearing and coolness in time of general chaos, bespeaking a care that is at once paternal and sympathic." This is a good description of the institution of TV and its stable, paternal anchors. Prince also describes the pattern

of disaster events which have stages, over time, which paradoxically embody change and usually preclude change.

49. Ibid., p. 53. In the aptly named *Disaster and the Millennium* by Michael Barkun (New Haven: Yale University Press, 1974), studies illustrate that the effects of Kennedy's assassination were "unique": that there was little difference between the Dallas spectators and TV spectators around the country, that the death of Kennedy was comparable to the loss of a parent or close relative. Eighty-two percent in Dallas, versus 68 percent nationally, experienced "extreme nervousness and tension." TV viewers had the following symptoms, which disappeared after the funeral: "loss of appetite, crying, difficulty sleeping, unusual fatigue." "Television temporarily created disaster victims." This is an intriguing assertion in a rather strange book; Barkun goes on to argue the effects of induced and constant catastrophe, for example, the Chinese Cultural Revolution, suggesting that the secret of permanent revolution is permanent disaster—which, from another political position, accords with Benjamin and Prince, who argue that disaster is one critical means of instigating revolution and change. Thus, there is a politics to catastrophe. Prince, quoting Professor Shailer Matthews, who distinguishes between a crisis and a revolution: "The difference between a revolution and a crisis is the difference between the fire and the moment when someone with a lighted match in hand pauses to decide whether a fire should be lighted." When I was a child, and older, we used to play the game of wondering what we would do if the bomb were dropped.

50. Sigmund Freud, *Standard Edition XX*, p. 170.

51. Rahul Sood, Geoffrey Stockdale, and Everett M. Rogers, "How the News Media Operate in Natural Disasters," *Journal of Communication* 37, no. 3 (Summer 1987): 28.

52. Mimi White, "Television: A Narrative—A History," *Cultural Studies* 3, no. 3 (October 1989): 51. White has been one of the most productive of the new television critics. Her assessment of history crosses many divides associated with television, particularly that between fiction and news, or in film, narrative versus documentary.

53. Sood, Stockdale, and Rogers, p. 36.

54. Ibid., p. 32.

55. Ibid., p. 34 (the authors are quoting another study).

56. Lee Wilkins and Phillip Patterson, "Risk Analysis and the Construction of the News," *Journal of Communication* (Summer 1987), p. 88.

57. Eleanor Singer and Phyllis Endreny, "Reporting Hazards: Their Benefits and Costs," *Journal of Communication* (Summer 1987), p. 10.

58. Mimi White, p. 291.

59. Schivelbusch, p. 131.

60. William C. Adams, "Whose Lives Count?: TV Coverage of Natural Disasters," *Journal of Communication* 36, no. 2 (Spring 1986): 113. (The flip side of this title is Meehan's "Why We Don't Count: The Commodity Audience.")

61. See Jameson reference above. For Jameson, the schizophrenic is "condemned" to live in the present; for some of us, particularly recovering addicts and followers of Eastern religions, living in the present is, perhaps, the highest attainment.

62. These quotations are from the text, Fagin's words which accompany the piece.

63. Stanley Karnow, *In Our Own Image: America's Empire in the Philippines* (New York: Random House, 1989). Karnow, a foreign news correspondent, is another version of Lansdale.

64. The kinship structure in the Philippines is not analogous to the Western notion of family. It involves a very extended family and an ethical commitment to kin which supersedes other structures. Along with land ownership, politics are determined by kinship structures. The custom of "favors" is another difference.

65. Homi K. Bhabha, "The Other Question—The Stereotype and Colonial Discourse," *Screen* 24, no. 2 (November/December 1983): 23, 29.

66. Homi K. Bhabha, "Sly Civility," *October* 43 (Fall 1985): 75.

67. Graham Pechey, "On the Borders of Bakhtin: Dialogization, Decolonialization," *Oxford Literary Review* 9, nos. 1/2 (1987): 69.

68. Benita Parry, "Problems in Current Theories of Colonial Discourse," *Oxford Literary Review* 9, nos. 1/2 (1987): 44. Parry compares the formulations of Bhabha and Gayatri Spivak, and reminds us that for Frantz Fanon, whose writings she is employing, "a native context initially enunciated in the invaders' language culminates in a rejection of imperialism's signifying system. This is a move which colonial discourse theory has not taken on board" (45). It would appear that communication scholars' "anti-imperialism" thesis regarding media in the Third World has, to a degree, heeded Fanon's analysis, and has indeed taken this work on board, however, not from the point of view of the colonized in the studies quoted in the prologue.

69. Gilles Deleuze and Felix Guattari, *On the Line* (New York: Semiotext[e], 1983), p. 2. Also see their *A Thousand Plateaus.*

70. Michael Shamberg, *Guerrilla TV* (New York: Holt, Rinehart, Winston, 1970), p. 33.

71. Fredric Jameson, "Postmodernism and Consumer Society," in *The Anti-Aesthetic*, p. 125.

72. I repeat these quotations by Benjamin—partially as a comparison with Jameson's assertions. Benjamin formulates an experience of the present as thoroughly inflected by history.

73. Benjamin argues personal experience inflected by memory, or living in the present *and* remembering the past, as a both/and logic which combines the intellect with affect; it is beyond the grasp of the intellect and more than sheer emotion. His theory of personal experience is a both/and logic and is thus pertinent to my argument and women.

74. Jameson, p. 125. This is, of course, his famous formulation.

75. Parry, p. 42.

76. Tzvetan Todorov, *Mikhail Bakhtin: The Dialogical Principle* (Minneapolis: University of Minnesota Press, 1984).

77. Mikhail Bakhtin, *The Dialogic Imagination*, ed. Michael Holquist (Austin: University of Texas Press, 1981); I cannot locate the page for this quotation.

78. Bhabha, "Sly Civility," p. 75. Also see "Of Mimicry and Man: The Ambivalence of Colonial Discourse," *October* 28 (Spring 1984).

79. Weber, p. 134: "Thus, if Freud's initial stories deal with men, betrayal, and ingratitude, death enters the scene with—as?—the passive female . . . a recurrent fatality linked to the female: she either eliminates the male or is eliminated by him. But nothing is more difficult to do away with than this persistent female." This is Weber's interpretation of *Beyond the Pleasure Principle.*

80. Weber, p. 130. Weber concludes with the Greeks, the myth, as it were, of our cultural origins or consciousness, back, along with Freud, to the *Symposium*; I prefer another direction.

81. Freud, *Inhibitions, Symptoms and Anxiety*, p. 129.

82. From the 1950s on, Bruce Conner, a San Francisco filmmaker and sculptor, recycled objects from mass culture and psychoanalysis, transforming them into fetishes *and* critiques of fetishism—fur, feathers, lace, dimestore jewelry, and film clips. He called these lost rather than found objects. In one unsettling piece, burned babies are bound with bits of nylon stockings and pubic hair, a work dealing with the horror of the gas ovens of World War II. These fetish objects linked the eroticism of violence to pornography. For Conner, the effects of masculine power were deadly and catastrophic.

Nowhere is this more succinctly realized in his films. *A Movie* (1958), like *Report*

(1965), consists entirely of bootlegged footage and found sound, materials which Conner reuses in later films. *Crossroads* is an elaboration of a short scene in *A Movie*—the Bikini Atoll nuclear footage; a few spectacular minutes are expanded into a film through repetition and reprinting. The banal—tails out, black leader, and credits—collides with the fatal, the scenes of catastrophe.

In *A Movie*, Conner edits movie chase scenes, sports racing scenes, and disaster footage—the nuclear blast, the explosion of the *Hindenburg*, and the collapse of a suspension bridge—all intercut with shots taken from *National Geographic* films of bare-breasted "primitives" and African animals. Here, the difference between ethnography and pornography (shots of Marilyn Monroe) is racism. The film is a history of cinema and technology as catastrophe and imperialism, a history of conquest by technology, resolutely linking sex, death, and cinema.

Report (thirteen minutes) replays the chaos of Kennedy's assassination. The motorcade dash to the hospital is accompanied by a frantic sound track taken from radio sound. Visibility is at stake, as the image frequently goes to black. Conner's strategy is the inverse of Ant Farm's visual re-creation. *Crossroads* is a thirty-six-minute stare or meditation on the Bikini Atoll explosion extended in time by slow motion and stop frame—a replay of "Scene 26, Take 2" taken from its context to a timeless rendering. While the film dramatizes the mesmerizing effects of media repetition, *Crossroads* walks a fine line between critiquing and aestheticizing the explosion. To return to the scene of the crime, and to make a film from the (Bikini) women's points of view, erased by history and aesthetics, would be quite another story.

83. "Nuclear Criticism," *Diacritics* 14, no. 2 (Summer 1984); additional contributors include Michael McCanles, Dean MacCannell, Zoe Sofia, Mary Ann Caws, and Derrick de Kerckhove.

84. Joyce Nelson, *The Perfect Machine: TV in the Nuclear Age* (Toronto: Between the Lines, 1987), thanks to Andrew Ross for this source.

85. David M. Rubin and Constance Cummings, "Nuclear War and Its Consequences on Television News," *Journal of Communication* (Winter 1987), p. 40.

86. Elizabeth Gross, "Lesbian Fetishism," unpublished paper delivered at a conference, "Queer Theory," at the University of California in Santa Cruz.

87. Paul G. Hayes, "This Is a Test! Wisconsin Residents Alerted to Accident at Nuclear Plant," *The Milwaukee Journal*, June 23, 1987, p. 1, then further back on June 24 and June 25, 1987.

88. Reported in *The Milwaukee Journal*, March 28, 1989, p. 2A.

89. Michael L. Smith, "Selling the Moon: The U.S. Manned Space Program and the Triumph of Commodity Scientism," in *The Culture of Consumption*, ed. T. J. Jackson Lears, p. 189.

90. Francis Ferguson, "The Nuclear Sublime," in *Diacritics*.

91. Jacques Derrida, "No Apocalypse, Not Now (full speed ahead, seven missiles, seven missives)," in *Diacritics*.

92. V. I. Arnold, *Catastrophe Theory* (Berlin, Heidelberg, New York, Tokyo: Springer Verlag, 1981, 1986), p. 89.

93. Michel de Certeau, *The Practice of Everyday Life*, trans. Steven Rendall (Los Angeles: University of California Press, 1984), p. 96.

94. Here I again intersect, as I did in the beginning, with Stephen Kern's opening chapter; I read several books on these early guys and, in the end, drew most of this *Reader's Digest*, condensed simplification from Loren Eiseley's *Doomsday: The Science of Catastrophe*, appropriately enough, like the progenitor of and model for the *National Enquirer*, published by Reader's Digest Press in 1977. So much for scholarship!

95. Strasser, p. 290.

96. Judith Allen, "Evidence and Silence: Feminism and the Limits of History," in *Feminist Challenges*, ed. Carole Pateman and Elizabeth Gross (Boston: Northeastern University Press, 1986), p. 178.

97. *High Anxiety* also moves from panic to laughter, away from fear and toward fearlessness, and for me, from the ridiculous (and imaginary) to the sublime (and reality, whatever that might be). However, my sublime is not that of male philosophers.

Part III: Inquiring Minds Want to Know

1. Dean MacCannell, *The Tourist: A New Theory of the Leisure Class* (New York: Schocken Books, 1976), pp. 47-48.

2. News coverage of Leona Helmsley portrayed her as "an abusive, imperious woman," whose income-tax crime was redecorating a country estate and paying for it out of her and her husband's company money. "Her 80-year old husband, Harry, was severed from the case because of a loss of memory." Lucky for Harry! The trial consisted of one negative testimonial after another, repeating the classic line—the reprise of "Let them eat cake!"—uttered within earshot of a servant: "We don't pay taxes, only the little people pay taxes." Her lawyer, going out of his way to point to her as a "tough bitch who was abrasive and demanding" as she tried to make it in a man's world, pointed out: "In the United States we don't put people in jail for being unpopular" (*The Milwaukee Journal*, July 23, 1989, p. 17A). The made-for-TV movie starring Suzanne Pleshette and Lloyd Bridges as Harry describes Leona's upward mobility through men and marriages, ending up with her ultimate dream, Harry Helmsley, wealthy owner of New York real estate. Leona's business acumen, her devotion to Harry, and her deployment of sexuality are there, along with her developing obsessions and irritations, for example, playing cards with her image on them. She starts out as a nice although manipulative woman, knowingly sleeping her way to the top, demanding marriage rather than mistress status for each upwardly mobile affair (the result of not receiving love or recognition from her mother, of course). As Leona ages in the film, she becomes what Freud calls an "old termagant." Her irascibility is directly linked to her aging, as well as to her success in business.

3. Sammye Johnson and William G. Christ, "Women through *Time*: Who Gets Covered?" *Journalism Quarterly* (1989), p. 289.

4. The Center for Media and Public Affairs in Washington, reprinted in *The Milwaukee Journal*, Feb. 8, 1991, A2.

5. Glenn G. Sparks and Christine L. Fehlner, "Faces in the News: Gender Comparisons of Magazine Photographs," *Journal of Communication* 36, no. 4 (Autumn 1986).

6. For several interesting analyses, see *Women in the News*, ed. Laviily Keir Epstein (New York: Hastings House, 1978).

7. Ibid. Trivialization is a tactic applied to women in the news—it involves the use of "less prestigious language and details, along with ridiculing legitimate claims." Other common tactics are the use of first names, the avoidance of professional titles, and an overemphasis on marital status. As the authors suggest on p. 101, naming has much to do with power.

8. Suzanne Pingnie and Robert P. Hawkins, "News Definitions and Their Effects on Women," in *Women in the News*, ed. Keir, p. 117.

9. "Gossiping about Gossip," *Harper's*, January 1986, pp. 37-50.

10. These comments were taken from a glossy mass mailing promoting status and a deal for being an initial subscriber, the privilege that would ensue from being "the first." The intimate, direct address of these brochures, couched in personal terms, as if this were a small in-group of friends rather than millions of complete strangers, amazes me. Does this imaginary of a small elite rather than mass readership work? TV has a comparable presumption of intimacy and togetherness; per-

haps more than anything, publicity is a challenge to the interpretation of the codes and decorum of friendship and intimacy, to their veracity. Perhaps the proliferation of the gestures of intimacy has led to an upping of the ante of the intimate and personal, the public confession, the inverse of Foucault's opening of *Discipline and Punish*—now anything is told without the slightest provocation, let alone being quartered alive. I would open my revision of Foucault with "readings" of some of the rejected tellers who wanted to be on Oprah, Phil, or Geraldo.

11. One of my students, Harry Wasserman, called Jay Shriver, the former producer's of Warhol's show, who provided this information on February 28, 1989.

VII. Gossip Theory

12. Max Gluckman, "Gossip and Scandal," *Current Anthropology* 4 (1963): 309.

13. Ulf Hannerz, "Gossip, Networks and Culture in a Black American Ghetto," *Ethos* 32 (1967): 36-60.

14. J. D. Logan, Ph.D., "The Psychology of Gossip," *Canadian Magazine* 31, no. 1 (May 1908): 106-11.

15. Ralph L. Rosnow, "Gossip and Marketplace Psychology," *Journal of Communication* (1977), pp. 158, 159.

16. Ralph L. Rosnow and Gary Alan Fine, *The Social Psychology of Hearsay* (New York: Elsevier, 1976).

17. Sally Yerkovich, "Gossip as a Way of Speaking," *Journal of Communication* (Winter 1977).

18. In Griffith films, as in the history of Hollywood until very recently, middle age didn't exist: characters, particularly women, were *either* young *or* old. Close scrutiny reveals, however, that young actresses playing old were merely stereotypical gestures, irascibility, or makeup, that age was a set of clichés, a masquerade. The history of the female star is a history of growing too old for parts, a reprise of Mary Pickford and Little Mary retiring to Pickfair behind closed doors; or dramatized as *Sunset Boulevard*, where Gloria Swanson is not old enough to be my grandmother, looking forty but playing around seventy-five, well over the hill of marketability and desirability, unlike her director, Cecil B. De Mille, who is still directing, still powerful, and looking substantially older than Swanson. Her counterpart is a younger woman, her vanity that of desiring a younger man who falls for the younger woman, ashamed of his affair, his prostitution, with the older woman. That women's desire for younger men is grotesque, an aberration, a kittenish burden and a demand, is a very different intepretation from the common and socially sanctioned scenario, the older man and the younger woman. Age shoves women to the margins, away from the limelight; men assume the center of the panopticon.

19. Jack Levin and Allan J. Kimmel, "Gossip Columns: Media Small Talk," *Journal of Communication* (Winter 1977), p. 169.

20. Alexander Rysman, "How the 'Gossip' Became a Woman," *Journal of Communication* (Winter 1977).

21. Homer Obed Brown, "The Errant Letter and the Whispering Gallery," *Genre* 10 (1977): 579; quoting Socrates, who said that "the problem of all writing is that it is parentless," Brown paraphrases "the parentless drift" which I use, unattributed, elsewhere.

22. Patricia Meyer Spacks, *Gossip* (Chicago: University of Chicago Press, 1985). This is a beautifully thought and written book that falls into the realm of pleasurable scholarship—for the reader, that is. Coming from film, aligned with mass reproducible culture as its history is, my premises regarding popular culture and its artifacts are frequently at odds with literary critics.

23. Mikhail Bakhtin, *Rabelais and His World*, trans. Helene Iswolsky (Bloomington: Indiana University Press, 1984), p. 139.

VII. Gossip Law

24. I took my arguments from reading specific cases and from two texts by legal scholars: "Libel and Slander," in *Prosser and Keeton on Torts*, 5th ed. (1984); and Michael F. Mayer's *The Libel Revolution: A New Look at Defamation and Privacy* (New York: Law Arts Publishers, 1987). Quotes from Prosser and Keeton are in numbers after 785.

25. *Newsweek*, December 8, 1980, p. 86. There is a certain tautology in using the popular press as data for an analysis of an even more populist press.

26. *Time*, April 6, 1981, p. 77.

27. *Newsweek*, p. 86.

28. Ibid., also mentioned in *The Libel Revolution*.

29. See William Boddy, "The Seven Dwarfs and the Money Grubbers: The Public Relations Crisis of US Television in the Late 1950s," in *Logics of Television*, ed. Mellencamp.

30. See Eileen Meehan, "Why We Don't Count: The Commodity Audience," in *Logics of Television*, ed. Mellencamp.

31. Jane Gaines, "Superman and the Protective Strength of the Trademark," in *Logics of Television*, ed. Mellencamp.

IX. Gossip and the Market

32. *Time*, February 21, 1972, pp. 64-65.

33. Michel Foucault, *Discipline and Punish: The Birth of the Prison*, trans. Alan Sheridan (New York: Vintage Books, 1979). The shock elicited by this opening chunk places us within a historical frame, before executions and death were placed behind closed doors or taken into the realm of privacy (often handled by strangers rather than friends and family). The scene is an attempt to elicit confession, the prize, and the story. Equally, Barthes analyzes the attempt to elicit story, and secret, in *S/Z*; it would appear that another theory needs to be devised for tellers eager to tell, with nothing left to hide and, then, perhaps nothing left to tell.

34. Andrew Ross, "Uses of Camp," in *No Respect: Intellectuals and Popular Culture* (New York and London: Routledge, 1989), p. 167.

35. *Time*, p. 64.

36. In *Jokes and Their Relation to the Unconscious*, the teller and the listener slip momentarily and mutually into the unconscious in the process of "getting" the joke; equally, disavowal functions in the unconscious. Like the fear of castration which the fetish (and disavowal) wards off, the joke, also indirectly, holds off the socially unacceptable. A comparison between the joke and the fetish (and their mutual techniques) is, in fact, quite illuminating.

37. *Forbes*, October 16, 1978, pp. 77-78.

38. *New York Times*, February 14, 1988, pp. 1, 9–10.

39. Felix Guattari, *Molecular Revolution: Psychiatry and Politics* (New York: Penguin Books, 1972), p. 52. "Familialism means magically denying the social reality . . . a miserable little area of identification" (54–55).

40. *Forbes*. Pope: "Out of our 35-cent-a-copy retail price, we usually give about 8 cents to the retailer and a little over 5 cents to the wholesaler," an early version of franchise (take-a-cut) culture or payola.

41. *Time*.

42. *Forbes*.

43. *New York Times*.

44. *Time*, April 9, 1990, p. 67.

45. *The Wall Street Journal*, May 20, 1991.

46. *New York Times*, p. 9.

47. *Forbes* presumes this is true. An analysis of these adverts, in the backs of the rags since I was born, reveals that they have changed very little, as have the products they push; reading them is like a time-warped return to the '50s and blackhead removers and magical muscle builders.

48. *The Wall Street Journal,* June 21, 1991, B1.

49. *New York Times.*

50. *Forbes.*

51. The fight was backstage; for further discussion of Barr, see the chapter on women and comedy.

52. *New York Times,* p. 9.

53. *National Examiner,* December 29, 1987.

54. *National Examiner,* May 10, 1988.

55. *Weekly World News,* August 18, 1987.

56. *Newsweek,* August 26, 1985, p. 43.

57. Edwin Diamond, "Celebrating Celebrity," *New York,* May 13, 1985, p. 23.

58. Peter Kaplan, "E.T.: The Latest Assault," *Esquire,* September 1983, pp. 245-46.

59. Mayer, *The Libel Revolution,* pp. 8-9.

60. Kevin Glynn, "Tabloid Television's Transgressive Aesthetic: *A Current Affair* and the 'Shows That Taste Forgot,' " *Wide Angle* 12, no. 2. It is exactly "transgressive" that suggests political trouble in this essay, just as Spacks's assessment of gossip's "subversion" triggers caution. Arguing transgression or subversion through gossip is tantamount to a politics of containment rather than power, the pleasure of remaining objects yet imagining oneself as a subject—this is the nonpower of the woman-behind-the-man ploy, an old and weary tale. Real power comes from speaking about oneself or one's position rather than the positions and behaviors of others. Gossiping is also a way to avoid talking about oneself, to evade affect and emotion, gossip as a form of displacement.

61. Richard W. Stevenson, "First Run Syndicators Find Tight TV Market," *New York Times,* February 27, 1988.

62. Bill Carter, *New York Times* news service, reprinted in *The Milwaukee Journal,* April 15, 1990, p. 3T.

63. Stevenson, p. 21.

64. Victor E. Ferrall, Jr., "The Impact of Television Deregulation on Private and Public Interests," p. 11 (in footnote 3).

65. Andy Warhol, *The Philosophy of Andy Warhol (From A to B and Back Again)* (New York and London: Harcourt, Brace, Jovanovich, 1975), pp. 24, 26. The context of the first comment is Warhol's returning from the psychiatrist's office and stopping at Macy's to buy his first television set, an RCA nineteen-inch black-and-white (which soon replaced his shrink). "I kept the TV on all the time, especially while people were telling me their problems, and the television I found to be just diverting enough so the problems people told me didn't really affect me anymore" (24). Warhol's theoretical object might have been the counterculture, which he revised or inverted. As he implies, the relationship between television and affect, often presumed, needs to be carefully reexamined. Warhol's comments on gossip are also prescient, and, of course, his grasp of commodity culture was apparent: "What's great about this country is that America started the tradition where the richest consumers buy essentially the same things as the poorest" (100). About waiting in line for movies, which reminded me of airports: "The idea of waiting for something makes it more exciting anyway" (115).

66. After daytime talk shows, a telephone number and a quick address are flashed for transcripts. The Investigative News Group is the publisher, which charges $3.00 cash or check, or $5.50 for credit card. For only $225, an annual subscription can be purchased. A FAX service is also available for transmission within twenty four hours, along with computer hookups through "CompuServe Informa-

tion Service." Thus, a fringe entrepreneur has sprung up around talk-news, including videotapes for *60 Minutes*. In addition, "research assistance" is available from over "20 major TV programs: Just call (212) 227-7323. With your major credit card . . . " We never need to leave our homes if we are TV critics, with credit (which can be either debt or credit these days), computers, and telephones.

67. Erica Jong, *Any Woman's Blues* (New York: Harper and Row, 1990), labeled "A Novel of Obsession" by the "author of *Fear of Flying*" on its very red cover.

68. *New York Times*, February 17, 1989, p. 21.

69. *The Milwaukee Journal*, March 10, 1991, 13; *The Wall Street Journal*, June 27, 1991, A1.

70. *Newsweek*, March 30, 1987, p. 28.

71. *Weekly World News*, August 18, 1987.

72. *People*, October 5, 1987, pp. 32-37.

73. *The Milwaukee Journal*, October 5, 1989, pp. 1, 6A.

74. Lawrence Grossberg, *It's a Sin* (Sydney: Power Publications, 1988).

X. Theorizing Affect

75. Jacques Lacan, "Seminar on the Purloined Letter," in "French Freud," *Yale French Studies*, ed. Jeffrey Mehlman, p. 44.

76. Strobe Talbott, "Rethinking the Red Menace," *Time*, January 1, 1990, pp. 66-72, the "Man of the Year" issue and essay about Mikhail Gorbachev. "Scenarios for a Soviet invasion of Western Europe have always had a touch of paranoid fantasy about them. . . . As for an attempted Soviet decapitating attack on American missiles, that danger has always been mired in a paradox. . . . In order to believe the Soviet Union is capable of waging and quite possibly winning a war against the West, one has to accept as gospel the hoary and dubious cliche about the U.S.S.R.: the place is a hopeless mess where nothing works, with the prominent and crucial exception of two institutions — the armed forces and the KGB." The intense military buildup of the last fifty years, plus the reservoir of public fear and loathing, was simply the result of an active imagination! This is quite an extraordinary revision of history and public policy.

77. Julia Lesage, "Why Christian Television Is Good TV," *Independent*, May 1987, p. 15.

78. Gilles Deleuze and Felix Guattari, "Becoming-Intense, Becoming-Animal," in *A Thousand Plateaus: Capitalism and Schizophrenia* (Minneapolis: University of Minnesota Press, 1987), p. 290.

79. Ibid., pp. 286–87, 288.

80. Ibid., p. 289. Right after this passage, Deleuze and Guattari inscribe sexual difference: "For women do not handle the secret in at all the same way as men [and 'virile secrecy']. . . . Men alternately fault them for their indiscretion, their gossiping, and for their solidarity, their betrayal. Yet it is curious how a woman can be secretive while at the same time hiding nothing. . . . They have no secret because they have become a secret themselves . . . a pure moving line." While this is presumably a very good thing (being a moving line), like the rest of their comments about the "becoming woman," it feels old-fashioned and unfamiliar, a bit gallant.

81. Andrew Ross, *No Respect*; Ross has taken his cue from Warhol, who, in *The Philosophy of Andy Warhol*, wrote: "I'm not saying that popular is bad so that what's left over from the bad taste is good. . . . But if you can take it and make it good . . . then you're not wasting. . . . You're recycling work and you're recycling people, and you're running your business as a byproduct of other businesses. . . . Leftovers are inherently funny" (93). (Indeed, women as leftovers of politicians or preachers were turned into jokes.) Here, Warhol intersects perfectly with Alliez and Feher and the new entrepreneurial spirit. The comparison between assailing Jim Bakker as a bad businessman (with the accompanying bad taste that entails) and praising

Warhol as a good artist (businessman) (although Robert Hughes, the art critic for *Time*, has consistently led the negative assessment of Warhol) with, against all his disclaimers, good taste is more than intriguing. If one has style, it permeates every aspect of life, or, good business is good taste.

82. Rebecca Birch Sterling, "Some Psychological Mechanisms Operative in Gossip," *Social Forces* 34: 1956, p. 26.

Part IV: Calculating Difference

1. Reine-Marie Paris, *Camille: The Life of Camille Claudel, Rodin's Muse and Mistress*, trans. Liliane Emery Tuck (New York: Henry Holt and Company, 1984/1988). The use of "muse" and "mistress" in the title suggests that the point of view is not necessarily that of a feminist, yet it inscribes a key female player; its goal, however, is to transform her into a genius, like the other art histories of geniuses.

2. Sigmund Freud, "The 'Uncanny,' " *Standard Edition* (London: Hogarth Press, 1955), Vol. 18, p. 248.

3. Mary Ann Doane, " . . . When the Direction of the Force Acting on the Body Is Changed: The Moving Image," in Mellencamp, ed., *Wide Angle 7*, nos. 1/2 (1985): 42-58.

4. Freud, *Standard Edition*, Vol. 10 (which also includes "Little Hans"). Many strands of "Rat Man" are picked up, amplified, and inverted in *Inhibitions, Symptoms and Anxiety*.

5. Jacques Lacan, *The Four Fundamental Concepts of Psycho-Analysis*, trans. Alan Sheridan (New York: Norton, 1978), p. 106.

6. Kathleen Woodward, *Aging and Its Discontents: Freud and Other Fictions* (Bloomington and Indianapolis: Indiana University Press, 1991). Because I wrote many of these ideas in May of 1987, I have taken quotations from an earlier paper by Woodward entitled "The Body in Age: Arguments and Scenes," which was broken up and mixed into her book; p. 11.

7. Many women do not become psychically or economically independent, separate, with their own boundaries or autonomy, transferring the same familial dependency to their children, thereby perpetuating what they experienced with and from their mothers. Separation and autonomy are not socially, economically, or libidinally easy for women within this culture.

8. Woodward, "Introduction," in *Aging and Its Discontents*.

9. Woodward, "Instant Repulsion: Decrepitude, the Mirror Stage, and the Literary Imagination," *Kenyon Review* 5, no. 4 (Fall 1983): 55.

10. Susan Suleiman, "Writing and Motherhood," in *The Mother Tongue: Essays in Feminist Psychoanalytic Interpretation*, ed. Shirley Nelson Garner, Claire Kahane, and Madelon Sprengnether (Ithaca and London: Cornell University Press, 1985), p. 358.

11. I cannot locate this quote by Suleiman; perhaps I paraphrased her insightful words rather than quoting them.

12. Sigmund Freud, "The Predisposition to Obsessional Neurosis" (1913), in *Sexuality and the Psychology of Love*, ed. Rieff, pp. 94–95. "The sweet maiden, the loving woman, the tender mother, has deteriorated" into the "old termagant."

13. Sigmund Freud, "Types of Neurotic Nosogenesis" (1912), in *Sexuality and the Psychology of Love*, p. 46.

14. Lois Banner, "The Meaning of Menopause: Aging and Its Historical Contexts in the Twentieth Century," paper delivered at a conference at the Center for Twentieth Century Studies, April 1989.

15. Marguerite Duras, *The Lover* (New York: Harper and Row, 1985), p. 46.

16. Freud, *Standard Edition*, Vol. 10, p. 206.

17. The first quotation is from Mary Russo, "Female Grotesques: Carnival and Theory," from her manuscript for *Feminist Studies/Critical Studies*, ed. Teresa de Lau-

retis (Bloomington: Indiana University Press, 1986); the second is from Mikhail Bakhtin, *Rabelais and His World*, trans. Helene Iswolsky (Bloomington: Indiana University Press, 1984), pp. 317-18.

18. Sigmund Freud, "Female Sexuality" (1931), in *Sexuality and the Psychology of Love*, p. 195.

19. Condit is my friend and colleague; these remarks came from a lengthy interview/discussion and from our team-teaching experiences.

20. Adrienne Rich, *On Lies, Secrets, and Silence: Selected Prose, 1966-1978* (New York: W. W. Norton, 1979), p. 13. When I first encountered her analogy, I was in opposition to its clichéd simplification. However, with obsessional neurosis in mind, the model of addiction does cohere around television in a more complex way.

21. See Part I, note 4.

22. Michel Foucault, *Disicipline and Punish: The Birth of the Prison*, trans. Alan Sheridan (New York: Vintage Books, 1979), pp. 137–38.

23. In "The Social Matrix of Television Invention in the United States," in *Regarding Television*, ed. E. Ann Kaplan, Jeanne Allen argues a more complex picture. I quote from my essay in *Screen*, "Situation and Simulation": "In the 1930s, television was a many sided machine: 1) radio movies to be shown on large screens in public theatres; 2) educator and advertiser for businesses and schools; 3) surveillance or "monitoring" devices for worker efficiency and military installations; and 4) two-way communication, developed by . . . AT&T." That it was manufactured as a piece of furniture, marketed for the family home (multiplying like rabbits in the newly developing suburbs), was an economic, not an ontologic, outcome.

24. Foucault, *Discipline and Punish*, pp. 164–65.

25. These comments were made during Morse's paper at the NEMLA conference in Providence, in March 1988.

26. Margaret Morse, "Artemis Aging: Exercise and the Female Body on Video," *Discourse* X.1 (Fall-Winter 1987-88): 21.

27. *The Wall Street Journal*, October 4, 1991, B1.

28. Judith Williamson, "It's Different for Girls," in *Consuming Passions: The Dynamics of Popular Culture* (London/New York: Marion Boyars, 1987), p. 49.

29. *The Milwaukee Journal*, April 11, 1990, p. 6E.

30. Jane Wagner, *The Search for Signs of Intelligent Life in the Universe* (New York: Harper and Row, 1986).

31. *The Wall Street Journal*, May 10, 1991, A7.

32. The video mourning bit was in *The Milwaukee Journal*, February 23, 1989, p. 8A; the video tribute reference was in *The Milwaukee Journal* sometime in 1989.

33. Neil Rosenberg, *The Milwaukee Journal*, October 20, 1987, pp. 1A, 6A. (This was a *front-page story*.)

34. *The Milwaukee Journal*, June 21, 1989, p. 2A.

XI. Obsessive Subjects

35. Sigmund Freud; this is a typical description of obsessional neurosis. In the case of the "old termagant," Freud had been discussing a patient who wanted to have children but "whose husband . . . could not satisfy this longing." "The content of her obsessional neurosis consisted in a tormenting obsession about washing and cleanliness . . . brought about by the impotence of her husband" ("Predisposition to Obsessional Neurosis," p. 91. Many behaviorists also tie OCD to sexual deprivations of various sorts.)

36. Jameson, "Postmodernism and Consumer Society," p. 125.

37. Deleuze and Guattari, *A Thousand Plateaus*, p. 34.

38. As Patrick Mahony argues in his meticulous, detailed re-creation and analysis of the case, "Freud furnished us with an explanation of the psychical mechanisms of obsessionals that can help us understand Freud himself and thus detect

obsessional traces contaminating his very explanation"—which Mahony does, symptomatically labeling them "contaminations" (165).

Freud described Lanzer as "an Oedipus type, loves his mother, hates his father (the original Oedipus was himself a case of obsessional neurosis—the riddle of the Sphinx)" (19). Because Freud aligned himself with Oedipus, "obsessional neurosis is unquestionably the most interesting and repaying subject of analytic research" (20). On the basis of his male/female, active/passive binarism, also the structuring opposition for feminist film theory, Freud eventually categorizes obsession as primarily the purview of men, with hysteria a female preserve, presumably forgetting his linkage of obsession with old, neurotic termagants. (This division is repeated, and repeatedly overturned, in *Inhibitions, Symptoms and Anxiety*.)

In keeping with the rest of his early theory, Freud attributes the cause to juvenile sexual activity. Hysteria was the result of shock to sex, and obsession the result of pleasure "transformed into [self-]*reproach*" (152). As I have argued, this libidinal/pleasure base changes in later Freud (1926) to anxiety. What remains consistent is women's inability to handle all this sex talk and experience, a structuring social difference of *Jokes and Their Relation to the Unconscious*.

Deleuze and Guattari's almost facile dismissal of another Freudian case study, the Wolf Man, is partially applicable to the Rat Man, although this was a more fragmented, less conclusive Oedipal reading. In "1914: One or Several Wolves," "No sooner does Freud discover the greatest art of the unconscious . . . than we find him tirelessly at work . . . reverting to his familiar themes of *the* father, *the* penis, *the* vagina, Castration with a capital C. . . . (On the verge of discovering a rhizome, Freud always returns to mere roots.)" As in their critique of "Little Hans," Deleuze and Guattari dissect enunciation: "The trap was set from the start. . . . Talk as he might about wolves . . . Freud does not even listen; he glances at his dog and answers, 'It's daddy.' For as long as that lasts, Freud calls it neurosis; when it cracks, it's psychosis'" (38).

Refutation aside, this case might have influenced Deleuze and Guattari more than they acknowledge. Rats sliding over one another as they move are, along with tuber plants, a central metaphor for rhizomatic movement and structures of thought. Because Lanzer's name was not revealed until 1986, he had been not an individual but a proper name of multiplicity, "a true proper name, an intimate first name linked to the becomings, infinitives, and intensities of a multiplied and depersonalized individual" (37–38). What Mahony sees as a weakness of Freud's unfinished, open-ended interpretation suggests why the Rat Man is more compatible with Deleuze and Guattari than the Wolf Man: "That disconnectedness . . . must be related . . . to the fact that Freud had not yet discovered the essence of obsessional neurosis to be a regression from oedipal conflict to anal eroticism" (Mahony, 217). For Mahony, the lack of a fully Oedipalized and narrativized explanation is a weakness; for Deleuze and Guattari, this would be a plus.

39. *The Wall Street Journal*, June 27, 1991, B1.

40. *The Wall Street Journal*, May 6, 1991, A1.

41. Hilary Radner, " 'This Time's For Me': Making Up and Feminine Practice," *Cultural Studies* 3, no. 3 (October 1989): 310.

XII. *Aging Bodies*

42. Woodward, "The Body in Age: Arguments and Scenes," p. 4.

43. Ibid., p. 12, quoting Freud letter of March 6, 1910. Woodward notes Freud's obsession not only with death but with dates.

44. See chapter 1.

45. See chapter 1.

46. Not only do I repeat quotes, here I repeat an argument from chapter 1.

47. Virginia Woolf, *Three Guineas* (New York: Harcourt, 1938), p. 18; this is a paraphrase.

48. Sigmund Freud, *Mourning and Melancholia, Standard Edition*, Vol. 14, p. 249. This is in Freud's comparison of the melancholic (a good description of an addict) and mourning, with the melancholic inflicting self-hatred as the result of a wretchedly low sense of self-esteem: "The patient represents his ego to us as worthless, incapable of any achievement. . . . He reproaches himself, vilifies himself" (p. 246).

49. Ibid., p. 151.

50. Jeremy Butler, "Notes on the Soap Opera Apparatus: Televisual Style and *As the World Turns*," *Cinema Journal* 25, no. 3 (Spring 1986): 67.

51. Sandy Flitterman-Lewis, "All's Well That Doesn't End—Soap Opera and the Marriage Motif," *Camera Obscura* 16 (January 1988): 120.

52. George Gerbner, Larry Gross, Nancy Signorielli, and Michael Morgan, "Aging with Television: Images on Television Drama and Conceptions of Social Reality," *Journal of Communication* 30, no. 1 (Winter 1980): 38/39.

53. Sigmund Freud, "Anxiety and Instinctual Life," *Standard Edition*, Vol. 22, p. 108.

54. An article in *The Village Voice*.

55. *Soap Opera Digest* 13, no. 21 (October 18, 1988): 1.

56. Cosmetic surgery brochures from Dr. Levy's office in Milwaukee.

57. Roland Barthes, *Roland Barthes*, trans. Richard Howard (New York: Hill and Wang, 1977), p. 159. "He has always regarded the (domestic) 'scene' as a pure experience of violence," which I refer to again later.

58. Rosalind Coward and Linda Semple, "Tracking Down the Past: Women and Detective Fiction," in *From My Guy to Sci-Fi: Genre and Women's Writing in the Postmodern World*, ed. Helen Carr (London: Pandora, 1989).

59. Amanda Cross, *Sweet Death, Kind Death* (New York: Ballantine, 1984), pp. 24-28.

Part V: Regime of Domiculture

1. Ross, p. 60.

2. I refer to Raymond Williams's notion of "privatized mobility" in relation to the family home and television, in *Television: Technology and Cultural Form* (New York: Schocken Books, 1975).

3. This is a referral back to Alliez and Feher, Part I.

4. As Lynn Spigel has described in *Logics of Television*.

XIII. Gracie

5. Jean Baudrillard, "Requiem for the Media," in *For a Critique of the Political Economy of the Sign*, trans. Charles Levin (St. Louis, Mo.: Telos, 1981), p. 184.

6. This transcription was taken from my videotape.

7. See my "Jokes and Their Relation to the Marx Brothers," in *Cinema and Language*, ed. Stephen Heath and Patricia Mellencamp (Frederick, Md.: University Publications of America, 1983).

8. Roland Barthes, "Writers, Intellectuals, Teachers," in *Image-Music-Text*, ed. Stephen Heath (London: Fontana/Collins, 1977), pp. 205-206.

9. Samuel Weber, *The Legend of Freud* (Minneapolis: University of Minnesota Press, 1982), p. 114.

XIV. Lucy

10. Bart Andrews, *Lucy & Ricky & Fred & Ethel* (New York: E. P. Dutton and Co., 1976). This invaluable sourcebook includes a concluding synopsis of shows by air

date and title without which I could not have historically organized my textual analyses; it was also used for anecdotes.

11. Charles Higham, *Lucy: The Real Life of Lucille Ball* (New York: St. Martin's Press, 1986).

12. Andrea Press, *Women Watching Television: Gender, Class and Generation in the American Television Experience* (Philadelphia: University of Pennsylvania Press, from proofsheets).

13. Raymond Williams, *Television: Technology and Cultural Form*.

14. See Higham.

15. See Andrews.

16. Jack Gould, TV critic for the *New York Times*.

17. For more on Lucy's history and image as a star in films, see Alex Doty, "The Cabinet of Lucy Ricardo: Lucille Ball's Star Image," *Cinema Journal* 29, no. 4 (Summer 1990). Presumably, Doty is in disagreement with me regarding Lucy's childish antics; yet I fail to see where he differs in theory, if at all.

18. Bart Andrews's book contains a synopsis of shows by air date and title, an invaluable listing.

XV. Jokes and Their Relation to TV

19. Hayden White, "The Value of Narrativity in the Representation of Reality," *Critical Inquiry* 7 (1980). Although there are no direct allusions, White uses enough terms to indicate that his essay was strongly influenced by Foucault as well as Lacan. For example, on pp. 23 and 24 he writes: "The history then, belongs to the category of what might be called the 'discourse of the real,' as against the 'discourse of the imaginary' or the 'discourse of desire.' The formulations are Lacanian, obviously, but I do not wish to push the Lacanian aspects of it too far."

20. Ibid., p. 10.

21. Freud, *Jokes and Their Relation to the Unconscious*, p. 196.

22. See, for example, Alex Doty.

23. Sigmund Freud, "Humour," *Standard Edition*, Vol. 21, pp. 162-63.

24. Susan Dworkin, "Roseanne Barr: The Disgruntled Housewife as Standup," *Ms.* 16 (July/August 1987): 106.

25. "Roseanne Barr: Domestic Goddess," *Vogue*, April 1988, p. 336.

26. Lenore Fleischer, *Publishers Weekly* 232 (October 23, 1987): 38.

27. Kathleen Rowe, "Roseanne: Domestic Goddess as Unruly Woman," paper presented at SCS annual meeting in Washington, D.C., May 1990; published in *Screen*, with revisions.

28. Nancy M. Henley, *Body Politics: Power, Sex, and Nonverbal Communication* (Englewood Cliffs, N.J.: Prentice-Hall, 1977).

29. Freud, *Jokes and Their Relation to the Unconscious*.

30. Judine Mayerle, "*Roseanne*—How Did You Get Inside My House? A Case Study of a Hit Blue-Collar Situation Comedy," *Journal of Popular Culture* 24, no. 4 (Spring 1991).

31. See Roland Barthes, *Roland Barthes*, p. 159.

32. *Newsweek*, March 13, 1989, p. 54.

Part VI: Countercultures

1. E. J. Dionne, *Why Americans Hate Politics*.

2. Susan Strasser, *Satisfaction Guaranteed* (New York: Pantheon Books, 1989), p. 15.

XVI. Women's Spaces/Women's Work

3. Susan Porter Benson, *Counter Cultures: Saleswomen, Managers, and Customers in*

American Department Stores, 1890-1940 (Urbana and Chicago: University of Illinois Press, 1986).

4. Anne Russell and Lorraine Calvacca, "Should You Be Funny at Work?" *Working Woman*, March 1991, pp. 74-75.

5. Susan Strasser, *Never Done: A History of American Housework* (New York: Pantheon Books, 1982).

XVII. Family Therapy

6. *Los Angeles Times*, June 13, 1991, p. F1.

7. Roby Rajan, "Rationality and Other Pathologies."

8. Fred Block, *Postindustrial Possibilities*.

9. Dolores Hayden, *Redesigning the American Dream: The Future of Housing, Work, and Family Life* (New York: W. W. Norton, 1984), pp. 145-56.

10. Thomas O'Boyle, "Fast-Track Kids Exhaust Their Parents," *The Wall Street Journal*, August 7, 1991, pp. B1, B8.

11. Cynthia Crossen, "Aquarius Generation Is Bane and Boon of Forecasters As It Grows Ever Older," *The Wall Street Journal*, September 16, 1991, pp. A1, A11.

XVIII. The Search for Signs of Intelligent Life

12. I want to express my gratitude to Jane Wagner for granting me permission to use so many of her words and ideas. I love the script so much that I wanted to reprint the entire text.

Index

♦

PATRICIA MELLENCAMP is Professor of Art History at the University of Wisconsin-Milwaukee. She is coeditor of three books on cinema and author of articles in *Screen, Afterimage, Wide Angle, Discourse,* and *Framework.* She is the editor of *Logics of Television: Essays in Cultural Criticism* and the author of *Indiscretions: Avant-Garde Film, Video, and Feminism.*